Religiöse Individualisierung in historischer Perspektive
Religious Individualisation in Historical Perspective

Religiöse Individualisierung in historischer Perspektive
Religious Individualisation in Historical Perspective

―

Abschlussbericht für die zweite Förderphase
der Kolleg-Forschungsgruppe 1013

Final Report of the Kolleg-Forschungsgruppe 1013
for the Second Funding Period

2013–2018

Herausgegeben von / Edited by
Riccarda Suitner, Martin Mulsow, Jörg Rüpke

DE GRUYTER

Die Drucklegung wurde durch die Deutsche Forschungsgemeinschaft (FOR 1080) finanziert.

ISBN 978-3-11-069637-0
e-ISBN (PDF) 978-3-11-069649-3
e-ISBN (EPUB) 978-3-11-069667-7
DOI https://doi.org/10.1515/9783110696493

Dieses Werk ist lizenziert unter der Creative Commons Attribution-NonCommercial-NoDerivatives 4.0 International Lizenz. Weitere Informationen finden Sie unter http://creativecommons.org/licenses/by-nc-nd/4.0/.

Library of Congress Control Number: 2020937740

Bibliografische Information der Deutschen Nationalbibliothek
Die Deutsche Nationalbibliothek verzeichnet diese Publikation in der Deutschen Nationalbibliografie; detaillierte bibliografische Daten sind im Internet über http://dnb.dnb.de abrufbar.

© 2020 Riccarda Suitner et al., publiziert von Walter de Gruyter GmbH, Berlin/Boston
Dieses Buch ist als Open-Access-Publikation verfügbar über www.degruyter.com.

Druck und Bindung: CPI books GmbH, Leck

www.degruyter.com

Contents

Riccarda Suitner, Martin Mulsow, Jörg Rüpke
Vorwort —— 1

Martin Fuchs, Antje Linkenbach, Martin Mulsow, Bernd-Christian Otto,
Rahul Bjørn Parson, Jörg Rüpke
1 Religious individualisation in historical perspective —— 3

Martin Fuchs, Antje Linkenbach, Martin Mulsow, Bernd-Christian Otto,
Rahul Bjørn Parson, Jörg Rüpke
2 Religiöse Individualisierung – und De-Individualisierung —— 6

Martin Fuchs, Antje Linkenbach, Martin Mulsow, Bernd-Christian Otto,
Rahul Bjørn Parson, Jörg Rüpke
3 Religious individualisation – and de-individualisation —— 36

4 Lived ancient religion: questioning cults and polis religion. A final report —— 57

5 Reports of fellows —— 67

6 ERC Advanced Grant "Lived Ancient Religion" —— 146

Janico Albrecht, Christopher Degelmann, Valentino Gasparini, Richard Gordon,
Maik Patzelt, Georgia Petridou, Rubina Raja, Anna-Katharina Rieger, Jörg Rüpke,
Benjamin Sippel, Emiliano Rubens Urciuoli, Lara Weiss
7 Article from the ERC project —— 155
   Religion in the making: The Lived Ancient Religion Approach

8 Tagungsberichte/Report on conferences —— 182

9 Publications of fellows and staff —— 267

Vorwort

Von 2008 bis 2018 förderte die Deutsche Forschungsgemeinschaft die Kolleg-Forschungsgruppe „Religiöse Individualisierung in historischer Perspektive". Über die erste Förderphase haben wir im Jahr 2013 bereits Bericht abgelegt.[1] Der vorliegende Bericht umfasst nun die zweite Förderperiode und stellt erneut inhaltliche Erträge, das ihnen zu Grunde liegende Forschungsprogramm, Berichte der Fellows und Berichte über Tagungen zusammen. Es ist ergänzt um die entsprechenden Berichte aus dem ERC Advanced Grant „Lived Ancient Religion", der das Forschungsprogramm der Kolleg-Forschungsgruppe um einen Antike-Schwerpunkt ergänzte. Wir danken an dieser Stelle noch einmal allen Beteiligten für ihre Mitwirkung am Programm wie an diesem Bericht. Ein besonderer Dank gilt Diana Püschel, die als Geschäftsführerin die gesamte Laufzeit hindurch den Rahmen für die inhaltliche Arbeit geschaffen hat. Dem Max-Weber-Kolleg, und insbesondere seiner wissenschaftlichen Geschäftsführerin, Frau PD Dr. Bettina Hollstein, gilt Dank für ihre unermüdliche und immer wieder inspirierende Anstrengung zur Einbettung der Arbeit beider Projekte in den größeren Rahmen des Max-Weber-Kollegs. Einen besseren Platz konnten sie nicht finden!

Der hier vorgelegte Bericht umfasst auch einen Beitrag des ERC-Projektes, der dessen Ergebnisse zusammenfasst. Die weiteren Arbeiten aus dem Gesamtprojekt sind in der Bibliographie am Ende dieses Bandes dokumentiert. In dem umfangreichen und ebenfalls *open access* gestellten Band „Religious Individualisation: Historical Dimensions and Comparative Perspectives"[2] sind zahlreiche Detailstudien und übergreifende Reflexionen zugänglich. Für die Schlussredaktion danken wir Johannes Benjamin Vonderschmidt sowie Antje Linkenbach und Martin Fuchs für letzte Korrekturen.

Riccarda Suitner, Martin Mulsow, Jörg Rüpke

---

[1] Bericht über die erste Förderperiode der Kolleg-Forschergruppe ‚Religiöse Individualisierung in historischer Perspektive' (2008–2012), hg. von Hans Joas und Jörg Rüpke, Erfurt: Universität Erfurt, 2013; zugänglich unter urn:nbn:de:gbv:547-201800238 (open access).
[2] Berlin: de Gruyter, 2020, hg. von Martin Fuchs, Antje Linkenbach, Martin Mulsow, Bernd-Christian Otto, Rahul Bjørn Parson und Jörg Rüpke.

Martin Fuchs, Antje Linkenbach, Martin Mulsow,
Bernd-Christian Otto, Rahul Bjørn Parson, Jörg Rüpke

1 Religious individualisation in historical perspective

The work of the research group 'Religious individualisation in historical perspective', which started in 2008 at the Max Weber Centre for Advanced Cultural and Social Study at the University of Erfurt (Germany) and has been financed by a generous grant of the DFG (German Science Foundation) in the format of a Kolleg-Forschungsgruppe (KFG), has ended on December 31st, 2018, after a second period of funding (directed by Hans Joas and Jörg Rüpke in the first, and Martin Mulsow and Jörg Rüpke in the second period).

The KFG started by formulating a critique of modernisation theory that was to be bolstered by demonstrating that phenomena that might well be called 'individualisation' were existent *and* important in pre-modern and non-Western cultures. During the subsequent years we have pushed forward in at least three directions:

- With regard to modernisation theory, the independence of 'individualisation' from other crucial factors all too quickly bundled together as 'modernisation' has been sufficiently demonstrated. 'Individualisation' thus has been set free as an analytical term that is useful also beyond Western or even multiple 'modernities'.
- With regard to the history of religion, hence, many phenomena and processes have come to the fore when we exchanged the lenses of collectivism by looking for anything comparable to 'individualisation'. In particular, narratives of ancient and post-ancient ('medieval' or 'early modern' in terms of West-European epochs) circum-Mediterranean, European as well as West and South Asian religions have changed and gained new facets far beyond the work of the group itself. Concepts like 'self' and 'agency', 'subject' and 'personhood', 'individuation' and 'personal identity' were taken on board, and were at the same time critically perused, in our attempt to develop more fine-grained concepts and descriptions.
- Reflection has turned onto the very concepts we started with. How are concepts of 'religion' shaped by the aforementioned master narrative of 'modern Western individualisation'? How is the normative character of the concept of the 'individual', whenever it is implied that one should *be* an individual, informed by such a narrative? How has the master narrative affected concepts of 'history' and 'change'? The paradoxical consequences of securing individuality by processes of institutionalisation (e.g., through ritualisation, group formation, the establishment of textual canons and traditions, etc.) as well as backlashes into de- or non-individualisation have come into view. Looking more closely at the individual has also brought to light features of personhood that do not easily comply with linear and uni-directional individualisation narratives. Even in (early) modernity

individualisation processes do not lead to a fully 'bounded' self-contained individual. The individual person always exhibits permeability, vulnerability and openness towards the outer and the social world in various degrees, as s/he is also capable of parting and pluralising him/herself in order to navigate multiple belongings, personalities and allegiances. Unravelling relational and partible aspects of the self has forced us to postulate a co-constitutive relation between what we call 'dividuality' and individuality.

All this has affected our view onto historical and contemporary societies and schools of thought, in a sociological and anthropological perspective as well as in terms of intellectual and ritual history. 'Religious individualisation', hence, understood as a polythetic umbrella term, has proved fruitful as a heuristic tool rather than a clear-cut semantic signifier of specific social dynamics. A summary of the research results produced by the more than one hundred members of the research group – the long-term fellows from all over the world, the core team at Erfurt, but also the many short-term fellows or participants in conferences –, is now published in open-access form, two volumes, co-edited by us, and focusing on transcending selves, dividual self, conventions and contentions and, authorities.[1]

The volume presented here will supplement our report on the first period of funding (2008–2012).[2] It will start with a summary of our findings, followed by the contributions published in a special issue of the journal *Religion* 45.3 in 2015, co-edited by Martin Fuchs and Jörg Rüpke and reprinted with the consent of the authors. Reports on the numerous workshops and conferences organised and co-organised by the Kolleg-Forschungsgruppe and the ERC Advanced Grant project "Lived Ancient Religion: Questioning Cult and Polis-Religion" (directed by Jörg Rüpke and co-directed by Rubina Raja), which grew out of the KFG and was funded by the European Research Council (Grant no. 295555, 2012–17) ensue. The publications resulting from these meetings and discussions, but above all by all the fellows and members of the research group are listed in the final bibliography.

The report – as much as the whole research group – is bilingual (and more). The 'executive summary' will be presented in German and English at the beginning, followed by further pieces in either English or German. Without denying the usefulness of one shared language, the introduction and this report are pleading for a culture of multilingual search for adequate terms in the rich repertoire of different *and* entangled traditions of concepts and experiences.

---

[1] doi 10.1515/9783110580853-001 (open access), edited by Martin Fuchs, Antje Linkenbach, Martin Mulsow, Bernd-Christian Otto, and Jörg Rüpke.
[2] https://www.db-thueringen.de/receive/dbt_mods_00034459 (urn:nbn:de:gbv:547-201800 238) (open access), edited by Hans Joas and Jörg Rüpke.

We wish to thank Riccarda Suitner, who undertook the burden of collecting and organising texts and reports and working until August 2018 on editing the volume, for her time and dedication. Carefully as ever, Diana Püschel, managing director of the group from the very first moment, oversaw the final production. Heartfelt thanks for ten years of intensive, extensive, empathic and patient work must be extended to her.

Martin Fuchs, Antje Linkenbach, Martin Mulsow,
Bernd-Christian Otto, Rahul Bjørn Parson, Jörg Rüpke

2 Religiöse Individualisierung – und De-Individualisierung

Die Arbeit der Forschungsgruppe „Religiöse Individualisierung in historischer Perspektive", die 2008 am Max-Weber-Kolleg für kultur- und sozialwissenschaftliche Studien der Universität Erfurt begann, ist endgültig beendet. Die Forschungsgruppe (oder Kolleg-Forschungsgruppe) wurde von der Deutschen Forschungsgemeinschaft (DFG) großzügig gefördert und war intellektuell in die lebendige und interdisziplinäre Atmosphäre und Diskussionskultur des Max-Weber-Kollegs eingebettet. Die Forschungsgruppe bestand aus mehr als hundert Mitgliedern, darunter das Kernteam in Erfurt, die langjährigen Fellows aus aller Welt, die ein oder mehrere Jahre bei uns waren, die vielen Kurzzeit-Stipendiaten, die Wochen oder Monate bei uns in Erfurt verbrachten, und die unzähligen Konferenzteilnehmer, die uns ihr Fachwissen für einige Tage zur Verfügung stellten.

In einem Abschlussband wurden wichtige Untersuchungslinien zusammengetragen, die die Forschungsgruppe in den letzten zehn Jahren von 2009 bis 2018 verfolgt hat. Über das Selbst hinaus, das geteilte Selbst, Konventionen und Infragestellungen und schließlich Autoritäten waren jene vier Perspektiven, die Prozesse der „religiösen Individualisierung" unserer Arbeit beeinflussten und erforschten, die wir in Fuchs et al. 2019 als Überschriften gewählt haben und die hier helfen können, unsere Arbeit zusammenzufassen. Ausgehend von den Mechanismen der *religiösen* Individualisierung haben wir die Akteure, Merkmale, Muster und Dynamiken solcher Prozesse untersucht. Der Fokus lag auf menschlichen Akteuren, sowohl bei Selbstbildern als auch bei ihrer Konstruktion oder Konzeption in verschiedenen Epochen und Regionen, und wir haben untersucht, wie sie in gesellschaftlichen Netzwerken eingebettet waren und wie Agency behauptet, zugeschrieben oder abgelehnt wurde. Die Gruppe hat diskutiert, wie die Agency durch ihre verschiedenen Kontexte appropriiert und modifiziert und gleichzeitig gestaltet und produziert wurde. Wir haben uns mit den wirtschaftlichen, politischen und rechtlichen Bedingungen und Einschränkungen, aber auch mit kulturellen Praktiken und Alltagsdiskursen beschäftigt, mit den Expertendiskursen von Philosophen und Theologen sowie lokal verankerten Intellektuellen und ihren translokalen Kolleginnen und Kollegen. Überall war es uns wichtig, die Räume und Muster der Individualisierung und Deindividualisierung sowie die Spannungen, die im Zuge dieser Entwicklungen entstanden sind, die Machtverhältnisse sowie Protest- und Marginalisierungsprozesse und schließlich die Prozesse der De-, Re- und Neo-Traditionalisierung anzusprechen.

Der Inhalt der einzelnen historischen Studien, die die Forschungsgruppe im laufenden Prozess der Anwendung und Neugestaltung des Konzepts der ‚Individualisierung' hervorgebracht hat, lässt sich weder hier noch im Abschlussband zusammenfassen, auch in seinen mehr als fünfzig Kapiteln nicht. Wenn man gezwungen ist, die Ergebnisse der Gruppe in Bezug auf den Begriff der ‚Individualisierung' zusammenzufassen, kann man sagen, dass der Kern unserer Arbeit sowohl kritisch als auch revisionistisch ist. Es ist insofern ‚kritisch', als er sich gegen die Monopolisierung des Begriffs ‚Individualisierung' durch Befürworter der Modernisierungstheorie richtet, die den Alltag dominiert. Er ist ‚revisionistisch', da wir uns oft gegen eine historiographische Perspektive ausgesprochen haben, die davon ausgeht, dass alle ‚vormodernen' Kulturen im Wesentlichen kollektiv oder kollektivistisch sind (mit Ausnahme einiger ‚großer Individuen'). So werden wir kurz unseren Ausgangspunkt skizzieren und dann das weitere Feld der behandelten Forschungsfragen sowie wichtige Ergebnisse vorstellen.

2.1 Meistererzählungen von Individualität und Individualisierung in der Religionsgeschichte

Im Gegensatz zu bestehenden Vorurteilen bietet die ‚Individualisierung' nicht nur ein Fenster in gegenwärtige Gesellschaften, sondern auch in die Vergangenheit sowie in die Religionsgeschichte im Allgemeinen (siehe Rüpke 2016a, im Folgenden verwendet). Es könnte hilfreich sein, noch einmal auf die Ursprünge dieser etablierten Meistererzählung zurückzublicken, deren Befragung der analytische Ausgangspunkt der Forschungsgruppe war. Thomas Luckmann hatte bereits Anfang der 1960er Jahre bei der Untersuchung empirischer Daten auf das Wachstum der amerikanischen Religion hingewiesen und diese als Indikator für Individualisierung verstanden (Luckmann 1967, erweiterte Version: Luckmann 1991). Individualisierung wird jedoch im soziologischen Diskurs weit über den Bereich der Religion hinaus allgemein als ein Unterscheidungsmerkmal der Moderne und als eines ihrer dominanten Merkmale angesehen. Solche Ansichten verlieren in der Regel – wenn auch nicht in Luckmanns Fall – den zeitgleichen und im Blick auf Individualisierung paradoxen Aufstieg der Massenkultur als begleitenden Modus der Integration in modernen Gesellschaften aus den Augen. Auch wenn man bedenkt, dass sich die soziologischen Theorien der Moderne in dem Gewicht, das sie der Individualisierung beimessen, unterscheiden, hat die Individualisierung dennoch einen festen Platz in allen klassischen soziologischen Modernisierungskonten (wie bei Flavia Kippele [1998], Kron und Horáček [2009] und anderen). Aus dieser Perspektive erscheint Religion als negativ mit dem Prozess der Individualisierung verbunden. Mit Ausnahme einiger weniger Denker, wie Georg Simmel (1968) und später Luckmann selbst, wurde die Religion als Opfer der von Individualisierung geprägten Prozesse angesehen.

Aus religionsgeschichtlicher Perspektive lohnt es sich, die Narrative historischer Prozesse genauer zu betrachten, die als Grundlage für die Gleichsetzung von Individualisierung und Moderne gedacht waren. Diese Narrative nehmen ganz unterschiedliche Formen an. In seiner berühmten Studie über die italienische Renaissance behauptete Jacob Burckhardt (1860, 141), dass das Interesse an Subjektivität im europäischen Kontext seit Ende des 13. Jahrhunderts erheblich gestiegen sei. Spätere Studien zeigten, wie in dieser Zeit neue und bahnbrechende philosophische, ästhetische, philologische und religiöse Alternativen sowie neue Institutionen dazu beitrugen, Räume der Kritik und Distanz zu dem zu schaffen, was als ‚traditionelle' Gesellschaft und Praxis angesehen wurde (z.B. Martin 2004). Mit dem Beginn der Renaissance wurde beispielsweise der Paganismus nicht nur zu einer ästhetischen Form, sondern auch zu einer religiösen Alternative (siehe Hanegraaff 2012; eine weitere Position siehe Stausberg 2009).

Die in diesen Kontexten zu identifizierenden Prozesse der religiösen Individualisierung wurden durch spätmittelalterliche Praktiken der religiösen Frömmigkeit inspiriert. Später, zu Beginn des 16. Jahrhunderts, machte die Reformation die Religion zum Gegenstand individueller Wahl. Während die dominanten aristotelischen und scholastischen Paradigmen in den frühen Jahren der Renaissance auf den Prüfstand kamen, stellten die Reformatoren nun eine weitere dominante religiöse Tradition, den Katholizismus, erneut in Frage. In diesem Fall wurden die orthodoxen Interpretationen jedoch nicht nur durch intellektuelle und künstlerische Unternehmen verdrängt, sondern vielmehr offen bekämpft. Max Webers (1864–1920) Dissertation über die protestantische Ethik nach der Reformation ist ein besonders pointiertes Beispiel für diesen Trend, mit seinem Schwerpunkt auf der Hinwendung zur innerweltlichen Askese, der Verantwortung jedes Einzelnen für sein Leben und der „Rationalisierung des *Lebensverhaltens*" – jetzt in der Welt und doch orientiert am *Jenseits* – als „Wirkung des Berufungskonzeptes des asketischen Protestantismus" (Weber [1920] 2011, 157).

Die ersten Risse im westlichen Selbstbild einer primär, wenn nicht gar ausschließlich modernen westlichen Herkunft der (religiösen) Individualisierung werden im Kontext von Webers vergleichender Analyse eurasischer Weltreligionen und Zivilisationen sichtbar. Insbesondere in Bezug auf Indien sah Weber seine Intellektuellenreligionen oder Soteriologien als ein Repertoire der am stärksten ausgeprägten und am systematischsten entwickelten Einstellungen von Weltindifferenz und Weltabweisung für das kultivierte Individuum. Was Weber leugnete, war, dass sich diese individualisierende Haltung auf das Leben in der Welt auswirkte. Er glaubte auch nicht, dass diese Formen der Religiosität die Mehrheit der Laien oder die unteren Schichten der Gesellschaft (was er die „Massen" nannte) erreichten. Weber sah die Entwicklungen in Indien und in allen anderen nicht-westlichen Zivilisationen als Sackgassen. Nur die protestantische Individualisierung ermöglichte für ihn den Durchbruch zur praktischen Individualisierung des Lebens in der Welt, der „Fähigkeit und Disposition des Menschen, bestimmte Arten von *praktischem* rationalem

Verhalten anzunehmen" (Weber 2004a, 109; siehe auch 1996, 250, 359/1958, 325; Fuchs 1988, 138ff. 277ff.; 2017, 227, 254).

Louis Dumont (1911–1998) entwickelte Webers Agenda in eine andere Richtung und schlug die Figur des indischen Weltentsagers (saṃnyāsin, śramaṇa) als wahrscheinlich die früheste Form der religiösen Individualisierung vor, wenn auch eine, die bereits sehr vielfältig war. Der idealtypische Entsagung Übende, der sich von sozialen Bindungen löste, wurde als das „Individuum außerhalb der Welt" konzipiert (Dumont 1980, 185, 267–86; dazu und zu den folgenden siehe Fuchs 1988, 417ff., 453–525). Dumont argumentierte, dass in Gesellschaften des „traditionellen, ganzheitlichen Typs" der Individualismus in der Regel nur in klarem Gegensatz zur (und damit für ihn „außerhalb") Gesellschaft stehen könnte (Dumont 1986, 26); Gesellschaften, die aus auf sich selbst orientierten Individualisten bestehen, sind ein modernes Phänomen. Dumont betrachtete jedoch auch das außerweltlich orientierte Individuum als den „Motor" und „Hauptakteur" der historischen Entwicklungen in Indien, nicht nur im religiösen, sondern auch im politischen und sogar wirtschaftlichen Bereich (Dumont 1965, 91; 1975a, 64; 1975b, 163). Darüber hinaus stellte Dumont die starke These auf, dass indische Formen der religiösen Individualisierung als wichtiger direkter oder indirekter Auslöser der religiösen Individualisierung im östlichen Mittelmeerraum in der Antike fungiert haben könnten. Sie hätten also griechische Philosophen und frühe Christen und damit den Westen noch weiter beeinflusst (hier geht es um die Gymnosophen oder „nackten Weisen", wie *Yogins* im Mittelmeer genannt wurden). Die Kategorie des (außerweltlich orientierten) Individuums, spekuliert Dumont, „hätte in der Geschichte nur einmal erfunden werden können", wodurch Indien als weltgeschichtlicher Ursprung der (religiösen) Individualisierung erscheint (Dumont 1975b, 168; 1986, 29). Seiner Ansicht nach wurde erst in der Geschichte des westlichen Christentums der Übergang vom „außerweltlichen" zum „innerweltlichen" Individualismus vollzogen. Die entscheidenden Schritte in diese Richtung wurden seiner Meinung nach zuerst von Calvin und dann von Luther unternommen. In einer ersten Phase wurden die religiösen Autoritäten der Kirche und des Papstes den weltzugewandteren Mächten des Kaisers und der Adligen übergeordnet; in einer zweiten Phase wurde der Wille des Einzelnen mit dem Willen Gottes identifiziert, so dass der individuelle Wille uneingeschränkt regieren konnte (1986, Kap. 1).

Dumonts Ansichten bleiben partiell und einseitig, da er die Religion strikt von der „traditionellen" Gesellschaft trennt. Die von ihm als streng „ganzheitlich" begriffene Gesellschaft spricht vor allem den Unterschichten jede Agency oder individuelle Subjektivität ab. Dies ist auf seine Abwertung anderer Quellen religiöser Individualisierung in Indien und anderswo zurückzuführen. In Bezug auf den indischen Fall hat Dumont, wie Weber vor ihm, vor allem die Relevanz von *bhakti* heruntergespielt. Dennoch räumte er ein, dass *bhakti* es im Kontext der „traditionellen" indischen Gesellschaft ermöglicht, dass „man die Welt *von innen* heraus verlassen kann" und dass alle Menschen „freie Individuen werden können" (Dumont 1980, 282f., unsere Kursivierung; vgl. Fuchs 2018).

Selbst derart elaborierte Analysen, die Formen der Individualisierung in der vormodernen und nicht-christlichen Welt aufspürten, waren noch immer von starken Spuren orientalistischer Stereotypisierung und der westlichen Tradition der Exotisierung, des *othering* der nicht-westlichen Welt geprägt (Fuchs 1988). Während sie dem asiatischen „Anderen" eine wichtige historische Rolle gegeben haben könnten, betrachteten sie sowohl die modernen religiösen als auch die säkularen Formen der Individualisierung weiterhin als authentischer und historisch fortschrittlicher. Während Wissenschaftler wie Weber und Dumont die Anfänge eines Bewusstseins für die vielfältigen Formen der religiösen Individualisierung widerspiegeln, blieb das Verständnis, dass Individualisierung ein Kennzeichen der einzigartigen westlichen Moderne sei, gleichwohl weitgehend verbreitet. Dies veranlasste andere Wissenschaftler zu behaupten, dass Personen, die zu bestimmten außereuropäischen oder vormodernen Kulturen gehören, nicht einmal die Möglichkeit hätten, einen Interessengegensatz zwischen „sich selbst" und „Gesellschaft" zu formulieren. Solche Ansichten wurden von Anthropologen massiv kritisiert (z.B. Spiro 1993). Die jüngsten Arbeiten zur Religion der vormodernen und vorchristlichen Antike, die in der Regel als „kollektiv" bezeichnet wird, haben zu ähnlichen Ergebnissen geführt. Die umfangreichen alten Diskussionen über religiöse Abweichungen und Versuche, religiöses Verhalten rechtlich zu standardisieren, zeugen von der Wahrnehmung und Akzeptanz einer umfangreichen religiösen Individualität, die in vielen verschiedenen Formen praktiziert wird (Rüpke 2011, 2016c).

Unterdessen wurde die exzeptionelle Selbstbeschreibung der westlichen Welt als „modern" im globalen Nicht-Westen kritisch hinterfragt. Diese Kritik nimmt entweder die Form eines Hinweises auf die historische Unangemessenheit solcher Singularitätsansprüche an oder die Form eines Gegensterotyps, das die östliche Kollektivität über die vermeintliche westliche Individualität stellt (vgl. Asad 1973, 1983). Die konzeptionelle Verknüpfung von Moderne und religiöser Individualität hat so das Studium vergleichbarer Phänomene in früheren Perioden außereuropäischer wie europäischer Geschichte behindert, so dass Individualität und Individualisierung bei der Untersuchung religiösen Wandels nur eine begrenzte Rolle gespielt haben.

Der Fall von *bhakti* in Indien wurde bereits erwähnt. *Bhakti* – ein Sammelbegriff für ein breites Spektrum von Phänomenen und Traditionen – ermöglicht individuelle Hingabe; verschiedene Formen von *bhakti* verbinden sich mit einer Kritik an sozialen und religiösen Einschränkungen. Für die mediterrane Antike haben einige Vorstellungen von Polis-Religion oder *civic religion* behauptet, dass die religiösen Praktiken der politischen Elite und ihre Definitionen von legitimen religiösen Handlungen der einzige bedeutsame Sektor von Religion in politischen Gemeinschaften seien. Die Vielfalt und Veränderbarkeit einzelner religiöser Handlungen und ihr tiefgreifender Einfluss auf die von der Elite als „öffentlich" bezeichneten Rituale wurden vernachlässigt. Das führte zu einer Betonung des kollektiven und grundsätzlich verschiedenen Charakters vormoderner Gesellschaften (Kritik siehe Rüpke 2007, 5–38; Kindt

2012, 12–35). In ähnlicher Weise ist das Stereotyp der religiösen Einheit des mittelalterlichen Europas (zur Kritik Borgolte 2001) nur ein stereotypes Gegenstück zur Selbstbeschreibung moderner Gesellschaften als pluralistisch, wie sie in der Säkularisierungsthese impliziert wird. Im Gegensatz zu solchen Stereotypen hat die jüngste Forschung, die sich auf die Geschichte der westlichen Esoterik und der Gelehrtenmagie konzentriert, eine Vielzahl von individualisierenden Impulsen und Strängen enthüllt, die die westliche Kultur- und Religionsgeschichte seit der Spätantike geprägt haben (siehe von Stuckrad 2010; Otto 2011; Hanegraaff 2012; Otto 2016, 2017; Bellingradt und Otto 2017; Otto 2018a, 2018b, 2018c). Die Diagnose der modernen Individualisierung und die Zuschreibung eines öffentlichen und kollektiven Charakters an die vormoderne Religion sind sich wechselseitig verstärkende Interpretationsrahmen.

Solche Beobachtungen und Kritiken dürfen jedoch nicht übersehen, dass die religiöse Individualität auch in Situationen, die durch Individualisierungsprozesse und entsprechenden religiösen Wandel gekennzeichnet sind, ungleich verteilt ist. Burckhardt hat bei der Identifizierung der Renaissance als Wendepunkt die Existenz von Dissidenten in den vorangegangenen Jahrhunderten nicht geleugnet. Was im 14. Jahrhundert neu war und Individualisierung als Prozess konstituierte, war nicht, wie die traditionelle historische Erzählung will, die Anwesenheit einzelner Intellektueller wie Petrarca (1304–1374). Vielmehr war die immer größer werdende Zahl von Menschen, die sich für technische und wirtschaftliche Fragen sowie für die subjektive Dimension der menschlichen Existenz interessieren, prägend. Bloße Zahlen können keinen Maßstab für die Beurteilung des Ausmaßes dieses Phänomens liefern. Man muss vielmehr die Kontexte, die intellektuellen, diskursiven und praktischen (zum Beispiel rituellen) Formen der Erscheinungsformen sowie ihre Folgen innerhalb einer gegebenen lokalen Gesellschaft identifizieren. Selbst in „modernen" und „westlichen" Gesellschaften kann sich die gefeierte Form der „Individualität" als sehr partiell oder sogar nur illusionär erweisen (siehe Kron und Horáček 2009, 151f.).

Die Betrachtung zeitgenössischer Religion in den Vereinigten Staaten von Amerika zeigt, dass „Individualität" kein einfaches Merkmal der „modernen" Religion ist, wie diejenigen behaupten, die die Privatisierung der Religion diagnostizieren. „Individualität" als Interpretationsrahmen und Verhaltensnorm findet sich vor allem bei mobilen Mitgliedern der weißen Mittelschicht. Individualität als Konzept wird für sie durch ihr eigenes Engagement und dessen soziale Folgen bestätigt (Madsen 2009, 1279–82). Dieses emische Konzept der „Individualität" ist keine willkürliche Option innerhalb einer Bandbreite möglicher privatisierter heiliger *Kosmoi*. Im Gegenteil, es ist ein von einer bestimmten Gruppe entwickeltes Konzept, wenn auch mit hegemonialem Charakter. Es ist eine Lebensweise, die in den Augen der gesamten Gesellschaft dominiert, auch wenn nicht die gesamte Gesellschaft daran teilhat (ebd.). Daraus ergibt sich eine wichtige Konsequenz, sowohl historisch als auch soziologisch: Bestimmte religiöse Traditionen könnten Praktiken der Selbstreflexion haben oder entwickeln, die in der Lage sind, Individualität zu fördern. Die Institutionalisierung solcher Tendenzen und ihre Konzeptualisierung *als* „Individualität" ist jedoch eine Frage von historischen Kontexten und sozialem Standort.

2.2 Ein Blick auf die religiöse Individualisierung – kurzgefasst

Bevor wir weiter ins Detail gehen, ist ein kurzer Überblick notwendig. Wie bereits erwähnt, begann die Kolleg-Forschungsgruppe – oder kurz KFG – mit einer Kritik an der Modernisierungstheorie. Die Absicht bestand darin, diese Kritik zu untermauern, indem wir zeigten, dass Phänomene, die man durchaus als „Individualisierung" bezeichnen könnte, in vormodernen und nicht-westlichen Kulturen vorhanden *und* wichtig waren. In den vergangenen Jahren haben wir jedoch diesen analytischen Ausgangspunkt in mindestens drei Richtungen weiterentwickelt und überschritten.

a) In Bezug auf die Modernisierungstheorie ist die Unabhängigkeit der Individualisierung von anderen entscheidenden Faktoren, die als Modernisierung gebündelt werden, nur allzu leicht nachzuweisen (z.B. Bellah und Joas 2012; Deuser und Wendel 2012; Joas 2012, 2013a, 2013b). Individualisierung wurde damit als analytischer Begriff freigesetzt, der über die westliche „Moderne" oder sogar der Rede von mehreren *modernities* hinaus nützlich ist (Fuchs, Linkenbach und Reinhard 2015; Fuchs und Rüpke 2015a; Mieth und Müller-Schauenburg 2012; Mieth 2014; Mieth 2016; Mulder-Bakker et al. 2017; Otto 2016, 2017, 2018a; Reinhardt 2014a, 2014b, 2016; Rosenberger 2013; Rüpke 2011, 2012b, 2012c, 2012d, 2013, 2014, 2015a, 2015b, 2016c; Rüpke und Spickermann 2012; Suitner 2016; Vinzent 2011; Vinzent 2014).

b) Religionsgeschichtlich traten viele Phänomene und Prozesse in den Vordergrund, als wir die Brille des Kollektivismus beiseite legten und stattdessen nach allem suchten, was mit „Individualisierung" vergleichbar ist (siehe Otto 2017 und weiter unten). Insbesondere die Erzählungen der antiken und nachantiken („mittelalterlichen" oder „frühen Neuzeit", im Sinne westeuropäischer Epochen) circum-mediterranen, europäischen, westlichen und südasiatischen Religionen haben sich verändert und neue Facetten weit über die Arbeit der Gruppe hinaus gewonnen. Konzepte wie „Selbst" und „Agency", „Subjekt" und „Persönlichkeit", „Individuation" und „persönliche Identität" wurden in unserem Versuch, präzisere Begriffe und Beschreibungen zu entwickeln, aufgegriffen und gleichzeitig kritisch hinterfragt (Fuchs 2015; Fuchs und Rüpke 2015b; Hartung und Schlette 2012; Hollstein, Jung und Knöbl 2011; Lichterman 2013; Messlin 2012; Ram 2013; Rebillard und Rüpke 2015b; Rüpke 2012a, 2015c, 2016b; Rüpke und Woolf 2013; Schlette 2013).

c) Schließlich hat sich die Reflexion genau auf die Begriffe konzentriert, mit denen wir begonnen haben. Wie werden Begriffe von „Religion" durch die oben genannte Meistererzählung der „modernen westlichen Individualisierung" geprägt (Otto, Rau und Rüpke 2015; Rüpke 2018b)? Wie ist der normative Charakter des

Begriffs des „Individuums", wenn impliziert wird, dass man durch eine solche Erzählung angehalten wird, ein Individuum *sein* zu *sollen*? Wie hat die Meistererzählung die Begriffe von „Geschichte" und „Wandel" beeinflusst? Die paradoxen Folgen der Sicherung der Individualität durch Institutionalisierungsprozesse (etwa durch Ritualisierung, Gruppenbildung, Etablierung von Textkanons und -traditionen) sowie Umschläge in die De- oder Nicht-Individualisierung sind in den Blick geraten. Die nähere Betrachtung des Individuums hat auch Merkmale der Persönlichkeit ans Licht gebracht, die nicht leicht mit linearen und unidirektionalen Individualisierungserzählungen übereinstimmen. Selbst in der (frühen) Moderne führen Individualisierungsprozesse nicht zu einem vollständig geschlossenen, selbstgenügsamen Individuum. Der Einzelne weist immer Durchlässigkeit, Verletzlichkeit und Offenheit gegenüber der äußeren und sozialen Welt in unterschiedlichem Maße auf, da er auch in der Lage ist, sich selbst zu teilen und zu pluralisieren, um durch multiple Besitztümer, Persönlichkeiten und Zugehörigkeiten zu navigieren (siehe Taylor 2007 und Beiträge zu Teil II von Fuchs et al. 2019). Die Entfesselung relationaler und partizipativer Aspekte des Selbst hat uns gezwungen, eine mitkonstituierende Beziehung zwischen dem, was wir *dividuality*, Dividualität, nennen, und Individualität zu postulieren. All dies hat unseren Blick auf historische und zeitgenössische Gesellschaften und Denkrichtungen beeinflusst, sowohl aus soziologischer und anthropologischer Sicht (Fuchs 2015; Rüpke 2015c) wie in Bezug auf *intellectual history* und Ritualgeschichte (zum Beispiel Mulsow 2012, 2015; Ben-Tov, Deutsch und Herzig 2013; Otto 2016; Bellingradt und Otto 2017; Otto 2018a, 2018b).

Zum Konzept der „religiösen Individualisierung" und im krassen Gegensatz zur oben genannten Meistererzählung – die die religiöse Individualisierung in der Regel als mehr oder weniger eindeutigen oder selbsterklärenden sozialen Prozess begreift – sind wir zu dem Schluss gekommen, dass die religiöse Individualisierung eher als polythetischer Oberbegriff, d.h. als heuristisches Werkzeug und nicht als klarer semantischer Signifikant einer spezifischen sozialen Dynamik verstanden werden sollte (Fuchs 2015; Fuchs und Rüpke 2015a; Otto 2017). Unsere Arbeit zeigte, dass religiöse Individualisierung, ähnlich wie andere polythetische Kategorien, eine große Anzahl von semantischen Begriffen mit sich bringt, die von verschiedenen Wissenschaftlern bei verschiedenen Gelegenheiten und in Bezug auf unterschiedliche Beobachtungen benutztwerden und so interdisziplinäre oder gar grundlegende interdisziplinäre Diskussionen des Gegenstandes erschweren. Inspiriert, aber auch frustriert von solchen Missverständnissen und durch den Vergleich einer Vielzahl von Fallstudien und Teilprojekten entstand eine begriffliche Matrix, die verschiedene Vorstellungen von religiöser Individualisierung abbildet, die in vier grundlegende Bereiche unterteilt sind. Diese Matrix wird hier in einer gekürzten Version (basierend auf der in Otto 2017, 33–6 veröffentlichten Originalversion) vorgestellt und aktualisiert.

Religiöse Individualisierung in diesem Sinne schließt ein oder begründet:

(A) Begriffe, die sich auf ein erweitertes Spektrum individueller Optionen oder Entscheidungen konzentrieren: Detraditionalisierung; Deinstitutionalisierung; Pluralisierung; Privatisierung (siehe Rüpke 2016a); Individualität kann zu einem normativen Ideal werden, einem „Kult" (Kron und Horáček 2009, 120-4), sie kann Mainstream und Pflicht werden; Streben nach Authentizität oder angeblicher Einzigartigkeit; verstärkte religiöse Selbstbestimmung (Mieth 2017); laufende Rekalibrierungen und Neuinterpretationen der Tradition (die zu vielfältigen Variationen und damit Pluralisierung führen: Renzi im Erscheinen); neuartige religiöse Synkretismen und Eklektizismen, die durch kulturelle Kontakte und Austausch initiiert wurden (siehe Fuchs, Linkenbach und Reinhard 2015); Konventionalisierungen (im Sinne stabiler, formalisierter und anerkannter Konventionen und Praktiken, die einzelne Initiativen in gesellschaftlichen Formen regeln und stabilisieren: siehe Mulder-Bakker in Fuchs et al. 2019); das religiöse Marktmodell (und damit Gewährung von religiöser Toleranz und Wettbewerb: siehe Hermann-Pillath in Fuchs et al. 2019); strategischer Einsatz der Teilung oder mehrerer Personen zur Erweiterung der Möglichkeiten.

(B) Begriffe, die sich auf das Selbst und Kreativität konzentrieren: kreatives, unabhängiges, originelles Denken über Religion; Entwicklung oder Schaffung religiöser Ideen, Konzepte, Entscheidungen, Normen, Praktiken; Reformierung oder Erfindung von Religionen; verstärkte Konzentration auf das „Selbst" oder die individuelle Erlösung; Entwicklung religiöser Selbstreflexion und der Idee einer individuellen religiösen Identität oder „Selbsterkenntnis", die schließlich von Momenten der Befreiung begleitet wird; Bemühen, sich vom religiös „Anderen" zu unterscheiden; Bewusstsein um die individuelle Verantwortung für das eigene Handeln, um moralische Verantwortung oder Bildung eines ausgefeilten Gewissenskonzeptes; Entwicklung eines Begriffs der Menschenwürde, der individuellen Menschenrechte oder der „Vorstellung vom einzigartigen Wert der eigenen Persönlichkeit" (Gordon 2015, 368); kreative Neuinterpretationen religiöser Selbstkonzepte in Krisensituationen wie Verfolgung, Diaspora oder Krieg (siehe Nijhawan zur „prekären Diaspora" in Fuchs et al. 2019); Entwicklung des Begriffs eines porösen oder multidimensionalen Selbst; Erzählungen von außergewöhnlichen, charismatischen oder herausragenden religiösen Figuren oder „Autoren" (siehe Becker, Rüpke 2018); biographische Transformationen des religiöse Selbst und religiöser Identitäten, etwa durch Bekehrung (siehe Suitner in Fuchs et al. 2019).

(C) Begriffe, die sich auf Devianz und Kritik konzentrieren: individuelle Aneignungen *(appropriations)*, die zu Abweichungen von etablierten religiösen oder rituellen Normen führen (oft unter dem Begriff der sogenannten „Volks"- oder „Volksreligion" zusammengefasst); soziale, kulturelle und/oder religiöse Entbettung und der vorübergehende Bruch sozialer Bindungen (Rüpke 2013, 13); intellektuelle „Autonomie" (im Gegensatz zur „Heteronomie") beim Denken über religiöse Angelegenheiten; die private Infragestellung oder gar offene Kritik etablierter religiöser Normen, Konzepte, Personen und/oder Institutionen; die bewusste Entscheidung, sich an religiöser Heterodoxie oder Heteropraxie zu beteiligen; das bewusste Schreiben oder Praktizieren des Verbotenen selbst unter dem Risiko der Verfolgung oder gar Todesgefahr; die offene Rebellion oder Revolte gegen etablierte religiöse Normen oder Institutionen.

(D) Erfahrungsorientierte Begriffe: Formen der Innerlichkeit (Fuchs 2015, 335); Fokussierung auf individuelle, erlebnisorientierte „Spiritualität"; besondere Aufmerksamkeit auf „Intuition" und andere Formen von inspiriertem Wissen; intensive religiöse Erfahrungen, beispielsweise direkte Begegnungen mit dem Göttlichen (auch durch Besessenheit: siehe Malik in Fuchs et al. 2019), oder in Form einer je individuellen Erforschung des inneren Selbst (siehe Parson, ebd.), was zu individualisierten und „abwegigen" Perspektiven auf religiöse Themen führen kann (teilweise inspiriert durch Prophezeiung oder Wahrsagerei); traditionelle erfahrungsbasierte religiöse Wege zur individuellen Befreiung, Erleuchtung oder göttlichen Vereinigung (z.B. in der christlichen Mystik, im monastischen Buddhismus oder in indischen *bhakti*-Traditionen); Ideen und Praktiken, die Selbsttranszendenz fördern.

Diese Matrix stellt keine „Typologie" oder gar eine vollwertige Theorie der religiösen Individualisierung dar. Sie ist vielmehr als eine Zusammenstellung von Bedeutungen, die der religiösen Individualisierung – innerhalb und außerhalb unserer Forschungsgruppe – zugeschrieben werden. Da diese Matrix auf den ersten Blick heterogen erscheint, hat sie sich als nützliches Werkzeug bei der Suche nach Anzeichen von Individualisierung sowie beim Vergleich verschiedener Fälle und Individuen erwiesen. Interpretiert man die Matrix als heuristisches „Netz von Begriffen", so kann sie auf religiöse Daten – ganz oder teilweise – angewandt werden, um zu klären, ob ein bestimmter Fall für die Erforschung der religiösen Individualisierung relevant ist, welche Bereiche und/oder Begriffe durch das Material selbst nahegelegt werden und welche dominant oder marginal sind. Dieses Verfahren, das auch als „polysemantische Analyse" bezeichnet wird (Otto 2017, 51), kann entweder von einzelnen Forschenden oder in Zusammenarbeit durchgeführt werden; die Zusammenarbeit unterschiedlicher Expertisen ermöglicht eine engmaschigere interkulturelle Komparatistik, zum Beispiel durch den Vergleich spezifischer Begriffe über Fallstudien aus verschiedenen religiösen, geografischen oder historischen Kontexten hinweg.

Ob sich diese unterschiedlichen Begriffe und Domänen tatsächlich auf ein kohärentes Feld beziehen (letztlich im Sinne eines „homöostatischen Clusters von Merkmalen": siehe Otto 2017, 39f. und Stausberg und Gardiner 2016) oder vielmehr auf verschiedene Arten von Phänomenen, die aus pragmatischen oder anderen Gründen unter einem Dach zusammengefasst sind, ist zu distkutieren. In gewisser Weise spiegelt die Matrix einen neuen Versuch wider, sich mit dem anhaltenden Problem der sogenannten „kritischen Kategorien" in der Religionswissenschaft auseinanderzusetzen, das heißt mit dem Problem, eine analytische Kategorie in den (post-) modernen Geisteswissenschaften zu definieren, ohne in die Fallen des Dekonstruktivismus oder der konzeptuellen Vagheit und Beliebigkeit zu geraten. Der Vorteil unseres polysemantischen Ansatzes besteht darin, dass erstens alle semantischen Facetten der Kategorie erhalten bleiben und somit in die Analyse einfließen (im Gegensatz zu monothetischen Arbeitsdefinitionen, die in der Regel unerwünschte semantische Begriffe unterdrücken), und zweitens das untersuchte Konzept nie fixiert oder stabil ist, sondern flexibel und offen bleibt für Revisionen, Rekalibrierungen und Erweiterungen im Lichte neuer Erkenntnisse. Trotz ihrer Mehrdeutigkeiten und fließenden Begriffsgrenzen hat sich die Matrix in unserer Arbeit als nützliches heuristisches Werkzeug erwiesen, um verschiedene Muster und Facetten der religiösen Individualisierung sowohl diachron als auch interkulturell zu identifizieren und zu vergleichen. Aus dieser Erfahrung heraus bieten wir sie hier auch für die weitere Arbeit an.

Wir differenzieren den Begriff der Religion für heuristische Zwecke in ähnlicher Weise. Um das Material zu erfassen und zu vergleichen, das religiöse Individualisierungen von der Antike bis zur Gegenwart, von Westeuropa bis in die west-asiatischen und indischen Regionen (mit kurzen Ausflügen in ostasiatische Kontexte) umfassen, von großen christlichen Organisationen bis hin zu Kontexten des religiösen Pluralismus und der diffusen Religiosität, von einzelnen Praktiken über Tempelrituale bis hin zur akademischen Theologie reichen kann, ist es notwendig, ein ausreichend breites Konzept von Religion als Arbeitsinstrument zur Verfügung zu haben. Ausreichend breit bedeutet jedoch nicht, dass so viele oder so wenige wie möglich der durch Religionsdefinitionen vorgegebenen üblichen *Topoi* zusammengeführt werden. Für die Zwecke dieses Projekts wird das Objekt „Religion" mit seinen laufenden Prozessen der individuellen Aneignung auf lokaler und translokaler Ebene als ein sich ständig veränderndes Orientierungssystem („Religion im Entstehen", *religion in the making*) verstanden, das innerhalb des kulturellen Kontextes, auf den es sich bezieht, einen je bestimmten, aber immer prekären Status hat. Wir gehen daher davon aus, dass „Religion":

- sich in ihrem Inhalt auf ein über den Alltag hinausgehendes Prinzip bezieht, das oft in Form von persönlichen Göttern erscheint, aber auch in verschiedenen Stufen des „Übernatürlichen" auftreten kann;
- diese Orientierung durch ein breites Spektrum von Medien kommuniziert, in denen Rituale und spezifische („heilige") Objekte und Geschichten eine herausragende Rolle spielen und in denen verschiedene Formen der Systematisierung („Lehre") auftreten können;
- Handlungsanweisungen in Form von Weltanschauungen und Normen zur Gestaltung des eigenen Lebens gibt; dennoch hängen die Auswirkungen und Folgen dieser Normen und Weltanschauungen immer von ihrer Aneignung (und damit auch Veränderung) durch den Einzelnen ab;

- einen verfestigten institutionellen Charakter in einer Vielzahl von Formen annehmen kann, die von einzelnen charismatischen „Anbietern" und ihren „Kunden" oder „Gläubigen" über „Laienvereinigungen" und andere Mitgliedschaftskonzepte bis hin zu religiösen Eliten reichen können, die Grenzen setzen oder Handlungsspielräume für individuelle Aneignungen eröffnen können; und schließlich,
- in ihrer konkreten Umsetzung einen Ort der intensiven Vernetzung über kulturelle, räumliche und zeitliche Grenzen hinweg darstellt. Der Begriff „Orientierungssystem" vereint dabei unter einer Überschrift Versuche, das Problem der Definition des Verhältnisses zwischen individuellem Handeln und sozialen Gruppierungen zu lösen.

2.3 Auseinandersetzung mit religiöser Individualisierung – Erweiterung der Perspektive

Die Entdeckung und Dokumentation dieser verschiedenen Facetten und Prozesse der religiösen Individualisierung aus anderen Zeiten und Orten eröffnet ein breites, aber vernachlässigtes Feld einer empirischen Forschung, in der dem Vergleich und der Verfolgung der Wechselwirkungen zwischen verschiedenen religiösen und kulturellen Traditionen besonderes Gewicht beigemessen wird. Dieser Ansatz erfordert aber auch, dass wir nach den Auswirkungen dieser Forschung auf die Sozialtheorie und die Religionsgeschichte fragen. Unser Zugriff wurde dabei durch die folgenden fünf Hypothesen bestimmt:

1) *Religiöse Individualisierung* ist nicht bloß ein spezifisches Phänomen des modernen Europas, sondern eine nützliche *heuristische Kategorie* für die Erforschung historischer Prozesse in sehr unterschiedlichen religiösen und kulturellen Kontexten, unabhängig davon, ob sie als Religionen (Islam, Buddhismus), Regionen (West-, Süd- und Ostasien, auch Gebiete in Europa wie die Iberische Halbinsel) und Zeiträume betrachtet werden. Dies erfordert einen kritischen Umgang mit Übersetzung und Terminologie und stimuliert eine Erweiterung und Überarbeitung der Konzepte durch die Einbeziehung anderer Erfahrungen und Erzählungen sowie anderer Formen und Wege der Individualisierung (Fuchs 2015). Die Anwendung der religiösen Individualisierung als Heuristik zur Interpretation verschiedener kultureller und historischer Kontexte (unabhängig davon, ob sie von der obigen Matrix inspiriert ist oder nicht) geht von der polemischen Absicht aus, in einer Weise zu suchen, die sich gegen die üblichen eurozentrischen und Modernitäts-fixierten Narrative richtet. Indem wir an anderen Orten andere Arten oder Facetten der religiösen Individualisierung aufdeckten, konnten wir geläufigere Arten von Individualisierungsprozessen kontextualisieren und sensibler miteinander in Beziehung setzen.

2) Diese Prozesse der religiösen Individualisierung sollten weniger als isolierte Phänomene verstanden werden, denn als Veränderungen von oder Reaktionen auf religiöse Erfahrungen, Traditionen und Diskurse. So bleiben die Kontexte, in denen Individualisierungsprozesse Gestalt annehmen, ebenso wie die Praktiken und Ideen, von denen sich bestimmte Akteure distanzieren oder die sie sich anzueignen versuchen, von Bedeutung. Gleichzeitig eröffnet die Suche nach den Kontexten von Prozessen der religiösen Individualisierung den Weg, zusätzliche (religiöse) Optionen und Traditionen sichtbar werden zu lassen. Entsprechend können auch Konstellationen kultureller Verflechtungen als wichtige Auslöser für individualisierende Entwicklungspfade in Erscheinung treten. Die Kapitel in Fuchs et al. 2019 zeigen, dass die Erforschung der Geschichte der Individualisierung in vielen Fällen eine *Erforschung der Geschichte der Zusammenhänge* ist, eine Forschung, die die verschiedenen Wege untersucht, auf denen kulturelle Grenzen überschritten wurden. Unter „Geschichte der Zusammenhänge" verstehen wir eine Untersuchung im Sinne von *entangled history* oder *histoire croisée*, die die wechselseitigen Wechselwirkungen und Transfers zwischen verschiedenen kulturellen Kontexten, Regionen, Religionen und Bezugssystemen analysiert. Eine solche Untersuchung beinhaltet einen verstärkten Fokus auf grenzüberschreitende Interaktionen und Austauschvorgänge, in denen verschiedene kulturelle und religiöse Traditionen aufeinander treffen und Ideen und Praktiken, die Individualisierungsprozesse stärken oder auslösen, transferiert werden. Neben der Frage, wie bestimmte Institutionen (zum Beispiele Rechte religiöser Gruppen) umgesetzt werden und wie vergessene Praktiken (Einzelbeichte) und Diskurse (Prophetie) wiederentdeckt werden, ist die Frage nach möglichen Wechselwirkungen besonders spannend. Migrationen von Ideen, Praktiken und deren Auswirkungen schufen komplexe Wechselwirkungen mit Folgen für die Religion, lange vor den großen Traditionszerfällen innerhalb und außerhalb Europas im 19. und 20. Jahrhundert. Aus diesem Blickwinkel betrachtet, können die von unserer Forschungsgruppe gewonnenen Erkenntnisse genutzt werden, um die vertikale oder zeitliche Tiefen-Dimension dieser Transformationsprozesse zu verfolgen. In der Gegenwart und für die Zukunft ist die immer stärkere Interaktion und Vernetzung zwischen kulturellen Traditionen und Trends unterschiedlicher Herkunft inmitten intensiver und divergierender Globalisierungsprozesse auffällig.

3) Da viele Prozesse der religiösen Individualisierung eng mit der Bildung von Institutionen, der Traditionalisierung und der Konventionalisierung verbunden sind, müssen die Wechselwirkungen zwischen diesen Prozessen systematisch untersucht werden. Solche Institutionalisierungsprozesse können (müssen aber nicht unbedingt) den paradoxen Effekt haben, dass sie den Individualisierungsgrad wieder einschränken. *Individualisierung und Deindividualisierung* sind in vielen Fällen miteinander verflochten. Der institutionelle Schutz einzelner Praktiken schafft gleichzeitig ein Bewusstsein für die Möglichkeiten von Heteropraxie oder Heterodoxie und die Instrumente, diesen durch Standardisierung entgegenzuwirken. Solche gegenseitigen

Reaktionen können dann die Macht des Dissens, aber auch die entschiedene Ablehnung von Alternativen noch einmal erhöhen. So können auch Prozesse wie die Schaffung von Kanons, Traditionen oder Formen des Fundamentalismus im Licht und im Kontext von Individualisierungsprozessen lohnend revidiert werden (Rüpke 2018c), wenn man die damit verbundenen Mehrdeutigkeiten im Auge behält. Religiöse Individualisierung – sofern sie nicht als Einbahnstraße zur Modernisierung verstanden wird – bezeichnet daher kontingente Prozesse des persönlichen religiösen Experimentierens und der kulturellen oder sozialen Grundlagen solchen Experimentierens und ihrer jeweiligen Artikulationen. Die Grenzüberschreitungen und Rückkopplungsschleifen sind Prozesse, die sowohl den einzelnen Handlungen als auch der Bildung von Gemeinschaften oder der Standardisierung auf institutioneller Ebene innewohnen. Darüber hinaus wird die Deindividualisierung nicht nur den Einzelnen einschränken, sondern kann auch Freiräume für neue Formen der Individualisierung schaffen. Genau aus diesem Grund strukturieren Begriffe wie „Selbst", „Individualismus" oder „religiöse Genies" unsere Arbeit *nicht*. Stattdessen wurden Formulierungen wie „Transcending Selves", „The Dividual Self", „Conventions and Contentions" und „Authorities" als Organisationsprinzipien etwa unseres Abschlussbandes gewählt.

4) Die soeben skizzierten Perspektiven ermöglichen die Entwicklung einer alternativen oder gar komplementären Erzählung zu der oben genannten Meistererzählung der „modernen westlichen Individualisierung". Hier kommt das Konzept der *dividuality* ins Spiel, nicht nur im Hinblick auf die „nicht-westlichen" Perspektiven, sondern auch durch den Vergleich der vielfältigen westlichen und nicht-westlichen Modernitäten. Verschiedene Autoren mit anthropologischem Hintergrund, wie Edward LiPuma (1998; 2001) und Alfred Gell (1999; 2013), aber auch Charles Taylor, der Philosoph des modernen Selbst (Taylor 1989, 2007), haben begonnen, (zwei) verschiedene, nebeneinander existierende Dimensionen der Persönlichkeit herauszuarbeiten, die über Zeiten und Räume, auch im modernen Westen, auffindbar sind. Von diesen ist der eine individueller und der andere „dividueller". Die veränderte Perspektive, das das Konzept der Dividualität, der Teilbarkeit der Person, hat sich gerade in unseren jüngsten Arbeiten niedergeschlagen (Fuchs et al. 2019). Individualität wird einerseits als dynamische Grundlage der menschlichen Sozialität und Individualität und andererseits als gelebte soziale Realität und konkrete soziale Praxis in bestimmten Gesellschaften und sozialen Kontexten verfolgt. Vor allem die sozialhistorische Perspektive trägt dazu bei, verborgene Geschichten der „Dividualisierung" aufzudecken, die mit der Individualisierung als Ergänzung einhergehen und paradoxerweise oft individuelle und sehr profilierte Standpunkte durch Strategien der Dividualisierung ermöglicht haben (etwa in Form von literarischen Praktiken, wie das Spiel mit verschiedenen Pseudonymen, die von einem einzelnen Autor verwendet werden, oder der Gegensatz zwischen Autor und Privatperson).

5) In der Theoriegeschichte hat das Konzept der Individualisierung meist als eurozentrische Strategie der Ausgrenzung gedient. Ebenso hat der Begriff der Religion das

Kollektiv oft in einen absoluten Wert verwandelt, der vor allem den vormodernen oder nicht-westlichen Gebieten zugeschrieben wird. Ausgehend von den Ergebnissen der KFG und durch die Auseinandersetzung mit der Forschungsgeschichte wurde ein *Religionskonzept* entwickelt, das es ermöglicht, die Geschichte der Religionswissenschaft im Kontext historischer Prozesse der Individualisierung und Vernetzung zu rekonstruieren und gleichzeitig die Fallstricke des Eurozentrismus zu vermeiden. Mit diesen theoretischen Überlegungen (Fuchs 2015; Rüpke 2015c; Otto 2017; Albrecht et al. 2018), neuen großformatigen Erzählungen (wie Joas 2012; Rüpke 2016d) und der im vorliegenden Band gesammelten Arbeit streben wir nicht weniger als eine Neudefinition des Religionsbegriffs an, indem wir die vorherrschende Sichtweise, die Religion im Kollektiv, im Institutionellen und im Standardisierten lokalisiert, in Frage stellen.

Diese vorherrschenden Annahmen über Religion haben die Wahl von Forschungsgegenständen beeinflusst, indem sie bestimmt haben, welche Themen analytische Aufmerksamkeit erhalten und welche Gruppierungen, Verhaltensweisen oder Überzeugungen es verdienen, als „Religion" bezeichnet zu werden. Sie haben auch einen entscheidenden Einfluss auf die Darstellung der Religion in anderen Disziplinen ausgeübt. Unsere Hypothese, die auf unseren bisherigen und den in Fuchs et al. 2019 dargelegten Erkenntnissen beruht, ist, dass eine neue Auffassung von Religion erforderlich ist, eine Auffassung, die eine intrinsische und wechselseitige Beziehung zwischen dem Einzelnen und dem Sozialen beinhaltet – vermittelt durch Zusammenhänge und Prozesse der Individualisierung und Deindividualisierung). Mit dem Konzept der religiösen Individualisierung als analytischem Ausgangspunkt einer sowohl Kontingenz- als auch Kontext-sensiblen Untersuchung ist es möglich, die Religionswissenschaft auf eine Perspektive auszurichten, die Prozesse der Individualisierung und Verstrickung systematisch einbezieht. Individuen handeln religiös, wenn sie mit zumindest situationsbedingt verfügbaren nicht-menschlichen Adressaten (unabhängig davon, ob diese innerhalb oder außerhalb dieses Kontextes angesiedelt sind) kommunizieren, denen Agency zuschreiben, und sie machen solche Handlungen sich selbst wie ihrem Umfeld plausibel, indem sie sich routinemäßig und strategisch traditionelle Semantiken aneignen. Folglich beinhaltet religiöses Handeln die Zuschreibung von Agency an Sponsoren solchen Handelns oder an das Publikum, umfasst Prozesse der Gruppenbildung wie Wettbewerb und Distinktion. Religion sollte daher analysiert und beschrieben werden als gelebte und stets neu entstehende Religion, *religion in the making*.

2.4 Implikationen und Perspektiven

Auf der Basis der publizierten Arbeit der KFG schlagen wir die Fortsetzung und Erweiterung der Forschung in fünf speziellen Bereichen vor:

2.4.1 Individualisierung und religiöse (und kulturelle) Verflechtungen

Ausgehend von lokalen Kontexten und spezifischen Formen der religiösen Individualisierung muss den Interaktionen und Vernetzungsprozessen zwischen gleichzeitigen religiösen Traditionsbildungen sowie der Übertragung von Praktiken und Überzeugungen über die Grenzen verschiedener sozialer Gruppen und Lebensweisen hinweg weitere Aufmerksamkeit geschenkt werden. Ob innerhalb oder zwischen kontinentalen oder subkontinentalen Räumen – detaillierte historische und ethnographische Studien müssen mit der Untersuchung von geografisch weitreichenden und langwierigen Transferprozessen kombiniert werden (Mulsow 2018). Was wir auf diesem Forschungsgebiet erwarten können, ist ein tieferes Verständnis der Wechselwirkungen zwischen Mikro- und Makrophänomenen, das von religiösen Ideosynkrasien intellektueller Vermittler, Nonkonformisten und Fernreisender bis hin zu Prozessen der Gruppenbildung reicht, die sich neuer Konzeptualisierungen und Formen individualisierter Praktiken bedienen. Zwei Aspekte verdienen hier besondere Aufmerksamkeit:

a) Kulturvermittler: Für Norbert Elias waren es die wandernden Gelehrten der Renaissance, die die ersten waren, denen Individualisierungsprozesse zugeschrieben werden können (Elias 2001). Im Gegensatz dazu hat unsere gemeinsame Arbeit gezeigt, dass solche Impulse keineswegs nur in Europa oder von der frühen Neuzeit an zu finden sind, sondern auch in alten und mittelalterlichen sowie außereuropäischen Gesellschaften, nicht zuletzt in Südasien. Im Kontext der Religion entstehen solche Prozesse vor allem dann, wenn sie mit Phasen der „Religionifizierung" (so Rüpke 2010) oder der religiösen Pluralisierung zusammenfallen, wie zum Beispiel in der römischen Kaiserzeit und über weite Teile der Religionsgeschichte Indiens. Indien war während des größten Teils seiner Geschichte durch ein hohes Maß an religiöser Vielfalt gekennzeichnet. Religiöse Ideen und religiöse Gruppen konnten nicht anders, als andere religiöse Modi und Konzepte im Blick zu haben, wenn sie ihre eigenen Praktiken und Perspektiven ausarbeiteten. Dies hat zu lebhaftem Austausch, zu Abgrenzungen, zu allen möglichen Kombinationen sowie zu Disputationen und Kämpfen geführt, und es gab viele Konstellationen, in denen soziale Akteure keine besondere Unterscheidung zwischen den verschiedenen religiösen Strängen oder Stammbäumen machten (Fuchs 2018, 141–3; Linkenbach 2016; Parson in Fuchs et al. 2019 und Parson im Erscheinen). Solche Konstellationen erlaubten einen unendlichen Strom neuer individualisierender Formen und Haltungen, die bisher noch nicht vollständig erforscht wurden. Im europäischen Kontext waren die Forderungen nach religiöser Individualisierung in abweichenden intellektuellen oder rituellen (und teilweise clandestinen) Traditionen, wie etwa bestimmten Traditionslinien der westlichen Esoterik oder gelehrter Magie (zu letzterer Otto 2016), immer präsent; aber auch in bestimmten Momenten und insbesondere an bestimmten Orten nahmen sie auf breiterer gesellschaftlicher Ebene zu, wie zum Beispiel in bestimmten Phasen des Mittelalters oder im 16. und 17. Jahrhundert in Mitteleuropa. In solchen Phasen kann man am

Beispiel des vormodernen Europas „pluralisierte Exilanten" (so Mulsow 2010) und entsprechend pluralisierte Migranten untersuchen, die ihre pluralen Identitäten nutzen könnten, um ihre eigenen Optionen für religiöses Handeln zu erweitern. Diese gebildeten Migranten waren sowohl Produkte von Verflechtungen und Verstrickungen als auch Akteure, die solche Verflechtungen durch die Entwicklung religiöser „Synkretismen" und sogar durch kulturelle „Missverständnisse", die Strömungen unterschiedlicher kultureller Hintergründe zusammenführten, weiter vorantrieben (App 2014, 11-23; Mulsow 2018, 22–6). Die Begegnung zwischen dem portugiesischen Jesuiten Monserrate und dem mogulischen Herrscher Akbar ist ein Beispiel für diese facettenreiche Pluralität im Kontext der zivilisationsübergreifenden Verbreitung millennaristischer Ideen im 16. Jahrhundert (Subrahmanyam 2005; s.a. Kouroshi 2015; Fuchs, Linkenbach und Reinhard 2015). Wie andere *marginal (wo)men* trugen sie das Wissen um ihre Herkunftskulturen in andere Regionen und besaßen gleichzeitig eine besondere Empfänglichkeit für fremde Ideen.

Die Untersuchung dieser speziellen Gruppen von *cultural brokers*, die oft Mitglieder von Eliten, aber manchmal auch von Unterklassen (Nath Yogis, Sufis, römisches Militärpersonal) sind, ermöglicht – soweit die Quellen vorhanden sind – die Untersuchung von Fragen, die sonst kaum zu beantworten sind. Ein Ausgangspunkt ist dabei die Frage, wie sich Erfahrungen aus religiösen Kontakten oder Verstrickungen in individuelle Aktivitäten umsetzen lassen, da das subjektive Bewusstsein für weitreichende Strukturen sehr unterschiedliche Formen annehmen kann.

Durch die Differenzierung der verschiedenen Facetten und Phänomene der religiösen Individualisierung und die Annahme, dass de- oder nichttraditionelles Verhalten zwischen Perfektion und Abweichung schwanken kann, ist es möglich, das Spektrum der uns zur Verfügung stehenden deskriptiven Begriffe zu erweitern. Mit einem solchen Ansatz können wir zuverlässiger feststellen, inwieweit Konzepte und Ideen (Mulsow 2017), die außerhalb einer bestimmten Gruppe oder eines bestimmten kulturellen Kontextes entstanden sind, Auswirkungen auf die Individualität in diesem Kontext und auf die spezifische Ausprägung dieser Form von Individualität hatten. Das sehen wir deutlich in Beiträgen unseres Abschlussbandes, die sich mit südasiatischen Persönlichkeiten wie Kabir, Akbar, Dara Shikoh, Banarsidas, Ramakrishna, Keshab Sen und Gandhi (Dey, Fuchs, Höke, Murphy, Parson, Sangari), mit dem europäischen Judentum (Facchini) und Papst Benedikt XIII. befassen, mit Pedro Martinez de Luna (Müller-Schauenburg), oder mit Albert dem Großen (Casteigt) und dem chinesischen buddhistischen Mönch Xuanzang (Deeg). Andere Fragen, die auch in den Vordergrund rücken können, sind Fälle von faktischen Zusammenhängen ("Hybridität"), die jedoch nicht mehr als Phänomene der Differenz wahrgenommen werden (etwa der radikale Pietismus, der über Religionszugehörigkeiten läuft, oder die Fusionen zwischen Sufi, Nath Yogi und *bhakti*-Ideen und -Praktiken im frühneuzeitlichen Punjab); schließlich könnte stereotypes Abwehrverhalten, wie das der religiösen Apologetik, religiöse Zusammenhänge und Hybriditäten tatsächlich verstärkt haben, obwohl man genau dies verhindern wollte. Methodisch sollte eine solche Forschung von gut dokumentierten Fällen von Individuen und ihren speziellen Formen individualisierter religiöser Praktiken ausgehen und dann Konsequenzen, soziale Diffusion und die diskursive Bewertung von „prekären" (Mulsow 2012) Formen religiöser Praxis und Wissen berücksichtigen.

Die Quellen offenbaren somit ein breites Spektrum von Akteuren, von religiös abweichenden Individuen in Mitteleuropa („Beginen", „Visionäre", „Hermetiker", „Spiritisten", Praktizierende der „Gelehrtenmagie" und so weiter), die sich nicht immer der vielfältigen transnationalen Wege bewusst waren, die ihre Quellen bis hin zu religiösen Kleinunternehmern, darunter Missionare (wie die Jesuitenmissionen in China, Japan und Indien; seit dem 19. Jahrhundert auch Missionarinnen), Kaufleute, Militärangehörige und Forscherinnen und Forscher in sehr unterschiedlichen Kulturen genommen hatten. Solche Menschen findet man über Epochen und Kontinente hinweg, angefangen bei „Chaldäern", „Zauberinnen", „Magi", alten Astrologen, unternehmerischen Asketen in Indien und anderswo, prominenten *Bhaktas*, *Gurus* oder *ācāryas*, und Heiligenpoeten, darunter einige aus Gruppen ohne jedes Ansehen und Frauen, im indischen Fall aber auch vielen einfachen Menschen, bis hin zu Zen-Spezialisten wie E. Herrigel und D. T. Suzuki.

b) Strukturelle Austausch- und Vernetzungsbeziehungen über kulturelle und religiöse Grenzen hinweg: Schon der Begriff „Jesuiten" verweist auf die Notwendigkeit, nicht nur Kontakte über einzelne Akteure, sondern auch Netzwerke und vernetzte Systeme sowie deren Entwicklungen zu berücksichtigen. Unter „Vernetzungsregimen" verstehen wir Netzstrukturen, in denen besondere strukturelle und habitualisierte Rahmen – Prinzipien, Regeln, Normen und Erwartungen auf beiden Seiten – langfristige Verbindungen ermöglichen. Beispiele für Vernetzungsregime sind Orden, Missionsgesellschaften und imperiale Formationen (Römisches Reich, Osmanisches Reich, Mogulreich), in denen verschiedene religiöse Strömungen, ethnische Gruppen und auch bestimmte Amtsträger interagieren. Lokale und überregionale Netzwerke werden durch solche Systeme miteinander verbunden und verfestigt; die rechtliche Klassifizierung von Gruppen bietet sowohl Grenzen als auch einen Freiraum für ihre jeweiligen Aktivitäten. Die Stereotypen von Außenstehenden über Gruppen können polemisch abgelehnt oder im Gegenteil als eigene Selbstbeschreibungen der Gruppen angenommen und kanonisiert werden.

Auch die Art der Interaktion und ihre individualisierende Wirkung sollten berücksichtigt werden. Sowohl Verbundprozesse als auch isolierte Entwicklungen sollten in einem geografischen Gebiet von Europa bis Südasien untersucht werden, wobei Westasien und islamische Reiche als Brücke in beide Richtungen dienen. Neben Strategien der Gruppen- und Netzwerkbildung und der gegenseitigen Differenzierung zählen auch individuelle Begegnungen. Zum Beispiel die Reaktionen zeitgenössischer „Beobachterinnen und Beobachter", die diese Fakten in ihrem jeweiligen Textgenre in ihrer Eigenschaft als Philosophinnen, Theologinnen, Juristinnen, Ethnographinnen, Hagiographinnen und Historikerinnen (und ihre männlichen Pendants) konzeptualisieren. Solche Prozesse sind für die Geschichte der Individualisierung von besonderem Interesse, zum einen durch ihr Verhältnis zu Traditionen der Selbstreflexion, die in Philosophie und Ethnographie seit der Antike präsent sind (sowohl in Europa als auch in West-, Süd-, Südost- und Ostasien) und zum anderen durch die von Mobilität geprägte Individualisierung der religiösen Erfahrung sowie durch die Übernahme fremder Traditionen durch den Einzelnen.

2.4.2 Die langfristigen Auswirkungen von Prozessen der religiösen Individualisierung und „De-individualisierung": Gegensätzliche Kräfte und Gegentrends

Wie Georg Simmel bereits vor vielen Jahren betonte, ist die Individualisierung immer von Prozessen der Institutionalisierung und Standardisierung begleitet. Die Individualisierung wurde daher immer von der Möglichkeit der De-individualisierung begleitet. Die wichtigsten Arten der „de-individualisierenden" Gegenkräfte sind Normung, Normalisierung, Kanonisierung, Ritualisierung, die Entwicklung von Dogmen und die Disziplinierung von Devianten – Prozesse, deren Resultate wir als „Konventionen" und „Autoritäten" bezeichnen. Ergänzende Dynamiken der Individualisierung und Deindividualisierung müssen weiter untersucht werden, um Formen und Konfigurationen von Stabilisierungsmechanismen ans Licht zu bringen:

Die Rolle des Rechts: Im spätantiken Mittelmeerraum ist beispielsweise die Entwicklung verschiedener Formen des religiösen Individualismus (von Wahlmitgliedsgruppen bis hin zu Einsiedlern) in einem wechselseitigen Prozess mit selbstverstärkenden Tendenzen zur Normierung verbunden, sei es im Strafrecht des *Codex Theodosianus* oder in talmudischen Texten. In jüngerer Zeit übersetzen sich solche Tendenzen beispielsweise in verfassungsrechtliche Regelungen zur individuellen oder korporativen Religionsfreiheit. In vielen Fällen forderten die Religionsgemeinschaften durch ihr Verhalten und ihre erklärten Verpflichtungen ein angemessenes Verhalten der Gruppenmitglieder. Angesichts der Bedeutung, die insbesondere seit der europäischen Aufklärung der Universalität der Rechtsnormen und der Gleichheit vor dem Gesetz als Individualisierungsmittel (statt der Deindividualisierung) beigemessen wird, erscheinen insbesondere das Recht und das religiöse Recht sowie die entsprechenden rechtsbildenden Institutionen als besonders interessante Forschungsgegenstände.

Konfessionalisierung: Paradoxerweise führt die Zunahme der Anzahl religiöser Optionen und des institutionellen Schutzes pluraler Modelle sowohl zur Verfügbarkeit von Alternativen und Entscheidungszwängen wie zu Uniformität aufzwingenden Prozessen der „Konfessionalisierung". Im Zuge solcher Prozesse können Religionen die Kritik an der Individualisierung bis hin zum Fundamentalismus verstärken. Darüber hinaus ist zu beobachten, dass die Entscheidung eines Einzelnen, bestimmte Optionen nicht auszuüben, oder das Fällen einer Entscheidung mit der Folge der Reduktion weitere Optionen einen notwendigen Teil seines Lebensstils und damit – paradoxerweise – auch seiner Individualisierung darstellt. Diese Form der Deindividualisierung ist also aufs engste mit Prozessen der religiösen Individualisierung verbunden.

Zusammenhänge zwischen räumlich entfernten Regionen: Auch hier erweitert der interkontinentale Ansatz das Spektrum der Fragen, die wir stellen können. Aufgrund der starken Tendenz zur Legitimierung und Standardisierung von Ideen und Institutionen kann das Produkt von Verknüpfungen in bestimmten Fällen zu einer institutionellen Homogenität werden, die die zugrunde liegende Verknüpfung bewusst verbirgt. Diese Form der Übertragung religiöser Strömungen und Ideen beinhaltet Prozesse der *longue durée*, die so weit gehen, dass sie auch die Grenzen einer lokalen Gemeinschaft überschreiten oder gar transkulturell werden. Da viele religiöse Akteure darauf achten zu bestätigen, dass ihr Handeln der Tradition entspricht, muss man sich mit der Bedeutung der Verbindung oder Trennung beziehungsweise der Bedeutung der vermeintlichen Ablehnung befassen. Solche Prozesse können für die Übertragung bestimmter Arten von Inhalten kausal sein, wie etwa bestimmte jüdische Elemente in „christlichen" traditionellen Konzepten (Sabbat, „Israel") oder „westliche" Elemente in orthodoxen Kirchen. Diese makrosoziologischen Fragen zielen darauf ab, zu untersuchen, inwieweit „Nichtkonformität" in einem bestimmten Umfeld (einschließlich der Rahmenbedingungen in bestimmten sozialer Schichten) möglich ist, und die Umstände zu verstehen, unter denen religiöse Individualisierung zu einer Art Standardisierung wird.

Religiöser Pluralismus und der Aufstieg der „Religionen": Die Individualisierung wirft immer die Frage auf, wie Grenzen gesteckt werden. Die „Religionen" selbst sind ein zentraler Bestandteil dieser Entwicklungen. Religionen erscheinen in diesem Zusammenhang als verfestigende Verkörperungen religiöser Praktiken und Überzeugungen – „Synkretismen" im ursprünglichen Sinne des Wortes –, die Gemeinschaft schaffen und Grenzen nach außen ziehen. Religiöser Pluralismus in Gesellschaften kann auch religiöse Praktiken und Überzeugungen von Minderheiten als stabile religiöse Optionen schützen.

2.4.3 Konzeptionelle Entwicklung und konzeptionelle Vergleiche – Selbstbefragung

Wie unsere Arbeit zeigt, sind explizite wie implizite Ideen über Persönlichkeit und Selbst, die in religiösen Kontexten entwickelt wurden, ein wichtiges Forschungsfeld und müssen systematischer erforscht werden (man denke an den Jainismus, an buddhistische und hinduistische Vorstellungen von „moralischem" Handeln, einschließlich der Karma-Theorien). Nicht-westliche Vorstellungen von Selbst oder Selbstbewusstsein sollten einem ausführlicheren Vergleich mit den modernen westlichen Konzepten unterzogen werden, die noch immer den meisten der global verhandelten

Theorien zugrunde liegen. Gefordert ist ein Sinn für die Prozesshaftigkeit und Veränderlichkeit der Selbstkonstitution.

Die Bemühungen, verschiedene philosophische Konzeptualisierungen in den Dialog miteinander zu bringen, wurden in jüngster Zeit mit neuer Kraft vorangetrieben (vgl. Fuchs 2015). Buddhistische, jainistische, vedantistische und westliche phänomenologische und analytische Traditionen wurden bisher gewinnbringend zusammengeführt (siehe unter anderem Siderits et al. 2011; Ganeri 2012; früher bereits Hacker 1978 a, b). Die primäre aktuelle Unterscheidung verläuft zwischen Positionen, die Vorstellungen eines minimalen Selbst verteidigen, und solchen, die für eine narrative Vorstellung von Selbst plädieren. Im Zusammenhang mit der ersten Gruppe von Positionen interessieren sich die laufenden Debatten für die Frage, ob das Selbst als Strom oder als Struktur zu verstehen ist; unter denen, die narrative Selbst-Konzepte unterstützen, besteht ein großer Streit zwischen denen, die behaupten, dass das Selbst narrativ verstärkt werde, und denen, die argumentieren, dass das Selbst narrativ konstituiert sei (Krueger 2011). Bisher haben jedoch komparative Diskussionen über verschiedene Stränge des philosophischen Denkens eine wichtige Frage unberührt gelassen: Inwieweit spiegeln die in einem bestimmten kulturellen und historischen Kontext auftauchenden Selbstkonzeptionen einfach soziale Vorstellungen der Zeit, in der sie entwickelt wurden, wider oder inwieweit konstituieren sie solche Vorstellungen und repräsentieren gesellschaftliche Individualisierungsprozesse? In Übereinstimmung mit Charles Taylors autoritativer Rekonstruktion von Wegen zu® modernen Vorstellung(en) des Selbst im „Westen" (Taylor 1989) schlagen wir weitere Studien vor, um andere Geschichten des „Selbst" zu rekonstruieren.

2.4.4 Die verborgenen Geschichten der Individualität

Anthropologische Debatten über die globale Variabilität der Vorstellungen von Selbst, Person, individueller Identität und Handlungsfähigkeit haben viel von unserer Arbeit inspiriert. Das spiegelt sich auch in unserem Fokus auf die Debatte über „individualistische" Formen der Persönlichkeitsentwicklung wider. Die Untersuchungen zu den vielfältigen Artikulationen des Selbst oder der Person zeigen deutlich, dass ein Verständnis von Selbst und Persönlichkeit in der Vormoderne wie auch in der Neuzeit nicht allein auf Individualität basieren kann, sondern durch eine Perspektive ergänzt werden muss, die auch die dividualistische Dimension erkennen kann. Wir halten drei weitere Forschungslinien für notwendig und vielversprechend.

Erstens schlagen wir vor zu untersuchen, wie die dividualistischen und die individualistischen Aspekte der Person zu verschiedenen Zeiten und an verschiedenen geografischen Orten koexistierten und koexistieren, und ob sich die Beziehungen unterscheiden je nach Lebensbereich (religiös, wirtschaftlich, sozial), in dem sie auftreten. Darüber hinaus ist es wichtig zu fragen, ob die Beziehung zwischen den beiden

Aspekten in einem bestimmten sozialen Umfeld nur eine gelebte Realität und stillschweigendes Wissen ist oder ob sie auch emisch konzeptualisiert und theoretisiert ist. Wenn letzteres der Fall ist, tritt diese Beziehung in diese Epistemologien ein oder fungiert sie gar als leitendes soziales Imaginaire?

Zweitens, inwieweit kann eine Analyse der Beziehung zwischen Individuellem und Dividuellem zu einer Anthropologie oder Lebensphilosophie beitragen und neue Impulse für Überlegungen zu den Bedingtheiten des Lebens liefern? Anthropologen und Philosophen haben die körperliche und soziale Verletzlichkeit des Menschen sowie seine materielle Abhängigkeit hervorgehoben. Trotz ihrer Einzigartigkeit hat ein einzelner Mensch nie die volle Kontrolle über sein Leben, handelt nie ganz nach seinem freien Willen, sondern arbeitet innerhalb der bestehenden Grenzen, die durch die notwendige Verstrickung von Körper und Umwelt (Butler 2006, Jackson 2008, 2013), einschließlich des Nicht-Unmittelbaren oder Transzendentalen, entstehen. Diese Verflechtungen spielen sich stärker ab unter Bedingungen der Prekarisierung und des sozialen Leidens und dort, wo Leben als ungleichwertig angesehen wird (Fassin 2009, 2010, Butler 2006).

Drittens, wie spielt sich das individuell-dividuelle Verhältnis in der größeren Erzählung von Staat, Nation und Bürger ab? Können wir tiefer in das Problem eindringen, mit mehreren Personen und mehreren Zugehörigkeiten zu navigieren (Pfaff-Czarnecka 2013), insbesondere unter den politischen Bedingungen von Flucht, Migration und Vertreibung, die oft durch religiöse Fundamentalismen und Konflikte ausgelöst werden?

2.4.5 Begriffserklärungen in der Religionsgeschichte

Wir schließen diese Reflexion ab, indem wir ein letztes Mal auf die Terminologie zurückkommen. Wie unsere Arbeiten gezeigt haben, enthalten die Begriffe „Individualisierung" und „Religion" eine implizite Agenda, die Europa oft mit säkularisierter Moderne verbindet, und Religion in Europa und anderswo mit Kollektivität. Diese Agenda wird häufig in Form von historischen Narrativen aktiviert, die für Individuen und religiöse Gruppen ein wichtiges Mittel darstellen, um sowohl Inklusion als auch Exklusion zu schaffen und damit ihre Identitäten zu konstruieren (Rüpke 2018b). Die „konfessionellen Prozesse" – bereits in der Zeit vom dritten bis sechsten Jahrhundert im gesamten Mittelmeerraum – führten zu Erzählungen über „Juden", „Heiden", „Christen" und „Manichäer", später über „Katholiken" und „Protestanten". Ebenso haben „kommunalisierende Prozesse" in Indien seit dem 19. Jahrhundert Kategorien von „Hindus", „Muslimen", „Sikhs" und anderen als typische Akteure und Triebkräfte des religiösen Wandels etabliert und gegenübergestellt (für konfessionelle Prozesse in der Antike: Rebillard 2012; Rebillard und Rüpke 2015a; Rebillard 2016; im späteren Europa: von Greyerz et al. 2003; van Lieburg 2006; für Kommunalisierungsprozesse: Pandey 1990; van der Veer 1994; Fuchs und Dalmia 2019). Zugegebenermaßen haben solche Erzählungen eine Perspektive auf vielfältige Interaktionen eröffnet und bilden heute eine Grundlage, von der aus wir über religiöse Pluralität sprechen können. Gleichzeitig haben sie aber auch Gruppengrenzen zementiert und fahren fort, sie buchstäblich festzuschreiben, die Gegenstand heftiger Kontroversen und einer Vielzahl von energischen Bemühungen religiöser Organisationen sind, geschlossene Gruppenidentitäten durchzusetzen. Klagen über Defizite in der religiösen Identität von Gruppenmitgliedern sind historisch weit verbreitet, in späteren Perioden sogar bei religiösen Gruppen mit eng geschlossener Mitgliedschaft. Individualität wird dann mit Abweichung gleichgesetzt. Aber auch Geschichtsschreibung und Erzählung im Allgemeinen bot und bietet seit der Antike eine wichtige Möglichkeit, die religiöse Individualität der beschriebenen Akteure zu betonen oder den religiösen Raum für den Autor selbst zu öffnen (Becker und Rüpke 2018). Erzählungen gelten als ein wichtiges Instrument der Individualisierung.

Und unsere eigenen Narrative? Während der Spätaufklärung (von Reinhart Koselleck als „Sattelzeit" bezeichnet) erfuhren bestimmte Schlüsselbegriffe in der Ideengeschichte („Frömmigkeit", „Kultur", „Zukunft" und sogar „Religion") inmitten der sozialen Umbrüche dieser Zeit eine Bedeutungsänderung. Mit dem Wandel des historischen Zeitverständnisses kam eine erneute Historisierung der Religion und die Entwicklung vielfältiger, individualisierter religiöser Kulte und Bewegungen (Feil 2007). Die Historisierung beeinflusste auch die Art und Weise, wie die intensiven Entwicklungen verschiedenster religiöser Traditionen in der Frühneuzeit und Kolonialzeit dargestellt wurden. Unsere eigene Arbeit ist Teil dieses Prozesses der Geschichte der untereinander verwandten Disziplinen. Die Verwendung von „historischen Perspektiven", die für unsere Forschung charakteristisch sind, um die Beziehung zwischen Religion und Individuum zu verstehen, ist selbst Teil eines Prozesses der Historisierung der Religionen. Das Studium des Christentums als Schlüsselkatalysator der religiösen Individualisierung, wie es von der frühen Forschung vorgeschlagen wurde, musste überschritten werden, um die Rolle anderer religiöser Traditionen als Kontext für Prozesse der religiösen Individualisierung zu erfassen. Gleichzeitig wurde durch diese Untersuchung die Bedeutung von Religion in gesellschaftlichen Prozessen deutlich erkennbar: Über verschiedene historische Epochen und Kulturräume hinweg war Religion ein bevorzugter Ort von Individualisierungsprozessen.

Diese historiographischen Ergebnisse bestätigen das Paradoxon der Religion, das im Mittelpunkt unserer Forschung steht: Religion zeigt sowohl individualisierende als auch deindividualisierende Tendenzen. Gleichzeitig sehen wir weder Religion als die einzige Quelle von Individualisierung noch sehen wir Religion als durchgängige Blockade oder Kampfmittel gegen Individualisierungsprozesse. Die Arbeit, die wir in unserer von der KFG inspirierten Arbeit geleistet haben, zeigt die Fruchtbarkeit des Fokussierens auf Individualisierung. Wie hier jedoch vorgeschlagen, müssen sowohl der Begriff der Religion als auch der Begriff der Individualisierung, insbesondere letzterer, viel sorgfältiger als bisher einer kontinuierlichen begrifflichen Reflexion unterzogen werden. Die Stoßrichtung der hier initiierten Arbeit schlägt weitere Wege für eine Forschung vor, die sich mit zusätzlichen Begriffen und Paradigmen in anderen Regionen und Epochen beschäftigt. Die bisher gewonnenen Erkenntnisse sowie die kritische Auseinandersetzung mit Religion und Individualisierung müssen durch die weitere Ausarbeitung von Konzepten erweitert werden, die sich mit den vielfältigen Phänomenen und historischen Prozessen über die Frühneuzeit und Europa hinaus befassen.

2.5 Literaturnachweise

Albrecht, Janico et al. 2018. 'Religion in the Making: The Lived Ancient Religion Approach', *Religion 48.2*. 1–27.

App, Urs. 2014. The Cult of Emptiness. The Western Discovery of Buddhist Thought and the Invention of Oriental Philosophy. Wil: University Media.

Asad, Talal. 1973. *Anthropology & the colonial encounter*. London: Ithaca Press.

Asad, Talal. 1983. 'Anthropological Conceptions of Religion: Reflections on Geertz', *Man NS 18*. 237–59.

Becker, Eve-Marie and Jörg Rüpke (eds.). 2018. *Autoren in religiösen literarischen Texten der späthellenistischen und der frühkaiserzeitlichen Welt: Zwölf Fallstudien*. Culture, Religion, and Politics in the Greco-Roman World 2. Tübingen: Mohr Siebeck.

Bellah, Robert N. and Hans Joas (eds.). 2012. *The Axial Age and Its Consequences*. Cambridge, MA: Harvard University Press.

Bellingradt, Daniel and Bernd-Christian Otto. 2017. *Magical Manuscripts in Early Modern Europe. The Clandestine Trade in illegal Book Collections*. New Directions in Book History. Basingstoke: Palgrave MacMillan.

Ben-Tov, Asaph, Yaacov Deutsch and Tamar Herzig (eds.). 2013. *Knowledge and religion in early modern Europe: Studies in honor of Michael Heyd*. Brill's studies in intellectual history. Leiden: Brill.

Borgolte, Michael (ed.). 2001. Unaufhebbare Pluralität der Kulturen? Zur Dekonstruktion und Konstruktion des mittelalterlichen Europa. Historische Zeitschrift Beihefte NF 32. Munich: Oldenbourg.

Burckhardt, Jacob. 1860. Die Cultur der Renaissance in Italien: Ein Versuch. Basel: Schweighauser.

Butler, Judith. 2006. Precarious life: The Powers of Mourning and Violence. London, New York: Verso.

Chakravarty, Uma. 1989. 'The world of the Bhaktin in South Indian traditions: The body and beyond', *Manushi* 50–52. 18–29.

Craddock, Elaine. 2007. 'The Anatomy of Devotion: The Life and Poetry of Karaikkal Ammaiyar'. In *Beyond the Circle: Women's Rituals, Women's Lives in Hindu Traditions*, ed. Tracy Pintchman, New York: Oxford University Press. 131–48.

Deuser, Hermann and Saskia Wendel (eds.). 2012. *Dialektik der Freiheit: Religiöse Individualisierung und theologische Dogmatik*. Religion in Philosophy and Theology 63. Tübingen: Mohr Siebeck.

Dumont, Louis. 1965. 'The functional equivalents of the individual in caste society', *Contributions to Indian Sociology 8*. 13–61.

Dumont, Louis. 1975a. *La civilisation indienne et nous*. Paris: Armand Colin.

Dumont, Louis. 1975b. 'On the comparative understanding of non-modern civilizations', *Daedalus* 104. 153–72.

Dumont, Louis. 1980. *Homo Hierarchicus. The Caste System and Its Implications.* Complete Revised English Edition. Chicago: University of Chicago Press.

Dumont, Louis. 1986. *Essays on Individualism. Modern Ideology in Anthropological Perspective.* Chicago: University of Chicago Press.

Eck, Diana L. and Françoise Mallison (eds.). 1991. *Devotion Divine: Bhakti Traditions from the Regions of India. Studies in Honor of Charlotte Vaudeville.* Groningen/Paris: Egbert Forsten/École Française d'Extrême Orient.

Elias, Norbert. 2001. *Die Gesellschaft der Individuen (Gesammelte Schriften).* Frankfurt am Main: Suhrkamp.

Fassin, Didier. 2009. 'Another Politics of Life is Possible', *Theory, Culture & Society 26/5.* 44–60.

Fassin, Didier. 2010. 'Ethics of Survival: A Democratic Approach to the Politics of Life', *Humanity, An International Journal of Human Rights, Humanitarianism and Development 1 (1).* 81–95.

Feil, Ernst. 2007. *Religio 4: Die Geschichte eines neuzeitlichen Grundbegriffs im 18. und frühen 19. Jahrhundert.* Göttingen: Vandenhoeck & Ruprecht.

Fuchs, Martin. 1988. *Theorie und Verfremdung: Max Weber, Louis Dumont und die Analyse der indischen Gesellschaft.* Europäische Hochschulschriften Reihe 20, Philosophie 241. Frankfurt am Main: Lang.

Fuchs, Martin. 2015. 'Processes of Religious Individualization: Stocktaking and Issues for the Future', *Religion 45.3.* 330–43.

Fuchs, Martin. 2017. 'India in comparison: Max Weber's analytical agenda'. In *Max Weber's Economic Ethic of the World Religions. An Analysis,* ed. Thomas Ertman. Cambridge: Cambridge University Press. 223–66.

Fuchs, Martin. 2018. 'Indian Imbroglios: *Bhakti* Neglected; Or: The Missed Opportunities for a New Approach to a Comparative Analysis of Civilizational Diversity'. In *Anthropology and Civilizational Analysis. Eurasian Explorations,* eds. Johann P. Arnason and Chris Hann. Albany, NY: SUNY Press. 121–54.

Fuchs, Martin and Vasudha Dalmia (eds.). 2019. *Religious Interactions in Modern India.* New Delhi: Oxford University Press.

Fuchs, Martin, Antje Linkenbach, Martin Mulsow, Bernd-Christian Otto, Rahul Björn Parson, and Jörg Rüpke (eds.) 2019. *Religious Individualisation: Historical Dimensions and Comparative Perspectives.* Berlin: de Gruyter.

Fuchs, Martin, Antje Linkenbach and Wolfgang Reinhard (eds.). 2015. *Individualisierung durch christliche Mission?* Studien zur außereuropäischen Christentumsgeschichte (Asien, Afrika, Lateinamerika)/Studies in the History of Christianity in the Non-Western World. Wiesbaden: Harrassowitz.

Fuchs, Martin and Jörg Rüpke 2015a. 'Religious Individualization in Historical Perspective', *Religion 45.3.* 323–9.

Fuchs, Martin and Jörg Rüpke. 2015b. ‚Religion: Versuch einer Begriffsbestimmung'. In *Religionen übersetzen: Klischees und Vorurteile im Religionsdiskurs.* Vorlesungen des Interdisziplinären Forums Religion der Universität Erfurt 11, eds. Christoph Bultmann and Antje Linkenbach. Münster: Aschendorff. 17–22.

Ganeri, Jonardon. 2012. *The Self. Naturalism, Consciousness, and the First-Person Stance.* Oxford: Oxford University Press.

Gell, Alfred. 1999. *The Art of Anthropology: Essays and Diagrams* (ed. E. Hirsch). London/New Brunswick, NJ: The Athlone Press.

Gell, Alfred. 2013. *Art and Agency: An Anthropological Theory* (Reprint). Oxford: Clarendon Press.

Gordon, Richard. 2015. 'Religious Competence and Individuality: Three Studies in the Roman Empire', *Religion* 45.3. 367–85.
Greyerz, Kaspar von et al. (eds.). 2003. Interkonfessionalität – Transkonfessionalität – binnenkonfessionelle Pluralität: Neue Forschungen zur Konfessionalisierungsthese. Gütersloh: Gütersloher Verlagshaus.
Hacker, Paul. 1978a. 'Sankara's Conception of Man'. In *Paul Hacker, Kleine Schriften*, ed. Lambert Schmithausen. Wiesbaden: Franz Steiner. 243–51.
Hacker, Paul. 1978b. ‚Die Idee Der Person Im Denken Von Vedanta-Philosophen'. In *Paul Hacker, Kleine Schriften*, ed. Lambert Schmithausen. Wiesbaden: Franz Steiner. 270–92.
Hanegraaff, Wouter. 2012. *Esotericism and the Academy: Rejected Knowledge in Western Culture*. Cambridge: Cambridge University Press.
Hartung, Gerald and Magnus Schlette (eds.). 2012. *Religiosität und intellektuelle Redlichkeit*. Religion und Aufklärung 21. Tübingen: Mohr Siebeck.
Hollstein, Bettina, Matthias Jung and Wolfgang Knöbl (eds.). 2011. Handlung und Erfahrung: Das Erbe von Historismus und Pragmatismus und die Zukunft der Sozialtheorie. Frankfurt am Main: Campus.
Jackson, Michael. 2008. Existential Anthropology: Events, Exigencies and Effects. New York: Berghahn Books.
Jackson, Michael. 2013. The Politics of Storytelling. Variations on a Theme by Hannah Arendt. Copenhagen: Museum Tusculanum.
Joas, Hans. 2012. Die Sakralität der Person: eine neue Genealogie der Menschenrechte. Berlin: Suhrkamp.
Joas, Hans. 2013a. *The Sacredness of the Person A New Genealogy of Human Rights*. Washington: Georgetown University Press.
Joas, Hans. 2013b. Glaube als Option : Zukunftsmöglichkeiten des Christentums. Freiburg im Breisgau: Herder.
Joas, Hans and Jörg Rüpke (eds.). 2013. Bericht über die erste Förderperiode der Kolleg-Forschergruppe 'Religiöse Individualisierung in historischer Perspektive' (2008–2012). Erfurt: Max-Weber-Kolleg.
Kindt, Julia. 2012. *Rethinking Greek Religion*. Cambridge: Cambridge University Press.
Kippele, Flavia. 1998. Was heißt Individualisierung? Die Antworten der soziologischen Klassiker. Opladen: Westdeutscher Verlag.
Kouroshi, Yahya. 2015. ‚Medialität und Modalität der Prophetie: Die Rezeption der Geschichte Christi am Hof der Großmogulherrscher in Indien um 1600 anhand von Schriften des Jesuiten Jeronimo Xavier'. In *Religionen in Bewegung: Interreligiöse Beziehungen im Wandel der Zeit*, eds. Michael Gabel, Jamal Malik and Justyna Okolowicz. Münster: Aschendorff. 123–41.
Kron, Thomas and Martin Horáček (eds.). 2009. *Individualisierung*. Bielefeld: transcript.
Krueger, Joel W. 2011. 'The Who and the How of Experience'. In *Self, No Self? Perspectives from Analytical, Phenomenological, and Indian Traditions*, ed. by Mark Siderits, Evan Thompson and Dan Zahavi. Oxford: Oxford University Press. 27–55.
Lichterman, Paul. 2013. 'Studying Public Religion: Beyond the Beliefs-Driven Actor'. In *Religion on the Edge: De-Centering and Re-Centering the Sociology of Religion*, eds. Courtney Bender et al. Oxford: Oxford University Press. 115–36.
Linkenbach, Antje. 2016. ‚Interreligiosität in Indien in historischer Perspektive'. In *Religionen in Bewegung: Interreligiöse Beziehungen im Wandel der Zeit*, eds. Michael Gabel, Jamal Malik and Justyna Okolowicz. Münster: Aschendorff. 99–122.
LiPuma, Edward. 1998. 'Modernity and Forms of Personhood in Melanesia'. In *Bodies and Persons: Comparative Perspectives from Africa and Melanesia*, eds. M. Lambek, A. Strathern, Cambridge: Cambridge University Press. 53–79.

LiPuma, Edward. 2001. *Encompassing Others: The Magic of Modernity in Melanesia*. Ann Arbor: The University of Michigan Press.

Luckmann, Thomas. 1967. The invisible religion: The problem of religion in modern society. New York, NY: Macmillan.

Luckmann, Thomas. 1991. *Die unsichtbare Religion*. Frankfurt am Main: Suhrkamp.

Madsen, Richard. 2009. 'The Archipelago of Faith: Religious Individualism and Faith Community in America Today', *American Journal of Sociology 114*. 1263–301.

Martin, John Jeffries. 2004. *Myths of Renaissance Individualism*. Basingstoke: Palgrave Macmillan.

Messlin, Dorit. 2012. '„Ich der Einzelne fürs Gemeinsame berufen": Friedrich Schlegels Poetik im Spannungsfeld von Individualisierung und Gemeinsinn'. In *Gemeinschaft in der Literatur – Mythos oder Wirklichkeit? Zur Aktualität poetisch-politischer Itnerventionen*, eds. Margot Brink and Sylvia Pritsch. Würzburg: Königshausen & Neumann. 49–61.

Mieth, Dietmar. 2014. *Meister Eckhart*. Munich: Beck.

Mieth, Diethmar. 2016. ‚Die individuelle Unmittelbarkeit der Mystik als Herausforderung der Religionen? Religiöse und nachreligiöse Perspektiven der Unmittelbarkeit, ausgehend von Meister Eckhart'. In *Meister Eckhart – interreligiös*, Meister-Eckhart-Jahrbuch 10, eds. Christine Büchner, Markus Enders and idem. Stuttgart: Kohlhammer. 9–23.

Mieth, Dietmar (ed.). 2017. *Anfänge der religiösen Selbstbestimmung im Mittelalter*. Theologische Quartalschrift 1. Tübingen: Schwabenverlag.

Mieth, Dietmar and Britta Müller-Schauenburg (eds.). 2012. Mystik, Recht und Freiheit: Religiöse Erfahrung und kirchliche Institutionen im Spätmittelalter. Stuttgart: Kohlhammer.

Mulder-Bakker, Anneke B. et al. 2017. The dedicated spiritual life of Upper Rhine noble women: A study and translation of a fourteenth-century spiritual biography of Gertrude Rickeldey of Ortenberg and Heilke of Staufenberg (Sanctimoniales). Turnhout: Brepols.

Mulsow, Martin. 2010. ‚Exil, Kulturkontakt und Ideenmigration in der Frühen Neuzeit'. In *Diskurse der Frühen Neuzeit*, ed. Herbert Jaumann. Berlin: de Gruyter. 441–464.

Mulsow, Martin. 2012. Prekäres Wissen: Eine andere Ideengeschichte der Frühen Neuzeit. Berlin: Suhrkamp.

Mulsow, Martin. 2015. *Enlightenment underground: Radical Germany, 1680–1720*, trans. H. C. Erik Midelfort. Charlottesville: University of Virginia Press.

Mulsow, Martin. 2017. 'A Reference Theory of Globalized Ideas', *Global Intellectual History 2/1*. 67–87.

Mulsow, Martin. 2018. ‚Elemente einer Globalen Ideengeschichte der Vormoderne', *Historische Zeitschrift 306*. 1–30.

Omvedt, Gail. 2008. Seeking Begumpura: The Social Vision of Anticaste Intellectuals. New Delhi: Navayana.

Otto, Bernd-Christian. 2011. *Magie. Rezeptions- und diskursgeschichtliche Analysen von der Antike bis zur Neuzeit*. Religionsgeschichtliche Versuche und Vorarbeiten 57. Berlin: de Gruyter.

Otto, Bernd-Christian. 2016. 'Historicising „Western learned magic": preliminary remarks', *Aries 16*. 161–240.

Otto, Bernd-Christian. 2017. 'Magic and Religious Individualization: On the construction and deconstruction of analytical categories in the Study of Religion', *Historia Religionum 9*. 29–52.

Otto, Bernd-Christian. 2018a. ‚„Magie im Islam" aus diskursgeschichtlicher Perspektive'. In *Die Geheimnisse der höheren und der niederen Welt: Magie im Islam zwischen Glauben und Wissenschaft*, eds. Sebastian Günther and Dorothee Lauer. Leiden: Brill. 515–46.

Otto, Bernd-Christian. 2018b. ‚Das Motiv der Perfektionierung im gelehrtenmagischen Diskurs des 20. Jahrhunderts'. In *Die Perfektionierung des Menschen? Religiöse und ethische Perspektiven*, eds. Thomas Bahne and Katharina Waldner. Vorlesungen des Interdisziplinären Forums Religion 13. Münster: Aschendorff. 81–105; 305–19.

Otto, Bernd-Christian. 2018c. 'A discourse historical approach towards medieval „learned magic"'. In *The Routledge History Handbook of Medieval Magic*, eds. Sophie Page and Catherine Rider. London: Routledge. 37–47.

Otto, Bernd-Christian, Susanne Rau and Jörg Rüpke (eds.). 2015. *History and religion: Narrating a religious past*. Religionsgeschichtliche Versuche und Vorarbeiten 68. Berlin: de Gruyter.

Pandey, Gyanendra. 1990. *The Construction of Communalism in Colonial North India*. Delhi: Oxford University Press.

Pfaff-Czarnecka, Joanna. 2013. *Multiple Belonging and the Challenges to Biographic Navigation*, Working Paper. Göttingen: Max Planck Institute for the Study of Religious and Ethnic Diversity.

Ram, Kalpana. 2013. Fertile Disorder: Spirit Possession in the Lives of Rural Tamil Women and the Limitations of Modern Subjectivity. Honolulu: University of Hawaii Press.

Rebillard, Éric. 2012. Christians and their many identities in late antiquity, North Africa, 200–450 CE. Ithaca: Cornell University Press.

Rebillard, Éric. 2016. 'Everyday Christianity in Third-Century Carthage', *Religion in the Roman Empire* 2.2. 91–102.

Rebillard, Éric and Jörg Rüpke. 2015a. 'Introduction: Groups, Individuals, and Religious Identity'. In *Group Identity and Religous Individuality in Late Antiquity*. CUA Studies in Early Christianity, eds. idem and idem. Washington, DC: Catholic University of America Press. 3–12.

Rebillard, Éric and Jörg Rüpke (eds.). 2015b. *Group Identity and Religious Individuality in Late Antiquity*. CUA Studies in Early Christianity. Washington, DC: Catholic University of America Press.

Reinhardt, Nicole. 2014a. 'Introduction: War, Conscience, and Counsel in Early Modern Catholic Europe', *Journal of Early Modern History* 18. 435–46.

Reinhardt, Nicole. 2014b. 'Just War, Royal Conscience and the Crisis of Theological Counsel in the Early Seventeenth Century', *Journal of Early Modern History* 18. 495–521.

Reinhardt, Nicole. 2016. Voices of Conscience. Royal Confessors and Political Counsel in Seventeenth-Century Spain and France. Oxford: Oxford University Press.

Renzi, Beatrice. Forthcoming. 'Religious individualisation and the collective self: Revisiting questions of agency through a study of religiosity in Central India'.

Rosenberger, Veit (ed.). 2013. *Divination in the Ancient World: Religious Options and the Individual*. Potsdamer Altertumswissenschaftliche Beiträge 46. Stuttgart: Steiner.

Rüpke, Jörg. 2007. *Religion of the Romans*, trans. Richard Gordon. Cambridge: Polity Press.

Rüpke, Jörg. 2010. 'Hellenistic and Roman Empires and Euro-Mediterranean Religion', *Journal of Religion in Europe* 3. 197–214.

Rüpke, Jörg. 2011. Aberglauben oder Individualität? Religiöse Abweichung im römischen Reich. Tübingen: Mohr Siebeck.

Rüpke, Jörg. 2012a. 'Lived Ancient Religion: Questioning „Cults" and „Polis Religion"', *Mythos* ns 5.2011. 191–204.

Rüpke, Jörg. 2012b. *Religion in Republican Rome: Rationalization and Ritual change*. Philadelphia: University of Pennsylvania Press.

Rüpke, Jörg. 2012c. ‚Religiöse Individualität in der Antike'. In *Der ganze Mensch: Zur Anthropologie der Antike und ihrer europäischen Nachgeschichte*, ed. Bernd Janowski. Berlin: Akademie-Verlag. 199–219.

Rüpke, Jörg. 2012d. ‚Religion und Individuum'. In *Religionswissenschaft*, ed. Michael Stausberg. Berlin: de Gruyter. 241–53.

Rüpke, Jörg. 2013. 'Individualization and Individuation as Concepts for Historical Research'. In *The Individual in the Religions of the Ancient Mediterranean*, ed. idem. Oxford: Oxford University Press. 3–38.

Rüpke, Jörg. 2014. *Religion: Antiquity and its Legacy*. London/New York: Tauris/Oxford University Press.

Rüpke, Jörg. 2015a. *Superstition ou individualité? Déviance religieuse dans l'Empire romain*, trans. Ludivine Beaurin. Bruxelles/Leuven: Latomus/Peeters.

Rüpke, Jörg. 2015b. 'Individual Choices and Individuality in the Archaeology of Ancient Religion'. In *A Companion to the Archaeology of Religion in the Ancient World*, eds. Rubina Raja and idem. Malden: Wiley. 437–50.

Rüpke, Jörg. 2015c. 'Religious Agency, Identity, and Communication: Reflecting on History and Theory of Religion', *Religion 45.3*. 344–66.

Rüpke, Jörg. 2016a. 'Privatization and Individualization'. In *The Oxford Handbook of the Study of Religion*, eds. Steven Engler and Michael Stausberg. Oxford: Oxford University Press.

Rüpke, Jörg. 2016b. *On Roman Religion: Lived Religion and the Individual in Ancient Rome*. Ithaca, NY: Cornell University Press.

Rüpke, Jörg. 2016c. *Religious Deviance in the Roman World: Superstition or Individuality*, trans. David M. B. Richardson, Cambridge: Cambridge University Press.

Rüpke, Jörg. 2016da. *Pantheon: Geschichte der antiken Religionen*. Historische Bibliothek. München: Beck.

Rüpke, Jörg. 2018a. *Pantheon: A New History of Roman Religion*. Princeton: Princeton University Press.

Rüpke, Jörg (ed.). 2018b. *Creating Religion(s) by Historiography* = Archiv für Religionsgeschichte 20. Berlin: de Gruyter. 1–184.

Rüpke, Jörg 2018c. 'Religious agency, sacralisation, and tradition in the ancient city', *Istrazivanya 29* (1), 22–38.

Rüpke, Jörg and Wolfgang Spickermann (eds.). 2012. *Reflections on Religious Individuality: Greco-Roman and Judaeo-Christian Texts and Practices*. Religionsgeschichtliche Versuche und Vorarbeiten 62. Berlin: de Gruyter.

Rüpke, Jörg and Greg Woolf (eds.). 2013. *Religious Dimensions of the Self in the Second Century CE*. Studien und Texte zu Antike und Christentum 76. Tübingen: Mohr Siebeck.

Said, Edward W. 1978. *Orientalism*. New York: Pantheon Books.

Schlette, Magnus. 2013. Die Idee der Selbstverwirklichung: zur Grammatik des modernen Individualismus. Frankfurt am Main: Campus.

Siderits, Mark, Evan Thompson, and Dan Zahavi (eds.). 2011. *Self, No Self? Perspectives from Analytical, Phenomenological, and Indian Traditions*. Oxford: Oxford University Press.

Simmel, Georg. 1968. *Soziologie: Untersuchungen über die Formen der Vergesellschaftung*. Gesammelte Werke 2. Berlin: Duncker & Humblot.

Spiro, Melford E. 1993. 'Is the Western Conception of the Self „Peculiar" within the Context of the World Cultures?', *Ethos 21.2*. 107–53.

Stausberg, Michael. 2009. ‚Renaissancen. Vermittlungsformen des Paganen'. In *Europäische Religionsgeschichte. Ein mehrfacher Pluralismus. Band 1*, eds. Hans G. Kippenberg, Jörg Rüpke, Kocku von Stuckrad. Vandenhoeck & Ruprecht. 695–722.

Stausberg, Michael and Mark Q. Gardiner. 2016. ‚Definition'. In *The Oxford Handbook of the Study of Religion*, eds. Michael Stausberg and Steven Engler. Oxford: Oxford University Press. 9–32.

Stuckrad, Kocku von. 2010. *Locations of Knowledge in Medieval and early modern Europe: Esoteric Discourse and Western Identities*. Leiden: Brill.

Suitner, Riccarda. 2016. *Die philosophischen Totengespräche der Frühaufklärung*. Studien zum achtzehnten Jahrhundert. Hamburg: Felix Meiner.

Suitner, Riccarda. 2019: 'The Good Citizen and the Heterodox Self: Turning to Protestantism and Anabaptism in Sixteenth-Century Venice.' In Martin Fuchs *et al.* (eds.), *Religious Individualisation: Historical Dimensions and Comparative Perspectives*. Berlin: de Gruyter. 459–474.

Subrahmanyam, Sanjay 2005. 'Sixteenth-Century Millenarianism from the Tagus to the Ganges'. In Sanjay Subrahmanyam, *Explorations in Connected History. From the Tagus to the Ganges*. Oxford: Oxford University Press. 102–137.

Taylor, Charles. 1989. *Sources of the Self: The Making of the Modern Identity*. Cambridge, Mass.: Harvard University Press.

Taylor, Charles. 2007. *A Secular Age*. Cambridge, Mass.: Harvard University Press.

van Lieburg, Fred (ed.). 2006. Confessionalism and pietism: Religious reform in early modern Europe. Mainz: von Zabern.

van der Veer, Peter. 1994. *Religious Nationalism. Hindus and Muslims in India*. Berkeley: University of California Press.

Vinzent, Markus. 2011. Christ's Resurrection in Early Christianity and the Making of the New Testament. Farnham: Ashgate.

Vinzent, Markus. 2014. *Marcion and the Dating of the Synoptic Gospels*. Studia patristica suppl. 2. Leuven: Peeters.

Weber, Max. 1958. *The Religion of India. The Sociology of Hinduism and Buddhism*, ed. and trans. by Hans H. Gerth and Don Martindale. Glencoe, IL: Free Press.

Weber, Max. [1921] 1996. *Die Wirtschaftsethik der Weltreligionen – Hinduismus und Buddhismus, Schriften 1915–1920*, ed. by Helwig Schmidt-Glintzer in collaboration with Karl-Heinz Golzio. Tübingen: Mohr Siebeck.

Weber, Max. 2004, 'Prefatory Remarks to the Collected Essays in the Sociology of Religion'. In *The Essential Weber. A Reader*, ed. Sam Whimster. London: Routledge. 101–12.

Weber, Max. 2011. *The Protestant Ethic and the Spirit of Capitalism. The Revised 1920 Edition*, translated and introduced by Stephen Kalberg. New York: Oxford University Press.

Martin Fuchs, Antje Linkenbach, Martin Mulsow,
Bernd-Christian Otto, Rahul Bjørn Parson, Jörg Rüpke

3 Religious individualisation – and de-individualisation

The work of the research group 'Religious individualisation in historical perspective', which began in 2008 at the Max Weber Centre for Advanced Cultural and Social Study at the University of Erfurt (Germany), has finally come to an end. The research group (or 'Kollegforschergruppe' in German) was generously funded by the German Science Foundation ('Deutsche Forschungsgemeinschaft', DFG) and was intellectually embedded in the vibrant and rigorous multi-disciplinary atmosphere and deliberative culture of the Max-Weber-Centre for Advanced Cultural and Social Studies at the University of Erfurt. The research group consisted of more than one hundred members, including the core team at Erfurt, the long-term fellows from all over the world who joined us for one or more years, the many short-term fellows who spent weeks or months with us in Erfurt, and the countless conferences participants who were kind enough to loan us their expertise for a few days at a time.

A final volume drew together important lines of investigation pursued by the research group during the last ten years from 2009 to 2018. Transcending selves, dividual self, conventions and contentions and, finally, authorities were those four of the perspectives that informed and explored processes of 'religious individualisation' our work, which we chose as headlines in Fuchs et al. 2019 and which can here help to summarise our work. Starting from the mechanisms of *religious* individualisation, we have been exploring the agents, characteristics, patterns, and dynamics of such processes. The focus was on human actors, both as they cast themselves and as they were constructed or conceived in different periods and across different regions, and we have examined how they were embedded in social webs and how agency was asserted, ascribed, or denied. The group havs been discussing how agency was appropriated and modified and, at the same time, shaped and produced by its various contexts. We have been looking into economic, political, and legal conditions and constraints, but also into cultural practices and everyday discourses, looking into the expert discourses of philosophers and theologians as well as locally embedded intellectuals and their trans-local counterparts. Throughout, it was important for us to address the spaces and patterns of individualisation and de-individualisation as well as the tensions produced in the course of these developments; power relationships as well as processes of protest and marginalisation; and, finally, the processes of de-, re-, and neo-traditionalisation.

The quantity of individual historical 'outputs' produced by the research group in the ongoing process of applying and reshaping the concept of 'individualisation' cannot be summarised neither here nor in the final volume even in its massive scale of more than fifty chapters. If forced to sum up the findings of the group with regard to the concept of 'individualisation', we might say that the gist of our work is both critical and revisionist. It is 'critical' in that it has been directed against the monopolisation of the term 'individualisation' by advocates of the modernisation theory that dominates everyday discourses. It is 'revisionist' in that we have often argued against a historiographical perspective that assumes all 'premodern' cultures to be essentially collective or collectivist (with the exception of a few 'big individuals'). Thus we will briefly sketch our starting point and then introduce the wider field of research questions tackled, as well as significant results.

3.1 Master narratives of individuality and individualisation in the history of religion

Contrary to received preconceptions and common assumptions, 'individualisation' offers a window not only into present societies but also into those of the past, as well as into the history of religions more generally (see Rüpke 2016a, used in the following). It might be helpful to once again look back at the origins of an established master narrative, the questioning of which was the analytical starting point of the research group. Examining empirical data back in the early 1960s, Thomas Luckmann pointed, in the context of his analysis of contemporary religion, to the growth of American churched religion and conceived of this as indicative of individualisation (Luckmann 1967, an enlarged version in German: Luckmann 1991). However, 'individualisation' is generally regarded in sociological discourse as a distinguishing feature of the modern age far beyond the realm of religion and as one of the dominant characteristics of 'modernity'. Such views usually – although not in Luckmann's case – lose sight of the paradoxical rise of mass culture as a concomitant mode of integration. Even when one takes into account that sociological theories of modernity differ in the degree of importance they assign to individualisation, individualisation nevertheless has a firm place within all classical sociological accounts of modernisation (as demonstrated by Flavia Kippele (1998), Kron and Horáček (2009), and others). Viewed from this perspective, religion appears as negatively related to the process of individualisation. With the exception of a few thinkers, such as Georg Simmel (1968) and later Luckmann himself, religion has been seen as having fallen prey to the processes characterised by individualisation.

From the perspective of 'History of Religion', it is worth taking a closer look at the narratives of historical processes that were thought to form the basis of the equation of individualisation with modernity. These narratives take quite different forms. In his famous study of the Italian Renaissance, Jacob Burckhardt (1860, 141) claimed that interest in subjectivity had risen considerably in the European context from the end of the thirteenth century. Later studies showed how in this period new and ground-breaking philosophical, aesthetic, philological, and religious alternatives, as well as new institutions, helped create spaces of critique and distance towards what became regarded as 'traditional' society and practices (e.g. Martin 2004). With the coming of the Renaissance, for instance, 'paganism' became not only an aesthetic form but also a religious alternative (see Hanegraaff 2012; for another position see Stausberg 2009).

The processes of religious individualisation that can be identified in these contexts drew inspiration from late medieval practices of religious piety. Later, in the early sixteenth century, the Reformation made religion the object of individual choice. While the dominant Aristotelian and Scholastic paradigms had come under scrutiny in the early years of the Renaissance, reformers now questioned again another dominant religious tradition, that is Catholicism. In this case, however, the orthodox interpretations were not only supplanted by intellectual and artistic enterprises but were, instead, openly fought against. Max Weber's (1864–1920) thesis on the post-Reformation Protestant ethic is an especially trenchant example of this trend, with its emphasis on the turn to inner-worldly asceticism, the responsibility of each individual for his/her life, and the 'rationalization of the conduct of life [*Lebensführung*] – now in the world yet still oriented to the supernatural [*Jenseits*] –' as the 'effect of ascetic Protestantism's concept of calling' (Weber [1920] 2011, 157).

The first cracks in the Western self-image of a primarily, if not exclusively, modern Western origin of (religious) individualisation become visible in the context of Weber's comparative analysis of Eurasian 'world-religions' and civilisations. With respect to India in particular, Weber made what he called its 'intellectual' religions, or soteriologies, a repository of the most pronounced and systematically developed attitudes of world-indifference and world-rejection available to the cultivated individual. What Weber denied was that this individualising attitude impacted life in the world and nor did he think that these modes of religiosity reached the majority of lay people or the lower sections of society (what he called the 'masses'). Weber saw developments in India, and in all other non-Western civilisations, as dead-ends. For him, only Protestant individualisation allowed a breakthrough to the practical individualisation of life in the world, the 'ability and disposition of men to adopt certain types of practical rational conduct [*praktisch-rationale Lebensführung*]' (Weber 2004a, 109; see also 1996, 250, 359/ 1958, 325;[1] Fuchs 1988, 138ff., 277ff.; 2017, 227, 254).

Louis Dumont (1911–1998) developed Weber's agenda in another direction and proposed the figure of the Indian world-renouncer (*saṃnyāsin, śramaṇa*) as probably the earliest form of religious individualisation, albeit one that was already highly diversified. The ideal-typical renouncer, who broke loose from social bonds, became conceived of as the 'individual-outside-the-world' (Dumont 1980, 185, 267–86; for

---

[1] N.B: The English translation of Weber [1921] 1996 – Weber 1958 – is not reliable.

this and the following see Fuchs 1988, 417ff., 453–525). Dumont argued that, in societies of the 'traditional, holistic type', individualism could generally only occur in clear opposition to (and thus for him 'outside') society (Dumont 1986, 26); societies composed of self-oriented individualists are a modern phenomenon. However, Dumont also regarded the 'otherworldly individual' as the 'motor' and 'main agent' of historical developments in India, not only in the religious field but also in the political and even economic realms (Dumont 1965, 91; 1975a, 64; 1975b, 163). In addition, Dumont advanced a strong thesis that Indian brands of religious individualisation might have functioned as an important direct or indirect trigger of religious individualisation in the eastern Mediterranean during antiquity. They would, thus, have influenced Greek philosophers and early Christians, and through this the West more broadly (the reference here is to the gymnosophists or 'naked sages', as *yogins* were called in the Mediterranean). The category of the (otherworldly) individual, Dumont speculates, 'might have been invented only once' in history, thus making India appear as the world-historical origin of (religious) individualisation (Dumont 1975b, 168; 1986, 29). In his view, it was only during the history of Western Christianity that the move from 'otherworldly' to 'innerworldly' individualism was made. The decisive steps in this direction were, he thought, taken first by Calvin and then, secondly, by Luther. In a first phase, the religious authorities of the church and the pope were made superior to the more worldly powers of the emperor and nobles; in a second phase, the will of the individual became identified with God's will, allowing the individual will to reign without restriction (1986, ch. 1). Dumont's views remain partial and one-sided due to his strict separation between individualizing religion and 'traditional' society. The society conceived by him as strictly 'holistic' denies especially the lower sections any agency or individual subjecthood. This is due to his depreciation of other sources of religious individualisation in India as well as elsewhere. Regarding the Indian case, Dumont, like Weber before him, especially downplayed the relevance of *bhakti*. Despite this, he acknowledged that *bhakti* makes it possible, in the context of 'traditional' Indian society, that 'one can leave the world *from within*' and that all people 'can become free individuals' (Dumont 1980, 282f., emphasis added; cf. Fuchs 2018).

Even elaborate analyses such as these, which detected forms of individualisation in the pre-modern and non-Christian world, were still imbued with strong traces of Orientalist stereotyping and of the Western tradition of 'othering' the non-Western world (Fuchs 1988). While they might have given an important historical role to the Asian 'other', they continued to consider both the modern religious and secular forms of individualisation to be more authentic and more historically advanced. While scholars such as Weber and Dumont reflect the beginnings of an awareness of the wide array of modes of religious individualisation, the understanding that individualisation is a distinguishing mark of the unique Western modernity nevertheless remained largely prevalent. This led other scholars to insinuate that individuals belonging to certain non-European or pre-modern cultures lack even the possibility of formulating any opposition of interests between 'themselves' and 'society'. Such views have been strongly and successfully criticised by anthropologists (e.g. Spiro 1993). Recent work on the religion of pre-modern and pre-Christian antiquity, usually characterised as 'collective', has produced similar results. The extensive ancient discussions about religious deviance and attempts to legally standardise religious behaviour attest to the perception and acceptance of an extensive religious individuality practiced in many different forms (Rüpke 2011, 2016c).

Meanwhile, the Western world's exceptional self-description as 'modern' has been critically challenged in the global non-West. This critique takes either the form of pointing to the historical inappropriateness of such claims to singularity, or the form of a counter-stereotype, elevating Eastern collectivity over supposed Western individuality (cf. Asad 1973, 1983). Conceptually linking the modern age and religious individuality has obstructed the study of comparable phenomena in earlier periods, so that individuality and individualisation have played only a limited role in the examination of the dynamics of religion in history. The case of *bhakti* in India has already been mentioned. *Bhakti* – a blanket term for a wide range of phenomena and strands – allows individual devotion; various forms of *bhakti* connect with a critique of both social and religious restrictions. For Mediterranean antiquity, some conceptions of *polis* religion or civic religion have claimed that the religious practices of the political elite and their definitions of legitimate religious actions were the only significant sector of religion in their polities. The variety and changeability of individual religious actions and their profound influence on those rituals called 'public' by the elite, have been disregarded, leading to an emphasis on the collective and the fundamentally different character of pre-modern societies (see Rüpke 2007, 5–38; Kindt 2012, 12–35 for criticism). In a similar vein, the stereotype of the religious unity of medieval Europe (see Borgolte 2001 for criticism) is just a stereotypical counterpart of the self-description of modern societies, implied in the secularisation thesis, as pluralistic. In contrast to such stereotypes, recent research focussing on the history of Western esotericism and learned magic has unveiled a variety of individualising impulses and strands that have informed Western cultural and religious history from late antiquity onwards (see von Stuckrad 2010; Otto 2011; Hanegraaff 2012; Otto 2016, 2017; Bellingradt and Otto 2017; Otto 2018a, 2018b, 2018c). The diagnosis of modern individualisation and the ascription of a public and collective character to pre-modern religion are mutually reinforcing frameworks.

However, such observations and criticisms cannot overlook the fact that religious individuality is distributed unevenly even in situations characterised by processes of individualisation which affect or transform religion. In identifying the Renaissance as a turning point, Burckhardt did not deny the existence of dissenters in the preceding centuries. What made a difference in the 14th century, and what constituted individualisation as a process, was not, as the traditional historical narrative has it, the presence of individual intellectuals such as Petrarch (1304–1374). Rather, the defining feature was the increasingly large number of people interested in technical and economic matters, as well as in the subjective dimension of human existence. Mere numbers cannot provide a scale for assessing the scale of this phenomenon. One needs to identify, rather, the contexts, the intellectual, discursive, and practical (e.g. ritual) forms of manifestation, as well as the consequences within a given local society. Even in 'modern' and 'Western' societies, the acclaimed form of 'individuality' might turn out to be very partial, or even only illusionary (see Kron and Horáček 2009, 151f.).

Consideration of contemporary religion in the United States of America shows that 'individuality' is not a straightforward characteristic of 'modern' religion, as is claimed by those who argue for the privatisation of religion. 'Individuality', as a framework of interpretation as well as a form of behaviour, is primarily found among mobile members of the white middle class. For them, 'individuality' as a concept is confirmed by their own commitment and its social consequences (Madsen 2009, 1279–82). This emic concept of 'individuality' is not an arbitrary option within a range of possible privatised sacred *cosmoi*. On the contrary, it is a concept developed by a specific group, albeit one that carries a hegemonic character. It is a way of life that is dominant in the eyes of the entire society, even if the whole society does not participate (*ibid.*). There is an important consequence to this, historically as well as sociologically: certain religious traditions might have or develop practices of self-reflection that are able to foster individuality. The institutionalisation of such tendencies, however, and its conceptualisation *as* 'individuality' is a matter of historical contexts and social location.

3.2 Looking into religious individualisation – in a nutshell

Before going into further detail, a brief overview is necessary. As indicated above, the 'Kolleg-Forschungsgruppe' – or in short KFG, as we used to call it – began by formulating a critique of modernisation theory. The intention was to then bolster this by demonstrating that phenomena that might well be called 'individualisation' were existent *and* important in pre-modern and non-Western cultures. However, in the years since we have pushed forward and beyond this analytical starting point in at least three directions.

a) With regard to modernisation theory, the independence of 'individualisation' from other crucial factors all too easily bundled together as 'modernisation' has been sufficiently demonstrated (e.g. Bellah and Joas 2012; Deuser and Wendel 2012; Joas 2012, 2013a, 2013b). 'Individualisation' has, thus, been set free as an analytical term that is useful beyond Western 'modernity', or even multiple 'modernities' (Fuchs, Linkenbach and Reinhard 2015; Fuchs and Rüpke 2015a; Mieth and Müller-Schauenburg 2012; Mieth 2014; Mieth 2016; Mulder-Bakker et al. 2017;

Otto 2016, 2017, 2018a; Reinhardt 2014a, 2014b, 2016; Rosenberger 2013; Rüpke 2011, 2012b, 2012c, 2012d, 2013, 2014, 2015a, 2015b, 2016c; Rüpke and Spickermann 2012; Suitner 2016; Vinzent 2011; Vinzent 2014).

b) With regard to the history of religion, many phenomena and processes came to the fore when we set aside the lenses of collectivism and looked instead for anything comparable to 'individualisation' (see Otto 2017 and further below). In particular, narratives of ancient and post-ancient ('medieval' or 'early modern', in terms of West-European epochs) circum-Mediterranean, European, and West and South Asian religions have changed and gained new facets far beyond the work of the group itself. Concepts such as 'self' and 'agency', 'subject' and 'personhood', 'individuation' and 'personal identity' have been taken on board, and at the same time critically examined, in our attempt to develop more fine-grained concepts and descriptions (Fuchs 2015; Fuchs and Rüpke 2015b; Hartung and Schlette 2012; Hollstein, Jung and Knöbl 2011; Lichterman 2013; Messlin 2012; Ram 2013; Rebillard and Rüpke 2015b; Rüpke 2012a, 2015c, 2016b; Rüpke and Woolf 2013; Schlette 2013).

c) Finally, reflection has turned towards the very concepts with which we started. How are concepts of 'religion' shaped by the aforementioned master narrative of 'modern Western individualisation' (Otto, Rau and Rüpke 2015; Rüpke 2018b)? How is the normative character of the concept of the 'individual', whenever it is implied that one should *be* an individual, informed by such a narrative? How has the master narrative affected concepts of 'history' and 'change'? The paradoxical consequences of securing individuality by processes of institutionalisation (e.g., through ritualisation, group formation, the establishment of textual canons and traditions, etc.) as well as backlashes into de- or non-individualisation have come into view. Looking more closely at the individual has also brought to light features of personhood that do not easily comply with linear and uni-directional individualisation narratives. Even in (early) modernity, individualisation processes do not lead to a fully 'bounded' self-contained individual. The individual person always exhibits permeability, vulnerability, and openness towards the outer and the social world in various degrees, as s/he is also capable of parting and pluralising him/herself in order to navigate multiple belongings, personalities, and allegiances (see Taylor 2007 and contributions to Part II of Fuchs et al. 2019). Unravelling relational and partible aspects of the self has forced us to postulate a co-constitutive relation between what we call 'dividuality' and individuality. All this has affected our view onto historical and contemporary societies and schools of thought, from a sociological and anthropological perspective (Fuchs 2015; Rüpke 2015c) as well as in terms of intellectual and ritual history (e.g. Mulsow 2012, 2015; Ben-Tov, Deutsch and Herzig 2013; Otto 2016; Bellingradt and Otto 2017; Otto 2018a, 2018b).

Regarding the very concept of 'religious individualisation', and in stark contrast to the master narrative referred to above – which usually conceives religious individualisation as a more or less unambiguous or self-explanatory social process –, we arrived at the conclusion that religious individualisation should rather be understood as a polythetic umbrella term, i.e. as a heuristic tool rather than a clear-cut semantic signifier of specific social dynamics (Fuchs 2015; Fuchs and Rüpke 2015a; Otto 2017). Our work revealed that religious individualisation, similar to other polythetic categories, entails a large number of semantic notions, which are evoked by different scholars on different occasions and with regard to different observations, thus hampering interdisciplinary or even basic inter-subjective understandings of the matter. Inspired but also frustrated by such misunderstandings, and through comparing a large number of case studies and sub-projects, a semantic matrix emerged that maps different notions of religious individualisation, grouped in four basic domains. This matrix is provided here in an abbreviated version (based on the original version published in Otto 2017, 33–6). This prose rendering of the matrix also includes more recent contributions.

Religious individualisation is said to encompass (or to underlie):

(A) Notions focusing on an enhanced range of individual options or choices: de-traditionalisation; de-institutionalisation; pluralisation; privatisation (see Rüpke 2016a); individuality may become a normative ideal, a 'cult' (Kron and Horáček 2009, 120–4), it may become mainstream and compulsory; striving for authenticity or alleged uniqueness; enhanced religious self-determination (Mieth 2017); ongoing recalibrations and reinterpretations of tradition (leading to manifold variations and thus pluralisation: Renzi forthcoming); novel religious syncretisms and eclecticisms initiated through cultural contacts and exchange (see Fuchs, Linkenbach, and Reinhard 2015, and below on 'interconnections'); conventionalisations (in the sense of stable, formalised and recognised conventions and practices, which regulate and stabilise individual initiatives in societal forms: see Mulder-Bakker in Fuchs et al. 2019); the religious market model (thus granting religious tolerance and competition: see Hermann-Pillath in Fuchs et al. 2019); strategic use of dividuality or of multiple personae to enhance one's options.

(B) Notions focusing on self and creativity: creative, independent, original thinking on religion; developing or creating religious ideas, concepts, choices, norms, practices; reforming or inventing religions; enhanced focus on the 'self' or individual salvation; development of religious self-reflection, and of the idea of an individual religious identity or 'selfhood', eventually accompanied by moments of liberation; struggle for distinctiveness from the religious 'other' (see also Murphy in Fuchs et al. 2019); awareness of individual responsibility for one's actions, of moral responsibility, or the formation of a sophisticated concept of conscience; development of the notion of human dignity and/or individual human rights, or of the 'conception of the unique value of one's own personhood' (Gordon 2015,

368); creative re-interpretations of religious self-concepts in the light of crisis, such as repressions, diaspora, or war (see Michael Nijhawan on 'precarious diasporas', ibid.); development of the notion of a permeable or multi-dimensional self; narratives of extraordinary, charismatic, or outstanding religious figures or 'authors' (see Becker, Rüpke 2018); biographic transformations with regard to religious selves and identities, e.g. through conversion (see Suitner in Fuchs et al. 2019).

(C) Notions focusing on deviance and critique: individual appropriations that lead to deviations from established religious or ritual norms (consider material often subsumed under the heading of so-called 'folk' or 'popular' religion); social, cultural, and/or religious 'dis-embeddedness, temporary rupture of social bonds' (Rüpke 2013, 13); intellectual 'autonomy' (as opposed to 'heteronomy') while thinking about religious matters; questioning established religious norms, concepts, persons, and/or institutions; openly criticising established religious norms, concepts, persons, and/or institutions (this notion is stronger than the former, which may be private); consciously choosing to engage in religious heterodoxy or heteropraxy; consciously writing or practicing the forbidden while risking persecution or even death; open rebellion or revolt against established religious norms or institutions.

(D) Notions focusing on experience: forms of inwardness ('Innerlichkeit': Fuchs 2015, 335); focus on individual, experience-based 'spirituality'; special attention given to 'intuition' and other forms of inspired knowledge; intense religious experiences, e.g. direct encounters with the divine (also through possessions: see Malik in Fuchs et al. 2019), or in the form of individually determined exploration of the inner self (see Parson, ibid.), which may lead to individualised off-book perspectives on religious matters (partly inspired by prophecy or divination); traditional experience-based religious paths towards individual liberation, enlightenment, or divine union (for example, in Christian mysticism, monastic Buddhism, or Indian *bhakti* traditions); ideas and practices that foster self-transcendence.

It is crucial to understand that this matrix does not represent a 'typology' or even a full-fledged theory of religious individualisation. We see it, rather, as a discursive collage of meanings that have been ascribed to religious individualisation within and beyond our research group. Heterogenous as this matrix may appear at first sight, it has proven to be a useful tool in scanning for indications of individualisation, as well as in comparing different cases and individuals. If one interprets the matrix as a heuristic 'net of notions', it may be applied to religious data – either partially or in its entirety – in order to elucidate whether a certain case is relevant for the study of religious individualisation, which domains and/or notions are triggered by the material, and which are dominant or marginal. This procedure, which has also been called 'polysemantic analysis' (Otto 2017, 51), may be carried out either individually or as a collaborative endeavour, with the latter approach allowing for a more fine-grained intercultural comparison – for instance, by comparing specific notions across case studies from different religious, geographical, or historical contexts.

Whether these different notions and domains actually refer to a coherent field (ultimately in the sense of a 'homeostatic property cluster': see Otto 2017, 39f., and further Stausberg and Gardiner 2016) or, rather, to various types of phenomena subsumed under the same umbrella for pragmatic or other reasons, is open to debate. In a way, the matrix reflects a new attempt to deal with the persistent problem of so-called 'critical categories' in the Study of Religion, i.e., with the problem of defining an analytical category in the (post-)modern humanities without falling into the traps of either deconstructionism or conceptual vagueness and arbitrariness. The advantage of our polysemantic approach is (1) that all semantic facets of the category are preserved and thus enter the analysis (in contrast to monothetic working definitions which usually suppress undesired semantic notions), and (2) that the concept under scrutiny is never fixed nor stable, but remains flexible and open to revisions, recalibrations, and extensions in the light of new findings. Despite its ambiguities and fluidities, the matrix has turned out to be a useful heuristic tool for identifying and comparing different patterns and facets of religious individualisation both diachronically and cross-culturally.

We differentiate the concept of religion in a similar fashion for heuristical purposes. In order to obtain a grasp of the subject that can comprehend and compare religious individualisations from antiquity to the present, from Western Europe to the west Asian and Indian regions (with brief forays into East Asian contexts), from large-scale Christian organisations to contexts of religious pluralism and diffuse religiosity, from individual practices to temple ritual to academic theology, it is necessary to have a sufficiently broad concept of religion available as a working tool. 'Sufficiently broad' does not, however, mean gathering together as many or as few as possible of the conventional *topoi* provided by definitions of religion. For the purposes of this project, the object 'religion', with its ongoing processes of individual appropriation on the local and trans-local levels, is understood as a permanently changing system of orientation ('religion in the making') that has a peculiar but always precarious status within the cultural context to which it relates. It is also understood that 'religion':
- in its content refers to some principle transcending the everyday that often appears in the form of personal gods but can also appear in different grades of the 'supernatural';
- communicates this orientation through a wide spectrum of media, in which rituals and specific ('holy') objects and stories play a prominent role and in which various forms of systematisation ('doctrine') can appear;
- provides directions for action in the form of both worldviews and norms about how to conduct one's life; nevertheless, the impact and consequences of these norms and worldviews always depends on their appropriation (and hence also modification) by individuals;

- can assume a solidified institutional character in a variety of forms, which may range from individual charismatic 'providers' and their 'clients' or 'students' to 'lay associations' and other membership concepts as well as religious elites which can set limits or open up manoeuvring room for individual appropriations; and finally,
- in its concrete implementation constitutes a place of intensive interconnection across cultural, spatial, and temporal boundaries. The term 'system of orientation' brings together under one heading attempts to answer the problem of defining the relationship between individual action and social groupings.

3.3 Looking into religious individualisation – widening the perspective

Discovering and documenting these different facets and processes of religious individualisation from other times and places opens up a broad but neglected field for empirical research in which special weight is placed on comparing and tracing the interactions between different religious and cultural traditions. Yet this approach also requires that we consider the implications this research has for social theory and the history of religion. Our central focus has been defined by the following five hypotheses:

1) *Religious individualisation* is not just a phenomenon specific to modern Europe but also a useful *heuristic category* for the study of historical processes across very different religious and cultural contexts, whether approached as religions (Islam, Buddhism), regions (Western, Southern and Eastern Asia, also areas in Europe such as the Iberian Peninsula), and time periods. This requires a critical approach to translation and terminology, and stimulates a broadening and rethinking the concepts by including other experiences and narratives and other forms and trajectories of individualisation (Fuchs 2015). The application of religious individualisation as a heuristic to interpret diverse cultural and historical contexts (whether or not inspired by the above matrix) starts from a polemical intention to search in a way that goes against the grain. As we uncovered other types or facets of religious individualisation originating in other places, we were increasingly able to contextualise the kinds of individualising processes that are more or less familiar to us and establish relationships among them with greater sensitivity.

2) These processes of religious individualisation should be understood less as isolated phenomena and more as reworkings of, or reactions to, religious experiences, traditions, and discourses. Thus, the contexts in which processes of individualisation take shape remain highly significant, as do the practices and ideas from which specific actors distance themselves or which they try to revise. At the same time, looking for the contexts of processes of religious individualisation opens the way for additional

(religious) options and traditions to become visible. Meanwhile, constellations of cultural entanglements can also come to the fore as important triggers of individualising strands. The chapters in Fuchs et al. 2019 demonstrate that the investigation of the history of individualisation is, in many cases, an *investigation of the history of interconnections* which examines the different ways in which cultural boundaries have been crossed. By 'history of interconnections' we mean an inquiry in the sense of 'entangled history' or 'histoire croisée', which analyses the reciprocal interactions and transfers between different cultural contexts, regions, religions, and reference systems. Such an inquiry involves an increased focus on 'boundary-crossing' interactions and exchanges, in which diverse cultural and religious traditions encounter one another and ideas and practices that strengthen or trigger individualisation processes are transferred. In addition to the question of how particular institutions (such as rights of religious groups) are implemented and how forgotten practices (individual confession) and discourses ('prophecy') are rediscovered, the question of possible interactions is particularly exciting. Migrations of ideas as well as practices and their effects created complex interactions with consequences for religion long before the great breakdowns of tradition within and outside Europe in the nineteenth and twentieth centuries. Seen from this angle, the insights gathered by our research group can be used to trace the vertical, or 'deep time', dimension of these processes of transformation. In the present and for the future, the ever-increasing interaction and interconnection among cultural strands and trends of diverse origin taking place amid intensified and divergent processes of globalisation is striking.

3) Given that many processes of religious individualisation are closely connected to the formation of institutions, traditionalisation, and conventionalisation, the interactions among these processes must be systematically examined. Such kinds of institutionalisation processes can (but need not necessarily) have the paradoxical effect of again limiting the scope of individualisation. *Individualisation and de-individualisation* are in many cases intertwined. Institutional protection of individual practices creates at one and the same time an awareness of the possibilities for heteropraxy or heterodoxy and the tools to counteract these through standardisation. Such mutual reactions may then again increase the power of dissent, but also the emphatic rejection of alternatives. Hence, even processes such as the creation of canons, traditions, or forms of fundamentalism can be revisited rewardingly in the light and in the context of individualisation processes (Rüpke 2018c), if one keeps an eye on the ambiguities involved in such processes. Religious individualisation – provided it is not taken to mean a one-way path to modernisation – thus designates contingent processes of personal religious exploration and of the cultural or social groundings of such explorations and their respective articulations. The boundary crossings and feedback loops are processes inherent to individual actions as well as to the creation of communities or standardisation at an institutional level. Furthermore, relapses into de-individualisation not only constrain individuals but may also create free spaces for new forms

of individualisation. This is precisely the reason why concepts such as 'self', 'individualism', or 'religious geniuses' do *not* structure our work. Formulations like 'Transcending Selves', 'The Dividual Self', 'Conventions and Contentions', and 'Authorities' have, instead, been chosen as the organising principles of it.

4) The perspectives just outlined allow for the development of an alternative or even complementary narrative to the aforementioned master narrative of 'modern Western individualisation'. Here, the concept of 'dividuality' comes into play, not only with regard to 'non-Western' perspectives but also by comparing the multiple Western and non-Western modernities. Various authors with an anthropological background, such as Edward LiPuma (1998; 2001) and Alfred Gell (1999; 2013), but also Charles Taylor, the philosopher of the modern self (Taylor 1989, 2007), have started to point out (two) different co-existing dimensions of personhood found across time and space, including in the modern West. Of these, one is more individual and the other more dividual. The altered awareness offered by the concept of dividuality is reflected in the outcome of our work (see Fuchs et al. 2019). Dividuality is, on the one hand, traced as the dynamic foundation of human sociality and individuality and, on the other hand, as a lived social reality and concrete social praxis in particular societies and social contexts. The socio-historical perspective in particular helps to reveal concealed histories of dividualisation that run alongside individualisation as its complement, and which have, paradoxically, often facilitated individual and distinct standpoints by means of dividualising strategies (for example, in the form of literary practices, such as the play with different pseudonymous used by a single author, or the opposition between author and private individual).

5) In the history of theory, the concept of individualisation has mostly served as a Eurocentric strategy of exclusion. Likewise, the concept of religion has often turned the collective into an absolute value that has been attributed especially to pre-modern or non-Western areas. Based on the KFG's results, and through confrontation with the history of scholarly research in this area, a *concept of religion* has been developed that makes it possible to reconstruct the study of religion in the context of historical processes of individualisation and interconnectedness while avoiding the pitfalls of Eurocentrism. With these theoretical reflections (Fuchs 2015; Rüpke 2015c; Otto 2017; Albrecht et al. 2018), new large-scale narratives (such as Joas 2012; Rüpke 2018a), and the work collected in the present volume, we are aiming at nothing less than a redefinition of the concept of religion by challenging the prevailing view, which locates religion in the collective, the institutional, and the standardised.

This prevailing supposition about religion has informed scholarly choices, determining what issues receive analytical attention and what groupings, behaviours, or beliefs merit being described as 'religion'. It has also had a decided influence on the portrayal of religion in other disciplines. Our hypothesis, based on our previous findings and those set out in Fuchs et al. 2019, is that a new conception of religion is needed, a conception that envisages an intrinsic and reciprocal relationship between the individual and the social (brokered by interconnections and processes of individualisation and de-individualisation). Taking the concept of religious individualisation as an analytical starting point of an inquiry that is sensitive to both contingency and context, it is possible to reorient the study of religion towards a perspective that systematically acknowledges processes of individualisation and entanglement. Individuals act religiously whenever they communicate with at least situationally available non-human addressees (whether those are situated within or beyond that context) to whom they ascribe agency and render such action plausible by routinely and strategically appropriating traditional semantics. As a consequence, religious action entails adscription of agency to patrons and/or audiences, processes of groupings, as well as competition and distinction. Religion, hence, should be analysed and described as lived religion and religion in the making.

3.4 Implications and perspectives

On the basis of our published work we propose the continuation and expansion of research in five particular fields:

3.4.1 Individualisation and Religious (and Cultural) Entanglements

While starting from local contexts and specific forms of religious individualisation, further attention must be given to interactions and interconnecting processes among concurrent religious strands, as well as to the transmission of practices and beliefs across the boundaries of different social groups and ways of life. Whether within or across continental or subcontinental spaces, detailed historical and ethnographical studies must be combined with the investigation of geographically wide-ranging and longue-durée processes of transferral (Mulsow 2018). What we can expect to emerge from this field of research is a deeper understanding of the reciprocal effects between micro- and macro-phenomena, ranging from religious idiosyncrasies of intellectual intermediaries, nonconformists, and long-distance travellers to processes of group formation that make use of new conceptualisations and forms of individualised practices. Two aspects deserve particular attention here:

a) Cultural brokers: For Norbert Elias, it was migrating scholars of the Renaissance period who were the first people to whom processes of individualisation can be ascribed (Elias 2001). By contrast, our combined work has shown that such impulses are by no means to be found only in Europe or from the early modern period onwards, but also in ancient and medieval as well as non-European societies, not least in South Asia. In the context of religion, such processes emerge above all when they coincide with phases of 'religionification' (thus Rüpke 2010) or religious pluralisation, as for example in the Roman imperial period and over broad stretches of the religious history of India. India was, for most of its history, characterised by a high degree of religious diversity. Religious ideas and religious groups could not but have other religious modes and concepts in view when elaborating their own practices and perspectives. This has led to lively exchanges, to demarcations, to all kinds of combinations, as well as to disputations and struggles, and there were many constellations in which social actors did not make any particular distinction between the various religious strands or pedigrees (Fuchs 2018, 141-3; Linkenbach 2016; Parson in Fuchs et al. 2019 and forthcoming). Such constellations allowed an unending stream of new individualising forms and stances that have not, so far, been exhaustively explored. In the European context, demands for religious individualisation have always been present in deviant intellectual or ritual (and partly underground) traditions, such as certain strands of Western esotericism or learned magic (see on the latter Otto 2016); yet, at certain moments and in particular places, they also increased on a broader societal scale, as, for instance, during certain phases of the Middle Ages or during the sixteenth and seventeenth centuries in Central Europe. In such phases one can investigate such things as, taking pre-modern Europe as an example, 'pluralised Exiles' (thus Mulsow 2010) and correspondingly pluralised migrants, who could use their plural identities to increase their own options for religious action. These learned migrants were both products of interconnections and entanglements and actors who pushed such interconnections further by developing religious 'syncretisms' and even by means of cultural 'misunderstandings', bringing together currents from different cultural backgrounds (App 2014, 11–23; Mulsow 2018, 22–6). The encounter between the Portuguese Jesuit Monserrate and the Moghul ruler Akbar provides an example of this multi-faceted plurality in the context of the cross-civilisational circulation of millenarian ideas in the sixteenth century (Subrahmanyam 2005; see also Kouroshi 2015; Fuchs, Linkenbach and Reinhard 2015). Like other 'marginal men', they carried knowledge of their cultures of origin into other regions and manifest simultaneously a special receptivity to foreign ideas.

The investigation of these special groups of 'cultural brokers', often members of elites but sometimes also of subaltern classes (Nath Yogis, Sufis, Roman military personnel), permits – where the sources are available – the examination of questions that can otherwise scarcely be answered. One starting point here is the question of how experiences of religious contacts or entanglements translate into individual activity, since subjective awareness of large-scale structures can take very diverse forms.

By differentiating the various facets and phenomena of religious individualisation, and by accepting that de- or non-traditionalised behaviour can oscillate between perfection and deviance, it is possible to widen the range of descriptive terms available to us. Taking such an approach allows us to more reliably ascertain the nature and degree to which concepts and ideas (Mulsow 2017) that originated outside a particular group or cultural context had an impact on individuality in that context and on the specific manifestation of that individuality. We see this clearly in the chapters of our final volume dealing with South Asian figures such as Kabir, Akbar, Dara Shikoh, Banarsidas, Ramakrishna, Keshab Sen, and Gandhi (Dey, Fuchs, Höke, Murphy, Parson, Sangari), with European Judaism (Facchini) and Pope Benedict XIII resp. Pedro Martinez de Luna (Müller-Schauenburg), or on Albert the Great (Casteigt) and the Chinese Buddhist Monk Xuanzang (Deeg). Other issues that may also come to the fore consider cases of factual interconnections ('hybridity') that are, however, no longer perceived as phenomena of difference (for example, radical pietism that runs across religious confessions, or the fusions between Sufi, Nath Yogi, and *bhakti* ideas and practices in early modern Punjab); finally, stereotypical defensive behaviour, such as that of religious apologetics, could actually reinforce religious interconnectedness and hybridities despite intending to prevent precisely this. Methodologically, such research should start from well-documented cases of individuals and their special forms of individualised religious practices and then move on to consider consequences, social diffusion, and the discursive evaluation of 'precarious' (Mulsow 2012) forms of religious practice and knowledge.

The sources thus reveal a broad spectrum of agents, from religiously deviant individuals in central Europe ('Beguines', 'visionaries', 'hermeticists', 'spiritualists', practitioners of 'learned magic', etc.) who were not always aware of the diverse transnational paths that their sources had taken, all the way through to religious entrepreneurs, including missionaries (such as the Jesuit missions in China, Japan, and India; since the nineteenth century also female missionaries), merchants, military personnel, and researchers across highly variegated cultures. Such people are found across periods and continents, beginning with 'Chaldeans', 'sorceresses', 'magi', ancient astrologers, entrepreneurial ascetics in India and elsewhere, prominent *bhaktas*, *gurus*, or *ācāryas*, and saint-poets, including some from disrespected groups and women but in the Indian case also many ordinary people, all the way up to Zen specialists such as E. Herrigel and D. T. Suzuki.

b) Structural relationships of exchange and interconnection across cultural and religious boundaries: The very term 'Jesuits' points to the necessity of considering not only contacts through individual actors but also networks and interconnectional regimes, as well as their evolutions. By 'interconnectional regimes', we understand network structures in which particular structural and habitual conditions – principles, rules, norms, and expectations on both sides – make long-term interconnections possible. Examples of interconnectional regimes include orders, missionary societies, and imperial formations (the Roman Empire, the Ottoman Empire, the Mughal Empire) in which various religious strands, ethnic groups, and also particular officeholders interact. Local and cross-regional networks are linked together and solidified by such regimes; the classification of groups in legal terms provides both limits and a free space for their particular activities. Outsiders' stereotypes of groups can be polemically rejected or, on the contrary, adopted and canonised as the groups' own self-descriptions.

Attention should also be given to the types of interaction and their individualising effects. Processes of interconnection as well, as isolated developments, should be investigated across a geographical area ranging from Europe to South Asia, with western Asia and Islamic empires serving as a bridge in both directions. In addition to strategies of group and network formation and reciprocal differentiation, individual encounters also matter. For instance, the reactions of contemporary 'observers' who conceptualise these facts in their in their respective textual genres in their capacities as philosophers, theologians, jurists, ethnographers, hagiographers, and historians. Such processes are of particular interest for the history of individualisation, on the one hand, through their relation to traditions of self-reflection that have been present in philosophy and ethnography ever since antiquity – European as well as West, South, Southeast, and East Asian – and, on the other hand, through the individualisation, shaped by mobility, of religious experience and through the adoption of foreign traditions by individuals.

3.4.2 The Long-Term Effects of Processes of Religious Individualisation and 'De-individualisation': Opposing Forces and Countertrends

As Georg Simmel emphasised many years ago, individualisation is always accompanied by processes of institutionalisation and standardisation. Individualisation was thus always complemented by the potential for de-individualisation. The most important types of 'de-individualising' counterforces might be said to be standardisation, normalisation, canonisation, ritualisation, the development of dogmas, and the disciplining of deviants – processes the outcome of which we address as 'conventions' and 'authorities'. Complementary dynamics of individualisation and de-individualisation need to be further explored in order to bring to light forms and configurations of stabilising mechanisms:

The role of law: In the late-antique Mediterranean, for example, the development of diverse forms of religious individualism (from elective-membership groups to hermits) is associated in a reciprocal process with self-reinforcing tendencies towards normalisation, whether in the criminal law of the *Codex Theodosianus* or in Talmudic texts. In more recent times such tendencies translate, for example, into regulations on individual or corporate religious freedom in constitutional law. In many cases, religious communities demanded, through their conduct and their stated commitments, appropriate behaviour from group members. In light of the significance that has been attributed, especially since the European Enlightenment, to the universality of legal rules and equality before the law as a means of individualisation (instead of de-individualising standardisation), law, and religious law in particular, as well as their corresponding law-forming institutions, appear to be particularly interesting objects of research.

Confessionalisation: Paradoxically, the increase in the number of religious options and in the institutional protection of plural models leads both to the availability of alternatives and choices and to uniformity-imposing processes of 'confessionalisation' (see Suitner 2019). In the wake of such processes, religions may enhance the criticism of individualisation to the point of fundamentalism. In addition, it must be kept in mind that an individual's decision not to exercise certain options, or an individual's making of decisions that have the effect of reducing further options, constitutes a necessary part of one's lifestyle and hence – paradoxically – also of individualisation. This form of de-individualisation is closely related to processes of religious individualisation.

Interconnections between spatially distant regions: Here, too, the interconnectional approach broadens the spectrum of questions we can ask. Due to a strong tendency to legitimise and standardise ideas and institutions, the product of interconnections may in certain cases turn into an institutional homogeneity that intentionally conceals the underlying interconnectedness. This form of transmission of religious currents and ideas involves *longue durée* processes to such an extent that they include transcending the limits of a local community or even becoming transcultural. Given that many religious actors take care to corroborate that their actions accord with tradition, one must look into the significance of interconnection or disconnection, or, as the case may be, the significance of the supposed refusal. Such processes may be causal for the transmission of specific kinds of content, as, for example, certain Jewish elements in 'Christian' traditional concepts (the Sabbath, 'Israel') or 'Western' elements in Orthodox churches. These macro-sociological questions seek to explore the extent to which 'nonconformity' is possible in a particular setting (including the settings of social classes) and to understand the circumstances in which religious individualisation turns into a kind of standardisation.

Religious pluralism and the rise of 'religions': Individualisation always raises the question of how boundaries are demarcated. 'Religions' themselves are a central ingredient in these developments. Religions appear in this context as solidifying nexuses of religious practices and convictions – 'syncretisms' in the original sense of the term – that create community and draw outward boundaries. Religious pluralism in societies can also safeguard religious practices and convictions of minorities as stable religious options.

3.4.3 Conceptual Development and Conceptual Comparisons – Questioning the Self

As our work demonstrates, ideas about personhood and self – explicit as well as implicit – that were developed in religious contexts are an important field of investigation and need to be more systematically explored (consider for instance Jain, Buddhist, and Hindu conceptions of 'moral' action, including *karma* theories). Non-Western ideas of self or selfhood should be subjected to a more elaborate comparison with the modern Western concepts that underlie most of our theories. What is required is a sense for the processuality and mutability of 'self'-constitution.

Efforts to bring different philosophical conceptualisations into dialogue with one another have recently been pursued with new vigour (cf. Fuchs 2015). Buddhist, Jain, Vedantist, and Western phenomenological and analytical traditions have so far been profitably brought together (see among others Siderits et al. 2011; Ganeri 2012; earlier already Hacker 1978 a and b). The primary current distinction is between positions that defend notions of a minimal self and those that plead for a narrative notion of self. In connection with the first group of positions, ongoing debates are interested in the question of whether the self is to be understood as a stream or as a structure; among those who support narrative notions of self, a major dispute is between those who claim that the self is narratively enhanced and those who argue that the self is narratively constituted (Krueger 2011). So far, however, comparative discussions of different strands of philosophical thought have left untouched an important question: to what extent do the conceptualisations of self that emerge in a particular cultural and historical context reflect and/or inform social ideas of the times in which they are developed and stand for societal processes of individualisation. In line with Charles Taylor's authoritative reconstruction of paths towards the modern notion(s) of self in 'the West' (Taylor 1989), we suggest further studies in order to reconstruct other histories of 'self'.

3.4.4 The Concealed Histories of Dividuality

Anthropological debates about the global variability of notions of the self, the person, individual identity, and agency have inspired a lot of our work, which is reflected also in our focus on the debate concerning 'dividualist' modes of personhood. The inquiries into the multiple articulations of the self or the person clearly show that an understanding of Self and personhood in pre-modern as well as in modern times cannot be based solely on individuality but has to be complemented by a perspective which can also detect the dividualist dimension. We consider three lines of further research to be necessary and promising.

Firstly, we propose investigating how the dividualist and the individualist aspects of the person are co-constituted and co-existing at different times and in different geographical places, and whether relationalities differ according to the spheres of life (religious, economic, social) in which they occur. In addition, it is important to ask if the relationship between the two aspects in a particular social setting is just a lived reality and tacit knowledge, or if it is also emically conceptualised and theorised. If the latter is the case, does this relationship enter these epistemologies or does it even functions as a guiding social imaginary?

Secondly, how far can an analysis of the individual-dividual relationship contribute to an anthropology or philosophy of life and provide new inputs for reflections on the conditionalities of life? Anthropologists and philosophers have emphasised the corporeal and social vulnerability of the human being, as well as its material dependency. Despite their singularity, an individual person is never fully in control of her/his life, never acts fully according to his/her free will, but works, rather, within the existing limits produced by the necessary entanglement of body and environment (Butler 2006, Jackson 2008, 2013), including the non-immediate or transcendental. These entanglements play out more forcefully under conditions of precarity and social suffering, and where life is considered of unequal worth (Fassin 2009, 2010, Butler 2006).

Thirdly, how does the individual–dividual relationship play out in the larger narrative of the state, the nation, and the citizen? Can we dive deeper into the problem of navigating multiple personae and multiple belongings (Pfaff-Czarnecka 2013), especially under political conditions of flight, migration, and displacement, often provoked by religious fundamentalisms and conflict?

3.4.5 Conceptual Terminology in the History of Religion

We close this reflection by returning one last time to terminology. As our research shows, the terms 'individualisation' and 'religion' contain an implicit agenda that often associates Europe with secularised modernity, and religion in Europe and elsewhere with collectivity. This agenda is often activated in the form of historical narratives, which constitute an important means for individuals and religious groups to create both inclusion and exclusion and, thus, to construct their identities (Rüpke 2018b). 'Confessionalising processes' – already in the period from the third to the sixth century across the entire Mediterranean region – gave rise to narratives about 'Jews', 'pagans', 'Christians', and 'Manicheans', and later about 'Catholics' and 'Protestants'. Similarly, 'communalising processes' in India since the 19th century have established and juxtaposed categories of 'Hindus', 'Muslims', 'Sikhs' and others as typical actors and driving forces of religious change (for confessionalising processes in antiquity: Rebillard 2012; Rebillard and Rüpke 2015a; Rebillard 2016; in later Europe: von Greyerz et al. 2003; van Lieburg 2006; for communalising processes: Pandey 1990; van der Veer 1994; Fuchs and Dalmia 2019). Admittedly, such narratives opened up a perspective on multifaceted interactions and today form a basis from which we can speak about religious plurality. At the same time, however, they also cemented (and continue to cement) group boundaries that are the objects of fierce controversy and a wide variety of forceful efforts on the part of religious organisations to impose closed group identities. Complaints about deficits in religious identity are historically widespread, in later periods even among religious groups with a closed membership. Individuality is equated with deviance. But historiography and narrative in general has also provided, since antiquity, an important opportunity for emphasising the religious individuality of the actors described or for opening up religious space for the author himself or herself (Becker and Rüpke 2018). Narratives figure as an important tool of individualisation.

And our own narratives? During the late Enlightenment (described as 'the saddle period' by Reinhart Koselleck), certain key concepts in the history of ideas ('piety', 'culture', 'future', and even 'religion') underwent a change in meaning amid the social upheavals of the period. Together with changes in the historical understanding of time came a renewed historicisation of religion and a development of diverse, individualised religious cults and movements (Feil 2007). Historicisation also affected the ways of representing the intensive developments of a wide range of religious traditions during the early modern and colonial periods. Our own work is a part of this trend within the history of the related disciplines. The use of 'historical perspectives', characteristic of our research, to understand the relationship between religion and the individual, is itself part of a process of historicisation of religions. The study of Christianity as a key catalyst of religious individualisation, as proposed by early scholarship, had to be transcended in order to grasp the role of other religious traditions as contexts for processes of religious individualisation. At the same time, this inquiry made the importance of religion in social processes clearly recognisable: across different historical periods and cultural regions, religion has been a privileged locus for individualising processes.

These historiographical findings confirm the paradox of religion that has been at the centre of our research: religion shows both individualising and de-individualising tendencies. At the same time, we neither see religion as the one and only seedbed of individualisation nor do we see religion as consistently discouraging or thwarting processes of individualisation. The work performed in our inspired by the KFG demonstrates the fruitfulness of zooming in on individualisation. As proposed here, however, both the concept of religion and the concept of individualisation, particularly the latter, must be used with much more care than has previously been the case, in the form of ongoing (conceptual) reflection. The trajectory of the work initiated here suggests further avenues for research that maintains an engagement with additional terms and paradigms, in other regions and epochs. The ground gained so far, along with the critical reflection on religion and individualisation, needs to be expanded by the further elaboration of concepts that attend to the manifold phenomena and historical processes beyond the early modern period and Europe.

(For references see the previous chapter)

4 Lived ancient religion: questioning cults and polis religion. A final report

The initial formulation of the Lived Ancient Religion project (Rüpke in Mythos 2011) was about rethinking the conceptualisation of the heterogeneous body of material known as 'the religion of the Roman Empire'. This was grounded in three specific challenges to existing approaches by questioning the implicit assumption that all inhabitants of the Empire were equally religious, the focus upon civic, i.e. collective, institutionalised religious practices, producing a series of sub-categories ('oriental cults', 'votive religion', 'funerary rites') in order to save phenomena, whose relation to civic practice is indeterminate, and the practice of treating 'pagan' religion, Judaism and Christianity as though they had existed historically in separate worlds.

The main thrust of LAR was to resist the easy reification of 'religion' in order to emphasise its ceaseless construction through individual action within the loose parameters provided by traditions and institutions – now summarised as a new introduction to Roman religion (Rüpke, On Roman Religion 2016, pb 2019). That is, to view religion as a precarious practice, whose referents ('gods') and communicative strategies are constantly in need of investment-labour of different kinds in order to maintain their plausibility. The paradigm of 'Lived Ancient Religion' provides the stimulus to integrate 'the' evidence on a new basis, invoke new types of evidence, challenge existing classifications of material, focus on neglected types of religious action. The long-term aim was from the beginning to provide new narratives of religious change in the Roman Empire. A massive account, relating change to religious innovation across social groups and individuals is summarizing these results for a broad audience (Rüpke, Pantheon 2016, Ital. 2017, Engl. 2018).

The expertise of team members in literary sources, in material culture studies, in theoretical approaches to history and religious studies allowed not only for the creation of these new narrative, but also for paradigmatic case studies (e.g. articles by L. Weiss, Female figurines at Karanis: An agentive approach 2015, G. Petridou, Becoming a doctor, becoming a god, Aelius Aristides as informed patient, 2016; J. Rüpke Knowledge of Religion in Valerius Maximus exempla: Roman historiography and Tiberian memory culture 2015). All in all, more than 100 publications and nearly 150 presentations for diverse audiences, civil society included, resulted out of the research project or were shaped by it. With eight programmatic conferences and invited speakers from disciplines outside Mediterranean Antiquity – from Sociology, Asian Studies, Jewish Studies, Religious Studies, South American Archaeology – the LAR-approach was tested and discussed within a large interdisciplinary horizon.

While invoking 'lived religion' as understood in modern contexts (R. Orsi; M. McGuire), LAR was neither restricted to 'everyday religion' nor focused on subjective experience. Instead it flagged four key terms aimed at straddling the dichotomy between subjectivity and communicative action within a general model of the historically contingent establishment of 'religion' as a socially-recognised field of action within the Empire (Rüpke, From Jupiter to Christ 2013): appropriation, agency, situational meaning and mediality (Raja, Rüpke in RRE 2015).

Appropriation denotes the situational adaptation and deployment of practices, institutions, norms and media to suit contingent individual or group needs and aims. 'Agency' underlines the priority of personal engagement, knowledge and skill in the provision of religious services, including public and private performance, teaching, networking (Rüpke in Religion 2015). In speaking of the situational construction of meaning, we assumed that religious meanings were not generated by worldviews but by the complex interplay of interests, beliefs and satisfactions in specific situations (Raja, Weiss in RRE 2015). Finally, the focus on communication required specific concern with the roles of material culture, embodiment and group-styles in the construction of religious experience, in short: mediality.

Thus LAR attended to communicated experience, to space in its various forms, to materiality, to ritual occasions, to imagery. Insofar as communication requires materiality, this demands for a new type of archaeology of religion (Raja, Rüpke, Companion 2015) as well as appropriations from the sociology of space. Inspired by phenomenology (Merleau-Ponty), we deliberately focused upon the role of bodily movements, actions and gestures in conveying culturally-coded meanings and emotions. Lived Ancient Religion emphasises the social context of religious action, and specifically the group-styles in specific cultural contexts, such as the family, neighbourhoods and associations (Lichterman. Raja, Rieger, Rüpke in RRE 2017). From this perspective, public cult appears less as a set of ideals, but more as a scheme of ordering priorities and distinctions whose effect is to outline (rather than define) an imagined community. Religious change starts from domestic and individual practices, not from competition of groups and cities. Among many achievements, objects like terracotta heads in Italy and dolls in Egypt has been demonstrated to be much more and much more ambivalent than 'votives', reports on epiphanies could be interpreted as enlarging agency in the case of Aelius Aristeides, confession-inscriptions as negotiation between women and temple professionals. Entrance tickets to priestly banquets at Palmyra opened a window into the role of religion in the dynamics of an urban society. All in all, LAR opened a window into the day-to-day working as long-term changes of religion that never is a fixed tradition but always religion in the making.

4.1 Achievements

The Lived Ancient Religion project as directed by Jörg Rüpke and co-directed by Rubina Raja, in close collaboration of (successively) five postdocs and four doctoral students addressed the research questions implied in its title by focusing on sub-projects on different social and communicative spaces from the domestic (a) over associations (b), public sanctuaries (c) and literary communication (d). The high risk and challenge of the project was to integrate findings from various geographical locations and periods within the Imperial Age into a new framework. Going beyond the focus on professional religious roles (priests, e) 'religious agency' has been developed as a perspective replacing a narrow focus on the political elite of civic religion and elaborated for religious studies in general.

Thus, the three original objectives have been fully met:

(1) Developing and establishing 'lived religion' as a new framework for the description and analysis of ancient Mediterranean religion and thus integrating the wealth of material and textual evidence of individual and collective behaviour, of popular and intellectual culture and above all material culture. A 'Companion on the Archaeology of Religion in the Ancient World' (published) and a handbook on Imperial Age Religion in a series on religion in the history of mankind ('Religionen der Menschheit', manuscripts in final stage) are making these findings accessible to comparative research on lived religion in other cultures and epochs, and thus re-introduce ancient religion into the research community of global history.

(2) Re-evaluating the history of religion in the Imperial period by developing a new narrative that has shifted the location of religious change in the lived practices of many religious agents instead of postulating a competition of more or less successful ‚religions' as acting units. The PI's massive narrative in 'Pantheon' (German published, trsl. in Engl. and Italian completed) has been included in the most prestigious series of German historical research.

(3) By addressing ancient religion as 'lived religion' LAR has contributed to (again) opening up Classical Studies to a wider field of disciplines by its theoretical contributions, comparative enterprises and a final conference programmatically dedicated to 'Leaving the disciplinary comfort zone' into theological, archaeological and historical disciplines beyond the Mediterranean and the ancient period (establishment of a new journal on Religion in the Roman Empire and multiple publications).

The research team had as constant members over the five years of the funding period the PI and director Jörg Rüpke, the co-director Rubina Raja, and the associated fellow Richard Gordon. Among the PhD- and PostDoc-researchers, the project experienced the normal and also inspiring fluctuation. Members in the first phase of the project were Marlis Arnhold (PostDoc), Christopher Degelmann (doctoral student), Valentino Gasparini (PostDoc, with a gap of employment for conduction research in his own DFG-funded project) and Lara Weiss (PostDoc). Later on Janico Albrecht, Maik Patzelt (doctoral students), Anna-Katharina Rieger, Georgia Petridou and Emiliano Urciuoli (PostDoc researchers) joined the team. Marlis Arnold left the team for an assistant researcher position at the University of Bonn in 2013, Lara Weiss for a permanent position at the Rijksmuseum van Oudeheden, Leiden, in 2015, while Christopher Degelmann got a position as assistant researcher at the Humboldt University Berlin (2015) and Georgia Petridou a permanent position as lecturer at the University Liverpool (2016). As associated doctoral student from the Sanctuary project of Greg Woolf, funded by the Alexander von Humboldt Foundation, Csaba Szabo finished his PhD in the course of the LAR-project.

PhD candidate Janico Albrecht (who submitted his thesis in 2019) is Ancient Historian with research interests in History of Roman Religion; History of the Roman Republic and Early Principate, History of Roman Germany; Latin Epigraphy; Strategies of Integration in Antiquity

Dr. Christopher Degelmann is an Ancient Historian with research interests in Religion and Politics of the Roman Republic and Early Principate, History of Rumors, Postmodern Theory in Historical disciplines

PD Dr. Valentino Gasparini is an Archaeologist with research interests in Isiac cults, Archaeology of the Senses, Pompeian Archaeology, Religious Experience and Embodiment; Visual Culture

Prof. Dr. Richard Gordon Classicist with research interests in Social History of Graeco-Roman Religion and Magic; Latin Epigraphy; Reception of Ancient (Greek and Roman) Religion in post-Enlightenment Germany.

Dr. Maik Patzelt is Ancient Historian with research interests in Performativity and Mediality; Gender and Embodiment; Religious Experience, (Social) Emotions and Feelings; Social Space(s), Milieus and Networks.

Dr. Georgia Petridou is Classicist, with research interests in Greek Literature; History of Greek and Roman Religion; History of Greek and Roman Medicine; Greek Epigraphy; Visual Culture.

Dr. Anna-Katharina Rieger is Archaeologist with research interest in Religion in the Roman Empire, Mediterranean Urbanism; Landscape Archaeology; Archaeology of Arid Regions; Material Culture Studies.

Prof. Dr. Rubina Raja is an Archaeologist and holds a chair at Aarhus University. Her research interests are in the culture and romanisation processes in the Roman Near East, conducting several excavations (recently Jerash); she is an expert on Palmyra.

PhD Candidate Benjamin Sippel (who submitted his thesis in 2019, too) is Ancient Historian with research interests in Social History of Roman Egypt and Lived Religion in Papyrology; Onomastics; Social functions of Sanctuaries; Financial networks in Villages; Religious Identities in Papyrological Sources.

Dr. Dr. Emiliano Rubens Urciuoli is Religious Historian, with research interests in Early Christianity; Social and Religious Identity; Poststructuralist Theory.

Dr. Lara Weiss is Egyptologist, with research interests in Funerary Archaeology; Daily Life Religion; Personal Piety; Cultural Landscapes.

Sub-project a) has been worked upon for Egypt (Lara Weiss, Benjamin Sippel) and domestic space, including the 'dependance' of tombs has been identified as a major place of religious innovation and change (PI). Focusing on lived religious practices rather than organisational forms in association (SP b) has led to the reconstruction of a wealth of practices, experiences and identities across different groups (Valentino Gasparini, Georgia Petridou, Emiliano Rubens Urciuoli, Jörg Rüpke). Shared spaces as offered by sanctuaries (SP c) enabled and enforced peculiar modes of individual appropriation and grouping (Rubina Raja, Anna-Katharina Rieger, Georgia Petridou, Csaba Szabo) rendering the architecturally denoted space a hub of open religious interaction, including the religious rhetoric of magistrates' prayers (Maik Patzelt). Literary communication (SP d), above all historiographic narrative, but also epigraphy and philosophy, has proven to be a centre-piece of lived religion, reflecting as well as transforming the latter (Janico Albrecht, Christopher Degelmann, Richard Gordon, Jörg Rüpke).

Fine-grained description of historical case studies have been combined with the reflection of old or the formulation of new methodologies and been distributed in the form of national and international conferences (eight international ones organized by the project team, ten international workshops, and numerous invited papers and organisation of sessions at national and international conferences and research institutions in Europe and USA), participation in an exposition ('Das Imperium der Götter', Badisches Landesmuseum Karlsruhe) or broadcasting/tv activities (interviews for The Classicist', shaping in consulting tv-series on religious places for 'kika') and last but not least a vast array of publications (27 monographs and edited volumes, many of them in series of high reputation, 36 articles in peer-reviewed journals, 95 chapters in books) in prestigious and highly visibile places.

The Lived Ancient Religion approach provides, we could demonstrate, an effective model for a new approach to the religious history of the long Roman Empire.

Neither a methodology nor a general theory of religion, Lived Ancient Religion is an eclectic approach marked by a specific range of interests. It aims to provide a critical complement to other possible approaches rather than simply replace them, by setting up new questions that, at any rate potentially, can be addressed to any empirical set of evidence throughout the Mediterranean basin. On the other hand, its application to Ancient Mediterranean religions should not be considered an end point: to leave the disciplinary comfort-zone has been part of its vision from the beginning. While taking its cue from inspiring research on contemporary religiosities and applying it to past religious contexts, Lived Ancient Religion aims in turn to contribute to mainstream religious studies. Its ambition is to 'give something back' to the wider scholarship of religion beyond the life-time of the project. By expanding the reach of the notion of 'lived religion' through the intensive historical and archeological examination of ancient religions, Lived Ancient Religion intends to provide points of connectivity for future scientific enterprises.

Returning to antiquity, we view the Lived Ancient Religion perspective as a major contribution to the creation of grand narratives of the religious history of the long Roman Empire. Here we can distinguish between city-based and overall perspectives.

In view of the intensity of its internal religious dynamics, contacts and exchanges, competition and distinction, Rome itself is a prime candidate for an account highlighting agency and mediality. But it also offers itself as a metaphor for all the other cities and regions that were more or less dramatically altered by larger cultural and political processes. Change here is cast as a narrative of agents coming to terms, collectively and individually, with both internal and external factors. Beyond that, the megalopolis of Rome will offer an important focus for a further line of inquiry on 'urban religion' based on the insights of Lived Ancient Religion. Equally one might frame the Empire as a whole as a dynamic field of action, a frame that contains a virtually unlimited range of religious phenomena. Themes here might be the resources available to religious actors, their affordances and potentials, the means through which individuals and groups created, institutionalised (and evaded) traditions, the perennial reality of religious change. The overall aim of these historiographical efforts would be to demonstrate the ability of the Lived Ancient Religion approach to provide an effective framework for synthetic histories of large periods and spaces.

The major effect of introducing the concepts of religious agency, instantiated religion and narrated religion is to reconfigurate current models of past religions. What are usually represented as static ensembles of religious symbols, beliefs and practices are better understood as complex dynamic processes, as interaction between historic agents and their changing material and spatial environments. The most important result of the project hence is that all we observe is religion in a permanent process of change by innumerous agents. It is religion in the making.

The numerous articles published by the project team demonstrates the many details in which we were able to move beyond the state of the art. The monographs, the impact of which can be seen for the time being only by the prestigious places of publishing and the numbers of translations commissioned or finalised, is indicative of how far our overall view of religion of the imperial period has been subjected to a massively new reconstruction and re-narration. 'Lived ancient religion' has not only been added to the methodological options of doing research on ancient religions, but could be accorded a prominent place among those. It has demonstrated that it is possible to include analysis of what was claimed by historical protagonists to be 'public' religion within an approach focusing on individual agents from all social positions.

4.2 Methodology

The initial formulation of the Lived Ancient Religion project was about rethinking the conceptualisation of the heterogeneous body of material that bears upon what is conventionally known as 'the religion of the Roman Empire'. The initiative was grounded in three specific challenges to existing approaches by questioning i) the implicit assumption that all inhabitants of the Empire were equally religious, ii) the focus upon civic, i.e. collective, institutionalised religious practices, producing a series of sub-categories ('oriental cults', 'votive religion', 'funerary rites') in order to save the phenomena, whose relation to civic practice is indeterminate and iii) the practice of treating 'pagan' religion, Judaism and Christianity as though they had existed historically in separate worlds – enshrined in a disciplinary division. The price paid for such commitments has been to uncouple the ancient world from approaches in the global study of religions, to the extent that it no longer has a place in many standard works.

Advances in knowledge and refinements in methodology were achieved in all individual projects and case studies. In three thematic fields – religious agency, dynamics of instantiated religion, and religion narrated / narrating religion – the team members obtained results dealing with textual and archaeological material. Curse tablets, analysed under the perspective of lived religion in antiquity offer a privileged insight into individual appropriations of religious resources (Gordon), while praying practices can best be studied as performances, goes beyond the essentialising grid of interpretations of this communicative act (Patzelt). The continuous interplay of religious and political rituals among the Roman (late republican) elite showed that the triggering of experiences by agents implementing ritual markers from f. e. funerary realm for other fields of discourse (election) could fail or not (Degelmann). From an archaeological point of view the negotiation of status among Palmyrene priest reflected in tokens and their iconographical choices (Raja) as well as the innovative capacities of Isiac cults in stimulating emotions in situational contexts (Gasparini) were cases for the aptness of LAR's methodology.

The creation of religious space, the appropriation, sacralisation and dynamic use of spaces could be narrowed down in a non-reifying way in a number of case studies. Looking at the spatial and material infrastructure in the Roman house (lamps, altars, wall painting) their character as inviting inhabitants and guests to imaginations, and triggering religious practices comes to the fore (PI). Practicing religion at Roman Karanis (Egypt) proves rather a phenomenon among elite families, transgressing the (inappropriate) distinction of public and domestic (Weiss). Situational aspects according to the agents grouping in shared sacred spaces are the crucial element for doing religion. The various motivations, interaction on various levels (personal, visual, spatial, temporal) change religious practices constantly (Rieger).

Narratives as a source of establishment of and orientation for groups and individuals are a field of permanent modification and (re-)production of position about religious knowledge (PI). A textualisation of religion in the second century CE is the resulst, which is reflected in works like the Hieroi Logoi of Aelius Aristides (Petridou). He as orator, author and person embodies in his texts his way of being religious. The various strategies of striving for legitimation and authority by operationalising religious practices among the Roman elite, either assumed exemplary or transgressive show the malleability of religion (Albrecht). Religious coding and ascriptions of meaning to objects or texts, is the field of discourses in the early Christian literature: Religious identities, 'right' or 'wrong' (religious) behavior depend not only on religious occupations, but on practical motivations, and situational-framings (Urciuoli).

4.3 Interdisciplinary and crossdisciplinary developments

Over the five years of the funding period a series of international conferences and workshops were at the core of the culture of interdisciplinary discourse LAR-project: From the opening conference 2013 and four more thematic large conference to workshops with scholars like Ann Taves (Religious Studies, Santa Barbara), Harriet Flower (Classics, Princeton), or Uffe Schjoedt (Religious and Cognitive Studies, Aarhus) and postgraduate courses on discourse analysis or agency of materiality, the contact to other fields of research and to neighbouring disciplines like Egyptology, Near Eastern Studies, Jewish and Christian Studies, Patristics, Ancient History, Classical Archaeology), but also within Sociology, Political, Indian and Chinese Studies, Theology and Geography were enhanced. The cross-disciplinary work was developed and in stays of guests (Paul Lichterman, Ann Taves, Nicola Denzey Lewis, Günther Schörner, Richard Neudecker) or guest lectures (Peter van Nueffelen, Annette Haug, Julietta Steinhauer). All in all, eight international conferences (Rome 2012, Erfurt 2013, Eisenach 2013, Ettersburg 2014, Copenhagen 2014, Erfurt 2015, Erfurt 2016, Eisenach 2017) and ten international workshops (on Isis 2013, on Medicine 2014, on LAR and Urban Religion with Princeton I 2015 and II 2016, on Experience 2016, on Materiality 2016, on Epochalisation 2016, on Religion of the Roman Empire, London 2016, on Lived Ancient Religion at Aarhus 2017, and on Magic at Erfurt in 2017) have been organised and published in adequate formats, from special issues through edited volumes to peer-reviewed open access repositories.

Inter- and cross-disciplinary developments gained momentum for example in the continuous exchange with the Kolleg-Forschergruppe based at the Max Weber Centre on 'Religious Individualisation in Historical Perspective' offered many opportunities to sharpen the aspects of individual appropriation and intentions in 'doing religion', and in the historical depth of practices.

The institutionalised and personal contact with the center of excellence 'Urbnet' at Aarhus University, directed by Rubina Raja, fostered the engagement with archaeological questions in the paradigm of 'Lived Ancient Religion', and lead to workshops on diachronic as well as methodological aspects (on epochalisation April 2016, on network analysis January 2017). A summer school organized by the *Studienstiftung des Deutschen Volkes*, which focused on the Augustan period as an exemplary field for religious change (August 2016) and doctoral courses at Aarhus (2016 and 2017), all held by PI and co-director, opened the approach of Lived Ancient Religion to young scholars from various fields of studies.

A research program on 'the role of cities in the history of religion', initiated by the Jörg Rüpke has its roots in the progress and results of the Lived Ancient Religion project. It focuses on the relationship of developments in religious practices in cities and the development of cities being confronted with and building on actors using religious practices in different phases of the history of religion. It is based at the Max Weber Centre, Erfurt, and has been integrated into a new 'Kolleg-Forschungsgruppe' on Religion and urbanity: Reciprocal formations (co-directed by Susanne Rau and Jörg Rüpke).

Ritual practices as means of individuals and groups to communicate, interact or react to the material, social but also transcendent world, and the role of such socio-religious practices in establishing or changing religious meaning found a new institutional setting in a joint Graduate School of the Max-Weber-Centre and the University of Graz, 'Resonant Self-World Relations in Ancient and Modern Socio-Religious Practices', with Jörg Rüpke being the spokesperson on the side of the MWK. The transdisciplinary collaboration of ancient studies with sociology and theology is at the heart of this research school, thus implementing results from the Lived Ancient Religion project in new fields of research.

4.4 Knowledge transfer

Primary audience to this type of basic research was the scientific community. Several times invitation of speakers to conferences have been combined with a call for papers or posters for young scholars, either doctoral students or early postdoc researchers. A number of research groups working on the ancient world have taken up the lived religion approach in case studies or conferences.

Additionally teachers of classical languages have been addressed in talks or a publication (PI in 'Latein und Griechisch in Berlin und Brandenburg').

Rubina Raja has organised an on-line exhibition at the Getty Research Institute (2016) and a live-exhibition on 'Harald Ingholt and Palmyra' 2015 at the Museum of Ancient Art at Aarhus University.

The favourable reception and taking up by other research groups has led to several ongoing cooperation and joint events; broader dissemination is assured by articles beyond academic journals and a TV series ('Schnitzeljagd', last 'Mit Christus um die Welt', previously 'Türkei', 'Griechenland', 'Holy Land' (also translated into English) by the German public children's channel 'kika') based on the lived religion approach.

4.5 Enhancing the immediate research environment

Over the course of LAR project the immediate host institution, the Max-Weber- Centre for Advanced Cultural and Social Research of the University of Erfurt, has developed beyond its international renown as an institute for cutting edge social theory and sociological research and history of religion into a hub for the study of ancient religion and its embedding into comparative research on religion. Beyond visiting experts in the framework of the ERC project a number of junior and senior researchers in the field of ancient religion (including early Christianity and ancient Judaism) have applied for and been accepted within the framework of the COFUND-Max Weber Fellowships. Based on the insights of the DFG-financed so-called Kolleg-Forschergruppe 'Religious Individualisation in Historical Perspective' the LAR team has stayed in close contacts with this group and influenced its research agenda. The results and visibility of both groups was vital in the Max-Weber-Centre's success in gaining a major grant from the national programme of Research Buildings, giving space for research on comparative historical and theoretical research on relationships with Self, social and material as well as overarching religiously conceptualised environments ('attractivity, indifference, and repulsion').

4.6 Further impact

The establishment and quick success of the new journal 'Religion in the Roman Empire' with its programmatic inclusion of a broad range of disciplines (bringing together anthropology, archaeology and literary studies) from fields that are treated as differentiated disciplines in universities (History of Religion/Storia delle religioni, Early Christianity, Ancient Judaism) held together by the Lived Ancient Religion paradigm has created a platform for an ongoing engagement with the topics and methods of the project. The composition of the editorial board as well as the contributors in published and current issues demonstrates the impact in the field. Together with colleagues from St Andrews and King's College, Jörg Rüpke has been the initiator of the journal and is now leading editor; team members Rubina Raja is on the editorial board, Richard Gordon on the advisory board. As stated in the editorial (RRE 1,1, 2015, 1–7), the journal invites papers from the whole field to a sharp peer review (about 40 to 60% of the submissions have been rejected so far). While the field is defined as 'Religion in the Roman Empire', the editorial stresses, new approaches 'starting from the notion of 'lived religion'' are expected. So far, seven issues have been dedicated in parts or as a whole to articles elaborated on the basis of papers held at LAR-conferences or workshops.

Kolleg-Forschungsgruppe
„Religiöse Individualisierung in historischer Perspektive"
5 Reports of fellows

Clifford Ando

My residence at the Max-Weber-Center (MWK) in summer 2013 was financed by the award of a *Friedrich Wilhelm Bessel-Forschungspreis* by the Alexander von Humboldt-Stiftung. During my stay, together with Jörg Rüpke of the MWK and Chris Faraone of the University of Chicago, I organized a conference under the title 'Public and private in Ancient Mediterranean law and religion. An historical and comparative conference'. The conference was jointly sponsored by the research group 'Religious Individualization in Historical Perspective' of the MWK and the Center for the Study of Ancient Religions of the University of Chicago. A volume arising from that conference is in progress. I also prepared a paper for the *Abschlusskolloquium* of the initial phase of the 'Religious Individualization' project. During this period I also prepared a working manuscript from a set of lectures that I delivered last year at the University of Toronto under the title, 'Roman Social Imaginaries'. This project studies the role of metaphor, metonymy, analogy and abstraction in Roman political and legal language, largely from the perspective of cognitive linguistic (rather than in respect to rhetorical studies of figure). It thus focuses not on the propositional content of Roman political speech or law, but on aspects of language susceptible of description as non-propositional operations through which other, properly propositional material is given voice.

Tomás Bartoletti

During my fellowship at Max-Weber-Kolleg as a member of the Research group „Religious individualisation in historical perspective", I could conclude my dissertation on Greek oracles in the early modern period in the context of humanist scholarship and its construction of Amerindian superstition. My PhD research examined the epistemological configuration of „Ancient Divination" between the representation of mantic practices in the Old comedy of Aristophanes and the way in which this source was interpreted to lay the basis of the modern discourse of „superstition", „irrationality" and „primitive thought", concepts that constituted this object in the field of Classical Studies and Anthropology. The ideas of „oracle", „myth" and „magic", among others, would cease to be „essentially" Greek, to be used epistemologically by Modernity. In this modern reconfiguration, „oracle" and „magic" are key concepts that will mark the limit that separates superstition from rationality, myth from logic, religion from science, the primitive from the civilized. All matters „irrational" (divination, magic, myths) were co-constructed between Classical Studies and Anthropology in opposition to „scientific-rational" knowledge. In this modern configuration, the Aristophanic comedy was usually appropiated in studies of ancient divination as evidence of prophetic fraud and political manipulation. For example, Anton van Dale in *De oraculis ethnicorum* (1683) quotes whole the oracle's scene of the comedy *Peace* with the aim of demonstrate the charlatanism of false prophets in Antiquity. Gerardus Vossius in *De Theologia Gentili* (1642, cap. IV) refers too to Aristophanes, when he explains the idea of *falsum numen*. On the contrary, the valuable testimony that a praxeological-constructivist analysis might offer as a work representing the performance of mantic practices in Aristophanic comedy was marginalized. In Aristophanes' comedy and by means of his particular anti-realist ethnography, it is possible to recover sociotechnical elements, materiality, historical references and cognitive dynamics tied to religion that other ancient sources do not portray. The analysis of Aristophanic sources under a praxeological-constructivist perspective has occupied the first part of my research and is the necessary complement for the study of the modern discourse of „superstition", „irrationality" and „primitive thought". The second part of my research that I developed at Max-Weber-Kolleg between October 2017 and September 2018 focused on the analysis of colonial chronicles of Americas, the projection of the European concepts of „idols" and „oracles" in these territories, and the appropriation and reception of such chronicles in the context of polemics on superstition and primitive thought in modern Europe. This second part of my research was fundamental for justifying epistemologically the novelty of a praxeological perspective applied to ancient Greek mantic practices. This perspective seeks to redefine the epistemological principles of the „divination" object both in Classical Studies and in Anthropology. As a consequence of this reflection, the possibility arises of using indigenous theories and Amerindian perspectives on rituality, agency, personhood, environment and relational epistemology for the analysis of ancient phenomena.

Eve-Marie Becker

In meiner Zeit als Fellow am Max-Weber-Kolleg habe ich verschiedene Forschungsprojekte vorantreiben oder abschließen können, die – in literaturgeschichtlicher Perspektivierung – der Einordnung der frühchristlichen Schriften in die hellenistisch-römische und -jüdische Literatur der frühen Kaiserzeit (1./2. Jh.) dienen. So habe ich einen ersten *draft* meiner Monographie 'The earliest Christian shape of historywriting. Tempus – memoria – historia' (Arbeitstitel; Yale University Press) zum Abschluss gebracht: In einer Linie, die vom Briefeschreiber Paulus und dem frühesten Evangelienschreiber Markus zum Verfasser des lukanischen Doppelwerkes führt, zeige ich in diesem Buch, wie frühchristliches Geschichtsdenken konstruiert wird. Erinnerungen an und Überlieferungen von Jesus werden narrativ erfasst und mit Hilfe prä-historiographischer Erzählformen zu einem innovativen literarischen *genre* – ‚Evangelium' – transformiert. Dieses *genre* tritt in den breiten Raum der hellenistischen Historiographie, die viele verschiedene micro- und sub*genres* kennt. Die Konstruktion dieser frühen Form von ‚historia' im sog. Urchristentum ist zunächst ein literarisches Unterfangen, das bestimmten narrativen Konventionen folgt, die einerseits für die frühjüdische Historiographie typisch sind (z.B. ‚personenzentrierte Darstellung'), andererseits aber auch Transfermöglichkeiten in die pagane Welt hellenistisch-römischer Leser erlauben (z.B. Quellenverarbeitung, Proömien, Reden). Doch über Memorisierung, Literarisierung und Narrativisierung hinaus dienen die frühesten Formen des Geschichtsdenkens und -schreibens im Christentum auch – im hermeneutischen Sinne – der Deutung von Zeit und Geschichte: Indem etwa vergangenes Geschehen narrativ erfasst, mit den Mitteln von *flash backs* and *flash forwards* zeitlich entwickelt, im Sinne einer *story* kausal geordnet und aus der Sicht des jeweiligen Autors mit der Zeit- und Weltgeschichte verbunden wird, dient es der Strukturierung von Zeit und Geschichte und damit auch der geschichtlichen Orientierung der ‚Christ believers' in der Zeit. Geschichtsschreibung dient auch im anthropologischen Sinne dem Zutrauen in die Erfahrung von Geschichte und läuft einer ‚Geschichtsflucht' zuwider. Die Konstruktion von Zeit und Geschichte ist letztlich also nicht nur eine literarische, sondern auch eine theologische Leistung mit ethischen Konsequenzen für die Welt- und Zeitdeutung.

Asaph Ben-Tov

Die aufkeimenden orientalischen Studien in der Gelehrtenrepublik der Frühen Neuzeit genießen in den letzten Jahren die zunehmende Aufmerksamkeit der Forschung als ein wichtiges Kapitel in der geistigen Geschichte Europas und als aufschlussreiches Beispiel für vormoderne Begegnungen mit außereuropäischen Kulturen. In meinem Forschungsprojekt befasse ich mich mit deutschen Orientalisten in der Zeit zwischen 1600 und 1750. Aus philologiegeschichtlicher Perspektive sind die Errungenschaften dieser Orientalisten meist von geringer Bedeutung, verglichen vor allem mit der Blüte der orientalischen Studien in Deutschland seit dem späten 18. Jahrhundert. Betrachtet man sie aber als ein ideengeschichtliches Kapitel der Frühen Neuzeit, werden der Quellen- und Ideenreichtum dieser Studien sowie ihre zeitgenössische Bedeutung klar. Das Jahr als Fellow am Max-Weber-Kolleg bot mir die Möglichkeit, diese quellennahen Untersuchungen weiterzuverfolgen. Der wichtigste Ertrag ist für mich mit der Fragestellung der Kollegforschergruppe »Religiöse Individualisierung in historischer Perspektive« eng verbunden: das religiös-individualisierende Potential der orientalischen Studien für einige Gelehrte im 17. Jahrhundert. Diese Fragestellung ist auch für die breitere historische Untersuchung von religiöser Individualisierung interessant, da die meisten Verfechter der studia orientalia im 17. Jahrhundert treue Anhänger ihrer jeweiligen Konfessionen waren. Somit stellt sich die Frage nach einer religiösen Individualisierung innerhalb einer gegebenen historischen Orthodoxie. Als Fallstudie für religiöse Individualisierung unter Orientalisten stand der Zwickauer Schulrektor und Arabist Johann Zechendorff (1580–1662). Anhand einer sorgfältigen Untersuchung seines handschriftlichen Nachlasses in der Zwickauer Ratsschulbibliothek bin ich der höchst individualisierten, gänzlich ungewöhnlichen »arabistischen« Frömmigkeit dieses lutherischen Gelehrten und Pädagogen nachgegangen. Die ersten Ergebnisse dieser Untersuchung der Individualisierungsräume, die durch eine (fromme und konfessionell konforme) Gelehrsamkeit geschaffen wurden, erscheinen demnächst im Sammelband der Forschergruppe.

Avner Ben-Zaken

My intellectual project aims at giving an alternative historical account to the rise of early modern science. Whereas traditional accounts mutually excluded adjacent scientific cultures, when Europeanist and Middle Eastern accounts disregard each other, I offered to focus on cross-cultural scientific exchanges, taking place at the culture margins. Such a focus on scientific practices at the cultural margins eventually results in exposing mundane networks that linked the neighboring cultures. The scholarly outcome was a culturally unified historical account, encompassing in I totality not only diverse cultures, but also various everyday practices and networks in which scientific activity transpire. In *Cross-Cultural Scientific Exchanges in the Eastern Mediterranean 1560–1660* (Johns Hopkins University Press, 2010), I focused on the rise of the heliocentric cosmology, as laying the foundation to the 'modern' revolutionary displacement of man from the center of the universe. I showed, however, that after the Copernican Revolution European practitioners engaged with the question of the relations of man and the cosmos by invoking, reconstructing and corroborating myths of ancient theology. In my more recent book, *Reading Hayy Ibn-Yaqzān: A Cross-Cultural History of Autodidacticism* (Johns Hopkins University Press, 2011), I continued to explore and reassess yet another fundamental concept of 'European modernity' – autodidacticism. This study unearths the deeply buried circulation of the Andalusian text through various and far-removed European contexts (Barcelona, Florence, and Oxford) in which early discussions on autodidacticism, empiricism and utopianism took place.

To complete a trilogy, I aimed at exposing the role of cross-cultural exchanges in transforming late medieval natural magic to early modern inductive scientific philosophy. My project at the Max-Weber-Kolleg 'Traveling with the *Picatrix*: Cultural Liminalities of Science and Magic' excavated the circulation of the *Picatrix*, an Andalusian *grimoire*, as it traveled across the Mediterranean in early modern Europe, stirring up natural magic not only as an alternative program for science, but also identifying it as an alternative scientific culture located in the East. In following the readings of Ficino, Agrippa and Campanella of the *Picatrix*, I unfolded a latent cultural process, beginning with Ficino who attempted to philosophize the concept of magic, through Agrippa who sought to legitimate the practice of magic and the persona of the magician, and up to Campanella who ventured to transform natural magic not only into the prime program for natural sciences, but into a political science as well. By stressing their reliance on a source that not only encouraged a competing program (natural magic), but was also written in a competing cultural space, my protagonists stressed that natural magic originated in the deep past, in the ancient space of the east. Thus, they further establishlits legitimacy by arguing thIin its essence, natural magic builds upon cross-cultural exchanges and on breaking disciplinary fences, fusing bodies of knowledge from different disciplines and from different cultures into each other, so to establish a new practical philosophy of science. The east, accordingly, was not only a space from which the philosophy of natural magic originated, but more particularly, the fictional cultural space where practice of natural magic acted as building an inductive bottom-top society.

Along the process of research, while completing this paper at the Max-Weber-Kolleg, I run across crucial evidence indicating that not only the aforementioned Renaissance figures read and were inspired by the *Picatrix*, but also the father of the heliocentric cosmology, Nicolaus Copernicus. I presented my preliminary findings in a talk at the Gotha Library, 'Clues beneath the Lamp: On Copernicus's magical 'other''. In this talk I stressed that the historiography of magic and the historiography of Copernicus have not yet intersected and that the aim of my paper is to enlist Copernicus into the 'magical-scientific' tradition, showing that not only mathematical-aesthetical or philosophical-physical concerns had driven Copernicus toward heliocentrism, but also astral-magical arguments regarding the governing power of the Sun over the other planets. I focused on a peculiar textual remark in *De revolutionibus*, in which Copernicus argued that 'others argue that the Sun governs the universe like a king', excavating the Picatrix as the 'silent' magical source for this crucial remark. I then used this finding as a clue and as a thread for exposing the cultural milieu of practitioners of magic in Cracow, who read the Picatrix, and the ways their magical practices where incorporated into the premises of the rising school of astronomy in Cracow, giving it an idiosyncratic character that was shaped by concerns regarding the power of the sun. The Cracovian blending of practices of astral magic and of the rising critique of the Ptolemaic model brought into light a conspicuous discrepancy between the functionalist centrality of the sun and its marginal location in the order of the planets. Copernicus's task, I argue, appeared to be the reconciling of this discrepancy by shifting the sun to center of the universe, turning the spatial center of the universe for the first time also the center of influences and forces.

Daniel Boyarin

I used my time at the Max-Weber-Kolleg to pursue a critical part of my work-in-progress, entitled "The History of Judaism: A Philological Investigation". The section that I worked on during my tenure at the Kolleg was the chapter on medieval Jewish usage (in Hebrew and Arabic), intended to show that Jewish writers did not have the abstraction "Judaism" (or any of its cognates) available to them. This endeavor was largely carried out through close study of the medieval Sephardic classical work of theology / philosophy / apologetic, known as the Kuzari, by Judah Halevi in both its Arabic original and contemporaneous Hebrew translation by Judah ibn Tibbon. The work on this chapter was completed by the time I left the MaxWeber-Kolleg and enabled me to finish a complete draft of the book during my tenure as Alexander von Humboldt Senior Fellow (Forschungspreisträger) at the Freie Universität Berlin for the next seven months. I am grateful for the time, space, colleagues, and especially the staff of the Max-Weber-Kolleg for all their support during my fellowship.

Jan N. Bremmer

It has been a great pleasure for me to have worked these past nine months at the Max-Weber-Kolleg within the framework of the Kolleg-Forschergruppe 'Religiöse Individualisierung in historischer Perspektive', but also in close alliance with the 'Lived Ancient Religion' (LAR) group. The highly stimulating intellectual environment of the Kolleg enabled me to complete a longer project and to advance a newer one. In the first months of my stay I completed my book *Initiation into the Mysteries of the Ancient World*, which appeared with De Gruyter (Berlin and Boston) in June 2014. The basis for the book were 4 lectures I had given in Munich in 2011-2012, in which I analysed the initiation proper into the Mysteries, as a 'thick description' of the main Mysteries had never been done. The final chapter and the Introduction, in particular, profited from a discussion in a Kolleg seminar in January 2014, which helped me to reformulate some methodological points and to add some references to the Mysteries in the Enlightenment.

The second part of my stay I worked especially on the theme of the descent into the underworld. This theme already appears in the Gilgamesh epic, and it is my aim to trace its progression from the Ancient Near East to Greece, where it was especially popular in Orphic and Pythagorean circles, but later was also adopted by the Jews and through them by the early Christians. The descent is a theme that is 'good to think with', as it enabled authors to reflect on what is ethically justified and what is punishable. In this way it also makes it possible to trace the development from transgressions to sins over a period of about 2 millennia. I gave a paper on the descent of Theseus and Peirithoos, one of the earliest such myths from ancient Greece, at the international conference 'Katabasis' in Montreal in May 2014.

In addition to my own projects, I also became very interested in Markus Vinzent's work on the early Christian thinker Marcion, whose work is not easy to reconstruct but whose influence was paramount in the first centuries of Christianity. I initiated a local seminar on 'Marcion of Sinope as Religious Entrepeneur', which took place on June 26, 2014 in cooperation with Jörg Rüpke and Markus Vinzent. It was one of the most exciting seminars I ever attended because of the conflicting views which made for intensive and highly stimulating discussions.

Last but not least I would like to mention the intellectual input I received through the seminars of the Kolleg-Forschergruppe, the meetings of the 'Lived Ancient Religion' group and the informal communal lunches and dinners. They have opened new vistas for me and made me conscious of new possibilities to approach the ancient world. Yet this was only possible because of the secretarial support of the Max-Weber-Kolleg. Their happy and always pleasant attitude made it a joy to go to the Kolleg every day.

Julie Casteigt

Das Ziel meiner Untersuchung [Ein mittelalterlicher Fall der religiösen Individualisierung als Anthropologisierung. *Super Iohannem* von Albert dem Großen] ist es zu zeigen, inwiefern Albert der Große einen Erkenntnisweg des göttlichen Prinzips vorschlägt, der vom Gesichtspunkt der Wissensdisziplinen her verschieden von der Metaphysik ist und vom Gesichtspunkt der implizierten Anthropologie her auf ein Verständnis des Menschen als Menschen, und nicht nur als ein von diesem getrennten Intellekt, beruht.

Hierbei geht es darum, das Spezifikum der Albertschen Überlegung in der Geschichte der mittelalterlichen lateinischen Welt zu verdeutlichen, und zwar in Bezug auf den Platz, der dem Individuum und seiner Handlungsfähigkeit in seiner Beziehung mit dem göttlichen Prinzip eingeräumt wird. Es zeigt sich, dass am Beginn dieser Untersuchung zwei Hauptbegriffe expliziert werden müssen: Individuum und Religion, im Sinn einer Beziehung mit einem göttlichen Prinzip.

Was den ersten Begriff betrifft, wird das Individuum in der Albertschen Sicht als Verbindung des Intellekts mit den Sinnen und der Vorstellungskraft, die beide mit dem Körper verknüpfen sind, verstanden – im Gegensatz zu einer Definition des Individuums, die allein von der spezifischen Natur des Menschen ausgeht, d.h. von dem vom Körper getrennten Intellekt. Darüber hinaus wird das Individuum nicht nur durch seine mehr oder weniger zahlreichen Fähigkeiten (Intellekt, Vorstellungskraft,

Sinne...), die in seiner Definition zugelassen werden, bestimmt, sondern auch von seiner Einschreibung in die Bedingungen, die außerhalb seiner *Psyche* sind, d.h. von Zeit und Raum, wie es weiter unten näher erläutert werden wird.

Folglich ist es meine Absicht, die Spezifizität der Albertschen Sicht der Individualisierung der Erkenntnis des göttlichen Prinzips aufzuzeigen, indem Individualisierung als Konzeption und Konstitution des individuellen Agents in der Erkenntnis des göttlichen Prinzips Verstanden wird. Auf der einen Seite impliziert die Individualisierung eine aktive Rolle des derart verstandenen Individuums in einer besonderen Modalität der Erkenntnis des Prinzips. Auf der anderen Seite konstituiert die Individualisierung die Identität des Individuums im Verhältnis zum göttlichen Prinzip im Erkenntnisakt mit.

Was den zweiten Begriff betrifft, verweist die Beziehung zum göttlichen Prinzip auf den Begriff der Religion. Allerdings wird ‚Religion' hier nicht im Sinn einer kontingenten Gesamtheit von Lehrsätzen, Texten, Glaubensaussagen, Riten, kollektiven oder individuellen Praxen und Institutionen verstanden, sondern als operativer Begriff. Hier wird ‚Religion' nämlich als Beziehungsoperator gesehen – genauer als Operator von Korrelationen, die eine reziproke Definition der Agenten (oder des Aktiven und des Passiven) im Akt, zu dem sie beide zusammengehören, enthalten. Die methodologischen Vorannahmen dieser Untersuchung bestehen einerseits in einer Abkehr von einer religiösen Perspektive im Sinn einer spezifischen dogmatischen, rituellen, institutionellen Gesamtheit und andererseits darin, den Begriff ‚Religion' im operativen Sinn, d.h. in der Bedeutung, Beziehungen zu erzeugen, zu verwenden.

Daher entwickelt sich meine Untersuchung eher auf der Erkenntnis- als auf der Praxisebene, insoweit die Erkenntnisebene die Voraussetzungen der Weise klar hervorhebt, in der sich der Agent im Akt, in dem er in eine kognitive Beziehung mit dem Prinzip eintritt, versteht Und konstituiert. Infolgedessen besteht die Herausforderung dieser Untersuchung darin zu zeigen, dass die Individualisierung, die im zur Metaphysik alternativen Erkenntnisweg, den Albert vorschlägt, inbegriffen ist, eine Metaphysik der Korrelationalität – oder der Quasi-Korrelationalität – voraussetzt. Der philosophische Essay, den ich vorbereite, beruht auf der kritischen Edition des *Super Iohannem* (Ioh. 1, 1-18), die ich gerade abschließe.

Max Deeg

Meine Arbeit am Max-Weber-Kolleg konzentrierte sich auf einen mit dem aktuellen Themenkomplex der Kolleg-Forschergruppe „Religiöse Individualisierung in historischer Perspektive" zusammenhängenden Aspekt, nämlich dem Verhältnis von Individualisierung und Institutionalisierung. Diesen untersuchte ich im Rahmen meines laufenden größeren Projektes, einer englischen Übersetzung mit ausführlichem historischen Kommentar des wohl bekanntesten „Reiseberichts" des frühen asiatischen

Mittelalters, des Datangxiyu-ji, „Bericht über die Westlichen Regionen aus der Großen Tang-Dynastie", des buddhistischen Mönchs und Indien-Reisenden Xuanzangs (600/602–664), der von dem zweiten chinesischen Tang-Kaiser Taizong in Auftrag gegeben worden war und im Jahre 646 dem Thron vorgelegt wurde. Der Fokus meiner Forschung war während meines Aufenthaltes in Erfurt auf die Fragestellung gerichtet, wie sich die verschiedenen Quellentexte, die auch die bio-hagiographischen Quellen zu Xuanzang – wie die von seinem Schüler Huili (aktiv 629–665) verfasste und von Yancong (aktiv 650–688) redigierte und erheblich erweiterte „Biographie des Hervorragenden Mönches [und] Tripitaka-Meister des Großen Cien-Kloster der Großen Tang-Dynastie" (Datang-Daciensi-sanzang-gaoseng-zhuan) – umfassen, im Kontext von (religiöser) Individualisierung verstehen lassen. Dabei habe ich mich u.a. von der Fragestellung leiten lassen, inwieweit autobiographische und biographische Quellen als Genres, die einen hohen Grad an narrativer Individualisierung suggerieren, tatsächlich eine solche Individualisierung des Protagonisten reflektieren und intendieren, oder ob sie nicht eher, ihrem hagiographischen Duktus gemäß, stark de-individualisierend wirken. Dabei lässt sich m.E. der Begriff der Funktion theoretisch nutzen, um die in den verschiedenen Quellen narrativ konstruierten Identitäten (Individualitäten?) herauszuarbeiten. Mein Fallbeispiel legt nahe, dass narrative Individualisierung in Form von Biographik (und Autobiographik) gleichzeitig auch eine Funktionalisierung im Sinne von auktoraler Intentionalität beinhaltet, die die zugeschriebene „Individualität" des Protagonisten durch die vorgegebenen funktionalen Parameter bestimmt und in gewissem Maße auch begrenzt. Entgegen dem herkömmlichen Verständnis, das den „Reisebericht" als eine Ich-Erzählung – und somit in gewisser Weise als ein teil-autobiographisches Werk – interpretiert, enthält Xuanzangs „Bericht" nur wenige Passagen, in denen der Mönch selbst agiert. Die biographischen Texte wiederum, allen voran die Einzelbiographie, werden i.d.R. als historische verlässliche Quellen über ein herausragendes religiöses Individuum (gaoseng, „eminent monk") interpretiert. Für meine eigene Arbeit zu Xuanzang in seinem historischen Kontext ist es dagegen wesentlich, die Vorstellung, dass die Biographie als historisch objektive Quelle zu werten sei, zu hinterfragen und auf die Funktionalität hinzuweisen, die bereits schon in ihrem hagiographischen Genre angelegt ist. Damit verbietet sich der übliche Ansatz, die „Individualitätslücken" des „Berichts" durch die vermeintlich biographisch-historischen Informationen der Biographik gleichsam auszugleichen und zu ergänzen. Im Falle von Xuanzang's biographischen Identitäten kann man, à longue durée und über den chinesisch-geographischen Kontext hinaus in Asien (Japan, Indien) und im Westen verschiedene Phasen und Formen von Identitätsfestschreibungen (Individualitäten?) erkennen, die m.E. bestimmten Funktionen entsprechen: 1. Institutionalisierung als Begründer einer buddhistischen philosophischen Schule; 2. Ästhetisierung als Mönch, der buddhistische Texte aus Indien nach China zurückbringt, in Form einer spezifischen Ikonographie und einer Verbildlichung des biographischen Narrativs; 3. Literarisierung durch die frühen Biographien, mittelalterliche und frühneuzeitliche Erzählungen und modernen Interpretationen, die gleichzeitig hagiographisierend, mythologisierend und somit de-individualisierend wirken; 4. Re-individualisierung und Verwissenschaftlichung Xuanzangs als Dokumentator der Geschichte Zentralasiens, Indiens und des Buddhismus ab dem 19. Jahrhundert; 5. Popularisierung von Xuanzang als paradigmatisch religiöser Suchender oder „Abenteurer" in Form von modernen Medien (Reiseberichte, Roman, Manga, Film), und 6. Politisierung, z.B. wenn Xuanzang als historischer Repräsentant indisch-chinesischer Kulturbeziehungen und Freundschaft interpretiert wird.

Hermann Deuser

Dass das Christentum in der Moderne unter massivem Veränderungsdruck stand und dass umgekehrt auch interne Entwicklungen der christlichen Theologien selbst, zumal im Einfluss der konfessionellen Differenzerfahrungen, dieselbe Moderne mitbestimmt haben, ist ein geschichtliches Faktum. Fraglich aber ist bis in die Gegenwart und deren Entscheidungsfragen für die Zukunft, wie und mit welcher Berechtigung bestimmte Veränderungen stattgefunden haben, provoziert wurden, zu vermeiden oder zu fördern wären. Die europäische *Moderne* um 1800 lebt bereits von dem etablierten Motiv der Entscheidung gegen eine *via antiqua* und für eine wissenschaftlich besser begründete *via moderna*; Renaissance, Humanismus und Reformation hatten dazu ihre spezifischen Beiträge geliefert. Neu aber ist jetzt im 18./19. Jh. die universale Instanz vernünftiger, empirischer, überprüfbarer Begründungen in den Wissenschaften wie im Blick auf Institutionen der Gesellschaft. Für Kirche und Theologie bedeutet dies bis heute die Herausforderung, diesem Forum zu entsprechen – oder aus guten Gründen und aufgrund der *Dialektik der Aufklärung* auch zu widersprechen. Es sind diese Linien von Tradition, Moderne und Gegenwart, denen in Entwürfen zur religionsgeschichtlichen, kulturtheoretischen, hermeneutischen, anthropologischen, sprachkritischen, wissenschaftstheoretischen Begründung theologischer Lehrstücke im Rahmen der Kolleg-Forschergruppe nachgegangen werden soll.
[Forschungsthema: Veränderungen der theologischen Dogmatik in der Religionsentwicklung der Moderne]

Hermann Deuser und Markus Kleinert

Die *Deutsche Søren Kierkegaard Edition (DSKE)* wird herausgegeben von Niels Jørgen Cappelørn, Hermann Deuser, Joachim Grage und Heiko Schulz und erscheint im Verlag De Gruyter (Berlin/Boston). Die Edition wird gefördert durch das Kulturministerium Kopenhagen, das Søren Kierkegaard Forschungszentrum Kopenhagen und die Carl Friedrich von Siemens Stiftung München. Die Kierkegaard-Forschungsstelle am Max-Weber-Kolleg wurde – ermöglicht durch Förderung der Carl Friedrich von Siemens Stiftung – im Herbst 2008 eingerichtet. Die *Deutsche Søren Kierkegaard Edition*

(DSKE) basiert auf der neuen dänischen Ausgabe *Søren Kierkegaards Skrifter (SKS)*, in der sämtliche Schriften Kierkegaards entsprechend gegenwärtigen editorischen Standards wiedergegeben und mit einem umfangreichen Realkommentar versehen werden. *DSKE* bietet den Text von *SKS* in sorgfältiger Übersetzung sowie einen adaptierten Kommentar. Da Kierkegaards literarischer Nachlass in deutscher Sprache bislang nur auszugsweise und entstellt zugänglich ist, soll die *DSKE* zunächst diesem Mangel abhelfen. Die deutsche Edition setzt folglich mit Kierkegaards Journalen, Notizbüchern und Aufzeichnungen ein, die einen Blick in Kierkegaards Werkstatt, in die Genese und Eigenart seines Denkens und Schreibens gewähren – was sowohl im Hinblick auf die veröffentlichten Werke als auch auf die Bedeutung der nachgelassenen Papiere als eigenständiger Teil des Gesamtwerks aufschlussreich ist. Für die KFG erwies sich die Auseinandersetzung mit Kierkegaard als in vielerlei Hinsicht fruchtbar.

Renate Dürr

The project "Global Knowledge, Religious Devotion, and the Making of Enlightenment Europe" focuses on the Jesuit journal Der Neue Welt-Bott, the premier Catholic missionary periodical in German-speaking lands and a household name among scholars working on the Society of Jesus. Modeled after the famous *Lettres Edifiantes et Curieuses*, *Der Neue Welt-Bott* initially featured translations of French letters but soon went beyond the French model and materials to become the first serialized publication of German Jesuit reports from all over the world in German. The periodical comprises 812 texts, arranged in 40 parts (with some scholars doubting the existence of parts 39 and 40) and published in five volumes between 1726 and 1761 (or 1758 for said scholars), amounting to over 4,500 densely printed folio pages. It further contains images, particularly new maps, cultural commentary and rich explanatory materials, such as a table that converts the Chinese calendar into a Christian framework.

Iconic figures like Bacon, Voltaire or Diderot have cast a long shadow on our understandings of the Enlightenment and its legacy, whether viewed positively in terms of rationality and modernity, or negatively in terms of European claims to superiority and dominance. Western European anti-clerical thinkers are still widely seen as the Enlightenment's standard-bearers. By contrast, this project approaches the Enlightenment from the Ottoman borderlands of the Habsburg Empire and a clerical context. We do so by examining a source base that has been widely yet uncritically used by historians. On the margins of Christian Europe, German Jesuits compiled missionary reports from into *The New* World Messenger (Der Neue Welt-Bott) an extraordinary publication of global scope as yet unexamined as a collection. It exemplifies the deep imbrication of religion and science, as well as reason and emotion that shaped the production of knowledge and European self-understandings in the Enlightenment. It also reveals how the missionary encounter with the "non-European world" – especially with the indigenous men and women who supplied extensive information about fauna, flora, geography, and their cultures – shaped the making of "European" science and epistemologies.

Esther Eidinow

My year in Erfurt, as a Junior Fellow within the framework of the Kolleg-Forschergruppe "Religiöse Individualisierung in historischer Perspektive", was both stimulating and productive allowing me to finish current projects and to begin new research. In terms of the latter, I was able to see through the final stages of publishing my monograph, Envy, Poison, and Death: Women on Trial in Classical Athens, which was published by Oxford University Press at the end of the first semester of my fellowship. The time also allowed for the completion of two other edited volumes of papers: Theologies of Ancient Greek Religion (with J. Kindt and R. Osborne), and Women's Ritual Competence in the Greco-Roman Mediterranean (with M. Dillon and L. Maurizio). In terms of new research, I was able to explore a number of new areas. Some of these moved quickly to become articles (one has been accepted by Numen); others were delivered as conference papers and will be developed for publication. In particular, the project I had come to the Kolleg to work on blossomed into a book proposal that has been accepted by Oxford University Press. A key part of the year for me was the Kolleg's seminar series: this was an invaluable space in which to try out new ideas. I am very grateful to the assembled fellows for their comments and insights on the two papers I offered there, which have certainly improved them. At the end of my Fellowship, Prof. Dr. Richard Gordon and I held an international conference on 'Narratives of Witchcraft', for which the Kolleg was kind enough to provide funds. It ran wonderfully smoothly thanks to the work of my co-organizer and the support of Doreen Hochberg and Ursula Birtel-Koltes, and I am extremely grateful to them all and to the Kolleg. The papers spanned time and place, from ancient Mesopotamia to contemporary East Cameroon, and we hope to publish them very soon. Overall, this time in Erfurt was invaluable, and I am indebted to the Kolleg for the time to work in this way and for the opportunity to meet so many inspiring people and collide with such a plethora of rich ideas. Finally, I was particularly glad that I was able to spend some time with Veit Rosenberger who first invited me to Erfurt.

Cristiana Facchini

Invited by Prof. Jörg Rüpke, I came to the Max-Weber-Kolleg Erfurt, in order to spend a sabbatical year, which started in November 2014 and ended in December 2015. I was invited as a recipient of three projects: 1) historiography of religion directed by J. Rüpke; 2) the Kolleg-Forschergruppe's project on religious individualization in historical perspective; 3) as one of the keynote speaker at the IAHR World Congress, held in Erfurt in August 2015. Within the framework of the Kolleg's project on religious individualization I have presented a book proposal whose tentative title is Entangled religions, aiming to write a history of religious representations on Judaism and Christianity as the result both of a dialogue and confrontation among scholars and intellectuals of different religious and political background, and of tangent proximity between the two religions. My research focuses on a set of different interconnections that are usually overlooked. The first one takes place at the crossroad between the early modern and modern period. The second one is relating to the interplay – real and symbolical – between Christian and Jewish culture. More precisely, my project aims at reconstructing representations of Judaism, as they were often entangled to representations of Christianity, from the early modern period to the first half of the 20th century. To add up, when focusing on agency, it is even more interesting to observe how the interaction among scholars and intellectuals of different religious, and later political, upbringing may shed new light on the role modern science, as applied to the study of religion, played even before the 'scientification' of religion. At Max-Weber-Kolleg Erfurt, I presented a paper on religious individualization focusing on early modern Judaism under the title „Entangled Histories. A Road Map to Individualization in Early Modern Judaism", in which I show how, against the background of a diaspora religion, individual agency shaped the religious system fueling its dynamism giving voice to different subjectivities and different locales. The overall picture, albeit not fully analyzed, combines recent historiographical trends such as connected biographies (Subrahmanyam) and transnational history, and discloses multiple possibilities to re-read the Jewish and Christian past. My contribution to the project of religious individualization continues with a project article on "Understanding 'prophets'. Possession, mysticism, and religious enthusiasm in the early modern period", in which I try to analyze cross-cultural phenomena of 'prophecy' among Jews and Christians of different denominations in the early modern period. I already presented a tentative paper („When the body speaks") at two different conferences (Villa Vigoni 2016 and Bertinoro 2016). In the article, I will try to analyze written reports of prophecy that fueled mystical experiences, which are to an extent radical form of religious individualization. Through the lenses of 'religious individualization', I wish to shed new light on the relationship between different forms of religious behavior and social experiences comprising mysticism, religious enthusiasm, and social criticism of established institutionalized religions focusing on the body and its ability to speak out. The second line of research that I pursued at the Max-Weber-Kolleg Erfurt is linked to the historiography of religion. I presented a paper entitled "'The immortal traveler'. How historiography saved Judaism" at the International Conference "Creating religions by historiography" held in Erfurt on 10–12 June 2015. The article is under evaluation and will be published in the Archiv für Religionsgeschichte (2017). In this contribution I explored the interconnection between the early modern and modern period investigating how German Jews from the Wissenschaft des Judentums appropriated texts, authors, and religious themes from earlier periods. More specifically, I analyzed how a set of themes – the historical Jesus and the interpretation of the Kabbalah – were instrumental to sustain the rise of Reform- and Liberal Judaism. While at the Max-Weber-Kolleg Erfurt, I also had the honor to be a keynote speaker at the IAHR Congress (23–29 August 2015), where I presented a paper entitled "Representing Judaism: Narrating, visualizing, performing, and feeling a religion", which has been turned into an article that will appear in print in 2016. In this article, I reflected upon a theme that has accompanied my research for years, that is the transformation of a religion under the impact of modernity. In this contribution, I focused on Judaism as an ideal case of study and tried to offer, accordingly, a new interpretation of how a religion changes and performs during times of acceleration. In doing so, I reflected upon different forms of representations, which span from historiography, scholarship and other textual narratives to performative arts, such as theatre and museums that interact with the various spheres of the public domain. Moreover, in the course of the year, I conducted a research and published a few articles on two other themes: focusing on the 19th and early 20th century, I wrote on the public consumption of religion, and reflecting upon the early modern period, I analyzed how influential are both space and place in defining religious practices. Ultimately, I took part to the organization of the conference "Describing and Explaining Ritual Dynamics" (26–28 October 2016) organized by the Research Centre "Dynamik ritueller Praktiken im Judentum in pluralistischen Kontexten von der Antike bis zur Gegenwart". During my stay as a fellow at the Max-Weber-Kolleg Erfurt, I have greatly enjoyed the discussions that took place during the seminars. My research has been greatly affected by the confrontations with colleagues and fellows and by the thriving intellectual atmosphere of the Kolleg. Although my book is still in the making, my research gained interest in new directions and perspectives that I will hopefully pursue in the coming years.

Peter Flügel

The twelve month long fellowship of the research group 'Religious individualization in historical perspective' of the Max-Weber-Center (MWK) gave me the opportunity to complete and newly pursue a variety of projects. The main outcome was the completion of my monograph *Die Sthānakavāsī Śvetāmbara Jaina-Orden in Nordindien*, based on the analysis of monastic biographies and epigraphic sources, which is in press with Harrassowitz publishers. Another monograph, *Askese und Devotion: Das rituelle System der Terāpanth Śvetāmbara Jains*, has been awarded funding by the Glasenapp-Foundation to be published in its Monograph-Series with Harrassowitz. Four edited volumes were edited and prepared for publication in autumn: *Jaina Law and Society* (Routledge), (with Gustaaf Houtman) *Asceticism and Power in South and Southeast Asia* (Routledge), (with Olle Qvarnström) *Jaina Scriptures and Philosophy* (Routledge), (with Olle Qvarnström) *Jaina Sacred Places* (Harrassowitz). Two public lectures were delivered during the year at the MWK: 'Emotion, Kognition und Handeln in der Jaina-Philosophie' (University of Hamburg 25 June 2013), and 'Max Webers Soziologie des Jainismus im Licht der neueren Forschung' (MWK Erfurt 8 July 2013), the latter of which is currently being prepared for publication. With generous co-funding of the research group 'Religious individualization in historical perspective', a conference on *Jaina Logic* was organised at SOAS in London. Videos of the presentations are published online, and some of the papers have been published already in the *International Journal of Jaina Studies*. Several conference papers were prepared at the MWK and are due to be published. The time at the MWK also gave me the opportunity to do archival research in the Staatsbibliothek in Berlin, where, somewhat unexpected, significant new facts for the history of Jaina Studies in the context of 19th century orientalism could be unearthed to be explored in a follow up project to the current Leverhulme Trust funded project on *Johannes Klatt's Jaina Onomasticon* at SOAS. Last but not least, the year at the MWK allowed – after more than 25 years abroad – to reconnect with the academic discourse in Germany, to learn more about Christianity, and to make many new friends. The relaxed and collegial atmosphere at the MWK, many stimulating discussions in seminars, over coffee, lunch and dinner, and the beautiful winter snow and continental summer have left a permanent positive impression.

Luise Marion Frenkel

I was fortunate to spend three months as a Junior Fellow at the Max-Weber-Kolleg Erfurt thanks to the DFG-funded project "Religious Individualization in Historical Perspective". I am extremely grateful to Jörg Rüpke for making this possible and also to colleagues and staff at the Max-Weber-Kolleg Erfurt, and the IBZ (Internationales Begegnungszentrum) for making this stay so pleasant and fruitful. Entitled "Transforming the Voice of Some into Collective Unanimous Clamour – Recording Acclamations for Christian and Imperial Institutionalization", my project focused on a wide range of late-antique texts from rough graffiti to tidy manuscripts of collections of conciliar documents. The fellowship began on a high note with the opportunity to present a guest lecture just two days after giving a paper at the Workshop "The Battle of Yarmuk (A.D. 636/A.H. 15). History and Memories of the Middle East" at the Eberhard-Karls-Universität in Tübingen. Both reflected the research carried out at Max-Weber-Kolleg Erfurt up to then, the available bibliographic resources, and its academic environment. During the two previous weeks, the first colloquia and conversations with members of the KFG and research projects on ancient lived religions and rituals drew my attention to further comparative sources and interpretations of inscriptions when orality, literacy, regional variation, and institutional mobilisation of the past are taken into account in the analysis of the narrative sources. The guest lecture at the Max-Weber-Kolleg Erfurt allowed me to present to its wider community also some of the conceptualisations developed over the previous three years. The research project led to a working manuscript of an article on the absence of individual voices in a representative selection of case studies of collective discourses and their narrative features. Less than half a year after the end of the fellowship, it has been published in Religion in the Roman Empire (RRE). The results of the critical interpretation of autobiographical narratives which refer to participation in unanimous discourse and consensual action, undertaken in the second half of the fellowship, will be presented at the closing conference of the KFG and submitted as a chapter. The paper presented in Tübingen, mentioned above, dealt with "Arab Conquerors in Greek Ecclesiastical Sources from Sozomen to the Lateran Council (649): Between Heresiology and Ethnography". The ongoing use for polemical purposes of narratives, in which unanimous and consensual discourses contribute decisively to impart identity, is thereby related to the paucity of mostly unrealistic literary presentations of early Arab military achievements and Muslim identities. The relevance of these texts both prior and contemporary to the early stages of the Arab invasions in processes of Christian institutionalisation around the Mediterranean contributed decisively to the consolidation of a repertory of tropes and narratives in political and religious discourses, such as Coptic hagiographies. The research done at Max-Weber-Kolleg Erfurt set the foundation for an offshoot of the project. Some early results are scheduled to be presented at major international conferences in the first semester of 2017. During my stay I also received the proofs of an article which has since appeared in the Journal of Aramaic Studies, and prepared a paper which was later accepted for publication in a volume of Studia Patristica. They address further case-studies of narratives of unanimous discourse and reassessments of theoretical foundations lingering behind overly literal interpretations. Communication problems hampered access to resources by Fernleihe at the Max-Weber-Kolleg Erfurt and unavoidable research and teaching commitments intervened: proofs of a chapter on language in the Nestorian controversy, reviewing graduate reports and the need to collect bibliography for the courses on Classical literature taught at the Universidade de São Paulo. Nevertheless, the Junior Fellowship was an excellent opportunity, not least to understand better German higher education. The Max-Weber-Kolleg Erfurt offered plenty of opportunities for young researchers' professional development, bringing together a truly international academic community having a commitment to a better understanding of societies past and present. That became clear in the colloquia, exhibition, conferences and the meetings of the Kolleg-Forschergruppe, in which academic dialogue ignored disciplinary boundaries. Echoing words already used in this publication, I acknowledge the debt to the many graduate students and Fellows in the KFG who informally shared their thoughts about higher education, their specialisms and life experiences, especially about religious initiation in various ancient cultures and better conditions for the preservation and publication of ancient and medieval texts, and whom I shall not embarrass by naming here. Still, the support and kindness of Doreen

Hochberg and Ursula Birtel-Koltes, the collegiality of Richard Gordon, and particularly the trust of Jörg Rüpke must not be left unmentioned.

Martin Fuchs

Religiöse Individualisierung in Indien wurde bislang vor allem mit Blick auf die Institution des samnayasa (,Weltentsagung') diskutiert. Demgegenüber richtet sich dieses Projekt auf solche Formen der religiösen Individualisierung, an die Reform-, Protest- und Selbstbehauptungsbewegungen insbesondere von Angehörigen der unteren Kasten und unterprivilegierter Gruppen anschließen konnten. Im Zentrum steht eine sozialphänomenologische Analyse von religiösen Konzeptionen des Selbst und seiner inter- wie transsubjektiven Relationen. Vor dem Hintergrund verschiedener bhakti-Traditionen (Formen persönlicher Zuwendung zu Gott) werden die Neukonzeptionen im 19. und 20. Jh. bis hin zur Neubelebung des Buddhismus untersucht. Angestrebt ist nicht nur, die Erforschung der (spirituellen) Erfahrungen und Perspektiven unterprivilegierter Gruppen, und damit letztlich der größeren Teile der indischen Bevölkerung, aus ihrer soziologischen Nische zu holen, sondern auch das universalistische Potential alternativer Religionsentwürfe sozialtheoretisch zu erschließen.

Dominik Fugger

Seit dem Jahr 2008 war Forschung zu Ferdinand Gregorovius (1821–1891) ein fester Bestandteil des wissenschaftlichen Programms am Max-Weber-Kolleg. Der Geschichtsschreiber der Städte Rom und Athen im Mittelalter interessierte dabei vor allem als paradigmatischer Schnittpunkt zeittypischer Konstellationen im 19. Jahrhundert, die wissenschaftliche Geschichtsschreibung als sinnstiftende Lebensaufgabe erscheinen lassen konnten. Dementsprechend standen die frühen Jahre des (späteren) Historikers im Vordergrund des Projektinteresses, mithin eine Lebensphase, in der Gregorovius sich selbst keineswegs als Geschichtsschreiber sah, noch ein solcher zu werden beabsichtigte. An der Königsberger Universität zum Theologen ausgebildet und bei Karl Rosenkranz zum Philosophen promoviert, engagierte er sich literarisch und publizistisch für die Revolution von 1848/1849. Wenn die vielseitigen Produkte dieser Jahre (mit einer Ausnahme) weder wissenschaftliche Geschichtsschreibung waren noch sein wollten, so zeigen gerade die Kommentare zum Tagesgeschehen, die er seit 1848 in Form von Leitartikeln für die Neue Königsberger Zeitung verfasste, ein von Hegel (und Herder) beeinflusstes geschichtsphilosophisches Denken, das nicht nur den späteren Historiker in seinen Perspektiven auf die Geschichte zum Teil vorwegnimmt, sondern durch seine existenzielle Auflading die spätere Hinwendung zum historischen Fach als geradezu folgerichtige Entwicklung erscheinen lassen kann. Das Wegbrechen der religiösen Verankerung im Luthertum gehört zu den wesentlichen Erfahrungen, die dieser Weltwahrnehmung vorausgingen und die Gregorovius mit vielen Intellektuellen seiner Generation teilte. Die genannten 92 Leitartikel, in denen Gregorovius das revolutionäre Tagesgeschehen einer fortlaufenden Deutung als notwendiger Teil eines notwendigen historischen Prozesses unterwirft, wurden im Rahmen eines eigenen Teilprojekts in den letzten Jahren ediert und mit einem erschließenden Kommentar versehen. Das Erscheinen dieses Bandes ist für Februar 2017 vorgesehen. Bereits zuvor hatte sich ein erstes Teilprojekt der Korrespondenz zugewandt, die Gregorovius nach seiner Emigration im Jahr 1852 mit Königsberger Bekannten und Freunden unterhielt. Zu den Briefpartnern gehörten u.a. sein Doktorvater Karl Rosenkranz, der Historiker Ludwig Friedländer und der Klavierpädagoge Louis Köhler. Die Briefe spiegeln den produktiven Durchbruch von Gregorovius' historiographischer Neigung unter dem Eindruck Roms. Mit ihrer Edition konnte 2013 die erste größere Briefausgabe zu Gregorovius seit über neunzig Jahren vorgelegt werden. Modellhafte Zugänge zu einem Verständnis von Geschichtsschreibung als Übersetzung erlebnishafter Erfahrung von Geschichtlichkeit erarbeitete schließlich eine Tagung, die Anfang 2014 in Erfurt veranstaltet werden konnte. Sie spannte den Bogen von den Voraussetzungen einer solchen, existenziell versichernden Geschichtserfahrung über das Erlebnis selbst, bis hin zu den historiographischen Verarbeitungen, die aus ihm hervorgehen, und untersuchte all diese Momente an ausgewählten (werk-)biographischen Stationen. Die Ergebnisse liegen seit 2015 unter dem Titel *Transformationen des Historischen* im Druck vor.

Gelegentliche Lehrveranstaltungen und auswärtige Präsentationen begleiteten und befruchteten die Arbeit. Der Dank des Projektleiters gilt der Staatsministerin für Kultur und Medien und ihrem Amtsvorgänger, die die Forschung wesentlich finanzierten. Er gilt nicht minder meinen zeitweiligen Mitarbeitern Nina Schlüter, Karsten Lorek und – immer wieder – Christian Scherer. Falls es mit all diesen Bemühungen gelungen sein sollte, einen neuen Blick auf Geschichtsschreibung als eine Form individueller wie kollektiver Lebensbewältigung anzubieten, so hätte sich der Zweck des Projekts erfüllt.

Richard Gordon

Geographische Mobilität und Schriftlichkeit sind die zwei wichtigsten Motoren der Individualisierungsprozesse in der Magie, die in diesem Projekt beleuchtet werden sollen. Eine wichtige Rolle bei solchen Innovationsprozessen spielen Techniken bzw. Modelle, die aus der Welt des kollektiv-legitimen Wissens übertragen werden (v.a. Sprüche, Redewendungen, Divinationstechniken, Krankheitsbilder, Götternamen).

Abgesehen von der Fixierung bzw. Inventarisierung von Rezepten und magischen Formeln und einer ganzen Reihe von paragraphischen Verstellungsmodi, ermöglicht Schriftlichkeit sowohl das Zusammenfügen bzw. Verschmelzen grundverschiedener magischer Traditionen und verwandter okkulter Wissenspraxis als auch die Artikulation neuer Theorien. Weitere Folgen sind die Entwicklung neuer Divinationsverfahren, die auf Schriftlichkeit basieren; die zunehmende Ausblendung der pharmakologischen Komponente ritueller Handlungen zugunsten der Invokation, insbesondere deren am leichtesten routinisierbares Charakteristikum, des *onoma barbarikon*; und die Verbreitung neuer Amulettentypen, deren Wirkung grundsätzlich eine schriftliche ist. Durch Schriftlichkeit wurde nicht nur das ‚magische Gedächtnis' enorm vergrößert, mit entsprechender Erweiterung der Verfahrensmöglichkeiten, die Praxis der Magie wurde zunehmend marktorientiert.

Elisabeth Gräb-Schmidt

Meine wunderbar intensive Zeit am Max-Weber-Kolleg war neben eigenen Arbeiten und Präsentationen – auch bei der zu Beginn stattfindenden DFG-Begehung der Kolleg-Forschergruppe – angefüllt mit anregendem Austausch nicht nur in den Kolloquien, sondern auch in informellen Gespräche. Mein Projekt zu Schleiermachers Verständnis von Individualisierung und der Rolle des Gefühls hat von diesem Austausch (etwa mit den Martin Fuchs und Vera Höke [Indien], oder mit Dietmar Mieth und Markus Vinzent bezüglich der unterschiedlichen Wahrnehmung der Innerlichkeitsdimension im Mittelalter bei Meister Eckhart) profitiert. Es wurde deutlich, dass Schleiermachers Theorie der religiösen Individualisierung, obwohl der Moderne zuzuordnen, gleichwohl durch seinen gefühlstheoretischen Ansatz die These unterstützen kann, dass das Konzept der Individualisierung keineswegs nur mit der Moderne oder der westlich-europäischen Zivilisation einhergeht, sondern antike und mittelalterliche Vorläufer hat, die nicht weniger valent sind, um das zu verstehen, was mit den Prozessen der Individualisierung gemeint ist. Kernpunkte der Theorie Schleiermacher sind 1. Die grundlagen-theoretische Position des Gefühls, die eine Unterscheidung von Religion und Religiosität ermöglicht durch die Anerkennung der vorrationalen Bedeutung der Affekte und 2. seine prinzipielle Verschränkung von Individuellem und Allgemeinem, das die Unterscheidung und Bestimmung in der Verflechtung von Einzelnem und Gemeinschaft erfordert. Diese Punkte wurden in zwei Richtungen untersucht: 1. in Auseinandersetzung mit den neueren politiktheoretischen Ansätzen (Cornelius Castoriadis, Claude Le Fort) durch deren (Wieder-)Entdeckung des Individuums und der Transzendenz im Imaginären und Kreativen als konstruktive Kritik an allein funktionalen Gesellschaftsmodellen und 2. als begriffliche Präzisierung der Bestimmung von Religion und Religiosität durch die grundlagentheoretische Position des Gefühls und der damit einhergehenden Bedeutung des Leiblichen.

Es hat sich anhand Schleiermachers Gefühlsbegriff gezeigt, dass das verengte Verständnis von Individualisierung der Moderne Kontinuitäten und Diskontinuitäten des Individualisierungs-verständnisses sowohl im Laufe der Geschichte als auch im Blick auf andere Kulturen verdeckt. Plausibilisiert werden kann die Verengung des modernen Individualisierungsverständnisses durch das Verschwinden des Begriffs der Seele aus der Wissenschaft, jedoch nicht aus der Literatur. Hier behält sie ihren Ort. Der in der Antike und im Mittelalter in der Philosophie geläufige Begriff der Seele, der in Schleiermachers Gefühlstheorie seine moderne Fortsetzung erfährt, bietet demgegenüber eine interkulturelle und interreligiöse Offenheit, in dem er das Moment der Verflechtung des Verhältnisses des Menschen zu sich und zum anderen, zur Sozialität abbilden kann, das in der Seele seine spezifische Ausrichtung erfährt, indem es sich in Riten und Praktiken der Gemeinschaft für die Einzelnen herausbildet. Diese interkulturelle und interreligiöse Offenheit des Begriffs der Seele würde es noch stärker ermöglichen, komparatistisch vorzugehen als es allein über den Begriff der Individualisierung möglich wäre, der eben dezidiert westlich-europäisch geprägt ist.

Eine solche begriffsgeschichtlich vergleichende Untersuchung gilt es allerdings noch fortzuführen, sowohl hinsichtlich der Verschiebungen, die durch die Moderne für die Thematik der religiösen Individualisierung vorgenommen wurden (Stichwort Säkularisierung, denn nicht von ungefähr sind es solche Untersuchen, die auch die gegenwärtige Infragestellung der Säkularisierungsthese in der sog. Wiederkehr der Religion plausibilisieren können) als auch hinsichtlich möglicher Anknüpfungspunkte an die Tradition der Antike und des Mittelalters (Meister Eckhart), sowie der Kultur Indiens, wie es nicht zuletzt auch während der Abschlusskonferenz im Juli deutlich wurde.

Knud Haakonssen

Als Fellow am Max-Weber-Kolleg möchte ich etwas zur Erforschung des neuzeitlichen Naturrechts beitragen. Dabei sind meine wichtigsten Arbeitshypothesen die Folgenden:
(1) Das ungeheuer umfangreiche Naturrecht des 17. und 18. Jahrhunderts lässt sich nicht einfach auf der Basis seines literarischen Nachlasses als ein Gedanken oder Lehrgebäude verstehen. Es war auch eine neue akademische Institution, die u.a. unterschiedlichsten politischen, theologischen, juristischen oder pädagogischen Aufgaben diente, und deren theoretische – oder philosophische – Grundlagen deshalb von Kontext zu Kontext stark variierten. Dennoch hatte es eine spezifische Identität als akademische Institution, als eine praktische Sprache und als eine Art literarisches Genre mit einem eigenen Kanon.
(2) Ein solches Phänomen lässt sich nicht allein mit Mitteln der Philosophie- oder Ideengeschichte verstehen; es erfordert mehrere historiographische Register. Zum Beispiel ist die alte Diskussion um die ‚Originalität' von Grotius und den nachfolgenden protestantischen Naturrechtlern im Verhältnis zu ihren scholastischen Vorgängern vielleicht von einem gewissen philosophischen Interesse; gleichzeitig ist diese Debatte aber auch ein Hindernis, will man die historische Bedeutung der allgemeinsten und am weitesten verbreiteten praxisbezogenen neuen Sprache in Europa vom Westfälischen Frieden bis zum Vormärz verstehen: das Naturrecht.

(3) Weitere Schwierigkeiten entstehen durch den Versuch, das frühmoderne Naturrecht in Kontinuität mit dem modernen Menschenrechtsdenken zu sehen und in diesem Zusammenhang das Naturrecht auf der Basis kantianischer oder nachkantianischer Perspektiven zu lesen und zu beurteilen. Das nach-grotianische Naturrecht ist einfach zu umfangreich, mannigfaltig und veränderlich, um auf diese Weise als Teil einer teleologischen Philosophiegeschichte betrachtet zu werden.

Ich bearbeite diese Thesen – meine Vorurteile – zum frühmodernen Naturrecht auf drei Ebenen. Erstens schreibe ich selbstständige Studien über einzelne Autoren. Gegenwärtig bereite ich die Publikation einer Auswahl meiner veröffentlichen Essays und unveröffentlichten Vorlesungen unter dem Titel ‚After Grotius, Before Kant: Studies in Natural Law' vor. Diese Arbeiten stellen eine Brücke dar zwischen meinen früheren Arbeiten zu Naturrecht und Aufklärung und dem, was meine Hauptaufgabe als Fellow der Kolleg-Forschergruppe ist, nämlich eine größere monographische Studie, die das Naturrecht im oben angedeuteten Sinn behandelt und dessen Titel ‚Natural Law, Theory and Practice from the Seventeenth to the Nineteenth Century' ist.

Zweitens bin ich seit vielen Jahren mit wissenschaftlichen Ausgaben von Naturrechtswerken und Werken, die mit dem Naturrecht in Verbindung stehen, beschäftigt. Diese Aktivitäten setze ich fort; gegenwärtig mit dem Abschluss einer komplexen Ausgabe der Politik und politische Ökonomie betreffenden Manuskriptnachlasses des schottischen Hume-Gegners Thomas Reid (1710–96) und der großen moralphilosophischen und naturrechtlichen Abhandlung ‚A System of Moral Philosophy (1755)' von Francis Hutcheson. Der erste Titel ist Teil meiner 10-bändigen ‚Edinburgh Edition of Thomas Reid', der zweite erscheint in meiner 44-bändigen Reihe ‚Natural Law and Enlightenment Classics'.

Drittens habe ich die Initiative für ein größeres europäisches Verbundvorhaben, ‚Natural Law 1625–1850', ergriffen, das ich jetzt zusammen mit Frank Grunert (IZEA, Halle) und Diethelm Klippel (Rechtsgeschichte, Bayreuth) leite. Das Projekt hat mehrere Teile. Es geht zum einen um ein breit angelegtes Digitalisierungsprojekt von allerlei Materialien, die die akademische Institutionalisierung des Naturrechts in ganz Europa im angezeigten Zeitraum dokumentieren. Dies wird zum anderen durch eine umfassende Bibliographie und Datenbank über Institutionen und Lehrer ergänzt. Im Rahmen eines internationalen Kongresses in Halle im Herbst 2013 laden wir außerdem zur Mitwirkung in einem internationalen Forschernetzwerk ein. Ein Schwerpunkt des Projekts ist die europäische Diaspora des protestantischen Naturrechts – auch in den katholischen Ländern. Gegenwärtig beteiligen sich Institutionen aus zwölf Ländern an dieser Arbeit.

Cornelia Haas

Von April 2010 bis Dezember 2013 am Kolleg als wissenschaftliche Mitarbeiterin in der Kolleg-Forschergruppe ‚Religiöse Individualisierung in historischer Perspektive', gefördert von der DFG. Was hat eine etwas ‚angestaubt' anmutende Gesellschaft, die mit Geistern und geheimen, im Himalaya ansässigen Meistern kommuniziert, mit der boomenden IT-Industrie Indiens zu tun?

Die Antwort auf diese Frage ergibt sich aus der Geschichte der 1875 in New York von Helena Blavatsky u.a. gegründete ‚Theosophical Society' (TS) und aus ihr hervorgegangenen Vereinigungen, sowie deren wichtiger Rolle im geistigen und politischen Geschehen im Indien vor der Unabhängigkeit. Auf mitunter subtile Weise setzt diese sich mancherorts bis in die heutige Zeit fort; ihre Sympathisanten sind und waren in gebildeten, oft einflussreichen Kreisen zu finden.

Ursprüngliches Ziel des Forschungsprojektes war es, mit Hilfe von Interviews exemplarisch Einsicht in gegenwärtige Aktivitäten und Lebenswelten der Splittergruppe *United Lodge of Theosophists (ULT) India* zu gewinnen. Spezielle Fragestellungen hierbei waren beispielsweise diejenigen nach möglicherweise unbewusster Modifikation eigener, (‚Familien-')Religion durch die Interpretation der Theosophen oder, dem tatsächlich relativ hohen Anteil von ‚Young IT-Professionals' geschuldet, die Frage nach Konsequenzen der Beschäftigung mit der Theosophie Blavatskys für das eigene Leben, v.a. im Hinblick auf ethisches Verhalten im Beruf. Ein Überblick der diesbezüglichen Ergebnisse in Kurzform befindet sich bereits im Druck.

Die zu einer genaueren Auswertung der o.g. Informationen notwendige detaillierte Aufarbeitung der Geschichte der ULT India seit ihren Anfängen im Jahre 1929 bis zur Gegenwart erhielt durch den Umzug des Projektes an das Max-Weber-Kolleg neue Perspektiven: Die Einbettung in die Kolleg-Forschergruppe ‚Religiöse Individualisierung in historischer Perspektive' eröffnete v.a. die Möglichkeit weitaus stärkerer Kontextualisierung der Geschichte der ULT India, sowie die Berücksichtigung des Aspektes religiöser Individualisierung. Dementsprechend wurden zunächst systematisch Interaktionen der theosophischen Bewegung mit indigen indischen Religionen untersucht, die sich bis in die heutige Zeit in theosophisch-hybriden Religionsformen, wie bspw. Der *Parsi-Theosophy* äußern und zum Teil Phänomene religiöser Individualisierung erkennen lassen.

Anschließend wurde innerhalb der theosophischen Bewegung ein *Stufenmodell religiöser Individualisierung* transparent gemacht, welches in der – theoretischen – Konzeption der ULT als Konsequenz vorangegangener Entwicklungen innerhalb der Gesamtbewegung einen Kulminationspunkt erreicht: Hierbei ergibt sich zunächst aus den sich scheinbar konträr verhaltenden Themen Wissenschaft, Spiritismus und Weltreligion ein unmittelbares Spannungsverhältnis, welches den Nährboden für die Genese der theosophischen Bewegung Blavatskys als ‚Vereinigung zur wissenschaftlichen Erforschung des Okkultismus und der Kabbalah' – so die Gründungsurkunde – bildet. Besonders hervorzuheben – und direkt dem Umfeld des Max-Weber-Kollegs geschuldet – ist hier die gewonnene Erkenntnis einer engen Verknüpfung mit den Ursprüngen der akademischen Psychologie: Deren Begründer, William James, war erwiesenermaßen TSMitglied; ein möglicher Einfluss auf sein Werk ist ein kaum beachtetes Feld und überaus interessant im Hinblick auf die Frage nach möglicher, wechselseitiger Inspiration. Die diesbezüglichen Aktivitäten William James' wären eine Anschlussuntersuchung wert. Entscheidend für das o.g. ‚Stufenmodell' ist jedoch die Strukturanalyse von Organisation und *theoretischem Anspruch* der ULT: Dieser manifestiert sich bis heute *in der Praxis* als organisierter Gemeinschaft anonym gedachter Einzelner, deren individueller Fortschritt durch eine nach außen geschlossene Gruppe gesichert werden soll.

Am fünften November 2010 organisierte ich im Rahmen des Projektes am Max-Weber-Kolleg einen interdisziplinären Workshop zum Thema ‚Theosophie in Indien' mit Experten verschiedener Disziplinen (Modern South Asian Studies, Religionswissenschaft, Musik, Theologie, Indologie), der sich der besonders der spezifisch südasiatischen Variante der Theosophie Helena Blavatskys und deren Wirkung widmete. Die insgesamt fünf Vorträge mit jeweils anschließender Diskussion repräsentierten inhaltlich wie methodisch die Vielfalt möglicher Herangehensweisen und Interessen, die dieses erst seit kurzer Zeit beachtete Forschungsfeld bietet: Zunächst stand die indigene Sicht mit einem Vortrag über ‚Bhagavan Das' Kritik an der Theosophischen Gesellschaft, 1913–1914' (Maria Moritz, Berlin; Bernadett Bigalke, Leipzig/Lausanne) und ‚Weltansichten von Akteuren der Theosophie im heutigen Indien' (Cornelia Haas, Erfurt) im Vordergrund. Im Anschluss wurden spezifisch indische Elemente der Lehren Blavatskys und deren Rezeption in Indien und Europa mit den Vorträgen von Sarah Heinrich (Heidelberg) über ‚Reinkarnation im Kontext der Theosophischen Gesellschaft: Anna Kingsford (1846–1888) und H. P. Blavatsky' sowie Karl Baier (Wien) über ‚Die Theosophische Rezeption der Yoga-Praxis in Indien' vorgestellt. Die Brücke in den Westen schließlich schlug Heinz Mürmel (Leipzig) mit dem Thema ‚Theosophie und Buddhismus in Leipzig vor dem ersten Weltkrieg'. Da die spezielle Thematik bisher kein Forum hat, dafür umso mehr Schnittstellen und Anknüpfungspunkte bietet, wurden weitere Aktivitäten der Vernetzung angedacht und auf den Weg gebracht.

Ich möchte mich bei allen für die lange und intensive Zeit am Max-Weber-Kolleg bedanken, die mir – fachlich, aber auch menschlich – wichtige Einsichten, Positionierungen und Konsequenzen ermöglichte. Vor allem aber gilt mein Dank den unschlagbaren Damen in den Sekretariaten, die mit Kompetenz, Kreativität und Hilfsbereitschaft nahezu jede ‚Katastrophe' – vom fehlenden Kaffeefilter bis zur Reisekostenabrechnung – zu beheben wussten!

Veronika Hoffmann

Mein Forschungsaufenthalt am Max-Weber-Kolleg und insbesondere innerhalb der Kolleg-Forschergruppe „Religiöse Individualisierung in historischer Perspektive" hat mir wesentliche konzeptuelle Klärungen für mein Projekt „Religiösen Zweifel denken" ermöglicht. Unter der Grundannahme, dass die Artikulation religiösen Glaubens und Zweifelns in signifikanter Weise vom jeweiligen historischen und kulturellen Kontext mitgeprägt ist, waren die Gespräche in der Kolleg-Forschergruppe zum einen hilfreich, um die Verhältnisbestimmung zwischen einer solchen Kontextualisierung im zeitgenössischen europäischen Kontext, wie ich sie unter Rückgriff auf Charles Taylor vornehmen will, und den systematisch-theologischen Anteilen des Projektes zu klären. Zum anderen haben mich die Diskussionen um das Konzept der Individualisierung angeregt, Zusammenhänge zwischen religiösem Zweifel und dem Erleben von Authentizität sowie zwischen Zweifel und Identität(skrisen) genauer in den Blick zu nehmen. Sie ließen zudem aufmerksam werden auf mögliche vorschnelle Vereinfachungen: Ist es immer der Einzelne, der zweifelt, gegenüber den Affirmationen einer Glaubensgemeinschaft? Welche weiteren, vielleicht produktiveren Strategien als solche der Ausgrenzung haben Glaubensgemeinschaften im Blick auf den Zweifel? Und was geschieht, wenn Zweifel als Marker von (individueller) Authentizität zu einem faktischen Mainstream wird? Diese und eine Reihe weiterer Fragen und Anregungen nehme ich von meiner Zeit mit für die Weiterarbeit an meinem Buchprojekt. Daneben habe ich im Rahmen der Kolleg-Forschergruppe eine Tagung zum Thema „Religiösen Zweifel denken" veranstalten können, die 2017 unter dem Titel „Nachdenken über den Zweifel. Theologische Perspektiven" publiziert wird. Überlegungen zum Verhältnis von Zweifel und Toleranz, deren Grundlagen ich im Rahmen meiner Fellowship erarbeitet habe, werde ich demnächst auf einer Tagung der deutschen Sektion der europäischen Gesellschaft für Theologie vorstellen. Die Gespräche und Diskussionen am Kolleg, formeller wie informeller Art, habe ich nicht nur als wissenschaftlich sehr anregend, sondern auch als menschlich immer angenehm empfunden. Dafür danke ich den Fellows und Kollegiatinnen und Kollegiaten, sowie auch den Mitarbeiterinnen des Kollegs für ihre Unterstützung.

Vera Höke

Das Projekt wird im Rahmen der Kolleg-Forschergruppe eine der nahezu ‚klassischen' indischen Reformbewegungen unter britischer Kolonialherrschaft, den Brahmo Samaj, sowie die aus ihr entstandene Church of the New Dispensation, thematisieren, also vor allem den von Keshab Chandra Sen begründeten Zweig untersuchen. Den historischen Rahmen bildet die Zeit zwischen ca. 1850 und 1880.

Besonders in der New Dispensation Church wird dem Individuum eine zentrale Bedeutung zugewiesen. Göttliche Inspiration und die menschliche Intuition bilden die primären Zugänge zum Göttlichen. Sie stehen als Autorität über allen Schriften, und gelten als Grundlage der Religionen. Auf ihrer Basis ist es Keshab Chandra Sen möglich, die in der Brahmo-Tradition so verachteten Hindu-Rituale nicht nur wieder aufzugreifen, sondern mit christlichen Ritualen zu einer integrierten, als stimmig empfundenen Entität zu konstruieren. Die evozierende Sprache in diesen neuen Ritualen sucht in den Anwesenden Bilder hervorzurufen, die eine Einfühlung in bestimmte religionshistorische Momente oder an relevante Orte bewirken sollen. Dieses

Zeit-, Raum- und Kulturgrenzen übergreifende Erleben zielt darauf ab, spezifische religiöse Inhalte zu verinnerlichen, und tritt an die Stelle intellektuellen Disputes. Die religiöse ‚Bildung' des Individuums (die auch und gerade moralische Aspekte und Aspekte der persönlichen Entwicklung umfasst) nimmt eine zentrale Rolle ein, die sich auch in den Strukturen der religiösen Gemeinschaft niederschlägt.

In der Konzeption dieser Lehre spielten christliche Impulse eine zentrale Rolle. Obwohl Keshab Chandra Sen schon früh einen regen Kontakt mit verschiedenen Missionaren in Kalkutta pflegte, war ihr Einfluss nicht unbedingt ausschlaggebend. Als wesentlicher kann die Rezeption unitarisch-transzendentalistischer Werke aus Amerika und England gelten. Keshab Chandra und andere Brahmos setzten sich v.a. mit den Schriften Theodore Parkers und Ralph Waldo Emersons auseinander. Vor diesem Hintergrund muss meines Erachtens der Rückgriff auf die Gaudiya-Vaishnava Rituale und bhakti betrachtet werden, die in der Bewegung seit 1876 deutlich an Bedeutung gewannen. Genau diese Kombination ‚westlich-christlicher' und ‚hinduistisch-traditioneller' Elemente hat die Bewegung historiographisch marginalisiert, da sie entweder als zu ‚christlich' oder als zu ‚traditionell' charakterisiert wurde, um wirklich von Interesse zu sein. Doch diese Verbindung erscheint mir keineswegs beliebig, oder rein dem Wunsch nach gesellschaftlicher Anerkennung geschuldet zu sein. Die potentiellen Gemeinsamkeiten zwischen transzendentalistischen Idealen und bhakti, die in der Individualität der Zugangsweise zum Göttlichen und der Emotionalität bestehen, sind bisher nicht erfasst worden.

Haiyan Hu-von Hinüber

Im Rahmen der Forschungsgruppe ‚Religiöse Individualisierung in historischer Perspektive' wurde das Projekt „Chinesische buddhistische Klöster in Deutschland. Zu Entwicklungen im 21. Jahrhundert" vom 15. April bis zum 30. September 2018 am Max-Weber-Kolleg durchgeführt. Es handelt sich um das erste Teilprojekt eines Gesamtprojektes „Chinesische buddhistische Klöster im 21. Jahrhundert". Auf historischer Grundlage wurde schwerpunktmäßig der für China charakteristische Aspekt der Individualisierung und Personifizierung bei der Herausbildung der buddhistischen Schulrichtungen (2.–6. Jh.) analysiert, die sich deutlich von der ursprünglichen Vorstellung des historischen Buddha unterscheiden. Dabei wurden auch die psychologischen Gründe für die rekonstruierte Genealogie der Meditationsschule *Chan-zong* behandelt, die seit dem 6. Jh. in China und später in Japan eine große Rolle für das geistliche und soziale Leben der Gesellschaft spielt.

Für den Synkretismus in China gilt die These von Max Weber nach wie vor: „Der alte Buddhismus ist in fast allen praktisch entscheidenden Punkten der charakteristische Gegenpol des Konfuzianismus". Die religionssoziologische Bedeutung dieses ‚Gegenpols' ist nach dem Ende der kommunistischen Zeit in China wieder voll zur Geltung gekommen. Seit der Öffnung und Reform des Landes (1978) hat der historisch einzigartige Zuwachs der Anzahl von Anhängern des Buddhismus in der chinesischen Gesellschaft zu tiefgreifenden Veränderungen geführt. Insbesondere bei der makroökonomischen Strategie ‚One Belt & One Road' (Seidenstraße zu Lande und zu Wasser), die von der chinesischen Regierung langfristig angelegt (2013–2025) und mit allen Mitteln vorangetrieben wird, handelt es sich um die historischen Routen, auf denen sich der Buddhismus seit der Zeitwende von Indien ausgehend über verschiedene zentralasiatische Länder nach China verbreitet hat. Dank der Rückbesinnung unzähliger Chinesen auf diese weit zurückreichende Tradition wird der praktizierte Buddhismus (lived religion) nochmals beflügelt. Die Auswirkungen dieser Entwicklung sind seit 2001 und vor allem in den letzten beiden Jahren selbst in Deutschland zu spüren.

Eine erste Bestandsaufnahme der buddhistischen Anhänger und Klöster (ca. 38.000) im gegenwärtigen China beruht auf den aktuellen wissenschaftlichen Publikationen und veröffentlichten Angaben aus den chinesischen Archiven sowie Sozialmedien. Ferner wurden Feldforschungen in sechs Klöstern und drei buddhistischen Akademien durchgeführt. Als Ausgangspunkt für die Fallstudien dient ein umfassender Einblick in die rechtliche Rahmenstruktur der regulierten „Religionsfreiheit" in der Volksrepublik China. Am Beispiel des Klosters ‚Liu-zu' (des sechsten Schulhauptes) in der Provinz Guangdong und in Deutschland (bei Göttingen) werden einige Aspekte des modernen Buddhismus exemplarisch untersucht, wie z.B. schulübergreifender Wiederaufbau der Klöster nach der verheerenden Zerstörung von 1949 bis 1977, Gründung der buddhistischen Stiftungen und Beginn der Kooperation mit Hochschulen, Verwaltung der Spendengelder durch die wiederbelebte Rechtstradition.

Annette Hupfloher

Meine Aufsätze zu den ‚Grenzen der Polisreligion' setzen der weit verbreiteten und forschungshistorisch vorherrschenden kollektivistischen Perspektive auf die antike griechische Religion eine dezidiert ‚individualisierende' entgegen. Während das Konzept der ‚Polisreligion' die Funktion der antiken griechischen Polis als Personenverband mit ihrem alles umfassenden Anspruch auf Regelung der Lebensführung ihrer Mitglieder betont, werden hier einzelne Akteure und ihre spezifischen Handlungsspielräume im Rahmen der antiken Poleis thematisiert (z.B. in der Fragestellung nach Kultgründungen), individuelle Praktiken (wie Divinationspraktiken, Heilungsrituale) herausgearbeitet und im Gegensatz zu traditionellen Forschungspositionen betont (statt marginalisiert). Personengruppen unterhalb der Ebene des Poliskollektivs mit ihren gruppenspezifischen Bedürfnisstrukturen (Gender- und Altersdifferenzierung) werden studiert, aber auch soziale Formationen, die die Polis transzendieren, indem sie größere Allianzen (Netzwerke) bilden. Insgesamt geht es also auch um Korrelationen zwischen Individuum und Gruppe(n) (verschiedener Ausdehnung). Dieser Ansatz trägt selbst dann, wenn die Rekonstruktion von Erlebniswelten (etwa Träume im Rahmen von Heilungs- und Divinationsritualen) unternommen wird, deren Inhalte ja sozial geformt sind.

Die Forschungen richten sich auf zwei Themenbereiche, in denen die Aktivitäten von Individuen in der Überlieferung antiker polytheistischer Systeme besonders gut fassbar sind, aber bisher nicht intensiv erforscht wurden: Handlungsspielräume und Erlebniswelten von Individuen. Die Überlieferungslage zu beiden Bereichen ist schon für die klassische Zeit in Griechenland gut; in hellenistischer Zeit und in der römischen Kaiserzeit nehmen die Zeugnisse (antike Literatur, Inschriften und archäologische Zeugnisse) zu und zeigen zum Teil sogar eine autobiographische Perspektive. Die Analyse dieses Materials zielt darauf, das Konzept der ‚Polisreligion' durch zusätzliche Perspektiven zu hinterfragen, zu modifizieren und nach Möglichkeit eine alternative Beschreibung der Relation zwischen Polis und Individuum zu erarbeiten. Die Analyse erfolgt mit historischen und kulturwissenschaftlichen Methoden (Text- und Kontextanalyse; Ikonologie) und mit vergleichenden Ansätzen, was die Ausarbeitung von Ähnlichkeiten und Unterschieden in Hinblick auf rezente und zeitgenössische religiöse Praktiken angeht. Diese Arbeiten zeigen, dass die öffentlich geübten und sichtbaren, kollektiv organisierten Riten im antiken Griechenland lediglich ein Teil des religiösen Feldes waren, dass es relativ breite Handlungsspielräume für individuelle Praktiken gab, dass sogar Anpassungen des tradierten Götterspektrums und der religiösen Riten an die Bedürfnisse einzelner Personen (Individualisierung religiöser Traditionen) gut bezeugt sind. Dies gilt nicht nur für die hellenistische Zeit, der von der Forschung traditionell die Betonung des Individuellen in allen Lebensbereichen zugeschrieben wird, sondern im Bereich der Religion schon für die klassische Zeit und auch für die römische Kaiserzeit.

Ute Hüsken

Das Jahr am Max-Weber-Kolleg in der Kolleg-Forschergruppe „Religiöse Individualisierung in historischer Perspektive" hat sich als ausgesprochen fruchtbar für mein Projekt „Changing Patterns of Women's Ritual Agency" erwiesen. In diesem Projekt gehe ich Fragen des Wandels in der Aneignung, der Zuschreibung und der Realisierung von religiöser und ritueller Handlungsmacht (agency) von weiblichen Ritualspezialisten in spezifischen hinduistischen und buddhistischen Traditionen nach. Hierbei handelt es sich um den erst jüngst wieder eingerichteten Nonnenorden in der buddhistischen Theravada Tradition und um eine recht rezente Entwicklung im indischen Sanskrit Hinduismus: Hier nehmen immer mehr Frauen die Rolle als Ritualspezialistin ein, obwohl dies nach den autoritativen Texten eine allein brahmanischen Männern vorbehaltene Aufgabe ist. Während ich für die buddhistischen Nonnen zunächst mit Fallstudien in Kalifornien begonnen hatte, konnte ich meine Arbeit im Rahmen von kurzen, aber intensiven Feldforschungsaufenthalten in der vorlesungsfreien Zeit auch auf Nonnengruppen in North Carolina, South Carolina und Colorado ausweiten. Dieser erweiterte Blickwinkel verdeutlichte die Dringlichkeit der Berücksichtigung der Intersektionalität der Kategorien gender, ethnicity und lokaler Mehrheitsreligion. Bei den hinduistischen Priesterinnen kommt Intersektionalität vor allem im Zusammenhang mit Kasten- und Klassenzugehörigkeit ins Spiel. Sehr deutlich wurde im Verlauf meiner Arbeit, dass es auch unter den Frauen, die als hinduistische Priesterinnen agieren, starke Unterschiede gibt, dass zum Teil sogar massive Rivalitäten bestehen. Es zeigte sich beispielsweise, dass die Ausübung der Sanskrit-Rituale für die brahmanischen Frauen der urbanen Mittelklasse auch den Versuch beinhaltet, die Ritualausführung in Sanskrit als brahmanisches Privileg zu erhalten.

Im Gegensatz dazu ist dies für Frauen der nicht-brahmanischen Kasten Mittel und Ausdruck von radikaler Sozialreform. Für beide Gruppen gilt jedoch gleichermaßen, dass die aus der Ausübung des Priesterberufes resultierende physische Mobilität im Verein mit zunehmender ökonomischer Unabhängigkeit ganz wesentlich zu individueller Ermächtigung (empowerment) beiträgt. Konformität mit der Tradition und vor allem mit den autoritativen Texten ist dabei in zunehmendem Maße verhandelbar – zumindest solange nicht das Neue und Individuelle in den Vordergrund gestellt wird, sondern als Rückgriff auf eine originale, jedoch in Vergessenheit geratene (bzw. unterdrückte) Tradition deklariert wird.

Noch während meiner Zeit am Max-Weber-Kolleg konnte ich einen ausführlichen Artikel zum Thema publizieren, zwei weitere Artikel befinden sich im Druck. Neben der ertragreichen Arbeit am eigenen Forschungsprojekt gelang es mir in der Zeit am Max-Weber-Kolleg, ein internationales Netzwerk zum Thema „Women as Leaders in World Religions" aufzubauen, das zur Grundlage der Beantragung eines ERC Advanced Grants werden soll. Ein ganz wesentlicher Faktor, der meinen Aufenthalt in Erfurt zu einem nicht nur akademischen Erfolg werden ließ, war die freundliche und kollegiale Atmosphäre am Max-Weber-Kolleg, der die intensive Arbeit auch in der Gruppe sehr gefördert hat. In diesem Zusammenhang hielt ich die Bereitschaft, sich mit der „academic acency" von weiblichen und jüngeren Mitgliedern innerhalb der Forschergruppe auseinanderzusetzen, für ausgesprochen fruchtbar und zukunftsweisend für deutsche Forschungsverbünde.

Priyanka Jha

The project "Buddhism and shaping of the Normative in Modern India" was undertaken as part of the research group (KFG) "Religious Individualisation in Historical Perspective". This project was to study the influence of Buddhism in shaping the normative of the Modern Indian State. For this, an attempt was made to contextualise the manner in which Buddhism came to shape the idea of India on the principles of Righteousness, Truth, Dignity and Equality. Buddhism has been invoked as political and social philosophy of emancipation. This was articulated in the writings by Dr B R Ambedkar (chairman of the Drafting Committee of Constituent Assembly and Law minister). This project attempted to locate Dr Ambedkar in reference to certain historical trajectory. This was informed by the writings and ideas of the thinkers who have not found their voice neither space in the larger canvas of nation and nationhood. These include: Anagarika Dharmapala, Dharmanand Kosambi, Ananda K Coomaraswamy and Mahapandit Rahul Sankrityayan.

This project attempted to read their writings and works as strands of Buddhism. This not only helped in breaking the homogeneous mould of emancipatory Buddhism but also of various other forms of Buddhism(s). This provided a certain frame of reference for post colonial invocation of religion in the shaping and creation of "the public" in South Asia. The strands identified were Identarian, Civilizational and Dialectical Buddhism. This project attempted to understand Politics of religion and the role that religion plays in foregrounding liberal values like Equality, Liberty, Justice and Dignity. The attempt was to understand a certain perspective of Religion as source of modern national self. The kind of role that this politics engineers in a post colonial context and the need to re-read the relationship of nation and religion. This project was interested in doing history of ideas from the lens of thinkers who invoke Buddhism primarily. This was done with the intention to:

Re-look at the understanding the normative of the nation, basing itself on "invocation of religion", this project attempted to move beyond dominant religions like Hinduism, Islam and, Christianity. To reading Emancipatory Buddhism and the heterogeneity in the same and tracing the genealogy.

The methodology included hermeneutics and history of ideas. Basing itself on interpretation of texts, writings, spaces of the thinkers, and its historical location.

Hans Joas

In der ersten Hälfte des Berichtszeitraums habe ich das Buch *Glaube als Option. Zukunftsmöglichkeiten des Christentums* in seine endgültige Form gebracht und im Juni 2012 veröffentlicht. Erneut waren die zahlreichen Verbesserungshinweise u.a. von Bettina Hollstein und von dem früheren Fellow Wolfgang Knöbl sehr hilfreich. Die Abschlussarbeiten konnte ich unter den exzellenten Arbeitsbedingungen des Freiburg Institute for Advanced Studies (FRIAS), an das ich im Frühjahr 2011 gewechselt bin, erledigen. Mit diesem Buch habe ich einen weiteren Beitrag zur Arbeit der Kolleg-Forschergruppe ‚Religiöse Individualisierung in historischer Perspektive' geleistet. Meine weitere Arbeit lässt sich in folgende drei Teilbereiche untergliedern:
1. Ich arbeite an einem Buch zu einer Theorie der Sakralisierung und Entsakralisierung. In diesem Buch werden, wie häufig bei mir, systematische und ideengeschichtliche Argumentationen miteinander verknüpft. In einer vorläufigen Gestalt habe ich den Gedankengang in Gestalt von sechs Vorträgen an der Universität Regensburg im Mai/Juni 2012 (als ‚Joseph Ratzinger-Papst Benedikt XVI-Gastprofessor') vorgetragen.

2. Zu den in den letzten Jahren entstandenen Aufsätzen zu den religionstheoretischen Arbeiten großer Denker des 19. und 20. Jahrhunderts kamen weitere hinzu, vor allem eine Auseinandersetzung mit der Theorie des ‚Heiligen' bei Rudolf Otto und mit den Werken von José Casanova und Wolfgang Huber.
3. Mein Buch zur Geschichte der Menschenrechte wird im Frühjahr 2013 in englischer Übersetzung erscheinen. Die Übersetzung wurde von mir korrigiert und für den Druck vorbereitet.

Karen Joisten

Meine Arbeit am Max-Weber-Kolleg war außerordentlich ertragreich und wichtig für mein Projekt „Freiheit und Verantwortung des Einzelnen in einer Geschichtenphilosophie". Es war im Rahmen der Kolleg-Forschergruppe „Religiöse Individualisierung in historischer Perspektive" angesiedelt. Es richtete den Fokus auf das Verhältnis des Einzelnen, der in einen narrativ bereits präfigurierten historischen Geschichtenkontext eingebunden ist, aber als Autor in diesen seine eigenen Geschichten produktiv einweben kann. In Anlehnung an Hannah Arendt gesagt, gelingt es ihm dabei unter Umständen, das Muster des bestehenden Bezugsgewebes menschlicher Angelegenheiten – in der Perspektive Wilhelm Schapps, des Vaters der Geschichtenphilosophie, gesagt: den lebendigen Geschichtenzusammenhang – zu verändern und ihm eine eigene Note einzuschreiben. Auf diese Weise kann die lesbare Welt immer wieder umgeschrieben und können Deutungsverschiebungen und Deutungsveränderungen vollzogen werden. Das Problem, das in diesem Spannungsverhältnis unhintergehbar ist, ist das der Notwendigkeit bestehender Narrationen als Totalität des bereits existenten Lebens-, Sprach- und Deutungszusammenhangs, das in Geschichten präsent ist, und das der Freiheit und Verantwortung des Einzelnen, der sich niemals voll und ganz aus dem Geschichtenzusammenhang seiner Zeit herauslösen kann. Hatte Aristoteles bereits darauf hingewiesen, dass der Mensch als der Handelnde Urheber seiner Handlungen ist, aber stets Miturheber bei den Handlungen beteiligt sind, konnte diese Perspektive nun kulturphilosophisch erweitert werden. Freiheit erweist sich in einem Geschichtenzusammenhang als absolut und relativ zugleich: Sie ist prinzipiell die Möglichkeit des Einzelnen, in Distanzierungsvollzüge einzutreten; sie kann aber stets nur relativ innerhalb des bestehenden Geschichtenbezugsgewebes sein. Der Prozess der Individualisierung tritt dergestalt als Prozess einer Freiheitserweiterung zum Vorschein (anders gesagt: als Prozess einer Freiheitsvertiefung), insofern der Einzelne – nicht zuletzt dank inter- und transkultureller Bezugnahmen – sich selbst anders fortzuschreiben vermag. Hand in Hand mit dieser Selbstveränderung – aus der Sicht Wilhelm Schapps gesagt: der „Eigengeschichte" – geht die Veränderung der Beziehungen zu den Mitmenschen und dergestalt der »Wirgeschichten«, die die untrennbare Verbindung zwischen Mensch und Mitmensch benennt. In der Zeit, in der ich am Max-Weber-Kolleg sein durfte, konnte ich diese Problemstellung anhand der

Geschichtentrilogie Wilhelm Schapps skizzieren und die Grundlage für eine Buchpublikation legen. Als Herausgeberin des Nachlasses von Wilhelm Schapp war es mir darüber hinaus möglich, in diesem Zeitraum den Nachlass auf diese Themenstellung hin zu sichten, um wichtige – über die Veröffentlichungen hinausweisende – Ergänzungen und Bedeutungsverschiebungen erfassen zu können.

Istvan Keul

Mein Projekt „Individualisierung und Institutionalisierung am Beispiel zweier rezenter asiatischer Neureligionen" befasste sich mit der Entstehung und Entwicklung zweier rezenter religiöser Formationen in Asien: der Verehrergruppe um Gururani und Yogiraj in Mumbai (Indien) und der religiösen Organisation Happy Science (Kofuku no kagaku) in Japan. Beide Formationen begannen in der zweiten Hälfte des 20. Jahrhunderts als Alleingänge religiös kreativer Individuen und verfestigten sich in wenigen Jahrzehnten zu stabilen Konfigurationen unterschiedlicher Ausprägung. Während es sich bei der Bewegung um Gururani um eine eher schwach konturierte und relativ kleine, jedoch sehr aktive transreligiöse Gruppe handelt, die am treffendsten mit dem religionswissenschaftlichen Kultbegriff beschrieben werden kann, ist Happy Science eine der zahlreichen neureligiösen Organisationen in Japan, deren Organisationsstruktur Ähnlichkeiten mit jener von Wirtschaftsunternehmen aufweist. Diese auf den ersten Blick disparaten religiösen Gruppen weisen eine ganze Reihe von Aspekten auf, deren vergleichende Untersuchung einerseits zu einem besseren Verständnis der jeweiligen Einzelfälle (Redeskription) beitragen kann, andererseits Möglichkeiten für metasprachliche Reflexion bietet. In beiden Fällen spielt in den einzelnen Etappen der Ausdifferenzierung individueller Sonderentwicklungen die Kombination kulturell unterschiedlicher Idiome eine wichtige Rolle. Der komparative Fokus insbesondere auf Entstehungskontexte, einzelbiographische Verläufe und frühe Institutionalisierungsprozesse leistet einen Beitrag zur Verfeinerung der Begrifflichkeit sowohl von religiöser Individualisierung als auch religiöser Vergemeinschaftung.

Julia Kindt

Die Zeit als *research fellow* am Max-Weber-Kolleg habe ich vor allem für die Arbeit an zwei Projekten genutzt:

Angeregt durch die vielen wunderbaren Diskussionen zur individuellen Religiosität in der Alten Welt am Kolleg habe ich einen Artikel zum Thema *Personal Religion: A Productive Conception for the Study of Ancient Greek Religion?* verfasst. Dieser Artikel wird nächstes Jahr im *Journal of Hellenic Studies* erscheinen. Ein Panel zum Thema der persönlichen Religion im alten Griechenland ist außerdem für das Jahrestreffen der *American Society of Classical Studies* (vormals *APA*) in San Francisco im Januar 2016 geplant (für weitere Informationen und Möglichkeiten zur Teilnahme, siehe http://apaclassics.org/annual-meeting/2016/ancient-greekpersonal-religion-orp-2016).

Außerdem habe ich an einem neuen Buchprojekt zum Thema *Anthropology and Animality in Ancient Greece* gearbeitet, welches die symbolische Beziehung zwischen Tieren, Menschen und Göttern in der griechischen Antike untersucht. Ein Kapitel zu *Gazing at Humans and Animals in Herodotus' Histories* wurde am Kolleg vorgetragen und hat sehr von den Kommentaren und Anmerkungen der Anwesenden profitiert.

Meine Familie und ich haben den Aufenthalt in Erfurt und vor allem auch die vielen netten Kontakte unter den Kollegiaten und Mitarbeitern am Max-Weber-Kolleg sehr genossen. In professioneller Hinsicht habe ich die Zeit am Kolleg als sehr produktiv empfunden. Ich möchte mich hierbei nochmals herzlich für die Einladung bedanken und der Hoffnung Ausdruck verleihen, mit dem Kolleg und seinen Mitgliedern auch in Zukunft in Kontakt zu bleiben.

Yahya Kouroshi

Während meiner Zeit am Max-Weber-Kolleg hatte ich die Gelegenheit, mit Forscherinnen und Forschern aus verschiedenen Disziplinen und aus der ganzen Welt in Kontakt zu kommen. Dies bedeutete für mich eine besondere Gelegenheit für den Austausch, die Diskussion, die Qualifizierung und die Vertiefung meiner Forschungsinteressen. Ich genoss die fachübergreifenden und interdisziplinären Diskussionen der an den Kolloquien Beteiligten v.a. in der Kolleg-Forschergruppe „Religiöse Individualisierung in historischer Perspektive". Darüber hinaus waren auch die Gespräche außerhalb der Kolloquien für mich sehr bedeutsam.

Während meiner Zeit am Max-Weber-Kolleg konnte ich verschiedene Forschungsprojekte vorantreiben, deren Schwerpunkt primär auf der Untersuchung von Materialien in der Forschungsbibliothek Gotha lag. Hierzu gehören Forschungen über die Zeitpraktiken „Kalender und Ordnung im interdisziplinären und interkulturellen Kontext um 1600" anhand der in der Forschungsbibliothek Gotha vorhandenen Manuskripte in arabischer, persischer und türkischer Sprache (noch unvollständig), sowie die Untersuchungen über die Erforschung ausgewählter persischer Handschriften von Jesuitenmissionaren in der Gothaer Forschungsbibliothek. Darüber hinaus habe ich es genossen, während meiner Zeit am Max-Weber-Kolleg viele Kollegiaten und Mitarbeiter des Max-Weber-Kollegs kennenzulernen. Dafür bin ich sehr dankbar und freue mich, auch in Zukunft mit dem Kolleg und seinen Mitgliedern in Kontakt zu bleiben.

Paul Michael Kurtz

My doctoral dissertation, submitted to the Department of Medieval and Modern History at the University of Göttingen, examined the entanglement of biblical studies, historicist philology, and cultural Protestantism in histories of ancient Israel at the time of the German Empire. It sought to what extent, in an age of "philological science", the very enterprise of reconstructing past religion was shaped by liberal Protestant values, shared by dominant historians at the turn of the twentieth century. It explored what scholars considered "religion" and "history" to be, how they proceeded to study these conceptual categories, and why they studied them the way that they did. To do so, it evaluated two representatives of distinct historiographical approaches: Julius Well hausen and Hermann Gunkel. Each of these major figures believed his own way of working represented what proper reconstruction of the past entailed, yet both reflected the shifting standards of writing on the past and the dramatic changes in university and society. Despite the real, often dramatic and polemical shifts in scholarship, the project exposed a fundamental continuity in how "history" and "religion" were conceived. Furthermore, it showed how the past was protestantized, that is, how these understandings directed the path to the ancient world. In consequence, the project disassembled investigations of Israel in particular to unearth the intellectual foundations of modern exploration of ancient religion in general. The work will be published, in revised form, next year by Mohr Siebeck in the series Forschungen zum Alten Testament I. The Max-Weber-Kolleg proved to be one of the most stimulating intellectual environments in which I have ever had the pleasure of working. Now a Marie Curie Fellow at the University of Cambridge, I found ready and able interlocutors at the Max-Weber-Kolleg who offered essential insight and critique as I developed my new research project and began to formulate grant applications.

Gesche Linde

Dieses Projekt zielt auf den Entwurf einer integrierten Sprach- und Handlungstheorie, basierend auf dem von dem amerikanischen Pragmatisten Charles S. Peirce 1905 entworfenen zehntrichotomischen Zeichenklassifikationssystem.

Interpretationsprozesse sind, Peirce zufolge, sämtlich so strukturiert, dass ein sog. Zeichen auf ein sog. Objekt bezogen wird und auf diese Weise ein sog. Interpretant (ein Interpretationsresultat) erzeugt wird. Zu den zentralen Ideen Peirces, denen ich folge, gehört erstens, dass dieses Grundmuster allen Bewusstseinsprozessen – Fühlen, Wollen, Handeln (eingeschlossen Sprechen), begrifflichem Verstehen (eingeschlossen Urteilen und Begründen) – zugrunde liegt, zweitens, dass Zeichen nach einem Konglomerat verschiedener Kriterien unterschieden werden können, so dass sich ein jeder Bewusstseinsprozess auf dieser Basis analysieren lässt. Diese Kriterien sind: die Binnenstruktur des Zeichens, die Binnenstruktur des Objekts, auf welches das Zeichen bezogen worden ist, die Art der Relation des Zeichens zum Objekt, die Binnenstruktur des Interpretanten und die Art der Relation des Zeichens (bzw. der Zeichen-Objekt-Relation) zum Interpretanten.

Peirce selbst hat die von dieser These verlangte Systematisierung in mehreren Schritten vorangetrieben, die zunächst 1903 in den Entwurf eines dreitrichotomischen Systems mündeten (d.h.: eines Systems, das für die drei Größen des Zeichens, des Objekts und des Interpretanten jeweils drei strukturelle Möglichkeiten ansetzt). 1904 erfolgte eine Erweiterung um drei auf sechs, 1905 um vier auf zehn Trichotomien. Das zehntrichotomische ist dasjenige System, mit dem ich arbeite, das Peirce selbst allerdings nie eingehend erläutert hat. Die Aufgabe, die ich mir gestellt habe, besteht deshalb darin, dieses System so auszugestalten, dass es zu einem funktionierenden Analyseinstrument sowohl von Handlungs- als auch von Sprachvollzügen wird. Seine Leistungsfähigkeit soll zum einen darin bestehen, dass es, indem es einen einheitlichen Analyserahmen für unterschiedliche Bewusstseinsvollzüge zur Verfügung stellt, strukturelle Ähnlichkeiten zwischen diesen sichtbar machen kann, zum anderen darin, dass es bislang unerreichte Differenzierungsmöglichkeiten an die Hand gibt, und schließlich darin, dass es den genetischen Zusammenhang zwischen verschieden strukturierten Interpretationsprozessen deutlich machen kann und auf diese Weise schlichte Entgegensetzungen (rational-emotional, Tier-Mensch, Individuum-Gemeinschaft etc.) unterläuft. Über den allgemeinen philosophischen Gewinn hinaus läge der spezifisch religionsphilosophische darin, dem im deutschen Sprachraum immer noch massiv dominierenden Schleiermacher-Paradigma bzw. einer Subjektivitätstheorie idealistischen Typs eine Theoriealternative gegenüberzustellen.

Antje Linkenbach

Das Menschenrechtsregime präsentiert sich als globale normative Ordnung mit universalistischem Anspruch und als positives Recht in Form internationaler Gerichtsbarkeit. Die globale Akzeptanz der Menschenrechte darf aber nicht darüber hinwegtäuschen, dass es sich bei ihrer Anerkennung oft nur um formale Zustimmung handelt, ohne konsequente praktische Umsetzung im politischen und lebensweltlichen Alltag. Dies auch weil das Menschenrechtspaket vielfach als ein primär westliches Produkt angesehen wird, welches kulturelle Differenz und alternative normative bzw. Wert-Vorstellungen zu ignorieren tendiere und dessen interkulturelle Legitimität dadurch nicht problemlos gegeben sei. Mein Projekt stellt daher die Frage nach der Anschlussfähigkeit bzw. Anschlussmöglichkeit anderer kultureller Traditionen an das bestehende Menschenrechtsregime sowie nach dem Potential zu dessen konzeptueller Erweiterung – beispielsweise durch vorangehende Prozesse interkategorieller Übersetzung und Wertegeneralisierung. Menschenrechte in der jetzigen Form sind kein ein für alle Mal festgeschriebenes und unveränderbares Produkt, sie sind vielmehr im Prinzip offen für Neu-Interpretationen, Reformulierungen und Erweiterungen, die sich aus dem interkulturellen Dialog ergeben können.

Eine erste Quelle zur Identifikation von potentiell anschlussfähigen Werten und Normen, wie auch solchen, die eine Reformulierung bzw. Erweiterung des bestehenden Menschenrechtsregimes nahelegen, sind – so die These – regionale Menschenrechtsentwürfe aus partikularen kulturellen Kontexten (z. B. *African (Banjul) Charter on Human and Peoples' Rights*, 1981; *Universal Islamic Declaration of Human Rights*, 1981; *Cairo Declaration on Human Rights in Islam*,1990; *Bangkok Declaration*, 1993). Die Regionalentwürfe kann man zum einen als Versuche ansehen, die UN-Menschenrechtserklärung in spezifische kulturelle Kontexte zu übersetzen, um sie dort verstehbar und annehmbar zu machen. Man kann sie aber auch – und dies erscheint mir von weiterführender Bedeutung – als Hinweise lesen auf leitende Ideale aus partikularen Kontexten, die, übersetzt in die Sprache des Rechts, den Anspruch auf universale Geltung und damit auch auf Einbezug in das globale Menschenrechtsregime erheben. Wertdimensionen, die aus regionaler Sicht stärker Berücksichtigung finden sollten, sind z. B. ökonomische und soziale Gerechtigkeit, die Stärkung/Resurrektion der Sozialität sowie eine konsequente Anerkennung von Pflichten als Basis der moralischen Gemeinschaft.

Mein Projekt verfolgt zwei Forschungsziele. Erstens versucht es, die Grundlinien des Wertehorizonts und des möglichen menschenrechtsrelevanten Wertespektrums ausgewählter zivilisatorisch-kultureller Kontexte (z. B. Südasien, Afrika) herauszuarbeiten; und zweitens, die Bedingungen und Möglichkeiten der Wertegeneralisierung kritisch auszuloten. Eine systematische Herausarbeitung der normativen bzw. Wert-Konstellationen erscheint mir die notwendige Grundlage für einen Diskurs der ‚Wertegeneralisierung' (Hans Joas), bei dem sich dann auch die westliche Tradition einer kritischen Revision unterziehen müsste. Für ein solches dialogisch-hermeneutisches Unterfangen lässt sich das Konzept der kulturellen ‚Übersetzung' und besonders das der ‚trans-categorical translation' methodisch fruchtbar machen (vgl. die Arbeiten von Doris Bachmann-Medick). Übersetzung – im Sinne einer kultursensitiven, hermeneutisch angeleiteten Analyse- und Kommunikationspraxis – ist in der Lage, auf eine Bezugsebene vorzustoßen, auf der Ausgangsbedingungen und Tiefenstrukturen interkultureller Kommunikation und Interaktion kritisch beleuchtet werden können. Nur wenn man die Theorien und Konzepte deseigenen wie des fremden Denksystems unter die Lupe nimmt, wenn man ihre Geltungsbereiche, Interpretationsdimensionen, Geschichte und Kontexte klärt, werden Schlüsselbegriffe der verschiedenen Traditionen erkennbar und ‚verhandelbar' und können als Basis für Universalisierungs- und Wertegeneralisierungsprozesse dienen. Menschenrechte erweisen sich damit auch als ein Übersetzungsproblem.

Harry Maier

The project 'Secret Places and Hidden Practices: Polemic. Imagination, and Deindividualisation in Early Christianity' take up the direction of the Kolleg-Forschergruppe by exploring space, deindividualisation, and entangled history. It develops what I have been working on in the last year, but with a new focus, namely on social identity and the creation of heresy as a mode of deindividualisation. I want to investigate entanglement by exploring how deindividualisation of opponents helps to form individuals in emerging Christian tradition, as requisite for sanctioned constructions of self and community. This helps to contest a simplistic orthodoxy vs. heresy model of Christian origins and shows how both together are implicated in the creation of social identity and practice.

The private household meetings of early Christians occasioned detractors to deploy a host of charges against an emerging new religious movement that ranged from cannibalism to sexual perversity. As Christianity emerged through the second century such charges were in turn deployed against its (now heretical) opponents. We can see this process already unfolding in the New Testament, in the vilification of 'the Jews' by Jewish and non-Jewish Christ followers. The Gospel of John, for example, both deindividualises Jewish opponents by casting them as offspring of the devil, or even as subjects of Caesar (rather than Yahweh); Matthew creates a typology of Pharisees for the same outcome; and Paul turns his opponents into circumcizing 'dogs' who preach a 'false Gospel' with infernal origins. Nowhere is this kind of polemic sharper than in John's Apocalypse where cosmic dualism, Hebrew Bible narratives that pit Israelites against Canaanites, and ideals of purity and impurity create enemies and deindividualise them as perverse monsters. As these polemical traditions developed they also drew on Greco-Roman ideas associated with illigitimate religious practices and religions. This we can see especially in creation of 'heretics' in the second century and accusations, by those laying claim to a normative Christianity, of secret and depraved ritual. The legislation of Constantine and his successors proscribing heresy developed this tradition in a new way, now outlawing the meetings of non-sanctioned groups and describing them with a series of terms (cosmic, medical, civic) to describe their identity.

Social geography furnishes useful tools for exploring how imagination creates spaces and populates them with various types of individuals. This project draws on its insights to consider how polemic functioned both to sanction and condemn spaces and promoted modes of orthodox individualisation even as it deployed imagination and vivid narrative to create counter sites for the erasure of legitimate religious identity, or deindividualisation. Consideration of space as source for the individual and its erasure shows how individualisation and deindividualisation work together in the creation of the social identity, normative institutions of belief and leadership, and orthodox practice.

Adelisa Malena

Im Oktober 2013 hatte ich das große Vergnügen, für einen Monat als Guest-Fellow der Kolleg-Forschergruppe 'Religiöse Individualisierung in historischer Perspektive' am Max-Weber-Kolleg zu meinem Projekt 'Die Rezeption der mittelalterlichen und frühneuzeitlichen Mystik im Radikalpietismus und in der antipietistischen Polemik' forschen zu dürfen. Ich konnte in der Universitätsbibliothek Erfurt und in der Forschungsbibliothek Gotha arbeiten.

Seit einigen Jahren beschäftige ich mich mit der Rezeption der mittelalterlichen und frühneuzeitlichen Mystik im deutschen Radikalpietismus lutherischer und reformierter Prägung und in der antipietistischen Polemik. Besonderes Augenmerk gilt dabei der Rezeption weiblicher Mystik.

Ich beabsichtige dabei diesen besonderen Aspekt kultureller Produktion im Pietismus in zweifacher Hinsicht zu analysieren: mittels einer Untersuchung 1) der Textproduktion (handschriftlich und gedruckt) innerhalb der Bewegung; 2) mittels einer Untersuchung der Vorwürfe, die in den polemischen Werken der Gegner des Pietismus vorgebracht wurden.

1) Bekannterweise wurde eine Reihe von Texten von mystischen AutorInnen im 17. und 18. Jahrhundert im pietistischen Milieu übersetzt und rezipiert (zum Beispiel: Caterina da Genova, Battistina Vernazza, Angela da Foligno, Teresa d'Avila, Pier Matteo Petrucci, Miguel de Molinos, Madame Guyon etc.). Dabei spielte das Engagement einiger Einzelfiguren für die kulturelle, sprachliche und konfessionelle Vermittlung eine entscheidende Rolle, so etwa von Friedrich Breckling, Gottfried Arnold, Pierre Poiret, August Hermann Francke und Gerhard Tersteegen. Biographien von MystikerInnen wurden in pietistischen Kreisen bekannt, u.a. auch dank der Tatsache, dass sie auf ‚unparteiische' Art und Weise – als Zeugnisse authentischer Glaubenserfahrungen – Eingang in einige wichtige Vitensammlungen fanden (wie z.B. in die *Historie der Wiedergebohrnen* des Reformierten Reitz, dessen erster Band 1698 in Offenbach erschien, und *Das Leben der Gläubigen* von Gottfried Arnold, Halle 1701).

Dabei verstehe ich die Übertragung der mystischen Tradition als Kulturtransfer; ich betrachte das Phänomen nicht nur, wie es in der Vergangenheit zumeist getan wurde, aus theologischer oder ideengeschichtlicher Perspektive, sondern fokussiere die Produktion, Zirkulation und Übersetzung von Texten, untersuche die sozialen und kulturellen Kontexte, in denen diese Texte über sprachliche und konfessionelle Grenzen hinweg rezipiert wurden, sowie die Netzwerke, die diese Übermittlungsprozesse unterstützten, und die entscheidenden Vermittlerfiguren, die auf unterschiedliche Weise zu diesem Transfer beigetragen haben. Ich versuche also, die interkonfessionelle Dimension des Radikalpietismus anhand von konkreten Hinweisen auf die Zirkulation von Texten und Beziehungen zwischen Menschen und Gruppen zu untersuchen. Besonderes Augenmerk wende ich auf die Analyse der Paratexte der deutschen Ausgaben der Schriften dieser Autoren/innen bzw. der über sie verfassten, ins Deutsche übertragenen Texte.

2) Zu den am häufigsten gegen den Pietismus und besonders gegen den radikalen Pietismus von seinen Gegnern vorgebrachten Vorwürfen gehört die ‚gefährliche Nähe' zur Mystik des Mittelalters und der frühen Neuzeit, insbesondere zur weiblichen Mystik. Dabei denke ich insbesondere an das berüchtigte *Gynaeceum haeretico fanaticum*, das 1704 von dem lutherischen Theologen Johann Heinrich Feustking in Frankfurt und Leipzig in Druck gegeben wurde. Dieses Werk lässt sich bekanntlich in eine Serie von theologischen und philosophischen antipietistischen Schriften einreihen, die im 17. und 18. Jahrhundert von der lutherischen Orthodoxie als Reaktion auf die wachsende Bedeutung des Pietismus verfasst wurden. Ich versuche, den Argumentationsstrang der übertriebenen Nähe zur weiblichen Mystik in einigen der wichtigsten antipietistischen polemischen Traktate zu verfolgen, um dabei nachzuvollziehen, inwiefern dieser Aspekt zur Stigmatisierung der Bewegung beitrug und welche spezifische Rolle den Mystikerinnen zugeschrieben wurde – innerhalb der geschlechtlich konnotierten Polemik von Seiten der Orthodoxien im Kampf gegen den radikalen Pietismus.

Meine Guest-Lecture am 22. Oktober 2013 und die darauffolgende Diskussion gaben mir die Gelegenheit, einige Aspekte meiner Arbeit mit ExpertInnen interdisziplinär zu diskutieren.

Aditya Malik

The primary concern of this research has been to establish theoretical and conceptual frameworks that aid in the analysis and translation of the texts that are the main focus of this project. These historical texts, like many other Indic texts, contain "mythical" and "legendary" materials together with a description of "historical" events.

The analysis and translation focuses on one particular text, namely the Hammira-Mahakavya (composed 1401) and on its reception in Hindi and English historiographical and philological studies from the mid-nineteenth to the mid-twentieth centuries. The initial conceptual question springs from the fact that the Hammira-Mahakavya, written by the Jaina poet Nayachand Suri, originates in a dream presented to the author of the text by the dead hero whose life and deeds lie at the center of the "great poem" (Sanskrit: *mahakavya*). The question that automatically arises here is whether history with its fundamental concern with empirical evidence, facts and what is considered "real" can originate in the subjective, inner world of dreams or what is considered "unreal". Is the "unreal" or imaginative fabric equally or more important here than the "real", empirical structure? But more pressing than this question is the question of the role of the imagination in the formulation of what is called history or historical "fact". In conceptual terms the project draws out the distinctions between and meanings of imagination and thinking about the past in tandem with Indian conceptual categories (Sanskrit: *kalpana, bhavana*). These conceptual linkages have, to my knowledge, not yet been satisfactorily undertaken in philosophical-historical scholarship in general, and in particular with reference to Indian ideas of history. This is important because many texts of historical value combine the imaginative with the empirical. In addition to the Hammira-Mahakavya, I also analyzed the Hammira-Raso, written in Hindi by the poet Jodha Raja (1701) as well as translations of the Persian works, Khaza'in al-Futuh of Amir Khusrau (1311) and the Tarikh-i-Firoz Shahi of Ziauddin Barani (1357). Besides this, I examined a work written in 1990 in English by L. S. Rathore with the title "The Glory of Ranthambore". The texts mentioned above, in Hindi and English, focus on the same set of events and the same protagonist of the Hammira-Mahakavya. The purpose of the project is to determine how these texts rework and refashion the historical and imaginative texture of the earlier, elaborate Sanskrit work. An analysis of all three texts together with the historical-philological studies of N. J. Kirtane (1879) in English and R. S. Sharma (1963/1968) in Hindi reveals how a temporal and cultural region is invented and memorialized through a singular series of events that provide a kind of "axial" moment in time. Moreover, these texts indicate the existence of a creative, "liberal" space of cosmopolitanism in terms of the intermingling of ideas, narratives, languages and the like, in which the protagonists occupy or rather embody and celebrate a nexus of values that underpins and allows such admixtures, interchanges and hybrid cultural forms to flourish that go beyond the compartmentalization provided by ethnic and religious identity.

Since taking up the fellowship, I have written 40,000 words toward the publication of a book. My research into conceptual issues regarding the idea of history, imagination and thinking about the past will complement the broader aim of the project, which is to understand shifting frameworks of historiography and the question of shared religious spaces and identities on the basis of seminal literary and historical texts, such as the Hammira-Mahakavya and other works mentioned above. In addition to the religio-historical analysis of texts written in Sanskrit, Rajasthani, Hindi and English, I was able to document spoken narratives as well as the architectural features (Hindu, Jain, Sufi and Buddhist temples and shrines) associated with the world heritage site of the fortress of Ranthambore in southern Rajasthan, which was the capital of King Hammira, the main protagonist of the texts I am studying. The inclusion of oral narratives from the site provides a unique research perspective that has not been attempted in any prior study. The opportunity to conduct ethnographic fieldwork in the region has enhanced the depth and range of the book. It is clear from my own previously published work, and from the work of other important scholars, that Indian / South Asian history, society and identity cannot be adequately understood without understanding the role, nature and function of the spoken word and its expression in oral traditions and narratives, and in ritual performance that continue to exist all over the subcontinent.

Angelika Malinar

The project focused on European women as interpreters of Hinduism in the colonial-modern period. From the last decades of the nineteenth century onward, women not only in India but also in Europe participated increasingly in the debates about Indian religion and society. Women like Annie Besant (1847–1933) and Margaret Noble (1867–1911) did not only pursue their own spiritual interests but were also actively engaged in socio-political and educational projects. In doing so, they challenged constructions of gender and regimes of power both in India and Europe, which resulted in complex biographies as well as in various interpretations of Hinduism. The latter have not received much scholarly attention. During my fellowship, I focused on the theoretical debates on the interpretation of the agency of European women in the colonial context, in particular on the issue of their individuality. The latter has become an object of debate in some post-colonial studies, which point out that these women lack independent agency and thus individuality. In an earlier study, I countered this view with respect to Annie Besant's biography. The theoretical approach pursued in my project has been developed in a larger theoretical framework that draws on notions of "entangled history" and "cultural translation". In this way, the discussion of biographical dimensions can be connected with the study of the concrete practices as well as practical results of the cultural translations at play. Furthermore, I worked on Annie Besant's interpretation of Hinduism, in particular the doctrines of *karman*, *bhakti* (devotion to God) and *dharma* (duty, religion) in her writings as well as in the textbooks on Hinduism she co-authored. The intertwining of political and spiritual agendas in Besant's interpretations is particularly obvious in her using the doctrine of *karman* for understanding the history of nations and current agendas of nation-building. The textbooks on Hinduism aim to give a general idea of India's "national religion" that accords generally with what is viewed as brahmanical or "orthodox" norms but is at the same time open to sectarian adjustments. In building the line of defence against all kinds of objections through a more or less undefined generality, the textbook delineates essential doctrines of the "eternal religion" (*sanātana dharma*) thus avoiding the term Hinduism. During my stay at the Max-Weber-Kolleg I again very much profited from the lively discussions and the critical engagement of the members of the Kolleg-Forschergruppe in a wide range of research topics. It gave me the opportunity to work intensively on my project and at the same time to participate in the very productive academic discourse at the Max-Weber-Kolleg. A first output of the research is an edited volume dealing with exchanges between Asia and Europe in the modern period. It will be published in spring 2018.

Katharina Ulrike Mersch

Im Oktober 2010 habe ich mein Habilitationsprojekt in der Kolleg-Forschergruppe ‚Religiöse Individualisierung in historischer Perspektive' am Max-Weber-Kolleg begonnen. Während meines zweijährigen Aufenthalts habe ich nicht nur eine umfassende Materialsichtung bewerkstelligen und Quellenkomplexe erarbeiten können, sondern habe vor allem konzeptionell vom interdisziplinären Austausch in der Kolleg-Forschergruppe und am Max-Weber-Kolleg profitiert.

Das Forschungsprojekt beleuchtet die Stellung laikaler Machthaber zur Kirche und ihren Institutionen vom 12. Jahrhundert bis zur Mitte des 14. Jahrhunderts. Zu diesem Zweck wird die Exkommunikation in den Blick genommen, mit der kirchliche Instanzen religiöses, soziales und politisches Verhalten ahndeten, das kirchlichen Normen und Interessen widersprach. Im Rahmen der Arbeiten am Kolleg konnten die zeitgenössischen kirchenrechtlichen Diskussionen und theologischen Leitlinien herausgearbeitet und in einem ersten Hauptabschnitt der Arbeit schriftlich niedergelegt werden. Im Sinne des übergreifenden Themas der Kolleg- Forschergruppe wurden die Bedeutung des individuellen Gewissens und persönlicher Entscheidungsfreiräume der Exkommunizierten im kanonistischen und theologischen Diskurs betont. Erste Hinweise auf Individualisierungs- und Individuierungstendenzen finden sich bereits in den kirchenrechtlichen Quellen des 12. Jahrhunderts, die bei der Frage, ob eine Exkommunikation vermieden oder riskiert werden solle, auf die auf dem Reflexionsvermögen gründende religiöse Integrität des einzelnen vom Kirchenbann bedrohten Laien setzte – im Zweifelsfall sollte er im Widerspruch zu den Vorgaben der Kleriker handeln. Dieser konzeptionelle Zugang erlaubt, im Hinblick auf die Kontrastierung von Norm und Praxis, die das Herzstück der Arbeit ausmachen wird, bislang wenig bekannte Wege zu beschreiten. Dieser Hauptteil der Arbeit widmet sich der Frage, wie sich Laien unter dem Eindruck des Kirchenbanns zu ihrer eigenen Person und zu ihrem sozialen Umfeld verhielten, wie sie gegen die Zensur aufbegehrten, wie sie sich Zugang zu kanonistischen und theologischen Wissensbeständen verschafft und der Exkommunikation zum Trotz an der christlichen Glaubenspraxis festgehalten haben. Im Zusammenhang mit den in den Kolloquien des Kollegs vorgestellten Fallbeispielen hat sich gezeigt, dass die sich aus moderner Perspektive aufdrängende Unterscheidung von religiösen und politischen Aspekten und Diskursen fehlgeht, vielmehr der Alterität mittelalterlicher Argumentation Rechnung zu tragen ist und in der *longue durée* neben den Individualisierungseben auch Säkularisierungsprozesse beobachtet werden müssen. Diskussionen über den politischen und sozialen Rang eines Exkommunizierten beinhalteten auch Debatten über die Einbindung dieser Positionen in das christliche Heilsgefüge. Sie waren außerdem verzahnt mit Reflexionen über die innere religiöse Haltung der Gebannten, wobei in den Quellen drei Ebenen dieses Diskurses zu unterscheiden sind: die Selbstäußerung der Exkommunizierten im Verfahren und im Austausch mit ihrem sozialen Umfeld, die Befunde ihrer Exkommunikatoren und anderer am Konflikt Beteiligter sowie sowohl zeitgenössische als auch retrospektive Deutungen des Konflikts durch Gelehrte, Geschichtsschreiber und sogar Mystikerinnen. In meiner Zeit am Kolleg konnte ich eine Reihe solcher Fallbeispiele bearbeiten, mich mit den Argumentationen der geistlichen und gelehrten Fürsprecher der Exkommunizierten vertraut machen und mir außerdem einen Überblick darüber verschaffen, wie Exkommunizierte sich die Teilhabe an der Messe, der christlichen Stiftungspraxis und der christlichen Bestattung verschafften und auf individuellen Wegen rechtliche Normen umgingen. Dafür möchte ich mich ebenso bedanken wie für die zahlreichen Denkanstösse, die ich aus Erfurt mitgenommen habe an die Universität Göttingen, wo ich mein Habilitationsprojekt weiterführe.

Dorit Messlin

Im Mittelpunkt des Habilitationsprojektes steht eine Normabweichungs- und Überschreitungsfigur, die in historischer und systematischer Perspektive unter dem Begriff des ‚Hyperbolischen' zum Gegenstand diskursgeschichtlicher und sozialphilosophischer Fragestellungen wird.

Eigentlich ist die Hyperbel ein rhetorischer Stilbegriff und bezeichnet allgemein jede übertriebene Darstellung eines Gegenstandes, bei der das *aptum* (im Sinne des Angemessenen, Wahrscheinlichen, Glaubwürdigen) zugunsten einer stärkeren Anschaulichkeit, Evidenz und Intensivierung überschritten wird. Da aus der klassischen Rhetorik die neuzeitliche Anthropologie hervorging, gewinnen die Begriffe des Angemessenen/Hyperbolischen auch als normative und verhaltensregulierende Kategorien an Bedeutung. In der Geschichte und im Sprachgebrauch des 17. und 18. Jahrhunderts führt der Begriff ‚Hyperbolik' vor allem auf Phänomene des Umgangs mit religiöser Digression, wobei er als Normabweichungstheorem eng mit dem Begriff des enthusiastischen Ingeniums verknüpft ist. Hier zeigt sich, dass der Begriff sehr lange eben nicht jene rein positive Bedeutung natürlich gegebener Kreativität hatte, wie er uns heute geläufig ist. Besonders in Deutschland überwiegen lange die negativen Konnotationen von Enthusiasmus als unberechenbare, ketzerische, fanatische Abweichung von den vernünftigen Lehren der (Staats-)Kirche und der Gesellschaft.

Die Arbeit untersucht historische Verhandlungen und Diskurse des Konzeptes der Angemessenheit (als normativer Maßstab) und seiner Überschreitung (Hyperbolik) auf dem Feld religiöser Erfahrungen und Kontroversen vom 17. Jahrhundert bis zur Gegenwart. In wechselnden Konstellationen und Kontexten geht es um Fragen nach den Operationalisierungen von Angemessenheit und ihrer Überschreitung, nach dem Anwendungsspektrum dieser Kategorien und ihrer Bewertungsmaßstäbe sowie nach thematischen Kontinuitäten und Diskontinuitäten in den Dynamiken der normativen Aushandlung von Angemessenheit bzw. von legitimer oder illegitimer Abweichung.

In den historischen Diskursen wird Hyperbolik zum einen als zentraler operationaler Faktor auf dem Feld religiöser Selbstentwürfe erkennbar, und äußert sich in viel fältiger Weise als Plädoyer für das Übermäßige, Überbordende, Regelverweigernde und als Ausdrucksform inkommensurabler Individualität. Von Seiten kultureller Normenkontrolle erscheinen Phänomene dieser Art aber auch als problematisch verhandelte ‚Abweichungen' von den majoritären Mustern gängiger Verhaltens- und Affektökonomien. Der Diskurs über ‚Hyperbolik', der im Verlauf des 17. Jahrhunderts einsetzt, macht Dynamiken der Diversifikation und der Digression sichtbar und dokumentiert ein starkes kulturelles Interesse an der Vermessung von Devianz.

Dietmar Mieth

Individualisierung bedeutet in den religiösen Bewegungen des Spätmittelalters die Suche nach religiöser Freiheit innerhalb eines sich immer mehr normativ verfestigenden staatlich-kirchlichen Bezugssystems (Juridifizierung, Bürokratisierung, Verschulung des Glaubens, Ausgrenzungen). Die Unmittelbarkeit des Individuums zu Gott, wie sie im 13. und 14. Jahrhundert in verschiedenen Varianten von den großen Mystikerinnen und Mystikern aus den Bettelorden gelehrt und gelebt wurde, wurde von der Suche nach dem ‚freien Geist' begleitet. Diese ‚Bewegung' in ihren Selbstlegitimationen von außen her, d.h. durch die Inquisition, zu erfassen, bildete die Hauptgrundlage für die bisherige Darstellung spätmittelalterlicher religiöser Bewegungen. Diesen Ansatz muss man problematisieren und durch den Versuch ersetzen, in den überlieferten Texten zu eruieren, was die ‚Abweichler' tatsächlich motiviert hat (s.u. dazu: Dietmar Mieth/Britta Müller-Schauenburg [Hg.], Mystik, Recht und Freiheit; Dietmar Mieth, Ketzer und Ketzerverfolger in Erfurt).

Auf dem Wege ist die Buchveröffentlichung *Meister Eckhart* in der Reihe ‚Denker' im Beck Verlag München. Für das Thema ‚Religiöse Individualisierung im Mittelalter', bezogen auf die religiösen Bewegungen des Spätmittelalters, wurden internationale Beziehungen verstärkt, u.a. durch die Beteiligung am Promotionsverfahren an der Sorbonne IV (Paris): Sebastian Maxim, 'Le *Moi* chez Maître Eckhart' (Oktober 2010), durch die Zusammenarbeit mit Prof. Ruedi Imbach, Sorbonne IV (Paris), dem Musée Cluny und mit einer französischen Mediävistentagung in Paris vom 28. Mai bis 1. Juni 2010 anlässlich des Gedächtnisses 1310–2010: der Prozess gegen die Begine Marguerite Porete (Förderung durch die DFG, die Sorbonne und das Heinrich Heine Haus), durch die Zusammenarbeit mit der internationalen ‚The Eckhart Society' (UK), u.a. mit einem Referat auf der Jahrestagung in Leeds (UK) vom 23. bis 25. September 2011, durch die Zusammenarbeit mit der Universität Lecce (Italien), der Universität Tokyo und der Universität Metz. Deutlich wurden auch im Rahmen dieses Projekts die interreligiösen Perspektiven, u.a. bei der Beteiligung an der Untersuchung von ‚Practical Mysticism' (Diss. 2012 über Eckhart und Rumi in Erfurt) und in der Zusammenarbeit mit japanischen Forschern zu Meister Eckhart („Meister Eckharts *Reden* an die Stadt', Symposium in Erfurt vom 15. bis 17. April 2011 unter internationaler deutsch-italienisch-japanischer Leitung). Erleichtert wurde das Projekt durch die Zusammenarbeit mit Akademien in München und Mainz, die für Tagungen und Vorträge Entgegenkommen zeigten. Die Tagung ‚Religiöse Individualisierung in der Mystik: Eckhart, Tauler, Seuse' wurde vom 23. bis 25. März 2012 in Kooperation mit der Akademie in München durchgeführt (vgl. *Zur Debatte* 7, München 2012).

Inzwischen hat sich am Max-Weber-Kolleg in Kooperation mit Kollegin Schmolinsky ein Arbeitskreis zur religiösen Frauenforschung im spätmittelalterlichen Europa etabliert. Er veranstaltete u. a einen Workshop ‚Typen der religiösen Individualisierung im Mittelalter' (15.11.2012).

Anneke B. Mulder-Bakker

Ever since my student days in 1965, when I unraveled Herbert Grundmann's masterpiece *Religiöse Bewegungen im Mittelalter* (published in 1935, but only widely read in the WB-edition of 1961), I have been fascinated by medieval laypeople who wanted to shape their own religious lives and sought spiritual perfection. It wasn't the professionals who interested me; the clerics and the 'religious' who led perfect lives in monasteries, since time immemorial, have already been studied by church historians (often clerics or monastics themselves). Nor was I intrigued by the efforts of simple lay folks tending to (so-called) 'idolatry', superstitious beliefs or downright heresies: they had been a favourite topic of scholars in the GDR.

Rather, I am fascinated by serious lay believers striving for devoted holiness in the lay world – and often playing leadership roles in the community of the faithful. I first started with hermits and wrote a book on the knighthermit Gerlach of Houthem (d. 1165), living in an oak tree near Maastricht and wandering around as a kind of *Wanderprediger*. I continued with anchoresses or recluses, living in cells attached to parish churches or urban chapels. From their solitary anchorholds in very public places, they acted as teachers, counsellors, and, in some cases, theological innovators for parishioners who would speak to them from the street. See my *Lives of the Anchoresses* (2005) and my *Verborgen Vrouwen* (2007).

Both the hermits and the recluses had stepped out of their ordinary lives in order to devote themselves full-time to God. In the context of the *Religiöse Individualisierung* project, I will focus on urban laywomen seeking devoted holiness in domestic households in the midst of cities. Living together in privately-owned houses, called *domus animarum* or *Gotshus* in the sources, earning their own money, inciting each other toward the good by mutual exhortation, they shaped their own religious lives and acted as spiritual leaders in the community. I focus on the case of Lady Gertrude Rickeldey of Ortenberg (d. 1335), who together with a younger companion, the young lady Heilke of Staufenberg (died after 1335), ran an aristocratic household first in Offenburg and then in Strasbourg in the time that famous mendicant preachers worked there (such as Meister Eckhart, well-known here in Erfurt). Gertrude herself lived in personal deprivation and rigorous asceticism while, at the same time, she enjoyed mystical experiences. Heilke, who was very well educated, managed the household and acted as her 'cleric'.

A younger laywoman from their immediate circle noted down the stories told by old Heilke in a spiritual biography: *Von dem Heiligen Leben der Seligen Frowen Genant die Ruckeldegen, und Waz Grosser Wunder Unser Lieber Her mit Jr Gewurcket Het* (c. 1340). This biography opens a window on the daily existence and the intellectual aspirations of the women. Nowhere do we hear a male voice, condescending or not, as we usually do in sources of ecclesiastical authors who wrote as outsiders. The *Leben* shows how God revealed the sins of fellow citizens to Gertrude, whom she reminded of their responsibility. She mediated in controversies and feuds, helped the sick and needy, and was an independent agent of salvation as Anneke B. Mulder-Bakker her holy presence had salvific qualities. The *Leben* concludes: 'Gertrude went out into the cities and villages of this world. The words that she spoke struck right to the heart. With her mild admonition and virtuous power she often outdid the mendicants'.

Together with two German scholars, Freimut Löser and Michael Hopf, I am working on an edition of the *Leben* in English translation. I will publish the text headed by a comprehensive historical study of Gertrude and Heilke's spirituality and agency, written by me, plus two literary studies by Löser and Hopf.

Martin Mulsow

Ich arbeite seit einiger Zeit an einer Monographie über ‚Historische Religionswissenschaft in der Frühen Neuzeit', in der ich in einzelnen Fallstudien die Theorien von Gelehrten des 16. bis 18. Jahrhunderts über antike Götter, Rituale und Institutionen analysiere. Solche Themen wurden in einer noch unprofessionalisierten Religionswissenschaft zumeist von Theologen, Philologen oder Historikern unter dem Titel ‚Idolatrie' bearbeitet.

Zugleich möchte ich durch die Verbindung mit der Kolleg-Forschergruppe ‚Religiöse Individualisierung in historischer Perspektive' meine Ideen über eine Ausweitung der Ideengeschichtsschreibung zur Frühen Neuzeit vorantreiben. Diese Historiographie ist immer noch sehr eurozentrisch angelegt, könnte aber, davon bin ich überzeugt, von einer Veränderung in Richtung auf eine ‚transkulturelle Ideengeschichte' sehr profitieren. In dieser Weise scheint mir auch die Suche nach einer Erweiterung der Thematik ‚religiöse Individualisierung' in Richtung auf eine Beschreibung religiöser ‚Entanglements' verschiedener Traditionen und ihrer Wirkung auf das Selbst von Akteuren fruchtbar zu sein. Die Verflechtung von Religionen in Kontaktzonen, durch Migranten und über gelehrte Aneignung konnte zu unvorhergesehenen Entwicklungen führen, die durch Individuen eingeleitet wurden, aber auch auf Individuen zurückgewirkt haben.

Bernd-Christian Otto

Etwa seit dem frühen 13. Jahrhundert sind lateinische Texte überliefert, die Ritualtechniken zur Beschwörung und Instrumentalisierung von Zwischenwesen beschreiben. Die in diesen Texten beobachtbare Verflechtung christlicher Liturgie- und Gebetstraditionen mit – aus christlicher Sicht – fremdartigen Elementen (etwa einer Vielzahl unbekannter Engelnamen oder Symbolfiguren) wirft die Frage nach dem Ursprung jener Elemente wie der ganzen Textgruppe auf. Ausgangshypothese (1) des Projekts ist, dass diese hoch- und spätmittelalterlichen lateinischen Beschwörungstexte das Produkt eines Rezeptionsprozesses aus dem arabischen Kulturraum darstellen. Diese Hypothese ist in der Forschungsliteratur vereinzelt geäußert, bislang allerdings nicht systematisch untersucht worden (im Unterschied zur mittlerweile gut rekonstruierten arabisch-lateinischen Transmission astrologischer und alchemistischer Texte). Tatsächlich sind aus dem arabischen Mittelalter – dieses schließt jüdische Milieus ein – deutlich früher Ritualtexte überliefert, die Techniken zur Beschwörung und Instrumentalisierung von Zwischenwesen beschreiben und große Ähnlichkeiten zu den lateinischen Texten aufweisen. Im Rahmen von Vorstudien wurde ein Korpus an mittelalterlichen arabischen und lateinischen Ritualtexten zusammengestellt (außerdem werden einige altkastilische und mittelgriechische sowie hebräische und aramäische Texte in Übers. einbezogen), das auf ein rezeptionsgeschichtliches Abhängigkeitsverhältnis hin untersucht werden soll. Als *tertium comparationis* dienen die Listen und Namen der adressierten Zwischenwesen, rituell genutzte Symbolzeichen (auch bezeichnet als ‚Sigillen' oder ‚Brillenbuchstaben'), pseudepigraphische und narrative Musterbildungen sowie einzelne Ritualtechniken und -elemente.

Darüber hinaus richtet das Projekt den Blick auf den sozialen Kontext der Beschwörungskunst im arabischen und lateinischen Mittelalter. Ausgangshypothese (2) ist, dass die Beschwörungskunst im arabischen Mittelalter zumindest in bestimmten Milieus offen praktiziert und als legitime Kunst bzw. ‚Wissenschaft' (arab. *'ilm*) erachtet wurde – trotz der auch in islamischen Kerntexten verankerten Magiepolemiken und -verbote. Darauf deuten u.a. der bereits quantitativ viel üppigere arabische Diskurs sowie die in den arabischen Texten häufig auftauchenden Narrative einer Aufwertung und Verwissenschaftlichung von arab. *sihr* (‚Magie') hin. Demgegenüber zeigt sich im lateinischen Spätmittelalter – trotz gewisser Freiräume in höfischen, universitären oder auch monastischen Milieus – ein insgesamt viel restriktiverer Umgang mit der Beschwörungskunst. In seiner weiteren Wirkungsgeschichte hat dieses neu verfügbare ‚prekäre Wissen' daher wichtige theologische Diskurse angestoßen: Hier ist an die Ausarbeitung einer elaborierten Sakramentslehre zur Stabilisierung christlicher ‚Orthopraxie' zu denken, an die konzeptionelle Weiterentwicklung des christlichen Nekromantie- und Häresieverständnisses, schließlich an die Wegbereitung der frühneuzeitlichen Hexenverfolgungen durch die Entwicklung komplexer Dämonologien und einer erstmals systematischen Magiegesetzgebung. Erweisen sich die Ausgangshypothesen als korrekt, widerfuhr der Beschwörungskunst im Zuge des

Transfers vom arabischen in das lateinische Mittelalter also eine massive Kontextverschiebung, die im Zuge des Projekts möglichst nuanciert rekonstruiert und beschrieben werden soll.

Parallel zu diesem Projekt arbeite ich seit mehreren Jahren an einer präzisen, kultur- und epochenübergreifenden, streng an Primärquellen orientierten und theoretisch fundierten Rekonstruktion der Geschichte westlicher Gelehrtenmagie; hierzu ist die Abfassung einer englischsprachigen Monographie vorgesehen.

Jennifer Otto

My postdoctoral research project came to an end in September 2017. The study, which I am preparing for publication as a monograph, consists of a socio-rhetorical analysis of the extant homilies preached by Origen in the Caesarean community, read in conversation with contemporary literary and archaeological evidence. It situates intra-Christian debates over the legitimacy of practices such as corporal punishment, military service, and voluntary martyrdom / sacrificial death within larger Christian and Greco-Roman discourses of legitimate violence. My work greatly benefited from the opportunity to present several guest lectures at the Max-Weber-Kolleg and in the colloquium "Locating Martyrs in Space and Time", organized by the Erfurt Spatio-Temporal research group. In addition to furthering my research, I also taught a master's level seminar, entitled "Violence in Early Christianity", in the Religious Studies department at the University. My stay in Erfurt also provided me the opportunity to revise my PhD dissertation, which will be published as Philo of Alexandria and the Construction of Jewishness in Early Christian Writings by Oxford University Press in Spring 2018. A major achievement of my time in Erfurt was the organization of an international research conference, entitled "Killing Christians, Christians Killing: Violence, Trauma, and Identity in Early Christianity", which was held from 14–16 July, 2017. Planned in collaboration with Professor Katharina Waldner, our meeting included paper presentations from twelve senior and emerging scholars from Germany, Italy, Denmark, the UK, and the United States. The papers proceeding from the conference will be published in a volume by Peeters Press, which will be co-edited by Katharina Waldner and myself. I am very grateful to have had the opportunity to learn from the remarkable group of scholars assembled by the Max-Weber-Kolleg.

Rahul Bjørn Parson

My project is part of the Kolleg-Forschergruppe 'Religiöse Individualisierung in historischer Perspektive'. We will publish the contributions of the KFG in 2018. I feel very fortunate to have been a part of this team. My research considers Jain merchant

Banārasīdās (1586–1643), best known as the author of the first South-Asian autobiography, the Ardhakathanaka or the Half-Tale. Banārasīdās was the central figure in the protestant movement of Jain spirituality called Adhyātma. He operated in a North Indian milieu enriched by Indo-Persian Islamic elements and the intractable variety of Indic cultural expressions of bhakti (devotional religion). I focus on Banārasīdās' Samayasāra Nāṭaka, a rendering of a Sanskrit / Prakrit classic into a vernacular poetic idiom, and an *Urtext* of Jain spiritualism. The Samayasāra Nāṭaka propels a mode of thinking about the Self and salvation which enables discourses and genres that had hitherto not existed in South Asia. Banārasīdās is in many ways an embodiment of individualization, evidenced in how he employs himself in philosophical texts and how he imagines his role in the career of the text. His work informs the way many poets and thinkers talk about the unconditioned Self in the subsequent centuries. Jain poets, like their Bhakti, Sufi and Sant contemporaries, found accommodation for strands of religious individualization within the cultural confluence that was Mughal North India (16th to 19th centuries). They began to apprehend an introspective, personal religious turn and calibrate it with their canonical, philosophical tenets, e.g. anekāntavād and syādavāda (non-absolutism and may-be-ism). Befitting the historical moment, this new literature appeared in a vernacular poetic idiom, thereby democratizing access to spiritual knowledge and emboldening further spiritual and literary innovation. This confidence coincided with non-religious spheres such as increased mobility, sociality and entrepreneurship, sharing family resemblances to non-Indian strands of individualization.

My time at the Max-Weber-Kolleg has allowed me to do this extended research, prepare some publications and vastly improve my knowledge of the required languages. I am indebted to my friends and colleagues at the Max-Weber-Kolleg for their warmth, intellectual support and camaraderie. The opportunity allowed me to expand my field of expertise and benefit from a stimulating scholarly environment. Aside from research time, I must acknowledge that the Max-Weber-Kolleg also propelled my career into a tenure-track professorship in the U.S. I look forward to future collaborations.

Marco Pasi

During the first months, I have been working on the theoretical and methodological aspects of my research. I have been focusing on the problems related to the concept of nationalism, especially in connection to religion, modernity and secularization. I have also looked at historical research on romantic socialism and messianism in the nineteenth century (e.g., Jacob L. Talmon, Paul Bénichou), because it is clearly the ideological backbone upon which the phenomenon I am studying has taken shape. Very recently, new research from Julian Strube (Sozialismus, Katholizismus und Okkultismus im Frankreich des 19. Jahrhunderts, Berlin 2016), even if not connected directly with the problem of nationalism, has made the connection between radical political ideas and esotericism in the first half of the nineteenth century emerge even more clearly and cogently. One of the most interesting aspects of the theoretical part of my research is that all three elements of the "triangle" I am studying (nationalism, esotericism and religious individualization) have been the object of similar discussions with respect to chronology and cultural context. All three are in fact related to the broader problem of "modernity", which entails the contested issues of uniqueness and particularity of modern western culture. Is, for instance, esotericism only western? Is it just a modern phenomenon? Such questions have received different answers from different scholars, and can be applied in analogous terms to nationalism and religious individualization as well. Apart from the theoretical and methodological aspects of my research, I have also begun to go deeper into the life and works of Adam Mickiewicz, the first author from my project. In the second part of the fellowship period, I have begun to do research on Giuseppe Mazzini, the second case study in my project. With respect to more concrete results of my project so far, I would like to mention that I already brought fresh attention to the understudied relationship between nationalism and esotericism by organizing a panel on "Western Esotericism and Nationalism: Strange Bedfellows or Happy Allies?" at the annual conference of the European Association for the Study of Religions (EASR), held at the University of Helsinki from 28 June to 1 July 2016. The panel included three other speakers apart from myself. My own paper presented the main lines of my research project, and was titled "Religious Individualization and Nationalism in Modern Europe through the Lens of Alternative Spirituality and Western Esotericism (1823–1939)".

With respect to publications, I plan to publish in two different peer-reviewed journals two papers I have prepared during the fellowship, one on the theoretical aspects of my project and one on Mazzini. The final goal of the project, however, remains the publication of a monograph. Finally, it is important to mention that I have submitted an application for the organization of a trilateral conference series at the Villa Vigoni, the German-Italian Centre for European Excellence. The application has been prepared in collaboration with Julian Strube (Ruprecht-Karls-Universität Heidelberg), Jean-Pierre Brach (École Pratique des Hautes Études) and Patricia Chiantera-Stutte (Università degli Studi di Bari Aldo Moro). The title of the proposed conference series, which is closely connected to my current research project, is "Esoterik und die Konstruktion politischer Identitäten in Europa: Historische Perspektiven und kritische Analysen". My experience at the Max-Weber-Kolleg has been quite positive on the whole. I have particularly appreciated the formula of the "colloquia", which allows fellows and staff members of the Max-Weber-Kolleg to present their research and profit from each other's feedback. This is where the multidisciplinary identity of the Max-WeberKolleg becomes a real, concrete asset. Some of the colloquia I have attended have given me inspiration and ideaswhich will stay with me and be quite useful in the future, whether for my own research project or for other future projects. On the other hand, the critical feedback received during my own colloquium presentation has been invaluable and has helped me to better conceptualize and refine some aspects of my work. The highlight of my activities during the semester break has been my participation in a conference and a round table workshop on theosophy and modern culture in Osaka and Kyoto, respectively. The two events have been organized by a team of Japanese colleagues who have received a large grant from the Japanese Council of Scientific Research for a three-year project on the theosophical movement. The roundtable workshop gave me the opportunity to present an overview of my current research project at the Max-Weber-Kolleg. During the rest of that period I have been working on the part of my research that focuses on Mazzini, with the reading of relevant literature and taking notes in view of the writing of the relevant chapter for my book project.

Ioanna Patera

In the two years I had the opportunity to spend at the Max Weber Center in Erfurt as a post-doctoral guest, I prepared my habilitation project, entitled *Objects within Ritual. Interpretations of ritual practices in ancient Greece*. The project has been presented and discussed in helpful and often enlightening discussions within the most stimulating Kolleg-Forschergruppe 'Religiöse Individualisierung in historischer Perspektive', under the supervision of Jörg Rüpke who helped me in avoiding numerous pitfalls and errors.

In this work I argue that modern nomenclature of ancient Greek object categories needs to be revised. Indeed what we call ritual objects is an all-encompassing category often applied in scholarship to various more or less coherent groups of objects. There is, however, no such category in ancient Greek sources. This inadequacy in terminology leads to a comparison of modern and ancient concepts relating to objects. More differences appear than equivalents and lead to a reconsideration of the whole concept of 'ritual objects'.

While ritual and objects were the main subject in the very beginning of this work, nomenclature has acquired an increasing significance. An examination of names in context, such as festivals named after specific objects, led me to reconsider the use and function of these objects within the occasions in question. In principle, we know that function is difficult to determine. The form of an object may give suggestions as to functionality, that is its potential use, without stating what actually happened. Therefore most of the times function assigned to objects is merely hypotheses.

Instead of building on the generally admitted hypotheses, I chose to proceed to a close reading of the sources. Whenever objects appear listed as a group that is given a name such as *chremata* (things that can/may be used), their function is unclear. Precious objects apart, the others are a melting pot of brand new and broken, pots, furniture, and even raw construction materials. Our sources rarely specify usage and this concerns very few objects. What are we to imagine about the others? Brought into ritual context to meet precise needs, they belong to a ready-touse stock that is stored in sanctuaries and forms the gods' wealth. As to the majority of 'sacred' or 'cult' objects, they appear to be far more ambiguous in ancient Greek sources than what modern scholarship admits. While modern readers conceptualized a category of sacred objects in many mystery cults, the ancient terms remain equivocal as to whether they refer to objects or to ritual practices.

Andrés Quero-Sánchez

Nachdem in verschiedenen in den letzten Jahren von mir publizierten Studien der – sowohl sachliche als auch historisch-philologische – Zusammenhang zwischen Eckharts Predigten und den Schriften Schellings nahegelegt worden ist, sollen nun weitere von Schelling nachweislich rezipierte ‚mystische' Autoren untersucht werden: Tauler (einschl. des anonymen ‚Buchs zur geistigen Armuth'), Böhme, Silesius, Oetinger, Hahn und Baader. Die Untersuchung all dieser Autoren soll *erstens* klären, ob sie als Vermittler der Schriften Eckharts in Frage kommen, womit ein wichtiger Beitrag zur Forschung der Eckhart-Rezeption geleistet werden soll. Es soll zudem *zweitens* die auf Schelling wirkende ‚mystische' Tradition einer an der Sache orientierten Analyse unterzogen werden, welche freilich im Lichte des relevanten historisch-philologischen Kontexts durchgeführt wird, und das heißt – was die ‚Mystik' Eckharts angeht – vor allem (wie die neueste Forschung gezeigt hat und gerade zeigt): im Lichte der philosophisch-theologischen Debatten an der Pariser Universität um 1300. Die letztlich sachliche Orientierung des freilich mittels konkreter kontextbezogener Untersuchungen durchzuführenden Projekts soll schließlich ermöglichen, die Frage nach der Rolle und den Chancen der ‚mystischen Vernunft' in aktuellen philosophisch-theologischen Debatten zu erörtern.

Benjamin Sippel

My project 'The Quotidian and Social Life of the Temple-Personnel in Roman Fayum' contests three fundamental premises that bias contemporary studies on Egyptian temples under Roman rule: (1) It rejects the preconception of Egyptian priests as "native elites" by determining situational capabilities and grouping strategies of priestly officials outside their sanctuaries; (2) it rejects the idea that we are able to tell a macroscopic history of Egyptian temples by pointing out that our sources are not sufficient to master such an enterprise; (3) it opposes the narrative of a "decline" of Egyptian temples in the 2nd and 3rd century by highlighting that this idea is primarily based on a misinterpretation of the historical record and outdated assumptions on Roman administrative practice.

To that end, the study compares five Egyptian temples by means of papyrological, epigraphical and archaeological evidence in a micro-historical approach. Main topics are (1) naming practices of priestly families, (2) interaction between temples, benefactors and clients, (3) secular income and alternative careers for priestly offspring, (4) conflicts in which temples or single priests were involved. The observation focuses on five settlements at the edge of the Middle-Egyptian Fayum: Bakchias, Narmouthis, Soknopaiou Nesos, Tebtunis and Theadelphia. All five villages bear enormous amount of historical evidence on Egyptian priests and temples and are currently under investigation by several international research-groups, thus the study contributes to a current and lively scientific discussion.

As a result, the study succeeds in contesting all three premises by drawing a more nuanced picture of social interactions, economic entanglement and cultural expression of priestly officials and their families within as well as outside temple – walls. One of the mayor results is the conclusion that there is no indication for a large-scale "crisis" or "extinction" of Egyptian temples in the 3rd century. Thus, some well-established premises on the situation of early Christianity or on the religious landscape of late antique Egypt may be reconsidered in future studies.

More general, the monograph offers a broad survey on Egyptian temples and priestly families in Roman Egypt. It points in several instances at fruitful aspects for future research and is an example how to adapt the micro-historical approach to ancient sources. The study addresses Ancient Historians, Papyrologists, Egyptologists, Historians of Religion, but also other social and historical researchers. Currently I revise the manuscript, targeting at a publication in 2020.

Rubina Raja

The aim of the project which I will undertake while being a fellow at the Max-Weber-Kolleg is to investigate the role of the sanctuaries in the zone between culture, religion and society in the Tetrapolis region of late Hellenistic and Roman Syria (app. 100 BC – AD 400) and to view them in a diachronic perspective. A focus will be to examine and compare, by way of the evidence (archaeological, epigraphic, numismatic and literary), the religious life of the Tetrapolis region in northern Syria/partly modern Turkey. Greater Syria was in antiquity as today, a hotspot for cultural, religious and political conflicts. The Tetrapolis in specific also played a pivotal role as a region located centrally in the Hellenistic world and also flowered in the Roman period. Through studying the region in antiquity it is possible to focus on what the background for these conflicts were and how conflict management and solutions were implemented. Furthermore the evidence from this region also provides an excellent opportunity to investigate religious life on the level of the individual and processes of individualization, both over shorter and longer periods of time, through written and archaeological evidence. Due to the nature of the political changes in Greater Syria in the Hellenistic and Roman periods provincial borders fluctuated and changed more than once during the period in concern and the aim of this project will among other things be to examine which changes we can trace in the religious life across changing provincial borders diachronically.

The Tetrapolis provides exemplary and important evidence, archaeological, epigraphic, numismatic and literary, which have not yet been collected, compared and analyzed in a major work. The rich and central Tetrapolis region, flourishing already in the Hellenistic period, was the home to prominent cults situated in its main cities, Antiochia, Seleucia, Laodicea and Apamea. However, due to the state of the archaeological evidence most evidence in the region comes from outside these cities and there have been no attempts to collect – both from the Tetrapolis cities and outside – what is known about the religious life and synthesize it. Such an endeavor might provide us with crucial information about the region as a whole and the single sites as such. The location of the Tetrapolis region is in northwestern Syria and partly modern Turkey. The Tetrapolis region was in close contact with Anatolia as well as the regions south and east of it, among these the Hauran that was a region transversed by trade routes from south to north as well as from east to west and the Decapolis region further south. However, the local situations still differed due to a number of factors, such as climate and topography. These are factors, which must be taken into consideration in a study of the religious life of this region. These three regions at one and the same time represent very different scenarios in terms of their economic, cultural and political as well as topographical situations, but in terms of the religious life they all three present us with plentiful evidence with which a useful intra- and interregional comparison can be undertaken. Through a study of the Tetrapolis region it is possible to trace both local and regional variations in the religious life and discuss these on the background of stabile or changing economic, cultural and political factors and fluctuating provincial boundaries within the wider framework of the Roman Empire.

Kalpana Ram

My period in Erfurt was for three months in the first half of 2018. During this time I worked on my project "Ornamentation as love: The aesthetics of 'Sringar' in the Indian performing arts and the production of the sacred" concerning the reform and re-choreographing of religious performing arts in India, with specific reference to dance and music. Affiliated to the overall project of "Religious individualisation in historical perspective", I concentrated on the sifting that occurred in the name of modernising India by middle class reformers who found unacceptable the actual custodians of religious dance and music. The female dancers of south India were unacceptable because they combined eroticism with religion; while the male musicians of north India were unacceptable because they were Muslims who paid scant attention to Sanskrit textual traditions or indeed, to textual traditions as such. The project aims to bring the traditions of north and south, music and dance into a single study that will concentrate not simply on the history of social reform but on the phenomenology of temporality as well as emotions and affects in different kinds of practices associated with the arts. For example, the reform movement is based on a vision of a highly compressed temporality which assumes it is possible to galvanise India into modernity. Unlike other areas of India's modern history, such as the replacement of Indian legal, educational, political and health institutions by British ones, the temporality of reform did not seek to effect a complete rupture with the past but rather sought to cut away unacceptable "excesses" in order to preserve a continuity with the past. This logic is specific to the performing arts in India. As a result, the deeper practices of training and performance have retained considerable continuity with the key features of Indian performance aesthetics.

The project explores both continuity and change as well as the forms of individuation this has made possible for individual performers who put their training to work in telling a variety of stories and even political messages, many of which re-interpret the received traditions.

Nicole Reinhardt

Nach meinem längeren Aufenthalt am Max-Weber-Kolleg im Kontext der Kolleg-Forschergruppe ‚Religiöse Individualisierung in historischer Perspektive' im Jahr 2011/12 war es mir vergönnt, erneut für einige Monate zurückzukehren, um mein Forschungsprojekt ‚Voices of Conscience. Royal confessors in seventeenth France and Spain' weiter voranzutreiben. Das in fünf Abschnitte gegliederte Buchprojekt, das inzwischen bei Oxford University Press unter Vertrag ist, widmet sich der Frage der Bedeutung des Gewissensrates in den katholischen Monarchien im 17. Jahrhundert. Nachdem ich während meines ersten Aufenthaltes die Kapitel zur Moraltheologie ausgearbeitet hatte, die sich mit dem Konzept königlicher Sünden und dem normativen Rahmen für königliche Beichtväter befassen, habe ich in diesem Jahr das Problemfeld der Kritik am königlichen Gewissensdiskurs verfolgt.

In einem ersten Schritt wird hier gezeigt, wie sich zunächst die Theorie und Praxis des ‚Gewissensrates' zu Beginn des 17. Jahrhunderts allmählich auflöste. Während dies in Frankreich vor allem im Kontext der Abwehr der ultra-katholischen ‚dévot'-Fraktion geschah und unter Richelieu's Ägide im Namen der Staatsräson durchgesetzt wurde, geriet die Frage des Gewissensrates in Spanien vor allem in das Kreuzfeuer theologischer Kritik. Es ging hier nicht, wie in Frankreich, um die ‚Illegitimität' moraltheologischer Orientierung für politische Entscheidung, sondern um die unzureichende Verankerung dieser Normen in der politischen Praxis auf Grund der Unzulänglichkeiten der Beichtväter oder ihrer Einbindung in den königlichen Räten. Gleichzeitig lässt sich eine ‚Klerikalisierung' des theologischen Diskurses nachzeichnen: die einst umfassend aufgefassten königlichen Sünden, die vor allem Aspekte der distributiven Gerechtigkeit im Auge hatten, wurden zunehmend auf die Verteidigung der klerikalen Immunität und Privilegien verengt. Damit agierten die Beichtväter allerdings immer weniger als Garanten umfassend verstandener gerechter Herrschaft, sondern als klerikale ‚Lobbyisten'. Vor dem Hintergrund dieser Auflösungstendenzen ist es nicht verwunderlich, dass auch die *persona* des Beichtvaters zunehmend kritisch dekonstruiert wurde.

Diese Frage habe ich unter dem Stichwort ‚der skandalöse Beichtvater' bearbeitet. Der Brennpunkt dieser Diskussionen lag hier eindeutig in Frankreich, obwohl Beichtväter hier kaum transparent in politischen Entscheidungsprozessen eingegliedert waren. Dennoch, oder vielleicht gerade deshalb, wurde hier die moralische Untauglichkeit des Beichtvaters in der Pamphlet-Literatur breit diskutiert. In der zweiten Hälfte des 17. Jahrhunderts verstärkte sich die Kritik vor allem im Zusammenhang mit der Jansenismuskrise, die mit einem sich radikalisierenden Anti-Jesuitismus einherging. Die anti-jesuitische Grundlage fokussierte stark auf den königlichen Beichtvater als ‚Agent' einer vermeintlichen globalen jesuitischen Verschwörung, doch verschoben sich die Schwerpunkte im Verlauf des 17. Jahrhunderts.

Wurde der Beichtvater zu Anfang noch als Element der Schwächung königlicher Herrschaft kritisiert, so geriet mit dem Aufkommen des Jansenismus immer deutlicher die Bedeutung der ‚schädlichen' Moraltheologie in den Blickpunkt. Diese Verschiebung fächerte sich in zwei Richtungen aus. Zum einen beförderte sie die Absolutismuskritik: dem unterstellten ‚Laxismus' der Beichtväter wurde zur Last gelegt, absolutistische Exzesse königlicher Machtausübung, vor allem jene Ludwigs XIV., abzusegnen.

Eine zweite Variante der Kritik am Laxismus der Jesuiten hob auf die moralische Pervertierung des Monarchen als Individuum ab. In Spanien wiederum blieben solche Diskurse ein Randphänomen und lassen sich allenfalls am Ende des 17. Jahrhunderts als Echo französischer Entwicklungen nachzeichnen; allerdings hatte sich dort die Beratungstätigkeit der Beichtväter deutlich reduziert. Der skandalöse Beichtvater war nunmehr ein Beichtvater, der sich nicht auf klerikale Interessenwahrung beschränkte. Dies war eine radikale Umkehrung und Verengung des ursprünglichen Modells des ‚guten Beichtvaters'.

Abschließend habe ich in einem dritten Schritt die theologischen und institutionellen Umwälzungen des ausgehenden 17. Jahrhunderts untersucht, in der sich eine zunehmende ‚Privatisierung' des königlichen Gewissens nachzeichnen lässt. Institutionell wurden die Beichtväter nun auch in Spanien aus politischen Gremien abgezogen, allerdings erlangten sie unter den Bourbonen den Status eines ‚Ministers' für Kirchenfragen, ähnlich wie in Frankreich unter Ludwig XIV. In Frankreich verlor der Beichtvater nach dem Tod Ludwigs XIV. auch diesen Einflussbereich und blieb fortan eine der Privatperson zugeordnete Instanz. Gleichzeitig lassen sich grundsätzliche Verschiebungen in der Moraltheologie ausmachen, die diese Entwicklungen vorbereiteten und begleiteten. Diese hoben nunmehr auf das ‚individuelle' Gewissen des

Fürsten ab, das im politischen Bereich keiner äußeren Instanz der Gewissensberatung mehr bedurfte. Damit war das königliche Gewissen endgültig eine private und keine öffentliche Frage.

Veit Rosenberger (†)

Speise und Trank dienen nicht nur dem Stillen von Hunger und Durst, sondern erlauben, sobald eine Gesellschaft Überschüsse erzielt, Aussagen über Religion, Schichtzugehörigkeit, Bildungsgrad und viele andere Aspekte. In unserer Welt verzichten die einen auf den Verzehr von Rind, andere auf das Essen von Schwein, wieder andere schränken sich zumindest zu bestimmten Zeiten ein. Auch in der Antike waren die Ess- und Trinkgewohnheiten Teil eines Habitus. In den homerischen Epen schmausten die Helden unendliche Mengen von gebratenem Fleisch, immer wieder begegnet einem die als mediterrane Trias bezeichnete Kombination aus Weizen, Wein und Ölbaum. Mit dem Aufkommen des Christentums entwickelten sich verschiedene Praktiken der Demut und der Entsagung. Peter Brown hat den Nexus zwischen der Askese des Körpers, dem Fasten und der sexuellen Entsagung meisterlich vorgeführt. In diesem Projekt soll der Blickwinkel umgedreht werden, soll es nicht um die Fastenpraxis, sondern um die Ess- und Trinkgewohnheiten der Protagonisten des Christentums gehen. So wie sich die Biographien der Heiligen und Bischöfe stark unterscheiden, so differieren auch die Nachrichten über deren Diät. Offensichtlich standen die Heiligen vor einer großen Bandbreite von Optionen, die vom Hungerkünstler bis zu einem von den Mitmenschen kaum variierenden Essverhalten reichten. Mir geht es darum, die möglichen diskursiven Begründungen für diese Unterschiede zu greifen und damit den Prozess einer religiös motivierten Individuierung zu beleuchten.

Jörg Rüpke

Für meine Arbeit in der Kolleg-Forschergruppe rückte in der zweiten Förderphase die Frage nach dem in antiker wie moderner Religionsgeschichtsschreibung implizierten Religionsbegriff weiter ins Zentrum. Für die Antike erwies sich dabei nach der Arbeit am spätrepublikanischen Autor Varro der frühkaiserzeitliche Historiker Valerius Maximus als Glücksgriff: Mit republikanischen Exempeln versucht er in Tiberianischer Zeit zu belegen, wie Religion zu einem ‚Wissen' wird, dessen Kenntnis individuelles Verhalten steuern muss; die Verwaltung dieses Wissens wird bei Priestern angesiedelt. Dieser Versuch, die Augusteischen Umbrüche und ihre Infragestellung traditioneller Autoritäten als Kontinuität zu rekonstruieren, wird für die mittelalterliche und frühneuzeitliche und selbst neuzeitliche Darstellung römischer Religion kanonisch. – Neben dieser Arbeit an historischem Material trat der Versuch, einen Religionsbegriff zu entwickeln, der es erlaubt, den individuellen Umgang mit religiösen Ressourcen als Religion (und nicht nur defizitäre Form von Religiosität) zu beschreiben. Die Diskussionen in- und außerhalb der Kolleg-Forschergruppe führten hier zu einem Begriff, der vor allem auf agency, Kommunikation und kollektive Identität abstellt. Religiöse Individualisierung wird damit als vielfältige Rahmenbedingung beschreibbar, die nicht einfach als Negation traditionaler Bindungen erscheint. Die systematische Ausarbeitung erlaubte einen kritischen Blick auf Definitionen, die Religion primär als kollektives Phänomen behandeln, sie bedarf aber noch weiterer Ausarbeitung im Blick auf das Auftreten von Religion als bestimmendem Weltbild und dem passiven Ausgesetztsein gegenüber Göttern oder Dämonen.

Kumkum Sangari

I participated in the research group on "Religious Individualization in Historical Perspective" for a few weeks from May to July 2017 and proposed to work on one chapter of my larger project on South Asian religious pluralism. The larger project was instigated by the increasing force of a chauvinist and exclusionary Hinduism and is intended to excavate the transnational, colonial, and nationalist contexts of the emergence of Hinduism as a single entity, and to study the lineages and practices of dissent. I was able to work on a chapter which looks comparatively at the early twentieth-century writings on Hindu- ism, dharma, and women by Mohandas Gandhi and Annie Besant within the entangled histories of colonial India and England at a time when both Hinduism and eosophy were in the making.

The project's focus on individualization introduced new complexities that centred on its definition, on the tension between the formulation of national collectives and personalized self-making, and most significantly, on the paradoxes of a transnational antimodernity that could propel otherwise dissenting historical actors into taking conservative positions on women and marriage. The responses I received at the colloquium, the discussions at the conference in Eisenach, and the informal discussions around these events were rich and suggestive. Apart from my own research, I engaged in discussions with several Max-Weber-Kolleg faculty, fellows, and graduate students on their research projects. I was also able to attend several lectures and colloquiums and participate in the conference on Dalits and religion. On the whole, it was a productive and enriching experience. I am very grateful for the extraordinary support and collegiality of everyone I encountered at the Max-Weber-Kolleg.

Dirk Sangmeister

In der Messestadt Leipzig sind in der Vergangenheit nicht nur viele Bücher gedruckt, verlegt und verhandelt, sondern auch viele Bücher verboten und beschlagnahmt worden. Die von der Leipziger Bücherkommission konfiszierten Werke wurden von der Mitte des 18. bis zur Mitte des 19. Jahrhunderts mehrheitlich auf den Dachböden des Leipziger Rathauses unter Verschluss gehalten, ehe man sich dann 1870 entschied, dieses ‚Gebeinhaus der verbotenen Literatur' zu vernichten, indem man (fast) alle Bücher zu Dachpappe verarbeiten ließ.

Vor der Vernichtung des Bestandes jedoch wurde ein höchst flüchtiges Inventar erstellt, das 360 Seiten umfasst, auf denen rund 67.000 Exemplare gebundener Bücher, ca. 7.500 Exemplare ungebundener Bücher, 110.000 einzelne Bogen, 12.500 einzelne Blätter, 2.300 Titelblätter und Umschläge, 36 Periodika in knapp 2.000 Exemplaren, 2.000 Musikalien und 5000 Bilder aus der Zeit von 1750 bis ca. 1860 datierend, ganz grob erfasst worden sind.

Dieser enorm umfangreiche Bestand an konfiszierten Büchern zerfällt, analytisch betrachtet, in zwei Gruppen, nämlich einerseits Werke, die beschlagnahmt worden waren, weil es sich aufgrund von Verletzungen von Druckprivilegien oder (später) Urheberrechten um unrechtmäßige Ausgaben handelte, und andererseits Werke, die aufgrund ihres Inhaltes Anstoß erregt hatten, d.h. vor allem heterodoxe, klandestine, revolutionäre, satirische oder erotisch-pornographische Werke, die nach Meinung der Obrigkeit ‚gegen die Religion, die Moral oder die guten Sitten' verstießen, wie die gängige Formel der Zensur damals lautete.

Die Theologica machten im 18. Jahrhundert einen beträchtlichen, im 19. Jahrhundert dann zunehmend geringeren Prozentsatz unter den beschlagnahmten Büchern aus. Im späten 18. Jahrhundert, als infolge der Aufklärung und der Französischen Revolution fast allerorten forcierte Schübe der Säkularisierung einsetzten, eröffneten sich neue Spielräume für Prozesse der religiösen Individualisierung, zugleich wurde aber eben dieser Prozess der Aufklärung durch das von Johann Christoph Wöllner initiierte ‚Edikt, die Religionsverfassung in den preußischen Staaten betreffend' (1788), das mittelbar Auswirkungen auf fast alle Territorien im Deutschen Reich hatte, massiv bekämpft.

Im Zuge dieser beiden gegensätzlichen Entwicklungen wurden zahlreiche Schriften von aufgeklärten Theologen, die eigene Pfade abseits der vorgeschriebenen Wege der Amtskirchen erkunden und beschreiben wollten, aber auch Streit- und Rechtfertigungsschriften, Autobiographien renegater Mönche, Klosterromane, Anklagen gegen den Klerus etc. geschrieben, die häufig zensiert oder konfisziert wurden. In Sachsen wurden heterodoxe Theologica genau in Augenschein genommen, weil die Leipziger Bücherkommission nicht nur der Landesregierung, sondern vor allem dem Oberkonsistorium in Dresden untergeordnet war, das die Federführung in allen Zensursachen hatte.

Das überlieferte Inventar der verbotenen Bücher mitsamt den dazu gehörigen Archivalien im Staatsarchiv Dresden dokumentieren den Prozess der allgemeinen Säkularisierung wie der religiösen Individualisierung in zahlreichen Facetten und fast allen Spielarten. Diese einzigartige Quelle ist bislang von allen Wissenschaftlern, die sich mit Zensur und Bücherverboten in Leipzig bzw. Sachsen oder dem deutschen Reich allgemein beschäftigt haben, übersehen worden, wird nun aber von mir im Rahmen eines Forschungsprojektes erschlossen und analytisch aufbereitet, das 2015–2016 von der Gerda Henkel Stiftung (Düsseldorf) getragen werden wird.

Christoph Schäfer

In dem Projekt ‚Konversion im Ostgotenreich. Glaubenswechsel als Indikatoren für Akkulturation und Religionspolitik' wurde, ausgehend von einer prosopographischen Grundlage, das Phänomen der Konversion in der ostgotisch-römischen Gesellschaft sowie deren Bedeutung für die innere Stabilität des von Theoderich d.Gr. gegründeten Reiches untersucht. Damit kann ein Beitrag zum besseren Verständnis der religiösen Verhältnisse geleistet werden, der über den Verbund mit dem Forschungsprojekt von Wolfgang Spickermann auch komparatistische Perspektiven im Kontext der Kolleg-Forschergruppe eröffnet.

Den Arianern in Theoderichs Reich ging missionarischer Eifer weitgehend ab. Das ermöglicht es orthodoxen Quellen etwa Konversionen zum Arianismus zu leugnen. Allein schon die geringe Zahl arianischer Gemeinden auf italischem Boden wird zwar die Zahl der Konvertiten in Grenzen gehalten haben, dennoch sind derartige Fälle belegt. In umgekehrter Richtung traten folgerichtig weitaus mehr Fälle auf, wobei mit Theoderichs Mutter Erelieva eine prominente Persönlichkeit in unmittelbarer Umgebung des Königs angeführt werden kann.

Während die Religionspolitik Theoderichs d.Gr. und seiner Nachfolger in der Forschung durchaus eine gewisse Aufmerksamkeit gefunden hat, ist das Phänomen der Konversion bislang nicht in den Mittelpunkt von Analysen gerückt worden. Dabei kulminieren gerade hierin Prozesse von Integration, Akkulturation und Kollaboration, wie wir sie ähnlich auch im Vandalenreich greifen können, wo allerdings die Religionspolitik zumindest zum Teil in eine andere Richtung zielte. Die unterschiedlichen Antworten auf die religiösen und gesellschaftlichen Herausforderungen in den beiden ostgermanischen Reichen zu vergleichen, erwies sich als ebenso reizvoll wie fruchtbar. Daher wird die Publikation gemeinsam mit der Studie von Wolfgang Spickermann erfolgen. Entscheidende Impulse hat die Untersuchung durch die Vorträge und Diskussionen im interdisziplinären Kontext des MWK erfahren. So konnten innovative Fragestellungen entwickelt und neue Perspektiven gewonnen werden.

Michael Seidler

I came to Max-Weber-Kolleg Erfurt with three main projects in mind. First, I wanted to complete my edition of Pufendorf's Latin *Dissertationes*, which will be part of the *Gesammelte Werke* published by Akademie/De Gruyter. This task is finished, in a sense, for I did complete my reading, editing, and annotating of the sixteen essays that will constitute this large volume. My work focused initially on several still untreated dissertations, but it also involved a return to pieces encountered years ago, which needed to comply with patterns developed in the meantime. The overall result was (for the first time) a unified text that must still be better integrated, provided with suitable appendices, indices, and synopses, and variously contextualized through a substantial volume introduction. Given my post-Max-Weber-Kolleg Erfurt return to the exigencies of normal life, as it were, I plan to have the manuscript ready for final submission in about a year. My second project was to be a collection of (my) previously published essays on Pufendorf, suitably cross-referenced, indexed, and introduced. Its point is not just republication and integration of sometimes hard-to-obtain pieces, but to provide new access points for further work. This project did not get far, at least directly, since my first and the third tasks took more time than anticipated. It remains a goal, however, and will be relatively easy to accomplish when the time is ripe(r).

My third goal was to begin a new, book-length study of Pufendorf interpreted as political realist and pragmatic naturalist (in contemporary terms). This requires a careful rereading and reinterpretation of his natural law approach as such, and also situating him in relation to contemporary moral and political debates in the manner that Hobbes, Hume, Kant, and others continue to be so placed. Early modern natural law (and natural law today) is an immensely variegated field, and Pufendorf offered a distinctive approach that is often lost in the muddle of superficially homologous discourse. My study will utilize many of the articles mentioned in the previous paragraph, but it needed also to address certain gaps. It is mainly in this last respect that my stay at Max-Weber-Kolleg Erfurt advanced the larger project, by providing several more platforms for the eventual chapters. These starting discussions emerged from specific undertakings.

First was a paper on dignity and respect, delivered at a natural law conference in Lausanne in September 2014. Pufendorf has a rather deflationary view of these notions, in my view, and so it was important to analyze them in the context of competing interpretations. Another, related venture also completed in the fall was a co-authored (with Knud Haakonssen) piece on natural law, rights, and duties. This will soon appear in a wide-ranging anthology on intellectual history (with Wiley). Third was a solicited paper on the relation of natural and international law, which will also appear this fall in a collection dedicated to the early modern history of the general topic. Fourth was my colloquium paper in May 2015, on „taking natural law seriously", which sought to update or contemporize the central notion of a 'natural state', so as to link Pufendorf's approach to natural law with current moral and legal concerns. Given its broad, stage-setting character, this paper will become part of my introduction to, or an early chapter of, the book.

I also devoted considerable effort to two other pieces that are only now seeing completion. One is the quintennial revision of my comprehensive entry on Pufendorf in the online *Stanford Encyclopedia of Philosophy*. This long and authoritative piece functions as a standard port of entry to the topic, especially in the English speaking world. The bibliographical work required for the update would have been much more difficult outside of Germany, without the (physical and electronic) resources in Erfurt and Gotha (and Berlin) at hand. At the same time, I was also collecting research materials toward the revision of a long article on 'economic' and 'mathematical' aspects of Pufendorf's method – in line with what may be called his natural law positivism – for a *Festschrift* to appear next year with Cambridge. Both these papers were remainders of my Max-Weber-Kolleg Erfurt stay, as it were, which nonetheless significantly furthered them.

Activities at Max-Weber-Kolleg Erfurt typically involve a dizzying array of projects and presentations, even if organized under general rubrics. I seldom found these distracting, however, and was able to link almost all of them with my own interests. Even getting temporarily derailed from my immediate concerns turned out to be useful, as I had to find my way 'back' from wherever someone's paper or talk had temporarily deposited me. This was both challenging and stimulating, and it broadened my perspective on my own work. Needless to say, as well, it was a constant pleasure to observe varying disciplinary approaches and personal styles, and to respond to challenges and suggestions from directions entirely different than the ones I am used to.

To praise and thank the staff, students, and colleagues at Max-Weber-Kolleg Erfurt for their support and friendship seems almost formulaic and unnecessary, since everyone who has been there does this: inevitably, profusely, and justifiably. For it is hard to imagine a better working and living environment, in both academic and human terms. Regrettably, given the constant exchange of students and fellows at the Kolleg, it is also an experience that cannot strictly speaking be repeated or revisited, at least not in a particular constellation. So I regard it as a fortunate singularity that not only lingers pleasantly in memory but has become part of me in many other ways as well.

Christopher Shaw

In what follows, I would like to offer a brief closing report on my residency with the Max-Weber-Kolleg. I was invited by Prof. Dr. Dietmar Mieth to take up a one-year residency with the Max-Weber-Kolleg from 1 September, 2013 to 31 August, 2014. During this time, my principal aims were to make significant progress on research and writing for my doctoral thesis and to study German. I can report that both of these aims were met, and that my home institution, the University of Oxford, is pleased with the work that I have submitted to them from this time.

My doctoral research is focused on the reception of the theology of Meister Eckhart in post-Kantian thought. My aim is to then apply my conclusions in order to develop a constructive theological engagement with various principles of secularity. During my residency with the Max-Weber-Kolleg I was able to collect and analyze a great deal of works on Eckhart, and then turn that research into a chapter for my thesis. Over the course of my 12-month stay I was able to produce 60,000 words of complete written work, which included chapters for my thesis on Eckhart, Hegel, Heidegger, and Gadamer. I was also able to enroll in German courses for the winter and summer semesters with the Universität Erfurt.

Aside from my research on Eckhart, I was also able to meet with other fellows such as Dr. Markus Kleinert and Prof. Dr. Jörg Rüpke. Dr. Kleinert and I were able to discuss our shared interest in Kierkegaard and translation. And, Prof. Dr. Rüpke and I established a professional link that can hopefully be used for future academic projects.

In conclusion, my time and experience in Erfurt and with the Max-Weber-Kolleg was, by all indexes, exceptional. Not only was I offered generous provisions for work and research, I was also fortunate to meet a great deal of very kind and welcoming people. And, for any future publications that I produce, I will be sure to include my thanks to the Max-Weber-Kolleg for its outstanding support. I sincerely hope that we will be able to work together in the future. Erfurt and the Max-Weber-Kolleg both proved to be excellent experiences for me, and I look forward to a sustained relationship with your fine institution.

Shunfu Shen

The main topic for this research stay in the Kolleg-Forschergruppe is the genealogy of human ideas, particularly among the three modes of myth, philosophy and religion.

It is widely granted that religion precedes philosophy. Does that genealogy conform to the fact? What is the scientific genealogy of human ideas? How about the relational order between religion and philosophy?

After intensive approaching into the characters of the three thinking ways, no one doubts the pioneering status of myth. The crucial issue is of the order of the occurrence between philosophy and religion. According to my assumption and analysis, philosophy precedes religion in the course of human thought. Religion follows philosophy and embraces the latter, which puts the latter forward to a new and higher level of thinking. Philosophy did not stem from the religion, but the vice versa. This is my assumptive genealogy of human ideas.

This genealogy is able to be applied to the development of Confucianism. Confucianism is not static, but dynamic. Its long history can be divided into four parts or stages at least, i.e., rational era, mythical era, philosophical era and religious era. The first era is the rational period. It is hard to find some independent authenticity for this period, owing to the metaphysical features of language.

The second mythical stage is represented by the Six Canons which were edited by Confucius. The canons are full of stories, myths, tales and legends. These myths concern either the relations between human being and gods, either the origin of the profane world. Some of them are cognate with the later philosophical topics, such as the Heaven and Earth gaping open.

The third period is Mencius' stage. This stage is characterized by its critique thinking mode, which is the typical mode of philosophical thinking. The feature of philosophical thinking is skepticism and critique. Mencius is the first Confucian philosopher in the history of Confucian philosophy. He doubted and criticized the canons, and proposed several metaphysical human natures which exist at the very beginning of human existence or by birth.

The fourth stage following the philosophical critical stage is the religious era. The mission for religious thinkers is to establish some absolute foundations for their inclining secular and finite beings such as social ideas. Some thinkers symbolize those unspeakable powers or beings, such as Heaven. Heaven is a natural phenomenon possessing some esoteric implications such as being universal, eternal and infinite. These features characterize Heaven as some symbols of some absolute and supernatural beings. As a result, Heaven is personalized as the greatest god in Chinese tradition, which is cognate with Christian God. He is the origin and archetype of the secular world. The secular human world is subject to the absolute sovereignty of the sacred Heaven. The existences on the earth follow the orders of the Heaven. Heaven is a symbol of the supernatural being, or supernatural power who is absolute and be able to determine the finite world. This is the main idea of Dong Zhongshu in Han Dynasty. And this personalization of Heaven hallmarked the transformation of Confucianism from a secular school of views to a divine, sacred and religious sect. Confucianism became a religious Confucianism.

From this point of view, Confucianism in Han dynasty finished its metamorphosis from a secular school of view through philosophy to a religious sect. Confucianism became a religious sect. From this case, it is obvious that Confucian philosophy preceded religious Confucianism. Philosophy preceded religion.

Christopher Smith

My project on the Roman kings was to look at how kingship is positioned with regard to religious activity, and to see monarchy as part of broader systems of power.

In the course of my time at the Max-Weber-Kolleg, I was able to develop two significant strands of this. First, by concentrating on the methodological underpinning of the project, I have extended the consideration of Roman kingship in three directions.

(1) I have gathered a number of approaches which allow the notion of power to be read more dynamically and co-operatively, and to continue my longstanding interest in the importance of heterarchic community formations in power structures. These models include Gramscian ideas of cultural hegemony, Arendt's notions of the public, Castoriadis and the social imaginary, Ranciere on difference and Serres and others on multiplicity.

(2) I also began to look more comparatively at the notion of kingship and chiefdoms, taking advantage of new work in the Pacific islands in particular. I was able to continue this after my time at the Max-Weber-Kolleg during a two month visiting lectureship in the University of Otago, New Zealand.

(3) I combined both these with notions of sovereignty, and how we understand the prehistory of a concept which is usually thought as a specifically modern notion. This will culminate in a conference in St Andrews in April 2019 (funded by the British Academy and the Academia Europaea), which will feature the work of Hartmut Rosa from the Max-Weber-Kolleg.

Second, I have been thinking increasingly about the role of the king in religion, and especially first as part of a mosaic of "watcher mechanisms" and arbitration processes and second as a figure within foundation myths which are, I will argue, implicit legitimations of community. I was able to present the first during my stay, and the second argument will be presented at the conference of "Religion and Urbanity. Theorising Mutual Formations" at the Max-Weber-Kolleg in November 2019.

Igor Sosa Mayor

Der Schwerpunkt meiner Forschungsarbeiten liegt in der Sozial- und Kulturgeschichte des europäischen Adels der Frühneuzeit. Dabei interessiert mich besonders das Wechselverhältnis dieser Gruppe mit den kirchlich-religiösen Entwicklungen der Zeit. Im Rahmen meines Aufenthaltes am Max-Weber-Kolleg möchte ich diese allgemeine Frage in Bezug auf das aristokratische religiöse Konsumverhalten untersuchen. Meine zentrale Forschungsfrage lässt sich folgendermaßen umreißen: Kann religiöses Konsumverhalten und der Umgang mit materiellen religiösen Gegenständen im frühneuzeitlichen Europa als Symptom und gleichzeitig als Ursache der Herausbildung von ‚Individualisierungsprozessen' gedeutet werden?

Neuere Arbeiten zum frühneuzeitlichen Adel betonen gerade die konfliktbeladenen Aspekte innerhalb der adeligen Häuser. Zudem ist auf die Experimentierfreudigkeit der Mitglieder dieser Gruppe hingewiesen worden, etwa hinsichtlich intimer Freundschaften, der Thematisierung des Selbst in ihren Schriften etc. Gerade die

Frage nach der Bildung individueller Praktiken durch das Medium Religion muss m.E. eigens thematisiert werden.

Religion wird meistens unter der Perspektive der Textualität analysiert. Dennoch bildet(e) Religion auf der ganzen Welt eine materielle Welt. Eine Vielzahl von Alltagsgegenständen religiöser Natur und unterschiedlichen materiellen Wertes, unterschiedlicher Größe, Beschaffenheit, usw. umgab die Menschen der Frühneuzeit: Kreuze, Rosenkränze, Halsbänder, Reliquien, Kleidungsstücke, Andachtsbildchen, Gemälde, Bücher, Heiligenstatuen usw. Viele dieser Objekte standen auch unter dem Einfluss normativer theologischer Diskurse in Bezug auf ihre Verwendung, Wirkungsmacht usw. Gleichzeitig haben Konsum und Materialität einen ambivalenten Bezug zur christlichen Religion (Luxuskritik, Weltabgewandtheit). Dies alles erfordert eine Analyse verschiedenartigster Aspekte: wie diese Gegenstände erworben, wo sie in den Wohnungen platziert, wie sie transportiert, wie sie an weitere Generationen vererbt wurden, welche Wirkungsmacht ihnen zugewiesen wurde usw. Praktiken und Diskurse treffen sich am religiösen Objekt. Gerade ihre Wechselbeziehung eröffnet uns einen Einblick in individuelle Praktiken und Erlebnisse.

Drei Themenkomplexe in den Beziehungen zwischen adeligen Gläubigen und religiösen Objekten in Bezug auf Individualisierungstendenzen scheinen zumindest zum jetzigen Zeitpunkt des Forschungsprojekts besonders untersuchenswert: 1) das weite Feld der Schriftlichkeit; 2) die komplexen Verhältnisse zwischen Gegenständen, religiöser Körpererfahrung und Individualisierung; 3) raumbezogene Dimensionen des religiösen Erlebnisses. Alle drei Themenkomplexe müssen vor dem Hintergrund konfessioneller und geschlechtsspezifischer Unterschiede hin untersucht werden.

Als Fallbeispiele werden das katholische Kastilien und das gemischtkonfessionelle Niederösterreich herangezogen, so dass vergleichende und kontrastierende Elemente mitberücksichtigt werden können. Der Untersuchungszeitraum (ca. 1550 – ca. 1750) umfasst beinahe die ganze Frühneuzeit, sodass etwaige langfristige Tendenzen beobachtbar sind. Die Pluralität der analysierten Quellentypen (Inventarliste, Autobiographien, Briefe, Gemälde, Stiche etc.) ergibt sich zwangsläufig aus dem untersuchten Gegenstand.

Wolfgang Spickermann

In den letzten Jahren habe ich meine Forschungen zu Lukian von Samosata, einem der Hauptvertreter der sogenannten zweiten Sophistik im Römischen Kaiserreich des 2. Jahrhunderts n. Chr. intensiv weitergeführt. Nach den nunmehr abgeschlossenen Arbeiten zum Verhältnis dieses Autors zu den im griechisch-römischen Kulturkreis ‚fremden' Gottheiten habe ich meine Fragestellung in Richtung der Kolleg-Forschergruppe ‚Religiöse Individualisierung in historischer Perspektive' erweitert und in mehreren Beiträgen im Rahmen von Workshops und Kolloquien die lukianische Haltung zu Magie, Aberglauben und besonders Orakel, die Schilderung des Freitodes des

Kynikers Peregrinos/Proteus und die Frage der Diskrepanz zwischen philosophischem Anspruch und individueller Lebensführung sowie Lukians Haltung zum Totenkult erörtert. Lukian ist ein Exponent der klassischen griechischen Bildung (Paideia), der seine Satiren mit dem moralischen Anspruch verfasst hat, dass die Gebildeten (Pepaideumenoi) ihre Lebensführung den eigenen Werten und denjenigen der Paideia anpassen müssten. So entlarvt er Scharlatane wie den erwähnten Peregrinos oder den ‚Lügenpropheten' Alexander von Abououteichos oder überzieht Abweichungen vom Ideal oder Inkonsequenzen des Handelns mit scharfem Spott. Meine weiteren Forschungen werden dem literarischen Ich im lukianischen Oeuvre gelten – redet der Autor tatsächlich über sich selbst oder schafft er lediglich eine fiktive Figur, die er mit seinem Namen verbunden wissen will, und wo liegen die Kriterien für den Leser, dies zu entscheiden?

Michael Stausberg

Mein Aufenthalt am Max-Weber-Kolleg war ein intellektuelles Abenteuer der angenehmen Sorte. Der Leitung des Max-Weber-Kollegs gebührt mein Dank und Respekt für das Bereitstellen eines inspirierenden intellektuellen Biotops mit einer optimalen Mischung aus Freiheit und Struktur, Begegnungen und Rückzugsmöglichkeiten. Die kollegiale und kooperative Arbeitsatmosphäre ist vorbildlich. Ich durfte mich nicht nur als Gast, sondern als Mitglied fühlen und einbringen. Die Teilnahme an den Kolloquien sowie an diversen Workshops, Tagungen und Arbeitstreffen habe ich seltenst als Ablenkung, sondern in der Regel als wichtig und bereichernd empfunden. Weiterhin hervorzuheben sind die Selbstverständlichkeit der Interdisziplinarität und der Einbindung von Promovierenden und Emeriti. Der Aufenthalt am Max-Weber-Kolleg hat es mir ermöglicht, mich in ein für mich neues Feld einzuarbeiten. Meine als serielle Biographik konzipierte Religionsgeschichte des 20. Jahrhunderts konnte ich auf den Weg bringen. Insgesamt konnte ich etwa ein Dutzend Teilkapitel schreiben im Umfang von etwa 350 Druckseiten; einige Teile wurden an verschiedenen Orten und Kontexten vorgestellt, darunter auch im Kolloquium.

Benjamin Steiner

Während des zweijährigen Aufenthalts als Fellow am Max-Weber-Kolleg konnte ich mich nach dem Erscheinen meiner Habilitationsschrift (*Colberts Afrika*) im Jahre 2014 weiter der Erforschung des französischen Kolonialreichs der Frühen Neuzeit widmen. Anders als in meiner Studie zur Wissens- und Begegnungsgeschichte in Afrika lenkte ich meine Aufmerksamkeit dem gesamten Kolonialraum zu, den die Franzosen im 17. und 18. Jahrhundert immer mehr zu einem Imperium bzw. Kolonialreich ausbauten.

Es war gerade die Frage nach globalhistorischen Kategorien, wie etwa dem Begriff des Imperiums (*empire*), die mich während meiner Erfurter Zeit am intensivsten beschäftigt hat. Neben zahlreichen Gesprächen und Diskussionen, die zwar hart am wissenschaftlichen Gegenstand, gleichzeitig aber immer in fairer und freundschaftlicher Atmosphäre geführt wurden, kam es außerdem zu verschiedenen Kooperationen mit anderen Forscherinnen und Forschern des Max-Weber-Kollegs. Hervorzuheben ist sicherlich die große Konferenz mit 15 Teilnehmern, die ich zusammen mit Martin Mulsow in Juli 2016 im Erfurter Augustinerkloster veranstaltet habe. Es ging dabei um den Austausch, die Verknüpfung, Verflechtung und andere Zusammenhänge, welche hinsichtlich einer globalen Ideengeschichte bzw. einer *global intellectual history* in der Frühen Neuzeit zu rekonstruieren sind.

Mit Martin Mulsow, den ich parallel zu meinem Fellowship als Lehrstuhlinhaber an der Erfurter Universität und Direktor der Forschungsbibliothek in Gotha vertreten habe, verband mich außerdem unser Interesse an materiellen Kulturen, denen ich in meinem Forschungsprojekt „Engineering Empire" besonderes Gewicht in einem alternativen Narrativ zum *empire building* aus materialhistorischer Perspektive beimesse. Auch hier war ich Teilnehmer einer zusammen von Martin Mulsow und Annette Cremer organisierten Gothaer Tagung, die sich dem Zusammenhang von Materialität und Geschichte widmete. Das Forschungsprojekt an Max-Weber-Kolleg „Engineering Empire. Large Projects, Global Material Cultures and Local Identities in the French Colonial Realm" experimentiert mit dem Ansatz der materiellen Kulturforschung und beabsichtigt, die aufgrund der mangelhaften schriftlichen Quellenlage vernachlässigte nicht-europäische agency durch eine mikrohistorische Verdichtung der Arbeitsprozesse beim Bau kolonialer Großprojekte, wie Festungen, Hafenanlagen, Stadtmauern etc. einzuholen. Dieses Ziel mag ein ehrgeiziges sein und provoziert Zweifel an den bislang üblichen historiographischen Kategorien, die auch immer wieder in den Diskussionen der Werkstattgespräche virulent wurden. Doch hat sich nach intensiven Archivrecherchen in Paris, London, Den Haag und Aix-en-Provence zu den kolonialen Bauvorhaben der Franzosen erwiesen, dass sich – gerade aus Sicht der Objekte und Akteure – die Geschichte nicht allein als europäische oder eurozentrierte Erzählung darstellen lässt. Vielmehr drängt es sich aufgrund der Globalität der Akteure und Objekte auf, von einer dezentralen Struktur des Empire auszugehen, die sich nicht mehr mit der bislang üblichen Unterscheidung von imperialen Zentren und Peripherien fassen lässt. Daher ist es notwendig, globalhistorische Betrachtungen nicht nur mikrohistorisch zu unterfüttern, indem dabei Differenz und Identität der jeweiligen Varianten der Globalisierungseffekte detailliert darstellt, sondern auch die globalen Kategorien, wie etwa des Kolonialreichs, des Imperiums oder der Differenz von europäischer und nicht-europäischer agency grundsätzlich auf den Prüfstand zu stellen.

Diesem Ziel um weite Schritte näher gekommen zu sein, verdanke ich zu großen Teilen meinem Aufenthalt am Max-Weber-Kolleg. Während der relativ langen Zeit meines Aufenthalts wurden wichtige Kooperationen auch außerhalb des Max-Weber-

Kollegs geschlossen und Forschungsergebnisse präsentiert und diskutiert. In Heidelberg wurden auf dem Treffen der Arbeitsgemeinschaft „Frühe Neuzeit" im VHD im September 2015 im Rahmen einer von mir und Susanne Friedrich organisierten Sektion die Rolle des Wissens bei der europäischen Expansion anhand verschiedener global agierender Institution in der Frühen Neuzeit diskutiert. Auf dem Hamburger Historikertag im September 2016 ging es indes in einer gemeinsam mit Kollegen aus Frankfurt am Main, Bielefeld und Basel organisierten Sektion um die strukturelle Frage nach der Funktion historischer Transformationen in der Geschichtsschreibung. Während einer kurzen Gastprofessur im März in Boulogne-sur-mer konnte ich zusammen mit Eric Roulet und anderen Kollegen aus Frankreich, Großbritannien, den Niederlanden und USA die Geschichte der europäischen Handelsgesellschaften in Amerika, Asien und Afrika diskutieren. Mit Susanne Rau von der Universität Erfurt habe ich damit begonnen, in unserer Funktion als Fachgebietsherausgeber der Online-Neuauflage der Enzyklopädie der Neuzeit, das Fachgebiet „Räume und Regionen" zu planen und im Zuge dieser Tätigkeit mehrere Schlüssel- und Forschungsartikel verfasst. Nach meinem Erfurter Aufenthalt kann ich somit auf mehrere Früchte erfolgreicher Zusammenarbeiten blicken. Sicherlich wäre diese Produktivität ohne die Ressourcen, die das Max-Weber-Kolleg mir zur Verfügung gestellt hat nicht möglich gewesen. Und auch in Zukunft hoffe ich, dem Max-Weber-Kolleg verbunden zu bleiben, da ich mit vielen der Kolleginnen und Kollegen weiterhin Gedanken und Arbeiten auszutauschen gedenke.

Julietta Steinhauer

During my stay at the Max-Weber-Kolleg (April–July 2018) I worked on my current project "migration on the margins". The project focuses on the lived experience of individuals migrating from the Near and Middle East and Italy to Hellenistic Greece. These migrants are recorded in sanctuaries, in which they created religious networks and worshipping communities. Such networks helped to continue religious traditions that individual migrants had brought with them and, at the same time, to create new religious identities in their new environments. While working in Erfurt, I presented a paper investigating the unusual prominence of female migrants within the religious networks on Delos (currently out for review with REA) and I participated in a conference on Neighbourhoods, organised by Emiliano Urciuoli and Jörg Rüpke, with a paper on the "religious" patterns of behaviour of foreign individuals in Hellenistic Delos (to be published in 2019).

Kocku von Stuckrad

Von Januar bis September 2013 war ich als Gastwissenschaftler im Rahmen der Kolleg-Forschergruppe ‚Religiöse Individualisierung in historischer Perspektive' am Max-Weber-Kolleg in Erfurt. Diese acht Monate waren für mich die ideale Gelegenheit, ein länger laufendes Projekt zu einem fruchtbaren Abschluss zu bringen. Mein Forschungsprojekt zum Thema ‚The Scientification of Religion: Discursive Reconfigurations between 1850 and 2000' hat inzwischen zu einer Monografie geführt, die 2014 bei De Gruyter (Berlin/Boston) unter dem Titel *The Scientification of Religion: A Historical Study of Discursive Change, 1800–2000* erscheinen wird. Im Rahmen des Projektes sind auch zwei Artikel erschienen ('Secular Religion: A Discourse-historical Approach to Religion in Contemporary Western Europe', in: *Journal of Contemporary Religion* 28 [2013]: 1–14; 'Discursive Study of Religion: Approaches, Definitions, Implications', in: *Method and Theory in the Study of Religion* 25 [2013]: 5–25). Ich hatte die Möglichkeit, meine Arbeit auf der Tagung der Kolleg-Forschergruppe in Modena (Italien) vorzustellen. Im November 2013 werde ich zum Thema außerdem auf der Jahrestagung der *American Academy of Religion* vortragen. Für 2014 organisiere ich eine *session* zum Thema ‚Diskursive Religionswissenschaft' auf der von mir organisierten Jahrestagung der *European Association for the Study of Religions* in Groningen.

Ohne die intensive Forschungsarbeit in Erfurt wären diese Publikationen nicht möglich gewesen. Von Anfang an war ich beeindruckt von der kollegialen Atmosphäre in Erfurt und von der intellektuellen Diskussionskultur, die interdisziplinäres Arbeiten möglich macht. Ich möchte mich sehr herzlich bedanken für die guten Gespräche und Anregungen, ebenso wie für die ausgezeichnete Unterstützung in allen administrativen Fragen. Ich freue mich sehr darauf, dass die Zusammenarbeit im nächsten Jahr fortgesetzt wird, und zwar im Rahmen einer *Summer School*, die ich mit Jörg Rüpke in Groningen organisiere, zum Thema ‚Mysticism and Esotericism in Pluralistic Perspective: Conflicting Claims of Knowledge and the Power of Individualism'. Dabei sind auch WissenschaftlerInnen aus Dänemark (Aarhus) und den USA (Rice University) beteiligt, sodass die Forschergruppe auch in diesen Netzwerken weiterwirken kann.

Riccarda Suitner

During the time I worked within the Kolleg-Forschergruppe on 'Religious Individualization in Historical Perspective', directed by Prof. Dr. Jörg Rüpke and Prof. Dr. Martin Mulsow, (6/2014–8/2018) I enjoyed above all the interdisciplinary methods and the numerous chances to discuss my research in an international research environment. Outcomes of this work are for instance the contribution "The Good Citizen and the Heterodox Self: Turning to Protestantism and Anabaptism in 16th-Century Venice" (2019), and articles I discussed during the colloquia and now published in collective volumes (e.g. "Reformation, Naturalism and Telesian Philosophy. The Case of Agostino Doni", in *Bernardino Telesio and the Natural Sciences in the Renaissance*, ed. by P. Omodeo, Leiden, Brill, 2019). These publications are results of a project I carried out during these years, which investigates the so-called "Radical Reformation" (Anabaptism, Antitrinitarianism), and considers primarily sources related to medicine such as medical treatises and *epistolae medicinales*. The approach and research program of the Kolleg-Forschergruppe gave me the chance to deepen in particular aspects related to the role of individual choice within the networks of religious dissenters I have closely taken into consideration.

The time at the Max-Weber-Kolleg gave me also the possibility to pursue collaborations with several institutions, in Erfurt and abroad: with the Gotha Research Center, with the Philosophical Faculty of Erfurt University, where I was a Teaching Fellow, with the Descartes Center of the University of Utrecht, where I was Junior Fellow (February–March 2018), with the Accademia degli Agiati (Italy), where I organized the conference 'Gli illuministi e i demoni. Il dibattito su magia e stregoneria nel Trentino del Settecento e i suoi legami con l'Europa', and with the International Research Network *Natural Law*, based at the Max-Weber-Kolleg as well.

Altogether, I have found my time at the Max-Weber-Kolleg highly productive and stimulating for my research; I appreciated in particular the chances of interaction with fellows and PhD students, and the lively activities organized, also beyond the strictly academic programme.

Kiran Sunar

During my time at the Max-Weber-Kolleg, I engaged three projects. The first was a paper entitled, "Sarāpās Across Contexts: Female Corporeality and the 'Elseworldly' in Early Modern South Asia". This paper focused on the sarāpā, or the place of the head-to-toe description of the heroine, within the Punjabi qissā. I argued that the sarāpā imageries located in the Punjabi qissā (the Punjabi romance-epic genre) were ones that moved across religious and linguistic registers and circulating literary traditions and into the qissā to imbricate a sense of an "elseworld" that did not fit previous norms of the fantastic. The second paper was entitled "Religious Individualization Through Religious Transformation: Rethinking Conversion and Disguise in Bhai Vīr Singh's Sundarī". This project suggested a different scale for thinking about religious convergences during the colonial period in Punjab, one that did not see religious conversions as outside of wider realms of religious transformations. I took up Bhai Vīr Singh's 1898 novel Sundarī, hailed as the first novel written in Punjabi, within which religious transformation is a central preoccupation in the text. Through an examination of the places of religious transformation within Sundarī, I argued that religious transformation, defined as conversion and as disguise, offer not only sites of religious conversation, but also spaces for questions of political and situational allegiance to emerge in a landscape that was undergoing immense flux. I furthered this project by engaging the question of gender as related to religious transformation. The third project engaged the question of residual rituals, through siyapaa, a cross-religion, cross-class, cross-caste Punjabi women's mourning ritual that underwent reform pressures by religious factions during the colonial period due to being seen as not appropriate religious behaviour. Tracing the siyapaa through its literary and cultural continuities, this project asked the question of how to engage ritual practices that continue to exist at the site of the gendered body in grief.

Emiliano Rubens Urciuoli

From October 2013 to February 2014 I have been invited at the Max-Weber-Kolleg as a *Gast-Postdoktorand* in History of Early Christianity. This research stay was framed within the cooperation program between the Max-Weber-Kolleg and the Scuola Internazionale di Alti Studi 'Scienze della cultura' of the Fondazione Collegio San Carlo in Modena. This School, which provides my Ph.D. scholarship, counts Professor Jörg Rüpke as a member of its Scientific Committee. Basically, my stay in Erfurt aimed at facilitating the supervision of my doctoral research by Prof. Rüpke, while taking the opportunity to attend Max-Weber-Kolleg's seminars and workshops, which were pertinent and close to my field of study. Furthermore, since the actual denomination of my Italian scholarship is 'Cultural Sciences', Max-Weber-Kolleg's was supposed to be a proper hosting institution for its renowned interdisciplinary structure, methodology and programs.

My current research is a genealogical inquiry on the participation of Christians in the political life before the process of 'Christianisation' of the Roman Empire (Title: 'Ego imperium huius saeculi [non] cognosco. A Genealogy of Christian Political Life [50–313 CE]'). Where did the 'Christian ruling class' preferably take place? How did these people concretely behave, insofar they were involved in such affairs that no Christian legitimate authority seems to have allowed and endorsed? Once introduced in the 'hard public sphere', did Christians conduct themselves exactly as non-Christian did? Or, conversely, may historians attempt to detect particular trajectories, attitudes and stances denoting the outcome of a specifically Christian 'feel for the public game' that will not outlast the legal, social and behavioural effects of the 'Constantinian turn'? I aim at answering to these questions, while outlining a new description of the Christian political forms of subjectivation before Constantine. The first part of the study focuses on some meta-hermeneutical problems in an attempt to evaluate and show how the ordinary understanding of the historical issue 'Early Christians and Politics' is framed by codified, standardised, and thus obstructive interpretations of the sources. The second part introduces the specific style of reasoning and method applied to the dataset, namely Pierre Bourdieu's 'general science of the economy of practices', profiting from the analytical worth of three of its main conceptual tools, i.e. fields, interests and strategies. Part Three deals with the proper genealogical core of the research, i.e. with the 'zero degree of the history' of Christian political life.

Staying at the Max-Weber-Kolleg gave me the precious opportunity to talk over this range of issues with specialists of Early Christianity, Roman Studies, and Religious Studies. The discussions of the papers embedded into the ERC research project on *Lived Ancient Religion (LAR)*, which have pointedly challenged both traditional and discursive approaches focused on normative religious behaviours by endeavouring to grasp religious appropriation by individual and collective agents, have been particularly stimulating. Indeed, my own sociological method of inquiry has been positively questioned by these groundbreaking self-centered perspectives. Furthermore, I have definitely benefited from the workshops on 'Religionsbegriff': these conversations, focused on texts troubled by definitory problems and non-imperialistic conceptualizations of religious representations and practices, has provided me with new critical lenses to investigate religious phenomena, and scrutinize my own epistemological approach to them alike. Finally, thanks to the invitation to the 4th LAR Conference in Copenhagen 'Grouping together in Lived Ancient Religion' (from 2nd to 4th June, 2014), a paper summarizing method and contents of my ongoing research (Title: 'Capitalizing on Bourdieu for a Genealogy of Christian Political Life [50–313 CE]') has been thoroughly discussed by some of the leading scholars in the discipline.

Rebecca Van Hove

During my fellowship at the Max-Weber-Kolleg I completed my doctoral thesis, which was a study of religion and authority in the legal and political speeches of fourth-century BCE Athens. The thesis explores not only *what* orators said about the divine but furthermore dissects *how* they could say what they do. To do so, it concentrates on the notion of "religious authority", which it takes as a dynamic and discursive constructed-and-contested process. Not only does such a sociologically sensitive conception of authority allow for a reading of oratory as a genre of performative texts in which orators speak persuasively, yet do so from an authoritative position; authority as a dynamic and constructed process is also a useful tool with which to approach religion in ancient Greece. This focus on religious authority allows namely for a recognition of both the asymmetry inherent in the relationship between orator and audience and the individual agency of orators, understanding their speeches as varied appropriations of religious ideas and notions and practices by individuals within a specific social context.

I completed the final part of the project during my stay in Erfurt, which examines oaths, questioning the dismissive treatment oaths in oratory have regularly received. It argues that they are not merely rhetorical tools of persuasion or casual interjections completely disconnected from their original function as a mechanism which makes binding an assertion, denial or promise. Rather, oaths are consequential performative speech acts considered efficacious, if risky, in nature. Ultimately, by dissecting the complex process of speaking authoritatively and persuasively about the gods in the law courts and the Assembly, this thesis contributes to our understanding of religious conceptions in the Athenian democracy. It questions the idea that religion was unimportant in oratory and shows instead how the relative infrequency of religious references should be understood as a consequence of the risk involved in making religiously authoritative claims about the unknowable gods.

The opportunity to be part of the welcoming, friendly and highly-stimulating research environment of the Max-Weber-Kolleg was a fantastic experience for me.

Jutta Vinzent

The research proposed to undertake is concerned with 'Concepts of space in 1930s Britain', a book project, which has grown out of my specialism of migration and its impact on visual representation.

Having worked on the ideas of space in constructivist and abstract sculpture and shown their differences between presenting and re-presenting space, I have been able to extend the findings to explore their limits, arguing that these, while applicable to art production, were not associated with exhibiting painting and sculpture, an activity which, like the book publication of *Circle*, was undertaken by those artists whose concept of space is the focus of the project (Gabo, Hepworth, Nicholson). In other words, theories of open and closed space do not seem to have any relevance for the conceptualisation of exhibition space.

By using a curatorial approach and installation photographs from the exhibitions of abstract and constructive art in the 1930s (some of these being published in *Circle*) as my source, I have been able to show in a paper presented at the MWK in the Summer Semester 2013 that the limits are those of the artists. Going beyond the artists' intention, abstract and constructive art exhibitions can be described as a Gesamtkunstwerk, as display strategies (including the colour of walls and the arrangement of objects) correspond with the works on show. On the basis of the distinction between Horizontal and Vertical Collectivism (Triandis and Gelfand, 1998; Singelis, Bhawuk and Michele, 1995), I developed a system to describe group exhibitions of abstract and constructive art further; while those in the 1920s (e.g. El Lissitzky's Abstract Cabinet) represent a vertical collective display, as the exhibits melt into one with the display strategies, those in the 1930s are horizontal collective displays, as there remains a certain distinction between both.

A reason for the change in display strategy might lie in the experience that collectivity could be abused politically, which also found its expression in exhibitions. A case in point is the 1937 Degenerate Art exhibition. Exploiting not only collective display strategies by showing abstract art as a *Gesamtkunstwerk*, it also used horizontal display strategies. However, it only mimicked these: the frames were left off for other purposes, while the labels identified the artists and a title, but the price was not the price for sale, but that for which the respective museum had bought it. Such deference was complimented by a hang either cluttered, compared to the single-line hang of the exhibits in the previously mentioned shows, or cascading to the ground, requiring the visitor to literally look down on the works. Furthermore, the use of slogans transformed the exhibition into a spectacle, a strategy by which the individual works are absorbed into a collective.

This means that the National Socialists exploited horizontal collective display strategies; but instead of emphasizing the individual, its effect was deindividualisation. Different from collectivity, which relies on an active participation of its members, deindividualisation can be seen as an act against others. As regards the installation of exhibitions, these two concepts are visibly distinct from each other: deindividualising exhibition displays are those like the Degenerate Art exhibition, exploiting cluttered hang and slogans, while the exhibitions listed in *Circle* use the collective only as a promotional strategy in order to enhance the individual and thus represent a horizontal collective display.

Markus Vinzent

Das laufende Projekt beschäftigt sich mit der Historisierung von Religion und Sakralisierung in zwei Schwerpunkten, die sich mit Individuen der christlichen Geschichte befassen, deren Kreativität Institutionalisierungen zur Folge hatte: Markion von Sinope im zweiten und Meister Eckhart im frühen vierzehnten Jahrhundert.
1. Die Textgrundlage von Markions eigenem kreativen literarischen Schaffen soll wieder hergestellt werden, und zwar beginnend mit seinem Evangelium, welches nicht isoliert, sondern in Synopse mit weiter verfügbaren Evangelien (kanonischen und nichtkanonischen) und weiteren Parallelen dargeboten wird. Auf dieser Grundlage wird zu zeigen sein, dass Markions Evangelium den Anstoß und die Grundlage für alle weitere Evangelienliteratur bildete. Über die Textgrundlage hinaus wird eine kommentierende Interpretation gewählt, die sich in aller Radikalität den möglichen Implikationen stellt.
2. Was das zweite Projekt betrifft, wird das philosophische Profil Eckharts im Zusammenhang mit dem Diskurs an den Universitäten Erfurt und Paris seiner Zeit entfaltet. Doch um dies nicht in Isolierung zum soziologischen, politischen, ökonomischen, theologischen und philosophischen Umfeld zu tun, werden derzeit auch Mitkollegen Eckharts gelesen und aus den Handschriften erhoben. Auch hier wird demnach die Frage nach dem Verhältnis von Innovation und Tradition, von Individualität und universitärer, kirchlicher und monastischer Institution gestellt und eingebunden in Eckharts prospektive Erwartung und retrospektive Reflexion diskutiert.

Katharina Waldner

Das Projekt ‚Mysterienkulte, Jenseitsvorstellungen und Individualisierung in der antiken Religionsgeschichte' wird im Rahmen der Kolleg-Forschergruppe ‚Religiöse Individualisierung in historischer Perspektive' in Kooperation mit Wolfgang Spickermann und Veit Rosenberger durchgeführt. Zu Beginn des 20. Jahrhunderts wurden die antiken Mysterienkulte als ein eigener Typ von Religion (re)konstruiert, der – im Gegensatz zu der kollektivistischen Polisreligion – individuelle Bedürfnisse nach ‚Erlösung' befriedigt habe und so als Vorläufer des Christentums gelten könne; dies verband sich für die Mysterienkulte der römischen Kaiserzeit mit der Behauptung, dass Mysterienkulte ein typisch ‚orientalisches' Phänomen seien. Allein die Rekonstruktion dieser Forschungsgeschichte ermöglicht es, den wichtigsten Beitrag der modernen antiken Religionsgeschichte zum Diskurs um Individualisierung von Religion zu erfassen. Nicht dies steht jedoch im Mittelpunkt des Projektes, sondern eine Relektüre der antiken Quellen insbesondere der archaischen und klassischen Zeit. Denn da die Begrifflichkeit der älteren Forschung (‚Mysterienreligionen', ‚Erlösungsreligion', ‚Orientalismus') zu Recht kritisiert und überwunden wurde, geriet die Frage nach der individuellen Dimension von Mysterienkulten, die bereits in der Antike als eigener Typus von Ritualen wahrgenommen wurden, in Vergessenheit. Dies gilt auch für deren Verbindung zu Jenseitsvorstellungen, die seit dem sechsten vorchristlichen Jahrhundert am deutlichsten im Fall der Mysterien von Eleusis und den Dionysos-Mysterien fassbar ist. Hier setzt mein Projekt erneut an und fragt, welcher Stellenwert der Option der Mysterien-Einweihung im System der antiken Polisreligion zukam. Die Mysterienrituale werden dabei im vielfältigen Diskurs über Jenseitsvorstellungen kontextualisiert. Diesen Diskurs selbst gilt es erneut zu rekonstruieren, denn er erlaubt Aussagen darüber, wie Persönlichkeit und Individuum in dieser Gesellschaft konzeptualisiert wurden. Die Einweihung in Mysterien erscheint so neben Bestattungsbräuchen als rituelle *performance* eben dieser Konzepte und damit auch von Individualität.

Jula Wildberger

Mein sechswöchiger Aufenthalt im Mai/Juni 2013 in der Kolleg-Forschergruppe war gekennzeichnet durch reichen und inspirierenden Austausch, der meinen Forschungen über eine mögliche Bedeutung des Stoizismus für die moderne Umweltethik nicht nur Impulse, sondern eine neue Richtung gab. Wie ich in meinem Vortrag ‚Individualismus vs. Holismus? Stoische Schönheit und die Paradoxa des erweiterten Selbst in der Tiefenökologie' zu Anfang des Aufenthaltes darlegte, scheint mir das systemische Denken der Stoa mit Konzepten wie dem des Schönen oder dem eines in allem Lebendigen angelegten, ja dieses überhaupt konstituierenden Gemeinsinns (soziale *oikeiōsis*; soziale Natur des aktiven Prinzips Gott) geeignet, Prinzipien für eine Umweltethik zu formulieren, die den Konflikt zwischen holistischen und individualistischen Ansätzen überwindet. Diese Überlegungen konnte ich entscheidend voran bringen durch präzisierende Forschung zur Natur dieses Gemeinsinns und die daraus resultierenden Einsichten zum Begriff *koinōnikos* nicht nur als Zum-Leben-in-einer-Gemeinschaft-disponiert-Sein und auch nicht nur als Altruismus, sondern schärfer als Liebe zum anderen, als Fähigkeit, mit dem anderen etwas Sinnvolles anzufangen (*khrēsthai*). Diesen Ansatz verfolge ich nunmehr weiter in einem Projekt ‚Beauty and Sociability in Stoic Accounts of Providence and Human Nature: A Foundation for an Environmental Ethic as Love of the Other?', die ich bei einer Konferenz ‚Greening the Gods: Ecology and Theology in the Ancient World' in Cambrige (März 2014) zur Diskussion stellen und im Anschluss daran auch schriftlich publizieren möchte.

Neu im Vergleich zu meinem ersten Besuch als Gastwissenschaftlerin am Max-Weber-Kolleg war, dass sorgfältige sowohl philologische als auch philosophische Analyse stoischer Begriffe von Individuum, Agent, Selbst oder auch Subjekt nun nicht mehr nur um des historischen Erkenntnisgewinns willen betrieben, sondern die Ergebnisse auf ihre Anschlussfähigkeit in modernen Debatten hin befragt wurden. Gerade was diese Weiterentwicklung meines Projekts betrifft, waren die intensiven, oft auch kritischen Diskussionen für mich sehr wichtig, da sie mir halfen, sowohl die Chancen als auch die methodologischen Probleme meines Unterfangens besser zu erkennen. Dies gilt besonders für meinen Beitrag zu der Konferenz ‚Forms of Religious Individualisation: Concepts and Processes' im Augustinerkloster Mitte Juli 2013. Die Publikation dieses Beitrags in einer überarbeiteten Fassung ist geplant.

Christopher Wojtulewicz

Contextualisation is key to this research project, which seeks to understand more clearly the intellectual relationships between Meister Eckhart and his interlocutors in the first two decades of the 14th century. Working through texts in the Amploniana, and alongside the research group in Erfurt during this stay is the focus of my time at the Max Weber Center. Jacobus de Aesculo is one of the masters who taught contemporaneously with Meister Eckhart at the University of Paris, but is also present in his theological questions in manuscripts and manuscript collections alongside those of Eckhart (most notably in the Vatican Library and in the Amploniana). In contextualising Eckhart within the early 14th century university environment, in order to better understand Eckhart's role in intellectual life in Paris, Erfurt and other important places of his career, but most specifically before, during and after his second regency (1311–1313), the project seeks to explore the individualistic and nuanced thought of the illustrious Dominican, not as an individual, separated from his social, cultural and intellectual roots, but as a key figure in the history of the development of philosophy and theology, connected to, and a part of, the development of the social, cultural and intellectual contexts in which he worked. In this sense the project brings to light a new ‚portrait' of Meister Eckhart, previously unseen. It also advances significantly knowledge of medieval European education, education methods, the production of texts, and the transmission of knowledge in this time of great intellectual activity.

Any significant study of the works of Jacobus de Aesculo has yet to be undertaken, and certainly his relationship to Meister Eckhart has yet to be explored. It is clear, however, from looking at the theological *quodlibeta* that we know to be authored by Jacobus, that a relationship exists between these two. Both masters are concerned with understanding the nature of God's power; but their convergence is not solely intellectual – both were influenced by the trial of Marguerite Porete (which Jacobus was involved with) and both had relations with suspect movements in their respective orders: the Franciscan Spirituals in the case of Jacobus, and the Beguines and Beghards with Eckhart. The project's interest in Jacobus in particular stems from being able to pose questions such as: what were the questions that the Franciscan Jacobus and the Dominican Eckhart shared in common? How do their individualities shape their (unique?) answers? In what ways did their ideas interact? And what sort of networks existed, intellectually, between the religious orders in Paris? These foci develop our understanding of this crucial period in the history of philosophy and theology, and enable us to think critically about the contextualization of these and other important thinkers in the history of ideas.

Paola von Wyss-Giacosa

Die einjährige Anstellung im Bereich „Verflechtungsgeschichte" hat es mir erlaubt, die im Sommer 2014 während einer Fellowship aufgenommene Arbeit zu Aspekten einer frühneuzeitlichen „idololatria illustrata" in der an wertvollen Gesprächen und Anregungen reichen Umgebung des Max-Weber-Kollegs fortzusetzen. Den Ausgangspunkt meines Projekts „Der Teufel in Asien. Wandernde Objekte und globale Religionswissenschaft" bildete zunächst Christian Hoffmanns 1667 in Jena erschienener, global angelegter Traktat *Umbra in luce*. Diese Abhandlung stellt einen bisher wenig beachteten Beitrag innerhalb eines zentralen religionsgeschichtlichen Diskurses der Zeit dar, in dem – mit Referenz auf patristische Argumente sowie zunehmendem Einbezug ethnographischer Literatur zu einem zeitgenössischen Heidentum Asiens und Amerikas – historisierende Narrative zu Ursprüngen und Diffusion der Idolatrie erarbeitet wurden.

Der Beweischarakter, den viele Gelehrte der materiellen Kultur zuschrieben, machte *antiquitates sacrae* wie *ethnographica* zu unabdingbaren Akteuren im angestrebten Erkenntnisprozess und verlieh der graphisch visuellen Umsetzung einzelner

Objekte im Buch eine entsprechend wichtige Rolle. In *Umbra in luce* finden sich denn auch äußerst interessante Illustrationen. Einzelne davon sind aus Werken einschlägiger Autoren übernommen, andere gehen, wie es im Text heißt, auf Stücke im „Antiquarium Gerhardinum" zurück. Aus dieser Sammlung des Jenaer Professors der Theologie Johann Ernst Gerhard, des Lehrers von Hoffmann, wurden demnach mehrere Objekte ins Bild gesetzt und dienten als Evidenz und ikonographische Referenz für die in *Umbra in luce* vorgetragenen Argumente. Der Verbleib der Gerhardschen Gegenstände ist bislang nicht bekannt, die Repräsentationen im Buch sind allerdings von bemerkenswerter Präzision und Qualität. Sie stellen auch in dieser sekundären Form wertvolles Anschauungs- und Studienmaterial für einen frühen Diskurs über die Religionen Süd- und Südostasiens dar. Zwar sind die Deutungen der Objekte in vielen Fällen falsch. Sie sind allerdings nicht beliebig oder lediglich prinzipielle Verurteilungen alles Nichtchristlichen, sondern das Ergebnis einer anhand vielschichtiger Quellen vorgenommenen Reflexion und der Rezeption von Gelehrtendiskursen der Zeit.

Dies kann etwa im Vergleich mit den Argumentationslinien anderer Autoren belegt werden, mit denen ich mich im letzten Jahr beschäftigt habe. Eine meiner Studien betraf die Abhandlung zur Idolatrie „West- und Ost-Indiens" des Paduaner Antiquars Lorenzo Pignoria, die er, eingegliedert in die von ihm edierte Neuauflage der *Imagini*, des bedeutenden mythographischen Werks von Vincenzo Cartari, 1615 veröffentlichte. Relevant ist der kurze Traktat Pignorias für mich deshalb, weil er nicht eine theologisch oder geographisch begründete Hypothese, sondern eine auf Objektstudium basierende Untersuchung vorlegte.

Pignoria hatte die bildliche Umsetzung sämtlicher von ihm analysierter Objekte in Auftrag gegeben, und diese *illustrationes* bildeten den Ausgangspunkt der von ihm vorgetragenen Gedanken. Der Paduaner Autor war damit in seiner Konsequenz, was die *demonstratio ad oculos* angeht, rigoros. Durch die getreue graphische Übertragung ins Bild wurden die in ihrer Provenienz genau rückführbaren „Abgötter" zu sichtbaren Akteuren, ja zu Protagonisten eines methodisch klar begründeten und bis heute nachvollziehbaren Arguments im Idolatrie-Diskurs der Zeit.

In frühneuzeitlichen Sammlungen lassen sich mehrfach Kultbilder asiatischen Ursprungs nachweisen. Einige davon sind bis heute erhalten. In einem Artikel habe ich mich mit einem dieser Artefakte beschäftigt, einem um 1600 zu datierenden thailändischen Buddha im Kopenhagener Nationalmuseum. Die Figur befand sich zunächst in Schleswig-Holstein, in der Kunstkammer des gottorfischen Herzogs Friedrich III. Im Jahr 1653 gegründet – zur selben Zeit wie die Gothaer Kunstkammer und die Kabinette in Brandenburg und Kopenhagen – war sie eine der bedeutenden Institutionen im nördlichen Europa. Was den Gottorfer Buddha so bemerkenswert erscheinen lässt, ist, dass dessen vielschichtige, durch mediale Wechselwirkung konstituierte Repräsentation im europäischen Kontext recht genau rekonstruiert werden kann. Dieses spezifische Kapitel in der Biographie und Rezeption der thailändischen

Figur im Westen, ihre Aufnahme und Einordnung in einer namhaften musealen Einrichtung der frühen Neuzeit, stellt eines der seltenen eindeutig identifizierbaren Beispiele der Praxis eines Objektdiskurses dar, wie er sich in Gelehrtenkreisen des 17. Jahrhunderts vor dem Hintergrund religionsgeschichtlicher Fragen entspann.

In dem Panel, das ich gemeinsam mit Daniela Bonanno anlässlich der IAHR-Konferenz organisierte (Re-presenting and Re-defining the Other Through the Ages: Images, Objects, and Texts in Interreligious Encounter), beschäftigte ich mich mit einem weiteren „thing-in-motion" (Arjun Appadurai) aus der gottorfischen Kunstkammer, diesmal mit einer javanischen Wayang-Figur, und mit der Frage, was geschieht, wenn ein fremder Gegenstand in den Deutungskreis westlicher Gelehrter tritt und über längere Zeit den wechselnden Vorstellungen folgend interpretiert und eingeordnet wird. Die noch in Arbeit befindliche Studie ist auch insofern relevant für die Beschäftigung mit *Umbra in luce*, als in Hoffmanns Traktat eine javanische Schattenspielfigur aus dem Gerhardinum besprochen und illustriert ist. Gleiches gilt für einen weiteren Artikel, an dem ich schreibe. Das Thema ist hier ein Objekttypus, der javanische Kris mit flammender Klinge und teilweise figürlich gestaltetem Griff, und die wechselhafte Aufnahme und Einordnung dieser Dolche in europäischen Reiseberichten und Abhandlungen. Gemeinsam ist meinen Untersuchungen der Kontextualisierung und Konvisualisierung von Objekten in frühneuzeitliche Sammlungen und religionshistorische Argumente das Interesse, die verschiedenen Bedeutungstransfers dieser im eigentlichen wie im diskursiven Sinne wandernden Gegenstände nachvollziehen zu können und damit ihre ideen- und verflechtungsgeschichtlichen Implikationen.

6 ERC Advanced Grant "Lived Ancient Religion"

Janico Albrecht

Roman discourse on religious behaviour can mostly be understood to centre on a negotiation of normative boundaries: In a religion not fixed on a set of authoritative texts, societal processes of communication had to occupy an equivalent role instead. These processes comprise efforts to construct, dispute, and affirm definitions of religious deviance (and norms) without necessarily relying on religious specialists or theological modes of discourse. Quite the contrary, they were based on the medium of narratives about famous individuals' exemplarity or deviance – the two often being interchangeable depending on the context and the target audience. It was a singular characteristic of the Roman Republic that these so-called 'construction-processes of deviance' were extensively tied to the social standing of those participating in them, namely, members of the senatorial elite. For them, taking part in those processes not only required a firm grasp of the often complicated and even conflicting mental outlooks on religious normativity. Furthermore, they were expected, to a certain degree, to 'live up to expectations' by embodying the values of their idealized communities.

This project is centred on these agents who as 'moral entrepreneurs' (Howard Becker) try to assert individual or group interests and claim authority over definitions of right and wrong. Focusing on such figures allows for further in-sights into the society: Who formulates norms, who may formulate norms, and what structural conditions were necessary in an elite keen to ensure its idea of consensus? Building upon a central assumption within the 'Sociology of Deviance' that changes to the normative boundaries of a society need not bear any correlation to the effective behaviour of deviants, the deviant agents themselves will play only a subordinate role. Instead the focus lies on processes of social stratification, strategies of identification, and the appropriation of religious roles.

My approach to the question begins by asking whether the emergence of discourses on individual religious deviance can be linked to the increased acuteness of inner-senatorial competition in the Middle Republican period and the resulting appropriation of religious modes of self-profiling. Historical agents who, at that time, led the way could – as exemplary figures – become fuel for the arguments of later generations as well as authoritative reference-points within such disputes. Late Republican and early Imperial successors (e.g. Cicero, Livy) used references to such earlier discourses, their content, and established results as a medium for anchoring an (imagined) normative senatorial cosmos. These well attested discourses represent the central sources, which can be used to track operative modes of deviance and their relationship to many of those 'moral entrepreneurs', several of whom also influenced the fate of the res publica as political authorities. At the same time, their often high degree of literary reflection on the emergence of religious normativity allows consideration of the likelihood that the authors themselves were influenced by and/or able to express constructionist interpretations of their own religious past and present.

In the second part of the project, I consider the way in which the domestic political and external changes wrought by the Principate of Augustus resulted in a shift of debates as well as a change of rules in the game of deviance construction. The original fronts of normative religious definitions became increasingly blurred, allowing for new actors, strategies, and areas of application for definitions of deviance. By including further exemplary cases, a more comprehensive picture will be drawn, which can be linked to the detectable change and changeability of Imperial Roman religion.

Marlis Arnhold

As member of the ERC-Research Group "Lived Ancient Religion: Questioning 'cults' and 'polis religion'" from June 2012 till May 2013 I started a research project on the sanctuaries of Roman Imperial Ostia, the harbour town of the city of Rome. The project aims for an analysis of the available material and written evidence of the cultsites beyond their differentiation according to architectural forms, cult identities, and their status as sacra private or sacra publica. All of these present criteria based on which the sites have been selected for investigations so far. In view of the program of the ERC-project the idea was to bring together in one study all sanctuaries which a contemporary of Roman Imperial times at least theoretically could have been able to see, know of, visit as well as live or work in or nearby (the phrasing is intended). Focusing thus on the various agents, a number of new questions have been raised for the analysis which result in a fundamentally new understanding of sacred space in Roman Antiquity: How was urban space shared and acquired in and through sanctuaries in Roman Imperial Ostia? Under which conditions was it even competed for? How was it conceptualized and transformed in consequence over time?

My research started with a compilation of the available evidence of the more than 80 known sanctuaries from Ostia from the period of the first four centuries CE. These comprise precincts with large podium temples as well as cult-rooms installed into domestic architectures and workshops but could also take the form of small shrines set into the corner of a courtyard or a niche placed into a wall. They were dedicated to all kinds of religious traditions known throughout Roman Imperial times including the Jewish and Christian cults. Taking into account the aspects of accessibility and visibility, the building phases of the known structures as well as the actions which once took place in and at the architectures were and are being analyzed. Indices for the latter can be obtained from the available finds and inscriptions, in particular, as well as a discussion of the possibilities provided by the available space in each case.

The research on this part of the project quickly resulted in a vast amount of material demonstrating the potentials of the changed perspective on the sanctuaries. All the same, further questions arose within the progressing studies, for instance, first of all the one of a terminology applicable to varying architectural forms which allows to address the structures precisely. Whereas some of the larger sanctuaries with Republican history were linked through the activities of various gentes, also "smaller" sites revealed links by means of the preserved inscriptions, which require further discussion of their character: Are we talking just about the presence of members of the same gens in different sanctuaries or were these connected in further ways?

What originally was intended not to exceed the length of a larger essay, soon took the scale of a monograph and even though its outline and scope are set, it is still far from finished. Nevertheless, several of the sanctuaries and aspects of this project have already been subjects of recent oral presentations and several articles are in progress of publication or preparation.

Christopher Degelmann

Scenes of mourning and pleading were omnipresent in ancient Rome. Our sources are full of passages in which burials are described with their specific gestures and signs. The rich archaeological tradition testifies to the importance that death and related ceremonies had in the life of the ancient Romans. In recent years research has devoted countless historical and archaeological publications to the subject.

Nevertheless, the ancient records show a wide range of cases where mourning and supplications are not directly related to death and burial. For example, senators wore mourning dresses in the curia to express their opposition to certain decisions and laws. As private individuals, they walked around the forum in mourning robes and asked the people to vote in their favour at the next meeting. Plaintiff and defendant could use signs of mourning in court to win over the jury. The defendants were even expected to behave in this way and it was a scandal if one of them refused to do so. This is only a selection of different fields of action in which mourning signs and gestures were combined with ritualized pleading, but it is already apparent that the use of semantics of death and burial were options for political strategies in the *res publica*.

My research focuses on the questions of how and why such signs and gestures worked or when they missed their target. It can be assumed that the scenes described in the sources so often promised success because they contained semantics that were familiar to the Romans from other settings of their everyday life. It is here that the desired emotions usually arose. The analysis of these ancient signs of sorrow and prayer outside their usual contexts assumes that the Roman basic value of *pietas*, which touched on the fields of family, community and gods, which were elementary for the Romans, was used in particular.

Based on these premises, I hope to not only gain a deeper understanding of a mechanism fundamental to the functioning of the Roman polity, but also to advance to the emotional side of Roman politics, far from clichés about instrumentalized religion in the late republic and the early principle.

Valentino Gasparini

"Small is beautiful". With this provocative title, likely inspired by his mentor Leopold Kohr, the economist Ernst Schumacher intended to criticise the sustainability of Western production systems and propose a human-scaled economic paradigm, thus anticipating several ecological issues with which, almost half a century later, we are still unsuccessfully struggling. Shifting from economics to religious studies, "small is beautiful" encapsulates the methodological approach championed by my project "Lived Ancient Religion (LAR): Questioning 'Cults' and 'Polis Religion'". This project was interested specifically in a "smaller" religion, yet not in the sense of "small gods" (to cite the title of Terry Prat chett's novel), that is, of deities allegedly occupying a lower position within the hierarchy of the Graeco-Roman pantheon. Rather, the study explores "the gods of small things" (citing now Arundhati Roy's novel), that is, the question of how human religiosity is affected by small things and how different local small-scale religious providers and entrepreneurs filtered, appropriated, adapted, instrumentalised or even invented new religious offers. In short, this study does not investigate elements of coherence and homogeneity within an allegedly shared religious worldview, but instead concerns itself with particularities, discrepancies and distortions within situational contexts.

The common topic that ties this project together is the Isiac cults. These are the cults (in the Graeco-Roman world from the beginning of the third century bCE to the beginning of the sixth century CE) of a dozen deities conceived of as originally worshipped in Egypt and belonging to the same mythical and liturgical circle: (Herma-)Anubis, Apis, Boubastis, Harpocrates, Horus, Hydreios, Isis, Neilos, Neph thys, Osiris and Serapis. Of course, the selection of the Isiac cults for this enterprise does not aim at reifying these cults as a quasi-religion, that is, as a self-sufficient system of religious belief and practices. Rather, it represents the arbitrary selection (within the wide spectrum of polytheistic options) of a heuristic tool encouraging the analysis of the different strategies by which the religious actors (individuals as well as smaller or larger social groups) built their own cultural idea of "Egypt" and used diverse materials (mediated orally, through texts or iconographies) to capitalise on the symbolic power of "Egypt" by incorporating and "othering" what they found. According to the LAR perspective, my research supports a methodological shift from the idea that the institutionalised civic religion is the dominant structure (based on the static and standardised performance of public, collective rites, and on elite-driven ideology) to a focus on theindividual as an active (often unpredictable) actor, capable of situational and creative innovation. This line of research is interested in the single cultic agents, not as "normalising" actors (that is, representatives of institutional entities or local oligarchies) but as individuals who (independently of their social position) act as decision-makers and conscious modifiers of established religious patterns. I provide a different account on the social dimension of Isiac religious practice, including variety, creativity, religious multiplicity, fluidity and flexibility of identities, changes in forms of individuality, and spaces for individual distinction. The Isiac cults can be investigated as a practical resource available to emergent or self-styled religious providers.

Maik Patzelt

Die vorliegende Dissertation hat sich um einen Quellenzugriff bemüht, der es erlaubt, eine Untersuchung des Betens im spätrepublikanischen und frühkaiserzeitlichen Rom in all seinen Facetten über eine Analyse verfügbarer Gebetstexte hinaus zu bestreiten. Während die bisherigen philologischen und historischen Modelle zur römischen Religion ein Verständnis für die Vielfältigkeit des Betens im antiken Rom verhindern und dieses auf normative und formalisierte Akte reduzieren, die von einem kulturellen oder kultischen Wissen diktiert und mit Hilfe eines schriftlichen Regelwerkes priesterlich verwaltet werden, erhebt die Studie das betende Individuum inmitten des ihn prägenden und umgebenden sozialen Kontextes zum Ausgangspunkt der Untersuchung. Dabei wird das Beten als ganzkörperliche und multidimensionale Kommunikation begriffen. Das Beten ist vor diesem Hintergrund als ein Ausdruck ‚gelebter Religion' erschlossen worden. Im Hinblick auf einen hierfür notwendigen Handlungsbegriff, der in einer Verkörperung gründet, hat sich das Konzept der Ritualisierung als geeignetes Instrument erwiesen, um den individuellen Handlungsmöglichkeiten nachzuspüren. Die theoretische und methodische Herausforderung bestand darin, aus dem herauskristallisierten kreativen Handeln eine religiöse Erfahrung erschließen zu können. Zu diesem Zweck wurde das handlungstheoretische Ritualisierungskonzept mit einer Bandbreite an anthropologischen, psychologischen und kognitionswissenschaftlichen Studien in Verbindung gebracht. Daraus ergab sich ein Schema, das ein stark verfremdetes bis selbstvergessen-exaltiertes Beten in Einheit mit erregenden bis ekstatischen Erfahrungen setzt. Der jeweilige Moment des Handelns evoziert in seiner Komplexität subjektive Erwartungshaltungen, die als eine religiöse Erfahrung oder als eine Erfahrung göttlicher Präsenz wahrgenommen werden können.

Die Untersuchung entlang dieses Schemas hat ergeben, dass dem Beten keine normativen und formalisiert-instruktiven Handlungsmuster innewohnten. Weder ließ sich das Gebet als eine geschlossene Handlungskategorie verifizieren, noch ließ sich die Existenz normativer Schriften in Form von Gebets- oder Ritualbüchern nachweisen. Demgegenüber konnte das kreative Potenzial eines betenden Römers offengelegt werden, der darum bemüht ist, für den jeweiligen Moment ein Gebet sprach-lich und körperlich zu ritualisieren. Ausgehend von verschiedenen Faktoren wie Publikum, Lebenssituation, Lebenserfahrung, persönliches Anliegen oder Götterbild etc., eröffnete sich eine nahezu unerschöpfliche Bandbreite, das eigene Beten zu gestalten. Am eindeutigsten ist dies bei den salutationes in römischen Tempeln zu beobachten. Diese hatten zum Ziel, eine persönliche Nähe zu einer Gottheit kommunikativ zu etablieren und zugleich zu erfahren. Eine Bandbreite an Ritualisierungen eröffnete sich etwa bei den Gebeten der Aristokraten, da diese versuchten, den eigenen Auftritt den Erwartungshaltungen eines Publikums anzupassen. Der betende Magistrat wurde vornehmlich kreativ tätig, indem er der priesterlichen Komposition auf lautlicher und körperlicher Ebene Gestalt verlieh. Die beistehenden pontifices vervollkommneten den Auftritt, indem sie dem Magistraten nicht lediglich die textliche Grundlage boten, sondern es ihm in darstellerischer Hinsicht gleichtaten. Ausgehend von diesen Beobachtungen kann ich grundlegende Einblicke in die Vielfalt des Betens im antiken Rom liefern und ein neues Bild religiöser Praxis in Rom entwerfen.

Georgia Petridou

The three years of research in the project "Lived Ancient Religion" at the Max-Weber-Kolleg have been a true revelation for me. I learned so much not only about history of religions but also about hard-working ethos and collaborative spirit within academia. My individual research area within the wider LAR project was "Interactions with Religious Specialists". Working with Jörg Rüpke, Richard Gordon, Rubina Raja, our distinguished research fellows (such as Jan Bremmer, Julia Kindt and Alexia Petsalis-Diomidis) and the rest of the LAR team in the field of history of Greek and Roman Religion has been a dream for me that has come true. The wider context of interaction with other specialists in the humanities and the social sciences at the Max-Weber-Kolleg has also been extremely beneficial for both my project within LAR and my personal development as a researcher. From the first month of my employment I took part in a long series of fascinating academic conferences. The conference that was focused on narratives was a true eyeopener for me, as it related both to my previous work on the divine epiphany and its emplotment in narratives and my current project on Aristides' self-conscious and "tormented" religious narrative, the Hieroi Logoi. In January 2015 I felt particularly privileged to be able to co-organise a three-day international conference on the religious professionals and their role in the cultic cosmos of the Imperial Era with Jörg Rüpke and Richard Gordon. Just before I left the Max-Weber-Kolleg I co-organised a workshop on the materiality of divine agency with Katharina Rieger. One year later I guest-edited a special issue (3.2) of the journal *Religion in the Roman Empire*. The issue is dedicated to embodiment and "lived ancient religion" and is entitled "Embodying Religion". I shared six different papers, all drafts of chapters from my forthcoming monograph on Aristides, with my colleagues at the

Max-Weber-Kolleg. The feedback I received every step of the way was extremely helpful and constructive. To say that I was very happy working for the LAR project would be an understatement. The Max-Weber-Kolleg inspired me to produce a significant number of research outputs that secured me a permanent Lectureship in Ancient Greek History at the University of Liverpool.

Anna-Katharina Rieger

Coming to the Max-Weber-Kolleg as an archaeologist was one of the most challenging opportunities along my way in academia. For three and a half years I enjoyed, as member of the project "Lived Ancient Religion", the unique qualities of this highly interdisciplinary and diverse, intellectually ambitious and constructively working place to study, meet and discuss topics in cultural and social studies. Within the frame of the project "Lived Ancient Religion" I dealt with sacred spaces in Roman provinces of Western Asia (today's Syria, Lebanon and Israel). Even though the topographical tailoring encompassed a desk-and-libraryoriented study, it offered even more the opportunity to look freshly onto sacred places which for decades were studied predominantly under aspects of provinciality or Romanness and religious syncretism. To overcome these interpretations, I applied an agent-based as well as a spatial approach that encompassed an investigation of how places are embedded in a larger socio-topographical context. Who invested in what parts of them and why; how places were internally organized and where can "hot spots" of ritual activity be marked off. By overcoming the dichotomies of elite vs. rural religion, provincial vs. Roman styles or nomadic vs. urban contexts, perspectives opened onto the differentiated and differentiating processes of growing and decreasing interest, fame, spatial functionalities and communication according to the people acting in the sacralised places. The agents organising and enlivening the sacred space at Seeia (Southern Syria) cannot be understood without the landscape features, spatial relations and resulting life-strategies around. A closer look onto the composition of the people, present in the sacred space, indicated the various interests and investments, not only in a rich architecture and dedications, but even more importantly in a complex water management system, covering and religiously imbuing a large territory. Investigating not only individual places but their relations helped pin down religious life in the making, often out of a continuous competition. The situational aspects of religious activities – where, who and when – were studied in roadside shrines along the routes of the Arabian Desert, used by passers-by. Inscriptions, graffiti and imagery revealed the spontaneous formation of the groupings for a religious act. The horizon of experience and expectation shaped the way in which they added their names and dedications in order to perpetuate the communication to their fellow agents. The limitations of discerning "lived religion" due to characteristics of archaeological material are clear-cut. However, the focus on the religious agents and on situational settings and contexts of objects, people, texts, reshaping religion and its spaces, lead to new interpretations of seemingly well-known sacred places, and revised the assumption of religion as a pre-set system.

Jörg Rüpke

The initial formulation of the Lived Ancient Religion project was a proposal about how one might rethink the conceptualisation of the vast, amorphous, heterogeneous body of material that bears upon what is conventionally known as "the religion of the Roman Empire". The very topic had itself hardly existed before the 1980s, being regularly confused with "ancient Roman religion" on the one hand, and the "Oriental religions of the Roman Empire" on the other. The initiative was grounded in three specific challenges to existing approaches:

(1) we criticised the implicit assumption that all inhabitants of the Empire, from the Republican "empire of booty" to the supposedly christianised empire of Theodosius I in the late 4th century CE, were equally religious (the "homo religiosus" fallacy).

(2) We also questioned the focus upon civic, i.e., collective, institutionalised religious practices. This is vital because that focus produced a series of supplementary subcategories (which are at the same time conceptual strategies), such as "mystery-religions", "oriental cults", "indigenous cults", "votive religion", "funerary rites", in order to save the phenomena, yet whose relation to civic practice is quite indeterminate – they are sub-categories that are neither empirically convincing nor analytically adequate.

(3) We criticised the practice of treating "pagan" religion, Judaism and Christianity as though they had existed historically in quite separate worlds – enshrined in a disciplinary division of labour that has been enforced since the rise of Neo-humanism in the late eighteenth century. Against a tradition of scholarship heavily invested in concepts of "tradition" and "sacral law", Lived Ancient Religion did not reconstruct local ancient religion as an ahistorical set of "symbols" of fixed meaning or from individual experiences ("belief"), but from the historical agents that are the producers of our "sources". It emphasised the social context of action deemed "religious", and specifically the "group-styles" that influence linguistic and behavioural patterns in specific cultural contexts, such as the (non-nuclear) family, neighbourhoods and associations. From this perspective, public cult appears less as a set of ideals that can in practice never be lived up to, but more as a scheme of ordering priorities and distinctions whose effect is to outline (rather than define) an imagined community. Apart from several monographs, many results have been published in issues of Religion in the Roman Empire. An article, co-authored by all members of the team and entitled "Religion in the Making", has been published in *Religion 48* (2018). Proceedings from the final conference at Eisenach will be published in April 2020.

Benjamin Sippel

Although numerous generations of ancient historians have rendered outstanding services to the study of the social and religious history of the Roman Empire, many details are still in the dark: What concrete socio-religious developments and constellations, for example, have contributed in the long run to the disappearance of polytheistic cults from a particular village and to Christian cult taking their place? A key to answering this question lies in the consideration of the temple personnel who performed public cult acts and were responsible for the maintenance of the sanctuaries: With these actors, the general cult activity stood and fell.

In my dissertation, I am therefore dealing with the question of which processes of change the Egyptian and Hellenistic rituals experienced in Egypt in the first centuries of Roman rule, which religious topography the spreading Christianity thus found in the rural regions of the country, and which factors favoured the decline of the one religion and the spread of the other, or made it possible at all, at the beginning of the fourth century CE. In this context, I examine the importance of the priestly offices in these persons' way of life and vice versa, the place of the cult functionaries in the village structures, and the extent to which changes in other areas of life affected the performance of their religious duties.

The villages of the Lower Egyptian Fayum Basin offer themselves first of all as a place of investigation, since on the one hand by far the most sources on polytheistic temple personnel come from this area and on the other hand some of the earliest traces of Christian practices and semantics can be found here. Should the work progress faster than planned, other regions of Egypt will be included in the study.

The papyrus fragments preserved from the Roman era offer the opportunity to gain a lively and varied insight into the life of the temple staff. Among other things, private letters, contracts and census declarations tell us about the everyday business, difficulties and life plans of the cult functionaries and document how they came to terms with the events of the day, sometimes resisted and with each of their actions determined anew the direction in which the future of the temple business on the knife edge leaned. Archaeological and epigraphic source material will also be included in the work, thus creating a cross-disciplinary work that brings together the findings of Egyptology, ancient history and religious studies, among others.

Janico Albrecht, Christopher Degelmann, Valentino Gasparini, Richard Gordon, Maik Patzelt, Georgia Petridou, Rubina Raja, Anna-Katharina Rieger, Jörg Rüpke, Benjamin Sippel, Emiliano Rubens Urciuoli, Lara Weiss

7 Article from the ERC-project

Religion in the making: The Lived Ancient Religion Approach*

For the past five years (2012–2017), the Max Weber Center of Erfurt University has hosted a project on 'Lived Ancient Religion: Questioning "cults" and "polis religion"', financed by the European Research Council and embedded in the research group on 'Religious individualisation in historical perspective' (see Fuchs and Rüpke 2015). It was designed to supplement existing accounts of the religious history of the Mediterranean area at the time of the long Roman Empire, accounts traditionally centred upon public or civic institutions. The new model focuses on the interaction of individuals with a variety of religious specialists and traditions, taking the form of material culture, spaces, and text. It emphasises religious experience, embodiment and 'culture in interaction' (section 1). On the basis of research into the history of religion of the Roman Empire, this co-authored article sets out to offer new tools for research into religion by formulating three major perspectives, namely religious agency, instantiated religion, and narrated religion (section 2). We have tried to illustrate their potential value by means of thirteen short case-studies deriving from different geographical areas of the central and eastern Mediterranean area, and almost all relating to the period 150 BCE to 300 CE (section 3). These short descriptions are summarising research pursued by the members of the team of authors, published or to be published in extended form elsewhere, as indicated by the references.

The aspirations of the LAR project

The initial formulation of the Lived Ancient Religion project ('LAR', cf. Rüpke 2011b) was a proposal about how one might re-think the conceptualisation of the vast, amorphous, heterogeneous body of material that bears upon what is conventionally known as 'the religion of the Roman Empire'. The very topic had itself hardly existed before the 1980s, being regularly confused with 'ancient Roman religion' on the one

---

* Originally published in *Religion* 48.4 (2018), 568–593 (Taylor & Francis), doi: 10.1080/0048721X.2018.1450305, CC-BY-NC-ND 4.0.

hand, and the 'Oriental religions of the Roman Empire' on the other (Bonnet and Rüpke 2009; Rüpke 2011c). The initiative was grounded in three specific challenges to existing approaches: a) We criticise the implicit assumption that all inhabitants of the Empire, from the Republican 'empire of booty' to the supposedly Christianised empire of Theodosius I in the late fourth century CE, were equally religious (the 'homo religiosus' fallacy). b) We also question the focus upon civic, i.e. collective, institutionalised religious practices. This is vital because that focus produced a series of supplementary sub-categories (which are at the same time conceptual strategies), in order to grasp, but also exclude phenomena that were very present, but neither collective nor necessarily institutionalised. These categories, such as 'mystery-religions', 'oriental cults', 'indigenous cults', 'votive religion', 'funerary rites', allowed to include the phenomena, yet did not determine the relation to civic practice. Thus, they are sub-categories that are neither empirically convincing nor analytically adequate. c) Thirdly, we criticise the practice of treating 'pagan' religion, Judaism and Christianity as though they had existed historically in quite separate worlds – enshrined in a disciplinary division of labour that has been enforced since the rise of Neo-humanism in the late eighteenth century.

The long-term price paid for such commitments has been to uncouple the ancient world from shifts of approach that have long since been established in the mainstream or global study of religions, to the extent that it no longer has a place in many standard works, and is at best confined to its own safe little corner (such as the excellent handbook edited by Salzman and Adler [2013]). Where are the individual religious agents in a framework fixated upon 'festivals' and 'collective practice'? What are we doing by making entities such as 'Roman religion' or 'Christianity' the subject of constative sentences? What is the historical value of an archaeological practice dominated by a concern for individual monuments and 'gods'?

The mantra of the Annales School was that 'the evidence only yields the answers if one knows how to pose the questions' (Bloch 1944, 77). A change of questions is a change of subject; fruitful new questions are stimulated by work in neighbouring disciplines. The main thrust of the Lived Ancient Religion initiative was to resist the easy reification of 'religion' (as though we all know what is involved) in order to emphasise its ceaseless construction through individual action within the loose parameters provided by traditions, ideals and institutions ('religion in the making', Rüpke 2016a). That is, to view religion as a precarious practice, whose referents ('gods') and communicative strategies are constantly in need of investment-labour of different kinds in order to maintain their plausibility. In the absence of a sufficiently broad indigenous concept of religion, the continuity of many practices and concepts later captured under incipient conceptualisations (*religio, thrêskeia, ta theia*), we opted for a wide substantialist definition, namely the *ascription of agency to non- or super-human agents* regarded as 'ancestors', 'gods' or 'demons', *usually performed in communicative action*. 'Religion in the making' was the title of the Lowell Lectures of Alfred North Whitehead as published in 1926. Apart from a formulation in the introduction, the phrase is never used again. Whitehead's account is of a universal history of religion, its necessary change in the course of development of a rational worldview and its permanent individual reproduction on the basis of aesthetic experiences that bring together the material and the noetic world. If it is philosophical critique that questions the stability of religion and dogmas in Whitehead, Rüpke's 'making', instead, focuses on the inherent dynamic quality of those cultural products that we identify as religion in the course of historical analyses.

'Lived Ancient Religion' does not pretend to be either a distinctive methodology or a general theory of religion, but is an eclectic approach marked by a specific range of interests. It seeks to complement other approaches by framing new questions that can be posed to a wide range of different types of evidence, deriving primarily but perhaps not exclusively from the Graeco-Roman world. Our approach is intended to provide the stimulus to integrate 'the' evidence on a new basis, invoke new types of evidence, challenge existing classifications of material, or focus on neglected types of religious action. In view of the development, reception and transfer of 'religious action' to different contexts and in relation to new concerns, we work with a general model of the historically-contingent establishment of 'religion' as a socially-recognised field of action within the Empire (Rüpke 2011b, 2011c; cf. Beyer 2009). The long-term aim was from the beginning to provide new narratives of religious change in the Roman Empire based upon the methodological points of departure and insights of the research thus inspired (see e.g. Rüpke 2018).

While invoking 'lived religion' as understood in modern contexts (e.g. Orsi 1997; McGuire 2008), there are clear differences in the application and implication of the concept. Starting from 'Lived Religion in America' (Hall 1997), the change of focus indicated by the concept was from a description of religion based on its dogmatic to religion as practiced. Nancy T. Ammerman thus choose a whole group characterised by ethics instead of dogmas (the 'Golden Rule Christians') as her point of departure (Ammerman 1997). The concept became more and more to be equivalent with 'everyday religion', paying close attention to subjective experience and meaning (see Ammerman 2008). 'Lived Ancient Religion' was neither restricted to 'everyday religion' (as opposed to organised or dogmatic religion) nor particularly focused on subjective experience, which is anyway hardly represented in the available evidence. Instead it flagged four key terms aimed at straddling the dichotomy between subjectivity and communicative action. These were appropriation, competence, situational meaning and mediality. All of these were intended to sharpen the accounts of the dynamics of ancient religious experiences, practices and beliefs.

Appropriation denotes the situational adaptation and deployment of existing practices and techniques, institutions, norms and media to suit contingent individual or group aims and needs (Raja and Rüpke 2015a; Arnhold and Rüpke 2016; Rüpke 2016b). Starting from the notion of ascription of agency, the catchword 'competence' was intended to underline the priority of personal engagement, knowledge and skill in the provision of services of all kinds, whether on an occasional or a professional basis, including public and private performance, authorship, teaching, networking (Gordon 2005; Hüsken 2009; Petridou 2013). In speaking of the situational construction of meaning, we assumed that religious meanings were not generated by worldviews but by the complex interplay of interests, beliefs and satisfactions in specific situations (Raja and Weiss 2015). Finally, the focus on communication (both vertical and horizontal) required specific concern with the roles of material culture, embodiment and group-styles in the construction of religious experience, in short: mediality (Malik, Rüpke, and Wobbe 2007; Meyer 2008; Hjarvard 2011; Lövheim 2011). Insofar as communication requires materiality, this amounts to a demand for a new approach in the archaeology of religion (the 'archaeology of religious experience', Raja and Rüpke 2015a).

Thus, against a tradition of scholarship heavily invested in concepts of 'tradition' and 'sacral law', Lived Ancient Religion does not reconstruct local ancient religion as an ahistorical set of 'symbols' of fixed meaning or from individual experiences (and so 'belief', cf. Scheid 2016), but from the historical agents that are the producers of our 'sources'. It emphasises the social context of action deemed 'religious', and specifically the 'group-styles' (based on Goffman's symbolic interactionism) that influence linguistic and behavioural patterns in specific cultural contexts, such as the (non-nuclear) family, neighbourhoods and associations (Lichterman et al. 2017). From this perspective, public cult appears less as a set of ideals that can in practice never be lived up to, but more as a scheme of ordering priorities and distinctions whose effect is to outline (rather than define) an imagined community.

Perspectives

In applying the initial conceptual tools to a variety of empirical material taken from across the Mediterranean world during the long Roman Empire, some perspectives emerged, which turned out to be particularly useful across the historical depth and geographical span of our inquiry, namely religious agency, instantiated religion and narrated religion. These three perspectives are laid out in summary fashion in this section. In the following section (3) they are illustrated and further fleshed out by means of the case-studies.

a) Religious agency
Within this grid we employ the concept of religious agency in order to capture the dynamics of practice and historical change. We understand 'religious agency' as a special type or aspect of the capacity to act in the historical societies under consideration, which results from the kind of agency involved in the context of communication with non- or superhuman addressees (or 'senders'; see Rüpke 2015a). We under-

stand such agency thus in a twofold sense, the powers ascribed to non- or superhuman addressees (which is the semantic or performative content of such communication), and the resultant modification of human action. To the extent that such communication ascribes agency to actors qualified as 'divine', that agency is privileged ('religious' in our definition), while the agency of the human initiators or principals of such communication is modified: mostly by being enlarged (e.g. acting in accordance with, or out of reverence for, the gods; as a legitimate descendant within a family cultic tradition etc.), but occasionally in being reduced, for example when agency is ascribed to the will of the gods only. Depending on their plausibility or degree of acceptance, the claims implied in such communication will also modify the wider social environment and so the agency attributed to an audience. From the point of view of social action, therefore, 'religious agency' opens up endless opportunities for both creating and managing complex scenarios. We also want to argue that it should be seen as a source of social and cultural change, including innovation in the realm of religious communication itself, its addressees, its forms, and its plausibility. Mediterranean antiquity offers abundant examples of the upscaling as well as attempts at controlling and restricting such agency.

Doing religious communication does not start *ab ovo*. We view human agents as embedded in multiple cultural frameworks that include traditions of communicating with or about divine communicators. At the same time these agents are constrained or supported by existing power relations. These structures are not simply abstract constraints but inform all situations in which competence is demonstrated. People perform religious communication in specific spatial and temporal contexts and in doing so produce specifically religious space and time: for instance, processions delimit territory, a complex ritual sequence transforms a day into a festival. Conversely a temple presents itself as the preferred place to contact the divine, a holiday demands gifts for the gods.

The spatio-temporal and the social context together afford agency. Religious agents feel empowered or empower themselves to act by drawing on divine agency; they are also driven by personal problems, economic needs, by political aspirations and moral codes. On their way to an important event, individuals might stop at some point and mark out a religious space by means of a simple prayer and offering, but such a claim could easily be ignored by others taking the same route, as the philosophic adventurer Apuleius pointed out in the second century CE (*Florida* 1). Drinking vessels repeatedly used in rituals may be marked as 'special' by carrying written invocations (e.g. the so-called 'Spruchbecher' of the north-western provinces). A patient might set up a small altar in thanksgiving, which might be seen for decades in a sanctuary. Objects form part of the ongoing sacralisation of specific spaces, that is, constitute investments in their character as sites particularly appropriate for religious communication (Rüpke 2016c), and advertises the principal's 'piety' and hence social standing – or might invite criticism of his or her 'superstition' (hence throwing doubt upon their competence).

The choice of place and time (Rüpke 2012) might be influenced by (imagined) inclusion in a group or could be instrumental in creating and sustaining such a group, for instance as followers of Isis or Christ (see Wedekind 2012). Religious action is however not confined to institutionalised religious contexts. The concept of 'grouping' is one of the more obvious possibilities here, whereby religious communication can be effected on a purely short-term basis without long-term consequences (Rebillard 2015; Rebillard and Rüpke 2015). An example here might be the invocation of divinatory signs (bird-flight or animal-entrails) by Greek or Roman generals in front of their soldiers to legitimate decisions about whether to engage or not (Patzelt 2018). Thus human religious agents and 'audiences' can ascribe agency to one other.

The consequences of situational religious agency go beyond immediate space and time. Roles are claimed and negotiated in ways that condition expectations in future situations. Media, whether in the form of objects or texts, may out-last their originary occasions. Grouping processes may establish lasting networks (Lichterman et al. 2017). Thus, religious agents do not only depend on, selectively use, and reproduce the resources they draw upon. They also modify them, both in the short and even in the long term. We use the concept of 'appropriation' (as outlined above) to refer to the adaptation and instrumentalisation of such resources. Religion from this point of view is a dynamic process, is always 'religion in the making'.

b) Dynamics of instantiated religion

Shifting the focus from the agents to the dialectics of expression and experience in religious communication and the many material or textual forms relevant in such connections, a second perspective emerges, which we term 'instantiation', thus shifting the focus from the agents themselves to the form and content of their actions.

Individual and group appropriations are approaches to, modifications or even inventions of practices, narratives or (informal) institutions, which re-enact and/or transform traditions (Rüpke 2011a, 2016b). This means that individual and group action draws upon shared knowledge but at the same time allows variation. The tension between existing knowledge and invention creates a dynamic, which is in principle never-ending (Gordon 2013a, 2013c). With respect to religious traditions – especially ancient ones – it is usually assumed that individuals and groups followed a strict set of existing pre-defined rules. However, even in antiquity individuals and groups disposed of a range of possible models for action depending on context and situation, quite apart from means of communicating with the other world. Just as today, not everybody was necessarily equally religious. The public performance of religious activity, for example setting up a statue or leaving a votive offering, correlates with expectations related to individual or group status – or, contrariwise, may break with them. In other words, resort to certain religious practices or narratives may be an important status marker within an (imagined) community, or it may assert difference. Physical mobility may increase the range of choices of modes of expression at a given location, if newcomers take objects and ideas along with them to a new place of residence or settlement (Tacoma 2016, passim). On the other hand, the experience of migration may transform selected religious practices and narratives into an important anchor of individual or group identity. In that case, the satisfaction of conformity may strongly reinforce membership of a(n imagined) community.

Fundamental to the instantiation of religious communication is recognition and acceptance of the types of expressive media available in a given context within specific cultural milieux. Such acknowledgement is the pre-condition for all religious action as manifested in the world, from spitting onto one's own breast to ward off ill-luck, through the offering of fruits to a deity, to the grandest possible individual euergetic gesture, such as the extremely rich donation of the Crypta Balbi at Rome or the sanctuary of Zeus Olympios at Gerasa/Jerash in modern Jordan. At the same time, the instantiation of the decision once made opens up options, quite limited in the case of how best to spit, virtually unlimited in the case of the grand gesture – for instance putting up further images of deities, organizing religious festivals or constructing further sacred spaces (de Polignac 2009; Rüpke 2013; Belayche 2014; Cooley 2015; Raja 2015c; Van Andringa 2015; Gordon 2017). Such options are themselves a form of power, and thus critical to the ascription of agency. In a word, instantiation, making some action manifest as 'religious action', requires resources, imaginative (i.e. competence) but also material. In a complex agrarian empire such as the Roman Empire, both types of resource were very unevenly distributed within the population as a whole, partly because of the massive concentration of the population in the agrarian sector, at the bottom of the chain of both information and wealth, but mainly because of the highly unequal distribution of status and wealth. It is above all in the density and diversity of urban environments that the investment choices within the elite condition and frame options lower down the social scale. The instantiation of motivations and experiences as 'religious' is thus inherently a matter not merely of desire but of resources.

Such instantiations are often taken at face value as direct expressions of intentions; they may, however, also be viewed as outcomes of complex processes involving a range of choices, intentions and negotiations. Previous instantiations, their scale and locations, are part of the conditioning environment. The final form, whether gesture, object, text or edifice, had their effects, great or small, upon contemporary and future ways of embarking on, or developing, religious initiatives. While choices or possibilities were of course closely linked to the scale of investment, and therefore also to social status and social styles, a wide range of instantiations, which did not in principle require heavy investment, might also come to have an immense impact on subsequent expressions of religious action and rituals (Rieger, 2016b). Gift practices might range from scattered individual offerings to accumulations of mass-produced terracotta votives offered over decades at one site. While the latter may give the impression that they all express the same intention, such motivations may in fact have differed immensely. The number of religious spaces within an urban context, whether monumentalised or not, may for example tell us about the long-term efforts of the political elite, but might also be expressions of individual aspirations to local and wider fame.

c) Religion narrated, narrating religion

'Instantiations' have been treated above all as synonyms of material forms in the previous paragraphs (cf. more generally Walker Bynum 2011; Droogan 2013; Mol and Versluys 2015; Raja and Rüpke 2015b; Knott, Krech, and Meyer 2016). Many instantiations of religion, however, from three line inscriptions to multi-volume literary texts, take the form of (at any rate implied) narratives. Indeed we might well say that narration, in both oral and written forms, is more or less omnipresent in religious practice, preparing, accompanying, and reflecting communication with ancestors or gods (Rüpke and Degelmann 2015). From a theoretical point of view, narrations have medial, communicative, and locative dimensions. They play a role in instantiating religion in three distinguishable ways.

Any experience that may be interpreted as a communication with the divine (whether in dreams, visions, epiphanies or prophecies), demands a choice whether it is to be revealed to others or not. In many cases, silence may be the preferred option (Smolak 2001). The choice to communicate, that is to say, to 'externalise' an experience interpreted as 'religious', in turn involves further choices: how is one to narrate the form of such an encounter and the divine presences involved? Whatever the choice made, we can properly understand the composition of such narratives as the production of religious knowledge. Such knowledge is however thoroughly ambiguous. Positively, it may open up opportunities for earning cultural, and specifically religious, capital (for this concept, see e.g. Urban 2003) of a recognised kind, which can be operationalised for strategic purposes in specific situations. Negatively, they may expose narrators to the risk of being accused of claiming an unmerited or unwarranted privilege, e.g. as 'false prophets' (Stroumsa 2013).

No narration begins from a *tabula rasa*: contextual knowledge plays an irreducible role in their creation. In the first place, the process of creating a narrative demands that one draw upon ready-made figures, tropes and schemes (see Koschorke 2012) that mediate between the 'original' experience, whatever it may have been, and the various products that emerge from it, whether (auto-)biography, historical works, (apocryphal) acts, informal stories, exhortative texts or even rhetorical performances. Secondly narrators may formulate, retell and re-arrange them more or less endlessly, and thus transfer them to new and different social or spatial settings. Religious narrations are thus dynamic elements in the communication between individuals, audiences and the divine agency they refer to, enabling the creation of new relationships and new imaginations (Rüpke 2018a).

Narratives are heard by audiences. Audiences too have choices: they may engage with the narrative, remain indifferent, or reject it in whole or in part. Either option allows the members of the audience to become in their turn religious agents, whether by re-telling, renewing, re-elaborating, or contesting the knowledge gained, in the light of their prior assumptions, knowledge and interests. By negotiating the narrative of a healing event to be set up in or near a temple, the individuals who financed such inscriptions could enlarge their own range of action and so reduce that of the priests (Gordon 2016; see also Petridou 2015). Thus claims to competence do not cease with the original narrative, but may be amplified, but also modified, in later communicative undertakings. Moreover, thanks to audience networks, the process of appropriation of the narrative message from the initial performance or reading can have no imaginable end (cf. Eidinow 2011).

By concentrating on an agentive approach to narrated religion we try to avoid treating narratives as though they offered stable meanings to reverent audiences. We understand the chiffre 'religion narrated/narrating religion' as a way of underlining the complexity of the communicative process and the inexhaustible variety of selective appropriations in 'making religion'.

Case studies

These three lines of enquiry, religious agency, instantiated religion and narrated religion, may now be used to structure the findings of the specific studies that have been produced in the course of the project that has now come to an end.

a) Studies thematising religious agency

The six studies grouped here, though evidently different in substance, focus on a number of common themes. They treat religious agency as a form of (self-)empowerment in specific social situations, in which the human actant stands to lose or gain a strategic good. At the same time, the degree of agency ascribed to deities varies sharply between the different cases, from the maximum implied by cursing (ascribing to the deity the power to punish or evil kill the target) to the minimum implied by negotiation for status within ad hoc dining groups where the deity addressed simply looks benignly upon the human initiative.

Cursing

The act of cursing offers an extreme example of individual religious agency acquired in the context of perceived threat to the principal's social or existential status. The issue here is not the 'objective' or 'juridical' justification for a curse against a target but rather the degree of anxiety, fear, anger or distress that subjectively warranted recourse to a curse. Such resort was an option realised at one specific moment in a longer, perhaps much longer, self-authored narrative, sometimes one repeatedly rehearsed before family, friends and supporters, in others perhaps a more spontaneous reaction, detailing a more or less serious threat to the social standing, honour, possessions, or integrity of the principal (Gordon 2015). This narrative provided the moral justification for the resort to a curse, one of the major sanctions available to individual agents, and might of course continue long after the actual utterance or (in the case of a written curse) deposition of the demand to the other world. Yet it is hardly ever drawn upon in formulating the curse itself, which is to be understood as a form of 'hard words' or 'hard thoughts' concentrating solely upon the rhetorical effect upon the explicit or implicit addressee. As a result, the precise aim of a curse is often quite uncertain (Alvar Nuño 2017). By invoking, explicitly or implicitly, the sanction of divine punishment, curses relied on a conception of a cosmos in which human action is subject to constant scrutiny by the other world, which was imagined as capable of direct action whose effect was to restore the socio-moral balance between the two (or more parties) parties involved in a conflict (Versnel 2010). In thus imagining the possibility of direct divine intervention, the private curse was a 'naïve' appropriation of a wider institution sanctioned by the dominant theodicy, 'naive' in the sense that the latter had long since rationalised the lack of fit between a nominally moral cosmos and individual deserts (cf. the argument of Plutarch's *De sera numinum vindicta:* 'the mills of the gods grind slowly but surely'; 'the wronged will be recompensed - in the world to come').

In the nature of things, no actual oral curses survive; what do survive are written curses, mainly written on lead or pewter sheet, a few on papyrus (e.g. Daniel and Maltomini 1990, nos. 37–41, 43–45, 56, 58–62). As is to be expected, given the sheer size and cultural diversity of the Empire, the textual strategies used vary greatly. The variety is partly related to levels of literacy and partly to different levels of ingenuity in appropriating discursive materials from the local stock of informal knowledge of 'how to do such things'. This informal knowledge might also include the notions of prayer and votive as suitable strategies. Curse tablets thus offer a privileged insight into individual appropriations of religious resources and lived religion in antiquity. The body is used as a key medium here: working from the representation of illness as a divine punishment, some curses seek to force the target to interpret illness as the consequence of having done wrong (Gordon 2013b); others attempt to attack the target's physical and social body by disarticulating it item by item, as in a cinematic panning shot. In other cases again, cult details are used as sources of persuasive comparison. If we turn to specialists, we find them exploiting new niches, such as the circus and the brothel, where clients again found themselves exposed to unpredictable hazard. Here we can speak of risk-minimisation (Eidinow 2007).

Performing prayer

By focusing on agency, we can highlight the performance of (public) prayer rather than its text. The distinction between profane and sacred gestures as well as public and private prayers is then secondary to the personal knowledge and competence that the agent activates when required. Rather than reproducing a fixed set of mandatory formulas and obligatory sequences of gestures, as allegedly required by civic institutions and traditions, it is up to the orant (the 'praying agent') to master the situation through performance.

The best example is a prayer by Clodius (mid-1st cent. BCE), which his contemporary Cicero alleges went disastrously wrong (Cicero, *On his House* 139–142). Clodius, just like other aristocrats in a similar situation, has to perform his prayer in public, as it were on stage. In general, we can say that in such cases the assisting pontiff composed a text, with which he prompted the orant, that is, the acting magistrate – or, in this case, the tribune of the people. The orant, however, has to activate his own physical resources in order to perform the text convincingly before the audience. These personal resources are of course not specified in any 'prayer book', nor are they a constituent of the religious knowledge transmitted by priests. Reading between the lines, we see that Clodius used his rhetorical skills in order to fulfil the expectations of the audience, which included, if we are to judge from the rhetorical manuals (e.g. Cicero, *On the rhetor* 3.151–156; 195–198), emotional arousal.. Whilst his colleagues seem to prefer gestures of raising one's hands up in the air, or covering one's head as devices to arouse the audience (Quintilian, *Institutes of Oratory* 11.3.114–116), Clodius opted for performing a wild dance, similar to that of the *Salii*, 'dancing' or jumping priests at Rome. Likewise, he enhances the dramatic modulation of the voice with uttering 'meaningless' sounds, 'just like women' (Patzelt 2018). Clodius, in other words, 'appropriated' a particular style of prayer performance in order to exceed ordinary expectations. The orant does evidently not merely 'convey' his or her concerns to a deity. As the example of Clodius shows, the orant needs to establish a communicative bond not just with the deity/ies addressed but also with a public, whether a regular audience or a momentary grouping. Since, as various CSR studies on prayer have shown, this communication relies on interaction rules rather than on mandatory liturgy (Schjødt 2009), we can say that such a situation ascribes a degree of agency to the audience. The agency ascribed to the deity, on the other hand, is essentially produced by the communication process and therefore admits of a huge variety of individual strategies, as Seneca's description of devotees on the Capitol at Rome exemplifies (*On superstition* fr. 36–37).

The performance of symbolic mourning

Using the LAR approach can also improve our understanding of Roman political culture, which was in many respects structured by rituals and ritualised by structures (Hölkeskamp 2010; Arena and Prag 2017). On this reading, significant actors could first appropriate signs and gestures from a 'primary' context and then adapt their usual meaning in keeping with their own aims (Lüdtke 1995). The case chosen here is 'symbolic mourning', a strategy sometimes employed, mainly by members of the political elite in Republican Rome, on occasions of existential personal or even more general crisis. This involved entering public spaces, for example the Forum or a lawcourt, dressed in soiled clothes, and allowing the beard grow (at a time when the norm was for adult men to be close shaven), both of them regular signs of mourning, though dark or dirty clothing might also be taken as a sign of low social status (Degelmann 2017). In other words signs and gestures of mourning were employed as strategies to negotiate (sometimes even to intensify) political conflicts.

Romans were acutely aware of the import of such strategies. Gossip and rumour flew fast. The 'mourner' might be demanding sympathy or abasing himself in public, both options requiring an emotional response from passers-by. Such strategies could save individuals from exile and death, but might be used before resort to violence or even at times of civil war. Sometimes however they failed (a regular risk in the case of all performative acts), for example when no one was willing to pay heed; and sometimes the principal had to amplify the range of his appeal by staging his children in court, or by weeping. It was not merely clothes, hair, performance and audience that were important, however: the specific associations of different locations in the city of Rome must have been significant, even though we know very little about this aspect.

Contextual appropriation of religious knowledge in Roman Egypt

In Roman Egypt, well-trained and -educated practitioners ('priests') dominated the tradition of cultic practice in temples by a variety of means including the production of texts and the organisation of festivals, thereby enlarging their own range of action. Whereas such activities were constrained by rather rigid rules, a few such individuals were also able to creatively appropriate elements from other religious traditions.

An excellent example is a papyrus written by an Egyptian cult-official named Pakysis early in the third century CE. This man was born about 166 CE and lived in Soknopaiou Nesos on the northern edge of the Fayum (c. 100 km south of modern Cairo) in Lower Egypt. As a *stolistes* of the main local temple, he had the prestigious task of dressing the cult-figures. When off-duty, however, he worked as a book-keeper for a large estate. So far, twenty accounts from this archive have been published (cf. Jördens 1998, 219–227; Geens 2015). One of these, written on reused papyrus and fairly chaotic in layout, is particularly interesting in the present connection. It begins with an invocation to four Greek deities: Agathe Tyche, Kerdon, Hermes and Aphrodite.

Such invocations are unknown from Egyptian temple-administration. The sequence of deities is highly exceptional and only found in three other published Greek papyri, all originating from second-century Fayum. Although all are very fragmentary, they seem to derive from the context of book-keeping and commerce. All four deities played a role in economic contexts: Agathe Tyche embodied Good Fortune, Kerdon was personified Gain, Hermes was the god of merchants and Aphrodite the goddess responsible for good relations. Perhaps Pakysis learned the formula from another bookkeeper or by studying other accounts in relation to his work.

Pakysis wrote the names on a private draft, and thus intended no human audience. It seems most likely that his (at any rate implicit) addressees were the four deities and that he was appropriating a practice already known among local accountants. We would then have a case in which a high-ranking Egyptian temple-official could assign religious agency to other, acculturated Greek, accountants and appropriate their knowledge for his own purposes. Context may here be crucial: Pakysis interacted with the Greek divine agents not in his temple but privately, while acting in a non-sacerdotal role.

Competing for status at Palmyra

Research undertaken on material from the oasis city of Palmyra in the Syrian Desert relating to the activities taking place in the various main sanctuaries of the city, has led to a more nuanced understanding of various aspects of religious life in this city (Raja 2015a). A large group of tiny religious dining 'tickets' (Latin: *tesserae*), mostly made of clay, provide an important case study, which impels us to review religious agency and the dynamics of instantiated religion in a different light (Raja 2015b, 2015c). More than 1,100 different types of these *tesserae* are known. Some have even been found in what is assumed to be complete series. The objects were used as entrance tickets to religious banquets, which were held by invitation in the main sanctuaries of the city. They carry detailed iconography and sometimes also inscriptions in Palmyrene Aramaic giving the name of the sponsor(s) of the event and in some cases also the names of deities as well as the date. Often Palmyrene priests, who were the sponsors of these banquets, are depicted on one side of the *tesserae*, with a variety of iconographic symbols on the other, ranging from depictions of deities, to astral symbols, measures of drink and food distributed at the banquet.

When scrutinised in detail, the iconographic language of the *tesserae* tells us about the ascription of religious agency in these situations, since the banquets were sponsored by a variety of Palmyrene priests. These were all depicted in a generic 'Palmyrene' fashion, but the rest of the iconographic language was chosen with much care from a varied visual repertoire, which was influenced by local, regional and imperial traditions and constantly in the making. While the *tesserae* seem to have had no importance once the guest had been admitted to the relevant banquet (they were often disposed of in the banqueting hall or nearby), considerable effort was expended in making each series unique (Raja 2016).

Through their detailed and individualised visual language, the Palmyran *tesserae* provide information about religious agency (the donor and the guest) in the city as well as being an instantiation of religion there. Each series is also a material expression of local tradition. As such, they seem to be specific to Palmyra itself, for none have been found in other locations where expatriate Palmyrenes lived, such as at Dura-Europos or Rome (Dirven 1999; Equini Schneider 1993).

Isiac cults and religious agency

The concept of religious agency is also of value in analysing religious practices related to Isis, Serapis, Osiris, Harpocrates, Anubis and several other Graeco-Roman deities supposed to have formed a divine 'family' originally worshipped in Egypt. It helps to explore the different strategies by which the agents involved (individuals as well as groups of varying sizes) constructed their personal idea of Egypt. We were interested in exploring how different small-time religious providers and entrepreneurs appropriated, instrumentalised or even invented religious offers, sometimes by avoiding tricky Egyptian themes, sometimes by drawing upon what they knew or imagined about 'Egyptian behaviour'.

Avoidance: whereas in Egypt Isis was one of numerous deities associated with *heka*, 'magic as a divine power', her Greek reception systematically avoided this aspect of her activity. Even in the Demotic and Graeco-Egyptian magical papyri, texts closely associated with the temple tradition, we can trace the attenuation of her association with magic, which disappears virtually without trace in her reception outside Egypt. In the only two *defixiones* (curse-tablets) in Latin that invoke her, she is viewed as an ordinary member of the local pantheon. This phenomenon is to be understood as a strategy of avoidance on the part of the mediators of the Isiac cults to the Graeco-Roman world, where 'magic' was criminalised, involving its deliberate re-presentation as marvel or wonder (Gordon and Gasparini 2014).

'Egyptian behaviour': one of the most intriguing fields explored is the 'spectacular' and ecstatic aspect of Isiac cultic practice, which involved multiple strategies of dramatisation and emotional saturation within different sensory domains: haptic stimuli (e.g. worshippers beating their chests to re-enact Isis' grief during the festival of the *Isia*) could arouse in the spectators latent physical impulses, giving them the impression of experiencing the 'same' pain; auditory stimuli (e.g. the shrill sound of the Isiac rattle, *sistrum*) had the potential to attract the attention of participants and passers-by and increase the emotional impact of the proceedings (Gasparini and Saura-Ziegelmeyer forthcoming); a variety of visual stimuli increased the dramatic intensity of the theatrical performances staged in these contexts (Gasparini 2018). In short, physical and emotional intensification created a lived 'Egyptian' experience.

b) Instantiated Religion

The following case studies focus on the use of objects or the modification of an environment that instantiates religion either directly or by physically commemorating religious experiences and practices, thus creating the infrastructure for further religious action by others. We treat these as spatial practices, but of course their social impact extended far beyond those spatial limits.

Creating religious space

Despite their different ritual forms and materialities, practices of communicating with the divine, instantiating and narrating religion all involved specific or imagined space. Such practices were learned by doing or listening, sometimes even reading. The religious competence thus acquired, as well as the agency often accorded the religious agent, made it possible to apply them to new spaces and new situations.

In several Italian cities the cult of the Lares, closely linked to the hearth as (one) religious focus of the private house, was instantiated on the external walls of houses or at cross-roads. The Lares thus became familiar to those (the great majority of the urban population) who lived over-crowded one-room apartments in some tenement building and for whom the street therefore functioned as a sort of extended multi-roomed home. The few owners or tenants of houses, on the other hand, as we know from Pompeii and Herculaneum, were able actively to configure the architectural features and decoration of their homes in order to create their own personal religious 'infrastructure', with living quarters decorated with scenes of religious practices and gardens full of mythic figures and gods (Rüpke 2018b, 229–234). This spatial infrastructure in turn surely triggered imaginative elaboration, perhaps even stimulated the performance of ritual, but could also be used by the permanent inhabitants, as well as by visitors, in many different ways.

Lighting played a large role here, for example in relation to the spatial elements, whether mural decoration or furniture, to be illuminated, and how. Religious agents used lamps as religious instantiations of the first order: the flames of oil-lamps, candelabras and braziers, often in considerable numbers, illuminated their bodies in action but also of course the figures of the gods they worshipped and other relevant objects. The suggestiveness of the play of shadows here should not be underestimated (Bielfeldt 2014, 202). Like circus scenes or erotic motifs, such objects became true 'eye-catchers', and the brilliant 'eyes' of flame might suggest the feeling that one were oneself actually the object of their gaze (Rüpke 2016c, 263–266).

Altars too are better seen as instantiations of religion rather than merely as cultic apparatus. For the person who caused an altar to be set up, it was an unmistakable sign of communication with a presence that was not otherwise immediately obvious to the eye, whether a 'god' or the dead. Its use was unthinkable without lighting a fire or pouring a libation: the upper surface was designed for just these modes of activation. Moreover, in most cases the lateral faces of an altar were themselves decorated with images of ritual instruments (usually a libation-dish and a water-jug) which alluded to blood-sacrifice. An altar was thus an instantiation of religion that expressed as much one's own competence and experience as it was part of an environment defined by other religious agents and negotiations of meaning. As such, it also alluded implied an endless sequence of similar rituals, extending from the remote past to the indefinite future. But an altar could also be 'activated' with a minimum of effort, just by placing a lighted lamp on it, and mumbling an invocation or a song. Altars of all sizes, and quantities of votive lamps, played an ever-larger role in the imperial period, at the expense of depositions of figural objects such as statuettes (Rüpke 2016c, 266–267).

Religious praxis in houses (or in the street) was also brought to bear in institutional spaces designed for religious communication, such as temple-areas and temple-buildings themselves, that is, spaces shared by many users and even regulated by staff. If graffiti were welcome in the home, as an expressive response on the part of invited guests and an instantiation of their relationship to the hosts, this minimal but durable form of instantiation may also have played a role within the precincts of temples. Such was demonstrably the case at Dura-Europos on the river Euphrates, at the most easterly point of the Roman Empire. There, in the temples and assembly buildings of Jews as well as worshippers of Christ and Mithras, graffiti-writers endeavoured to perpetuate themselves with their requests to be remembered or blessed, as close as possible to the focal point of the original providers' religious instantiatiation, that is, the cult image, or on mural paintings, or in the corridors. In this way they also appropriated the great two- or three-dimensional instantiations of religious communication and experiences set up by others, thus entering into the process of loose grouping mentioned above.

Transcending the categories of public and private?

Lived ancient religion in the domestic space has also been studied under the rubric of instantiation in Karanis, a Roman town or large village again in the Fayum area of Lower Egypt. What was surprising, however, is how scattered and limited the archaeological evidence was. One influential view has it that later Roman Egypt was a period when religious practice gradually shifted from major temples to villages, and mainly the domestic sphere, since many larger temples had been closed (Frankfurter 1998, 97–144). However the idea that religion 'moved into the domestic sphere' is historically questionable, since there is plenty of evidence for domestic religious practice already in Pharaonic times (Weiss 2015). More important for the present issue, however, is that the surviving evidence for domestic religious practice in Roman Karanis was found mainly in houses belonging to relatively wealthy individuals.

Despite the enormous number of finds recovered by the American excavation of Roman Karanis, the character of religious practice there remains nevertheless somewhat enigmatic. A case in point concerns the decorated wall-niches in the better-off houses, which contained images, whether two- or three-dimensional (Gottry 1995; Weiss forthcoming). Traces of fire-emplacements suggest that offerings were performed in front of some at least of these niches, as in Italy. Relatively wealthy families, including veterans from the army, manifested their good fortune by means of the tasteful decoration and architecture of their houses, but evidently also by performing appropriate (religious) practices. It seems probable that these practices also included other village-groups, such that the assumption that 'domestic religion' equates with 'private religion' may be inaccurate. Despite the late date of abandonment (in the fifth century CE), there were no clear signs of Christian practice.

'Doing religion' in sanctuaries and grouping for religious practices in the eastern Mediterranean

The religious agents we can trace in shared sacred spaces of the Graeco-Roman Eastern Mediterranean, in the form of dedications, built structures and inscriptions, came there for different reasons, and with different interests. In order to reconstruct religious practices and their socio-spatial settings in larger spatial entities such as a region, a city or an oasis one needs to be clear about the cultural framework the religious agents living there could draw on (their 'horizon of experience' and their 'horizon of expectation'). These horizons have an impact on actors' interests and motivations for instantiating religion: ideas about how to depict a deity, how to address him, her or it, how to make an offering or stage a festival differed widely. Moreover, given the fluidity of the ways in which people practised religion or established short- and longer-term groupings, we can analyse these shared sacred spaces in modern Syria, Israel and Lebanon from two different points of view, a) in terms of individual sites, such as Caesarea Philippi, and b) under the rubric of short-term 'grouping' (Lichterman and Eliasoph 2003; Lichterman et al. 2017).

By viewing religion as continuously in the making, we can perhaps re-think the difficult archaeological issues of why a specific site came to be heavily sacralised, and the significance of the shifts and changes effected over time by a variety of different agents. At the highly evocative sanctuary at Banias, the source of the river Baniyas (one of the major tributaries of the river Jordan at the foot of Mount Hermon) near ancient Caesarea Philippi, inscriptions and niches cut into the rock-face, statuary, buildings, and courtyards together created a spatially-differentiated sacralisation of the rock-face and the terrace in front of it, which reaches down to the river. Over a period of several generations, religious agents there invested in innumerable alterations, major and minor, thus creating dozens of individual sites of particular personal significance: The most intense interaction of these visitors with the divine, however, took place not in, or in front of, the buildings but in front of the rock-face, i.e. not in the closed articulated spaces, as we might expect, but in the open spaces (Rieger 2016). At the individual level, the most memorable and effective investments were the brief inscriptions and small niches cut into the rock-face, rather than the marble images of deities (Friedland 2012; Rieger 2016). It was in the interplay between spaces, materials and media, that religion was instantiated at this site, and the place sacralised.

As for 'grouping', regular inscriptions, graffiti, figural *schizzi* on stone surfaces, and dedications of objects at small road-side shrines along the routes criss-crossing the Arabian Desert reveal the temporary comings-together of travellers and caravans for a brief religious act, a whole variety of strategies (motives too) for gaining the aid of gods or spirits. While on the move, people stopped at sites where others before them had instantiated religion, and in their turn added yet another 'trace', and so on and on, over many generations – truly 'religion in the making'. Each person's horizon of experience and expectation shaped the way in which they added their names and dedications, thus establishing 'thin' communication with their largely unknown fellow-agents (see above on graffiti at Dura-Europos). The concept of 'grouping' helps to highlight how the situational aspects of religious action – time, place and agents – condition choices of how to establish contact with the divine. This is especially valuable for the archaeologist trying to find ways of moving beyond mere dry description of small, scattered, rather insignificant religious sites.

c) Narrated Religion

Grouping through narration

Narratives are a powerful instrument for the formation of groups. The very process of narrative emplotment renders persons, objects, and events meaningful by setting them into temporal, spatial, and social frames. Narratives however are rarely 'closed': the biographical narrative of the individual, for example, necessarily alludes to, even incorporates, the 'public' narratives of families, groups, and polities, thus creating a complex narrative identity, which is not the mere sum of all the narrative vectors, but has been filtered through a variety of institutions and interests, each of which can be understood as itself a complex network of narratives and practices, whose ramifications have no natural limits. In the case of a citizen of Athens, such a dense 'bio-narrative', if limited to *ta theia* or *thrêskeia* ('religion'), might result in something that we would call 'Greek religion' (Eidinow 2011). As such, narratives, the 'emplotment' of events and actions, embedded in time, space and personal relationships, were a major source of orientation for groups (Rüpke 2016d).

For the first and second centuries CE, two insights are of particular importance for narratological approaches in History of Religion. If we view religious narrative as a transformation of religious practices into knowledge, we cannot be satisfied with mere content-analysis. We should rather understand narratives as exercises in communication, and thus engaged in network-formation beyond ritual. Granted that in our sources such narratives are generally unique, we should not be misled into dismissing them for that reason. For the uniqueness of a transmitted text is often merely apparent: it had its antecedents, whether typological or substantive, and its very existence was an invitation to future re-telling (Rüpke and Degelmann 2015).

Formation of a network depended as much on consensus, on which schemata and shared traditions could build, as on the framing of relevant contexts in which the imagined group ('we') could elaborate a shared past. Such a 'we' was not simply given but needed to be sustained by unremitting effort on the part of religious agents and their instantiations. The degree of explicitness and exclusivity could vary widely, depending on the choice of subject, the self-definition of the narrator (whether implicit or explicit), the choice of literary convention (genre being itself a mode of communication always related to a specific social context) and the assessments offered. The implicit reader of Greek or Latin fables was less narrowly defined than the implicit reader of a grand historical narrative such as that of Livy, or the fully 'connected' reader of Ovid's Augustan commentary on contemporary rituals in his *Fasti*, 'On the calendar' (Rüpke 2015b).

As can be seen from many historiographical or so-called antiquarian texts, narratives engaged with a preceding discourse on norms and knowledge, reproducing, modifying or actually challenging previous positions, be they consensual, hegemonic or conflicting; but they might even inaugurate quite new discourses, for example with reference to the figure of Christ. We can thus find plenty of strategies of authentication in ancient religious narratives even if we can hardly judge their efficacy. Extra-textual references might reinforce the narrative's claim to veridicality, but plausibility was achieved rather by internal coherence in addition to the degree of conformity with common knowledge and authoritative grand narratives. Indicating the author's correct name (the 'orthonym'), though widespread, was neither a necessary nor a necessarily successful strategy. Attributing the text to someone else, or even a fictitious author (pseudepigraphy; pseudonymity), were important mimetic strategies that claimed authority by virtue of the narrative form and content rather than the author's personal writ (Becker 2009, 377–378).

Narrating the suffering body

Approaching the body (human and divine alike) as a bio-cultural product certainly constitutes a major advance over earlier views. In the now-dominant Foucauldian conceptual framework of the 'care of the self' (Foucault 1986), the body is accorded a central place in the literary and cultural production of the so-called Second Sophistic, a major response of Greek intellectuals in the High Empire to the fact of Roman colonial power. However, our emphasis on embodiment in the religious field was an attempt to take a step back and look afresh at the surge of interest about the body and its care in Second-Sophistic narratives. We saw this not as a new development but as an intensification of much older ideas about the body and its dependence on the gods' care during illness. By engaging closely with the correlation between medical terminology and mystery-cult imagery in flagship narratives of the Second Sophistic, such as Aelius' Aristides' *Hieroi Logoi* [the 'Sacred Tales'] (after 145 CE), Lucian's *Alexander, the Pseudo-prophet* (after 165 CE), we can construe medical practice in the Empire as embodied knowledge experienced and expressed in religious terms; while serious or 'major' illness can be thought of as challenging a patient's identity, a challenge experienced as crises requiring repeated, mainly oneiric, therapeutic communication with a privileged and persistent divine interlocutor (Petridou 2017b).

No less important is how Aelius Aristides appropriates many of the ritual schemata and performances of the cult-officials of the Asclepieion (temple-hospital sacred to Asclepius) at Pergamon in Asia Minor (Petridou 2016), and uses his membership of the tightly-knit community of high-born 'therapeutae' (patients/worshippers) there to contest current religious and medical expertise and establish himself as an expert in both fields (Petridou 2017a). The 'Sacred Tales', once thought of as a purely private text, is more properly seen as an open, public one.

Narrating religious transgression
Several key scenes of Late Republican and Imperial Roman elite interaction can be analysed regarding their contemporary religious meaning and its impact on the emerging discourses. Concepts taken from the sociology of deviance (esp. Becker 1973; Schur 1980) afford an interactionist perspective that allows us to reject traditional ideas that assumed the existence of a-priori norms and thought of behaviour as determined by membership of a specific group. Interactionism emphasises that the construction of religious meanings is an on-going process, affected *inter alia* by political and social debates, literary discourses, and encounters with authoritative or model figures and the strategies (and implicit mechanisms) they deploy. Applied to the political elite of the Roman Republic, the interactionist approach allows for a wider understanding of the appropriation of religious motifs by its members as well as their need to ground religious claims for (non-elite) audiences. In this connection, given its boundary-crossing and -affirming potentialities, the theme of religious transgression presents an especially fruitful point of entry.

An early key scene is the murder of the *tribunus plebis* ('tribune of the plebs') Tiberius Sempronius Gracchus, whose office nominally granted him the most extraordinary protection that Roman law had to offer: When in 133 BCE Gracchus' political ambitions scandalised many senators, it was of all people P. Cornelius Scipio Nasica, the pontifex maximus ('supreme pontiff'), i.e. the head of one of the two major colleges of priests at Rome, who instigated the mob that lynched him in the Forum. In doing so, Nasica explicitly used the authority of his priesthood as symbolic capital to challenge the moderate course advised by the consul P. Mucius Scaevola. Nasica claimed that Gracchus had himself violated the law with respect to another (opposing) tribune, but is also supposed to have represented Gracchus as a (proper) sacrificial victim. He thus not only mobilised the religious capital deriving from his office but even insinuated that murdering an enemy of the state might actually be a fitting offering to a heaven eager to preserve the Republic, identified with the interests of the senators opposed to Gracchus.

Narrating religion to police the religious
The religious character of an action is, by and large, a matter of argument (Rüpke 2015a). Consensus regarding the ascription of agency to the divine world depends on

a variety of factors, ranging, in a polytheistic system, from the very awareness of the 'existence' of a given deity through the degree of commitment to any member of the pantheon, to the assessment of the relevance and salience of a single such religious identity in a given situation. In consequence, what is instantiated may be deemed religious as well non-religious depending on the definition of a situation by the different agents involved. Narratives, whether oral or written, can enable such ascriptions to out-last the specific event (see also p.000 above).

Surveying the history of ancient Mediterranean religions, now including Chriatianity, it is not rare to find that only one of the framings that made it into a narrative version has survived in textual form, while others are either lost or reported only from the perspective of the narrative that has survived. But what if a narrative has survived precisely *because* it strives hard to convince a contemporary audience that a given practice should be considered religiously laden, being a direct expression of good/bad, strong/weak religious motivations? This circumstance is pretty much the norm when it comes to early Christian literature.

How-to-die-gloriously booklets ('martyr acts') and how-to-live-truly hand-books (pastoral treatises) seek to instantiate religious meanings as the only possible outcome of discursive and non-discursive practices. The utterances 'God is my Lord' (*Acts of the Scillitan Martyrs* 6) and 'Caesar is the Lord' (*Martyrium of Polycarp* 8.2) are presented as alternative answers to the demand: 'To whom are you ultimately obedient?' The first would express a good/strong religious motivation; the second a bad/weak one. Yet it is possible to argue that, in extra-textual reality, the two statements did not necessarily share the same religious coding/connotation, the latter in some cases being either a declaration of a mere political deference, thereby refusing to interpret the situation in religious terms (Rebillard 2012), or a strategic tergiversation, issuing from a desire to minimise commitment in a power-laden context (Scott 1990). The obligation to offer sacrifice, e.g. to the emperor's statue, would be a stumbling-block only in the case of the second option.

Conclusion: offering new perspectives

The three guiding perspectives set out here, religious agency, instantiated religion, and narrated religion, together with the thirteen thumb-nail case-studies based on a relatively wide variety of empirical evidence, are intended to illustrate the claim of the Lived Ancient Religion approach to provide an effective model for a new approach to the religious history of the long Roman Empire.

As we have said, Lived Ancient Religion is neither a methodology nor a general theory of religion but an eclectic approach marked by a specific range of interests. It aims to provide a critical complement to other possible approaches rather than simply replace them, by setting up new questions that, at any rate potentially, can be addressed to any empirical set of evidence throughout the Mediterranean basin in antiquity. On the other hand, its application to Ancient Mediterranean religions should not be considered an end point: 'leaving the disciplinary comfort-zone' has been part of its vision from the beginning. While taking its cue from inspiring research on contemporary religiosities and applying it to past religious contexts, Lived Ancient Religion aims in turn to contribute to mainstream religious studies. Its ambition is to 'give something back' to the wider scholarship of religion beyond the life-time of the project. By expanding the reach of the notion of 'lived religion' through the intensive historical and archaeological examination of ancient religions, Lived Ancient Religion hopes to provide points of connectivity for future scientific enterprises.

Returning to antiquity, we view the Lived Ancient Religion perspective as a significant contribution to the creation of future grand narratives of the religious history of the long Roman Empire. Here we can distinguish between city-based and overall perspectives. In view of the intensity of its internal religious dynamics, contacts and exchanges, competition and distinction, Rome itself is a prime candidate for an account highlighting agency and mediality (Rüpke 2016c). But that does not mean that it can be taken as a direct model for all the other cities and regions that were more or less dramatically altered by larger cultural and political processes initiated by the fiscal and administrative order imposed from Rome. Each of them has its own trajectory. Beyond that, the megalopolis of Rome will offer an important focus for a further line of inquiry on 'urban religion' based on the insights of Lived Ancient Religion. Equally, one might frame the Empire as a whole as a dynamic field of action, a frame that contains a virtually unlimited range of religious phenomena. Themes here might be the resources available to religious actors, their affordances and potentials, the means through which individuals and groups created, institutionalised (and evaded) traditions, the perennial reality of religious change. The overall effect of these historiographical efforts would be to demonstrate the ability of the Lived Ancient Religion approach to provide an effective framework not merely for individual cities but also for synthetic histories of large periods and spaces.

The major aim of introducing the concepts of religious agency, instantiated religion and narrated religion is to reconfigurate current models of past religions. In our view, what are usually represented as static (or even crisis-ridden) ensembles of religious symbols, beliefs and practices are better understood as complex dynamic processes, as interaction between historical agents and their changing material and spatial environments. In a word, religion is to be viewed as ever in the making.

References

Alvar Nuño, A. 2017. *Cadenas invisibles. Los usos de la magia entre los esclavos en el Imperio romano*. Besançon: Presses Universitaires du Franche-Comté.
Ammerman, N. T. 1997. 'Golden Rule Christianity: Lived Religion in the American Mainstream'. In *Lived Religion in America: Toward a History of Practice*, ed. by D. D. Hall. Princeton: Princeton University Press. 196–216.
Ammerman, N. T., ed. 2007. *Everyday religion: Observing modern religious lives*. Oxford: Oxford University Press.
Arena V., and J. W. Prag, eds. 2017. *A Companion to the Political Culture of the Roman Republic*. Chichester: Wiley Blackwell.
Arnhold, M., and J. Rüpke. 2016. „Appropriating and Shaping Religious Practices in the Roman Republic". In *Politische Kultur und soziale Struktur der Römischen Republik: Bilanzen und Perspektiven*, edited by M. Haake, and A.-C. Harders, 413–428. Stuttgart: Steiner.
Becker, H. S. 1973. *Outsiders. Studies in the Sociology of Deviance*. New York: The Free Press.
Becker, E.-M. 2009. „Von Paulus zu 'Paulus': Paulinische Pseudepigraphie-Forschung als literaturgeschichtliche Aufgabe". In *Pseudepigraphie und Verfasserfiktion in frühchristlichen Briefen*, edited by J. Frey, J. Herzer, M. Jannssen, and M. Engelmann, 363–386. Tübingen: Mohr Siebeck.
Belayche, N. 2014. „From Personal Experience to Public Display: A look into the therapeutic sanctuary of Gadara". In *Öffentlichkeit. Monument. Text*, edited by W. Eck, & P. Funke, 615-617. Berlin: de Gruyter.
Beyer, P. 2009. „Religion as Communication: On Niklas Luhmann, The Religion of Society (2000)". In *Contemporary Theories of Religion*, edited by M. Stausberg, 99–114. Abingdon: Routledge.
Bielfeldt, R. 2014. „Lichtblicke-Sehstrahlen: Zur Präsenz römischer Figuren- und Bildlampen". In *Ding und Mensch in der Antike: Gegenwart und Vergegenwärtigung*, edited by R. Bielfeldt, 195–238. Heidelberg: Winter.
Bloch, M. (1944) 1997. *Apologie pour l'histoire ou Métier d'historien*. Reprint, Paris: Armand Colin.
Bonnet, C., and J. Rüpke, eds. 2009. *Les religions orientales dans les mondes grec et romain*. Paris: Maison des sciences de l'homme.
Cooley, A. 2015. „Multiple Meanings in the Sanctuary of the Magna Mater at Ostia". *Religion in the Roman Empire* 1 (2): 242–262.
Daniel, R. W., and F. Maltomini, eds. 1990. *Supplementum magicum*. 2 vols. Opladen: Westdeutscher Verlag.
Degelmann, Chr. 2017. *SQUALOR. Symbolisches Trauern und Selbsterniedrigen in der politischen Kommunikation der römischen Republik und frühen Kaiserzeit*. Stuttgart: Steiner.
de Polignac, F. 2009. „Sanctuaries and Festivals". In *A Companion to Archaic Greece*, edited by K. A. Raaflaub, and H. van Wees, 427–443. Chichester: Wiley Blackwell.
Dirven, L. 1999. *The Palmyrenes of Dura-Europos: A Study of Religious Interaction in Roman Syria*. Leiden: Brill.
Droogan, Julian 2013, *Religion, Material Culture and Archaeology*. London: Bloomsbury.
Eidinow, E. 2007. *Oracles, Curses, and Risk among the Ancient Greeks*. Oxford: Oxford University Press.
Eidinow, E. 2011. „Networks and Narratives: A Model for Ancient Greek Religion". *Kernos* 24: 9–38.
Equini Schneider, E. 1993. *Septimia Zenobia Sebaste*. Rome: L'Erma di Bretschneider.
Foucault, M. 1986. *The Care of the Self*. Vol. 3 of *The History of Sexuality*. Translated by R. Hurley. New York: Pantheon Books.
Frankfurter, D. 1998. *Religion in Roman Egypt: Assimilation and Resistance*. Princeton: University Press.

Friedland, E. A. 2012. The Roman Marble Sculptures from the Sanctuary of Pan at Caesarea Philippi/Panias (Israel). Boston: American Schools of Oriental Research.

Fuchs, M., and J. Rüpke. 2015. „Religious Individualisation in Historical Perspective". *Religion* 45 (3): 323–329. doi: 10.1080/0048721X.2015.1041795.

Gottry, H. C. 1995. *Domestic Religion in Graeco-Roman Karanis: Origins, Theories, and New Approaches*. Unpublished Undergraduate Honors Thesis, University of Michigan.

Gasparini, V. 2018. „Les acteurs sur scène. Théâtre et théâtralisation dans les cultes isiaques". In *The Greco-Roman Cults of Isis. Agents, Images and Practices*, edited by V. Gasparini, and R. Veymiers. Leiden: Brill.

Gasparini, V. and A. Saura-Ziegelmeyer. Forthcoming. „Les cultes isiaques. Stratégies de dramatisation et saturation émotionnelle".

Geens, K. 2015. „Pakysis son of Tesenouphis, Priest". In *Graeco-Roman Archives from the Fayum*, edited by K. Vandorpe, W. Clarysse, and H. Verreth, 267–268. Leuven: Peeters.

Gordon, R. L. 2005. „Competence and 'Felicity Conditions' in Two Sets of North African Curse-tablets (DTAud nos. 275–85; 286–98)". *MHNH. Revista Internacional de Investigación sobre Magia y Astrología Antiguas* 5: 61–86.

Gordon, R. L. 2013a. „Cosmology, Astrology, and Magic: Discourse, Schemes, Power, and Literacy". In *Panthée: Religious Transformations in the Graeco-Roman Empire*, edited by L. Bricault, and C. Bonnet, 85–111. Leiden: Brill.

Gordon, R. L. 2013b. „Gods, Guilt and Suffering: Psychological Aspects of Cursing in the North-Western Provinces of the Roman Empire". *Acta Classica Universitatis Scientiarum Debreceniensis* 49: 255–281.

Gordon, R. L. 2013c. „The Religious Anthropology of Late-Antique 'High' Magical Practice". In *The Individual in the Religions of the Ancient Mediterranean*, edited by J. Rüpke, 163–186. Oxford: Oxford University Press.

Gordon, R. L. 2015. „Showing the Gods the Way: Curse-tablets as Deictic Persuasion". *Religion in the Roman Empire* 1 (2): 148–180.

Gordon, R. L. 2016. „Negotiating the Temple-Script: Women's Narratives among the Mysian-Lydian 'Confession-Texts'". *Religion in the Roman Empire* 2 (2): 227–255.

Gordon, R. L. 2017. „From East to West: Staging Religious Experience in the Mithraic Temple". In *Entangled Worlds: Religious Confluences Between East and West in the Roman Empire*, edited by S. Nagel, J. F. Quack, and Chr. Witschel, 413–442. Tübingen: Mohr Siebeck.

Gordon, R. L., and V. Gasparini. 2014. „Looking for Isis 'the Magician' (ḥk3y.t) in the Graeco-Roman World". In *Bibliotheca Isiaca III*, edited by L. Bricault, and R. Veymiers, 39–53. Bordeaux: Ausonius Éditions.

Gordon, R. L., G. Petridou, and J. Rüpke. 2017. „Introduction". In *Beyond Priesthood: Religious Entrepreneurs and Innovators in the Roman Empire*, edited by R. L. Gordon, G. Petridou, and J. Rüpke, 5–11. Berlin: de Gruyter.

Hall, D.D., ed., 1997. *Lived Religion in America: Toward a History of Practice*, Princeton: Princeton University Press.

Hjarvard, S. 2011. „The Mediatisation of Religion: Theorising Religion, Media and Social Change". *Culture and Religion* 12 (2): 119–135.

Hölkeskamp, K.-J. 2010. Reconstructing the Roman Republic: An Ancient Political Culture and Modern Research. Princeton: Princeton University Press.

Hüsken, U. 2009. „Ritual Competence as Embodied Knowledge". *The Body in India: Ritual, Transgression, Performativity*, edited by A. Michaels, and Chr. Wulf, 200–220. Berlin: de Gruyter.

Jördens, A., ed. 1998. Griechische Papyri aus Soknopaiu Nesos (P. Louvre I). Bonn: Habelt.

Knott, K., V. Krech, and B. Meyer. 2016. „Iconic Religion in Urban Space". *Material Religion* 12 (2): 123–136.

Koschorke, A. 2012. Wahrheit und Erfindung: Grundzüge einer Allgemeinen Erzähltheorie. Frankfurt/Main: S. Fischer.
Lichterman, P., and N. Elisoph. 2003. „Culture in Interaction 1". *American Journal of Sociology* 108 (4): 735–794.
Lichterman, P., R. Raja, A.-K. Rieger, and J. Rüpke. 2017. „Grouping Together in Lived Ancient Religion". *Religion in the Roman Empire* 3 (1): 3–10.
Lövheim, M. 2011. „Mediatisation of Religion: A Critical Appraisal". *Culture and Religion* 12 (2): 153–166.
Lüdtke, A., ed. 1995. *History of Everyday Life: Reconstructing Historical Experiences and Ways of Life*. Translated by W. Templer. Princeton: Princeton University Press.
Malik, J., J. Rüpke, and Th. Wobbe, eds. 2007. *„Religion und Medien: Vom Kultbild zum Internetritual"*. Münster: Aschendorff.
Meyer, B. 2008. „Media and the Senses in the Making of Religious Experience: An Introduction". *Material Religion* 4: 124–135.
McGuire, M. B. 2008. *Lived Religion: Faith and Practice in Everyday Life*. New York: Oxford University Press.
Mol, E., and Versluys, M. J. 2015. „Material Culture and Imagined Communities in the Roman World." In *A Companion to the Archaeology of Religion in the Ancient World*, edited by R. Raja, and J. Rüpke, 451–461. Chichester: Wiley Blackwell.
Orsi, R. 1997. „Everyday Miracles: The Study of Lived Religion". In *Lived Religion in America: Toward a History of Practice*, edited by D. Hall, 3–21. Princeton: Princeton University Press.
Patzelt, M. 2018. Über das Beten der Römer: Gebete im antiken Rom im Spiegel von Ritualisierung und religiöser Erfahrung (ca. 1. Jh. v.Chr.–2. Jh. n.Chr.). Berlin: de Gruyter.
Petridou, G. 2013. „'Blessed Is He, Who Has Seen': The Power of Ritual Viewing and Ritual Framing in Eleusis". *Helios* 40 (1–2): 309–343.
Petridou, G. 2015. „Emplotting the Divine: Epiphanic Narratives as Means of Enhancing Agency". *Religion in the Roman Empire* 1 (3): 321–342.
Petridou, G. 2016. „Becoming a Doctor, Becoming a God: Religion and Medicine in Aelius Aristides' Hieroi Logoi." In *Religion and Illness*, edited by A. Weissenrieder, and G. Etzelmüller, 306–335. Eugene, OR: Cascade Books.
Petridou, G. 2017a. „Contesting Medical and Religious Expertise in the Hieroi Logoi: The therapeutae of Pergamum as Religious and Medical Entrepreneurs". In *Beyond Priesthood. Religious Entrepreneurs and Innovators in the Imperial Era*, edited by R. L. Gordon, G. Petridou, and J. Rüpke, 183–211. Berlin: de Gruyter.
Petridou, G. 2017b. „What is Divine about Medicine? Religious Imagery and Bodily Knowledge in Aelius Aristides and Lucian." *Religion of the Roman Empire* 3 (2): 242–264.
Raja, R. 2015a. „Staging 'Private' Religion in Roman 'Public' Palmyra: The Role of the Religious Dining Tickets (Banqueting Tesserae)." In *Public and Private in Ancient Mediterranean Law and Religion*, edited by C. Ando, and J. Rüpke, 165–186. Berlin: de Gruyter.
Raja, R. 2015b. „Cultic Dining and Religious Patterns in Palmyra: The Case of the Palmyrene Banqueting Tesserae." In *Antike. Architektur. Geschichte*, edited by S. Faust, M. Seifert, and L. Ziemer, 181–200. Herzogenrath: Shaker Verlag.
Raja, R. 2015c. „Complex Sanctuaries in the Roman Period". In *A Companion to the Archaeology of Religion in the Ancient World*, edited by R. Raja, and J. Rüpke, 307–319. Chichester: Wiley Blackwell.
Raja, R. 2016. „In and Out of Contexts: Explaining Religious Complexity through the Banqueting Tesserae from Palmyra". *Religion in the Roman Empire* 2 (3): 340–371. doi: 10.1628/219944616X14770583541445.

Raja, R., and J. Rüpke, eds. 2015a. A Companion to the Archaeology of Religion in the Ancient World. Chichester: Wiley Blackwell.

Raja, R., and J. Rüpke. 2015b. „Archaeology of Religion, Material Religion, and the Ancient World". in *A Companion to the Archaeology of Religion in the Ancient World*, edited by R. Raja, and J. Rüpke, 1–25. Chichester: Wiley Blackwell.

Raja, R., and J. Rüpke. 2015c. „Appropriating Religion: Methodological Issues in Testing the 'Lived Ancient Religion' Approach". *Religion in the Roman Empire* 1 (1): 11–19. doi: 10.1628/219944615X14234960199632.

Raja, R., and L. Weiss. 2015. „The Role of Objects: Meaning, Situations and Interaction". *Religion in the Roman Empire* 1 (2): 137–147.

Rebillard, É. (2012). Christians and Their Many Identities in Late Antiquity, North Africa, 200–450 CE. Ithaca: Cornell University Press.

Rebillard, É. 2015. „Material Culture and Religious Identity in Late Antiquity". In *A Companion to the Archaeology of Religion in the Ancient World*, edited by R. Raja, and J. Rüpke, 427–436. Chichester: Wiley Blackwell.

Rebillard, É., and J. Rüpke, eds. 2015, *Group Identity and Religious Individuality in Late Antiquity*. Washington, DC: Catholic University of America Press.

Rieger, A.-K. 2016.a „Gods on the Rocks – Material Approaches to the Rock-face at Caesaraea Philippi (Mount Hermon)". In *Borders. Terminologies, Ideologies, and Performances*, edited by A. Weissenrieder, 173–199. Tübingen: Mohr Siebeck.

Rieger, A.-K. 2016b. „'Waste matters': Life cycle and agency of pottery employed in Graeco-Roman sacred spaces". *Religion in the Roman Empire* 2, no. 3 (2016): 307–339.

Rüpke, J. 2011a. „Individual Appropriation and Institutional Changes: Roman Priesthoods in the Later Empire". In *Politiche religiose nel mondo antico e tardo antico: poteri e indirizzi, forme del controllo, idee e prassi di tolleranza*, edited by G. A. Cecconi, and Ch. Gabrielli, 261–273. Bari: Edipuglia.

Rüpke, J. 2011b. „Lived Ancient Religion: Questioning 'Cults' and 'Polis Religion'". *Mythos: Rivista di Storia delle Religioni* 5 (18): 191–204.

Rüpke, J. 2011c. „Reichsreligion? Überlegungen zur Religionsgeschichte des antiken Mittelmeerraums in römischer Zeit." *Historische Zeitschrift* 292: 297–322.

Rüpke, J. 2012. „Sakralisierung von Zeit in Rom und Italien: Produktionsstrategien und Aneignungen von Heiligkeit". In *Heilige, Heiliges und Heiligkeit in spätantiken Religionskulturen*, edited by P. Gemeinhardt, and K. Heyden, 231–247. Berlin: de Gruyter.

Rüpke, J. 2013. „Introduction: Individualisation and Individuation as Concepts for Historical Research". In *The Individual in the Religions of the Ancient Mediterranean*, edited by J. Rüpke, 3–28. Oxford: Oxford University Press.

Rüpke, J. 2015a. „Religious Agency, Identity, and Communication: Reflecting on History and Theory of Religion". *Religion* 45 (3): 344–366.

Rüpke, J. 2015b. „The 'Connected Reader' as a Window into Lived Ancient Religion: A Case Study of Ovid's Libri fastorum". *Religion in the Roman Empire* 1 (1): 95–113.

Rüpke, J. 2016a. „Ancient Lived Religion and the History of Religion in the Roman Empire". In *Studia Patristica 74*, edited by M. Vinzent, and A. Brent, 1–20. Leuven: Peeters.

Rüpke, J. 2016b. „Individual Appropriation of Sacred Space". In *Espaces sacrés dans la Méditerranée antique*, edited by Y. Lafond, and V. Michel, 69–80. Rennes: Presses universitaires de Rennes.

Rüpke, J. 2016c. *On Roman Religion*. Ithaca, NY: Cornell University Press.

Rüpke, J. 2016d. „The Role of Texts in Processes of Religious Grouping during the Principate". *Religion in the Roman Empire* 2 (2): 170–195.

Rüpke, J. 2018a. „Narratives as Factor and Indicator of Religious Change in the Roman Empire (1st and 2nd centuries)". In *El platonismo en los Padres de la Iglesia*. Vol. 2 of *Studia Patristica 76*, edited by M. Vinzent, and R. Pereto Rivas, forthcoming. Leuven: Peeters.

Rüpke, J. 2018b. *Pantheon: A New History of Roman Religion*. Princeton: Princeton University Press.

Rüpke, J., and C. Degelmann. 2015. „Narratives as a Lens into Lived Ancient Religion, Individual Agency and Collective Identity". *Religion in the Roman Empire* 1 (3): 289–296.

Salzman, M., and W. Adler, eds. 2013. *The Cambridge History of Religions in the Ancient World*. Cambridge: Cambridge University Press.

Scheid, J. 2016. *The Gods, the State, and the Individual: Reflections on Civic Religion in Rome*. Translated by C. Ando. Philadelphia: University of Pennsylvania Press.

Schjødt, U. 2009. „The Religious Brain: A General Introduction to the Experimental Neuroscience of Religion". *Method and Theory in the Study of Religion* 21: 310–339.

Schur, E. M. 1980. The Politics of Deviance. Stigma Contests and the Uses of Power. Englewood Cliffs: Prentice-Hall.

Scott, J. C. 1990. Domination and the Arts of Resistance: Hidden Transcripts. New Haven: Yale University Press

Smolak, K. 2001. „Interius cogitando et loquendo: Zum Phänomen des Schweigens in der Spätantike." In *The language of silence*, edited by S. Jäkel, and A. Timonen, 171–181. Turku: Turun Yliopisto.

Stroumsa, G. G. 2013. „False Prophets of Early Christianity". In *Priests and Prophets among Pagans, Jews and Christians*, edited by B. Dignas, R. Parker, and G. G. Stroumsa, 208–229. Leuven: Peeters.

Tacoma, L. E. 2016. *Moving Romans: Migration to Rome in the Principate*. Oxford: Oxford University Press.

Urban, H. B. 2003. „Sacred Capital: Pierre Bourdieu and the Study of Religion". *Method & Theory in the Study of Religion* 15: 354–389.

Van Andringa, W. 2015. „The Archaeology of Ancient Sanctuaries". In *A Companion to the Archaeology of Religion in the Ancient World*, edited by R. Raja, and J. Rüpke, 29–40. Chichester: Wiley Blackwell.

Versnel, H. S. 2010. „Prayers for Justice in East and West: Recent Finds and Publications". In *Magical Practice in the Latin West*, edited by R. L. Gordon, and F. Marco Simón, 275–355. Leiden: Brill.

Walker Bynum, C. 2011. Christian Materiality: An Essay on Religion in Late Medieval Europe. New York: Zone Books.

Wedekind, K. 2012. Religiöse Experten im lokalen Kontext: Kommunikationsmodelle in christlichen Quellen des 1.–3. Jh. n.Chr. Gutenberg: Computus.

Weiss, L. 2015. Religious Practice at Deir el-Medina. Leiden: Peeters.

Weiss, L. Forthcoming. „Domestic Cults and Family Religion in Roman Times". In *The Blackwell Companion to Ancient Egyptian Religion*, edited by M. Bommas. Chichester: Wiley Blackwell.

Whitehead, A. N. 1926. *Religion in the making*, Lowell lectures. New York: Macmillan.

8 Tagungsberichte/Report on conferences

8.1 Kolleg-Forschergruppe „Religiöse Individualisierung in historischer Perspektive"

Tagung vom 17. bis 19. September 2012 am Max-Weber-Kolleg: ‚Burial Rituals, Ideas of Afterlife, and the Individual in the Hellenistic World and the Roman Empire' (Richard Gordon, Wolfgang Spickermann, Katharina Waldner)

Die internationale Tagung wurde im Rahmen der Kolleg-Forschergruppe ‚Religiöse Individualisierung in historischer Perspektive' veranstaltet und finanziell von der Fritz-Thyssen-Stiftung unterstützt. Hierzu trafen sich vom 17. bis 19. September 2012 im Augustinerkloster zwanzig Althistoriker, Archäologen, Altphilologen, Religionswissenschaftler und Ägyptologen, um interdisziplinäre Zugangsweisen zur Thematik zu entwickeln.

Die Vielfalt der Bestattungspraktiken in antiken und modernen Kulturen hat ihren Ursprung in der einfachen Tatsache der Sterblichkeit des Menschen. Darüber hinaus provoziert Tod in jeder Kultur (und jeder Religion) Vorstellungen darüber, was danach geschieht, also über eine postmortale Existenz. Wenn auch jeder Tod höchst individuell ist, ist die Bestattung der Toten immer ein großes sozio-religiöses Anliegen. In gleicher Weise sind diesbezügliche Praktiken auch in einer bestimmten Kultur nie standardisiert oder homogen, sondern sie beruhen auf kontingenten Schemata und Möglichkeiten. Auf dieser Basis soll eine Verbindung zwischen den drei Bereichen Bestattung, Eschatologie und Individuation fruchtbar gemacht werden.

Die Tagung sollte daher die Wechselbeziehungen zwischen Bestattungspraktiken, Vorstellungen von Leben nach dem Tod und deren Verhältnis zum Individuum in hellenistischer und römischer Zeit untersuchen. Wenn die ersten beiden Begriffe relativ eindeutig sind, gilt dies nicht für den dritten. Wir verstehen den Begriff des Individuums in einem zweifachen Sinn: 1) In dem elementaren Sinne von ‚einer Person', die sich der Tatsache ihrer Sterblichkeit bewusst ist und möglicherweise Vorbereitungen für ihre Bestattung trifft (z.B. Auswahl einer bestimmten Art von Grab, Grabstele, Sarkophag etc.) und vielleicht auch versucht, ein Leben nach dem Tod für sich selbst und Angehörige (z.B. durch Initiation in einen oder mehrere Mysterienkulte) zu gewährleisten; 2) als Mittel der Konzeption einer individuellen Identität (Person), die im Laufe der Bestattungsriten eine Transformation erfährt und so in der Lage ist, über den Moment des physischen Todes hinaus zu existieren. Um dieses facettenreiche Feld zu untersuchen, hat die Konferenz drei große Themenkomplexe behandelt:

1. Archäologie und die Anthropologie von Tod und Sterben,
2. Erinnerung an die Toten: Praktiken des Totengedenkens und Jenseitsvorstellungen,
3. Rituale über den Tod hinaus? Mysterienkulte und Grabriten.

Ein von den drei Veranstaltern herausgegebener Sammelband ist in Vorbereitung.

ESF-LiU Conference vom 10. bis 14. September 2012 in Norrköping (Schweden): 'Historiography of Religion' (Jörg Rüpke, Susanne Rau, Bernd-Christian Otto)

The conference focused on the question "How, under which conditions and with which consequences are religions historicized?". It aimed at furthering the study of religion as of historiography by analysing how religious groups (or their adversaries) employ historical narratives in the construction of their identities. Likewise it asked how such groups were invented by later historiography and are continued in modern research. Thus it also focused on the biases and elisions of current analytical and descriptive frames. Combining disciplinary competences of Religious Studies and History of Religion, Confessional Theologies, History, History of Science, and Literary Studies, the participants initiated a *comparative historiography of religion*. Furthermore, *a history of historical research* on religion was stimulated by identifying key steps in the early modern and modern history of research. The agenda of the conference was therefore highly comparative and interdisciplinary.

Numerous scholars from different fields of historical and religious research, from Circum-Mediterranean and European as well as Asian religious traditions from the first millennium BCE to the present came together. The conference was structured by a series of six sessions in three days (including one poster session) which combined impulses from short (10 minutes) and long (20 minutes) lectures with plenary discussions. Here, the impulse of the initial question was driven forward by further questions developed in the opening lecture by the organizers like "Which contexts do provoke processes of historicization and the development of historiography in particular?"; "Which practices to historicize the past, i.e. to acknowledge and sequence the pastness of the past, have been used in historicizing religions?"; "How do religions make themselves immune against historicist claims?" The conference programme included some 26 papers focusing on the above-mentioned questions and covered a variety of topics and religious traditions. A first group of papers dealt with narrations of 'origins and developments'. In this group, among others, specialists on the ancient Mediterranean (Ingvild Gilhus), on Hinduism (Johannes Bronkhorst), Islam (Chase Robinson), Buddhism (Sylvie Hureau; Per Sørensen), the European middle ages (Pekka Tolonen), and Early modern Europe (Yves Krumenacker) presented lectures on their topics. A second group dealt with the topic of 'writing histories' and included papers on Islam (Ulrika Mårtensson, Shahzad Bashir), Hinduism (Jon Keune), Early modern and modern Europe (Susanne Rau; Hannah Schneider; Franziska Metzger), and modern China (Philipp Hetmanczyk). Finally, a third group focussed on the interconnectedness between pre-academic and academic discourses dealing with the historiography of religion: 'Transforming narratives: scholars, methods, disciplines'. In this group, papers on Judaism and Jewish Studies (Reinhard G. Kratz, Christiana Facchini), on modern interpretations of ancient polytheism (Renée Koch-Piettre, Gabriella Gustafsson), and on the modern History of Christianity in Italy (Giovanni Filoramo) were presented. A poster session offered the opportunity to present case studies as contributions to the other sessions. It was used by nearly twenty young scholars.

Tagung vom 22. bis 24. November 2012 am Max-Weber-Kolleg im Rahmen der Kolleg-Forschergruppe 'Religiöse Individualisierung in historischer Perspektive' und in Kooperation mit der Forschungsstätte der Evangelischen Studiengemeinschaft (FEST), Heidelberg: ‚Metamorphosen des Heiligen. Vergemeinschaftung durch Sakralisierung der Kunst' (Markus Kleinert)

In der Einführung wurden zunächst drei zentrale Aspekte des Tagungsthemas erläutert: erstens, die methodisch grundlegende Thematisierung des Heiligen als Kommunikationsgeschehen, als *Zuschreibung* von Heiligkeit mittels habitualisierter Deutungsverfahren und Handlungsformen; zweitens, die soziale Funktion solcher Sakralisierungen, die durch sie bewirkte *Identitätsstiftung* und *Vergemeinschaftung*; drittens, der *Wandel* solcher Sakralisierungen, in diesem Fall die tendenzielle Verlagerung der Kommunikation des Heiligen von der Institution der Religion auf die Institution der Kunst, die sich kurz mit dem Begriff der Kunstreligion bezeichnen lässt (Magnus Schlette). Als ein Musterbeispiel für diesen Themenkomplex, für die Vergemeinschaftung durch Sakralisierung der Kunst wie für die Kritik eben dieses Prozesses wurde kurz die Deutungs- und Aufführungsgeschichte von Beethovens letzter Klaviersonate op. 111 vor Augen geführt (Markus Kleinert).

In seinem Eröffnungsvortrag stellte Volkhard Krech das Heilige nach phänomenologischen und begriffs- bzw. wissenschaftsgeschichtlichen Anmerkungen als eine besondere Kommunikation dar, durch die die letztlich paradoxe Verfasstheit sozialer Systeme kommuniziert werden könne und die die Voraussetzung religiöser wie kunstreligiöser Kommunikation bilde (welche sich dann in ihren Gewichtungen, nicht aber grundsätzlich voneinander unterscheiden). Im Hinblick auf die Unterscheidung von religiöser und kunstreligiöser Kommunikation wurde in der Diskussion unter anderem die Frage nach der jeweiligen Verträglichkeit von Ironie aufgeworfen, auf die, wenngleich damit kein Unterscheidungsmerkmal benannt ist, im Tagungsverlauf noch mehrfach zurückgekommen wurde. Stefan Alkier wies mit Bezug auf Diskurse über das Wunder (am Beispiel von Gregor von Nyssas Lebensbeschreibung seiner Schwester Makrina) auf die der religiösen Kommunikation immanente

Rationalität hin, die mit der bloßen Entgegensetzung von Wunderglauben und Wissenschaft verkannt wird und auf die wechselseitige Abhängigkeit von Wunderdiskursen und Wirklichkeitskonzepten verweist. Dagegen entwickelte Reinhard Brandt unter Bezugnahme auf die Konzepte des Erhabenen bei Pseudo-Longinos und Kant (hier unter besonderer Berücksichtigung der begründungstheoretischen ‚Figur des Vierten') einen emphatischen Vernunftbegriff, vor dem eine Sakralisierung als fahrlässige Ermäßigung erscheint, so erkennbar etwa in Burkes Konzept des Erhabenen. Nach diesen grundsätzlichen Beiträgen zum Sakralen wurde die Sakralisierung speziell der Kunst bzw. der Künste und deren soziale Funktion behandelt.

In seiner detaillierten Analyse von Elvis Presleys Bühnenshow in Los Angeles deutete Heinrich Detering diese Auftrittsserie als ein popkulturelles kunstreligiöses *Ritual*, dessen allmählich perfektionierter Verlauf auf eine universale Kultursynthese abzielt und in dem der Künstler die Funktion eines Schamanen übernimmt.

Wolfgang Braungart deutete anhand von Lessings *Minna von Barnhelm* und *Nathan der Weise* einen der Kunst *eigenen religiös-utopischen* Zug an, der darin besteht, dass das Subjekt in der ritualisierten Auseinandersetzung mit einem autonomen Kunstwerk seiner eigenen Unbedingtheit innewerden könne, und der in der Vorstellung einer künstlerischen *Kompensation* des schwindenden Einflusses traditioneller Religionen gerade verfehlt wird. Er leitete mit diesen Thesen eine Reihe literaturwissenschaftlicher Beiträge ein. Bernd Auerochs demonstrierte die Spannung zwischen kunstreligiösen Ansätzen und der Kritik einer Ästhetisierung von Religion im Werk Martin Bubers, was nebenbei verdeutlichte, dass das Thema der Vergemeinschaftung durch Sakralisierung der Kunst keinesfalls auf die christliche Tradition beschränkt ist. Danach wurden zwei Extrempositionen innerhalb der christlichen Tradition behandelt: auf der einen Seite die bei aller Differenzierung vorherrschende Reserve gegenüber der Kunst in der Literatur des Pietismus, bei August Hermann Francke und Gottfried Arnold (Joachim Jacob), auf der anderen Seite die in einem emphatischen Wort- und Sprachverständnis begründete Kunstreligion Hölderlins (Johann Kreuzer). Schließlich demonstrierte Günter Häntzschel, wie in den im neunzehnten Jahrhundert außerordentlich populären Lyrikanthologien eine diffuse religiöse Stimmung erzeugt wurde und zu diesem Zweck auch profane Texte (durch strategische Präsentation und mehr oder weniger unauffällige Manipulationen der Herausgeber) sakralisiert wurden.

Neben diese literaturbezogenen Studien traten drei Vorträge, die Anspruch und Wirklichkeit der Sakralisierung von Kunst am Beispiel der Musik untersuchten. Peter Steinacker rekonstruierte Wagners kunstreligiöses Programm und gab einen Ausblick auf dessen Musealisierung im Wagnerismus. Dietrich Korsch deutete Mozarts *Così fan tutte* als Experiment auf die ordnungsstiftende Kraft der Liebe, dessen Ausgang im Kunstwerk als Ambivalenz festgehalten werden könne und gerade darin ein Analogon moderner, nur in Gegensätzen explizierbarer Religiosität bilde. Elisabete M. de Sousa widmete sich in einer detaillierten Analyse dem Mozart-Kapitel in Kierkegaards *Entweder/Oder*, um unter Hinzuziehung der zeitgenössischen musikkritischen Kontexte (Schumann, Berlioz, Wagner) einen emphatischen Begriff von Virtuosität herauszuarbeiten, als dessen Verkörperung Liszt erscheint und der sich auf Grund der darin enthaltenen Ambivalenzen wiederum in eine Analogie zu moderner Religiosität bringen lässt.

Überblickscharakter hatten die Vorträge von Werner Hofmann, der das Verhältnis von Religion und bildender Kunst in Anlehnung an Hegels Ausführungen über die Auflösung der romantischen Kunstform (die Dialektik von Nachahmung des Objektiven in seiner Kontingenz einerseits und subjektivem Humor andererseits) darstellte, und von Bernhard Schäfers, der aus architektursoziologischer Perspektive die Vorstellung von Transformationsprozessen innerhalb des Verhältnisses von Kunst und Religion – im Gegensatz zu Kompensationsmodellen – stützte.

Der für die Tagung gewählte Ansatz, das vielfach thematisierte Verhältnis von Kunst und Religion auf der Grundlage der Kommunikation des Heiligen, von sozialen, identitätsstiftenden Praktiken der Zuschreibung von Heiligkeit zu untersuchen, erwies sich so insgesamt als sehr produktiv. Zu der Tagung konnte neben den Referenten eine ungefähr gleich große Zahl von Gästen begrüßt werden. Die Tagungsbeiträge sollen in einem Sammelband innerhalb der von der FEST herausgegebenen Reihe *Religion und Aufklärung* des Tübinger Verlags Mohr Siebeck veröffentlicht werden. Im Hinblick auf eine systematisch vollständige Darstellung des Forschungsansatzes werden in diesen Sammelband einige zusätzliche Beiträge aufgenommen, zum Beispiel zur Vermittlung der die Sakralisierung der Kunst bewirkenden Einstellungs- und Handlungsmuster in der Pädagogik (so erscheint darin auch der auf der Tagung wegen Krankheit entfallene Beitrag von Jürgen Oelkers).

Tagung vom 14. bis 16. Februar 2013 am Max-Weber-Kolleg, in Kooperation mit dem Deutschen Literaturarchiv Marbach und im Rahmen der Kolleg-Forschergruppe ‚Religiöse Individualisierung in historischer Perspektive': Sokratische Ortlosigkeit. Kierkegaards Idee des religiösen Schriftstellers' (Markus Kleinert)

In der Einführung wurde die Problematik entwickelt, die in Kierkegaards Selbstverständnis als religiöser Schriftsteller impliziert ist: die Zwiespältigkeit und das Wagnis eines literarischen Unternehmens, das eine ästhetische Existenz religiös begründen und eine religiöse Existenz ästhetisch absichern will, sich dabei aber auf keine kirchlich-religiöse Vollmacht stützt und sich auch nicht dem etablierten Wissenschaftssystem zuordnen lässt, ja insbesondere gegenüber der Universitätsphilosophie und -theologie auf Distanz geht. Die Spannung in Kierkegaards Selbstverständnis zeigt sich zum Beispiel daran, dass er seine Tätigkeit als Schriftsteller einerseits in Anlehnung an die eigene Sokrates- Darstellung und unter Hervorhebung der Sokrates bei Platon zugeschriebenen Ortlosigkeit kennzeichnet, andererseits für sich metaphorisch Polizeigewalt in Anspruch nimmt. Vor diesem Hintergrund sollte auf der Tagung zunächst Kierkegaards Idee des religiösen Schriftstellers im Spannungsfeld von Religion, Dichtung und Wissenschaft genauer betrachtet werden; dann sollte untersucht werden, welche Paradigmen die literarische und auch die literaturwissenschaftliche Rezeption dieses Schriftstellers bestimmen und ob dabei sein Selbstverständnis von Belang ist; schließlich sollte die Aktualität der Idee des religiösen Schriftstellers im Hinblick auf Religiosität und religiöse Rede in der Moderne thematisiert werden (Markus Kleinert).

In seinem Eröffnungsvortrag arbeitete Heiko Schulz akribisch heraus, wie der religiöse Schriftsteller in Kierkegaards Werk bestimmt ist: Die Spezifizierung nahm ihren Ausgang von wissenschafts-theoretischen Überlegungen zu der von Kierkegaard konzipierten Existenzwissenschaft; die christliche Redekunst, die Kierkegaard im kritischen Anschluss an die antike Rhetorik entwirft, steht im Dienst der Existenzwissenschaft; der religiöse Schriftsteller wiederum bedient sich der christlichen Redekunst auf eine Weise, die philosophische Metaphysik und theologische Dogmatik als für das religiöse Selbstverhältnis des Einzelnen gleichermaßen irrelevant suspendiert. Vor diesem Hintergrund wurde die besondere Problematik des religiösen Schriftstellers erkennbar. Anschließend wurde Kierkegaards Idee des religiösen Schriftstellers zu antiken und modernen Traditionen in Beziehung gesetzt. Rasmus Sevelsted parallelisierte das Verhältnis von Platon zu Sokrates mit dem von Kierkegaard zu seinen Pseudonymen, unter Hervorhebung der Notwendigkeit poetischer Veranschaulichung (dabei erläuterte er auch die Bedeutung der Atopie bei Platon). Wolfgang Spickermann nahm Kierkegaards positive Bezugnahmen auf Lukian zum Anlass, die Eigenschaften im Werk dieses historisch schwer fassbaren spätantiken Autors herauszustellen, die Kierkegaards Sympathie hervorgerufen haben müssen, insbesondere die ironisch- übermütige negative Dialektik im Zusammenhang von Philosophie- und Religionskritik. Magnus Schlette untersuchte die Bedeutung der Autobiographie für den religiösen Schriftsteller Kierkegaard, vor allem anhand der wechselseitigen Beziehung von im engeren Sinne autobiographischen und pseudonymen Schriften und unter vergleichender Hinzuziehung der pietistischen Autobiographie, hier der Lebensgeschichte von August Hermann Francke; das Verhältnis von Werk und Existenz erfährt bei Kierkegaard demnach folgende Zuspitzung: Die literarische Imagination wird zu einem für die Selbstwerdung notwendigen Akt der Bewährung, das Werk wird zum notwendigen Medium des Christwerdens.

Eine Reihe von Vorträgen beschäftigte sich dann mit der literarischen Rezeption Kierkegaards und seiner Idee des religiösen Schriftstellers. In der von Christian Wiebe entworfenen Typologie der Rezeptionsformen in der Literatur um 1910 zeichnete sich eine Skala literarischer Umgangsweisen mit Kierkegaards Selbstverständnis ab: von der absichtlichen oder unabsichtlichen Vernachlässigung über die mehr oder weniger stark modifizierende Aneignung bis hin zur Verfälschung (wobei selbst die *Proklamationen* von Ludwig Derleth ihrer ästhetisch-politischen Zweideutigkeit wegen als Reflex auf Kierkegaards ähnlich zweideutige Schriften des Kirchenkampfs verstanden werden können). Das Thema wurde von Charles Cahill fortgeführt, der Kierkegaards Präsenz in der späten Weimarer Republik untersuchte; die Bezugnahme auf Kierkegaard bewirkte bisweilen überraschende Allianzen, wie die von Wilhelm Kütemeyer und Alfred Baeumler mit ihren Versuchen, den religiösen Schriftsteller gegen bzw. für den Nationalsozialismus zu mobilisieren; Kierkegaards Anziehungskraft beruht in solchen Zusammenhängen mit darauf, dass sich die zentrale Kategorie des Einzelnen für die Kritik an Institutionen eignet, der derart losgelöste Einzelne aber wieder beliebigen Zwecken untergeordnet werden kann. Jan Bürger führte das Thema schließlich mit Blick auf die Literatur des späteren zwanzigsten Jahrhunderts aus, indem er verschiedene Rezeptionsweisen vorstellte und dabei zugleich das Potential des Literaturarchivs demonstrierte, so dass bekannte Kierkegaard-Rezeptionen wie die von Max Frisch in neuem Licht erschienen und gänzlich neue Wirkungsgeschichten sichtbar wurden, so etwa ein Einfluss von Kierkegaards Wiederholung auf Paul Celans *Todesfuge*. In zwei weiteren Beiträgen wurden für die literarische Rezeption entscheidende Strukturen der Kierkegaardschen Texte behandelt. Angelika Jacobs zeigte, wie Kierkegaards Texte durch eine fundamentale Unruhe auf einen Schock hinwirken, der mit dem Konzept des Erhabenen verbunden werden kann und auf die Selbstaufhebung der Ästhetik und ein religiöses Selbstverhältnis des Lesers angelegt ist. Mit diesem ästhetisch induzierten Schock verwandt ist die Sprach- und Denkfigur des Paradoxen, der sich Mathias Mayer widmete: in einem geeigneten mentalitätsgeschichtlichen Kontext konnten die in Kierkegaards Texten entfalteten Paradoxien als Impuls zu einer so fundamentalen wie ungesicherten, ins Offene weisenden ethischen Reflexion der Moral wirken, zum Beispiel bei Broch und Kafka, doch lässt sich Kierkegaard auf diese Weise auch zum utopischen Potential der mystischen Paradoxie bei Musil in Beziehung setzen.

Mit einem Seitenblick wurde das Verhältnis der skandinavistischen Literaturwissenschaft zu Kierkegaard betrachtet. In seinem diesbezüglichen Überblick verdeutlichte Joachim Grage die Schwierigkeit eines genuin literaturwissenschaftlichen Umgangs mit Kierkegaard, wobei in den einschlägigen Arbeiten Kierkegaards Selbstverständnis als religiöser Schriftsteller entweder beiseitegelassen oder übernommen, kaum aber in seiner Problematik untersucht wird.

Abschließend wurde nach der Aktualität der Idee des religiösen Schriftstellers gefragt. Peter Tschuggnall erkannte in der Poesie grundsätzlich eine Möglichkeit religiöser Rede, die der seit der Jahrhundertwende artikulierten Sprachkrise Rechnung trägt; er vergegenwärtigte diese Theopoesie durch Werke aus den verschiedenen Künsten, insbesondere der Musik. George Pattison beantwortete die Frage, wie sich das Christ-Sein in einem post-christlichen Zeitalter literarisch zum Ausdruck bringen lasse, zunächst mit einer doppelten Verlusterklärung: Kierkegaards Zeitalter sei in religiöser Hinsicht durch das Ende des theistischen Konsenses gekennzeichnet, in ästhetischer Hinsicht durch das Ende der Kunst, deren Stelle das Ästhetische als Zeitgeist einnehme; daher stelle sich Kierkegaard die Aufgabe, die christliche Idee in der alltäglichen Existenz darzustellen, unter Verzicht auf metaphysische Absicherungen und in der Orientierung an der Lebensgeschichte Jesu, eine Aufgabe, der Kierkegaard mit all seinen schriftlichen Ausdrucksformen, mit den pseudonymen und erbaulichen Schriften wie mit den Journalen und Notizbüchern nachzukommen versuche. Schlussvortrag und Eröffnungsvortrag griffen so ineinander: Während der religiöse Schriftsteller eingangs anhand der Kierkegaardschen Konzepte der Existenzwissenschaft und christlichen Redekunst genau spezifiziert wurde, erschien er abschließend als die Idee, die das gesamte Werk Kierkegaards umfasst und zusammenhält.

Das Thema der Tagung, die so zentrale wie problematische Idee des religiösen Schriftstellers, und der entsprechend interdisziplinäre Ansatz erwiesen sich damit als sehr fruchtbar, zumal der 200. Geburtstag Kierkegaards so Anlass für eine kritische Auseinandersetzung mit seinem Werk war, wodurch die Problematik wie das utopische Potential von Kierkegaards Version der Sokratischen Atopie deutlich wurden. Neben den Referenten konnte eine große Zahl an Gästen auf der Tagung begrüßt werden, darunter von diplomatischer Seite Per Erik Veng, Botschafts-Rat an der Dänischen Botschaft in Berlin, und von journalistischer Seite Nikolaus Halmer (ORF) und Maximilian Krämer (F.A.Z.), die beide ausführlich über die Tagung berichteten. Eine Veröffentlichung der Tagungsbeiträge ist in Arbeit.

Wissenschaftliche Tagung der Kolleg-Forschergruppe ‚Religiöse Individualisierung in historischer Perspektive' am Max-Weber-Kolleg in Verbindung mit der Akademie der Diözese Mainz und der Meister Eckhart-Gesellschaft vom 19. bis 21. April 2013 im Haus am Dom in Mainz: ‚Sprachbilder und Bildersprache bei Meister Eckhart und in seiner Zeit. Strategien des Sprechens über das Unsagbare' (Dietmar Mieth)

In der Mystik begegnen uns Sprachbilder, ja eine ganze Bildersprache. Mystik bewegt sich an den Grenzen von sprachlicher Ausdrucksfähigkeit – und entfaltet gerade darin ihre Anziehungskraft. Das Interesse an Meister Eckhart, dessen sprachliche Faszination auch noch in den Übersetzungen in andere Sprachen erhalten bleibt, geht oft auf seine Sprachbilder zurück. Er setzt sie bewusst ein, um die scharfe Begrifflichkeit und die spekulative Kraft seines Denkens anschaulich umzusetzen und der Erfahrungswelt seiner Zuhörer und Zuhörerinnen anzupassen. So spricht er vom Siegeldruck des Wachses, vom Echo als Widerhall einer Stimme, die man nicht hört, vom Prozess des Sehens, der Holz und Auge zusammenschließt, von der Überblendung durch das Licht, von Bildern, die sich wechselseitig spiegeln, aber nicht fixiert sind. Sein Programm ist, wie es später Heinrich Seuse ausdrücken wird, Bilder mit Bildern zu überwinden und damit einen Bereich zu öffnen, in welchem unser Vorstellungsvermögen zugleich entfaltet und überschritten wird.

Diese Thematik ist bisher nur fallweise in den Forschungen, in deren Zentrum oft Eckharts philosophischtheologische Bildtheorie stand, behandelt worden. Die Tagung hat versucht, diesen Stand der wissenschaftlichen Bemühungen zu erweitern.

Zugleich aber verfolgt sie die Absicht, solche Erkundungen mit den breiteren Interessen an den Sprachbildern in der europäischen Mystik zu verbinden und in diesem Sinne den Charakter einer reinen Fachtagung zu überschreiten.

Wolfgang Achtner, Gießen, hinterfragte das Tagungsthema kritisch, indem er die Bildkritik und das Motiv der Bildlosigkeit der ‚Bildersprache' Eckharts gegenüberstellte. Eckharts oft in Bildern ausgedrückte Bildkritik, d.h. seine Überzeugung, dass eine bildhaft vermittelte Erkenntnis für die Gotteserkenntnis nicht hinreichend ist, wurde vor den Hintergrund ihrer ideengeschichtlichen Voraussetzungen gestellt. Der Vortrag leuchtete die Bandbreite der verschiedenen Kontexte aus, in denen diese Bildkritik als Erkenntnismodus eingesetzt wird. Die scholastische Erkenntnistheorie, der aristotelische Vernunftbegriff und die apophatische Theologie wurden in ihrem Zusammenspiel und in ihrem Verhältnis zu Eckharts Theorie von der Gottesgeburt in der Seele vorgeführt. Mit Blick auf transkulturelle Analogien und einschlägige psychologische Mechanismen wurde die Frage erörtert, ob und wenn ja in welchem Sinne Eckhart überhaupt als Mystiker bezeichnet werden kann.

Martina Roesner, Wien, untersuchte ‚Bilder der Eigenschaftslosigkeit. Die Verwendung relationaler Metaphorik in Meister Eckharts lateinischen Schriften'. Mit Blick auf Eckharts lateinische Schriften fällt auf, dass die Vergleiche, die er im Rahmen seiner theologisch-exegetischen Darlegungen verwendet, zwar häufig dem Bereich der Natur entstammen, aber nicht so sehr einzelne Naturdinge als vielmehr deren Grundstrukturen betreffen, wie etwa die Abfolge von Blüte, Zeugung und Frucht, die Beziehung des Herzens bzw. der Seele zum Organismus als Ganzem, das Verhältnis von Licht und Wärme zu ihrem Ausbreitungsmedium oder die Deutung der Schöpfung als ‚Übersprudeln' einer kochenden Flüssigkeit. In all diesen Fällen betrifft die bildhafte Analogie keine einzelne, dingliche Eigenschaft, sondern gilt der jeweils zum Tragen kommenden Verhältnisbestimmung zwischen gewissen Grundprinzipien wie Materie und Form, Ursache und Wirkung, Zentrum und Peripherie.

‚Dô gedâhte ich ein glîchnisse [...] Vergleich und Gleichnis in den deutschen Predigten Meister Eckharts' lautete der Titel des Vortrags von Dagmar Gottschall, Salento. Der Beitrag stellte das Vergleichsrepertoire aus Eckharts deutschem Predigtwerk und mögliche Quellen vor: Es entstammt überwiegend dem Bereich der Naturphänomene, der Physik und der Optik. Ein Blick auf andere zeitgenössische Prediger zeigte die Auffälligkeit oder Unauffälligkeit Eckhartscher Vergleiche. Jeweils ist zu fragen: Inwieweit spielt das Publikum, inwieweit seine Selbstverständigung jeweils für einen Vergleich eine Rolle?

Stephan Grotz, Regensburg/Mainz, stellte ‚Wie zerbricht man Gleichnisse? Bemerkungen zur Struktur von Meister Eckharts Bildersprache' vor. Der Beitrag zeigte auf, dass Eckharts Bildersprache nicht so sehr darauf abzielt, das per se Unanschauliche doch noch etwas anschaulicher zu machen. Insofern hat Eckharts Bildersprache auch keinen vergleichenden Charakter in dem herkömmlichen Sinn. Eckharts Gleichnisse vergleichen nicht so sehr (also z.B. Gott mit irgendetwas); sie sprechen vielmehr von Gleichheit, und zwar vor allem von einer Gleichheit mit Gott. Der Vortrag entfaltete besonders Eckharts Umgang mit biblischen Vergleichen anhand der berühmten Predigt 9 ‚Quasi (!) stella matutina'. Hier ist das Wort ‚quasi' gleichsam eine Leitfigur. In seinem Vortrag ‚Meister Eckharts vünkelîn der sêle – Bild oder Begriff?' ging Alois Haas, Zürich, zunächst auf das Bild des Feuers und des Funkens in unterschiedlichen Kulturen und Religionen ein. Dabei ging es ihm vor allem historisch um die Bedeutung des Feuers in der Elementenlehre und deren Symbolfunktionen in der ‚Achsenzeit'. Feuer und Funken stehen für Tiefe und positive Entfaltung aus einem Kern heraus. In der Zuspitzung auf Meister Eckharts Grundgedanke wurde von ihm eine Bündelung vieler vorhergehender begrifflicher und bildlicher Pointierungen beschrieben: in der Stoa, im Neuplatonismus, in der Lehre vom aufsteigenden Intellekt. Die Alternative von Begriff und Bild ist also falsch: Hinter allen Begriffen ist zugleich eine bildliche Fassung präsent, und alle Bilder sind mit begrifflichem Denken ausgestattet.

Markus Vinzent, London, stellte ‚Eckharts Bildsprache in seinen lateinischen Predigten' vor. Er konnte mit Beispielen aufzeigen, wie Texte missverstanden und falsch übersetzt werden können, wenn man die Bildseite nicht korrekt darstellt und analysiert. Zudem konnte er zeigen, dass die Rhythmik in Eckharts lateinischem Sprach-Duktus verloren geht, wenn man übersieht, dass die Worte nur in einer bestimmten Abfolge eine besondere klangliche Struktur erzeugen. Insofern zeigte der Vortrag das rhythmische Sprechen in Eckharts lateinischen Sermones auf. Offensichtlich wurden hier nicht nur Texte als inhaltliche Vorlagen entwickelt, sondern zugleich enthielten sei für den Prediger Anleitungen dazu, wie etwas elegant vorzutragen war. Damit steht die lateinische Eckhart-Philologie vor neuen Aufgaben, die ihrerseits wiederum mit den systematischen Funktionen abzugleichen sind.

Die Reihe der Vorträge zu theologischen und mystischen Schriften aus dem Umkreis Eckharts eröffnete der Beitrag von Regina Schiewer, Eichstätt, zu den St. Georgener Predigten. An den von ihr präsentierten Beispieltexten konnte sie zeigen, wie weit die Reichhaltigkeit metaphorischer Sprache bereits im Anfang des 13. Jahrhunderts entwickelt war. René Wetzel, Genf, beschäftigte sich mit den Engelberger Predigten, die Johannes Tauler nahe stehen. Sie benutzen u.a. Gleichnisse der Natur (Sonnenablauf) für geistliche Vorgänge. Die Metaphern des Fließens und Zerfließens, des verborgenen Weins in der Traube, der Wüste und der Grundlosigkeit sind hier bereits als Routine fassbar. Eine ausführliche Untersuchung der Illuminationen von Seuse-Handschriften durch Ingrid Falque, Leiden, vermochte es, Verbindungen und auch Spannungen zwischen der bildhaften Sprache Seuses, die sich entscheidend von der Eckharts unterscheidet, und den Illustrationen aufzudecken. Die Illuminationen übernehmen eine Kommentarfunktion, die deutliche Rückschlüsse auf die Rezeption und die Gebrauchskontexte der Seuse-Texte erlauben. Ben Morgan, Oxford, und Cora Dietl, Gießen, beschäftigten sich in ihren jeweiligen Beiträgen mit Eckharts Bildersprache im Spiegel der zeitgenössischen Rezeption.

Den Abschluss der Tagung bildete eine Erweiterung des Horizonts von Eckhart und seinem Umkreis auf die Mystik in der Ostkirche. ‚Die Sprachkunst Eckharts und Gregorios' Palamas – ein struktureller Vergleich' war das Thema von Thomas Daiber, Gießen. Ähnlichkeiten zwischen Eckhart und Palamas (1296–1359) werden unter Hinweis auf eine gemeinsame Quelle, Ps. Dionys, ebenso bemerkt, wie offenkundige Unterschiede in ihrer Stellung und in der Haltung der jeweiligen Kirche zu ihnen. Palamas setzt sich in der orthodoxen Kirche weitgehend durch und wird zum anerkannten Bezug. Gott kann nach Eckhart nicht mit Eigenschaften (adjektivisch) bezeichnet werden, weil er die reine Substanz bezeichnet. Die für die Gottwerdung notwendige ‚Eigenschaftslosigkeit' des Menschen wird hier begründet. Daiber spricht von einer ‚linguistischen Gotteskonzeption' bei Eckhart, in der Gott nicht ‚kategorisierbar' sei. Palamas überbrückt das Problem der Unerkennbarkeit Gottes, indem der Mensch in die Energie Gottes hineingenommen wird und an ihr deshalb partizipiert. Vielleicht ergeben sich aber, so die Diskussion, hier mehr Möglichkeiten des Vergleichs, insofern Eckhart ja auch eine ‚Einheit mit Gott im Wirken' vorschwebt.

International conference of the research group 'Religious Individualization in Historical Perspective' at the Max-Weber-Center, May 6–8, 2013: 'The Agents of Isiac Cults. Identities, Functions and Modes of Representation' (Valentino Gasparini)

While the cultic networks established in the Egyptian, Greek and Roman worlds are familiar, as research-topics, to the historians of ancient religions, those relating to the Isiac deities have only recently aroused, somewhat limited, interest. Despite the works of experts such as Françoise Dunand, Sharon Kelly Heyob, Michel Malaise or Fabio Mora, the identities, functions and ways of representing the participants in those cults, whether priests, initiates, pilgrims or simple devotees, irrespective of their gender or status, are still largely unclear.

Our conference aimed to fill this gap by identifying the distinctive features of the actors of Isiac cults, both individually and as groups, without removing them from their context, one in which they interact with the actors of the other Graeco-Roman cults. For this purpose, a theoretical approach, specific to the history of religions of the ancient world, has been combined with a more empirical perspective, based on literary, epigraphic, archaeological and iconographic material.

The conference (financed by the German Research Foundation [DFG] and the Fonds de la Recherche Scientifique – FNRS de l'Université de Liège) has been organized by a scientific committee including Dr. Valentino Gasparini (Max-Weber-Center – Universität Erfurt) and Dr. Richard Veymiers (F.R.S.-FNRS – Université de Liège), with the cooperation of Prof. Jörg Rüpke (Max-Weber-Kolleg – Universität Erfurt), Prof. Françoise Van Haeperen (Université Catholique de Louvain), Dr. Thomas Morard (Université de Liège) and Prof. Vinciane Pirenne-Delforge (F.R.S.-FNRS – Université de Liège). 39 speakers have been invited from 8 different countries.

The first part of the double meeting has been held at the University of Erfurt the 6th-8th of May 2013, building on the recent research on 'religious individualization in a historical perspective' at the Max-Weber-Center. The aim of this event was to re-incorporate the Isiac cults in the historico-sociological discourse concerning religious pluralism. To what extent are we able to outline a sociology of the actors or Isiac cults? Who are the actors in these cults, where do they come from, what do they do and how do they interact with one another? These issues need to be tackled without preconceptions, taking due account of variations linked to geographic and chronological factors. The conference has begun with a discussion of the *status quaestionis* and with an introduction to the theoretical issues. The first section has been about the Isiac devotees and their attitude to religious choices. Specific issues to be discussed included: the significance of theophoric names, the degrees of exclusivity, the respect for the priestly or regional traditions and the different degrees of personal investment (pilgrimages, associations of devotees such as *melanephoroi* or *hypostoloi*, mystery-initiation).

The second section dealt with the members of the Isiac priesthood: priests and priestesses, as well as *oneirokritai*, aretalogists and *hierophonoi*, *neokoroi* and *zakoroi*, *stolistai* and *kleidouchoi*, *kannephoroi*, *lampterophoroi* and *pastophoroi*. This led to an examination of their terminology and prosopography, and an attempt to specify their identities (origins, gender and status) and functions in different contexts, in order to decide the extent to which it is appropriate to speak of the 'Isiac priesthood'. The third and final section dealt with spaces and ritual activities. The aim here was to identify the different locations, public or private, in which the Isiac devotees performed their rituals, on a daily or occasional basis, especially during major festivals.

The second part of the conference has been held at the University of Liège the 23th–24th of September 2013. With regard to iconography, although the way of representing the divinities of the Isiac circle has been the subject of a great number of studies, the images of the Isiac community have not received the same degree of attention, with the exception of a few specific studies. The aim of the second episode in Liège was to examine to what extent it is possible to construct a panorama of the iconography of the actors of the Isiac cults. Following the same pattern as in Erfurt, after an introductory session on the *status quaestionis* and methodology, it has been possible to examine the appearance of the devotees based on particular media, such as funerary stelae, or on certain iconographic types, such as children with the 'Horus lock', before turning to the iconography of office-holders ('priests'). A third and final section dealt with the representations of Isiac ceremonies, such as processions, banquets, sacrifices and dances, showing these actors, namely devotees and priests, in full interaction with one another. Valentino Gasparini as well as *oneirokritai*, aretalogists and *hierophonoi*, *neokoroi* and *zakoroi*, *stolistai* and *kleidouchoi*, *kannephoroi*, *lampterophoroi* and *pastophoroi*. This led to an examination of their terminology and prosopography, and an attempt to specify their identities (origins, gender and status) and functions in different contexts, in order to decide the extent to which it is appropriate to speak of the 'Isiac priesthood'. The third and final section dealt with spaces and ritual activities. The aim here was to identify the different locations, public or private, in which the Isiac devotees performed their rituals, on a daily or occasional basis, especially during major festivals.

Tagung vom 24. bis 25. Mai 2013 am Max-Weber-Kolleg: „Pragmatismus und/oder Theorie sozialer Praktiken. Potentiale einer Theoriedifferenz" (Andreas Pettenkofer)

Soziologische Erklärungen brauchen eine Sozialtheorie, die nicht nur den rationalen Akteur kennt, der – in souveräner Distanz zur jeweiligen Situation – kalkulierend seine Zwecke verfolgt. Einen wichtigen Beitrag, gerade was kultursoziologische Fragen angeht, leistet hier die Diskussion über ‚soziale Praktiken'. Sie rückt das Moment des nichtreflektierten Handelns in den Vordergrund; die Körperlichkeit des Handelns; sowie die Rolle der Dingwelt in Prozessen sozialer Ordnungsbildung. Damit zielt sie darauf, die handelnden ‚Subjekte' ihrerseits als soziale Produkte zu begreifen. Mit dem Erfolg dieser Perspektive zeigen sich aber ihre Probleme: Wird die Entstehung personaler Identitäten und entsprechender Handlungsmuster hier nicht zu rasch auf Machtverhältnisse zurückgeführt? Führt die Idee, dass soziale Ordnung auf nichtreflektierten Routinen aufbaut, die durch die Körperlichkeit des Handelns und die Materialität der Situation gestützt werden, nicht zu übertriebenen Stabilitätsannahmen? Muss dieses Verständnis der Körperlichkeit des Handelns, wie auch das Verständnis der Rolle materieller Artefakte, nicht zumindest ergänzt werden? Hier scheint es lohnend, die pragmatistische Tradition aufzunehmen, die von einer ähnlichen Problemstellung ausgeht, aber andere Lösungen vorschlägt: ein Konzept nichtreflektierten Handelns, das auf das Wechselspiel von Routine und Reflexion achtet; ein anderes Verständnis der Körperlichkeit des Handelns und der basalen Sozialität des Subjekts; jeweils mit Konsequenzen für die Analyse sozialer Ordnungsbildung. Zu fragen wäre dann: Welche Potentiale und welche Grenzen der pragmatistischen Perspektive zeigen sich, wenn man sie mit der Debatte über ‚soziale Praktiken' konfrontiert? Bieten diese Perspektiven Konzepte an, die einander ergänzen und sich verbinden lassen? Gibt es bereits Ansätze einer geglückten Verbindung? Wo handelt es sich um unvereinbare Theorieoptionen, deren Kenntnis aber zur Schärfung der Konzepte und zur Klärung der möglichen Theoriestrategien beiträgt?

Zur Diskussion solcher Fragen fand im Mai am Max-Weber-Kolleg eine Tagung statt, organisiert von Hella Dietz (Göttingen), Frithjof Nungesser (Graz) und Andreas Pettenkofer (MWK), mit Unterstützung der Sektion Kultursoziologie in der Deutschen Gesellschaft für Soziologie. Nach einem kurzen Einführungsvortrag (Hella Dietz, Frithjof Nungesser) argumentierte Andreas Pettenkofer (Erfurt) dafür, das Konzept ‚Praktiken' – unter Nutzung von Elementen der durkheimianischen wie der pragmatistischen Tradition – nicht im Sinne eine Theorie über bestimmte (präreflexive etc.)

Handlungsmuster zu verstehen, sondern im Sinne einer Theorie über einen bestimmten Situationstyp, nämlich über Beweissituationen. Gegen derartige Integrationsvorschläge betonte Jörg Potthast (Berlin), am Fall der techniksoziologischen Diskussion, den seines Erachtens voreiligen Charakter der im Kontext des ‚Praktiken'-Konzepts stattfindenden Pragmatismusrezeption, die – scheinbar paradoxerweise – gerade dazu führe, dass das Bild eines unproblematischen, reflexions- und konfliktfreien Normalbetriebs des Sozialen aufrechterhalten werde. Jörg Strübing (Tübingen) und Frithjof Nungesser (Graz) unternahmen beide einen Vergleich der wesentlich an Bourdieu orientierten Varianten einer ‚Theorie sozialer Praktiken' mit pragmatistischen Ansätzen, die an Mead anknüpften. Dabei betonte Strübing – unter dem Titel „Practice Theory: Where Is the Mead/t?" – vor allem die Defizite dieses PraktikenKonzepts, indem er vorführte, dass die pragmatistische Tradition jene Phänomene von Routinehandeln, die das ‚Praktikten'-Konzept ins Zentrum rückt, differenzierter beschreibt. Dagegen hob Nungesser, mit Verweis auf die „Janusköpfigkeit der Sozialität", eher die Komplementarität der beiden Herangehensweisen vor und unterstrich, dass gerade für die Erklärung von Konfliktphänomenen die vorliegenden pragmatistisch inspirierten Konzepte nicht ausreichen. Die letzten beiden Vorträge des ersten Tages zielten darauf, den Nutzen der diskutierten Konzepte anhand empirischer Fallstudien zu prüfen: Tanja Bogusz (Berlin) berichtete über ihre ethnographische Begleitung eines Biodiversitäts-Projekts in Papua Neuguinea; sie versuchte – mit Blick auf Durkheim und Dewey – herauszuarbeiten, wie die Konzepte, die diese unterschiedlichen Theorietraditionen anbieten, an je unterschiedlichen Punkten des Forschungsprozesses nützlich werden. Hella Dietz (Göttingen) berichtete über ein laufendes Projekt zur südamerikanischen Wahrheitskommission; ihr ging es darum zu zeigen, wie Überlegungen von Dewey und Boltanski helfen, über eine enge machttheoretische Beschreibung solcher Phänomene hinauszukommen – wobei die Diskussion dann unter anderem die Frage betraf, ob sich Deweys Perspektive auch eignet, solche Machtphänomene zu erfassen.

Der zweite Tag begann mit einem Vortrag von Henning Laux (Bremen), der dafür plädierte, dass auch die Soziologie sich stärker mit der Philosophie Richard Rortys auseinandersetzen sollte, die – mit ihrer Aufwertung der Kontingenz und ihrem Konzept eines ironischen Engagements – sogar einen gesellschaftstheoretischen Nutzen biete; eine solchermaßen informierte Theorieperspektive sei speziell für heutige, nicht mehr durch hohe Stabilität gekennzeichnete Gesellschaften angemessen. Hannes Krämer (Frankfurt/Oder) kontrastierte anhand des Problemfelds ‚Kreativität' die pragmatistische mit der ethnomethodologischen Herangehensweise; ausgehend von einem kürzlich abgeschlossenen Projekt zur Marketingbranche zeigte er, wie die Ethnomethodologie an die Stelle der Frage, welche Handlungsprozesse tatsächlich kreativen Charakter haben, die Frage setzt, wie die Beteiligten bestimmte Handlungsweisen als kreativ markieren (‚doing creativity'). Hilmar Schäfer (Frankfurt/Oder) widmete sich den theoretischen wie methodischen Konvergenzen von pragmatistischer Soziologie und ‚ActorNetwork Theory' (Callon, Latour); er illustrierte das mit

Überlegungen aus einem gerade begonnenen Projekt, das sich dem Problem des ‚kulturellen Erbes' im Bereich der Architektur widmet. – Die letzten beiden Vorträge der Tagung konzentrierten sich auf die Frage, welche methodologischen Konsequenzen aus diesen sozialtheoretischen Überlegungen zu ziehen wären. Alexander Antony (Erlangen) berichtete über sein Dissertationsprojekt, das sich am Fall der Atemtherapie mit der Frage beschäftigt, wie Phänomene eines körpernahen ‚impliziten Wissens' in soziologischen Forschungen erfasst werden können; seine These lautete, dass man Deweys Analysen dieser Wissensform und der mit ihr verbundenen Handlungsweisen am besten mit einer ‚autoethnographischen' Methode gerecht wird. Robert Schmidt (Erlangen) betonte zunächst nochmals – ausgehend von den Themen ‚Körperlichkeit des Handelns', ‚Materialität' und ‚implizites Wissen' – die Komplementarität der auf der Tagung verhandelten Theorieströmungen und plädierte dann dafür, dass nur ein ethnographisches – oder jedenfalls: einem ethnographischen Erkenntnisstil folgendes – Vorgehen geeignet sei, diese theoretischen Einsichten umzusetzen. Da alle Beteiligten die Diskussionen sehr interessant fanden, endete die Tagung mit der Entscheidung, sich nächstes Jahr wieder zu treffen. Eine Buchveröffentlichung ist in Planung.

Tagung im Rahmen der Kolleg-Forschergruppe ‚Religiöse Individualisierung in historischer Perspektive' vom 20. bis 21. Juni 2013 am Max-Weber-Kolleg: ‚Transplantation – Transmortalität – Transparenz' (Andrea M. Esser)

Das philosophische Verständnis des Todes und dessen praktische Bedeutungen sowie damit einhergehende ethische Konsequenzen sind zentrale Gegenstände der Forschung von Prof. Dr. Andrea M. Esser, mit denen sie sich als Fellow am Max-Weber-Kolleg und als Leiterin des philosophischen Teilprojekts des durch die Volkswagen-Stiftung geförderten interdisziplinären Forschungsprojekts ‚Tod und toter Körper' befasst. Dabei bezieht sich ihre Forschung nicht nur auf eine begrifflich-theoretische Reflexion über den Tod und den Hirntod, sondern auch auf deren praktische Implikationen und Konsequenzen für die Organspendepraxis, deren rechtliche Normierung und gesellschaftliche Verwirklichung praktische Probleme einer philosophisch-ethischen Beurteilung darstellen.

Anlass für die Konzeption der Tagung war die im Sommer 2012 verabschiedete Neuregelung des Transplantationsgesetzes in Deutschland. Dieses Gesetz sieht vor, alle Bürgerinnen und Bürger umfassend über Ablauf und Organisation der Organspende zu informieren, und sie in regelmäßigen Abständen dazu aufzufordern, ihre Entscheidung für oder gegen eine Organspende zu dokumentieren. *Welche* Institutionen das Informationsmaterial für diese Aufklärungskampagnen erarbeiten und nach *welchen* Maßgaben sie die dafür vorgesehenen Materialien jeweils gestalten, war bislang kaum Gegenstand kritischer öffentlicher Diskussionen. Um eine solche

Diskussion kritisch führen zu können, bedarf es zunächst der Erarbeitung empirischer Erkenntnisse darüber, welches Wissen über die Organspende gesellschaftlich vorherrscht, wie die rechtlich gebotene Aufklärung institutionell umgesetzt wird, welcher medialen Ästhetisierungsformen sich dabei bedient wird und wie die normativ wirksamen Inhalte darin zum Ausdruck kommen. An der Erarbeitung dieser Erkenntnisse besteht nach Auffassung der Mitglieder des Forschungsprojekts ‚Tod und toter Körper' nicht nur ein wissenschaftliches, sondern auch ein öffentliches Interesse. Aus diesem Grund hat das philosophische Teilprojekt unter der Leitung von Andrea Esser am 20. und 21. Juni 2013 Expertinnen und Experten der Debatte in das Max-Weber-Kolleg eingeladen, um im Rahmen der Tagung die Frage zu diskutieren, was die in der öffentlichen Diskussion aufgestellten Schlagworte ‚Transparenz', ‚Information' und ‚Aufklärung' im Kontext der Organspende überhaupt bedeuten können und welche Praxis als ‚Aufklärung über die Organspende' verstanden werden kann (und soll).

Den Auftakt der Tagung bildeten zwei öffentliche Abendvorträge. Der Philosoph Prof. Dr. Matthias Vogel (Gießen) leistete in seinem Vortrag eine erste Klärung eines der Grundbegriffe der Debatte. Aufklärung stellt, so Vogel, einen offenen und sozialen Lern- und Erfahrungsprozess dar, der darauf angelegt ist, praktische Bedingungen unserer Möglichkeiten des Verstehens zu entwickeln. Insofern sich unser Verstehen aber nicht nur im Medium der Sprache, sondern auch durch andere Medien vollziehe, seien Verstehensprozesse auch durch visuelle und andere ästhetische Darstellungsformen strukturiert. Diese medial vermittelten Inhalte, wie sie z.B. in Werbekampagnen zur Organspende zu beobachten seien, prägten wesentlich die Entwürfe unserer Selbst-Bilder, an denen wir uns normativ in Entscheidungen orientieren. Wie solche Entscheidungen als selbstbestimmte oder autonome gelten könnten, entwickelte Vogel durch die Explikation der normativen Bedingungen eines Aufklärungsprozesses. Der Anwalt und Journalist Dr. Oliver Tolmein (Hamburg) nahm das Stichwort der ‚Selbstbestimmung' auf und führte in seinem Vortrag die These aus, dass Vorab-Erklärungen zur Organspende im Grunde den juristischen Status von Patientenverfügungen hätten. Damit sei aber eine zentrale Schwachstelle des Transplantationsgesetzes in der Novellierung nicht behoben, sondern in Teilen sogar verschärft worden. Solange sich diese Erklärung nämlich in einer bloßen Zustimmung zur Organspende erschöpfe, sei sie ungeeignet, medizinische Maßnahmen im Vorfeld der Organentnahme, in denen die Patientinnen und Patienten zwar bereits einwilligungsunfähig seien, aber nicht als tot gelten würden, hinreichend bestimmt zu normieren und regulieren. Darüber hinaus wies Tolmein darauf hin, dass allein schon die ‚Bitte des Staates' an seine Bürgerinnen und Bürger, sich zu entscheiden, das Neutralitätsgebot des Staates unterlaufe, da dieses Ansinnen eine materiale Wertentscheidung für die Organspende impliziere.

Den als intensives Arbeitsgespräch konzipierten Workshop am darauf folgenden Tag eröffnete der Medienwissenschaftler Prof. Dr. Rainer Leschke (Siegen) mit einer medientheoretischen Reflexion auf wirkmächtige kulturelle Bilder, die u.a. eine stark negative Codierung leiblicher Fragmentierung aufweisen, so dass realistische visuelle Darstellung von Organspenden seiner Meinung nach zu einem Problem für die Bereitschaft zur Spende führen müssten.

Dass wir uns in unserem Urteilen und Handeln auch zu solchen realistischen Darstellungsformen und Bildern und deren negativer Codierung kritisch reflektierend ins Verhältnis setzen können und im Sinne einer angemessenen Aufklärungspraxis auch müssen, stellte Andrea Esser in ihrem Beitrag heraus. Auf der Basis eines pragmatistischen Verständnisses von Bedeutungsklärung diagnostizierte und kritisierte sie in den aktuellen Werbekampagnen das Vorherrschen von ‚Individualismus', ‚Moralischem Dogmatismus' und einem ‚Magisch-mythischen Denken'. Damit aber leisteten die Kampagnen einem ‚abstrakten Denken' Vorschub, welches eine selbstbestimmte und kritische Entscheidung über die Zustimmung oder Ablehnung der Organspende schwerlich ermögliche.

In eine ähnliche Richtung argumentierte auch die Philosophin PD Dr. Theda Rehbock (Dresden/Marburg), die in ihrem Beitrag *vernünftige* Selbstbestimmung an Bedingungen einer kritischen Aufklärung band. Das bedeute konkret, die Bürgerinnen und Bürger über die besondere Situation des Hirntodes und die praktischen Implikationen der Organentnahme (aggressive Hirntoddiagnostik, lebendige Anmutung Hirntoter, erschwerte Abschiednahme usw.) umfassend und ohne moralisierenden Druck zu informieren, damit diese sich vor diesem Hintergrund ein Urteil bilden könnten, in dem nicht schon von vornherein entschieden ist, ob Organspende per se gut oder schlecht ist.

Die Leiterin des rechtswissenschaftlichen Teilprojekts Prof. Dr. Brigitte Tag (Zürich) informierte in ihrem Beitrag über die rechtlichen Rahmenbedingungen der Aufklärung über die Organspende in Deutschland und stellte klar, dass dem Staat zwar qua Gesetz ein Aufklärungsauftrag obliege, dies aber nicht bedeute, dass nicht auch andere Institutionen als die Krankenkassen und die Deutsche Stiftung Organspende (DSO) Kampagnen starten dürften.

Mit welchen medialen Mitteln und Informationsmaterialien z.B. die Techniker Krankenkasse oder die Werbekampagnen der BZgA arbeiten, wie sie dabei gezielt eine Pro-Einstellung zum Hirntodkonzept sowie zur Organspendepraxis herstellen und welche strukturellen und individuellen Interessen den Hintergrund dieser Kampagnen darstellen, war Untersuchungsgegenstand der Beiträge des Journalisten und Soziologen Dr. Ludger Fittkau (Darmstadt) sowie der medienanalytischen Untersuchung der dem Teilprojekt Soziologie angehörenden Forscherinnen Dr. Antje Kahl und Dr. Tina Weber (beide Berlin).

Zum Abschluss des Workshops nahm die Philosophin Prof. Dr. Barbara Merker (Frankfurt a. M.) noch einmal die Frage nach dem Hirntod auf und diagnostizierte ein folgenreiches ‚Missverständnis', dem die Hirntoddebatte ihrem Urteil zufolge bis heute aufsäße. So sei die Grundfrage der Debatte, ob ein hirntoter Mensch *wirklich* tot sei, falsch gestellt, da sie unterstelle, dass es eine reale Grenze zwischen Leben und

Tod in der Natur gäbe. Diese Auffassung beruhe aber, wie sie argumentativ herausstellte, auf einem begrifflichen Klassifikationsproblem. Da, so Merker, die Grenze nicht in der Natur gegeben ist, sondern die Natur und deren individuelle oder allgemeine Normen in einer zunächst kontingenten, dann aber sozial vorgeschriebenen oder noch zu bestimmenden normativen Relation stünden, gingen diese grundsätzlichen Überlegungen der erneuten Frage nach Definition, Kriterium und Feststellung des Hirntodes und den normativen Regulierungen unserer Praxis voraus.

Dass die gegenwärtig vorherrschenden medial vermittelten Bilder und Formen der Aufklärung über Organspende zumeist unzureichend sind, um einen Begriff von Aufklärung zu realisieren, der den entwickelten normativen Geltungsbedingungen genügt, kann als ein Resultat der Tagung gelten. Welche Bedingungen und Kriterien für ein kritisches Verständnis des Hirntods und einer angemessenen Aufklärung der Organspende gelten sollen, konnte in Grundzügen auf dieser Tagung entwickelt werden. Die weitere Entwicklung dieser Geltungsbedingungen und konkrete Empfehlungen zur Ausgestaltung öffentlicher, politischer und rechtlicher Praxen bleiben aber weiterhin gewichtige Aufgaben der wissenschaftlichen und öffentlichen Diskurse. Um hieran weiter zu wirken sei darauf verwiesen, dass Radiomitschnitte dieser Tagung Anfang 2014 in der Sendung ‚Hörsaal' von DRadio Wissen zu hören sein sollen. Darüber hinaus ist für Mitte 2014 eine Publikation des Forschungsprojekts ‚Tod und toter Körper' mit dem Titel ‚Die Krise der Organspende – Anspruch, Analyse und Kritik aktueller Aufklärungsbemühungen im Kontext der postmortalen Organspende' geplant. Hier sollen die Erträge der Tagung durch weitere empirische Analysen untermauert und mit ethischen Reflexionen verbunden werden.

Meister Eckhart-Tage vom 4. bis 6. Juli 2013 in Erfurt (Dietmar Mieth)

Die Zusammenarbeit an der Kolleg-Forschergruppe am Max-Weber-Kolleg (MWK) der Universität Erfurt ermöglicht Synergie-Effekte zwischen den Programmen und Projekten der Meister Eckhart Gesellschaft (MEG), des MWK sowie den Katholischen Akademien in Bayern und in Mainz.

In Erfurt fand sich 2012 zusätzlich ein Initiativkreis Meister Eckhart (www.meister-eckhart-erfurt.de) zusammen, der damit begann, für 2013 Eckhart-Tage in Erfurt zu planen. Vertreten waren die Predigergemeinde, die MEG, die Universität Erfurt durch das MWK, die Evangelische Stadtakademie Meister Eckhart, das Katholische Forum, und eine Reihe von engagierten Einzelpersonen.

Begleitend zur Initiative für 2013 wurden Broschüren für eine Eckhart-Initiative im Bildungs-Tourismus bzw. spirituellen Tourismus erstellt. Die Broschüre *Meister Eckharts Faszination heute* liegt inzwischen nicht nur in Erfurt (Predigerkirche, Tourismusbüro) aus, sondern sie ist inzwischen auch auf Englisch erhältlich. Sie wird auch im englischsprachigen Raum verteilt. Eine zweite Broschüre, ebenfalls in beiden Sprachen, beschreibt *Einen Weg der Erfahrung mit Meister Eckhart durch Erfurt* (für die Broschüren: Autor: Mieth, Übersetzung: Vinzent, Fotograf: Schmidt). Das Datum der Eckhart-Tage 2013 erinnert auch an Eckharts Weg nach seiner zweiten Pariser Professur 2013 an den Rhein. Dem Thema ‚1313–2013: Der Thüringer Meister Eckhart als Begründer der Rheinischen Mystik?' widmete sich ein zweitägiger wissenschaftlicher Workshop, veranstaltet vom MWK im Predigerkloster (s. dazu der eigene Bericht).

In Straßburg fand dann ebenfalls unter Leitung von Frau Prof. Vannier ein ähnlicher Workshop am 19. September 2013 statt. Auch dieser wurde von einer öffentlichen Veranstaltung mit Musik und Lektüre von Eckhart-Texten in der Krypta des Straßburger Münsters begleitet. Für die Erfurter Eckhart-Tage wurde die renommierte Schauspielerin Martina Gedeck zu einer Eckhart-Lesung in der Predigerkirche mit Hilfe der Herbstlese e.V. und zugleich als Schirmherrin des Programms eingeladen. Diese Lesung am Donnerstagabend, den 4. Juli 2013, in der Predigerkirche war ausverkauft und sehr eindrucksvoll. Frau Gedeck verstand es, in einer von innen getragenen Intensität die Gedanken Meister Eckharts, trotz ihres hohen philosophischen Anspruches, mit viel Einsicht und Einfühlung in einer direkt das Herz ansprechenden Unmittelbarkeit vorzutragen.

Zu den Eckhart-Tagen gehörte ein Einkehrtag am Samstag, den 6. Juli 2013, im Predigerkloster, den Frau Morawietz, Erfurter Theologin, vorbereitet und durchgeführt hat, mit der innerlichen und schweigenden Verarbeitung von Texten im Chorgestühl der Kirche (ca. 50 Teilnehmer/innen). Den Abschluss bildete ein festlicher, ökumenischer Gottesdienst, umrahmt von Liedern Mechthilds von Magdeburg, in der Predigerkirche am Samstag, den 6. Juli, mit Pfarrer Dr. Holger Kaffka, der evangelischen Landesbischöfin Ilse Junkermann, Weihbischof/Diözesanadministrator Dr. Reinhard Hauke und Kardinal Professor Dr. Walter Kasper aus Rom, der zu Eckharts Predigt zur Geschichte der Tempelreinigung Jesu im Neuen Testament (bei Eckhart die Predigt Nr. 1) predigte. Auch diese Veranstaltung fand eine vollbesetzte Kirche.

Die *Meister Eckhart-Tage* in Erfurt werden eine Fortsetzung finden, voraussichtlich 2016. Dazwischen sind weitere Veranstaltungen und Initiativen zu Meister Eckhart in Erfurt zu erwarten. Ein Büro für Eckhart-Initiativen wurde in der Predigerstr. 9 eröffnet. Den Abschluss für das Jahr 2013 wird die Einweihung eines Bodendenkmales vor dem Portal der Predigerkirche dienen mit in den Boden eingelassenen Zitaten Meister Eckharts.

Tagung in Zusammenarbeit mit der Meister Eckhart-Gesellschaft und der Èquipe de Recherches sur les Mystics Rhénans (Université de Metz) vom 4. bis 5. Juli 2013 im Predigerkloster Erfurt: ‚1313–2013: Der Thüringer Meister Eckhart als Begründer der Rheinischen Mystik?' (Dietmar Mieth)

Vom 4. bis 5. Juli fand im Rahmen der *Eckhart Tage 2013*, organisiert von Professor Dr. Dietmar Mieth, Präsident der Meister Eckhart-Gesellschaft, in Zusammenarbeit mit der Équipe de Recherches sur les Mystics Rhénans (Université de Metz) und der Kolleg-Forschergruppe ‚Religiöse Individualisierung in historischer Perspektive' eine Tagung zum Thema ‚1313–2013: Der Thüringer Meister Eckhart als Begründer der Rheinischen Mystik?' statt. Nach einer kurzen Begrüßung durch Prof. Wolfgang Spickermann, Leiter des Max-Weber-Kollegs, an dem die Kolleg-Forschergruppe angesiedelt ist, hielt Prof. Volker Leppin aus Tübingen den ersten Vortrag: ‚Eckhart und Luther'. In Bezug auf das Verhältnis von Eckhart zum Protestantismus galt er einerseits als Vorbereiter der Reformation, andererseits aber auch als (schlechter) Scholastiker der ‚alten' Kirche.

Prof. Marie-Anne Vannier von der Universität Metz stellte Eckhart als Begründer der Rheinischen Mystik vor. ‚Rheinische Mystik' wurde nach dem 2. Weltkrieg eine Begriffsprägung gegen die Vereinnahmung der ‚Deutschen Mystik' durch den Nationalsozialismus. ‚Mystik' betont hier gegen philosophische Reduktionen die religiöse Erfahrung. Die Mystik der drei Dominikaner, Eckhart, Tauler, Seuse, bildet den Kern der ‚Rheinischen Mystik' als ‚spekulative' Mystik.

Die beiden darauf folgenden Vorträge befassten sich mit der Rezeptionsgeschichte von Eckharts Gedanken. Dr. Maxime Mauriège, Universität Köln, Thomas Institut, untersuchte die ‚compilatio mystica' als Fortsetzung der Anliegen Meister Eckharts. Die aus dem 15. Jahrhundert stammenden, aber erst im 17. Jahrhundert zusammengestellten Texte (Hamburger Codex 1614), auch ‚Mosaiktraktate' wegen ihrer Disparatheit genannt, enthalten überwiegend Gedanken Eckharts oder der ‚Eckhartisten'. Das ist am Inhalt und an der Sprache nachweisbar. Die Intention der Kompilation ist nicht klar, aber sie beweist, dass es eine kontinuierliche, wenn auch nicht genaue, Überlieferung der Gedanken Eckharts gegeben hat und dass diese weiter rezipiert wurden. PD Dr. Andrés Quero-Sánchez, Universität Regensburg und Max-Weber-Kolleg, untersuchte die Wirkung Eckharts im deutschen Idealismus in seinem Vortrag: ‚Die neuzeitliche Wiederaufnahme der ‚mystischen' Vernunft: Fichte, Schelling, Hegel'. Eckharts ‚Warumlosigkeit', seine Betonung der ‚Grundlosigkeit' und der 'Unmittelbarkeit', in welchen Ziel- und Wirkursachen ausgeschlossen werden, können in einer Dialektik von Modernität betrachtet werden: die ‚konkrete' Moderne, die vom empirischen Einzelding ausgeht und Überhöhungen entlarvt (,aufklärt') und die idealistische Moderne, die sich gerade dagegen richtet, und die durch Eckhart bzw. seine Reprise im Idealismus vorbereitet ist.

Der Bibelwissenschaftler Prof. Christoph Bultmann, Universität Erfurt, stellte die Frage: ‚Wie legt Eckhart die Bibel aus? Bezüge zur alttestamentlichen Weisheit'. Mit den historischen Entstehungskontexten der Predigten Eckharts befasste sich Prof. Freimut Löser, Universität Augsburg, in seinem Vortrag: ‚Thüringer Predigten Meister Eckharts – Vorschlag für eine Edition'. Wie ist der Bezug von Predigten zu Thüringen bzw. Erfurt zu klären? Zwei thüringische Predigten (in mitteldeutscher Sprache) finden sich in London: Pr. 32 (Elisabeth) und Pr. 95. Bei der Elisabeth-Predigt lässt sich der Thüringer Bezug besonders gut zeigen. Prof. Katharina Bracht, Universität Jena, untersuchte ein Gedicht, das Eckhart zugeschrieben wird: Das ‚Granum Sinapis' und die Väter-Theologie. Das Gedicht ist in Thüringen entstanden. Von Ruh wird es Meister Eckhart zugeschrieben. Dr. Chris Wojtulewicz, King's College London, sprach zu: ‚Leading the debates? Eckhart in the Context of Early Fourteenth Century Paris'. Dabei ging es darum zu zeigen, welche Prägungen, die aus Eckharts lateinisch verfassten Pariser Quaestionen (1311–1313) stammen, sich in die deutschen Predigten hinein verfolgen lassen. Das britische Forschungsprojekt, dass Eckharts Pariser Quaestiones und Disputationes neu erschließen will, verfolgt Spuren in die Predigten des ‚späten' Eckharts am Rhein.

Dr. Saeed Zarrabi Zadeh, Universität Erfurt, ging in seinem Vortrag ‚Practical Mysticism – Eckhart and Sufism' den Beziehungen zwischen Rheinischer Mystik und Sufismus nach. Zwischen Eckhart und dem islamischen Sufismus hat man gern unter dem leitenden Gesichtspunkt von Parallelen bzw. Ähnlichkeiten geforscht. Für Parallelen verwies man in der Struktur des spekulativen ‚Systems' auf Ibn Arrabi (geb. 1240). Der Vergleich Eckhart–Rumi, den der Referent vorgenommen hat, beruht auf einer anderen Hermeneutik: Gerade die Unterschiedlichkeit zwischen einer poetischen und affektiven Mystik (Rumi) und einer intellektiven Mystik (Eckhart) erlaubt es, die praktischen Methoden des Nachvollzuges sich wechselseitig spiegeln zu lassen.

‚Unmittelbarkeit und Vermittlungsstrukturen göttlicher Gegenwart in der mystischen Theologie Eckharts von Hochheim und Nikolaus' von Kues' war das Thema von Dr. Christian Ströbele, Universität Tübingen. Eckhart bekam Probleme, die in den theologischen Gutachten der Avignonenser Gutachten sichtbar sind, weil ihm eine vorbehaltlose Identifizierung von Mensch und Gott vorgehalten wurde. Bei der Relecture, die Cusanus den Texten angedeihen ließ, hat er die Intentionen Eckharts als Zielvorstellungen ‚sub specie aeternitatis' bewahrt, zugleich aber die bleibende irdische ‚Alterität' zwischen göttlichem und menschlichen Erkennen, Sein und Leben hervorgehoben. Im Unterschied zu Eckhart baut er explizite Sicherungen gegen Missverständnisse ein, die von den Avignonenser Gutachern repräsentiert werden, welche Eckharts eigene Absicherungen – etwa die Lehre von der bleibenden Kontingenz oder seine deutliche Berufung auf die Worte der Schrift – vermutlich als Alibi verstanden haben. Auch für Prof. Dietmar Mieth, Universität Tübingen und Max-Weber-Kolleg, war das Thema Unmittelbarkeit bei Meister Eckart zentral für seinen Vortrag: ‚Die individuelle Unmittelbarkeit der Mystik als Herausforderung der Religionen'. Die historischen Konflikte der individuellen Mystik, die man an den Beispielen Meister Eckhart und deutlicher noch am Prozess gegen Marguerite Porete aufzeigen kann, verweisen auf wiederholbare Konstellationen. Im katholischen Bereich ist es eher die Ekklesiologie, in welcher die Kirche als Ursakrament die Heilsmittel allein bereit hält, im Protestantismus ist später eher der Konflikt zwischen Erfahrung und gläubiger Orthodoxie, die sich alles von ‚extra nos' her sagen lässt. Während im Pietismus z.B. bis heute die Erfahrung höher eingeschätzt wird als das Sakrament, ist das in der Orthodoxie umgekehrt. Diese Konflikte sind im Islam als Spannung zwischen Sufismus und rechtstheologischer Regulierung von Praktiken ebenso zu beobachten wie im Judentum, wo man die Spannung an der zunächst sehr ambivalenten Behandlung des Moses Maimonides bis ins 14. Jahrhundert hinein ablesen kann. Das Problem verschärfte sich, als sich Mystik Anfang des 20. Jahrhunderts vom Monotheismus als Religion löste (vgl. die ‚gottlose Mystik', die einflussreich von Fritz Mauthner thematisiert wurde) und neureligiöse Reprisen der Mystik diese noch eher gegen Institution und Dogma kehrten. Dies kommt auch in der Forderung des Eckhart-Preisträgers Ernst Tugendhat (2007) zum Ausdruck, Mystik aus humanistischen Gründen an die Stelle von Religion zu setzen.

Tagung vom 15. bis 17. Juli 2013 am Max-Weber-Kolleg: ‚Forms of Religious Individualisation. Concepts and Processes' (Asaph Ben-Tov)

Seit 2009 hat die Kolleg-Forschergruppe ‚Religiöse Individualisierung in historischer Perspektive' in kritischer Auseinandersetzung mit dem Bild von Individualisierung, das Modernisierungstheorien entwickelt haben, in unterschiedlichen historischen Kontexten religiöse Individualisierungsprozesse untersucht. Anlässlich des Abschlusses der ersten DFG-Förderphase veranstaltete die Kolleg-Forschergruppe eine Tagung zu ihrem Kernthema. Vor allem diente diese Tagung als Gelegenheit, über die bisherige Forschung jetziger und ehemaliger Kollegiaten zu reflektieren: durch eine Betrachtung der thematischen Vielfalt der Forschungsarbeiten in der Forschergruppe in den ersten vier Jahren und gleichzeitig durch eine vorsichtige Überlegung zu überspannenden Typologien.

Während der dreitägigen Tagung (15.–17. Juli 2013) wurden zahlreiche abgeschlossene wie laufende Arbeiten vorgestellt und diskutiert. Die Beiträge, die sich über eine große Bandbreite dehnten, befassten sich u.a. mit der methodologischen Herausforderung archäologischer Spuren religiöser Individualisierung in der griechischrömischen Antike, religiöser Kompetenz und individualisierten Praktiken in der Antike, der Mystik und religiöser Individualisierung und Heterodoxie im christlichen Mittelalter, Individualisierung und Gewissen in der Frühen Neuzeit sowie mit weiteren Fallstudien, die die Diskussion bis zum frühen 20. Jahrhundert führten. Die nicht-europäischen Schwerpunkte mehrerer Fellows und Kollegiaten fanden sich in Beiträgen zur religiösen Individualisierung im Hinduismus, im Jainismus und in der konfuzianischen Lehre. Die breit gefächerte Tagung diente zugleich als Zwischenfazit im Übergang von der ersten zur zweiten Förderphase sowie auch als ein reflektierter Impuls für die weitere Entwicklung der Forschergruppe.

Tagung in Kooperation mit der University of Chicago vom 3. bis 5. Juli 2013 am Max-Weber-Kolleg: ‚Public and Private in Ancient Mediterranean Law and Religion' (Jörg Rüpke)

Diese Tagung im Rahmen der Kolleg-Forschergruppe ‚Religiöse Individualisierung in historischer Perspektive' fand in Kooperation mit dem Classics Department der University of Chicago statt. Ausgangspunkt war die Rolle, die der Begriff ‚privat' im modernen Denken über das Individuum spielt, im Vergleich mit der antiken Konzeptualisierung von ‚privatus' und ‚publicus'. Während Religion etwa im liberalen angloamerikanischen Diskurs vielfach als Privatangelegenheit begriffen wird, spricht Cicero in seinem Dialog *Über die Gesetze* allen Individuen gerade private und öffentliche religiöse Rollen zu (2,19). Um eine Engführung zu vermeiden, aber zugleich intensive kulturelle und soziale Konstellationen untersuchen zu können, konzentrierte sich die Tagung auf die Antike, war hier aber mit der Einbeziehung von rabbinischem Judentum und frühem Islam zeitlich breit und komparativ angelegt.

Fokus war in allen untersuchten Fallbeispielen die Frage nach der Leistung der Unterscheidung von ‚öffentlich' und ‚privat' und den Veränderungen, wie Clifford Ando und Jörg Rüpke in ihrer Einleitung erläuterten. Eine erste Gruppe von Diskussionen auf der Basis der vorab gelesenen Beiträge befasste sich mit rechtlichen Konstruktionen. Edward Harris (Manchester) fragte nach der Rollenabgrenzung von Familie und Staat im attischen Recht bei Mord, Judith Evans-Grubbs (Emory University) untersuchte den Übergang von Privatem in Öffentliches im Falle von illegitimer Nachkommenschaft und Inzest. Natalie Dohrmann aus Philadelphia thematisierte die Durchdringung von privater und öffentlicher Sphäre in rabbinischer Rechtskultur. Ahmed El-Shamsy (Chicago) lenkte den Blick auf dasselbe Problem im frühen islamischen Recht.

Eine zweite Gruppe von Fällen fragte nach der öffentlichen Thematisierung und Normierung von Religion im Medium des Rechts. Rubina Raja (Aarhus) stellte die Nutzung öffentlichen Raumes für private religiöse Ereignisse (und die daraus resultierende Problematisierung der Unterscheidung) für das syrische Palmyra vor, William van Andringa (Lille) legte den Fall privater Tempelstiftungen in römischen Kolonien vor. Dieses Beispiel konnte dann mit dem hauptstädtischen Rechtsdiskurs im Kampf Ciceros um sein den Göttern von Dritten geweihtes Eigentum (Elisabeth Begemann, Erfurt) abgeglichen warden. Salvatore Randazzo aus Catania führte den komplexen Fall religiöser Vereine und der diesbezüglichen Rechtsbildung vor.

Religiöse Vorstellungen und Diskurse bildeten den Gegenstand der dritten Gruppe, in der Claudia Bergmann (Erfurt) eschatologische Zuspitzungen von öffentlich oder privat in Bankett-Vorstellungen, Catherine Hezser (SOAS, London) Überlegungen zu Funktionen einer neutralen Zone zwischen öffentlich und privat im rabbinischen Denken und Esther Eidinow (Manchester) Fragen nach der Zugänglichkeit des privaten Denkens bei Menschen und Göttern zur Diskussion stellte.

Die Notwendigkeit, die je unterschiedlichen begrifflichen und sozialen Strategien zu unterscheiden, fügte sich gut mit dem vergleichenden Befund ähnlicher Lösungen und Probleme zusammen: Ort und Stellenwert individueller Intention und Reflexionen sowie die Komplexitätssteigerung in städtischen Gesellschaften bildeten dabei die Pole der Diskussion und die wichtigsten Erträge der Tagung.

Workshop der Kolleg-Forschergruppe ‚Religiöse Individualisierung in historischer Perspektive' am Max-Weber-Kolleg und des Großprojektes ‚Meister Eckhart und die Pariser Universität' am King's College London vom 14. bis 15. November 2013 in Erfurt, gefördert vom britischen AHRC, in Verbindung mit der Meister Eckhart-Gesellschaft: ‚Thomas von Erfurt und Meister Eckhart' (Markus Vinzent)

Thomas von Erfurt wurde bekannt als Verfasser einer an der Universität Paris vielgelesenen philosophisch-systematischen Grammatik (veröffentlicht um 1310). Er war aber mehr als nur Autor dieses systematischen Lehrbuches. Als Magister in Erfurt an St. Severus und vermutlich auch am Schottenkloster und an anderen Stiftsschulen, deren Rektor er zeitweise war, machte er sich als Zeitgenosse Meister Eckharts einen Namen, der damals in Erfurt als Provinzial der Dominikaner residierte. Trotz seiner Bedeutung blieb Thomas in seiner eigenen Wirkstätte Erfurt bislang weithin unbekannt, seine Beziehung zu Meister Eckhart ist noch ungeklärt, und innerhalb der philosophischen Forschung ist sein Werk in Europa unterbeleuchtet, während in den USA Thomas von Erfurt schon länger untersucht wird. Dass er gerade in seiner Heimat und in Europa wenig beachtet wird, ist umso erstaunlicher, als bekanntermaßen seine spekulative Grammatik (die bis ins 20. Jh. unter dem Namen des Duns Scotus bekannt war) eine wichtige Anregung für Ch. Pierce und seine Ausbildung der Semiotik bildete und dieses Werk (wenn auch noch vermeintlich als Schrift Duns Scotus') den Ausgangspunkt für die Habilitationsschrift Martin Heideggers darstellte. Thomas hat folglich Heidegger einen wesentlichen Anstoß für die Ausbildung seiner Philosophie gegeben.

Der Workshop beabsichtigte, in interdisziplinärer Kooperation auf Thomas von Erfurt aufmerksam zu machen und insbesondere die Diskursbeziehung zwischen Thomas und Eckhart und die Verbindung von Erfurt und Paris herauszustellen und inhaltlich die Verschränkung von Grammatik, Metaphysik und Bibelexegese in Erfahrung zu bringen.

Der Workshop fand im Max-Weber-Kolleg vom 14. bis 15. November 2013 statt, organisiert von Markus Vinzent und Dietmar Mieth. Die Eröffnung übernahm Christian Lehmann (Sprachwissenschaft, Erfurt) mit einem einführenden Einblick in die

Grammatik des Thomas von Erfurt. Gefolgt wurde er von einer ersten Sektion, die die Bedeutung Thomas' in der philosophischen Rezeption beleuchtete: Andrés Quero-Sánchez (Philosoph, MWK) referierte über Thomas von Erfurt bei Martin Heidegger, Gesche Linde (Theologin, Darmstadt, Fellow MWK) über Thomas von Erfurt bei Charles Peirce und Stephan Grotz (Philosoph, Hamburg) über Spuren der modistischen Grammatik in der Metaphysik Eckharts. In einem Abendvortrag sprach Oliver Davies (King's College, London) zur Hermeneutik, Metaphysik und Mystik.

Am zweiten Tag wurde das Verhältnis zwischen Thomas von Erfurt und Meister Eckhart näher betrachtet. Claire Taylor Jones (Germanistik, Notre Dame, USA) wies auf Einflüsse des Thomas auf Eckhart, Dietmar Mieth (Theologe, Tübingen, Fellow MWK) sprach über den Einfluss der Modistik auf Meister Eckharts Bibelexegese und Markus Vinzent (Theologe und Historiker, Fellow MWK) über Thomas, Eckhart und Paris mit Blick auf die Bedeutung von Personalpronomen im Denken beider.

Tagung an der Katholischen Akademie in Bayern vom 28. bis 30. März 2014 in Zusammenarbeit mit der Meister Eckhart Gesellschaft und dem Max-Weber-Kolleg, gefördert durch die Deutsche Forschungsgemeinschaft: ‚Meister Eckhart interreligiös' (Dietmar Mieth)

Die Unmittelbarkeit der individuellen religiösen Einsicht ist etwas, das alle Religionen prägt. Was ist dabei das Einzigartige, das Meister Eckhart heute zu einem religiösen Botschafter überall in der Welt macht? Der Name ‚Meister Eckhart' ist wie ein Schlüssel, der die Tür zum Gespräch öffnet.

Die Tagung erörtert in verschiedenen fachlichen Zugängen die Grundlagen eines interreligiösen Diskurses. Eckhart ist ein Prüfstein dieses Gespräches, u.a. auch am Max-Weber-Kolleg. Das Einzigartige in der interreligiösen Aufmerksamkeit für Meister Eckhart könnte u.a. darin bestehen: Es ist Meister Eckharts Absicht, in der Menschwerdung Gottes das Menschentum jedes Menschen zu würdigen. Maßgebliche Grundzüge seines eigenen Denkens verdankt Meister Eckhart zudem nicht nur der christlichen Tradition, sondern dem jüdischen Religionsphilosophen Moses Maimonides und islamischen Philosophen.

Hinsichtlich der interreligiösen Wirkung Meister Eckharts wird oft nach dem Buddhismus gefragt. Daher hat Shizuteru Ueda, der 1965 über Meister Eckhart promoviert hat, der langjährige dritte Leiter des Zen-buddhistischen Instituts in Kyoto, den öffentlichen Abendvortrag gehalten.

Die Verbindung der indischen Religiosität in ihren unterschiedlichen Ausprägungen mit Meister Eckhart ist seit dem 19. Jahrhundert ein Thema, teilweise auch über die Theosophie vermittelt. Sowohl in Indien, z.B. im Bhakti, als auch im Islam, im Sufismus, ist die Liebe mit Selbsthingabe und Offenheit für das Göttliche verbunden. Islamische Wissenschaftler suchen etwa, Ibn Arrabi und Rumi mit Meister Eckhart ins Gespräch zu bringen. Aber es gibt auch Differenzen, z.B. in der Wahrnehmung des Körpers in den Formen der mystischen Versenkung, im Verständnis des Göttlichen und in Bezug auf die Institutionen der Gesellschaft.

Meister Eckhart wird auch in einer literarischen ‚Mystik' auf jeweils eigene Weise rezipiert, z.B. auch in der deutschen Literatur (genannt werden hier gern Rilke, Musil, Celan). ‚Mystik statt Religion' sehen manche als Weg in die Zukunft.

Die Zusammenarbeit der beteiligten Institutionen (Kolleg-Forschergruppe am Max-Weber-Kolleg, Meister Eckhart-Gesellschaft, Katholische Akademie in Bayern) war reibungslos und vorzüglich. Die Betreuung der Referent/inn/en, die Versorgung der Teilnehmer/innen und die Organisation des Programmablaufs wurden sehr gut aufgenommen. Vor allem das Niveau, zugleich die Bemühung um Verständlichkeit und die konstruktive Stimmung in den Debatten wurden sehr gelobt. Für alle Vorträge standen auch Kurztexte zur Verfügung. Die Diskussion war stets rege. Der Zuspruch von akademischen Teilnehmer/inn/en war darüber hinaus sehr groß, stets über 200, beim Abendvortrag Uedas 300 Personen.

Internationale Tagung vom 11. bis 13. Juni 2014 am Max-Weber-Kolleg, gefördert durch die Deutsche Forschungsgemeinschaft: ‚Realizing Justice? Encountering Normative Justice and the Realities of (In)Justice in South Asia' (Antje Linkenbach-Fuchs)

Vom 11. bis 13. Juni 2014 fand in den Räumen des MaxWeber-Kollegs der Universität Erfurt die Tagung „Realizing Justice? Encountering Normative Justice and the Realities of (In)Justice in South Asia" statt. An der interdisziplinären Tagung nahmen 25 Wissenschaftlerinnen und Wissenschaftler aus Deutschland, Indien, Neuseeland, Großbritannien und der Schweiz teil; das Spektrum der Disziplinen umfasste Philosophie, Rechtswissenschaft, Soziologie, Ethnologie, Religionswissenschaft und Indologie. Die einzelnen Sitzungen wurden von einer Reihe interessierter Kolleginnen und Kollegen sowie Doktoranden besucht. Insgesamt stieß die Tagung auf erhebliche Resonanz, was sich u.a. an der hohen Teilnahmebereitschaft der von den Organisatoren eingeladenen Personen zeigte, sowie an den intensiven und ergiebigen Diskussionen nach den Vorträgen und in der Abschlusssitzung. Die Veranstaltung zeichnete sich aus durch verschiedene Zugangsweisen zu der Tagungsthematik. Einige Beiträge stellten normativ-theoretische und konzeptionelle Überlegungen zu den Begriffen von Gerechtigkeit und Recht aus westlicher und indischer (textwissenschaftlicher) Perspektive in den Mittelpunkt; die überwiegende Zahl der Referenten und Referentinnen aber widmete sich der Frage nach Gerechtigkeit aus einer realitäts- und realisierungsorientierten Perspektive. Sie präsentierten Überlegungen, die auf eigener historischer bzw. gegenwartsbezogener empirischer Forschung zum Thema Gerechtigkeit in unterschiedlichen gesellschaftlichen Feldern sowie Regionen Indiens basierte. Stark thematisiert wurden die Pluralität von Gerechtigkeitsvorstellungen und

Gerechtigkeitsakteuren, die vielfältigen institutionellen und nicht-institutionellen Versuche der Realisierung von Gerechtigkeit (staatliche, nicht-staatliche), sowie die verschiedenen Formen existierender Ungerechtigkeit und die Reaktionen darauf.

Mit einem systematisierenden Überblick über vier zentrale und jeweils in sich plurale Dimensionen von Gerechtigkeit eröffnete Gunnar Folke Schuppert (Rechtswissenschaft) die Tagung. Andreas Pettenkofer (Soziologie) plädierte für einen pragmatistisch-soziologischen Umgang mit der Gerechtigkeitsfrage und verlangte, neben einer Betrachtung der normativen Ordnungen verstärkt die interaktive Situation von Gesellschaftssubjekten (real world situations) in den Blick zu nehmen. Der vergleichende Beitrag von Winfried Hinsch (Philosophie) und Dorothea Schulz (Ethnologie) konzentrierte sich auf Probleme, die sich für universalistische Gerechtigkeitskonzeptionen in post-kolonialen Kontexten mit dem für sie spezifischen Pluralismus religiöser und weltanschaulicher Zugehörigkeiten ergeben. Mahendra Singh (Rechtswissenschaft) leitete mit seinem Beitrag zum Konzept der Gerechtigkeit in der indischen Verfassung zu normativen Ordnungen und Realitäten auf dem südasiatischen Subkontinent über. Er betonte vor allem, dass die Indian Constitution die Idee von Gerechtigkeit bereits in ihrer (verpflichtenden) Präambel aufgreift und sich dabei vor allem an marginalisierte Gruppen richtet.

Vier Beiträge befassten sich mit Normen und Realitäten von Gerechtigkeit in Indien aus textwissenschaftlicher und/oder historischer Sicht. Nach deutlicher Kritik an Amartya Sens Fokus auf *niti* und *nyaya* als zentrale Rechtsbegriffe im hinduistischen Indien präsentierte Patrick Olivelle (Indologie) *dharma* als das Konzept, welches es erlaube, Vorstellungen von Recht, Pflicht und Gerechtigkeit im hinduistischen Kontext auszudrücken. Auch Timothy Lubin (Religion Südasiens) rückte *dharma* ins Zentrum seines Beitrags. Er konfrontierte spätmittelalterliche Inschriften zu Eigentumstransaktionen mit normativ-theoretischen Aussagen in der Sanskrit Dharmashastra Literatur. Bei den Beiträgen von Lindsey Harlan und Peter Gottschalk (beide Religionswissenschaft) standen lokale Geschichte(n), Heldenerzählungen und Erinnerungskultur im Mittelpunkt. Harlan konzentrierte sich auf die Repräsentation und Verehrung zweier Heldenfiguren im urbanen Rajasthan und diskutierte Gerechtigkeitsvorstellungen im Kontext von Gewalt. Gottschalk thematisierte die narrative bzw. mythische Rekonstruktion von Aspekten der Ungerechtigkeit in der sozialen Ordnung am Beispiel eines Dorfes in Bihar.

Die Situation der indischen Dalit lässt die Widersprüche zwischen normativ geforderter Gerechtigkeit und realen Verhältnissen der Marginalisierung und sogar Gewalt in Indien besonders deutlich erscheinen. Daniel Gold (Religionswissenschaft) stellte zwei Dalit-Gruppen vor, die auf ihre sozio-ökonomische Situation unterschiedlich reagieren und damit auf ein unterschiedliches Verständnis von Gerechtigkeit (partikular vs. universal) verweisen. Beatrice Renzi (Ethnologie) verdeutlichte die Intersektionalität der Diskriminierung und die daraus erwachsende Dynamik der Ungerechtigkeit. Julia Eckert (Ethnologie) griff erneut die Frage nach alternativen Norm-vorstellungen und Gerechtigkeitskonzeptionen auf. Sie konfrontierte unterschiedliche Begründungsstrategien und zeigte, dass die von einer Gruppe eingeforderten Rechte (auf Land, Menschenwürde, citizenship etc.) von anderen Teilen der Gesellschaft nicht notwendig akzeptiert werden müssen. Shalini Randeria (Ethnologie) versuchte in ihrem Beitrag eine Analyse institutionalisierter Agenten des Rechts und der Gerechtigkeit. Bezogen auf zwei Entwicklungsgroßprojekte in Indien im ländlichen und im urbanen Raum thematisierte sie die Dynamiken, die im Kontext von Neoliberalismus und Globalisierung zu einer fundamentalen Veränderung der Funktionen und Aufgaben von NGOs, Gerichten und Administration und damit auch zu einem Wandel im der Bedeutung von Recht und Gerechtigkeit geführt haben. Normative Ideen und praktische Formen der Gerechtigkeitsfindung existieren nicht nur im säkularen Kontext, sie sind auch für den religiösen Bereich prägend.

Zwei Beiträge der Konferenz haben sich mit dem Phänomen der göttlichen Gerechtigkeit in Kumaon (Zentralhimalaya) befasst. Monika Krengel (Ethnologie) verwies zunächst auf das Nebeneinander und die gleichzeitige Inanspruchnahme verschiedener Alternativen der Gerechtigkeitsfindung (staatliche Gerichte, customary law, Gottheiten). Eine Gottheit der Gerechtigkeit (*nyay ka devta*) mit Namen Goludev stand bei Aditya Malik (Religionswissenschaft) im Zentrum seines Beitrags. Goludevs Sensibilität für Ungerechtigkeit habe seine Quelle in der eigenen Unrechtserfahrung, eine Tatsache, die ihn auch für Niedrigkastige und Frauen attraktiv mache. Der letzte Beitrag von Antje Linkenbach-Fuchs (Ethnologie) widmete sich dem Thema der Umweltgerechtigkeit. Sie hinterfragte die dem Begriff implizite Annahme einer Vereinbarkeit von Sorge um die Umwelt und Wunsch nach sozialer Gerechtigkeit und spürte dem Verhältnis beider Forderungen am Beispiel zweier aktueller tribaler (international unterstützter) Umweltbewegungen in Indien nach. Das Zusammenspiel von Gerechtigkeitssuche und sustainability in diesen beiden Fällen rührt aus ihrer Sicht daher, dass beide Forderungen Teil sind von Ansprüchen auf höherer Ebene: dem Anspruch auf Anerkennung (von Differenz) und dem Ideal eines selbstbestimmten guten und würdevollen Lebens, das auf einem respektvollen Umgang mit der natürlichen Umwelt basiert.

Unter den Tagungsteilnehmern bestand Konsens, dass es sinnvoll und ergiebig war, den Blick auf die Formen gelebter, realisierter Gerechtigkeit bzw. Ungerechtigkeit in nicht-westlichen Ländern (hier: Südasien) zu lenken, ohne die normative Ebene aus den Augen zu verlieren. Als besonders positiv erschien es, dass Normen und Realitäten in historischer und regionaler Perspektive betrachtet, d.h. Begrifflichkeiten sowie Praktiken in ihrer jeweiligen zeitlich spezifischen Ausformung und Entwicklung, aber auch in ihrer regionalen Partikularität analysiert wurden. Durch diese Vorgehensweise konnten neue Erkenntnisse gewonnen und weiterführende Problemstellungen identifiziert werden. Die Tagungsergebnisse sollen in einer Publikation einer breiteren Öffentlichkeit zugänglich gemacht werden.

Internationale Konferenz vom 24. bis 26. September 2014 an der Bergischen Universität Wuppertal in Kooperation mit dem Max-Weber-Kolleg, gefördert durch die DFG: „‚... man könnte fast sagen: die Satire flucht und der Humor betet.' Humor und Religiosität in der Moderne" (Markus Kleinert)

In der Einführung wurde zunächst in Anlehnung an Wittgenstein das Verhältnis von der gegenwärtig gewöhnlichen Verwendung des Humorbegriffs und jener emphatischen Bedeutung erörtert, die der Humor in der Kunst und Philosophie seit der Aufklärung erhalten hat und die primärer Anlass ist, den Humor auf dieser Tagung als Artikulation von Religiosität unter den Bedingungen der Moderne zu thematisieren. (Gerald Hartung, Wuppertal) Dann wurden zwei Aspekte des Tagungsthemas hervorgehoben: zum einen die Rekonstruktion, die Untersuchung kanonischer wie vernachlässigter Beiträge zum modernen Humor unter besonderer Berücksichtigung religiöser Implikationen; zum anderen die Gegenwartsrelevanz dieser Rekonstruktion, insofern sie zu einer Klärung anhält, was unter spezifisch moderner Religiosität zu verstehen ist; so kann die Beschäftigung mit dem Humor – in kritischer Reflexion der großen Narrative zur Moderne (Rationalisierung, Säkularisierung, Individualisierung) – zu einer Theorie der modernen Kultur beitragen (Markus Kleinert, Erfurt).

Um Humor und Religiosität als Habitus zueinander ins Verhältnis setzen zu können, ging Volkhard Krech (Bochum) von der Untersuchung des jeweiligen Wortfelds aus, wobei er gegenüber der Konzentration auf den vor allem in der Tradition Jean Pauls metaphysizierten ‚Welt-Humor' für die Berücksichtigung auch bescheidenerer, banaler bzw. banalisierter Erscheinungsformen des Humors plädierte. Auf dieser Basis wurden dann verschiedene Verbindungen von humoristischem und religiösem Habitus dargestellt, von der einseitigen Integration (etwa der mystische Begriff von Gelassenheit als humoristisches Moment innerhalb einer religiösen Haltung) bis zum wechselseitigen Korrektiv (wenn Humor und Religiosität als eigenständige Formen des Umgangs mit Kontingenz der Verabsolutierung einer Form entgegenwirken). Zu dieser Darstellung bot der Vortrag von Gerhard Danzer (Berlin) insofern ein Gegenstück, als darin gerade der – mit Harald Höffdings Begriff – ‚große Humor' behandelt wurde, und zwar in exemplarischer Abgrenzung von dem mit Freud gedeuteten Witz und dem mit Bergson gedeuteten Komischen. Die humoristische Weltanschauung äußert sich demnach nicht im Verlachen des an eine dreigliedrige Sozialstruktur gebundenen Witzes oder dem auf Wiedereinbeziehung des Gegenübers zielenden Lachen der Komik, sondern im Lächeln einer souveränen Persönlichkeit, die sich der gewöhnlichen Wirklichkeit bewusst und ihr zugleich spielerisch überlegen ist. Die Frage, ob dieses Lächeln als Sinnbild des Humors gelten kann und inwieweit es ggf. affirmative oder subversive Züge hat, sowie die Frage nach dem Verhältnis zwischen dem Humor als Weltanschauung und den alltäglichen Formen des Humors wurden im weiteren Verlauf der Tagung wiederholt diskutiert.

Nach den beiden systematisch überblickshaften Darstellungen beleuchtete eine Reihe von Vorträgen einzelne philosophische und künstlerische Beiträge zum Humor in der Moderne. Oliver Koch (Bochum) erläuterte Jean Pauls Humorkonzept, das sich durch den emphatischen Transzendenzbezug von der vorangehenden englischen Tradition abhebt und – in Übereinstimmung mit Jacobis Philosophie – in einer Doppelstellung gegen die bloße Differenz negativer Theologie und die bloße Identität des Pantheismus behauptet. Michael Scheffel (Wuppertal) deutete E.T.A. Hoffmanns Prinzessin Brambilla in einer detaillierten Textinterpretation als gelungene Umsetzung des frühromantischen Entwurfs einer Tranzendentalpoesie, insofern darin Reflexivität auf allen Erzählebenen verwirklicht und zugleich – unter den Stichworten Humor und Einbildungskraft – aus der Statik der Spiegelung in einen allumfassenden Prozess überführt wird, in den nicht zuletzt der Rezipient einbezogen ist. Lydia B. Amir (Rishon LeZion) untersuchte vor allem die epistemologische Funktion des Humors bei Shaftesbury, Hamann und Kierkegaard: vom ‚test of ridicule' über die Kritik eines verabsolutierten Verstandes bis zum Komikverständnis als Indikator der jeweiligen Existenzweise.

Einer vergleichsweise vernachlässigten Position der Philosophiegeschichte wandte sich Gerald Hartung zu, indem er die Humortheorie von Moritz Lazarus als Verhaltenslehre für den Menschen der säkularen Moderne deutete: an die Stelle einer Aufhebung tritt darin das humoristische Ausgleichen bestehenbleibender Gegensätze, metaphorisch: der Friedensschluss. Auf einen solchen Frieden zielt auch das Humorkonzept von Hermann Cohen, dessen Herausbildung Andrea Poma (Turin) nachzeichnete; der Humor verhindert demnach als übergeordnete temperierende Instanz die Verabsolutierung einzelner ästhetischer, ethischer oder religiöser Positionen. In schroffem Gegensatz zum befriedenden Humor bei Lazarus und Cohen steht Nietzsches radikal kritisches und selbstkritisches Lachen, wie Silvia Stoller (Wien) mit Bezug auf ‚Die Fröhliche Wissenschaft' und ‚Also sprach Zarathustra' ausführte (wobei die Gefährdung solcher Radikalität durch einen Verweis auf Canettis Blendung angedeutet wurde). Mittels begriffsgeschichtlicher Rekonstruktion arbeitete Markus Kleinert an Werken von Jean Paul, Peter Hille und Fontane heraus, welche religiösen Implikationen in der gängigen Rede von ‚verklärendem Humor' und ‚humoristischer Verklärung' enthalten sein können.

Klaus-Dieter Osthövener (Wuppertal) untersuchte das Verhältnis von Humor und Religion in der klassischen Moderne anhand von mythologischen und gleichnishaften Texten Kafkas, Musils Mann ohne Eigenschaften sowie Thomas Manns Doktor Faustus, wobei – neben verschiedenen Weisen der Wechselwirkung zwischen Kunst und Religion – auch die zur humoristischen Referenz auf Religion gegenläufige Tendenz zur Wiedergewinnung unbedingten Ernstes deutlich wurde. Ebenfalls dem Zeitraum der klassischen Moderne widmete sich Harald Tausch (Gießen), allerdings anhand einer Familiengeschichte: der des Kunsthistorikers Gustav Friedrich Hartlaub und seines Sohnes, des Schriftstellers und Künstlers Felix Hartlaub (sowie des persönlichen Umfelds, zu dem etwa der Kunsthistoriker Wilhelm Fraenger zählt); zu den in diesem Kreis verhandelten Themen gehört auch der Humor, letztlich ein Versuch, den Autonomieanspruch des Subjekts mit dessen geschichtlicher Bestimmtheit zusammenzubringen – und das mit praktischen Konsequenzen, wie an den sozialen Strukturen, Publikationswegen und Texten gezeigt wurde, die im Kreis der Hartlaubs während des Nationalsozialismus entstehen.

Eine wichtige Ergänzung zu diesen primär philosophisch und literarisch ausgerichteten Beiträgen bot Wolfgang Rathert (München), der – nach einem allgemeinen Überblick über das Verhältnis von Musik und Religion – anhand von Werken Robert Schumanns (z.B. der Humoreske op. 20 mit der unhörbaren „Inneren Stimme") und Gustav Mahlers erörterte, in welchen Hinsichten sich die Kennzeichnungen humoristisch und religiös überhaupt auf musikalische Werke anwenden lassen. Will man die Referate und Diskussionen auf eine Formel bringen, so könnte man sagen: der Humor ist ein ebenso vertrautes wie strittiges Mittel zur Idealisierung der Realität – wobei Wesensbestimmungen, Erscheinungsformen und Bewertungen dieser Idealisierung thematisiert wurden. Eine besondere Attraktion bildete die Lesung von Brigitte Kronauer aus ihrem im Vorjahr erschienenen Roman ‚Gewäsch und Gewimmel', die als öffentliche Veranstaltung im Von der Heydt-Museum Wuppertal stattfand. Der Journalist Nikolaus Halmer verfasste für den Österreichischen Rundfunk einen Bericht über die Tagung (http://science.orf.at/stories/1747532/). Gefördert wurde die Tagung durch die Deutsche Forschungsgemeinschaft (DFG), die Gesellschaft der Freunde der Bergischen Universität sowie von der Stadtsparkasse Wuppertal. Eine Veröffentlichung der Tagungsbeiträge ist geplant.

‚Meister Eckhart-Forschung und religiöse Individualisierung im Spätmittelalter', Workshop am 11. Dezember 2014 im Rahmen der KFG-Forschergruppe ‚Religiöse Individualisierung in historischer Perspektive' (Dietmar Mieth)

Die Absicht dieses eintägigen Workshops war es, Forschungsstände miteinander ins Gespräch zu bringen. Zum einen ging es dabei in Ergänzung zur Meister Eckhart-Tagung in München 2012 darum, die Untersuchungen zur ‚Religiösen Individualisierung' im deutschen und lateinischen Werk Eckharts zu erweitern. Zum anderen sollten auch andere Spuren der religiösen Individualisierung im Mittelalter ergänzt und damit ins Gespräch gebracht werden. Dazu dienten die beiden Beiträge von Anneke Mulder-Bakker (Religionshistorikerin, Groningen, Fellow am Max-Weber-Kolleg) und Martina Roesner (Philosophin, Wien). Beide bezogen sich auf das Eucharistie-Verständnis. Frau Mulder-Bakker entfaltete anhand des Lebenswerkes der Begründerin der Fronleichnamsprozession (Juliana von Lüttich) deren Initiative zu einer volksnahen und öffentlichen Begegnung mit der leibhaft sichtbaren Eucharistie sowie die fördernde und zugleich einschränkende Behandlung dieser Initiative durch Papst Urban IV, der Erzdiakon in Lüttich gewesen war. Das Fest wurde 1264 eingeführt, die Liturgie aber – durch Thomas von Aquin – im Auftrag umgeschrieben. Frau Roesner zeichnete anhand der einschlägigen deutschen Werke Eckharts eine sehr spezielle

Eucharistielehre nach, die von vorneherein als Entfaltung der naturalen Schöpfungsmacht Gottes betrachtet wird und den iterativen Vorgang der Gottesgeburt in einem wirkmächtigen Zeichen pointiert und exemplifiziert. Chris Wojtulewicz (London) machte mit den Reaktionen auf Eckhart und seine Pariser *Quaestionen* vertraut, indem er anhand verschiedener handschriftlicher Notizen in Kompilationen von *Quaestionen* nachwies, inwieweit Eckharts Themen aufgegriffen wurden. Jana Ilnicka (Rom, Saarbrücken) behandelte insbesondere den Begriff ‚relatio' in der für Eckhart typischen Form der Beziehungslehre, die (nicht nur bei ihm) in Spannung zum Substanzbegriff steht, den Eckhart unter anderen Voraussetzungen beibehält. Hierbei behandelte sie insbesondere die erste der beiden Pariser *Quaestionen* (enthalten in den von Markus Vinzent wiederentdeckten *Quaestionen* Eckharts), die das Thema der ‚relatio' behandeln. Andres Quero-Sánchez (Philosophie, Max-Weber-Kolleg) erarbeitete anhand der Texte zur ‚Spekulativen Grammatik' (Boethius von Dacia, Thomas von Erfurt) deren Beziehungen und Spannungen zu Meister Eckhart, vor allem unter der Perspektive des Realismus und des Idealismus bzw. der ‚mystischen Vernunft' (bei Eckhart). Christian Ströbele (Fundamentaltheologie, Tübingen) verfolgte in Korrespondenz das Thema der Vernunft bei Anselm von Canterbury und Meister Eckhart als wechselseitige Implikation von Wahrheit, Rechtheit und Gerechtigkeit. Dabei beleuchtete er auch sprachgeschichtlich den Zusammenhang von ‚gerade ausgerichtet' und ‚gerecht'. Dietmar Mieth behandelte das Verhältnis von Interiorisierung (‚Innerlichkeit') und Individualisierung am Beispiel der Unmittelbarkeit der spirituellen Erfahrung bei Eckhart aber auch bei den signifikanten Beginn, insbesondere Marguerite Porete. Mit dem Workshop wurde auch das Interesse an den religiösen Frauenbewegungen verstärkt. Dazu wurde der Arbeitskreis am Max-Weber-Kolleg (mit Sabine Schmolinsky), der sich mit diesem Thema beschäftigt, zur aktiven Teilnahme eingeladen.

Internationale Jahrestagung der Meister-Eckhart-Gesellschaft und der Albert-Ludwigs-Universität Freiburg in Kooperation mit der Katholischen Akademie der Erzdiözese Freiburg in Freiburg i.Br. und dem Max-Weber-Kolleg vom 13. bis 15. März 2015: „Von ‚Schwester Katrei' bis zum ‚Frankfurter' – Meister Eckharts Wirkung im 14. und 15. Jahrhundert" (Dietmar Mieth)

Die Tagung war international hochgradig besetzt (London, Bern, Paris, Colmar, Lecce, Moskau). Sie zeigte insbesondere, welche Dynamik sich schon in der frühen Eckhart-Überlieferung erkennen lässt, wenn sich verschiedene Fächer (Germanistik, Philosophie, Geschichte, Theologie) interdisziplinär der Eckhart-Rezeption widmen. Das Eckhart-Bild der Moderne hat seine Vorläufer schon in den Redaktoren und Schreibern während und kurz nach Eckharts Lebenszeit. Dabei treffen Eckharts Texte auf individualisierte Konzepte ihrer Schreiber und anderer Rezeptoren. Besondere Aufmerksamkeit wurde daher auf der Tagung den Schreibstuben zuteil. Es ging um die Individualitäten der Schreiber, um die Ökonomie des Schreibens, um die Handschriften als „Wissensspeicher", um die Selektion für bestimmte Zwecke, z.B. für die Moral im Kloster, insbesondere auch aufgrund der Volkssprache für Laienbrüder. Die Volkssprache avanciert dabei zur Formelsprache. Hier war bereits der Ansatzpunkt für das Eröffnungsreferat von Freimut Löser (Augsburg): „Unser Eckhart", wie Schreiber „ihren" deutschen Eckhart bezeichnen. Bereits im „Paradisus animae intelligentis" (vor 1341), der 32 Eckhart-Predigten enthält, findet man seitens der Thüringer Dominikaner eine Akademisierung und Latinisierung als Konzeption vor. Eckharts Text über die „minne" DW III, Pr. 60, 22,3-7 kann geradezu als Widerspruch zu dieser thematischen Ausrichtung und Profilierung gelesen werden.

Die germanistische Forschung brachte weitere Erträge in die Tagung ein, die das lebendige Weiterwirken Eckharts im spirituellen Schriftgut aufzeigen. Regina Schiewers (Eichstätt) Beitrag über den „Seelenwinkel" (eine Straßburger Hs. des 15. Jh.) verwies auf eine namentliche Zuordnung zu Eckhart in einer Spruchsammlung. Michael Hopf (Augsburg) untersuchte Eckhart-Legenden, also Textzeugen, die Eckhart als inszenierte literarische Figur narrativ behandeln. Echten Rezeptionen der Lehre Eckharts stehen Simplifizierungen in der Sache und in Bildern gegenüber. Eckhart dient als Figur einer „dramatisierten Theologie". Lydia Wegner (Bern/Berlin) behandelte die sog. Mosaik-Traktate, insbesondere Pfeiffer Nr. XI und XIII. Im Vordergrund steht das Erlernen der Indifferenz und die gewagte Formel „den Tugenden Sterben", die an Marguerite Porete erinnert. Dagmar Gottschall (Lecce) ging auf anonyme Traktate des 14. Jahrhunderts ein, z.B. das sog. „Geistbuch". Teile stammen noch aus der Lebenszeit Meister Eckharts. Das gilt auch für Handschriften zu der Erzählung „Schwester Kathrei" (ca. 1320). Die Exzerpte werden immer wieder verkürzt weiter gereicht. Laurentiu Gafiuc (Augsburg) zeigte auf, dass die Handschriften in weitaus überwiegender Zahl im Südwesten entstanden sind. Durch das Handschriften-Händlerwesen wurden sie dann oft erst im 19. Jahrhundert anders verteilt. Sie haben ihren „Sitz im Leben" in Klöstern, insbesondere von Dominikanerinnen. Die ältesten verweisen auf 1350 in Straßburg oder Basel. Ihr jeweiliger spiritueller Zweck und Gebrauch hat Vorrang vor dem Autoren-Nachweis, den es jedoch an wenigen Stellen für Eckhart gibt. Balácz Nemes (Freiburg i.Br.) zeigte die Eckhart-Lektüre von Augustiner-Chorherren im Kloster Rebdorf im 15. Jahrhundert. Hier werden auch Kommentare geschrieben. Die Bewegung zur „devotio moderna" ist spürbar. Eckharts Verabschiedung der „gratia creata" stößt auf dogmatische Kritik.

Die Verzahnung des deutschen und des lateinischen Eckhart in der Rezeption behandelte Markus Vinzent (London/Erfurt) am Beispiel der neu zur Kenntnis genommenen und erstmals bearbeiteten Handschriften auf der Wartburg (1. Drittel 14. Jahrhundert). Dort findet sich ein ähnlicher Fall wie Eckharts lat. Vaterunser-Kommentar, der auch noch zu untersuchende Parallelen in deutschen Vaterunser-Kommentaren in handschriftlicher Eckhartumgebung aufweist. In der Wartburghandschrift finden sich Verweise auf Thomas von Aquin und Pariser Diskurse sowie auf die Eckhartschen Bibelkommentare (In Gen., In Sap.). Vinzent verweist auch auf die eigenständigen und dem Vortrag angepassten Bibelübersetzungen Eckharts aus dem Lateinischen. Dabei werde der biblische Text zugespitzt und existentiell gesteigert. Klaus-Bernwart Springer (Erfurt/Köln) behandelte Eckharts Wirkungen im Dominikanerorden im 14. und 15. Jahrhundert. Er listete vielfältige Zeugnisse auf, die z.T. noch in Eckharts Lebenszeit gehören. Der (Buch-)Historiker Gilbert Fournier (Colmar/Paris) lieferte neue und überraschende Erkenntnisse zur Eckhart-Rezeption bei Nikolaus Cusanus. Er hat die Handschrift Bernkastel-Kues, St. Nikolaus Hospital 21 genauer untersucht. Diese zeigt den lateinischen Eckhart in einem neuen Licht und eröffnet den Zugang zu einer widersprüchlichen Rezeption der Bulle „In agro dominico", die auch im 15. Jahrhundert übersetzt wurde. Mikhail Korkhov (Moskau) beschrieb die lateinischen Übersetzungen deutscher Schriften von Meister Eckhart. Bei Johannes Wenck im 15. Jahrhundert finden sich Zitate z.B. aus dem Buch der göttlichen Tröstung und aus der Predigt DW 2. Eine Koblenzer Handschrift enthält die Übersetzungen ins Lateinische: Pr. 2, 6 und 52 (geistl. Armut), von der Geburt (Pfeiffer 475–478), ferner die Legende von Meister Eckharts „Wirtschaft". Wenck sieht 1430 in Heidelberg den verurteilten Eckhart in einer Linie mit Wyclif, Hus und den Begarden. Abschließende aktualisierende Bemerkungen (Dietmar Mieth, Tübingen/Erfurt): Die vielfältige Rezeption Meister Eckharts ist oft über geflügelte Worte bekannt. So z.B. in Bezug auf die Gottesgeburt. Gern wird Angelus Silesius zitiert: „Und wäre Christus tausendmal geboren und nicht in dir, du wärest doch verloren." Was bei Meister Eckhart eine Ansage für die Gemeinschaft des Menschen mit Gott ist, wird hier zu einer Drohung ausgedeutet. Daran kann man erkennen, wie sehr Rezeptionen verändern können, indem sie scheinbar ein Motiv erhalten. Die Erkenntnis, dass Rezeptionen ambivalent sind, zog sich wie ein roter Faden durch die Tagung.

,Die Stimme des Autors. Religiöse Innovation in hellenistisch-römischer Zeit', internationale Tagung vom 20. bis 22. Mai 2015 im Rahmen der Kolleg-Forschergruppe ,Religiöse Individualisierung in historischer Perspektive' im Augustinerkloster in Erfurt mit Unterstützung der DFG, der Fritz-Thyssen-Stiftung und in Zusammenarbeit mit ,Homines novi', Aarhus/AUFF (Eve-Marie Becker, Jörg Rüpke)

Eminente Texte der antiken literarischen *kanones* sind durch ihre Verfasser nicht nur – historisch und literarisch – ,autorisiert', sondern das jeweilige Konzept von Autorschaft wirkt auf die Produktion und Rezeption eines Textes direkt ein. Die Autorkonzeption ist damit – ähnlich dem literarischen *genre* – eine Art *template*, das literarische Texte generiert. Autorkonzeptionen erweisen sich dabei aber nicht als starre Formate, sondern sind in ihrer Rückbindung an Autoren-Personen immer auch dem Wandel und der Veränderung unterworfen. Insofern machen Autorkonzepte ein erhebliches literarisches Potential in der (antiken) Literatur aus. Das gilt, wie die Tagung zeigen konnte, besonders für den Bereich der *religiösen Literatur*. Für die Religionsgeschichte der Kaiserzeit mit ihrer enormen religiösen Produktivität, die sich ebenso in einer intensivierten religiösen Kommunikation wie in zahllosen, oft kurzlebigen, aber eben auch langfristig erfolgreichen Gruppenbildungen niederschlug, ist die Frage der literarischen Autorschaft von besonderer, auch sozio-politischer Bedeutung: Autoren waren hier nämlich vielfach auch religiöse ‚(Klein-) Unternehmer'. Die Tagung ging der Frage nach, wie bestimmte Autoren, die wir als ‚reale Autoren' bezeichnen können, sich selbst als ‚Autoren' zu erkennen und dabei ein religiöses und literarisches Profil geben. Leitenden Fragestellungen waren: Welche Elemente der literarischen Profilgebung begegnen uns? Welche ‚Autorenkonzepte' und Erzählerfiguren und -positionen werden dadurch im Bereich von religiöser Literatur geschaffen? Welcher literarischen *genres* bedienen sich die jeweiligen Autoren? Stehen Autorkonzeption und *genre* in einem inneren Zusammenhang? Findet die Autor-Profilierung innerhalb und/oder außerhalb (auto-)biographischer Texte bzw. Textteile statt? Welche erkennbaren oder verschleierten Intentionen verfolgen die Autoren mit ihrer (literarischen) Profilgebung? Geben sie selbst Hinweise auf intendierte Rezeptionsprozesse (Rezeptionsanweisungen) – gibt es ggf. selbst-kanonisierende literarische Elemente? Woran machen Zeitgenossen religiöse Innovation oder Devianz fest? Tragen Autorenprofile und deren mögliche Imitierung zur ‚religiösen Individualisierung' bei? Welche Rollenmodelle, welche Autoritätsrelationen bieten sie an? Welche Rezeptionsformen und -institutionalisierungen legen sie nahe?

Die Tagung griff diese Fragen in einer religionsgeschichtlichen Breite auf, die zeitlich bei dem ersten frühjüdischen ‚Autor' (*Ben Sira*) einsetzt und bis zum Ende des zweiten Jahrhunderts n.Chr. reichte und sich räumlich auf das Imperium Romanum richtete. Sie konzentrierte sich auf jene Sprachen und Sprachtraditionen (Griechisch, Latein, mit Seitenblicken auf das Hebräische und Syrische), die in großem Umfang den Austausch von literarischen Modellen, Institutionen literarischer Kommunikation und schließlich auch – durch Zweisprachigkeit, vor allem aber zahllose Übersetzungen – den Austausch von Textinhalten ermöglichten. Dabei wurden grundlegende Fragestellungen zum kultur- und ideengeschichtlichen Kontext der antiken Autoren mit konkreten Textinterpretationen verbunden. Als Ergebnis lässt sich festhalten: Die Frage nach Autoren in religiösen Texten zielt auf Formen und Veränderung von Autorenkonzepten in religiösen Texten des antiken Mittelmeerraums. Vorstellungen von individueller Produktion von und Verantwortung für Texte und die Orthonymie, die Angabe eines Verfassers bzw. einer Verfasserin mit Namen spielen hier eine große Rolle – eine erstaunlich große Rolle sogar, wenn man die vielen Alternativen von anonymer oder geteilter Textproduktion oder die Modifikation von Texten während des immer wieder notwendigen Abschreibens von Texten oder während der Performanz solcher Texte bedenkt.

Religiöse Texte verkomplizieren diese Situation, indem sie neben der oder dem menschlichen Textproduzenten gerade transzendenten Stimmen Platz einräumen. Gottheiten, Engel oder Gestalten der Unterwelt können als ‚eigentliche' Autoren so hinzutreten. Wenn solche Texte in einem rituellen Kontext zu Gehör gebracht werden, tritt eine weitere Rolle hinzu: die von rituellen Akteuren, seien das religiöse Spezialistinnen oder Schauspieler. Dabei mag es sich um Rezitationen in großen Auditorien vor offenem Publikum oder um das Verlesen und Interpretieren von Texten in geschlossenen kleinen Zirkeln handeln. In dieser Situation wird das explizite oder implizite Bild, das der Text oder der oder die textimmanente Erzählerin vom Autoren entwerfen, selbst zu einer Strategie, dem Text Autorität und einen bestimmten Status zu verleihen. Im engeren Sinne haben der oder die Verfasserin – dass die Gender-Komponente bei diesen Prozessen eine große Rolle spielt, steht außer Frage – damit eine große Bedeutung für die Wahrheitsansprüche oder die Relevanzansprüche des Textes. Im weiteren Sinne wird er oder sie damit zu einem zentralen Akteur in der gesellschaftlichen Wirklichkeit. Ob als religiöser Spezialist oder gar ‚religious entrepreneur' (mit Interessen an Gefolgschaft und Lebensunterhalt) betreten sie so das weite Feld von religiösen Diskursen und religiösen Praktiken.

'Creating Religion(s) by Historiography', international conference of the research group 'Religious Individualization in Historical Perspective' at the Augustinerkloster in Erfurt, June 10–12, 2015 (Jörg Rüpke)

The conference, organized by Martin Mulsow and Jörg Rüpke, was part of the research of the Kolleg-Forschergruppe 'Religious Individualisation in Historical Perspective' and financed by the German Science Foundation (DFG). To narrate one's past is one of the most important tools to define one's identity. This holds true for individuals in genealogies or conversion narratives as well as for groups and nations, bolstering their coherence and claims by national histories. Religious groups use similar tools as recent research has stressed. Given the lack or rudimentary state of religious organization, the lack of membership concepts, the contested character of orthodoxy and heresy, phenomena of 'civil religion' or widely shared practices and beliefs in many regions and epochs, the definition of the subject of a history is of paramount importance. It is by the very narrating of origins, conflicts, exclusions and alliances that the identity of the narratives' subjects, their characteristics and boundaries are defined. This is as crucial in separating believers and non-believers as in dressing the balance between religion as a collective enterprise ('religions') and religion as an individual practice ('spirituality'). If this seems typical of emic historical narratives, a closer look betrays that etic, scientific historiography usually follow these frameworks and divisions.

The conference addressed questions like: How instrumental is historiography of religion – emic and etic – in creating religions and the concept of a plural of religions as accountable social units with a history of its own? What are the terminological tools (religions, confessions, schools, sects)? What are the narrative tools (stories of oaths and treaties, of deviance, of contenders...)? What are compositional decisions to that purpose (ingroup-outgroup changes of perspectives, comparison, successions as organizing principle, definition and treatment of epochs)? Are individual or institutional historiographers reacting to or shaping processes of group formation? Are they empowering or censuring individuals? These questions were applied to the historiographical rise traditions like 'Judaism', 'Christianity', 'Buddhism' and 'Gelugpa-Buddhism' in particular, but also on founding figures like 'Moses' or 'Zoroaster'. A crucial result was the insight that such inventions were not unique but were part of ancient, medieval or modern and contemporary situations and interests, interests in genealogies or 'pureness' as well as interests of particular groups and professional agents. Such situations are responsible for very different epistemological conditions for narrating 'religion' as 'history'.

„Geschichtsschreibung (Storiografia)", Workshop vom 18. bis 19. Juni 2015 in Zusammenarbeit mit Fondazione Collegio San Carlo di Modena und École Pratique des Hautes Études Paris in Modena (Veit Rosenberger)

An der Fondazione San Carlo in Modena, mit der das Max-Weber-Kolleg seit einigen Jahren eine Kooperation verbindet, fand am 18. und 19. Juni 2015 eine Tagung unter dem Titel „Storiografia. Ricerca storica e scrittura del passato" statt. Vortragende kamen aus dem Umfeld der Fondazione San Carlo und aus der École Pratique des Hautes Études (Paris); aus Erfurt waren Dominik Fugger, Maik Patzelt und Veit Rosenberger mit von der Partie. Die Fondazione San Carlo, 1954 eingerichtet, befindet sich in den altehrwürdigen Räumen ihrer Vorgängerinstitution, dem im 17. Jahrhundert installierten „Collegio dei Nobili di San Carlo", aus dem Bischöfe und Kardinäle hervorgegangen sind. Heute ist die Fondazione San Carlo eine geisteswissenschaftlich ausgerichtete Institution, unabhängig von der Universität und deren Politik. Ferner verfügt die Fondazione San Carlo nicht nur über eine herausragende Bibliothek, barocke Prunkräume und endlose Gänge, in denen die herausragenden Absolventen vergangener Jahrhunderte in Öl portraitiert sind, sondern auch über einen weiteren streng gehüteten Schatz. Im Speicher reifen einige Liter des berühmten aceto balsamico di Modena. Der Essig ruht je ein Jahr in sieben Fässern aus verschiedenen Holzarten. Angesichts der Dauer und angesichts des Verdunstungsverlustes über sieben Jahre hinweg wird der hohe Preis für den traditionell hergestellten Balsamico-Essig verständlich. In den Vorträgen wurden zwei Themenfelder behandelt: Zum einen die Möglichkeiten einer Geschichtsschreibung der Antike, zum anderen Ansätze in der Historiographie von Ferdinand Gregorovius über Michel Foucault und Michel de Certeau bis Isaiah Berlin. Carlo Altini, Direttore scientifico der Fondazione, skizzierte in seinem Grußwort die Situation der Geisteswissenschaften, die sich allerorten in der Defensive befinden. Wenn man bedenkt, dass zu Lebzeiten Max Webers die Geschichte als Leitwissenschaft fungierte, so ist die Fallhöhe beträchtlich.

'XXI. World Congress of the International Association for the History of Religions' at the University of Erfurt, August 23–29, 2015 (Elisabeth Begemann)

From August 23 to 29, the XXI. Quinquennial World Congress of the *International Association for the History of Religions* (IAHR) was hosted at the University of Erfurt. More than 1300 scholars of religions were scheduled to present their research in almost 400 parallel panels and sessions over a period of four days. The topic of the congress, 'Dynamics of Religions: Past and Present', was outlined and presented by eighteen keynotes of leading scholars in the field of religious studies. In four daily parallel keynotes, they discussed the changes and continuities of religions and religious studies in their various fields, reflecting the four thematic areas of the congress, 'Religious Communities in Society: Adaptation and Transformation', 'Practices and Discourses: Innovation and Tradition', 'The Individual: Religiosity, Spiritualities and Individualization' and 'Methodology: Representations and Interpretations'. Keynote speakers were:

Peter Beyer (Ottawa): 'Forms of Religious Communities in Global Society: Tradition, Invention, and Transformation'
Vasudha Dalmia (Berkeley): 'Homogenizing Hinduism: A Watershed'
Cristiana Facchini (Bologna): 'Representing Judaism: Narrating, Visualizing, Performing, and Feeling a Religion'
Ingvild Saelid Gilhus (Bergen): 'Bodies, Texts and Otherness – Religious Change in Antiquity and Today'
Wouter Hanegraaff (Amsterdam): 'Fantastic Religion: Esoteric Fictionality and the Invention of Tradition'
Jeppe Sinding Jensen (Aarhus): 'No Human is an Island: Natures, Norms and Narratives'
Kim Knott (Lancaster): 'Inside Out? The (In)visibility of Religious Communities in Contemporary Societies'
Karénina Kollmar-Paulenz (Bern): 'Of Yellow Teaching and Black Faith: Entangled Knowledge Cultures and the Creation of Religious Traditions'
Suzanne Marchand (Louisiana State): 'Herodotus, Historian of World Religions: How the Reception-History of the Father of Lies Can Help Move the Conversation beyond 'Orientalism"
Sylvia Marcos (Cuernavaca): 'Transformation and Revitalization: Mesoamerican Religious Traditions'
Martin Mulsow (Erfurt/Gotha): 'Global Intellectual History and the Dynamics of Religion'
Kalpana Ram (Macquarie): 'Religion, Human Agency and Change: The Importance of Intermediary Experiences'
Hubert Seiwert (Leipzig): 'Dynamics of Religion and Cultural Evolution'

Susumu Shimazono (Tokio): 'Religion and Public Space in Contemporary Japan: The Reactivation of State Shinto and Buddhism as Public Religion'

Dianne Marie Stewart (Emory): 'From Syncretism to Social Belonging: Retheorizing Tradition and Innovation in African Heritage Religious Cultures of the Caribbean and the Americas'

Abdulkader Tayob (Kapstadt): 'The Biographical Trajectories of Political Islam'

Gerald West (Kwazulu Natal): 'Religion Intersecting De-nationalisation and Re-nationalisation in Post-Apartheid South Africa'

Xiaoyun Zheng (Peking): 'On the Management Mode of Chinese Theravada Buddhism'

The findings have been compiled in a publication, to which the abstracts of the panels and papers are added in an electronic open access version to serve as the congress proceedings (https://www.degruyter.com/view/title/516446).

The congress was preceded by two pre-conferences, of the SAMR and AESToR Net, which met on Saturday and Sunday at the Max-Weber-Kolleg Erfurt. Approximate sixty participants (invited speakers and guests) attended these conferences. The congress proper was opened Sunday, August 23, by the formal opening and keynote lecture at the Theater Erfurt. Among the guests were the Thuringian Minister President Ramelow and various honorary consuls to honor the occasion. The keynote 'Dynamics of Religion and Cultural Evolution' by Hubert Seiwert (Leipzig) was sponsored by a generous contribution by the family of the late Gary Lease and appeared in the program as Opening Keynote and Gary Lease Memorial Lecture, followed by a reception.

Congress participants came from all over the world to attend the Erfurt meeting. An approximate 50 per cent were Europeans, with the second largest percentage from Asia, followed by the Americas, Africa and c. 3 % from Australia and New Zealand. With a grant by the German Research Foundation (DFG) and by the Ernst Abbe Stiftung, Jena, organizers were able to keep the participation fee to a relatively low € 150,00 (early registration), even with a green fee added to offset some of the carbon dioxide produced during travel to and from the Congress. A total of more than thirty travel grants were awarded to allow scholars from less affluent regions and universities from all over the globe to attend the congress and present their research.

The organizers were also committed to reduce waste material and therefore to forego printed products, including a printed program, session guide or abstract book. These were only available in online versions for download from the IAHR Congress website, to which was added the congress app, sponsored by the publishing house de Gruyter. As most participants were equipped with notebooks, tablets and smart phones and because the congress provided free WiFi, this was an easy and widely accepted way of finding sessions, speakers and venues.

The academic program was supplemented by a number of receptions in the evening hours that were hosted by national associations of religious studies and publishing houses. These receptions are and were a welcome opportunity to meet colleagues and friends in a more informal atmosphere. The congress barbecue on Wednesday evening – after the traditional tour day, which gave our guests the opportunity to discover Erfurt and Thuringia – was the largest of these events, with more than 800 participants enjoying the food, drink and music.

The program of the IAHR Congress was made up of proposed panels and individually submitted papers. All papers submitted to the congress underwent anonymous peer review in order to ensure a high academic standard. The local organizing team, headed by congress directors Christoph Bochinger, Bayreuth, and Jörg Rüpke, Erfurt, approached sixteen leading scholars to act as program committee, reviewing more than 1600 proposals, most of which could, fortunately, be accepted. This policy produced a varied, stimulating and diverse program, the high quality of which many of our participants commented on.

The more than one hundred helpers from German and international universities ensured a smooth running of the congress, not only in the sessions, but in helping participants find their way around campus and helping and advising in numerous larger and smaller matters.

The congress ended Saturday, August 29, with the closing keynote 'Gilhus: Bodies, Texts and Otherness – Religious Change in Antiquity and Today' by Ingvild Gilhus, Bergen, and the General Assembly at the Altes Heizkraftwerk, Erfurt, which was generously made available for our use by the Achava-Festival.

Though a new executive committee of the IAHR was elected during the congress and the previous executive committee concluded their term of office, the host of the next IAHR Congress has not yet been decided on.

Tagung vom 8. bis 10. September 2015 in Manchester: 'Experiences of Sanctuaries, Experiences of Empire' (Anna-Katharina Rieger)

A joint research meeting of the Curere Network ("Cultural Responses to the Roman Empire") (resp. Katell Berthelot) and the "Sanctuary Project" (resp. Greg Woolf, financed by the Humboldt Foundation) was organized by Peter Oakes, a member of the network at Manchester. In a very convenient and concentrated atmosphere, about 25 participants discussed the religious dimension of the Roman Empire embracing Judaism, Christianity and Roman Eastern Mediterranean traditions. In particular, sanctuaries as places of 'condensed' religious and political activity and the reflections of such activities in texts were the focus of the contributions. The papers covered topics from the Jerusalem temple and its architectural language (S. Rocca) as well as its religio-political operationalisation in Graeco-Roman texts, mainly Flavius Josephus, and Midrashic texts (M. B. Shahar, V. Noam, M. Morgenstern) to traces of Christian communities in archaeological and epigraphical evidence at Philippi/Greece (P. Oakes). The Graeco-Roman religion was represented by papers on social networks and agents in two Dacian sanctuaries of Iupiter Dolichenus (C. Szabó), the role of literary production and collection in the functioning of Asklepieia in Asia Minor (G. Petridou) and the evidence in architecture but not in ritual practices of the emperors' worship in Southern Syria (A.-K. Rieger). A contribution on the Augusteum at a Pan sanctuary, built by king Herodes, discussed the ways of how Graeco-Roman traditions could merge with Jewish ones (R. Deines). The worship of gods modelled along the salutatio of the Roman elite and creating intimate experiences stimulated thoughts about the intertwined social and religious realms in the society of the urbs Roma (M. Patzelt). Some recurring issues were the value and end of architectural analogies, the definition of worship in Roman and Jewish contexts, as well as the aim and function of Midrashic texts, while aspects of economic entanglements of sanctuaries as well as a differentiation of templum in the sense of jurdical and spiritual templa were not covered by the papers. A highlight was the afternoon in the John Rylands Library, where Philip Alexander, expert in Jewish Literature, together with a curator explained an amazing selection of objects and manuscripts ranging from an Assyrian clay tablet to a Coptic papyrus, to coloured Bible and Tora manuscripts, and to a 19th century collection of Jewish amulets. The day ended with a tour through the reading rooms of the neo-Gothic library.

"Interrelational Selves and Individualization", Winter School Max-Weber-Kolleg, 5–9 January 2016 (Martin Fuchs)

What do we mean when we talk of "the Self"? What do terms like self-realization, self-awareness, self-transformation, self-esteem, self-determination, self-surrender or self-transcendence refer to? What do images of an unfolding self, or of the cultivation of a self, connote? The Winter School examined philosophical debates on notions of self-hood against the backdrop of historical and comparative research about cultural concepts of selves. This includes processes of (religious) individualization. Instead of discussing authoritative conceptualizations of the self and selves, we focused on the difficulties, and on the debates involved, in exploring (or constructing) notions of self-hood. Thus we took up and discussed suggestions of a minimal self in relation or opposition to propositions of narrative, dialogical, relational or experiential selves. One assumption underlying the discussion was that the formation and/or exploration of (notions of) selves has to be seen within an interactionist frame, i.e. interactional relationships with other selves, as well as with the "world", including dimensions and selves that transcend what is directly accessible. (In this wide sense, the self can be understood as social.)

The questions arising from these considerations included the processuality (versus stability) of selves, the question of the non-self, as well as denials of the reality of selfhood, the relationship between concepts of self and concepts of identity (as well as non-identity), personhood and subjectivity (including self-responsibility), the role of, and relationship to, the body (one's own and the bodies of others), and the ownership of self. Thus, we investigated the modalities of selfhood. These reach from mutuality and respect, including identification with one's other, to somewhat antagonistic delineations of selves, to constellations characterized by the lack and need for recognition of selfhood and the power of self-determination of social beings. Aspects of passivity were included – the self as recipient of the activities of others – , as they encompass the dynamics of self-perception and perception by others. The winter school was organized by Martin Fuchs, Max-Weber-Kolleg, and Magnus Schlette, FEST, Heidelberg (Philosophy) with the participation of Thomas Fuchs, University of Heidelberg (Psychiatry, Philosophy), Jonardon Ganeri, New York University (Philosophy), Karen Joisten, University of Kassel (Philosophy), Angelika Malinar, University of Zürich (Indology, Philosophy), Chakravarthi Ram-Prasad (Lancaster, Philosophy) and Dan Zahavi, University of Copenhagen (Philosophy).

„Zum Verhältnis von Erfahrung und Normativität. Interdisziplinäre Perspektiven", Workshop anlässlich des 75. Geburtstags von Prof. Dr. Dietmar Mieth vom 21. bis 22. Januar 2016 am Max-Weber-Kolleg (Antje Linkenbach)

Mit der Frage nach dem Verhältnis von Normativität und Erfahrung griff der Workshop ein Thema auf, das für den Theologen und Sozialethiker Dietmar Mieth, langjähriger Fellow des Max-Weber-Kollegs, eine zentrale Herausforderung darstellt. Das Phänomen Erfahrung wurde im Kontext des Workshops in einem lebensweltlich-alltäglichen Sinn einerseits und in einem außeralltäglichen signifikanten Sinn andererseits thematisiert (und nicht in seiner Relevanz für die positivistischen Wissenschaften). Die Veranstaltung hatte einen explorativen Charakter; sie näherte sich dem Thema aus interdisziplinärer Perspektive und war auch interessiert, die empirische Relevanz theoretischer Überlegungen zu berücksichtigen. Mit Theologie, Philosophie, Soziologie, Anthropologie, Ökonomie und Religionswissenschaft repräsentierten die teilnehmenden Wissenschaftlerinnen und Wissenschaftler ein breites disziplinäres Spektrum. Der Workshop versuchte eine Verständigung über den hier relevanten Normenbegriff, der im Kern moralisch gedeutet wurde (Dietmar Mieth, Max-Weber-Kolleg). Weiterhin wurde der Erfahrungsbegriff in seinen Formen, Dimensionen, Hierarchien, Intensitäten und Dramatisierungen vor allem aus pragmatistischer Sicht und damit als Resultat von Situation und Kontingenz diskutiert (Matthias Jung, Universität Koblenz; Andreas Pettenkofer, Max-Weber-Kolleg). Die Frage nach der Handlungs- und Gestaltungskraft von Erfahrung schlug die Brücke zu der Ebene der Normen und reflektierte ihre Fähigkeit zu Begründung, Erhalt, aber auch zu Kritik und Transformation normativer Ordnungen (Ludwig Siep, Universität Münster; Andrea Esser, Universität Jena; Bettina Hollstein, Max-Weber-Kolleg). Eher skeptische

Sichtweisen auf den Erfahrungsbegriff kamen aus dem Kontext der protestantischen Erfahrungs- und Erlebniskritik und der Max-Weber-Forschung (Gesche Linde, Universität Rostock; Johannes Weiß, Universität Kassel; Carsten Hermann-Pillath, Max-Weber-Kolleg). Für die Bestimmung des Verhältnisses von Normativität und Erfahrung besitzt das Phänomen der Kontrasterfahrung als Wurzel von Gesellschaftskritik besondere Relevanz (Christoph Henning, Max-Weber-Kolleg). Diese These konnte anhand von Exklusions- und Missachtungserfahrungen marginalisierter Gruppen in Indien vertieft und konkretisiert werden (Martin Fuchs, Antje Linkenbach, beide Max-Weber-Kolleg). Die Tagung ging mit einer abschließenden Gesprächsrunde zum Thema „Normativität und Gesellschaftskritik" zu Ende, in der die Erkenntnisse des Workshops im Lichte zukünftiger Projektplanung am Max-Weber-Kolleg ausgewertet wurden.

„Religiösen Zweifel denken", Tagung im Rahmen der Kolleg-Forschergruppe „Religiöse Individualisierung in historischer Perspektive" vom 11. bis 12. Februar 2016 am Max-Weber-Kolleg (Veronika Hoffmann)

Traditionell galt religiöser Zweifel im Christentum in aller Regel als eine Bedrohung des Glaubens. Diese Sicht wird jedoch in jüngerer Zeit zunehmend in Frage gestellt und der Zweifel demgegenüber z.B. als Sicherungsmechanismus gegen fundamentalistisch-intolerante Engführungen oder als kritischer Begleiter einer intellektuell redlichen religiösen Überzeugung verstanden. In der theologischen Reflexion ist diese Frage bisher nur begrenzt aufgegriffen worden. Unter den Bedingungen aktueller religiöser Pluralisierung und Individualisierung und eines aggressiv auftretenden atheistischen Naturalismus muss sie jedoch als ein wesentlicher Aspekt wissenschaftlicher Reflexion auf Religion betrachtet werden. Dazu wollte die Tagung „Religiösen Zweifel denken" einen Beitrag leisten, die am 11./12. Februar 2016 am Max-Weber-Kolleg stattfand.

Das Augenmerk richtete sich dabei zum einen auf die Vielfalt der möglichen Perspektiven und Zugänge, die sich aus der Mehrdeutigkeit des Begriffs „Zweifel" ergeben: So kann Zweifel aus erkenntnistheoretischer Sicht in seiner Anfrage an bestehende Vorstellungen und Grundannahmen neue Räume der Interpretation öffnen. Er kann sich aber auch in stärker existenzieller Hinsicht äußern: als verunsichernde Infragestellung von etwas, das zentrale Bedeutsamkeit besitzt, oder als Vertrauenskrise. Zum anderen lassen sich mehrere mögliche Deutungshorizonte unterscheiden, die unter Umständen miteinander in Spannung treten. Deutungen aus einer religiösen Innensicht heraus, die beispielsweise auf der Linie der reformatorischen Konzeption der „Anfechtung" Zweifel als Glaubensprüfung verstehen, versuchen in der Regel, dem Zweifel einen Ort im Raum des Glaubens zu geben. Solche Innendeutungen lassen sich aber heute nicht mehr von den zugleich möglichen Außendeutungen einer kritischen Anfrage an den Glauben abschotten. Dementsprechend sind auch theologische Gewissheitskonzepte unter Bedingungen verschärften Pluralitäts- und Kontingenzbewusstseins nicht mehr in traditioneller Weise zugänglich. Eine Neukonzeption des religiösen Gewissheitsbegriffes – möglicherweise in Fortführung von Überlegungen zur „kontingenten Gewissheit" (Joas) oder der „zweiten Naivität" (Ricœur) – ist, so zeigten die Diskussionen der Tagung, ein theologisches Desiderat.

In den Blick rückte außerdem das Verhältnis religiösen Zweifels zu einem Verständnis individueller „Authentizität". Das Ideal einer Treue zu sich selbst verbietet das Festhalten an einem Glauben, der einem zutiefst zweifelhaft geworden ist. Aber wie genau wären hier Elemente des Willentlichen und des Widerfahrenden im Blick auf Glaube und Zweifel zueinander ins Verhältnis zu setzen? Und in welcher Weise wäre die theologische Dimension der Gnade einzutragen, die Gott auch dem Zweifelnden oder den Glauben Verlierenden nicht entzieht?

Die Tagung ging diesen Fragen aus unterschiedlichen konfessionellen, theologischen und religionsphilosophischen Perspektiven nach. Veronika Hoffmann (Erfurt/Siegen) skizzierte einleitend „veränderte Bedingungen des Zweifels" unter der Perspektive der von Charles Taylor analysierten „veränderten Bedingungen des Glaubens". Jürgen Werbick (Münster) lotete traditionelle Umgangsweisen mit dem Zweifel in der lutherischen Anfechtung und der Mystik auf ihr Anregungs-, aber auch Irritationspotenzial für den aktuellen Zweifelsdiskurs aus. Im Blick auf aktuelle soziologische „Dekonversions"-Studien widmete sich Karsten Lehmkühler (Straßburg) dem Thema eines von der Wahrhaftigkeit gegenüber sich selbst geforderten Glaubensverlustes und seinen theologischen Deutungen, während Andreas Koritensky (Paderborn) Ansätze einer virtue epistemology im Blick auf mögliche Fehlformen religiöser Urteilsbildung vorstellte. In einer „Theorie imaginativer Rationalität", wie sie Gregor Maria Hoff (Salzburg) skizzierte, lässt sich der Zweifel epistemologisch als Erweiterung von Interpretations- und Handlungsmöglichkeiten lesen. Maureen Junker-Kenny (Dublin) zeigte kritisch insbesondere an Habermas' Verständnis von Religion, wie dieses von Gewissheitsunterstellung ausgeht, und stellte ihm differenzierende Zugänge Paul Ricœurs in der Figur der „Bezeugung" (attestation) und einer „zweiten Naivität" nach dem Durchgang durch die „Wüste der Kritik" entgegen. Abschließend entwarf Michael Bongardt (Berlin) eine dreifache Phänomenologie des Zweifels: an der Kirche, am Glauben, an Gott, und akzentuierte gegenüber einem Zweifel an Glaubensvorstellungen die dem religiösen Glauben eigentümlichen Dimensionen der Beziehung und des Vertrauens, die möglicherweise das Zerbrechen bestimmter religiöser Konzepte sogar voraussetzten.

„Eine Lichtung des deutschen Waldes – Mystik, Idealismus und Romantik", Tagung der Meister Eckhart-Forschungsstelle vom 19. bis 21. Mai 2016 am Max-Weber-Kolleg (Andrés Quero-Sánchez)

Die Tagung fand im Rahmen des von der Deutschen Forschungsgemeinschaft finanzierten Forschungsprojekts: „Der ewige Begriff des Individuums": Eine historisch-philologisch-systematische Untersuchung der ‚mystischen Vernunft' und deren Rezeption im Werk Schellings (QU 258/3–1) sowie in Zusammenarbeit mit der Kolleg-Forschergruppe „Religiöse Individualisierung in historischer Perspektive" (KFOR 1013) im Erfurter Predigerkloster und IBZ statt. Die Internationale Tagung hat die interdisziplinäre Diskussion zwischen Historikern, Germanisten, Theologen und Philosophen aus verschiedenen Ländern (Deutschland, Österreich, Spanien, Frankreich, Großbritannien; USA und der Schweiz) ermöglicht sowie die folgenden Themenkomplexe untersucht:

(1) Kann man Eckharts ‚Mystik' als eine idealistische Form des Denkens auffassen? Wenn ja, inwieweit (Dietmar Mieth [Erfurt]: Bild und Begriff bei Meister Eckhart; Marie-Anne Vannier [Metz]: Eckhart und der Idealismus)?

(2) Die Frage nach den konkreten Editionen der Schriften Meister Eckharts, die dessen Rezeption im 18./19. Jahrhundert ermöglicht haben (Janina Franzke [Augsburg]: Der Baseler Taulerdruck; Rudolf Weigand [Eichstätt]: Speners Tauler-Ausgabe).

(3) Die nationalsozialistische Rezeption Meister Eckharts (Henning Dörr [Köln]: Meister Eckhart in Rosenbergs ‚Mythos des 20. Jahrhunderts'; Martina Roesner [Wien]: Vom ‚deutschen Geist' zum ‚deutschen Willen'; Christoph Henning [Erfurt]: Meister Eckhart und Hermann Schwarz; Maxime Mauriège [Köln]: Die Frage nach der nationalsozialistischen ‚Rechtgläubigkeit' Eckharts in den 30er Jahren).

(4) Der Zusammenhang zwischen Mystik und Romantik (Peter Nickl [Regensburg]: Brentano und die Mystik; Bärbel Frischmann [Erfurt]: Friedrich Schlegel und die Mystik; Alexandra Besson [Université de Lorraine]: Novalis und die negative Theologie).

(5) Der Zusammenhang zwischen Platonismus, Idealismus und Mystik (Theo Kobusch [Bonn]: Der Begriff ‚Selbstentäußerung'; Andrés Quero-Sánchez [Erfurt]: Der Begriff ‚Korruption'; Jens Halfwassen [Heidelberg]: Die Anfänge des Deutschen Idealismus im Tübinger Stift).

(6) Die Rolle der Mystik in Fichte (Ives Radrizzani [München]: Fichtes Kritik am Mystischen; Christoph Asmuth [Berlin]: Meister Eckhart und Fichte).

(7) Die Rolle der Mystik im Werk Schellings (Markus Enders [Freiburg]: Die Freiheit Gottes bei Eckhart und Schelling; Ben Morgan [Oxford]: Eckhart, Schelling und Heidegger; Lore Hühn [Freiburg]: Der Begriff ‚Gelassenheit' in Schellings Spätwerk; Harald Schwaetzer [Bernkastel-Kues: Franz von Baader; Christian Jung [London]: Emanuel Swedenborg; Christian Danz [Wien]: Schellings ‚Stuttgarter Privatvorlesungen').

(8) Die Rolle der Mystik in Hegel (Glenn Magee [New York]: Hegel und Böhme).

(9) Die Rolle der Mystik in Hölderlin (Markus Vinzent [London/Erfurt]: Eckhart und Hölderlin).

Der Tagungsband wird von A. Quero-Sánchez herausgegeben, er erscheint im Jahre 2017 bei Brill (Leiden/Boston) (Reihe: Studies on Mysticism, Idealism and Phenomenology/Studien zu Mystik, Idealismus und Phänomenologie).

"Storiografia II", Tagung mit FSC Modena und EPHE Paris vom 16. bis 17. Juni 2016 in Modena (Jörg Rüpke)

Unter dem Titel "Storiografia: Ricerca storica e scrittura del passato II" wurden am 16. und 17. Juni 2016 an der Fondazione San Calo in Modena die Zusammenarbeit von FSC, Ecole Pratique des Hautes Etudes, Paris, und dem Max-Weber-Kolleg Erfurt mit einer weiteren gemeinsamen Tagung der Doktorandenprogramme fortgesetzt. Zwei Tage lang wurden klassische Werke der Historiographie und Probleme der Geschichtsschreibung in Vorträgen und Diskussionen beleuchtet. Dabei ging es etwa um Philosophiegeschichtsschreibung seit der Antike (etwa bei Plotin und Simplicius), um Geschichtsbilder bei Nietzsche und eschatologische Motive in der zeitgenössischen französischen Philosophie. Für die historiographische Tradition Italiens wurde nach der faschistischen Nutzung der Anthropologie des 19. Jahrhunderts wie der Memorialkultur des 20. gefragt, für Ungarn nach den internationalen Netzwerken der eigenen Nationalgeschichtsschreibung. Beiträge aus Erfurt betrafen die These, dass "Christentum" ein Konstrukt der Historiographie des 2. Jahrhunderts sei (J. Rüpke), die Umdeutungen der Geschichte des Samaritaners (D. Mieth) und jüngere methodische Reflexionen zur Verflechtungsgeschichte in Deutschland (R. Suitner). Für 2017 wurde das Thema "Tradition und Traditionskritik" ins Auge gefasst. Geplant ist die Tagung für den 22. und 23. Juni 2017.

"Bhakti and Self", Tagung vom 21. bis 24. Juni 2016 am Max-Weber-Kolleg (Martin Fuchs)

Insofar as one can generalize about bhakti, one aspect that seems to stand out is the element of creativity and innovation characteristic of this religious strand. Over long stretches of Indian history, bhakti was recurrently renewed, exemplifying new forms of experience and inventing new modes of articulation. Observed from a certain angle, bhakti exhibits potentials for religious individualization that many (though not all) forms of bhakti have tapped into and that differ from the forms of individualization represented by the figure of the renouncer elaborately discussed elsewhere (notwithstanding cases in which both modes of religious individualization can be combined). A particularly characteristic of bhakti is the emphasis put on the relational aspects of human experience manifested in (imageries of) continual interactions with the divine, or the divine's representative, as well as in continual interactions with other bhaktas. It is this kind of inner social dynamics that lends itself to an exploration of the inter-relational dimensions of self/selves, and of individual identity and personhood as they have been or still are articulated by different formats of bhakti. As lived religion(s), this perspective on bhakti provides an angle different from largely philosophical or theological debates over concepts of selfhood, soul, or atman. While research on bhakti has been burgeoning over the last two or three decades, particularly in India and North America, the aspect of relationality of selves has so far not received the attention it deserves.

The conference on "Bhakti and Self", held at the Max-Weber-Kolleg Erfurt, in the context of the research group "Religious Individualization in Historical Perspective" (KFG) and organized by Martin Fuchs together with Rahul Parson, discussed notions of selfhood, individualization and inter-subjectivity articulated in bhakti contexts covering different periods and regions of South Asian history. In his introductory presentation, Martin Fuchs (Max-Weber-Kolleg Erfurt) focused on the dimensions and implications of the triangular relationship between a bhakti devotee (bhakta), the divine and other bhaktas, and its resonances with certain modes of sociological thinking. Karen Pechilis (Drew University) discussed the relationship between ordinary and extraordinary people and the possibility of an ordinary, everyday individualism taking up a comparison within Tamil religious intertextuality between the 6th-century female bhakti poet Kāraikkāl Ammaiyār's poetry and the authoritative 12th-century biography of her authored by Cēkkilār. Anne Feldhaus (Arizona State University) engaged with 13th-century Marathi literature of the Mahānubhāvs and their views of the selfhood of divine incarnations focussing on devotees' views of the subjectivity of the group's two principal divine incarnations: Cakradhar, the founder of the group, and Gundam Rāūl, his guru. Again with respect to Maharashtra, in this case Jnandev and his work known as the Jnaneshwari, a commentary on the Bhagavad Gita (c. 1290 CE); Christian Novetzke (University of Washington) discussed the work's soteriological critique of inequality and the conceptual field where unequivocal demands for social equality meet the complications of social distinction endemic to everyday life. Like Novetzke, Purushottam Agrawal (Delhi) started from questioning the idea that concepts of freedom attached to notions of the individual is the sole purview of the modern West. Focussing on Kabir who is known for his unique poetic power and his outright and sarcastically expressed rejection of the varnashrama hierarchy, he depicted his idea of 'Self' as the most articulate expression of the philosophical notion of the individual in the early modern north India. Vasudha Dalmia (University of California, Berkeley) discussed the Vallabha Sampradaya 16th-century compendium, the Do sau Bavan Vaishnavan ki Varta, emphasizing the tension between community belonging and the depiction of the model devotees as different from the ordinary people, between reciprocity and excess. With respect to the transregional lyrical networks of bhakti saint-poets of the 16th and 17th century, John Stratton Hawley (Barnard College) discussed the ways in which the saliency of selfhood was both affirmed and denied. In her presentation on Tulsidas, Vasudha Paramasivan (University of California, Berkeley) raised the question whether it is possible to speak about the fashioning of a "poetic self". Jon Keune (Michigan State University) highlighted how bhakti theology shaped the ways that Marathi authors represented the selves and voices of Untouchables, referring in particular to Eknath and Chokhamela. On the background of changing narratives of the Bavari panth, Till Luge (Orient Institute, Istanbul) discussed the relationship between the construction of both social distinctions and spiritual practice. Heidi Pauwel's (University of Washington) presentation on the 18th-century autobiographical pilgrimage report of the Krishna bhakta Nagaridas (Savant Singh) discussed his depiction of his self-transformation. Taking the case of the autobiography of Piro, a Muslim prostitute who joined the Gulabdasi dera (19th century), Anshu Malhotra (Delhi University) followed up on how Piro deployed and expanded on bhakti's repository of stories and legends as a resource that allowed her to "imagine herself otherwise", envisage a soteriological path for herself and take her place next to her guru as an ostensible consort in the dera. Turning to the 20th century and somewhat reversing the perspective, Denis Matringe (École des Hautes Études en Sciences Sociales, Paris) discussed the bhakti of a French 20th-century Indologist, Lilian Silburn who became a follower of a Hindu Sufi (Naqshbandi) guru in Kanpur, Radha Mohan Lal Adhauliya. Rinku Lamba (Jawaharlal Nehru University, New Delhi) undertook a comparison of the approach to self in (sant) bhakti with the kind of subject/self envisioned in the writings of Gandhi, Tagore, and Ambedkar on the question of religion. In the final paper, Kumkum Sangari (University of Wisconsin) deliberated on the contingency and instability of the self as mode of continuation; she emphasized that bhaktas did not express a given self but sought producing a self. The final discussion addressed the diversity and potientialities and the wide range of explorations of the relationality of self in the field of bhakti, a field that calls for further explorations. The intention is to publish the papers.

„Towards a Global History of Ideas", Tagung der Kolleg-Forschergruppe „Religiöse Individualisierung in historischer Perspektive", in Kooperation mit dem Forschungszentrum Gotha vom 7. bis 9. Juli 2016 im Augustinerkloster in Erfurt (Martin Mulsow)

In den vergangenen Jahren war zu beobachten, wie eine ganze Reihe wissensgeschichtlicher Disziplinen sich „globalifizieren" (Jürgen Osterhammel), d.h. auf die Globalisierung mit einer Ausweitung ihrer Agenda reagieren. Man spricht von einer „Global History of Science", von „World Antiquarianism", „World Philology", „Global Art History" und neuerdings auch von einer „Global Intellectual History", angeregt nicht zuletzt von Christopher Bayly. Der Tagung ging es darum zu konkretisieren, was denn eine solche globale Ideengeschichte sein könne, wie sie sich von den anderen Globalgeschichten abgrenzt und welche Kategorien sie benötigt. Sie konzentrierte sich auf drei Aspekte: (1) Erfahrungen mit der Globalifizierung von Wissens- und Ideengeschichte, Probleme, institutionelle Konsequenzen. (2) Spezifische Probleme, wenn es um eine Globalifizierung der Forschung zur Vormoderne geht, also vor der Zeit der akuten Globalisierung des 19. und 20. Jahrhunderts. Wie sind die „entanglements" dieser frühen Phasen weltweiter Interdependenz, insbesondere in der Frühen Neuzeit, zu analysieren? (3) Wechselwirkungen zwischen den diversen Bereichen globalifizierter Wissensgeschichte. Eingeladen waren zahlreiche prominente Forscher der internationalen Diskussion.

Nachdem Martin Mulsow (Erfurt/Gotha) den Entwurf einer Referenztheorie der Globalisierung vorgestellt hatte, gab Sebastian Conrad (Berlin) am Beispiel der Rezeption von Zolas Nana einen Eindruck von den vielfältigen globalen Aneignungen kultureller Stoffe im 19. Jahrhundert. Jürgen Renn (Berlin) stellte die komplexe Kategorien-Matrix vor, mit der am MPI für Wissenschaftsgeschichte in Berlin Globalisierung des Wissens erforscht wird, und Hans Medick (Göttingen) zeigte anhand von chinesischen Erfahrungen die globalen Potentiale von Mikrohistorie auf. Als Abendvortrag sprach Jan Assmann (Konstanz) von Offenbarung als globalem Phänomen. Am nächsten Tag begannen Iris Schröder (Erfurt) und Benjamin Steiner (Erfurt) mit Vorträgen über Afrika: Schröder erörterte die Problematik von kartographischen Grenzziehungen am Fall von Äthiopien, Steiner die Schwierigkeiten, eine intellectual history von oralen und kolonial durchwirkten Kulturen zu erstellen. Dominic Sachsenmaier (Göttingen) nahm sich danach der paradoxen Ungleichheit an, mit der Globalgeschichtsschreibung heute praktiziert wird: an angloamerikanischer Forschung wird alles rezipiert, doch Forschungen aus exotischen Ländern oder Ostasien werden nicht wahrgenommen. Stefan Hanß (Cambridge) stellte ein Skizzenbuch aus dem Istanbul des 16. Jahrhunderts vor, das als wahres islamisch-europäisches Hybridprodukt in diplomatischen Zirkeln entstanden war, dessen Bilder aber in diverse westeuropäische Türkentraktate Eingang fanden. Auch Carlo Ginzburg (Pisa) ging es um Hybridphänomene. Er zeigte am Beispiel des Inka-Historiographen Garcilaso de la Vega, welche intrikaten Fragen linguistischen Transfers sich in Fällen stellen, in denen Ideen zwischen den Kulturen ausgetauscht werden, so dass es einer „Ethnophilologie" bedürfe, die sich ihrer annimmt. Kapil Raj (Paris) untersuchte die Vielfalt der Akteure, die sich in der Kartenproduktion insbesondere in Indien zusammengefunden hat. Anna Akasoy lenkte schließlich die Aufmerksamkeit auf die islamische Welt: Ist das intellektuelle „Erbe" des Islams aus Sicht der Europäer vorgeprägt durch deren Wahrnehmungsraster?

Am letzten Tag erwies Knud Haakonssen (Erfurt/St. Andrews) dem großen Ideenhistoriker John G.A. Pocock die Ehre, indem er den Neuseeländer als „Insel-Theoretiker" beschrieb, der als solcher eine besondere Sensibilität für Globalgeschichte und Transmissionen entwickelt habe. Paola Molino (München) stellte ihr Projekt einer vergleichenden Geschichte der Bibliotheks-Katalogisierungen vor und verstärkte damit das Moment der Praktiken, auf das heutige Ideengeschichte immer zurückkommt, um sich vor unangebrachten „Höhenflügen" und Gipfelgeschichten zu schützen. Abschließend kam dann Gerhard Wolf (Florenz) mit einhundert Bildern von asiatisch-europäischen Mischformen und Transferphänomenen aus Kunst und materieller Kultur auf die visuellen Aspekte zurück, die schon zuvor thematisch waren. Er schlug vor, an Panofskys Idea und an Warburg anzuknüpfen, wenn man den ideengeschichtlichen Aspekt von visueller Kultur fassen wolle. Insgesamt eröffnete die Konferenz damit einen bunten Strauß von Fragen und Forschungsansätzen, die alle noch weiter diskutiert werden müssen. Es wurde deutlich, dass hier noch keine Disziplin vorliegt, sondern ein neues und undefiniertes Feld, auf das Beiträge von verschiedensten Richtungen getragen werden. So aber war die Tagung auch gemeint gewesen: als ein erstes Vermessen eines künftigen Faches, das noch seine Kontur sucht. Einige der Beiträge werden als erstes Heft der neuen Zeitschrift Global Intellectual History veröffentlicht werden.

„Wolveramus dicitur. Neue Überlegungen zu Entstehungskontexten und Funktionen der ältesten lebensgroßen Bronzestatue des deutschen Mittelalters", Tagung am 25. August 2016 am Max-Weber-Kolleg (Matthias Engmann)

Unter der Leitung von Jörg Rüpke, Dietmar Mieth und Julie Casteigt haben sich am 25. August 2016 im Internationalen Begegnungszentrum der Universität Erfurt (IBZ) dreizehn Wissenschaftler aus den Gebieten der Kunsthistorie, Werkstoffwissenschaft, Theologie, Philosophie, antiker und mittelalterlicher Geschichte zusammengefunden, um die Entstehung und Verwendung des Kandelabers „Wolfram" im Mariendom zu Erfurt zu erörtern und anhand von neuen Daten zu diskutieren.

In der ersten Sektion der Tagung – Das Objekt – hebt zunächst Norbert Schmidt die stilistischen Merkmale des Wolfram hervor. An ausgewählten Beispielen zeigt er, dass man sowohl aus der Physiognomie, der Haar- und Bartgestaltung als auch aus der dargestellten Bekleidung und dem speziellen Faltenwurf, die so oder ähnlich auch woanders in der Kunstgeschichte zu finden sind, kaum ein bestimmtes Jahrzehnt und sogar nur mit Vorsicht ein bestimmtes Jahrhundert der Entstehungszeit ablesen lässt. Darüber hinaus könne man versucht sein, dem Künstler/Stifter/Auftraggeber zu unterstellen, dass (abgesehen von dem kleinen Futteral) sämtliche zur Identifikation und Interpretation der Figur nötigen Attribute bewusst weggelassen worden sind, um tatsächlich ein anthropomorphes Gerät (Leuchter) ohne persönliche Zuschreibung zu schaffen. Hiltrud Westermann-Angerhausen vergleicht den Wolfram mit anderen Bronzen aus dem gleichen Zeitraum und stellt unter anderem die Hypothese auf, dass es einzig den Überlieferungsumständen (Kriege, Wiederverwendung von Bronze) zugeschrieben werden muss, dass nur ein einziger mittelalterlicher, freistehender Personenleuchter überliefert ist. Außerdem stelle er lediglich eine

Anthropomorphisierung dar und keine Personifizierung, was für die Memorialkultur normal war und auf keine weitere Funktion schließen lassen muss als die, dass er ein Kandelaber ist. Schließlich zeigt Bernhard Mai anhand seiner metallurgischen Untersuchungsergebnisse, dass Kopf und Hände des Wolfram separat und dass die Inschrift zusammen mit dem Torso gegossen wurde (und nicht im Nachhinein eingestanzt worden sei).

In der zweiten Sektion der Tagung – Die Inschrift – stellt zunächst Franz Jäger im Vergleich mit anderen Bronze-Inschriften heraus, dass die Buchstabenform des Wolfram romanische Merkmale aufweist und nicht nach dem 12. Jh. hergestellt worden sei. Michael Matscha erwähnt, dass Wolfram und Hildeburg die Namen der Stifter sind (wobei die einnamige Nennung seit dem 12. Jh. üblich ist). Durch philologische Untersuchung und Kontextualisierung der Inschrift, die in Teilen sogar bis auf das 10. Jh. zurückverfolgt werden kann, wird diese zwischen das 12. Jh. und (nicht später als) Mitte des 14. Jh. datiert. Dietmar Mieth plädiert sodann auf die Hermeneutik der Untersuchung: Was bedeutet der Wolfram? Dabei wird Wolfram in den liturgischen Kontext des Stundengebets und Responsoriums gestellt, wobei zwischen einem okkasionellen und rituellen Gebrauch des Wolfram unterschieden wird. Und er plädiert anhand einer historisch-liturgischen Deutung der Inschrift darauf, dass diese um das 14. Jh. entstanden ist. In der anschließenden Diskussion wird mehrfach darauf hingewiesen, dass der Wolfram zwar erst 1425 genannt wird, aber schon davor in Gebrauch gewesen sein muss, und zwar an verschiedensten Orten/Kirchen Erfurts.

In der dritten Sektion der Tagung – Leuchter, Licht – präsentiert Frank Joachim Stehwig, die vorhergehende Diskussion aufgreifend, zunächst seine Ergebnisse zur Recherche der Statuten der juristischen Fakultät. In deren Beschreibung der Feierlichkeiten für das Patronatsfest der Fakultät am Tag des hl. Ivo (am 19. Mai im Chor der Erfurter Stiftskirche St. Marien, heute Dom) wird der Wolfram-Leuchter erstmals erwähnt. Diese Quelle wird sodann mit den 1270/1280 entstandenen Statuten der Stiftskirche abgeglichen. Dort ist im Zusammenhang mit einem Statut ein großer Leuchter erwähnt, der in der Nähe des Hochaltars im Chor der Kirche an exponierter Stelle stand und dem eine wichtige liturgische Funktion zukam. Vera Henkelmann erörtert sodann die symbolisch-funktionale Bedeutung der Beleuchtung im kirchlichen Kontext und verortet den Erfurter Leuchter in der Tradition der mittelalterlichen Sakralleuchter. Der sogenannte Wolfram erweist sich hierbei als Memorialleuchter, der jedoch nicht zwingend an einem Grab gestanden haben muss. Johannes Tripps unterstreicht schließlich die Zugehörigkeit des Wolfram-Leuchters zu den sogenannten „stummen Gehilfen" (anthropomorphe Altargeräte), die zwischen 1150 und 1250 entstanden sind und im Laufe des 13. Jh. durch angelomorphe Altargeräte abgelöst werden. Im Gegensatz zu allen anderen Beispielen der „stummen Gehilfen" trägt der Wolfram z.B. kein liturgisches Gewand, das rein stilistisch unter dem „Druck" der Konstruktion steht (der Faltenwurf ist aus Gründen der Stabilität so gestaltet). In der vierten Sektion der Tagung – Rituale/Judeneid – interpretiert Jörg Rüpke die an den Erfurter Judeneid geknüpften Rituale als solche zwischen öffentlichem und privatem

Raum. In diese Spannung verortet er den Wolfram als zwischen Kontexten und Orten changierenden Funktionsträger von öffentlichen Ritualen. Er vertritt die Thesen, dass Wolfram, neben seiner Funktion als Kandelaber auch die Funktion einer vor der Kirche stehenden Torarollenhalters innehatte, wie auch, dass Wolfram (teils prozessionsartig) die religiösen Räume wechselte und deshalb mobil sein musste (und deshalb nicht am Sockel festgemacht sein durfte). Letztlich laufe diese Betrachtungsweise auf eine Methodik hinaus, die materiale Befunde mit zeitgenössischen Praktiken zusammendenken will. In der fünften Sektion der Tagung – Bilderwelt – unterstreicht Naomi Feuchtwanger-Sarig, dass zunächst das Problem besteht, dass es keine Vergleichsobjekte zum Wolfram gibt, betont aber ihre Überzeugung, dass er nur in einem christlichen Kontext denkbar ist und nicht als Torarollenhalter fungiert haben kann, was – neben einer detaillierten Analyse der Attribute des Wolfram – auf ihr Hauptargument zurück geht, dass die Tora das Heiligste ist, das weder berührt werden darf noch (öffentlich) ausgerollt wird. Markus Vinzent unternimmt sodann (ebenso wie der darauffolgenden Vortrag von Julie Casteigt) einen Wechsel zu einer allgemeineren Perspektive. Er insistiert auf eine methodologische Fokussierung der hermeneutisch-kontextualisierenden Entschlüsselung der Wolframfigur. Während Vinzent anhand von Meister Eckharts Umgang mit Bibelexegese und Schriftpraxen eine hermeneutische Bewegung betont, die zwischen jüdischem und christlichem Denken changiert, hebt Casteigt – anhand von Albert dem Großen – eine Bewegung heraus, die vom jüdischen auf das christliche Denken hingeht. Hierbei wird letztlich keine synthetische, sondern eine „kondensative" Betrachtungsperspektive verfolgt (Casteigt), also eine, die Möglichkeiten eröffnet, bereitstellt und ernstnimmt und dabei auch von dem Grundsatz geleitet ist, dass es sowohl im hochkulturellen wie auch sozialem Bereich mittelalterlichen Lebens keine Trennung zwischen christlicher und jüdischer Kultur (in Erfurt) gab (Vinzent). Am Schluss einigten sich die Experten und Teilnehmer auf das Ergebnis, dass der Wolfram nicht jüdischen, sondern definitiv christlichen Ursprungs ist und aus dem 12. Jh. stammt. Über die Frage, ob der Wolfram-Leuchter als „reiner" Kandelaber genutzt wurde oder nicht, gab die Tagung wichtige Anregungen und zeigte den weiteren Forschungs- und Diskussionsbedarf.

Tagung in Zusammenarbeit mit SOAS der University of London vom 8. bis 10. September 2016 in London: 'Max Weber's Hinduism and Buddhism. Reflections on a Sociological Classic 100 Years on' (Martin Fuchs)

Max Weber's study of *Hinduism and Buddhism*, published as the second volume of his *Gesammelte Aufsätze zur Religionssoziologie* (Collected Essays on the Sociology of Religion) and touching upon, besides religion, social structure, political and economic history, and scientific achievements of the Indian civilizational region, while outdated and controversial in several respects, has not received the attention it deserves, neither among scholars of South Asia, who often do not understand the place of the study within Weber's œuvre, nor among sociologists who have engaged with Weber's theories and agendas but usually lack knowledge and an understanding of the religious and the general history of the Indian subcontinent and its social structures. The conference on the occasion of the 100th anniversary of Weber's "India study" brought together scholars from both these backgrounds who, to a lesser or greater degree, have been involved in attempts to overcome this lacuna. Scholars from South Asian countries, however, remained underrepresented, the reason being that, other than his general sociology, Weber's comparative sociology of religion and his work on India have never attained much interest in South Asian scholarship.

The keynote, at least, was given by one of the most renowned Indian scholars, the historian Romila Thapar (Jawaharlal Nehru University, New Delhi), who made a fresh attempt to come to terms with Weber's India and demanded an empirically and historically much more refined and sensitive approach to the study of South Asia. Several contributors took up concepts of Weber or engaged with his depiction of specific dimensions of Indian civilizational history. Stephan Kalberg (Boston) reconstructed Weber's depiction of the different life orders in the Indian context. Wolfgang Schluchter (Heidelberg) discussed Weber's multiple intra- and trans-civilizational comparisons. Andreas Buss (Ottawa) and Hans Kippenberg (Bremen) took up core concepts of Weber, *Eigengesetzlichkeit* and *Entzauberung* (often translated as disenchantment). Peter Flügel critically discussed Weber's rendering of Jainism against the background of modern scholarship. Sam Whimster (London) reconstructed the transition to capitalism with regard to Weber's views and with a special focus on the agrarian sector. Helwig Schmidt-Glintzer (Lichtenberg-Kolleg Göttingen) discussed Weber's understanding of the role of the literati in Hinduism and Buddhism borrowing from his knowledge of the Chinese case. Laura Ford (New York) reconstructed Weber's distinction between formal and substantive rationality and read Weber's inadequate understanding of the Indian legal tradition against his understanding of European natural law traditions. Hermann Kulke (Kiel) made a strong argument for the relevance of Weber's notion of legitimization for an understanding of state formation processes in Indian history. In a similar vein, David Gellner (Oxford) took issue with Sheldon Pollock and his critique of Weber's legitimation concept.

Other contributions went beyond Weber. Richard Gombrich (Oxford) applied Weberian ideas to an analysis of three Buddhist movements in modern Taiwan. Susantha Goonatilake (Colombo) attacked the Orientalism and Euro-centrism of Western scholars. Meghnad Jagdishchandra discussed Indian modernity from an economic angle. At the end, taking Weber's difficulties of doing justice to *bhakti* as a case in point, Martin Fuchs (MaxWeber-Kolleg Erfurt) discussed the potentialities and limitations of Weber's approach to intercultural comparison and the study of world religions and suggested a new conceptualization of Indian religious dynamics. Revisiting Weber's concept of "world" and of attitudes and relations to the world, he discussed possibilities of connecting certain dimension of Weber's conceptualization with the concept of world relations and articulations of the world of the likes of Maurice Merleau-

Ponty, Johann Arnason, and Hartmut Rosa. The contributions of the conference will be published.

Sixth International Conference of the Society for the Study of Western Esotericism vom 1. bis 3. Juni 2017 (Bernd-Christian Otto)

Die sechste internationale Tagung der Society for the Study of Western Esotericism fand vom 1. bis 3. Juni im Augustinerkloster in Erfurt statt. Insgesamt nahmen etwa 160 Wissenschaftler aus aller Welt an der Tagung teil. Das Tagungsprogramm umfasste drei volle Tage, insgesamt etwa hundert Einzelvorträge, die gestaffelt in vier parallelen Panels stattfanden. Ferner gab es an jedem der drei Tage eine Keynote Session, in der jeweils drei etablierte Wissenschaftler kürzere, ineinander verzahnte Vorträge hielten, die in der zweiten Stunde mittels einer strukturierten Plenardiskussion besprochen wurden. Am zweiten Tag wurden zudem ein Workshop zu Kompetenzen von Nachwuchswissenschaftlern sowie zwei kürzere Führungen (eine Kloster- und eine Stadtführung) angeboten. Am ersten Abend gab es einen von der Foundation of the Chair of Hermetic Philosophy and Related Currents finanzierten Empfang im Renaissancehof des Augustinerklosters.

Die Tagung war nicht nur aufgrund der insgesamt geglückten Organisation, des tollen Ambientes, des guten Wetters und der großen nationalen wie internationalen Resonanz und Teilnehmerzahl ein großer Erfolg. Es war insbesondere das Konferenzthema – „Western Esotericism and Deviance" –, das offenbar einen Nerv der gegenwärtigen Debatte getroffen hatte und zu fundierten wie fruchtbaren Diskussionen führte. Zum einen wurde das Meisternarrativ einer prinzipiellen kulturellen Ausgegrenztheit und Marginalität westlicher Esoterik (Stichwort „Rejected Knowledge") neu aufgerollt und aufgebrochen; zum anderen wurden zahlreiche Fallstudien vorgestellt, die vor dem Hintergrund des Tagungsthemas viel nuanciertere Befunde boten, die nicht nur unterschiedliche Grade, sondern auch zeit- und ortsabhängige Progressions- und Dekadenzdynamiken hinsichtlich der kulturellen Akzeptanz oder Ausgegrenztheit esoterischer Strömungen anzeigten.

Namentlich zu nennen sind nicht nur die inspirierenden Beiträge der Keynote Speaker, etwa von Olav Hammer, Jay Johnston, Richard Gordon, Claire Fanger, Marion Gibson oder Martin Mulsow. Auch die Panels über „The Cultic Milieu Reconsidered" (Egil Asprem, Kevin Whitesides), „Deviance and Orthodoxy in Islamic Esotericism" (Mark Sedgwick, Alexandre Toumarkine) oder „Esotericists Embracing Deviance" (Allison P. Coudert) konnten wichtige Denkanstöße zur Thematik liefern.

Der große Erfolg der Tagung zeigte sich zudem in der Presseresonanz (u.a. Radio- und Fernsehinterviews für den MDR) sowie zahlreichen positiven Rückmeldungen von Teilnehmern im Nachgang des Kongresses. Eine Veröffentlichung der wichtigsten (etwa 25) Beiträge ist bereits in Vorbereitung und wird von mir und Marco Pasi (Amsterdam) in der Aries Book Series des Brill-Verlags herausgegeben werden.

Tradizione. La costruzione dell'identità in prospettiva storica, Tagung vom 22. bis 23. Juni 2017 in Modena (Jörg Rüpke)

Vom 22. bis 23. Juni 2017 fand an der Fondazione San Carlo in Modena und auf Einladung von Professor Carlo Altini die nun schon fünfte gemeinsame Tagung des dortigen Doktoranden- und Postdoktorandenkollegs mit der Section sciences religieuses der École Pratique des Hautes Études Paris und dem Max-Weber-Kolleg statt. In Vorträgen und dreisprachigen Diskussionen wurden von Angehörigen dieser Institutionen Fallstudien und Reflexionen über zentrale Begriffe vorgestellt. Die Beiträge reichten von der Antike bis zur französischen Kant-Rezeption und Traditionen französischer Laicité. Von den Erfurter Teilnehmer/inne/n stellte Sarah Al-Taher Überlegungen zur menschlichen Identität als defizitäre Wesen in der Anthropologie von Platons Mythen vor, Tilo Wesche beschäftigte sich mit Aristoteles' Eigentumskonzept, und Maik Patzelt sprach über spätantike Witwenbilder und die ihnen zugeschriebenen Praktiken. Roberto Alciati, COFUND-Fellow am Max-Weber-Kolleg, stellte westliche Mönchstraditionen und -genealogien vor. Erneut boten die historischen Räume im Stadtzentrum von Modena einen guten Rahmen, über Alters- und Sprachgrenzen hinweg ins Gespräch zu kommen und gemeinsame Begriffsarbeit zu betreiben.

Religious Individualization in Historical Perspective: Types and Concepts, KFG-Abschlusstagung vom 27. bis 30. Juni 2017 (Jörg Rüpke)

Als Auftakt der letzten Arbeitsphase und mit dem Ziel, die unterschiedlichen individuellen Teilprojekte der Kolleg-Forschergruppe zu bündeln, fand zum Semesterende eine dreieinhalbtägige Tagung mit über vierzig Mitgliedern statt. Das gewählte Format war ungewöhnlich: Im stetigen Wechsel von Plenartreffen und Sitzungen unterschiedlicher Arbeitsgruppen wurden die letzten, noch nicht in den wöchentlichen Kolloquien diskutierten Texte für Kapitel eines gemeinsamen, mehrere ‚Bände' umfassenden Buches zu Dimensionen, Formen und Folgen religiöser Individualisierung diskutiert. Wichtiger noch war die Verklammerung dieser Beiträge durch gemeinsame Reflexionstexte von jeweils drei bis vier Autor/inn/en, deren Kapitel so durch eine gemeinsam verfasste Abschlussreflexion zusammengebunden und selbst noch einmal geschärft wurden. Bandweise trafen sich dann wiederum mehrere dieser Kleingruppen, um über Struktur und Titel ihrer Kapitelsammlung zu diskutieren. Nicht mit neuen Aufgaben von der Tagung zurückzukehren, sondern im Gefühl, eine Aufgabe erledigt zu haben, war die Zielsetzung.

Zuerst mit Skepsis betrachtet, war die Befriedigung doch groß, in wenigen Tagen diese neuen „Nachworte" verfasst und damit die Reflexion des Gesamtvorhabens deutlich vorangebracht zu haben. Dass Restaufgaben noch zu erledigen waren, soll nicht verschwiegen werden. Das Gesamtergebnis soll zur Jahresmitte 2018 in Druck und parallel im Open-access-Modus online gehen.

Tagung vom 4. bis 6. Juli 2017: ‚Dalit and Religion' (Martin Fuchs)

An interdisciplinary group of researchers from India, Mexico, the United States, Canada, Sweden and Germany met in the premises of the Augustinerkloster in Erfurt between 4th and 6th of July 2017 to discuss the topic *Dalit and Religion*.

Dalits (a modern self-designation for "Untouchables") and other disadvantaged people had to negotiate modes of religiosity and religious power structures continuously. Dalits had to face the denial of inclusion, and encountered severe problems when trying to establish spaces for themselves. At the same time Dalits invented ideas, practices and agendas of their own. Throughout Indian history the socio-religious hierarchy and the dominant, even hegemonic religious strands and traditions have been accompanied by counter-imaginaries, which represent universalistic concepts, but have never become dominant.

This conference had set itself the task to approach the field of religion in India from the perspective of discriminated, although differently positioned groups of people, and, therefore, from an angle that differs from the perspectives enshrined in the dominant religious discourses. It also put forward the ways religious practices and ideas are being articulated and appropriated by the various actors as well as on the ways new experiences and imaginaries are being formulated and expressed both historically and contemporaneously.

The religious traditions and strands covered included forms of Hinduism and forms of *bhakti*, forms of Islam, forms of Christianity and the new or Navayana Buddhism. Martin Fuchs (Max-Weber-Kolleg) gave an introduction into the topic. G. Aloysius (Puducherry) focused on the dilemmas facing excluded social groups in India and the ways their sense of religiosity changes. Saurabh Dube (Mexico) insisted that the question of religiosity for Dalits does not admit singular solutions.

Prithvi Datta Chandra Shobhi (Karnataka) discussed the relationship between Virashaiva *bhakti* and Untouchability in the twelfth century; he followed this up by discussing how Untouchables themselves in a later period, since the sixteenth century, produced critical epics. Ishita Banerjee-Dube (Mexico) foregrounded the ambivalences of (graded) inclusion, taking the case of Mahima Dharma (Odisha). She asked to what extent a change of faith could guarantee dignity and an erasure of negative discrimination. Beatrice Renzi (Max-Weber-Kolleg) explored Dalit counter-discourses and their relation to Brahmanical Hinduism in Madhya Pradesh and highlighted the critical importance of re-appropriating the divine to reclaim rights and dignity. Sanjay Jothe (Mumbai) focused on the contradiction among followers of the Kabirpanth between notions of a "mystic" Kabir and a "social revolutionary" Kabir. In contrast, Valerian Rodrigues (Mangalore) elaborated on the presence of Kabir as the "absent guru" in the life and work of B.R. Ambedkar.

Milind Wakankar (New Delhi) took up the instance of the seventeenth-century poet of the Qadiri Sufi sect, Sheikh Muhammad, who wrote Varkari (i.e., *bhakti*) poetry in Marathi, focusing on interiority and negativity. Joel Lee (Massachusetts), taking the case of the Halalkhor, Dalit Muslims in Eastern Uttar Pradesh, discussed the ambivalence of dissent and resistance, swaying between intimate untouchability and intimate touchability. Ajay Bhardwaj (Vancouver) presented both a documentary and a paper in which he highlighted a case of close association of Dalits with Sufi shrines in Punjab.

Joseph M.T. (Mumbai) covered the variants of positions among Dalit Buddhists in Aurangabad (Maharashtra). Jon Keune (Michigan) discussed the relationship of Dalit Buddhism with transnational Buddhist activity in Nagpur (Maharashtra). P. Sanal Mohan (Kerala) discussed the case of autonomous Dalit churches in Kerala, new forms of prayer and a new concept of the body, reviving pre-Christian traditions. Heinz Werner Wessler (Uppsala) presented various positions regarding the question of conversion among North-Indian Dalits who resist the call to Buddhism as part of the Dalit awareness movement.

A thorough study of Dalit experiences with the different modes of religiosity is important beyond India and South Asia. Within the field of religious studies it will realign the focus on inter-subjectivity and the quality of human relationships, paying particular attention to the significance that dimensions which transcend the world of materiality and immediacy have for the people concerned.

Conference, 8–10 November 2017: 'Urban Religion in Late Antiquity'
(Emiliano Urciuoli)

Organized through the collaboration between the MaxWeber-Kolleg and the Centre for Urban Network Evolutions at Aarhus University, the international conference "Urban Religion in Late Antiquity" (Augustinerkloster, Erfurt) invited scholars from different disciplinary backgrounds (classics, Roman and early modern history, early Christian studies, Byzantine studies, religious studies, archeology and sociology of religion) to explore late antique Mediterranean city spaces in order to address such questions as: How is religion used by different agents to appropriate and "craft" urban space over time? How do religious practices and imaginaries produce a transcending global that is different from other projections of the trans-urban? How does the urban context change different or even competing practices of religious communication and the ensuing forms of sacralization?

Within the framework of a larger comparative approach, the conference focused on these processes in the historical context of the advanced imperial and late antique Mediterranean space (2nd – 8th century CE). This is a period of sustained change and ever new appropriation of urban spaces by ever different agents within clearly articulated and monumentalized built environments. Interested in the individuals' making of urban space and in the processes of grouping following on, or directed against, such built environments, the papers looked for archeological evidence not only of new structures but also of rebuilding, ignoring or actively avoiding spaces, as well as of creating urban spaces by patterns of movements or marking in religious terms. Textual evidence for such strategies, as well as for imaginations of urban spaces, ritual practices, religious narratives or norms of reinterpreting and transcending them, were also specifically sought after. Without assuming an easy evolutionary path, the papers assumed and showcased high variability in the mutually productive relationship between the developments of urban-based religious practices and the developments of cities confronted with, and building on, agents who used religious practices in different phases of the history of religion. Both the mutual constitution and the mutual critique of the urban and the religious have emerged from the city-to-city investigations; they were further emphasized within the round-table and the final general discussions. The publication of the conference proceedings in the series "Religionsgeschichtliche Versuche und Vorarbeiten" (de Gruyter) is forthcoming.

Meister Eckhart in Köln, Internationale Jahrestagung der Meister Eckhart-Gesellschaft vom 15. bis 18. März 2018 in Köln (Markus Vinzent)

Die Meister-Eckhart-Gesellschaft zusammen mit dem Thomas-Institut der Universität zu Köln organisierte ihre Internationale Jahrestagung 2018 zum Thema „Meister Eckhart in Köln". Die wissenschaftliche Leitung und Organisation lag bei Andreas Speer, Direktor des ThomasInstituts der Universität zu Köln, Maxime Mauriège, Beauftragter für das Meister-Eckhart-Archiv am ThomasInstitut, und Freimut Löser, Professor für Deutsche Sprache und Literatur des Mittelalters, Universität Augsburg. Meister Eckharts Kölner Jahre stehen zumeist im Schlagschatten des Prozesses, der in dieser Stadt gegen ihn angestrengt wurde. Sein Wirken als Lektor am dominikanischen Generalstudium in Köln findet über das bloße Faktum hinaus kaum Beachtung, während seine dortige Predigttätigkeit häufig im Lichte des Prozesses wahrgenommen wird. Hierzu bieten die Prozessdokumente reichen Anlass und ebenso Eckharts Verteidigungsschriften. Nicht zuletzt hat die von Joseph Quint gewählte Editionsstrategie zu einem Bild des Kölner Eckhart beigetragen, das in wesentlichen Teilen von den Häresievorwürfen gegen den Meister geprägt ist.

Diese Leserichtung vom Ende her ist – ungeachtet ihrer Verdienste für die philologische Evidenz – nicht zuletzt deshalb problematisch, da die auf diese Weise intendierte oder gar erzeugte Teleologie nicht zwangsläufig mit den Intentionen und Fakten übereinstimmen muss, die Eckharts letztes großes Wirkungsfeld in Köln bis zum Beginn des Prozesses charakterisieren. In mehreren Vorträgen behandelte die Tagung die Frage, wodurch diese Jahre geprägt sind. Auffällig ist etwa, dass Eckhart seine Kölner Predigttätigkeit offenbar systematisch angelegt hat. Hiervon zeugen die zahlreichen Bezugnahmen auf Themen, Orte und Anlässe. Gibt es einen Kölner Predigtzyklus, wie ist dieser im Kirchenjahr einzuordnen und wie steht es um die Datierung? Auffällig sind auch die vielfältigen Bezüge auf Paris. Offensichtlich setzt sich

Eckhart noch intensiv mit den scholastischen Debatten an der Sorbonne auseinander. Wer sind seine potentiellen Gesprächspartner? Lassen sich hier Unterschiede zu seiner Pariser Zeit als Student, Lektor und Magister feststellen? Gibt es besondere theologische Themen in den Kölner Predigten? Gibt es darin Anzeichen für Diskontinuitäten mit seinen früheren Lehren? Wie steht es um die relative, wie um die absolute Chronologie der Texte? Kann man von einer Entwicklung Eckharts oder gar von einem Spätwerk sprechen? Wie spricht Eckhart konkret in Köln? Welche Hinweise gibt es auf den Zusammenhang zwischen Schreibsprache und Oralität sowie auf den Dialekt? Wer liest wann in welcher Form und in welcher Zusammenstellung die Kölner Texte? Hier stellt sich die Frage von Rezeption und Redaktion. Was lässt sich über die Wirkung der Kölner Texte sagen? Wie weitreichend sind sie? Fungiert Köln als Schaltstelle einer Verbindung zu den Niederlanden?

Eckharts eigene Übersetzungen zentraler Passagen seiner Kölner Predigten ins Lateinische im Rahmen seiner Verteidigung bieten einen Zugang zur Terminologie und zum Zusammenhang von lateinischem und deutschem Werk. Schließlich stellt sich die Frage nach dem historischen Kontext von Eckharts Kölner Zeit: die Situation und Form der Seelsorge, das dominikanische Generalstudium und die deutsche Dominikanerschule, der Einfluss Alberts des Großen, die Stellung der Dominikaner in der Stadt und im Verhältnis zu den anderen Orden sowie zum Erzbischof von Köln. Was ergibt der Vergleich mit anderen volkssprachigen Texten aus Köln (etwa den „Kölner Klosterpredigten")? Darf man ein „Eckhart-Publikum" in Köln annehmen? Lassen sich Spuren von Eckharts Tätigkeit auch außerhalb der Predigten und Prozessmaterialien (etwa in Texten wie „Meister Eckharts Wirtschaft") finden? Lassen sich Schüler Eckharts (z.B. Tauler, der im Kölner Dominikanerinnenkloster St. Gertrud gepredigt hat) oder Kölner ‚Eckhartisten', d.h. Anhänger des Meisters identifizieren und somit Hinweise auf eine mittelbare Überlieferung finden? Wie steht es mit Kölner häretischen Kreisen und speziellen Seelsorgestrategien? Ziel der Tagung war es, eine differenzierte Sicht auf Meister Eckharts Kölner Zeit und eine sorgfältige Spurensuche in den historischen, philosophisch-theologischen und institutionellen Milieus zu bieten.

Tagung vom 16. bis 17. Mai 2018 in Metz: 'Maître Eckhart: Lecteur des Pères de l'Église' (Sarah Al-Taher, Markus Vinzent)

Im März 2018 wurde das DFG-ANR-Kooperationsprojekt „Lehren und Predigen mit patristischen *auctoritates*. Meister Eckhart, Brückenbildner zwischen Frankreich und Deutschland, Vergangenheit und Gegenwart" unter der Leitung von Markus Vinzent (Max-Weber-Kolleg Erfurt) und Marie-Anne Vannier (Université de Lorraine) aufgenommen. In dieser Kooperation sollen Fragen nach Prozessen von Rezeption bzw. Appropriation, der Verschiebung von Autoritäten und Nutzung von Referenzen und der kreativen Dynamik von Lektüre und Relektüre untersucht werden. Neben Monographien und gesammelten Studien wird unter anderem ein kritischer Index der patristischen Quellen Eckharts erarbeitet. Anlässlich dieser Kooperation, innerhalb deren das deutsche und französische Team gemeinsam die Quellen Meister Eckharts erforschen und der Wissenschaft zur Verfügung stellen wird, fand die erste gemeinsame Tagung zum Thema „Maître Eckhart: Lecteur des Pères de l'Église" in Metz statt. Vertreten wurde das Max-Weber-Kolleg durch Markus Vinzent, Julie Casteigt, Jana Ilnicka, Dietmar Mieth und Sarah Al-Taher.

In französischer und deutscher Sprache wurden zahlreiche Vorträge rund um das Thema „Eckhart und die Kirchenväter" gehalten – besonderer Schwerpunkt war die Bedeutung und Vielseitigkeit der verschiedenen Quellen Eckharts. Neben einem historischen Erkenntnisgewinn ermöglicht die Erforschung der bislang vernachlässigten Quellen ein tieferes und vielseitigeres Verständnis der Nomenklatur zur Erfassung der verschiedenen Prozesse in der Literaturaneignung eines mittelalterlichen Autors wie Eckhart.

Julie Casteigt sprach zum Beispiel über den Einfluss der Kirchenväter in Eckharts Denken; Jana Ilnicka hielt einen Vortrag zum Thema „Boethius als Gewährsdenker für die Trinität"; Dietmar Mieth stellte die Nutzung patristischer Quellen Eckharts in den Bezug zur Gegenwart; Markus Vinzent nutzte das Beispiel der Referenz auf die Bekenntnisse des Augustinus bei Eckhart zur Frage nach Reziklat und Zitat. Zusammen mit den Beiträgen der französischen Kolleg/innen aus den historischen, sprachlichen und literaturwissenschaftlichen Disziplinen vor allem zu einzelnen patristischen Autoren (Hieronymus, Isidor von Sevilla etc.) wurde deutlich, dass zunächst Grundfragen etwa zu den Themen Zitat, Verweis, Referat etc. geklärt werden müssen, bevor zielgerichtet nach Eckharts möglichen Verwendungen von *auctoritates* gefragt werden kann. Durch diese erste, erfolgreiche gemeinsame Tagung in Metz konnte eine Plattform für eine produktive und anhaltende Zusammenarbeit geschaffen werden, die demnächst auch digital unterstützt wird. Das Auftakttreffen in Metz bot darüber hinaus einen guten Rahmen, um auch persönlich miteinander ins Gespräch zu kommen und sich gegenseitig zu bereichern. Im Rahmen des Kooperationsprojekts werden in Zukunft weitere gemeinsame Veranstaltungen stattfinden.

Conference, 4–6 July 2018: 'Religion of Quarters: Practicing Religion on a Neighborhood Scale in the Hellenistic and Imperial Periods' (Emiliano Urciuoli)

The International Conference "Religion of Quarters: Practicing Religion on a Neighborhood Scale in the Hellenistic and Imperial Periods" posited that the assumption that basic units of dwelling, working and gathering in densely populated quarters of the cities of the empire form a privileged focus of investigation for the study of ancient Mediterranean religions. Often devoid of monumental complexes, the kind of religion taking place on this scale of the urban fabric is traditionally grouped under the questionable rubric of "private religion". Questioning conventional dichotomies for the classification and spatialization of phenomena deemed religious (such as "public / private", "polis religion / cults"), the conference gathered together scholars from different fields in order to discuss how inner-city spaces affected the shape of religious representations, conducts and experiences during the Hellenistic and Roman Periods ("Urban Religion").

The topic of the conference comprised a rich variety of urban settlements: (a) multi-story crowded tenements with several rental apartments functioning as space for a variety of religious practices; (b) grand houses organized into portions whose physical setting could occasionally accommodate non-resident and extra-familial worshippers; (c) different non-residential locales (shops, halls, clubhouses etc.) belonging to the same city block and run by family members, leased to private individuals and / or used as meeting places for associations; (d) privately owned but publicly used facilities (neighborhood baths, cookshops and bars) functioning as neighborhood highlights and landmarks and forming the focus of the local communal life; (e) side-streets and crossroads with their relatively small-scaled religious material environments.

The program raised a number of questions: How and to what extent did the varying spatial features of domestic units and street networks affect the imagination and practice of religion? Which was the interplay between urban layout, locational aspect and occupancy patterns of buildings, and the construction of neighborhood-based religious networks? What forms of rivalry among religious specialists did such locations prompt? What codes of religious conduct became necessary and persuasive in such settings? Although the participants agreed that several critical problems still need to be solved and questions reassessed on both a theoretical and empirical level (e.g., What boundaries do neighborhoods delineate? How does localism and "locative religion" map onto "neighborhood religion"? Which are the most suitable comparative models for the study of neighborhood religion at a crosscultural level?), the conference has eventually probed and gauged the potentiality of a neighborhood-scale analysis of religious communication in ancient Mediterranean cities. The publication of the conference proceedings is planned for the second half of 2019.

8.2 ERC Advanced Grant "Lived Ancient Religion"

Koordinatorin: Dr. Anna-Katharina Rieger

Internationale wissenschaftliche Tagung des ‚Lived Ancient Religion'-Projekts vom 4. bis 7. November 2012 am Deutschen Archäologischen Institut und der British School in Rom: „Archäologie gelebter Religion in der Antike" (Jörg Rüpke)

Religionsarchäologie hat sich in den vergangenen Jahren mit Hilfe neuer Methoden in der Archäologie zu einem wichtigen Arbeitsfeld entwickelt. Materielle Überreste werden als Spuren von Ritualen oder Ausdrucksformen religiöser Erfahrungen gedeutet. Die innovativste Forschung wird zweifelsohne in sehr konkreten Bereichen wie in der Archäologie des (Opfer-)Rituals und des Todes betrieben. Der *Lived-Ancient-Religion*-Ansatz lenkt die Aufmerksamkeit auf Praktiken und Alltagsreligion. In Form einer internationalen Tagung an zwei wichtigen Standorten archäologisch-altertumswissenschaftlicher Forschung und in Kooperation mit dem Istituto Svizzera wie der Universitet Aarhus (Henner von Hesberg, Rubina Raja, Christoph Riedweg, Jörg Rüpke, Christopher Smith) wurden auf der Basis vorab ausgetauschter Texte grundsätzliche methodische Probleme der Religionsarchäologie wie die neuen Perspektiven und die für sie notwendige Datengrundlage diskutiert, die die Frage nach gelebter Religion bietet und sich von einer „archaeology of belief" oder kognitionswissenschaftlichen Ansätzen (T. Insoll, H. Whitehouse) grundsätzlich unterscheidet.

Ein erster Blick galt der Perspektive des „Embodiment", konkretisiert durch Laura Gawlinski (Loyola) an Bekleidung, Gideon Bohak (Jerusalem) an Amuletten und durch Thierry Luginbühl (Lausanne) an Prozessionsritualen im gallorömischen und indischen Bereich. Frederick G. Naerebout (Leiden) ergänzte das mit dem Blick auf Tanz, Robin Jensen (Vanderbilt) in ihrer Analyse von Bauten für Initiationsrituale, insbesondere die Taufe. Ein zweiter Blick galt den Formen religiöser Erfahrung, so des gemeinsamen Mahls (Marleen Martens, Brüssel) und Formen temporärer Deprivation (Richard Gordon, Erfurt), ein dritter Austauschprozessen und Modifikationen in Randzonen oder außerhalb des römischen Reiches, in Britannien, Nordafrika und Ägypten (Greg Woolf, St. Andrews; Valentino Gasparini und Lara Weiss, Erfurt).

Den räumlichen und materialen Bedingungen religiöser Erfahrung wurden expressive Formen gegenübergestellt: Alexandra Busch (Rom) untersuchte Altäre, Günther Schörner (Wien) Votive, die Körperteile darstellen, Wolfgang Spickermann (Erfurt, jetzt Graz) monumentale Inschriften. Marlis Arnhold (Erfurt, jetzt Bonn) schuf mit dem Blick auf die Kultanlagen, die von kleineren religiösen Vereinen errichtet wurden, einen Übergang zur folgenden Gruppe von Beiträgen. Hier fragten nach Räumen religiöser Erfahrungen Richard Neudecker (Rom), der antike Gärten vorstellte, wie Joannis Mylonopoulos (New York), der Formen der Erstellung sakraler Landschaften vorführte. Miguel John Versluys und Eva Mol (Leiden) ergänzten das mit einem Blick auf „imagined communities", Christopher Smith (Rom/St. Andrews) mit der Frage nach der Schaffung von Erinnerungsräumen in Städten wie Rom. Die klassischen Formen sakraler Räume bildeten den Abschluss dieser Sektion: Tempel (Henner von Hesberg, Rom), komplexe Heiligtumsanlagen, besonders in den nordwestlichen Provinzen (William van Andringa, Rennes), und offene Heiligtümer (Rubina Raja, Aarhus). Inge Nielsen (Hamburg) und Susanne Gödde (München) ergänzten die Befunde um Gebäude religiöser Gruppen und Theater.

Abschließend standen übergreifende analytische Probleme im Vordergrund. Die verschiedenen Etappen der religionsarchäologischen Gender-Forschung stellte Zsuzsa Varhelyi (Boston) vor, Steven Fine (New York) erläuterte exemplarisch das Problem des häufig faktischen Verlusts und der auf Graustufen fixierten Theoriebildung, Eric Rebillard (Ithaca) behandelte die Probleme, religiöse Identitäten aus archäologischen Befunden zu erhellen. Jörg Rüpke (Erfurt) vertiefte das Problem von kollektiv oder individualisierend orientierten analytischen Perspektiven. Zum Abschluss der Tagung behandelte John North (London) in der ersten „Roma/London Lecture" das Thema „Göttinnen und Sibyllen".

Die Ergebnisse der Diskussionen sollen in einen gemeinsamen und durch weitere Beiträge ergänzten „Companion to the Archaeology of Religion in the Ancient World" einfließen, der sich inzwischen in der Schlussphase redaktioneller Bearbeitung befindet.

Opening conference for the ERC research project "Lived Ancient Religion: Questioning 'Cults' and 'Polis Religion'", 11th –14th June 2013, at the Max-Weber-Center: "Sharpening the Knife: Making Religion Effective in Everyday Life" (Marlis Arnhold)

With this conference, the project funded by the European Union within the 7th Framework Programme which is located at the Max Weber Center of the University of Erfurt and directed by Prof. Dr. Jörg Rüpke (Erfurt, Germany) and Prof. Dr. Rubina Raja (Aarhus, Denmark) was publicly opened. Thus a series of consultations of experts was started. The conference pursued a twofold aim which focused both on the introduction to the project and its various aspects as well as the methodological issues raised by it. In order to "sharpen the knife" in regard to methodology, scholars from three continents, representing a wide range of subjects such as Archaeology, Ancient History, Philology, Religious Studies, and Theology, came together to contribute presentations from the perspective of their specific fields and to discuss their methodological approaches.

The conference started on 11 June with the ceremonial opening at the Thueringen State Chancellery which was attended by approximately 70 participants. They were welcomed by the patron of the conference, Marion Walsmann, Thueringen Minister for European Affairs and Head of the State Chancellery. Jörg Rüpke introduced the issues of the project before Rubina Raja concluded with a first insight into the scope of the project in her public lecture titled "Look at me! My Father was Famous: Priestly

Self-Representations in the Roman Near East as Media Creating Meaning in Situations".

During the following days the conference continued at the Augustinerkloster, Erfurt. The first session on Wednesday, 12 June, brought the aspect of "The Role of Objects" to attention which was first addressed by Lucinda Dirven (Amsterdam). In her presentation "Imagining Religion in Mithraic Cults. The Case of Dura-Europos" she particularly stressed the issue of cult attendents staging rituals and myths and thus shed new light on the diversity of a cult that is generally perceived as rather uniform. The objects of this presentation can be found depicted on the walls of the Dura Europos-mithraeum itself. Lara Weiss, herself member of the ERC-project at Erfurt, spoke about "Conceptualizing the Creation of the Sacred: Mass Production vs. Handmade Figurines". Showing examples from her investigations at Karanis in Egypt she discussed what different kinds of meaning the same object could have for different persons in different situations. A toy from the perspective of a child could very well have been a figurine for religious purposes from the standpoint of its parents. The session continued with the contribution of Michael Satlow (Providence, RI). Speaking about "Searching for Jewish Votive Objects in Roman Palestine", Michael Satlow dealt with the question under which conditions objects received a sacred meaning and were perceived as sacred by the authors of various Jewish texts. Particularly interesting was the temporal shift from referring to an object as "sacred" to "put into higher service" which Michael Satlow noted. The papers of this session thus discussed new methods illustrated in case studies and pinpointed the variety of experiences and memories stimulated.

The second session was dedicated to the issue "Group Styles" and likewise comprised three presentations. Markus Vinzent (London) contributed a critical view of the topic from the perspective of his studies on Marcion, titled "Practical and Cognitive Dissonance: Jewish Liturgical Traditions, Innovations and Counter-Rites in Marcion's Roman Community". Then, Marlis Arnhold (Erfurt) raised the questions of the lack of visibility and limited visual accesses as well as the consequences of these for the understanding of cult-groups. For this, she analysed the archaeological, epigraphic and literary evidence of the Bona Dea cult at Ostia for her presentation "The Last One Shuts the Door: Cult-Groups Communicating Through (In)Visibility". Finally the topic of the session was addressed by John North (London) in his investigation on the "Funeral Rituals and the Significance of the *Nenia*" which focused on the ritual lamentation at the end of Roman funerals and the views of various authors on it. The contributions to this session thus all shed a critical view on the term group and underlined the temporally limited, situational visibility and construction of the collective identities that defined them. This session raised the most controversial opinions during the final discussion. The topic is highly important as the modern notion of the term "group" still persists in scholarship and the questions, what makes a group actually a group, when, and how often, do require much discussion.

Session III comprised four presentations on the topic "Meaning in Situations" and started with Anton Bierl (Basel) and his contribution on "Lived Religion and Construction of Meaning in Greek Literary Texts and Contexts". He focused on the situational construction of new meanings by various Greek authors using among others mythical stories problematising the notion of literary texts as "sources". Eric Rebillard (Ithaca, NY) spoke about "Everyday Christianity in Third-Century Carthage". In reference to "everyday nationhood" he proposed a theoretical framework that could be used to analyze sites "where Christianness might, but need not, be at work". In the third contribution to the session, Vered Noam (Tel Aviv) addressed the Jewish views of what was perceived as impure ritual in various situations – and what not in others – in her presentation "Ritual Impurity and Human Intention". And finally, Christopher Smith (Rome) raised the question of what role prayers and other ritualised speech acts played in Roman religion drawing attention to the ideas of Eduard Norden's Œuvre „Aus altrömischen Priesterbüchern". The title of this book also served as title of his contribution. The session's contributions hence explored "meaning" in situational constructs and examined the effectiveness of religious instruments as employed in order to create, change, and enhance meanings.

It was followed by a poster session of altogether ten doctoral and postdoctoral researchers who had been invited to attend the conference.

The afternoon continued with the fourth session on "Appropriation" which drew attention on the individuals behind the actions that led to the construction of rituals and buildings as well as the production of meanings in difference to established traditions. Karen King (Harvard) started with her contribution "Religion(s) of the Book"/"Textual Communities" asking which of the lived practices actually had the potential to make it into 'book religion' and what authority the written word had in light of illiteracy. Michal Bar-Asher Siegal (Beer Sheva) continued with a presentation on "The Transmission and Collections of Traditions in Anthologies" which revealed her passion for the issue how traditions from anthologies were later on loaded with authority by religious communities. Under the title "Just Like the Emperor and his Family: Appropriating the Emperors' Religion in the Roman Empire" Zsuzsa Varhelyi (Boston) then drew attention of what can be termed "(implicit) religious trend-setting" through the emperors and their families. Independent of their specific topic, all of the contributions from this session explore the processual character of religious practice and underline that actually every agent is provider and acquisant at the same time which shows how complex religious change in fact is. This also accounts for the last presentation of this session, given by Angela Standhartinger (Marburg) on "The Beginning of the Eucharist or Constructing the Lord's Supper". It centered on the "words of institution", 1 Cor 11:22-25/Mk 14,22-24 par., and their meaning and function in the context of the Eucharist, proposing an origin in the context of ritual lamentation at funerals.

The last session held on the morning of Friday, 14 June, dealt with „Learning and Memory" from the perspective of lived religion. The contributions here addressed the questions how individual religious practice depended upon the intellectual as well as the embodied availability and the situational salience of "traditions", that is, complex belief systems or simple sequences of ritual action. The terms "learning" and "memory" here refered to processes of acquireing knowledge by formal training or constant repetition and to instances of recalling emotions, complex patterns, cognitive or bodily knowledge. Asking for "The Implicit Reader of Antiquarian Literature: Questions in Ovid's Libri fastorum" Jörg Rüpke (Erfurt) shed new light on an extensively studied literary text from the time of Augustus. Katharina Waldner (Erfurt) analysed the rituals described and explained in the text of the Derveni Papyrus. Under the title "Reading, Knowledge and Religious Practice: The Derveni Papyrus and its Context" she discussed the contents of the texts in regard of its find context, that is burials which reveal a highly individualized burial practice, as well as in relation to presocratic philosophy.

The conference thus brought many aspects, methodological issues, and perspectives related to "Lived Ancient Religion" up, which provide a fruitful base both for further investigations by the various participants as well as the general approach of the overall ERC-project. With the knife thus sharpened connection points between the topics of the single sessions and with them, the complexity of the issue under investigation, have become much more visible.

„The Role of Objects – Creating Meaning in Situations", internationale Tagung im Rahmen des ERC-Projekts „Lived Ancient Religion: Questioning ,Cults' and ,Polis Religion',, vom 9. bis 11. Oktober 2013 im Haus Hainstein/Wartburg in Eisenach (Lara Weiss)

Im Rahmen des von Jörg Rüpke initiierten Projekts *Lived Ancient Religion* (LAR) zur religionswissenschaftlichen Grundlagenforschung fand vom 9. bis 11. Oktober in der Eisenacher Tagungsstätte Haus Hainstein die von Rubina Raja und Lara Weiss organisierte internationale Tagung „The role of objects-creating meaning in situations" statt. Sie war Richard Gordon zum 70. Geburtstag gewidmet.

Hintergrund für die Tagung war die Beobachtung, dass religiöse Objekte in der Antike einen gegenständlichen und visuellen Rahmen für gelebte Religion bildeten. Je nach Situation und Person konnten z.B. dieselben Dinge unterschiedliche Rollen spielen oder auch selbst zu bestimmenden Faktoren von religiösen Handlungen werden. Das Spektrum der Vorträge der Tagung des Max-Weber-Kollegs der Universität Erfurt umfasste jedoch nicht nur die mitteleuropäische Antike, sondern auch den vorderen Orient, Indien und Mesoamerika. Genauso international waren die geladenen Sprecher, die aus zehn Ländern (USA, Frankreich, Niederlande, Schweiz, Spanien, Bulgarien, Großbritannien, Italien, Dänemark und Israel) angereist waren und in regen Diskussionen der Frage auf den Grund gingen, wie genau verschiedene Dinge je nach Gebrauchskontext Sinn stifteten und wie sie bestehende Bedeutungen veränderten oder auch verstärkten.

In vier thematischen Folgen wurden jeweils verschiedene Themenkomplexe abgearbeitet. Die erste Session „Identifying Objects in Contemporary Discourse" konzentrierte sich auf den Diskurs verschiedener Objekte. Während Patricia McAnany (Chapel Hill) die unterschiedlichen Bedeutungen von Knochenresten in verschiedenen Grabtypen diskutierte, zeigte Ioanna Patera (Paris) die Undefinierbarkeit von Opfergaben bzw. eben gerade nicht deren Ersatz auf. Die zweite Session „Transferable Meanings in Space and Time" zeigte den Imperator Augustus als religiöses Objekt (Frank Daubner/Stuttgart) sowie Keramikware, aber auch -scherben als sichtbare Erinnerung an die im Tempel vollzogenen Opfer (Anna-Katharina Rieger/Erfurt). In der dritten Session „Objects, Spaces and Time" diskutierte Richard Gordon (Erfurt) die Rolle von Fluchtafeln und Drew Wilburn (Oberlin) die Bedeutung von Straußeneiern als religiöse Objekte. In „Multiple Meanings" konnte gezeigt werden, in welchen Situationen und unter welchen Bedingungen Objekte auch verschiedene Bedeutungen annehmen können. U.a. gelten solche vielfachen Bedeutungen für Opfergaben im Sanktuar der Magna Mater in Ostia (Alison Cooley/Warwick), die Gürtelschnalle römischer Soldaten (Stephanie Hoss/ Sheffield), beim Abendmahl ausgeteiltes Brot/Eucharistie (Volker Menze/Budapest), Textilfigürchen aus Ägypten (Karen Johnson/ Ann Arbor), Terrakottas aus Beit Nattif (Achim Lichtenberger/Bochum), die sogenannten Bankett-tesserae aus Palmyra (Rubina Raja/Aarhus) sowie die Amtstracht der jüdischen Hohepriester (Gideon Bohak/Tel Aviv). Die Session „Mobility and Immobility as Change Factors" schließlich, ging der Frage nach, ob (Im)mobilität einen konzeptuellen Unterschied im Gebrauch von Objekten macht, was anhand von goldenen Glasmedallions im Grab- bzw. Hauskontext (Hallie Meredith/Dartmouth), der Ikonographie der Göttin Tyche auf phönizischen Münzen (Andreas Kropp/Nottingham), dem Banner von Indra im altvedischen Ritual (Angelika Malinar/Zürich) sowie für feste und bewegliche Hausaltare im römischen Ägypten (Lara Weiss/Erfurt) gezeigt werden konnte. Den Festvortrag hielt Francisco Marco Simon (Zaragoza) zu Objekten, die Freundschaftsverträge zwischen Städten religiös symbolisierten.

Die Tagung darf als voller Erfolg gelten. Es gab nicht nur zahlreiche Anknüpfungspunkte zwischen den einzelnen Beiträgen und Gesichtspunkten, sondern es kam auch schon gleich zu Beginn eine wunderbare Stimmung und Dynamik zwischen den Teilnehmern auf, die sicherlich nicht zuletzt auf die mitten im Wald gelegene Tagungsstätte mit einem malerischen Blick auf die Wartburg zurückzuführen ist. Nicht zuletzt durch die verschiedenen methodischen Ansätze konnte z.T. bekanntes Material neu definiert und verstanden werden. Es wurden aber auch einige Fragen für die weitere Forschung aufgeworfen, z.B. inwieweit man Objekte als Konzept jenseits ihrer Dinglichkeit verstehen könne. Als wichtigstes Ergebnis der Konferenz darf genannt werden, dass die Bedeutung religiöser Objekte keineswegs statisch ist. Im Gegenteil: Die Bedeutungen von Objekten unterscheiden sich nicht nur zwischen den jeweiligen Religionen, sondern können auch innerhalb bestimmter Kulturräume je nach Kontext verschieden sein, da die Objekte von den jeweiligen Akteuren in jeder Situation neu angeeignet werden und sich ihre Bedeutung dabei verändern kann. Damit inspirierte die Konferenz nicht nur alle Teilnehmer, sondern auch die laufende Forschung der Lived Ancient Religion-Mitarbeiter auf allen Ebenen, d.h. sowohl die eher archäologisch ausgerichteten als auch die eher historisch und philologisch ausgerichteten Forschungsprojekte.

Internationale Konferenz im Rahmen des ERC-Projekts „Lived Ancient Religion" vom 29. bis 31. Januar 2014 auf Schloss Ettersburg bei Weimar: „Stories told – Memories uttered" (Christopher Degelmann)

Zwischen dem 29. und 31. Januar 2014 traf sich in Schloss Ettersburg bei Weimar eine internationale und interdisziplinäre Gruppe im Rahmen des vom *European Research Council* geförderten Projekts *Lived Ancient Religion: Questioning ‚cults' and ‚polis religion'*. Die inzwischen dritte Tagung der Erfurter Forschergruppe mit dem Titel „Stories told – Memories uttered", organisiert von Christopher Degelmann und Jörg Rüpke, befasste sich mit der Bedeutung von Narrativen für die Erfahrung von Ritualen im griechisch-römischen Altertum und den Nachbarkulturen. Anhand von vornehmlich textlichen Quellen fragte sie nach der Art und Weise, wie Erzählungen von der eigenen, aber auch über fremde Religion das religiöse Individuum beeinflussen konnten oder zur Konstruktion einer kollektiven religiösen Identität beitrugen. Besonderes Augenmerk lag neben den zeitlichen und räumlichen Aspekten vor allem auf den damit einhergehenden sozialen, historischen und kognitiven Auswirkungen von religiösen Narrativen: Wie lang waren einzelne Geschichten, Fabeln und Sagen in Gebrauch? Wie weit verbreiteten sie sich? Welche Faktoren trugen zu ihrer Lang- oder Kurzlebigkeit bei? Wem dienten sie wozu und welche Machtverhältnisse wurden dadurch konfiguriert? Dabei bildeten nicht zuletzt die Struktur von Narrativen und die Suche nach den Konsequenzen der Beschaffenheit von Texten und Erzählungen einen zentralen Untersuchungsgegenstand.

Diese Fragen wurden entlang von Fallstudien überprüft. So untersuchte man Biographien, Pilgerberichte, Briefwechsel, Ritualtexte und Inschriften sowie viele andere Formen des verschriftlichen Wortes auf ihren Wert für die Bildung von kleineren und größeren Narrativen. Deutlich wurde ein Unterschied zwischen den griechisch-römischen Traditionen und den älteren Kulturen des antiken Nahen Ostens, für den identitätsbildende Erzählungen aufgrund einer vor allem archäologisch, weniger textlich fundierten Quellenbasis kaum festzustellen sind. Aber auch christliche Zeugnisse bewegen sich zwischen eigener, auf Abgrenzung und Polemik bedachter Traditionsbildung und der Aneignung zahlreicher paganer Motive, die den Anhängern ein Gefühl der Vertrautheit in einer als religiös zumindest als feindlich konstruierten Umwelt vermitteln sollten. Allgemein deutet dieses Phänomen in eine Richtung, die auch für andere religiöse Gruppen beansprucht werden kann: Sie wurden sowohl von außen als auch von innen mit einem Label versehen, das sich in den Erzählungen von und über die jeweilige Religionsgemeinschaft niederschlug und narrativ kodiert war.

Außerdem kam mehrfach zur Sprache, wie limitiert unser Blick auf Narrative vor dem Hintergrund des gesprochenen Wortes ist. Zahlreiche, wirkmächtige – im eigentlichen Sinn des Wortes – Erzählungen können wir nicht mehr fassen, da man sie nicht verschriftlichte. Dazu zählten nicht nur langlebige Motive, die über Rhapsoden und dergleichen vermittelt wurden, sondern auch humorvolle Geschichten und Witze, die man etwa über siegreiche Feldherren zum Besten gab. Sie spiegelten häufig die persönlichen Erfahrungen der kleinen Leute wider, wie man sie auch in dem für die Antike nur marginal beleuchteten Phänomen des Gerüchts greifen kann. Die Untersuchung von entsprechenden Graffiti und Dipinti mag eine Alternative sein zu einer textwissenschaftlichen Annäherung an das Problem des ‚gesprochenen Narratives' und seiner Auswirkung wie Ausbreitung in verschiedene Textgruppen; doch sie ist nicht in der Lage, den narrativen Kontext einzubinden oder gar zu rekonstruieren. So wurde konstatiert, dass diese Erscheinung eine der zentralen Herausforderungen kommender Auseinandersetzung mit der Rolle religiöser Narrative in den Kulturen des antiken Mittelmeerraums darstellt.

International conference of the ERC project 'Lived Ancient Religion', 2nd to 4th June, 2014 at the Royal Academy of Sciences and Letters, Copenhagen: 'Grouping together in Lived Ancient Religion' (Anna-Katharina Rieger)

How do groups come into being? How do the members interact, internally and externally? What is the role of groups in changing societal and political situations? These were the main questions posed by the 4th LAR-conference "Grouping together in lived ancient religion", a conference, which offered new insights into the nature and dynamics of groups in religious contexts.

Focusing on situational communication in and of groups, the conference drew on the concept of "culture in interaction", implying the shaping of "group styles" for understanding formation, unity or diversity of religious groups (Lichterman – Eliasoph 2003). These concepts allow for theorising situational differences in creating and reproducing religious representations, knowledge and practices – away from public norms. Speech and text, selection of objects, dress and gesture, as well as choice of time and place might be significant in order to establish groups at least on a temporary basis. The six sessions of the conference were dedicated to the different situations and strategies by which people unify and specialize in, establish authority by or enunciate religious groups. Classicists, archaeologists, sociologists as well as scholars from Theology, Judaic studies and Ancient History gathered at the Royal Academy of Science and Letters of Denmark to discuss these issues.

Paul Lichterman (Los Angeles) opened the first session by providing a rich discussion of the "sociological perspective on groups in religions contexts". He broadened his and N. Eliasoph's concept of group style (embracing *group boundaries*, *group ties* and *speech norms*) by *group scenes* that form the collective (religious) practice and can be appropriated depending on the individual situation. Many of the following contributions referred to his concepts and explored in how far they might bear on religiously defined groups in antiquity. Emiliano Urciuoli (Modena) utilized the field-theory of Pierre Bourdieu and looked at how Christians behaved as members of the political elite of pre-Constantinian Rome. The in principle contradictory fields of "power" and "Christian religion" were merged in the political and economic interest of these individuals, who belonged simultaneously to different "social universes". The contribution of Urciuoli raised the general issue of identities determined by the belonging to a group: Our terminological distinction of "Christ" and "Roman" was an entity *in personam*.

The second session – "Encounters in travelling" – focused on how groups may form and on how existing groups may (inter)act in the special situation of being on the move. Philippe Bornet (Lausanne) showed how Rabbis established their authority and fostered the spread of ideas or rules by travelling around. Changing places and coming into contact with different groups helped to build up a network where they were active as guests, teachers and arbitrators. Katharina Rieger (Erfurt) analysed Late Hellenistic and Roman sacred places along the routes of the Arab Desert that are both adapted to and formed by travelling individuals and groups. Through religious practices as dedications and graffiti these travellers communicated to others (individuals or groups). Without being present at the same moment they formed groups – beyond time and space. Tim Whitmarsh (Oxford) dealt with a "mental community", the *atheoi*. He focused on the Late Hellenistic times where reflections in texts show that these *atheoi* are not formed by social interaction but by their renunciation of the gods. He argued that the *doxographia* of that time structured the knowledge and facilitated the formation of networks of intellectuals – unified in the negation of the gods – in Early Imperial times.

The contribution of Eric Rebillard (Ithaca) in the third session of the conference on "Encounters in public and private spaces" inquired into the strategies employed by Christians in third century Carthage to distinguish themselves from their fellow Carthaginians. Rather unexpectedly, the followers of Christ attached importance to distinction by means of dress, naming or gestures only internally. Yet, in situations among other Carthaginian citizen, these distinctions did not play any role. Those "separate worlds" did not exist socially and spatially, but only temporarily in the contexts of religious gatherings. Arja Karivieri (Stockholm) with her paper on cave sanctuaries in Attica raised the question of cult practices, their religious affiliation, (intellectual) motivation and density, especially in Late Antiquity. The increase of the objects (lamps) as opposed to the decrease in the variety in Late Antiquity and Early Byzantine times is evidence of large gatherings in those caves and/or with a higher frequency. Karivieri related this phenomenon to the neo-platonic philosophy and the religious groups related to it. On the other hand, the mere increase of population in that time could be the reason for a surge of activity in the caves.

Aspects of gender were the topic of the fourth session, "Gender specific strategies and situations". Here Kate Cooper (Manchester) developed further her thoughts on "subordinate members" (of a household, a group, a society) and their vulnerability. By comparing late antique female martyrs, *defixiones* and the kidnapping of Syrian nuns in the year 2013, she explored the possible ways women can oppose to violence and (male) dominance. Darja Šterbenc Erker (Berlin) addressed the role of the Roman *matrones* as powerful group in religious and thus political concerns in Augustan times. A close reading of official documents of the *ludi saeculares* of 17 BCE (CIL 6, 32323) reveals the disobedience of the matrons as group, who decided not to fulfill their part in the rites. Conscious negation of authority along the lines of different religious duties (mourning, *ludi*) of one societal group leads to a reformulation of the ritual rules of the *ludi*.

The fifth session was dedicated to "Textual communities", where Karen L. King (Harvard) offered an example on how to apply group style to ancient groups that formed around reading, hearing and interpreting texts. Referring to Pauline literature and the understanding of text as practice, she argued that a religion like Christianity, based on texts, varies widely through the different situations where the texts are enacted, and what practices are played out. This view allows for assessing the impact of putative texts as well. Françoise van Haeperen (Louvain-la-Neuve) interpreted epigraphical evidence (taken as speech norm) from Ostian guilds as example for groups using texts as forming and unifying element (ties and boundaries). Via these practises, van Haeperen maintained, not only did they establish their internal cohesion, but also communicated their external references (city, Imperial court). Even though highly formalized, these epigraphic documents were used in a highly refined manner by the *collegae* to clear their position in the social network of Ostia. Jörg Rüpke (Erfurt) questioned the concept of textual communities as strong momentum also for religious groupings, especially in times of political and cultural change. Referring to texts from different genres that span across the first centuries CE he claimed that it were more local and transient networks that formed around textual practices, rather than strong, textual communities, unified through a canon of texts. Speech norms can be detected in texts from the first century CE onwards, nonetheless, group ties and boundaries were transmitted only to a limited extent.

The focus on "Short term ritual communities" in the sixth session offered us the opportunity to look at temporarily limited groupings, how they were constituted and perpetuated. Maura K. Heyn (Greensboro) explored the signs and styles priests on Palmyrene tomb reliefs used to represent themselves by choosing distinct features of dress, gesture and attributes that set them apart from others Palmyrenians. The depictions in the tombs were used to remind of communal (religious) gatherings, thus strengthening both, the prestige of the deceased and the community identity of Palmyra. Aspects of time and point in time were addressed by Michael Satlow (Providence) in his contribution on the Jewish New Moon celebrations. By comparing the rules for this periodical practice from The Hebrew Bible with the ones of Late Antique Rabbinic texts, he showed how variable and flexible a calendric festival can be and the ways the importance of a ritually correct observance of the New Moon had changed. Lived religious practices and centralized rules (temple/rabbi) are highly interwoven with local variations to which Rabbis responded as having great importance. Clemens Leonhard (Münster) discussed the gradual differences of adherence to Christian groups – a characteristic of Late Antiquity. Participation and access to rituals was on a temporary basis (Eucharist); or it was only seen as a potential (Baptism). "Extra-liturgical benefits such as access to informal social networks" was of more importance in the second/third century than a fully established membership, as developed in the fourth/fifth century CE. Differentiation by group styles and internal bonding was of limited interest for early Christians. Rubina Raja (Aarhus) addressed the issue of banqueting groups in Palmyra. Mirrored in the *tesserae* – entrance tickets to their ritual banquets – these groupings appear as temporarily, spatially and socially highly restricted and exclusive. This phenomenon – comparable to associations – allows for questioning the heuristically hampering categories of public and private cultic activities and the related static groups of a public or a private body of people. Such short term communities served as link between other social groupings in the society, thus establishing at the same time distinction and connection.

The participants engaged in a lively and highly interrelated discussion, thus narrowing down the questions that remained, the helpful sociological concepts or terminological problems. As a result most participants agreed to the suitability of a definition of groups via *styles* and *scenes* that takes account of groups as highly fluid and unstable entities of societies. However, the distinction of group from, for example, network, community or association has yet to be determined. On this definition depends how to assess the quality and types of interaction which all groupings substantially are based on. Depending on the variety and simultaneously the limitedness of ancient sources (texts, objects, spaces, reconstructed practices) their distinctive characteristics and qualities have to be clearly delineated. Moreover, the individual and his/her choices (out of a culturally given set) as an influential factor of a group's constitution must not be neglected either.

The range of methodological approaches and scholarly backgrounds offered in the fourth LAR conference inspired thoughts that will bear on the approach of *Lived Ancient Religion*, emphasizing ways of interaction, contrasting the authoritative rules and local practices, and focusing on situational differences.

"Beyond Duty. Interacting with Religious Professionals and Appropriating Tradition in the Imperial Era", ERC-Tagung vom 14. bis 16. Januar 2015 im Augustinerkloster Erfurt (Georgia Petridou)

The fifth 'Lived Ancient Religion' (henceforth LAR) conference in January 2015 focused on religious practitioners and providers of specialized religious knowledge and their interaction with lay people in the Ancient Mediterranean. A good number of our contributors (esp. Jan Bremmer, Esther Eidinow, Valentino Gasparini, Richard Gordon and Jörg Rüpke) dealt with the strategies these religious experts employed to lure in lay people (wider public and political authorities) and either take advantage of their emotional and physical needs or logically convince them about their own entitlement to power. Other contributions (like those delivered by Nicola Denzey-Lewis, AnneMarie Luijendijk, Georgia Petridou and Angela Standhartinger) concentrated more on issues of frequency of their interaction with lay people and the visibility of these religious professionals: how often did they interact with people and how accessible were they and to whom? Rubina Raja, Jörg Rüpke, Federico Santangelo and Markus Vinzent, in particular, focused on the question how easily religious knowledge and expertise lent itself to political contestation and how often religious titles and offices became part of the wider economic system of symbolic capital of prestige and honour. In this view, religious offices and titles became instruments of societal elevation rather than recognitions of religious expertise. Moreover, several of our contributors (esp. Jan Bremmer, Nicola Denzey-Lewis, Richard Gordon, Georgia Petridou, Jörg Rüpke and Annette Weissenrieder) examined further the related but thematically distinct issue of deprofessionalisation of religious expertise and wider dissemination of religious knowledge. Additional emphasis on the educational background of these religious was laid in the contributions of Anne Marie Luijendijk and Michael Swartz. Finally, the body as locus of contestation and signification of religious power was another important thematic thread that was explored in the contributions of Anja Klöckner, Valentino Gasparini, Ivana and Andrej Petrovic, Rubina Raja and Annette Weissenrieder. The last decade has seen a surge of scholarly interest in these religious professionals. Our meeting, however, was substantially different due to its unique intercultural character and its explicit focus on appropriation and contestation of religious expertise in the Imperial Era. The papers presented in LAR V examined the religious professionals, their dynamic interplay with pre-established religious schemata and authorities, as well as their proneness to religious interventionism and revisionism all around the ancient Mediterranean. A further but equally significant advantage of our meeting was its wide range of media of transmission considered here. Our contributors looked at both old and new materials, which derive not only from literary sources, but also from papyri, inscriptions, and material culture. Above all, the LAR V conference went well beyond pre-existing discussions not only in terms of the original sources, but also in terms of modern scholarly categories and terminology. In fact, problematizing the established and prima facie self-explanatory modern scholarly categories of priests and priesthood was one of the common themes that ran throughout the papers presented. Hence, we felt fully justified in adopting the rather provocative title Beyond Priesthood: Religious Entrepreneurs and Innovators in the

Imperial Era for the resulting publication, which is edited by the organizers and has appeared with the RGVV series of De Gruyter in 2017 (open access).

„Lived Ancient Religion and Medicine", ERC-Workshop am 28. Mai 2015 am Max-Weber-Kolleg (Georgia Petridou)

Our workshop brought together several international experts with a diverse backgrounds in classical studies, material culture, history of medicine, theology, ancient history and history of religions to look afresh at the individual as a sufferer/patient in conjunction with his personal religious/magical/alchemical (modern distinctions not ancient) beliefs/practices. More specifically, Patricia Baker (Conceptions of Salubrious Environments: Asclepia in their Natural Environments) embarked on an interdisciplinary survey of what Greeks and Romans would identify as salubrious locations in terms of their views, access to fresh air and water, and their positions away from places that were malodorous or cacophonous. For Baker, a thorough examination of these landscapes, or 'healthscapes', as she calls them, would provide us with an understanding of the desired sensual experiences sanctuaries offered that helped in the formation of health. The contribution of Jane Draycott (When Lived Ancient Religion and Lived Ancient Medicine Meet: Roman Domestic Medical Practice and its Practitioners) shifted the focus from the community and the group to the individual and the household. Draycott combined religious and medical historical approaches and examined the role that Roman private religious belief and practice played in domestic medical practice in Italy during the Late Republic and the Principate. With the paper of our keynote speaker, Richard L. Gordon (Knowing the signs: Pliny's herbarii, Lydian confession texts and somatic curses), we remained in the field of domestic medicine and herbalism and discussed the dynamics and problematics of the "folk-body". Gordon selectively discussed three different types of Imperial evidence for the "folk-body": a) Pliny's books on plant and animal remedies, b) the use of illness as an anamnesic device in the Lydian "temple script", and c) some curses that demand the forfeit of "blood" (i.e. life-force) as a punishment for theft and other wrong-doing. All of these themes, as Gordon maintained, were closely linked to religious representations. The contribution of Jessica Hughes ('Found' Objects and Lived Ancient Religion) moved the agenda of our meeting to the much promising area of material evidence and looked at yet another of the intersections of medicine and lived religion, a category of very special sanctuary dedications, which were not made explicitly to be votives, but which were 'repurposed' as offerings after having served a range of other functions, such as personal adornment and tools for work. These objects, Hughes argued, provide us with a unique opportunity to peep through the curtains and discover aspects of the individual experiences of illness and healing. The contributions of Matteo Martelli (Religion, Alchemy and Medicine in Zosimus of Panopolis' writings) and Antoine Pietrobelli (Galen's Religious Itinerary) grounded the discussion even more firmly on the realm of the individual. Martelli looked at the junctures of Egyptian religious practice and medicine as they are portrayed in the alchemical writings of Zosimus of Panopolis. Zosimus, as Martelli argued, criticized Egyptian religious ideas and contrasted them with a 'rational' practice of alchemy and medicine only to highlight some key aspects of his own syncretic methodological framework. Pietrobelli, on the other hand, examined thoroughly the complexities that lay behind extracts of Galen's work, which gives us glimpses into his private religious and philosophical realm. As Pietrobelli rightly argued, scholars find it difficult to comprehend how the multiple religious identities of a pagan worshipper (therapeutes) of Asclepius, a believer in a monotheistic demiurge and an avowed agnostic, could all be combined in the same person. The conceptual frame- work of Lived Ancient Religion, may in fact prove extremely helpful, Pietrobelli maintained in reconciling the singularity of Galen's religious evolution with his unique philosophical profile. The contribution of Georgia Petridou (What is Divine About Medicine? Mysteric Imagery and Bodily Knowledge in the Second Sophistic) recapped some of the themes discussed earlier and looked further into the intersections of medicine and religion in Imperial literature. Petridou asked why religious imagery and terminology drawn from mystery cults were employed to describe bodily knowledge in two of the most emblematic narratives of the second sophistic: Aelius Aristides' Hieroi Logoi and Lucian's Alexander the Pseudo-Prophet. Her argument was that those texts and many others from the same period dealt with a new kind of physiology, a physiology that is religiously experienced and religiously expressed. Finally, the crossroads between medicine and lived religion as they manifest themselves in the early Christian literature were explored by Annette Weissenrieder (Disease and Healing in a Changing World: "Medical" Vocabulary and the "Female Patient" in the Vetus Latina Mark and Luke). Weissenrieder looked at the Vetus Latina, or "Old Latin Bible", a diverse collection of Latin biblical texts used by Christian churches probably from the second century on, and focused on the narratives of healing of "female patients", especially the bloodletting woman and Jairus' daughter in VL Mark 5 and Luke 8. She showed that along with the spread of medical knowledge beyond medical circles, there come medical designations, which are similar or strikingly different from those current in the medical discourse and are taken up in the manuscripts found and related to the so-called "African" text that is close to Cyprian and different in the so-called European text tradition. Back in 1988, Arthur Kleinmann (The Illness Narratives. Suffering, Healing and the Human Condition) defined illness as "the lived experience of monitoring bodily processes", and thus bridged the gap between externally defined medical categories of illness and the more personal experience that illness is for the individual patient. Within the methodological framework of the LAR, illness can be thought of as a personal crisis, often reveals hidden cracks in the socio-political nexus. It offers a unique opportunity for the individual to make adjustments to pre-established political, healing and religious schemata and to create new ones. Thus, illness and its counterpart (healing religious and secular), this workshop argued, offer a unique insight into the 'Lived Religion' in the Graeco-Roman world.

"Seeing the Gods", Tagung vom 3. bis 4. Juni 2015 am Max-Weber-Kolleg
(Marlis Arnhold)

On June 3 and 4, 2015, scholars of Classical Studies, New Testament Studies, and Religious Studies met at the University of Bonn for the international conference "Seeing the Gods. Image, Space, Performance and Vision in the Religion of the Roman Empire" conducted by Dr. des. Marlis Arnhold (Bonn), Prof. Dr. Harry Maier (Vancouver, BC), and Prof. Dr. Jörg Rüpke (Erfurt). The scope of this conference was to shed new light on the dialectics of imagination and illustration of the divine in texts and pictures. The individual contributions thus analyzed how meaning was coded and recoded in visual cues in order to create images of the divine. Not only was shown how meanings and visual cues could alter over time independently from each other, but also that the use of particular cues in specific contexts followed purposes (the one of legitimation, for instance). But also the disposition of the individual viewer towards an image of a divine being as well as his or her socio-cultural and religious background proofed crucial for the perception of an image's meaning. The conference thus revealed the strong entanglement of Christian and Non-Christian imagery on the one hand since these shared the same cultural background. On the other hand, it brought to light a number of issues, which provide potential for a continuation of the discussions: As such, the impact of the creative process in the imagemaking or the interdependency of an individual's cultural knowledge and experiences and his or her reaction to images of the divine appeared as very interesting aspects. The conference was realized with the generous support of the German Research Foundation, the Faculty of Arts of the University of Bonn, and the Max-Weber-Kolleg Erfurt, for which we would like to express our gratitude. Revised proceedings have been published with Mohr Siebeck in 2019.

"Epochalisation and Periodization: The Augustan Age", ERC-Workshop in Zusammenarbeit mit der Universität Aarhus vom 4. bis 5. April 2016 in Aarhus
(Anna-Katharina Rieger)

Epochs and periods are our tools to describe and cope with developments and trends in history. However, there is a need to critically approach these terms in order to revise the ways in which they are applied in scholarship and often hamper how we look and write about certain times, individuals, and phenomena in history. Distinguishing epochs and periods makes historical phenomena comparable and comprehensive, but it is a retrospective act creating boundaries, which inhibit to see the processual, transgressing elements.

In this workshop, the Augustan period as one of the best studied periods of Roman and more general Mediterranean and European history served as example to ask about a revision of the concepts of epochalisation and periodization through the lens of strategies within the religious sphere. Contributors were asked to consider a) a critique of periodization, b) innovation and tradition of religion, c) politicization of religion.

With a focus on the time between 45 BC and AD 15, the participants dealt with problems of the (trans-)formation of religion in the time of Octavian and later Augustus. The small circle allowed for an intensive discussion of individual papers.

Karl Galsinky ("hic nec tempora pono: Tua, Caesar, aetas") discussed concepts of periodization in the times of Augustus by looking mainly at poetry, or the involvement of people in religious affairs (ludi saeculares). The more cosmopolitical frame in the Empire lead to a memory creation linked to the emperor and oriented towards the future and not the past. Hence, the notion of saeculum becomes qualitative rather than chronological in the times of Augustus.

New insights into the recent findings of one of the earliest temples for the veneration of Augustus (Tiberian) in Ostia came with the paper of Roberta Geremia ("The temple of Rome and Augustus in Ostia: new elements for its dating"). A close revision of iconographical elements (clipeus, capricorn), entries in the fasti and historical setting under the successor of August lead her to this early dating.

With Jesper Majbom Madsen ("When their leaders became gods: Ruler cult in a Roman political context") the roots of the emperor's worship were questioned. Against the general opinion that the emperor's worship emerged from the Hellenistic ruler cult in the Greek East – and not earlier than 29 BCE – he claimed that it started earlier referring to Roman traditions in the last years of Caesar's dictatorship.

The margins were the topic of Rubina Raja's paper on the „Creation of an epoch: Octavian, Herod and the epochalisation seen from the East". She focused on the active role Herod played in Augustus' politics in a time when his sovereignty was not yet assured. Herod did not only copy Roman models but was in some aspects a forerunner to developments in Rome.

Christopher Hallet revised in an overview of "Octavian's renewal of Rome's earliest temples and shrines in the late 30's and early 20's BC: An Archaic Revival" the prevailing view on the "Augustan Classicism". He could show convincingly how slow architecture and sculpture was modelled along the lines of Classical Greek imagery, ornaments, and buildings, and how big and important the interest in Etruscan and Italic exempla was.

A phenomenon in Rome itself was tackled by Katharina Rieger ("Religion at grassroots, religion in Apollinic spheres: A look at some altars and bases in Augustan Rome"). Analysing the chronological range of altars and bases (of the quindecemviri and the vicomagistri), she showed how short-lived or tentative some phenomena in objects and iconography were. Only scholars' retrospective views make these objects being cores of the changes in art and religion, but might have had an ephemeral role in their time.

Jörg Rüpke focused on the "Augustan History of the Roman calendar" and argued that the changes in the times of Augustus opened the calendar for further meanings as well as determined it for the purposes related to Augustan politics and Roman imperialism. Hence, the Augustan phase between the Julian reform and Julio-Claudian routinization was more influential than the fixed distinction of reforms make us think.

All papers, based on variegated evidence, showed that manifold strands of religious representations, the power of marginality as well as memory and the past were present as driving forces in the pre-Augustan and Augustan time. Thus, the participants added aspects to the conditions prevailing in this time that gave politics the chance to change and use religion to a much higher degree allowing for a soft religious innovation and change of how "history" was employed by exceptional politicians like Octavian and later Augustus.

"Religious Experience", ERC-Workshop vom 19. bis 20. Mai 2016 am Max-Weber-Kolleg (Maik Patzelt)

The Max-Weber-Kolleg Erfurt, and especially the "Lived Ancient Religion" project was pleased to host Ann Taves, a world specialist on religious experience, for a period of over three weeks, including a two-day workshop on "Religious Experience". Religious experience is a key concept of the Lived Ancient Religion approach, but simultaneously, religious experience is the most difficult concept to work with. The problem lies in the vast range of possible approaches ranging from philosophy and sociology to psychology and cognitive science. Whereas one still debated problem lies in the curious idea of having a religious experience sui generis, another line of discourse debates the impossibility of analyzing something as deeply personal as somebody's experiences. With a clear emphasis on cognitive approaches, Ann Taves' approach discusses philosophical, sociological and psychological discourses in a way that allows his- torians to rethink the aspect of religious experience expressed in their mostly very fragmentary material in these terms. Ann Taves' approach both provides methods to pinpoint the variety of religious experiences (or experiences 'deemed religious') in historical texts as well as to illuminate the various ritual strategies to that end. The first day was dedicated to Ann Taves and her recent work on religious experience and its role for constituting religious communities, such as Alcoholics Anonymous and the Latter Day Saints movement ('Mormons'). Ann Taves pointed out how experiences deemed religious serve as crucial communicative elements in forming communities. Again, her contribution helped to reconfigure how the Lived Ancient Religion project could approach religious experience. On the second day, two contributors of the Lived Ancient Religion project, Georgia Petridou and Maik Patzelt, illustrated the richness of the ancient material in these terms. Both reconsidered the importance of religious experience in antiquity. By introducing the hieroi logoi of Aelius Aristides, Georgia Petridou illustrated the variety of religious experiences in ancient pilgrimage. Maik Patzelt illustrated the variety of techniques for trance in ancient Rome. The lively discussions shed new light on well-known material and illuminated the way in which new concepts and methods can be fruitfully applied to the religions of the ancient world. In result, religious experience appeared as a central concern in ancient religions. A deeper investigation of religious experiences in antiquity thus remains a highly recommended task.

"Urban Religion", ERC-Workshop in Kooperation mit dem Classics Department of Princeton University vom 2. bis 3. Juni 2016 am Max-Weber-Kolleg (Maik Patzelt)

Once again, the Lived Ancient Religion project and the Classics Department of Princeton came together in order to discuss new approaches to ancient religions. After fruitful discussions of lived ancient religion at Princeton University in January 2015, Erfurt now hosted a group of six guests from Princeton University. One further participant, Dan-el Padilla Peralta, presented his paper via Skype. For two intensive days, this workshop examined and developed the idea of urban religion in antiquity. Urban religion was seen as a specific constellation of materiality and communication that finds its expression most of all in the emergence of public spaces. From this starting point, the workshop explored religious interactions, degrees of institutionalization, innovation, imitation, and mutual influence of practices as well as identities. Whereas the first day was dedicated to Roman material, the second day concentrated on Greek and Egyptian evidence. Concerning the Roman material, three contributions (Maik Patzelt, Carolyn Tobin, and Caroline Mann) explored the problems of ritual transgression and how these transgressions could be regarded as expressions of ritual innovation, of religious and political interactions, and of new identities. Richard Neudecker and Harriet Flower dedicated their efforts to aspects of architectural strategies and the individual use of religious spaces, while Dan-el Padilla Peralta offered an insight into the broader problem of the human resources needed in the construction processes of religious architecture. The second day started with Michael Flower challenging anew the concept of religion as used in Greek sources to draw attention to key aspects of urban religion on a broader scale. This attempt was followed by archaeological approaches of Valentino Gasparini and Margaret Kurkoski who both concentrated on aspects of architectonic and representational innovation within and beyond certain communities. After Myrthe Bartels considered pseudo-Aristotelian reflections on religious epithets, Jonathan Henry pointed out the degrees of institutionalization and innovation in the field of late ancient exorcism. Common dinners helped to further discuss and develop our idea of urban religion. The workshop brought up many aspects, methodological issues, and perspectives, which provide a fruitful basis for further investigations of urban religion. The workshop thus served as a good basis on which to continue and increase our corporation with Princeton to further new and fruitful approaches to the religions of the ancient world beyond common dichotomies, such as private and public religion.

"Lived Religion in Metropoleis. A Comparative Approach", ERC-Tagung vom 21. bis 23. Juni 2016 im Augustinerkloster in Erfurt (Emiliano Rubens Urciuoli)

Organized through the collaboration between the Max-Weber-Kolleg Erfurt, and the Centre for Urban Network Evolutions at Aarhus University, the conference Lived Religion in Metropoleis: A comparative view (21–23 June 2016, Erfurt, Augustinerkloster) explored the mutual constitution of religious and urban spaces by focusing on big cities. Both the comparative approach on early modern and contemporary metropoleis and the cross-disciplinary (ancient history, early Christian studies, archaeology, sociology, social geography) training of the participants were capitalized for answering the following set of questions: How did urbanization processes and urban facets translate into religious agency, communication and identities within the megacities? What would ancient religion have looked like without the specific contribution of these centres to the shaping of religion and religious traditions? Are we able to narrate religious change in a way that pays sufficient attention to it? A gender- and age-balanced group of specialists, the high number of the contributors (19) advises against a fully detailed report of the conference, which deliberately shuffled the chronological order as well as the theoretical vs. historical-empirical partition of the talks, and benefited from cases studies and micro-level analyses without losing touch with its broader problematic and specific scopes. All sessions were chaired by members of the "Lived Ancient Religion" project and followed by a final discussion meant to critically assess the meeting and imagine possible future appointments for elaborating on the subject. While arguing for a more precise definition of the research object (metropoleis) and wondering whether to sharpen the overall theoretical framework, the contributors shared the feeling that a new promising field has been opened for self-centred perspectives on religions. In this sense, a follow-up conference is planned for November 2017.

"Narrating Witchcraft. Agency, Discourse and Power", ERC-Tagung vom 30. Juni bis 1. Juli 2016 am Max-Weber-Kolleg (Richard Gordon)

Once a staple of UK African anthropology, witchcraft became a non-topic with the debate over 'magic' in the 1970s. But the irresistible rise of witch-finding movements all over sub-Saharan Africa, among many other events, made the topic of such beliefs, and their major vehicle, witchcraft narratives, an increasingly important focus of current anthropological research. Post-modern approaches to narrative mean that we no longer need to decide about 'truth' or 'falsehood' but can be content with negotiation, ragged ends, and variable strategies in complex social situations. Early-modern historians are exploring similar approaches to their trial material.

Given this background Esther Eidinow (Junior Fellow, Max-Weber-Kolleg Erfurt) and Richard Gordon (Associate Fellow, Max-Weber-Kolleg Erfurt), both historians of antiquity, set up an international conference at the end of the Summer semester 2016 within the framework of the ERC 'Lived Ancient Religion' project, directed by Jörg Rüpke and Rubina Raja, to explore the possible extra-value provide by a comparative perspective on such narratives. To that end, we invited ten international speakers: an African anthropologist, three early-modern historians, an expert on Kabbalah, two authorities on the ancient Near East (Babylonia, Egypt), two commentators on early Christian material, and a philologist. Given the differences between the types and extent of the primary material available in these different historical periods, the contributors played to their strengths.

Peter Geschiere (Amsterdam) emphasized the moral ambiguity of healers/witches in the territory of eastern Cameroon, the waves of new fashions and crazes of mystical protection, the ceaselessly inventive bricolage of new witchcraft narratives, and the fears of attacks emanating from one's own family expressed in the new rumours of zombie-workers. He also underlined the need, if we are to do comparative research at all, to ignore minor differences between different areas and periods and look for dominant patterns. Above all, 'witchcraft' is not an explanation, as is so often claimed, but a black hole requiring to be filled. Marion Gibson (Exeter) used two of the English witchcraft pamphlets arising from trial-proceedings, a genre that exists nowhere else, to show how variable the narratives relating to the self-same case might be. Stories of witchcraft events and the roles adopted in them by the principals are/were in constant flux in accordance with the shortterm needs of the tellers, to say nothing of the judges and the pamphlet-writers, so that there never could be a 'final' version. Alison Rowlands (Essex) used the extensive documentation from Rothenburg ob der Tauber concerning the case of Margaretha Horn (1652) to provide a memorable account of one peasant woman's long struggle to resist an accusation of witchcraft. Here again, the elusiveness of the charge, the ambivalence of every claim and every item of evidence, and the central importance of framings were beautifully brought out. Wolfgang Behringer (Saarbrücken) showed how the authors of demonological treatises manipulated narratives they found in trial records in order to fit their own truth and fully appreciated the value of such 'first-hand' mini-narratives in granting credibility to their demonological scenarios. The evidence available for the ancient Near East offers virtually no witchcraft narratives of these types, though they surely once existed, yet a comparative perspective enables us to draw out certain common themes. Thus Greta van Buylaere (Würzburg) showed that suspicion of one's own family was characteristic of witchcraftfears in Babylonia while direct accusation was avoided by 'materialising' the witch as a figurine that could then be destroyed, and that from the mid-second millennium the 'standard-image witch' becomes female. Svenja Nagel (Würzburg) suggested that private witchcraft attacks seem to have been adapted from temple recipes, while the very existence of textual amulets suggests that fear of witchcraft was relatively widespread. We know that wisefolk existed but cannot estimate their role, which in other societies is of key importance. In the case of the Graeco-Roman world, Esther Eidinow (Nottingham/Erfurt) raised the gender-question in relation to the trials of women, especially metics (i.e. resident but foreign) in fourth-century BCE Athens: Virilocal marriage and widespread concubinage meant that women, the Other inside, might easily be the target of accusations particularly in the aftermath of the Peloponnesian War. Richard Gordon (Erfurt) emphasised the many different forms of what we can broadly call witchcraft narratives in the Roman Empire, the value of the impalpability of 'magic', and the ability of actors in fraught situations to create narratives adapted to their strategic aims. Jan Bremmer (Groningen/Erfurt) showed how the figure of Simon Magus ballooned in the Christian imaginaire from the mid-first to the early third century acquiring ever more fantastical contours, while Almuth Lotz (Potsdam) contrasted the ability of top-class rhetors in the late-antique eastern Mediterranean to use accusations of witchcraft to emphasise their own status with the Christian saint whose intervention spreads an idealized harmony in a divided village. Perhaps the most curious case was that produced by Yuval Harari (Negev): the evidence of several curses written by Kabbalists to kill Hitler and other leading Nazis in the dangerous period of Rommel's advance on Cairo in 1942 before the first battle of El Alamein. If such curses were produced by rabbis, they were not considered 'magic' but as the effective use of divine power. This point emphasizes the relationality of all such narratives, the need for finer contextualizations, and the awareness of the levels of 'interference' that go into their construction. But, as Geschiere emphasised so forcefully, there is always the big story, the wider situation, which gives such narratives their social power. Negotiations with the Pennsylvania University Press are under way with the aim of publishing the proceedings in their Magic in History series.

"Materiality of Divine Agency in the Graeco-Roman World", ERC-Workshop vom 29. August bis 2. September 2016 am Max-Weber-Kolleg (Anna-Katharina Rieger)

Within the framework of the ERC Advanced Grant "Lived Ancient Religion", directed by Jörg Rüpke, a Postgraduate Workshop on the "Materiality of the Divine Agency in the Graeco-Roman World" took place between 29th August and 2nd September 2016. The Postgraduate Workshop aimed to investigate archaeological evidence and textual sources in a comparative way to unearth the multiplicity and richness with which divine agency is depicted and presented in narratives, religious practices and ideas, as well as in iconographical evidence. How well grounded in ritual action and cultural production was it to imagine the gods and goddesses in an aniconic or hybrid form?

Why was there ever the need to communicate in writing with the gods? Why did the gods need food, clothing, and material gifts? How did curses work? What deities were able to heal, and how did they realize it? The workshop attracted more than 20 doctoral students and early career researchers from Classics, Religious Studies, Archaeology, Ancient History, and Theology to come to Erfurt. The invited guest speakers Emma Aston, Nicola Denzey Lewis, Esther Eidinow, Amy Smith, Ian Rutherford, und Greg Woolf from the University of Reading, Nottingham, London, and Brown, introduced topics like the materiality of the divine body, of tombs and the dead, the hybridity of divine beings, anatomical offerings and libations, cursing and curse tablets, the agency of images and objects. They were seconded by lectures given by Georgia Petridou, Katharina Rieger, and Jörg Rüpke from the Max-Weber-Kolleg Erfurt. The participants from the US, UK, Finland, Basque Country, Spain, Italy, Hungary, France, Austria, and Germany filled the four study days with lively discussions in a very open atmosphere. All engaged closely with the extensive methodological and thematic agenda that focused on aspects of the materiality of divine agency. Papers on concepts of the divine, on strategies of communication (divination, cursing, sacrifice) and their transformation into physically perceivable objects or texts (altars, dedications, buildings) were presented. Marginal areas of religious practices (invention of new gods and religious specialists) but also variations of epiphanies and embodiment of the deities in image and text throughout Classical Antiquity were explored in various papers. A base line in the discussion was the question what in particular the concept of "agency" might mean in various contexts, and what its employment can add to our understanding of religious processes and practices. Apart from the contacts to our colleagues from Reading, we got into contact with collaborators of the project "Empire of Faith" (University Oxford) and of the Center of Excellence "Changes in Sacred Texts and Traditions" (Finland University, Helsinki), which might be interesting for future exchanges. Many of the participants, especially those in the stage of writing their Ph.D. theses, took off with stimulating input on how to analyze religious phenomena in antiquity as preserved in texts and (image)-objects.

Klausurtagung des ERC-Projektes „Lived Ancient Religion" vom 8. bis 9. Dezember 2016 (Jörg Rüpke)

Nach fünf erfolgreichen und ertragreichen Jahren kamen gegenwärtige und ehemalige Mitarbeiter/innen des ERC-Projektes „Lived Ancient Religion: Questioning ‚Cults' and ‚Polis Religion'" am 8. und 9. Dezember 2016 im Schloss Ettersburg in Weimar zusammen, um gemeinsam in die Vergangenheit und Zukunft zu blicken. Eröffnet wurde die Klausurtagung des im Mai 2017 ausgelaufenen Projektes mit der Rekapitulation des Erreichten. Zahlreiche Publikationen, ausgerichtete Konferenzen und eine eigene Fachzeitschrift (Religion in the Roman Empire) hat das Projekt unter der Leitung von Jörg Rüpke hervorgebracht und somit nachhaltig die Forschungslandschaft in den einzelnen altertumswissenschaftlichen Fachgebieten geprägt. Ein Rückblick auf die verschiedenen Einzelprojekte der jeweiligen Mitglieder hat bewiesen, wie vielseitig die Suche nach gelebter antiker Religion gestaltet werden kann. Diese Erkenntnis hat alle Beteiligten dazu angeregt, das Konzept der Lived Ancient Religion weiterzuverfolgen und auszudifferenzieren. In Anbetracht dieses Erfolges verstand sich die Tagung als Wegbereiter künftiger Herausforderungen, neue Akzente der Lived Ancient Religion zu setzen und neue Perspektiven zu gewinnen. Mit diesem Ziel vor Augen wurde einhellig das Interesse bekundet, auch in Zukunft persönliche und institutionelle Kooperationen mit den jeweiligen Mitgliedern zu pflegen und auszubauen. Das jüngst unterzeichnete Memorandum for Understanding zwischen dem Max-Weber-Kolleg und dem Centre for Urban Network Evolutions in Aarhus, unter der Leitung des Projektmitglieds Rubina Raja, hat diese Bemühungen in erste Bahnen gelenkt. Das Ende des Lived-Ancient-Religion-Projektes kann vor diesem Hintergrund nur der Anfang umfassenderer Forschungen zu den Religionen von der Archaik bis zum Hochmittelalter sein. Es bleibt viel zu tun, und mit dieser Gewissheit blicken die gegenwärtigen und ehemaligen Mitarbeiter/innen erwartungsvoll in die Zukunft.

Leaving the (Disciplinary) Comfort Zone: Lived Ancient Religion AD 1 to 800, Final Conference of the ERC Advanced Grant "Lived Ancient Religion", 3rd to 5th April 2017 (Jörg Rüpke, Rubina Raja)

With a final conference bridging time periods and disciplines, the ERC Advanced Grant "Lived Ancient Religion", directed by Jörg Rüpke and Rubina Raja, concluded its five years of intense research. Under the topic of "Leaving the (Disciplinary) Comfort Zone: Lived Ancient Religion Ad 1 to 800", about 25 internationally renowned colleagues were invited to Eisenach from 3rd to 5th April. The conference aimed at an implementation and adaptation of the project's results into the larger field of religious studies of the Mediterranean rather than on presenting achievements. Therefore, the invited speakers came from a variety of disciplinary contexts (Jewish Studies, Theology, Late Antiquity, Early Christian Studies) and not only from the inner circles of the LAR project. They were asked to test, criticize and contextualize definitions or results from the LAR project in their fields of research. Chronologically and topographically, topics ranged from the Mediterranean, North Africa and Europe to Western Asia, from Hellenistic times to Early Medieval times.

Among the speakers were Barbara Borg (University of Exeter), David Frankfurter (University of Boston), Nicola Denzey Lewis (Brown University), Rebecca Flemming (Cambridge), Alexia Petsalis-Diomidis (Oxford), Angela Kim Harkins (Boston College), Ian Rutherford (University of Reading), Moulie Vidas (Princeton) as well as members of the Max-Weber-Kolleg (Emiliano Urciuoli, Katharina Rieger, Richard Gordon, Maik Patzelt and Valentino Gasparini). They reflected in their contributions about the four main thematic fields of the conference: "A 'Thing' Called Body", "Commemorating the Moment: Individual Modification and Appropriation of Sacralized Spaces and Objects", "Experiencing the Religious" and "Switching the Code: Individual Appropriation of Religious Texts".

Whereas the panel "Experiencing the Religious" aimed at bringing to the fore experiences underlying religious action and identifying the discourses about the dangers or values of true or false religious experiences, "Switching the Code" wanted to reconsider the techniques and procedures by which meanings, discourses and writings are performed, controlled and reproduced in religious settings and/or for theological purposes. Coming from the corner of materiality, "A 'Thing' Called Body" emphasized the situational meaning of material artefacts in religious contexts. Likewise, the panel "Commemorating the Moment" focused on the individual appropriation and modification of (mainly public) norms in the religious field, including rituals, but particularly objects and spaces, in order to disclose "micro-strategies of sacralization". In a round-table discussion Corinne Bonnet (Toulouse), Jan Bremmer (Groningen), Zsuzsanna Varhelyi (Boston) and Judith Lieu (Cambridge) commented Jörg Rüpke's recently published book Pantheon: Geschichte der antiken Religionen (München: C. H. Beck) under the perspective of long-term developments in religious studies of the Mediterranean. They together with the vivid discussions in all four panels highlighted the benefits and the prospective potential of the "lived religion" approach, which continues by shedding light on urban space and urban religion.

The very intense and, at times, controversial discussions are published as an issue of the journal *Religion in the Roman Empire 4.1* (2018) (round-table contributions) and in two volumes published in an open-access format with De Gruyter (contributions to the thematic fields of the conference, doi: 10.1515/9783110557596).

9 Publications of fellows and staff

Ando, Clifford

– 2013: „Subjects, gods and empire, or Monarchism as a theological problem", in: Jörg Rüpke (ed.), *The Individual in the Religions of the Ancient Mediterranean*, Oxford: Oxford University Press, 86–111.
– 2014: „Postscript: Cities, citizenship and the work of empire", in: Claudia Rapp and H. A. Drake, (eds.), *The city in the classical and post-classical world. Changing contexts of power and identity*. Cambridge: Cambridge University Press, 240–256.
– 2015: „Three revolutions in government", in: Lucian Reinfandt, Stephan Prochazka and Sven Tost, (eds.), *Official epistolography and the languages of power*, Vienna: Verlag der Österreichischen Akademie der Wissenschaften, 163–172.
– 2016: „The rites of others", in: Jonathan Edmondson and Alison Keith (eds.), *Roman Literary Cultures: Domestic Politics, Revolutionary Poetics, Civic Spectacles*. Toronto/Buffalo/London: University of Toronto Press, 254–277.
– 2016: „Religiöse und politische Zugehörigkeit von Caracalla bis Theodosius." Translated by Leif Scheuermann. Keryx – *Zeitschrift für Antike 4 (2016)*, 61–73.

Arnhold, Marlis

– 2020: „Transformationen stadtrömischer Heiligtümer während der späten Republik und Kaiserzeit". Contextualizing the Sacred. Turnhout: Brepols.
–; Harry O. Maier, Jörg Rüpke (eds.) 2019: „Seeing the god: image, space, performance and vision in the religion of the Roman Empire". Tübingen: Mohr Siebeck.

– 2013: „Group Settings and Religious Experiences", in: Cusumano, N. et al. (eds.), *Memory and Religious Experience in the Greco-Roman World*. Stuttgart: Steiner, 145–165.
– 2015: „Male Worshippers and the Cult of Bona Dea", *Religion in the Roman Empire 1.1*, 51–70.
– 2015: „Sanctuaries and Urban Spatial Settings in Roman Imperial Ostia", in: Rüpke, J.; Raja, R. (eds.), *A Companion to the Archaeology of Religion in the Ancient World*. Malden, MA: John Wiley & Sons.
– 2016: (together with Jörg Rüpke) „Appropriating and shaping religious practices in the Roman Republic", in: Haake, Matthias; Harders, Ann-Cathrin (eds.), *Politische Kultur und soziale Struktur im Republikanischen Rom*. Steiner: Stuttgart, 416–432.
– 2018: „Republikanische Heiligtümer im kaiserzeitlichen Rom", in: Blömer, Michael; Eckhardt, Benedikt (eds.), *Transformationen paganer Religion in der Kaiserzeit. Rahmenbedingungen und Konzepte*, RGVV vol. 72, Berlin: de Gruyter, 175–198.
– 2019: „Imagining Mithras in light of iconographic standardization and individual accentuation", in: Arnhold, Marlis; Maier, Harry O.; Rüpke, Jörg (eds.), *Seeing the god: image, space, performance and vision in the religion of the Roman Empire*. Tübingen: Mohr Siebeck, 125–147.

Banerjee-Dube, Ishita

– 2019: Religious individualisation and collective bhakti: Sarala Dasa and Bhima Bhoi, in: Martin Fuchs et al. (eds.), Religious Individualisation: Historical Dimensions and Comparative Perspectives, Berlin: de Gruyter, 847–864.

Bashir, Shahzad

– 2019: Reading the self in Persian prose and poetry, in: Martin Fuchs et al. (eds.), Religious Individualisation: Historical Dimensions and Comparative Perspectives, Berlin: de Gruyter, 443–458.

Becker, Eve-Marie

– 2017. The Birth of Christian History: Memory and Time from Mark to Luke-Acts. New Haven: Yale University Press.

– 2015: „Historiography: II. Greco-Roman Antiquity", *Encyclopedia of the Bible and Its Reception vol. 11*. Berlin/Boston: de Gruyter. 1129–1135.
– 2016: „Shaping Identity by Writing History: Earliest Christianity in its Making", *Religion in the Roman Empire 2, 2*. 152–169.

Ben-Tov, Asaph

2019: Early modern erudition and religious individualisation: the case of Johann Zechendorff (1580–1662), in: Martin Fuchs *et al.* (eds.), *Religious Individualisation: Historical Dimensions and Comparative Perspectives*, Berlin: de Gruyter, 1255–1268.

Ben-Zaken, Avner

– 2017: „No Place for Regrets: Heidegger and Thomas of Erfurt", *Haaretz Literary Supplement*, 28.12.2017 (in Hebrew).
– 2019: „Traveling with the *Picatrix*: On the Cultural Liminalities of Science and Magic", in: Martin Fuchs *et al.* (eds.), *Religious Individualisation: Historical Dimensions and Comparative Perspectives*, Berlin: de Gruyter, 1033–1064.

Boyarin, Daniel

– 2018. *Judaism: the genealogy of a modern notion*, Key Words in Jewish Studies, New Brunswick NJ: Rutgers University Press.

Bremmer, Jan

– 2014. *Initiation into the Mysteries of the Ancient World*, Hardback and ebook: Berlin and Boston: de Gruyter.
–; Boschung, Dietrich (eds.) 2015. *The Materiality of Magic*, Munich: Wilhelm Fink.
– et al. (eds.) 2016. *The Ascension of Isaiah*, Leuven: Peeters.
– 2017. Maidens, Magic and Martyrs in Early Christianity: Collected Essays I, Tübingen: Mohr Siebeck.

– 2014: Religious Violence between Greeks, Romans, Christians and Jews, in: A.-K. Geljon and R. Roukema (eds), *Violence in Early Christianity: Victims and Perpetrators*, Leiden: Brill, 8–30.

- 2014: Conversion in the Oldest Apocryphal Acts, in: B.S. Bøgh (ed.), *Conversion and Initiation in Antiquity: shifting identities – creating change*, Bern: Peter Lang, 59–76.
- 2015: Preface: The Materiality of Magic, in: J. Bremmer and D. Boschung (eds.), *The Materiality of Magic*, Munich: Wilhelm Fink, 7–19.
- 2015: From Books with Magic to Magical Books in Ancient Greece and Rome, in: D. Boschung and J. Bremmer (eds.), *The Materiality of Magic*, Munich: Wilhelm Fink, 241–269.
- 2015: God against the Gods: Early Christians and the Worship of Statues, in: D. Boschung and A. Schaefer (eds), *Götterbilder der mittleren und späten Kaiserzeit*, Munich: Wilhelm Fink, 139–58.
- 2015: The Passion of Perpetua und Felicitas, *Reallexikon für Antike und Christentum*, vol. 27, Lief. 211, 178–190.
- 2016: The Domestication of Early Christian Prophecy and the *Ascension of Isaiah*, in: J. Bremmer et al. (eds.), *The Ascension of Isaiah*, Leuven: Peeters, 1–23.
- 2016: Shamanism in Classical Scholarship: where are we now?, in P. Jackson (ed.), *Horizons of Shamanism: A Triangular Approach:* Stockholm Studies in Comparative Religion 35, Stockholm, 52–78.
- 2016: Ancient Necromancy: Fact or Fiction?, in: K. Bielawski (ed.), *Mantic Perspectives – oracles, prophecy and performance*, Gardzienice, Warsaw, Lublin: Ośrodek Praktyk Teatralnych 'Gardzienice', 119–141.
- 2016: Body Politics: Imagining Human Sacrifice in Euripides' Iphigeneia in Aulis, in: K. Bielawski (ed.), *Mantic Perspectives – oracles, prophecy and performance*, Gardzienice, Warsaw, Lublin: Ośrodek Praktyk Teatralnych 'Gardzienice', 35–56.
- 2016: The Construction of an Individual Eschatology: the Case of the Orphic Gold Leaves, in: K. Waldner et al. (eds), *Burial Rituals, Ideas of Afterlife, and the Individual in the Hellenistic World and the Roman Empire*, Stuttgart: Steiner, 31–52.
- 2016: Arthur Darby Nock's Conversion (1933): a balance, in: J. Weitbrecht, W. Röcke and R. von Bernuth (eds), *Zwischen Ereignis und Erzählung. Konversion als Medium der Selbstbeschreibung in Mittelalter und Früher Neuzeit*, Berlin/Boston: de Gruyter, 9–29.
- 2016: Richard Reitzenstein, Pythagoras and the *Life of Antony*, in: A.-B. Renger and A. Stavru (eds), *Forms and Transformations of Pythagorean Knowledge*, Wiesbaden: Harassowitz, 227–245.
- 2016: Theseus' and Peirithoos' Descent into the Underworld, *Les Études Classiques* 83, 35–49.
- 2016: Imperial Mysteries, *Mètis* 14, 21–34.
- 2017: Lucian on Peregrinus and Alexander of Abonuteichos: A Sceptical View of Two Religious Entrepreneurs, in: R.L. Gordon et al. (eds), *Beyond Priesthood: Religious Entrepreneurs and Innovators in the Roman Empire*, Berlin and Boston: de Gruyter, 47–76.
- 2017: Philosophy and the Mysteries, in: C. Riedweg (ed.), PHILOSOPHIA in der Konkurrenz von Schulen, Wissenschaften und Religionen. Zur Pluralisierung des Philosophiebegriffs in Kaiserzeit und Spätantike, Berlin/Boston: de Gruyter, 99–126.
- 2017: Cult Spaces in a Longue Durée Perspective, in: H.-U. Wiemer (ed.), *Kulträume. Studien zum Verhältnis von Kult und Raum in alten Kulturen*. Stuttgart: Steiner, 285–296.
- 2017: Pilgrimage Progress?, in: T.M. Kristensen and W. Friese (eds), *Excavating Pilgrimage*, Abingdon and New York: Routledge, 275–284.
- ; van der Lans, Birgit 2018: Tacitus and the Persecution of the Christians: An Invention of Tradition?, *Eirene* 53, 299–231.
- 2018: Jews, Pagans and Christians in the Apocryphal Acts, in: St. Alkier and H. Leppin (eds), *Juden – Heiden – Christen?* Tübingen: Mohr Siebeck, 333–362.

- 2018: Religious Violence and its Roots. A View from Antiquity, in: W. Mayer and C.L. de Wet (eds), *Reconceiving Religious Conflict. New Views from the Formative Centuries of Christianity*, Abingdon and New York, 30–42.
- 2018: Review: Jörg Rüpke's Pantheon, Munich: Beck, 2016, in *Religion in the Roman Empire* 4, 107–112.
- 2019: Religion and the limits of individualisation in ancient Athens: Andocides, Socrates, and the fair-breasted Phryne, in: Martin Fuchs et al. (eds.), *Religious Individualisation: Historical Dimensions and Comparative Perspectives*, Berlin: de Gruyter, 1009–1032.

Bueno, Arthur

- 2019: Simmel and the forms of in-dividuality, in: Martin Fuchs *et al.* (eds.), *Religious Individualisation: Historical Dimensions and Comparative Perspectives*, Berlin: de Gruyter, 409–436.

Casteigt, Julie

- Forthcoming. Métaphysique et connaissance testimoniale. Une lecture figurale du Super Iohannem (Jn 1, 7) d'Albert le Grand, Leuven: Peeters, (Eckhart: Texts and Studies 11).
- 2019. *Albertus Magnus, Super Iohannem (Ioh. 1, 1-18)*, Leuven: Peeters, (Eckhart: Texts and Studies 10).
- (ed.) 2019. *Verbe et chair: le sens de l'union dans la réception philosophique de l'Évangile de Jean (Jn 1, 12-14)*, Münster, Berlin, Wien, Zürich and London: LIT Verlag, (Théologie biblique).

- 2013: „Au-delà du sujet, l'impersonnel?", *Archives de Philosophie*, Cahier n. 76/3, automne 2013, 371–374.
- 2013: „Comment passer de l'ignorance à la connaissance? Une figure du maître *manuductor* selon Albert le Grand", in: Noacco, C./Bonnet, C./Marot, P./Orfanos, Ch. (eds.), *Figures du maître*, (Interférences), Rennes: PUR, 45–59.
- 2013: „Deux exemples de rencontres entre philosophes juifs, musulmans et chrétiens: Thomas d'Aquin/ Averroès et Maître Eckhart/Maïmonide", in: *Controverses religieuses au Moyen Âge et enjeux contemporains – autour de Ramon Llull, Maïmonide, Averroès, Thomas d'Aquin*, Centre théologique Ramon Llull de Perpignan, Diocèse de Perpignan, colloque des 5–6 octobre 2007, Girona: Gràfiques Alzamora, 63–92.
- 2013: „Le *De anima* dans l'*Expositio sancti Evangelii secundum Iohannem* de Maître Eckhart: une révolution aristotélicienne dans la noétique eckhartienne?", in: Friedman, R./Counet, J.-M. (eds.), *Medieval Perspectives on Aristotle's De Anima*, Institut Supérieur de Philosophie, Louvain-la-Neuve/Leuven: Peeters, 121–144.
- 2013: „Ni Conrad, ni Henri': le fond de la personne est-il personnel, impersonnel ou sans fond dans les sermons allemands de Maître Eckhart?", *Archives de Philosophie*, Cahier n. 76/3 (automne 2013), 425–440.
- 2014: „Coexistence et médiation dans le Prologue de l'Évangile selon saint Jean commenté par Albert le Grand" in: Musco, A./Musotto, G. (eds.), Coesistenza e Cooperazione nel Medioevo. Coexistence and Cooperation in the Middle Ages. In Memoriam Leonardo E. Boyle (1923–1999). IV European Congress of Medieval Studies F.I.D.E.M. (Fédération Internationale des Instituts d'Études Médiévales), Palermo, 23–37 june 2009, Palermo: Officina di Studi Medievali, 1–24.

- 2014: „Quelques propositions synthétiques pour une lecture des interprétations albertienne et eckhartienne de Jn 1, 6-8", in: Amerini, F. (ed.), *'In Principio erat Verbum'. Philosophy and Theology in the Commentaries of the Gospel of John (II–XIV Century)*, Archa Verbi. Subsidia, vol. 11, Münster: Aschendorff Verlag, 159–176.
- 2015: „Condamnés à une connaissance de chauve-souris? Albert le Grand et l'intellect humain conjoint aux sens et à l'imagination", in: Bouchet, Fl./Klinger-Dollé, A.-H. (eds.), *Penser les cinq sens au Moyen Âge: poétique, esthétique, éthique*, (Rencontres, Civilisation médiévale), Paris: éditions Classiques Garnier, 37–54.
- 2015: „Contre une idée reçue selon laquelle Maître Eckhart ne parle pas d'amour...", *Recherches philosophiques* 1 (septembre 2015), 31–56.
- 2015: „Le principe est-il indétermination ou principe de différenciation selon le commentaire eckhartien de l'*Évangile de Jean*? „, in: J.-Ch. Lemaître & É. Rigal, *Jean-Marie Vaysse – Cartographies de le pensée à la fin de la métaphysique*, (Europaea Memoria), Hildesheim: Olms, 199–216.
- ; avec Dietmar Mieth et Jörg Rüpke 2016: „Der Träger der Erfurter Riesenthorarolle. Eine religionsgeschichtliche Hypothese zu einem übersehenen Judaicum, *Zeitschrift für Religion und Geistesgeschichte* 68/2 (Mai 2016), 97–118.
- 2016: „Énonciation et indétermination. Au-delà de la lecture derridienne de la théologie négative de Maître Eckhart?", *Ephemerides Theologicae Lovanienses* 92/2 (2016), 229–250.
- 2016: „Le lieu, principe d'individualisation ou d'intériorité réciproque dans le commentaire johannique de Maître Eckhart?", in: Ch. Wojtulewicz, J. Vinzent (eds.), *Performing Bodies. Time and Space in Meister Eckhart and in the Performances and Video Installations of Taery Kim*, (Eckhart: Texts and Studies 6), Leuven: Peeters Publishers, 115–141.
- 2016: „Welcher individuelle Erkenntnisweg zum Göttlichen ist für den Menschen nach Albert dem Großen möglich", *Theologische Quartalschrift*, n.196, Heft 3/2016, 249–275
- 2017: „Aimer l'un dans l'autre ou d'un désordre amoureux condamné: une lecture de l'article 25 de la bulle pontificale *In agro dominico*", in: D.Mieth, M-A. Vannier, M. Vinzent and C.M. Wojtulewicz (eds.), *Meister Eckhart in Paris and Strasbourg*, (Eckhart: Texts and Studies 4), Leuven: Peeters, 177–208.
- 2017: „Identité du témoin et accomplissement des figures: le modèle de la voix et du Verbe dans la lecture albertienne de Jn 1, 19-24", *Annali di Storia dell'Esegesi* 34/1 (2017), 125–144.
- 2017: „La fonction des médiations matérielles dans l'acte baptismal: Entre discours exégétique (*Super Iohannem*, Jn 1, 25-28) et discours théologique chez Albert le Grand", in: J. Casteigt (ed.), *Le Témoin dans la tradition johannique*, Revue de sciences philosophiques et théologiques101 (2017/1), 69–92.
- 2017: „*Le Témoin dans la tradition johannique*", Revue de sciences philosophiques et théologiques 101 (2017/1)
- 2017: „*Malum bonum et lucem tenebras*. Die göttliche Bestimmung des menschlichen Seins und Handelns in der Auseinandersetzung der Avignoneser Theologenkommission mit Meister Eckhart", *Theologische Quartalschrift*, n.197, Heft 1/2017, 72–95.
- 2018: „Metaphysics and testimonial knowledge in the Super Iohannem of Albert the Great", *Traditio* 73, 255–289.
- 2018: „'Soleil noir'. La théologie négative de Maître Eckhart jugée malsonnante dans l'article 5 du *Votum Avenionense*", in: Rodolphe Calin, Tobias Dangel und Roberto Vinco (Hrsg.), *Die Tradition der negativen Theologie in der deutschen und französischen Philosophie*, Universitätsverlag Winter, Heidelberg, (Heidelberger Forschungen 41), 67–90.
- 2018: „Incarnation et témoignage: l'économie des médiations dans le commentaire du Prologue de l'*Évangile de Jean* par Albert le Grand", in: J. Casteigt (éd.), *Verbe et chair: le sens de l'union*

dans la réception philosophique de l'Évangile de Jean (Jn 1, 12-14), Münster, Berlin, Wien, Zürich and London: LIT Verlag, 75–106.
- 2019: „'Vase of light': from the exceptional individuality to the individualisation process as influenced by Greek-Arabic cosmology in Albert the Great's Super Iohannem", in: Martin Fuchs *et al.* (eds.), *Religious Individualisation: Historical Dimensions and Comparative Perspectives.* Berlin: de Gruyter, 53–72.
- 2019: „The subject as *totum potestativum* in Albert the Great's *Œuvre*: cultural transfer and relational identity", in: Martin Fuchs *et al.* (eds.), *Religious Individualisation: Historical Dimensions and Comparative Perspectives*, Berlin: de Gruyter, 347–362.
- 2020: „Selbstbestimmung vor dem religiösen Gesetz: die Auseinandersetzung Meister Eckharts mit der Avignoneser Kommission", in: D. Mieth (Hrsg.), *Religiöse Selbstbestimmung – die Anfänge im Mittelalter und das Konzept Meister Eckharts, Beiheft des Meister Eckhart Jahrbuches*, Aschendorff: Kohlhammer.

Conolly, John

- 2016: „Eckhart and the Will of God: A Reply to Stump", *Medieval Mystical Theology*, 25, 1, May 2016, 6–20.
- 2017: „Tatort Garten Eden: Eigennutz und Individualisierung in der Ursündenlehre Meister Eckharts", *Theologische Quartalschrift*, 197, 1 (2017), 48–71.
- 2018: „Freiheit und Wille bei Eckhart und Kant", *Meister-Eckhart-Jahrbuch* 12, Spring 2018, 293–318.
- 2019: „'Von den guten wercken': Eckhart und Luther über die Werkgerechtigkeit und die rechte Motivation als 'Springbrunnen'" under review for publication in the *Meister-Eckhart-Jahrbuch* 13, Spring 2019.
- 2016: „Book Review of Kurt Flasch, Meister Eckhart: Philosopher of Christianity", in: *The Catholic Historical Review*, Fall 2016, Vol. 102, No. 4, 831–32.

Dalmia, Vasudha

2019: Being Hindu in India: culture, religion, and the Gita Press (1950), in Martin Fuchs *et al.* (eds.), *Religious Individualisation: Historical Dimensions and Comparative Perspectives*, Berlin: de Gruyter, 1097–1120.

Deeg, Max

- 2019: Many biographies – multiple individualities: the identities of the Chinese Buddhist monk Xuanzang, in: Martin Fuchs *et al.* (eds.), *Religious Individualisation: Historical Dimensions and Comparative Perspectives*, Berlin: de Gruyter, 913–938.

Deuser, Hermann

- –; Saskia Wendel (eds.) 2012. *Dialektik der Freiheit*, Tübingen: Mohr Siebeck.
- –; Markus Kleinert, Magnus Schlette (eds.) 2015. *Metamorphosen des Heiligen*, Religion und Aufklärung 25, Tübingen: Mohr Siebeck.
- 2013: „Marvels, Miracles, Signs and the Real. Peirce's Semiotics in Religion and Art", in: Stefan Alkier/Annette Weissenrieder (eds.), *Miracles Revisited*, Berlin/Boston: de Gruyter, 377–390.

– 2016: „Theology of Nature", in: *Holy Light Theological Journal*, Taiwan, No. 1, December 2016, 13–53.

Dey, Amit

– 2019: Islamic mystical responses to hegemonic orthodoxy: the subcontinental perspective, in: Martin Fuchs et al. (eds.), *Religious Individualisation: Historical Dimensions and Comparative Perspectives*, Berlin: de Gruyter, 1269–1290.

Dube, Saurabh

– 2019: Subjects of conversion in colonial central India, in: Martin Fuchs et al. (eds.), Religious Individualisation: Historical Dimensions and Comparative Perspectives, Berlin: de Gruyter, 895–912.

Dureau, Christine

– 2019: 'Greater love …': Methodist missionaries, self-sacrifice and relational personhood, in: Martin Fuchs et al. (eds.), Religious Individualisation: Historical Dimensions and Comparative Perspectives, Berlin: de Gruyter, 583–602.

Eidinow, Esther

– 2019: Self as other: distanciation and reflexivity in ancient Greek divination, in: Martin Fuchs et al. (eds.), Religious Individualisation: Historical Dimensions and Comparative Perspectives, Berlin: de Gruyter, 541–558.

Engmann, Matthias

– 2019: Taking Job as an example. Kierkegaard: traces of religious individualization, in: Martin Fuchs et al. (eds.), *Religious Individualisation: Historical Dimensions and Comparative Perspectives*, Berlin: de Gruyter, 159–184.
– 2019: Disunited identity. Kierkegaard: traces towards dividuality, in: Martin Fuchs et al. (eds.), *Religious Individualisation: Historical Dimensions and Comparative Perspectives*, Berlin: de Gruyter, 497–512.

Facchini, Cristiana

–; T. Catalan (eds.) 2015. „Portrait of Italian Jews (1800s–1930s)" = Quest. Issues in Contemporary Jewish History 8 (2015).
–; Lannoy A. (eds.) 2019. The other Jesus. Alternative histories of Jesus and the religious world of the past from the nineteenth and early twentieth centuries, Brepols: Turnhout (collection of 12 articles & introduction, forthcoming).
– 2013: „Voci ebraiche sulla tolleranza religiosa. Pratiche e teorie nella Venezia barocca", *Annali di storia dell'esegesi* 2/30 (2013), 393–419.

- 2014: „Orientalistica ed Ebraismo. Una storia ai margini. David Castelli e Giorgio Levi della Vida", in: M. Mazza, N. Spineto, *La storiografia storico-religiosa italiana tra la fine dell'800 e la seconda guerra mondiale*, Alessandria: Edizioni dell'Orso, 111–139.
- 2014: „Predicare nel ghetto. Riflessioni su riti orali e performance rituale nel mondo ebraico di età barocca", in: M. Del Bianco Cotrozzi, R. Di Segni, M. Massenzio (eds.), *Non solo verso Oriente. Studi sull'ebraismo in onore di Pier Cesare Ioly Zorattini*, Firenze: L.S. Olschki, 173–196.
- 2015: „Judaism. An Inquiry into the Historical Discourse", in: B.-C. Otto, S. Rau, J. Rüpke (eds.), *History and Religion: Narrating a Religious Past* (Religionsgeschichtliche Versuche und Vorarbeiten 68), Berlin: De Gruyter, 371–392.
- 2015: „Six Authors in Search of a Narrative, in Portrait of Italian Jews (1800s–1930s)", T. Catalan and C. Facchini (eds.), *Quest Issues in Contemporary Jewish History* 8 (2015), I–XX.
- 2016: „Luigi Luzzatti and the Oriental Front: Jewish Agency and the Politics of Religious Toleration", in: M. Dogo and T. Catalan (eds.), *The Jews and the Nation-States of Southeastern Europe from the 19th Century to the Great Depression: Combining Viewpoints on a Controversial Story*, Newcastle: Cambridge Scholars, 2016, 227–245.
- 2016: „Luigi Luzzatti e la teoria della tolleranza religiosa. Per una storia del consumo pubblico delle scienze delle religioni" *Annali di storia dell'esegesi* 33/1 (2016), 275–300.
- 2016: „Narrating, Visualizing, Performing, and Feeling a Religion. On representations of Judaism", in *Dynamics of Religion. Past and Present*, edited by C. Bochinger, J. Rüpke together with Elisabeth Begemann (Religionsgeschichtliche Versuche und Vorarbeiten 67), Berlin: de Gruyter, 273–296.
- 2017: „Entangled histories. A road map to religious individualization in early modern Judaism", *Annali di storia dell'esegesi* 34/1, 145–174.
- 2018: „Il Gesù di Leon Modena. Per una storia materiale ed urbana del Magen we-herev di Leon Modena", *Annali di storia dell'esegesi* 35/1 (2018), 163–187.
- 2018: „Living in Exile: Wissenschaft des Judentums and the study of religion in Italy (1890s–1930s)" in: F. Bregoli, C. Ferrara degli Uberti, G. Schwarz (eds.), *Italian Jews in Context*, Palgrave (forthcoming 2018)
- 2018: „'The immortal traveler'. How historiography changed Judaism", in: J. Rüpke (ed.), *Creating Religions by Historiography*, *Archiv für Religionsgeschichte* 20.1 (2018), 111–134.
- 2018/19: „The 'war zone' of the historical Jesus. Scholarship, politics, and religion in Italy 1890s–1930s)", in: Ead., Lannoy A. (eds.) *The other Jesus. Alternative histories of Jesus and the religious world of the past from the nineteenth and early twentieth centuries*, Brepols: Turnhout.
- 2019: „Jewish Preaching, Space, and the Baroque", in: A. Guetta, P. Savy (eds.), *Non contrarii, ma diversi*, Rome: Viella (delivered January 2018).
- 2019: „Religious polemics and 'regimes of historicity'. Interpreting the Magen ve-herev of Leon Modena", in: A. Destro, M. Pesce (eds.), *Proceeding of the 2nd Annual Meeting on Christian Origins*, Brepols: Turnhout (Delivered November 2017).
- 2019: „The Making of Wissenschaft des Judentums in a Catholic Country. The Case of Italy", in: Christian Wiese, Mirjam Thulin (eds.), *Wissenschaft des Judentums in Europe: Comparative and Transnational Perspectives*, (Studia Judaica 76) de Gruyter, Berlin 2018 (delivered 2013, revised twice between 2014 and 2015).
- 2019: „Understanding 'prophecy': charisma, religious enthusiasm, and religious individualisation in the 17th century. A cross-cultural approach", in Martin Fuchs *et al.* (eds.), *Religious Individualisation: Historical Dimensions and Comparative Perspectives*, Berlin: de Gruyter, 1299–1320.
- 2018: Books discussion: Aaron W. Hughes, *Jacob Neusner. An American Jewish Iconoclast*, New York: New York University Press, 2016, pp. 1–319; Amir Engel, *Gershom Scholem. An Intellectual Biography*, Chicago–London, The University of Chicago Press, 2017; George Prochnick,

Stranger in a Strange Land: Searching for Gershom Scholem in Jerusalem, London: Granta, 2017 in *Quest – Issues in Contemporary Jewish history* 12/2 (2018)

Feldhaus, Anne

– 2018: „The Significance of Place in Early Mahānubhāv Literature", in: B. Sengar and L. McMillin (eds.), *Spaces and Places in Western India: Formations and Delineations*, New Delhi: Routledge.
– 2019: „Individualisation, Deindividualisation, and Institutionalisation among the Early Mahānubhāvs", in: Martin Fuchs *et al.* (eds.), *Religious Individualisation: Historical Dimensions and Comparative Perspectives*, Berlin: de Gruyter, 831–846.

Flügel, Peter

–; Kornelius Krümpelmann (eds.) 2016. *Johannes Klatt: Jaina-Onomasticon*, Wiesbaden: Harrassowitz.
–; Sam Whimster (eds.) 2017. Special Issue (Part I): Max Weber's Hinduism and Buddhism: Reflections on a Sociological Classic 100 Years On, London: Max Weber Studies Office (Max Weber Studies 17, 2).
–; Sam Whimster (eds.) 2018. Special Issue (Part II): Max Weber's Hinduism and Buddhism: Reflections on a Sociological Classic 100 Years On, London: Max Weber Studies Office (Max Weber Studies 18, 1).
– 2019. Die Sthānakavāsī Śvetāmbara Jaina-Orden in Nordindien: Protestantische und Post-Protestantische Jaina-Reformbewegungen, Wiesbaden: Harrassowitz.
–; Sam Whimster (eds.) 2019. Max Weber's Hinduism and Buddhism: Reflections on a Sociological Classic 100 Years On. London, London: Max Weber Studies.

– 2016. „Life and Work of Johannes Klatt.", in: Peter Flügel & Kornelius Krümpelmann (eds.), *Johannes Klatt: Jaina-Onomasticon* Wiesbaden: Harrassowitz (Jaina Studies 1), 9–164.
– 2017: „Johannes Emil Otto Klatt (1852–1903). Forgotten Chronicler of Jainism and Bibliographer of Oriental Literature: Letters to Albrecht Weber 1874–1882, Ernst Kuhn 1881–1889, Charles Rockwell Lanman 1889 and Eberhardt Karras 1891, with Curriculum Vitae, and a Complete Bibliography of Johannes Klatt's Works.", *Berliner Indologische Studien* 23, 69–141.
– 2018: „Social-Differentiation and Self-Differentiation: The Jaina Concept of the Individual and Sociological Individualisation-Paradigms", Max Weber Studies 18, 2.
– 2018: „Reflexive Mechanisms and Agency in Jaina Law. The Maryādā Paṭṭaka and Ācārya Sohanlāls Reforms of the Pañjāb Lavjī Ṛṣi Sampradāya 1895–1911", *International Journal of Jaina Studies* 14.

Frenkel, Luise Marion

– 2016: „Individual Christian voices in the narratives of late-antique acclamations", *RRE 2:2* (2016) 196–226, doi: http://dx.doi.org/10.1628/219944616X14655421286095.
– 2016: „The record of acclamations and cries in the Acts of Ephesus (431)", in: Vinzent, M. & Brent, A. (eds.) *Studia Patristica*. Vol. LXXIV – Including Papers presented at the Fifth British Patristics Conference, London, 3–5 September 2014. Leuven: Peeters, 303–316.

- 2017: „The imperial identity of senatorial rituals in Late Antiquity.", in: A. Zuiderhoek and W. Vanacker (eds.), *Imperial identities in the Roman World*, New York City: Routlegde, 199–218.
- 2018: „Procedural similarities between fourth and fifth-century Christian synods and the Roman Senates: myth, politics or cultural identity?", in: Markus Vinzent (ed.), *Studia Patristica*. Vol. XCII – Papers presented at the Seventeenth International Conference on Patristic Studies held in Oxford 2015. Volume 18: Liturgica and Tractatus Symboli; Orientalia; Critica et Philologica; Historica. Studia Patristica 92. Leuven: Peeters, 293–302.
- 2018: „Mustering sources and vindication: Theodoret of Cyrrhus' sources and the models of Greek ecclesiastical historiography", in: O. Devillers and B. B. Sebastiani (eds.), *Les historiens grecs et romains: entre sources et modèles*. Scripta Antiqua 109, Bordeaux: Ausonius Éditions, 349–358.
- 2018: „Peace and Harmony at Church Councils and in the Roman Empire under Theodosius II.", *AHC 48* (1), Brill, 70–86.
- 2019: „Institutionalisation of the tradition and individualised lived Christian religion in Late Antiquity", in: Martin Fuchs et al. (eds.), *Religious Individualisation: Historical Dimensions and Comparative Perspectives*, Berlin: de Gruyter, 1223–1254.

Fuchs, Martin

–; Antje Linkenbach, Wolfgang Reinhard, (eds.) 2015. *Individualisierung durch christliche Mission?*, Wiesbaden: Harrassowitz.
–; Vasudha Dalmia (eds.) 2019. *Religious Interactions in Modern India*, New Delhi: Oxford University Press.
– et al. (eds.) 2019. Religious Individualisation: Historical Dimensions and Comparative Perspectives. Berlin: de Gruyter.

- 2013: „Foreword", in: Robinson, Rowena, *Boundaries of Religion: Essays on Christianity, Ethnic Conflict, and Violence*, New Delhi: Oxford Univ. Press, 11–15.
- 2013: „Vorwort", in: Voigt, Viola, Interkulturelles Mentoring made in Germany: zum Cultural Diversity Management in multinationalen Unternehmen, Springer VS, 13–17.
- 2014: „Slum als Lebenswelt", in: Karlheinz Sonntag (ed.), *Arm und reich* [Sammelband der Vorträge des Studium Generale der Ruprecht-Karls-Universität Heidelberg im Wintersemester 2012/2013], Heidelberg: Universitätsverlag Winter, 129–55.
- 2015: „Einleitung", in: *Individualisierung durch christliche Mission?*, Wiesbaden: Harrassowitz, 13–37.
- 2015: „Introduction", in: *Individualisierung durch christliche Mission?*, Wiesbaden: Harrassowitz, 38–63.
–; Jörg Rüpke 2015: „Religious individualization in historical perspective", *Religion* 45.3 (2015), 323–329.
- 2015: „Processes of religious individualisation: Stocktaking and issues for the future", *Religion* 45 (3), 330–43.
–; Jörg Rüpke 2015: „Religion: Versuch einer Begriffsbestimmung", in: Bultmann, Christoph and Antje Linkenbach (eds.), *Religionen übersetzen. Klischees und Vorurteile im Religionsdiskurs*, Vorlesungen des Interdisziplinären Forums Religion der Universität Erfurt 11, Münster: Aschendorff, 17–21.
- 2016: „Alternative Genealogien von „Menschenwürde" und „Menschenrechten"?: das universalistische Potential indischer Religionen und das Problem des übersetzerischen Anschlusses", in: Esposito, Anna Aurelia; Oberlin, Heike; Viveka Rai, B.A. and Karin Juliana Steiner (eds.), *In ihrer*

rechten Hand hielt sie ein silbernes Messer mit Glöckchen ...": Studien zur indischen Kultur und Literatur, Wiesbaden: Harrassowitz, 75–87.
- 2016: „Institutionalzing informal socialities: Dalit urban poor in Dharavi", in: Hugo Gorringe et.al. (eds.), From the Margins to the Mainstream: Institutionalising Minorities in South Asia, London: Sage, 245–60.
- 2015: „Worldview and relations to the world: The concepts of karman and bhakti in Weber's study of Hinduism and Buddhism", Sociological Problems 47 (3–4), 147–162 [in Bulgarian].
- 2016: „Worldview and relationships to the world: the concepts of karma(n) and bhakti in Weber's study on Hinduism and Buddhism", Max Weber studies 16 (2), 211–27.
- 2017: „India in Comparison: Max Weber's Analytical Agenda", in: Thomas C. Ertman (ed.), Max Weber's Economic Ethic of the World Religions: An Analysis, Cambridge: Cambridge University Press, 223–266.
- 2017: „Recognition across difference: conceptual considerations against an Indian background", in: Dieter Gosewinkel, Dieter Rucht (eds.), Transnational struggles for Recognition. New perspectives on civil society since the twentieth century, New York/Oxford: Berghahn, 252–76.
- 2017: „Sociology of World Relations: Confronting the Complexities of Hindu Religions. A Perspective beyond Max Weber'", Max Weber Studies 17 (2), 196–211.
- 2017: „'Hermeneutik des Neuen'. Ruptures and Innovations of Interpretation – Reflections from Indian Religious History: The Case of Bhakti, Social Imaginaries 3 (2), 57–75.
- 2017: „'Hermeneutik des Neuen'. Rotture e innovazioni nell'interpretazione religiosa. Rifessioni dalla storia religiosa indiana: il caso della bhakti", in: Carlo Altini, Philippe Hoffmann and Jörg Rüpke (eds.), Issues of Interpretation. Texts, Images, Rites, Stuttgart: Franz Steiner, 225–242.
- 2018: „Indian Imbroglios: Bhakti Neglected, Or: the Missed Opportunities for a New Approach to a Comparative Analysis of Civilizational Diversity", in: Arnason, Johann and Chris Hann (eds.), Anthropology and Civilizational Analysis. Eurasian Explorations, Albany (NY): SUNY Press, 121–154.
–; Antje Linkenbach, 2018: „Critique of Conversion – Conversion as Critique: M.K. Gandhi, B.R. Ambedkar and the Prerogative of Interpretation", in: Rafael Klöber and Manju Ludwig (eds.), HerStory. Historical Scholarship between South Asia and Europe. Festschrift in Honour of Gita Dharampal-Frick, Heidelberg: CrossAsia-eBooks, 313–330.
- 2019: „Dhamma and the Common Good: Religion as Problem and Answer – Ambedkar's Critical Theory of Social Relationality", in: Martin Fuchs and Vasudha Dalmia (eds.), Religious Interactions in Modern India, New Delhi: Oxford University Press, 364–413.
- 2019: „Transcending Selves, Introduction to Part I", in: Martin Fuchs et al. (eds.), Religious Individualisation: Historical Dimensions and Comparative Perspectives, Berlin: de Gruyter, 35–49.
- 2019: „Self-affirmation, Self-transcendence and the Relationality of Selves: The Social Embedment of Individualisation in Bhakti", in Martin Fuchs et al. (eds.), Religious Individualisation: Historical Dimensions and Comparative Perspectives, Berlin: de Gruyter, 257–288.

Gordon, Richard L.

- 2013: „Gods, guilt and suffering: Psychological aspects of cursing in the north-western provinces of the Roman Empire", Acta Classica Universitatis Scientiarum Debreceniensis 49 (2013), 255–81.
- 2013: „Individuality, selfhood and power in the Second Century: The mystagogue as a mediator of religious options", in: J. Rüpke and G. Woolf (eds.), Religious Dimensions of the Self in the Second century CE, STAC 76, Tübingen: Mohr-Siebeck, 146–172.

- 2013: „The Religious anthropology of Late-antique 'high' Magical Practice", in: J. Rüpke (ed.), *Individualization in the Religions of the Ancient Mediterranean*, Oxford: Oxford University Press 163–86.
- 2013: „'Will my child have a big nose?': Uncertainty, authority and narrative in katarchic astrology", in: V. Rosenberger (ed.), *Divination in the Ancient World: Religious Options and the Individual*, Stuttgart: PawB 46, 93–137.
- 2015: „Religious competence and individuality: Three studies in the Roman Empire", *Religion* 45.3 (2015), 367–385.
- 2015: „Showing the gods the way: Curse-tablets as deictic persuasion", *RRE* 1.2 (2015), 148–180.
- 2016: „Den Jungstier auf der goldenen Schulter zu tragen. Mythos, Ritual und Jenseitsvorstellungen im Mithraskult", in: K. Waldner, W. Spickermann, R.L. Gordon (eds.), Burial Rituals, Ideas of Afterlife, and the Individual in the Hellenistic World and the Roman Empire, Stuttgart: PawB 57, 219–253.
- 2016: „Negotiating the temple-script: Women's narratives among the 'confession-texts' of western Asia Minor", in: *RRE* 2.2 (2016), 227–255.
- 2017: „Nature, order and well-being in the Roman cult of Mithras", in: A. Hintze and A. Williams (eds.), *Holy Wealth: Accounting for this World and the Next in Religious Belief and Practice: Festschrift for John R. Hinnells*, Iranica 24, Wiesbaden: Harrassowitz, 93–130.
- 2017: „From East to West: Staging Religious Experience in the Mithraic Temple", in: S. Nagel, J.-F. Quack and C. Witschel (eds.), *Entangled Worlds: Religious Confluences between East and West in the Roman Empire. The Cults of Isis, Mithras and Jupiter Dolichenus*. Proceedings of the Colloquium held at Heidelberg 26–29 Nov. 2009, Orientalische Religionen in der Antike 22, Tübingen: Mohr Siebeck, 413–442.
- 2017: „'Straightening the paths': Inductive Divination, Materiality and Imagination in the Graeco-Roman Period", in: Claudia Moser and Jennifer Knust (eds.), *Ritual Matters: Material Remains and Ancient Religion*, Memoirs of the American Academy in Rome, Supplementary vol. 13 Ann Arbor: University of Michigan Press, 119–143.
- 2019: „Subordinated religious specialism and individuation in the Graeco-Roman world", in: Martin Fuchs *et al.* (eds.), *Religious Individualisation: Historical Dimensions and Comparative Perspectives*, Berlin: de Gruyter, 985–1008.

Gräb-Schmidt, Elisabeth

- 2013: „Säkularisierung und der Ruf nach Werten. Zur kategorialen Bedeutung der Freiheit im Zeitalter ihrer Gefährdungen", in: N. Slenczka, (Hrsg.), *Was sind legitime außenpolitische Interessen? Unverfügbare Voraussetzungen des säkularen Staates. Umgang mit Schuld in der Öffentlichkeit. (BThZ 2013)*, Leipzig: EVA Leipzig, 96–113.
- 2013: „Time and Eternity – The ontological impact of Kiergegaard's conception of time as a contribution to the question of the reality of time and human freedom", in: A. Nicolaidis, W. Achtner (Hrsg.), *The Evolution of Time. Studies of Time in Science, Anthropology, Theology*, Oak Park, 162–184.
- 2014: „Wie kommt das Gute in die Welt? Natur und Freiheit des Menschen im Spannungsfeld von Soziobiologie, Ethik und Religion", in: Th. Schlag, H. Simojoki (Hrsg.), *Mensch – Religion – Bildung. Religionspädagogik in anthropologischen Spannungsfeldern*. Gütersloh: Gütersloher Verlagshaus, 340–351.
- 2015: „Der Mensch – seine Natur als Freiheit. Zu den Bestimmungen des Verhältnisses von Natur und Freiheit in anthropologischer, kosmologischer und verantwortungsethischer Absicht", in: dies., R. Preul (Hrsg.), *Natur (MJTh 27 / MThSt 122)*, Leipzig: EVA Leipzig, 29–50.

- 2015: „Der lebendige Grund personaler Identität. Überlegungen zu einem leibbezogenen Personkonzept im Anschluss an Wilhelm Dilthey", in: E. Gräb-Schmidt, M. Heesch, F. Lohmann, D. Schlenke, Ch. Seibert (Hrsg.), *Leibhaftes Personsein. Theologische und interdisziplinäre Perspektiven. (MThSt 123)*, Leipzig: EVA, 77–96.
- 2016: „Religion und Freiheit. Zur emanzipativen Kraft der Transzendenz", in *ZThK 113 (2016) 2*, 195–233.
- 2017: „Autonome Systeme. Autonomie im Spiegel menschlicher Freiheit und ihrer technischen Errungenschaften", *Zeitschrift für Evangelische Ethik (ZEE) 61*, Gütersloh: Gütersloher Verlagshaus, 163–170.
- 2017: „Freiheit als Freiwerden. Phänomenologische Bestimmungen der neuzeitlichen Freiheit", in: T. Söding, B. Oberdorfer (Hrsg.), *Kontroverse Freiheit*, Freiburg: Herder, 16–32.
- 2017: „Nachhaltigkeit im Zeichen reformatorischer Freiheit", in: T. Jähnichen u.a. (Hrsg.), *Rechtfertigung – Folgenlos? Jahrbuch Sozialer Protestantismus, Bd. 10*, Leipzig: Evangelische Verlagsanstalt, 113–129.
- 2017: „Das Gleichgewicht zwischen dem Ästhetischen und dem Ethischen in der Herausarbeitung der Persönlichkeit: Das Versteckspiel des Lebens und der Ernst der Authentizität", in: H. Deuser, M. Kleinert (Hrsg.), *Søren Kierkegaard: Entweder – Oder (Klassiker Auslegen 67)*, Berlin/New York: de Gruyter, 193–211.
- 2017: „Menschenrechte und Christentum. Metaphysische und rechtssystematische Überlegungen zur Frage ihrer Geltung und Universalisierung", in: S. Altmeyer u.a. (Hrsg.), *Menschenrechte und Religionsunterricht (JRP 33)*, Göttingen: Vandenhoeck & Ruprecht, 26–37.
- 2017: „Gerechtigkeit und Freiheit in den Institutionen", in: U.Heckel, J.Kampmann, V.Leppin, Ch.Schwöbel (Hrsg.), *Luther heute: Ausstrahlungen der Wittenberger Reformation*, Tübingen: Mohr Siebeck, 319–350.
- 2018: „Freiheit und Selbsterkenntnis. Zur Bedeutung der Buße in der Anthropologie Luthers", in *Theologische Literaturzeitung (ThLZ) 143 Nr.6*, 571–588.
- 2018: „Der Wirklichkeits- und Normativitätsanspruch der Ethik. Überlegungen zu Grundlegungsfragen der Ethik in reformatorischer Sicht", in: M. Roth, M. Held (Hrsg.), *„Was ist theologische Ethik? Grundbestimmungen und Grundvorstellungen"*, Berlin/Boston: de Gruyter, 41–62.
- 2019: „Transcendence and Freedom: On the Anthropological and Cultural Centrality of Religion", in Martin Fuchs et al. (eds.), *Religious Individualisation: Historical Dimensions and Comparative Perspectives*, Berlin: de Gruyter, 141–158.

Haakonssen, Knud

- (co-ed.) 2013. *„David Hume"*, International Library of Essays in the History of Political Thought, Aldershot, Hamps.: Ashgate, 2013.
- (ed.) 2014. „Modern International Thought. A symposium occasioned by David Armitage's Foundations of Modern International Thought", special issue of History of European Ideas, 40 (2014).
- (co-ed.) 2015. *„Thomas Reid on Society and Politics"*, edited with an introduction. Edinburgh: Edinburgh UP.
- (ed.) 2016. „Language in Intellectual History: The Work of Hans Aarsleff", special issue of History of European Ideas, 42 (2016).
- (co-ed.) 2017. „Ludvig Holberg (1684–1754). Learning and Literature in the Nordic Enlightenment", London: Routledge.

- 2013: „Five questions to Knud Haakonssen", in: *Intellectual History: 5 Questions*, ed F. Stjernfelt, M. Haugaard Jeppesen and M. Thorup, Copenhagen: Automatic Press, 71–77.

- 2013: „Natural rights or political prudence? Toleration in Francis Hutcheson", in: *Natural Law and Toleration in the Early Enlightenment*, eds J. Parkin and T. Stanton, Oxford: Oxford UP (Proceedings of the British Academy), 183–200.
- 2016: Indledning [Introduction], Ludvig Holberg, *Introduction til Naturens og Folkerettens Kundskab*, in: Ludvig Holbergs Skrifter: http://holbergsskrifter.dk/holberg-public/view?docId=NF/NF_innl.page&doc.view=minimal (2016).
- 2016: (co-author), „Natural law: Law, rights and duties", in: *A Companion to Intellectual History*, ed R. Whatmore, Chicester, W. Sussex: Wiley-Blackwell, 2016, 377–401.
- 2016: „The *Lectures on Jurisprudence*", in: *Adam Smith. His Life, Thought and Legacy*, ed Ryan Hanley, Princeton: Princeton UP, 48–66.
- 2017: „Early-modern natural law theories", in: *Cambridge Companion to Natural Law Jurisprudence*, ed George Duke and Robert P. George, Cambridge: Cambridge UP, 76–102.
- 2017: Introduction, part 2: The author and the work, in: *Ludvig Holberg (1684–1754). Learning and Literature in the Nordic Enlightenment*, ed K. Haakonssen & S. Olden Jørgensen, London & New York: Routledge, 2017, 13–26.
- 2017: „Holberg's Law of Nature and Nations", in: Ludvig Holberg (1684–1754). Learning and Literature in the Nordic Enlightenment, ed K. Haakonssen & S. Olden Jørgensen, London & New York: Routledge, 59–79.
- 2017: „Pufendorf on power and liberty", On-line discussion forum (January 2017): http://oll.libertyfund.org/pages/lm-pufendorf.
- 2018: „Natural law and moral philosophy", in: *Cambridge Companion to the Scottish Enlightenment*, ed Alexander Broadie & Craig Smith, Cambridge: Cambridge UP, forthcoming 2018.
- 2018: „Om *Natur- og folkeretten*", in: Ludvig Holberg, *Natur- og folkeretten* (*Ludvig Holbergs Hovedværker*, vol. 19), Copenhagen & Aarhus: Det Danske Sprog- og Litteraturselskab & Aarhus Universitetsforlag, 11–35.

- 2016: Review article of Benjamin Straumann, *Roman Law in the State of Nature*, in: *Bryn Mawr Classical Review*, 2016: http://bmcr.brynmawr.edu/2016/2016-01-32.html

Haas, Cornelia

- 2013: „Jagadamba tanzt. Rukmini Devi und das World-Mother-Movement", in: Stephan Koehn und Heike Moser (Hg.): *Frauenkörper/Frauenbilder. Inszenierungen des Weiblichen in den Gesellschaften Süd- und Ostasiens*. Wiesbaden: Harrassowitz, 161–177.
- 2014: „The Logoi and the Dragon in der „vergleichenden Mythologie" Helena Blavatskys", in: Cyril Brosch und Annick Payne (Hg.): *Na-wa/i-VIR.ZI/A. MAGNUS.SCRIBA. Festschrift für Helmut Nowicki zum 70. Geburtstag*. Herausgegeben von Cyril Brosch und Annick Payne. Wiesbaden: Harrassowitz (Dresdner Beiträge zur Hethitologie 45), 79–94.
- 2015: „From Theosophy to Indian Religions – The Conversions of Helena Blavatsky and Henry Steel Olcott to Buddhism", in: Antje Linkenbach / Martin Fuchs / Wolfgang Reinhard (Hg.): *Individualisierung durch christliche Mission?* Wiesbaden: Harrassowitz, 505–515.
- 2015: „United Lodge of Theosophists India – Transcultural Re-Definition of Indian History of Ideas in the Urban Context of the High-Tech-Metropolises Mumbai and Bangalore", in: *Capitales de l'ésoterisme européen et dialogue des cultures*. Paris: Orizons, 197–209.
- 2019: „Varieties of spiritual individualisation in the theosophical movement: the United Lodge of theosophists India as climax of individualisation-processes within the theosophical movement", in: Martin Fuchs *et al.* (eds.), *Religious Individualisation: Historical Dimensions and Comparative Perspectives*, Berlin: de Gruyter, 1365–1380.

Henderson, Ian H.

– 2013: „Mark's Gospel and the Pre-History of Individuation", in: (ed.) Jörg Rüpke, *Religious individuation in the Ancient Mediterranean*, Oxford: Oxford University Press, 269–297.
– 2015: „The Child, Death and the Human in Mark's Gospel", in: (eds.) Ulrike Mittmann and Beate Ego, *Evil and Death: Conceptions of the Human in Biblical, Early Jewish, Early Christian, Greco-Roman and Egyptian Literature* (Deuterocanonical and Cognate Literature 18; Berlin: de Gruyter, 2015), 199–219.
– 2019. „,… quod nolo, illud facio' (Romans 7:20): institutionalizing the unstable self", in: Martin Fuchs *et al.* (eds.), *Religious Individualisation: Historical Dimensions and Comparative Perspectives*, Berlin: de Gruyter, 807–830.

Herrmann-Pillath, Carsten

– 2015. Culture: The Ritual Order of State and Markets, London: Routledge.
– 2017. Wachstum, Macht und Ordnung. Eine wirtschaftsphilosophische Auseinandersetzung mit China, Marburg: Metropolis.

– 2016: „Fei Xiaotong's comparative theory of Chinese culture: Its relevance for contemporary cross-disciplinary research on Chinese 'collectivism'", *Copenhagen Journal of Asian Studies* 34(1), 25–57.
–; Man Guo 2016: „Ritual and property: Theorizing a Chinese case", *Man and the Economy 4(1)*, doi: 10.1515/me-2017-0004.
–; Björn Vollan, Zhou Yexin, Andreas Landmann & Hu Biliang 2017: „Cooperation and Authoritarian Values: An Experimental Study in China", *European Economic Review 93*, April 2017, 90–105.
– 2016: „Performativity, Performance and Politics: Towards an Evolutionary Taxonomy of Economic Systems", *Schmollers Jahrbuch 136(3)*, 257–284.
–; Feng, Xingyuan 2017: „Cultural Entrepreneurship in China (February 21, 2017) „, Available at SSRN: https://ssrn.com/abstract=3040490.
–; Guo, Man 2017: „Power, Property and Governmentality in South China: The Case of the Wen (Man) Clan in Hong Kong and Shenzhen (December 18, 2017) „, Available at SSRN: https://ssrn.com/abstract=3089728.
– 2018: 'Iclan': „The Chinese Ritual Economy in the 21st Century (April 22, 2018)", Available at SSRN: https://ssrn.com/abstract=3166765.
–; Man Guo 2019. „Lineage, Food and Ritual in a Chinese Metropolis", *Anthropos 114*. 195–207.
– 2019: „Religious individualisation in China: a two-modal approach", in: Martin Fuchs *et al.* (eds.), *Religious Individualisation: Historical Dimensions and Comparative Perspectives*, Berlin: de Gruyter, 643–668.

Höke, Vera

– 2019: Individualisation in conformity: Keshab Chandra Sen and canons of the self, in: Martin Fuchs *et al.* (eds.), *Religious Individualisation: Historical Dimensions and Comparative Perspectives*, Berlin: de Gruyter, 1381–1400.

Hoffmann, Veronika

– (ed.) 2017. Nachdenken über den Zweifel. Theologische Perspektiven, Ostfildern.

– 2017: Einleitung, in: Ead. (Hg.): *Nachdenken über den Zweifel. Theologische Perspektiven*, Ostfildern, 7–20.
– 2017: „Zweifel, Säkularität und Identität", in: Ead. (Hg.): *Nachdenken über den Zweifel. Theologische Perspektiven*, Ostfildern, 21–35.
– 2018: „,Zu gläubig', um tolerant zu sein? Erkundungen im Spannungsfeld von Glaubensgewissheit, Zweifel und Toleranz", in: Kirschner, Martin; Ruhstorfer, Karlheinz (Hgg.): *Die gegenwärtige Krise Europas. Theologische Antwortversuche*, Freiburg (QD 291), 274–293.
– 2019: „Individualised versus institutional religion: Is there a mediating position?" in: Martin Fuchs et al. (eds.), *Religious Individualisation: Historical Dimensions and Comparative Perspectives*, Berlin: de Gruyter, 1121–1138.

Hu-von Hinüber, Haiyan

– 2018: „What to do if the Owner of a Monastry is put in jail? The Saṃgha's Begging Area according to Early Vinaya Texts", in: *Saddharmāmṛtam. Festschrift für Jens-Uwe Hartmann zum 65. Geburtstag*, herausgegeben von O. von Criegern, G. Melzer und J. Schneider, Wien 2018 (Wiener Studien zur Tibetologie und Buddhismuskunde, Heft 93), 201–213.

Kleinert, Matthias

–; Gerald Hartung (eds.) 2017. *Humor und Religiosität in der Moderne*, Wiesbaden: Springer.

Klostergaard Petersen, Anders

2019: Suifaction: typological reflections on the evolution of the self, in: Martin Fuchs et al. (eds.), *Religious Individualisation: Historical Dimensions and Comparative Perspectives*, Berlin: de Gruyter, 185–214.

Kouroshi, Yahya

– 2016: „Medialität und Modalität der Prophetie. Die Rezeption der Geschichte Christi am Hof der Großmogulherrscher in Indien um 1600 anhand von Schriften des Jesuiten Jeronimo Xavier", in: Jamal Malik et al. (Hgg.), *Religionen in Bewegung. Interreligiöse Beziehungen im Wandel der Zeit*, Münster: Aschendorff, 123–141.
– 2018: „Poetik und Grammatik des Blicks: Goethes Symbol-Begriff vom Euphrat aus betrachtet", in: Christine Maillard/Hamid Tafazoli (Hgg.), *Persien im Spiegel Deutschlands. Konstruktionsvarianten der Persienbilder in der deutschsprachigen Literatur vom 18. bis in das 20. Jahrhundert*, Strasbourg: Presses universitaires de Strasbourg, 243–263.

Liedhegener, Antonius

- 2012: „,Neue Religionspolitik' in der verfassungsstaatlichen Demokratie? Religionsfreiheit als Schranke und Ziel politischen Entscheidens in religiös-kulturellen Konflikten", in: Bogner, Daniel/Heimbach-Steins, Marianne (Hg.), *Freiheit – Gleichheit – Religion. Orientierungen moderner Religionspolitik* (= Religion und Politik, Bd. 4) Würzburg, 111–130.
- 2014: „Religion, Bürgergesellschaft und Pluralismus. Gesellschaftliche und politische Integration aus der Perspektive demokratischer politischer Systeme", in: Arens, Edmund (Hgg.), *Integration durch Religion? Geschichtliche Befunde, gesellschaftliche Analysen, rechtliche Perspektiven* (= Religion – Wirtschaft – Politik, Bd. 10) Baden-Baden – Zürich, 63–84.
- 2014: „Säkularisierung als Entkirchlichung. Trends und Konjunkturen in Deutschland von der Mitte des 19. Jahrhunderts bis zur Gegenwart", in: Gabriel, Karl/Gärtner, Christel/Pollack, Detlef (Hg.), *Umstrittene Säkularisierung. Soziologische und historische Analysen zur Differenzierung von Religion und Politik*, 2. durchges. und um ein Reg. erg. Aufl., Berlin, 481–531.
- 2015: „Nachkriegszeit (1945–1960)", in: Hölscher, Lucian/Krech, Volkhard (Hg.), *Handbuch der Religionsgeschichte im deutschsprachigen Raum, Bd. 6,1: 20. Jahrhundert – Epochen und Themen*, Paderborn, 135–174, 449–455 und 554–559.
- 2016: „Ein kleiner, aber feiner Unterschied. Religion, zivilgesellschaftliches Engagement und soziale Integration in der Schweiz", in: Arens, Edmund (Hgg.), *Integrationspotenziale von Religion und Zivilgesellschaft. Theoretische und empirische Befunde* (= Religion – Wirtschaft – Politik, Bd. 14) Baden-Baden – Zürich, 121–181.
- 2016: „Religiöse Identitäten als Problem wechselseitiger Identifizierungen und Kategorisierungen. Aktuelle theoretische Konzepte und Fragen ihrer Operationalisierung in der empirischen Religionsforschung", in: Werkner, Ines-Jacqueline/Hidalgo, Oliver (Hg.), *Religiöse Identitäten in politischen Konflikten* (= Politik und Religion), Wiesbaden, 65–82.
- 2018: „Pluralisierung", in: Krech, Volkhard/Pollack, Detlef/Hero, Markus/Müller, Olaf (Hg.), *Handbuch Religionssoziologie*, Wiesbaden, 347–382.

Linkenbach, Antje

- –; Martin Fuchs; Wolfgang Reinhard (eds.) 2015, *Individualisierung durch Christliche Mission?*, Wiesbaden: Harrassowitz, (Studien zur Außereuropäischen Christentumsgeschichte – Asien, Afrika, Lateinamerika).
- –; Christoph Bultmann (eds.) 2015, *Religionen Übersetzen: Klischees und Vorurteile im Religionsdiskurs*, Münster: Aschendorff.
- – et al. (eds.) 2019. *Religious Individualisation: Historical Dimensions and Comparative Perspectives*. Berlin: de Gruyter.

- 2014: „Religion, Säkularisierung und Rechtspluralismus im modernen Indien", in: Benedikt Kranemann, Christof Mandry, Hans-Friedrich Müller (Hrsg), *Religion und Recht*, Münster: Aschendorff, 137–162.
- 2015: „The World Religion of Hinduism: On the Construction of the Image of India in German Textbooks", in *Eckert.bulletin* 15, 14–17.
- 2015: „Weltreligion Hinduismus: Zur Konstruktion des Indienbildes in deutschen Schulbüchern", in: Christoph Bultmann, Antje Linkenbach (Hrsg.), 2015, *Religionen Übersetzen: Klischees und Vorurteile im Religionsdiskurs*, Münster: Aschendorff, 23–44.

- 2016: „Bewegungen für Umweltgerechtigkeit in Indien", in: *Handbuch Entwicklungsforschung*, hrsg. von Manuela Boatca, Karin Fischer und Gerhard Hauck; Springer NachschlageWissen (online) 2015. Druckversion 2016.
- 2016: „Interreligiosität in Indien in historischer Perspektive", in: Michael Gabel, Jamal Malik, Justyna Okolowicz (Hrsg.), *Religionen in Bewegung: Interreligiöse Beziehungen im Wandel der Zeit*, Münster: Aschendorff, 99–122.
- 2016: „Soziale Bewegungen und selbstbestimmte Entwicklung", in: *Handbuch Entwicklungsforschung*, hrsg. von Manuela Boatca, Karin Fischer und Gerhard Hauck; Springer Nachschlage-Wissen (online), 2015. Druckversion 2016.
- 2017: „Environmental Justice in India? Examining the Compatibility between Sustainability, Social Justice and the Gandhian legacy", in *Journal of Social and Economic Studies (ANSISS)*, 2017, 27.1.
- 2017: „Gender Dynamics and Equality in India: A Plea for an Integrative Approach to Social Justice", in *RDWU Journal of Social Sciences and Humanities*, 2017, Vol. 2, 5–21.
- 2017: „Sustainable Development in a Dharmic Land? Environmental and Political Protest in Uttarakhand", in: Joshi, B.K. and Joshi, Maheshwar P. (eds.), *Unfolding Central Himalaya: The Cradle of Culture*, Dehra Dun: Doon Library and Research Center; Almora: Almora Book Depot, 296–324.
- –; Martin Fuchs, 2018: „Critique of Conversion – Conversion as Critique: M.K. Gandhi, B.R. Ambedkar and the Prerogative of Interpretation", in: Rafael Klöber and Manju Ludwig (eds.), *HerStory. Historical Scholarship between South Asia and Europe. Festschrift in Honour of Gita Dharampal-Frick*, Heidelberg: CrossAsia-eBooks, 313–330.
- 2018: „Travelling Deities: Ritual, Territory and Authority in the Central Himalayas (India). The Hermeneutics of Ethnographic Research", in: Carlo Altini, Philippe Hoffmann, Jorg Rüpke (eds.), *Issues of Interpretation. Texts, Images, Rites*, Stuttgart: Franz Steiner, 253–268.
- 2018: „Projecting a New Anthropology? Some reflections on Lawrence Krader's contribution to the discipline of anthropology and his significance today", in: Cyril Levitt and Sabine Sander (eds.), *Beyond the Juxtaposition of Nature and Culture. Lawrence Krader, Interdisciplinarity, and the Human Being*, New York: Peter Lang (New York), 133–149.
- 2019: „Der Tod der Muttersprache" –Sprache und Sprachpolitik in Indien, in: Südasien 39.2, 7–12.
- 2019: „The Empathic Subject and the Question of Dividuality", in: Martin Fuchs *et al.* (eds.), *Religious Individualisation: Historical Dimensions and Comparative Perspectives*, Berlin: de Gruyter, 383–408.
- –; Martin Mulsow, 2019: „The Dividual Self: Introduction to Part 2", in: Martin Fuchs *et al.* (eds.), *Religious Individualisation: Historical Dimensions and Comparative Perspectives*, Berlin: de Gruyter, 323–344.

Maier, Harry O.

- 2019: Paul's Letter to Philemon: a case study in individualisation, dividuation, and partibility in Imperial spatial contexts, in: Martin Fuchs *et al.* (eds.), *Religious Individualisation: Historical Dimensions and Comparative Perspectives*, Berlin: de Gruyter, 519–540.

Malik, Aditya

- –; Sweetman, Will (eds.) 2016. *Hinduism in India: Modern and Contemporary Movements*. New Delhi: Sage Publications.

– 2016. Tales of Justice and Rituals of Divine Embodiment: Oral Narratives from the Central Himalayas. New York: Oxford University Press (pb 2018).

– 2015: „The *darbar* of Goludev: Possession, Petitions, and Modernity", in: William S. Sax and Helene Basu (eds.) *The Law of Possession. Ritual, Healing, and the Secular State* (193–225). New York: Oxford University Press.
– 2016: „Folk Hinduism: The Middle Ground?", in: Will Sweetman and Aditya Malik (eds.) *Hinduism in India: Modern and Contemporary Movements* (176–193). New Delhi: Sage Publications.
– 2016: „Possession, Alterity, Modernity", Introductory chapter in: Sekhar Bandyopadhyay and Aloka Parashar Sen (eds.) *Religion and Modernity in India.* (36–63). New Delhi: Oxford University Press.
– 2019. „The swirl of worlds: possession, porosity and embodiment", in Martin Fuchs *et al.* (eds.), *Religious Individualisation: Historical Dimensions and Comparative Perspectives*, Berlin: de Gruyter, 559–582.

Malinar, Angelika

–; S. Müller (eds.) 2018. Asia and Europe – Interconnected: Agents, Concepts, and Things, Wiesbaden: Harrassowitz.
– 2013: „Mohandas Karamchand Gandhi", in: K. A. Jacobsen, H. Basu, A. Malinar & V. Narayanan (eds.) *Brill's Encyclopedia of Hinduism. Vol. V*, Leiden, Brill, 542–551.
– 2013: „,… western-born but in spirit eastern …' – Annie Besant between Colonial and Spiritual Realms", in: *Asiatische Studien/Études Asiatiques* 67, 4: 1115–1155.
– 2014: „'Following one's Desire' (*kāmacāra*): On a Characterisation of Freedom in Vedic literature and the Mahābhārata", in: *Asiatische Studien/Études Asiatiques* 68, 4, 757–782.
– 2014: „Sensory Perception and Notions of the Senses in Sāṃkhya Philosophy", in: A. Michaels, Ch. Wulf (eds.), *Exploring the Senses, Asian and European Perspectives on Ritual and Performativity*, London: Routledge, 34–51.
– 2015: „Religion", in: G. Dharampal-Frick et al. (eds.). Key Concepts in Modern Indian Studies, New York, Oxford: Oxford University Press, 289–297.
– 2015: „Religionsfreiheit und Hinduismus", in: H. Ziebertz (ed.). *Religionsfreiheit: Positionen, Konflikte, Herausforderungen*, Würzburg: Echter, 183–210.
– 2015: „Religious Pluralism and Processes of Individualization in Hinduism", in: *Religion* 45, 3, 386–408.
– 2016: „Konfigurationen von Mystik zwischen Indien und Europa", in: *Meister Eckhart Jahrbuch 10*, 103–120.
– 2017: „Narrating Sāṃkhya Philosophy: Bhīṣma, Janaka and Pañcaśikha at *Mahābhārata* 12.211–12", in: *Journal of Indian Philosophy* 45, 4, 609–649.
– 2017: „Philosophy in the *Mahābhārata* and the History of Indian Philosophy", in: *Journal of Indian Philosophy* 45, 4, 587–604.
– 2017: „Religious Pathways: Social and Ritual Activity (*karman*), Knowledge (*jñāna*), Devotion (*bhakti*)", in: G. Oddie and G. Bailey (eds.), *Handbook of Hinduism*, New Delhi: Sage.
– 2018: „Karmic Histories and the Synthesis of 'East and West'. Annie Besant on Hinduism", in: A. Malinar & S. Müller (eds.), *Asia and Europe – Interconnected: Agents, Concepts, and Things*, Wiesbaden: Harrassowitz.
– 2019: „Religious plurality and individual authority in the *Mahahbharata*", in: Martin Fuchs *et al.* (eds.), *Religious Individualisation: Historical Dimensions and Comparative Perspectives*, Berlin: de Gruyter. 1173–1200.

Mersch, Katharina

- 2013: „Göttlich legitimierter Eigensinn. Gewissensfreiheit als Option im Umgang mit dem exkommunizierten Ludwig dem Bayern und dem Interdikt", in *Frühmittelalterliche Studien 47 (2013)*, 209–238.
- 2018: „Überlegungen zum Verhältnis von Schuld, Reue und Intention am Beispiel der Ermordung des Erzbischofs Burchard III. von Magdeburg", in: hrsg. von Jan-Hendryk de Boer und Marcel Bubert (Kontingenzgeschichten), *Absichten, Pläne, Strategien. Erkundungen eines Problems der Vormoderneforschung*, 141–174.
- 2019: „Out of bounds, still in control. Exclusion, religious individuation and individualisation during the later Middle Ages", in: Martin Fuchs et al. (eds.), *Religious Individualisation: Historical Dimensions and Comparative Perspectives*, Berlin: de Gruyter. 1321–1350.

- 2014: Rezension: Jaser, Christian, „Ecclesia maledicens. Rituelle und zeremonielle Exkommunikationsformen im Mittelalter", Tübingen: Mohr Siebeck 2013, in *sehepunkte 14 (2014), Nr. 4* [15.04.2014]. http://www.sehepunkte.de/2014/04/24545.html.
- 2014: Rezension: „hrsg. von Letha Böhringer, Jennifer Kolpacoff Deane, Hildo van Engen, „Labels and Libels. Naming Beguines in Northern Medieval Europe (Sanctimoniales 1)", Turnhout 2014, in *Archa Verbi 11 (2014)*, 210–212.
- 2017: Rezension: Franz-Josef Arlinghaus (ed.), „Forms of Individuality and Literacy in the Medieval and Early Modern Periods", Turnhout: Brepols Publishers, 2015, in *Historische Zeitschrift 304/2 (2017)*, 432f.

Mieth, Dietmar

- 2013. Ein Weg der Erfahrung mit Meister Eckhart durch Erfurt. Erfurt (engl. Übers.: Markus Vinzent).
- –; Dagmar Gottschall in Zusammenarbeit mit Katharina Mersch (eds.) 2013, *Meister Eckharts „Reden an die Stadt" (Meister Eckhart Jahrbuch, Bd.6)*, Stuttgart: Kohlhammer.
- 2013. Meister Eckharts Faszination heute. Erfurt (englische Übers.: Markus Vinzent).
- 2014. *Meister Eckhart*. München: Beck.
- 2018. Im Wirken schauen. Die Einheit von vita activa und vita contemplativa bei Meister Eckhart und Johannes Tauler. Neu mit Text, Übersetzung und Kommentar zur Predigt Meister Eckharts über Maria und Martha (2003). Darmstadt: Wiss. Buchgesellschaft. Neudruck (first ed. 1969).
- –; Irene Mieth 2019. Sterben und Lieben. Selbstbestimmung bis zuletzt. Freiburg i.Br.: Herder.

- –; Britta Müller-Schauenburg (eds.) 2012, Mystik, Recht und Freiheit. Religiöse Erfahrung und kirchliche Instituionen im Spätmittelalter. Stuttgart: Kohlhammer.
- (ed.) 2014. Meister Eckhart, Einheit mit Gott. Die bedeutendsten Schriften zur Mystik. 2. Aufl. der Neuausgabe. Ostfildern: Patmos.
- (ed.) 2014, Meister Eckhart. Vom Atmen der Seele. Stuttgart: Reclam.
- –; Marcus Düwell, Jens Braarwig, Peter Brownsword (eds.) 2014. *The Cambridge Handbook of Human Dignity, Interdisciplinary Perspestives*. Cambridge: University Press.
- –; Monika Bobbert (eds.) 2015. *Das Proprium der christlichen Ethik*. Luzern: Exodus
- –; Christine Büchner, Markus Enders (eds.) 2016. Meister Eckhart interreligiös = Jahrbuch der Meister Eckhart Gesellschaft, Bd. 10. Stuttgart: Kohlhammer.
- –; Marie-Anne Vannier, Markus Vinzent Christoph Wojtulewicz (eds.) 2016. *Meister Eckhart in Paris and Strasbourg (Eckhart Texts and Studies, vol. 5)*. Louvain: Peeters.

- (ed.) 2017. Anfänge der religiösen Selbstbestimmung im Mittelalter = special issue Theologische Quartalschrift 197, 1. Ostfildern: Schwabenverlag.
-; Freimut Löser (eds.) 2019. Unterscheiden lernen. Meister Eckharts Erfurter Lehrgespräche, Text, Übersetzung, Kommentar. Ostfildern: Grünewald.
-; Regina Schiewer (eds.) 2019. *Religiöse Selbstbestimmung, Anfänge im Spätmittelalter*, Beiheft 7 zum Meister-Eckhart-Jahrbuch Gesellschaft, Stuttgart: Kohlhammer.

- 2013: „Die individuelle Unmittelbarkeit der Mystik als Herausforderung der Religionen", in: Evangelischer Pressedienst (EPD) Dokumentation Nr. 34 *„Nachdenken über Meister Eckhart"*, vom 20.8. 2013, Frankfurt a.M., 30–38.
- 2013: „Die Meister sagen – die Leute fragen. Denken, rhetorische Intensität und Didaktik in den Reden der Unterweisung Meister Eckharts", in: Dagmar Gottschall, Dietmar Mieth (Hrsg.), *Meister Eckhart Jahrbuch 7, Meister Eckharts Reden an die Stadt*, Stuttgart: Kohlhammer, 325–346.
- 2013: „Meister Eckhart als interreligiöse Integrationsfigur", Zuerst in: hg.v. Katja Becker, Frank-Thilo Becher, Wolfgang Achtner, *Magister, Mystiker, Manager. Meister Eckharts integrale Spiritualität*, Giessen 2012, 74–85, ferner in: Rainer Funk zum 70. Geburtstag, hg. v. Helmut Johach und Burkhard Bierhoff, *Humanismus in der Postmoderne*, Pfungstadt, 129–141.
- 2013: „Meister Eckhart's God", in: Jeanine Diller, Asa Kasher (eds.), *Models of God and Alternative Realities*, Dordrecht: Springer, 801–810.
- 2013: „Menschenwürde – vormoderne Perspektiven am Beispiel zweier Impulse des Spätmittelalters", in: Klaus Ridder, Steffen Patzold (Hg.), *Die Aktualität der Vormoderne. Epochen-Entwürfe zwischen Alterität und Kontinuität*. Berlin: Akademie-Verlag, 319–340.
- 2013: „Reichtum und Armut bei Meister Eckhart", in *Theologische Quartalsschrift 193 (2013)*, 209–219.
- 2013: „Wert und Zeit. Über den richtigen Umgang mit der Zeit", in *Jahrbuch für Biblische Theologie* 28 (2013), 271–294.
- 2014: „Das Freiheitsmotiv bei Meister Eckhart", in: Freimut Löser/Dietmar Mieth, Hg., *Der Meister im Original, Jahrbuch der MEG 7*, Stuttgart: Kohlhammer, 79–104.
- 2014: „Der Umgang mit sich Selbst. Anselm Grüns Anleitungen zum guten Leben", in: Thomas Philipp, Jörg Schwaratzki, Francois Xaver Amherdt (Hg.), *Theologie und Sprache bei Anselm, Grün*. Freiburg-Basel-Wien: Herder, 140–155.
- 2014: „Gelassenheit", in: Erbe und Auftrag, Monastische Welt 90 (2014), 246–255.
- 2014: „Human Dignity in Late Medieval Spiritual and Political Conflicts", in: Düwell, Brownsword, Braavig, Mieth, (eds.), *The Cambridge Handbook on Human Dignity*, Cambridge: University press 74–85.
- 2014: „Meister Eckhart interreligiös", (Zusammenfassung) in: *Zur Debatte*, München 7/2014, 9–12.
- 2014: „Weisheit", in: *Anselm Grün begegnen*. Münsterschwarzach: Vier Türme, 243–249.
- 2015: „Maria und Marta", in: Rudolf Walter (Hg.), *Inspiration für das Leben. Im Dialog mit der Bibel*, Freiburg-Basel-Wien: Herder, 126–135.
- 2015: „The Outer and Inner Constitution of Human Dignity in Meister Eckhart", in: Ulrich Schmiedel, James Matarazzo Jr. (eds.), *Dynamics of Difference. Christianity and Alterity, a Festschrift for Werner G. Jeanrond*, London: Bloomsbury, 71–78.
- 2016: „Der barmherzige Samariter und die narrative Ethik Jesu (Lk 10,25-37). Ein Essay über die Grundidee der Nächstenliebe, ihr Missverständnisse und ihre politische Bedeutung", in: Paul Chummar Chittilappilly (Hg.), *Horizonte gegenwärtiger Ethik*, Freiburg i.Br.: Herder, 229–238.

- 2016: „Der Himmel in mir. Die Interiorisierung des Himmels bei Meister Eckhart. ‚Was oben war, ist innen'", in: Harald Lesch, Bernd Oberndorfer (Hg.), *Der Himmel als transkultureller ethischer Raum*, Göttingen: Vandenhoek, 105–126.
- –; Julie Casteigt, Jörg Rüpke 2016: „Der Träger der Erfurter Riesenthorahrolle. Eine religionsgeschichtliche Hypothese zu einem übersehenen Judaicum", in *Zeitschrift für Religions- und Geistesgeschichte* 68,2, 98–118.
- 2016: „Die individuelle Unmittelbarkeit der Mystik als Herausforderung der Religionen? – Religiöse und nachreligiöse Perspektiven der Unmittelbarkeit, ausgehend von Meister Eckhart", in: Büchner, Enders Mieth (Hg.) *Meister Eckhart – interreligiös*, Meister-Eckhart-Jahrbuch, Bd. 10, Stuttgart: Kohlhammer, 9–24.
- 2016: „Die Tugend der Gelassenheit", in: *Sei gelassen, Gedanken, Anregungen, Ruheplätze*, Stuttgart: Reclam, 28–31.
- 2016: „Dynamics of Meister Eckhart – Past and Present", in: Jutta Vinzent and Christopher Wojtulewiccz (eds.), Performing Bodies. Time and Space in Meister Eckhart and Taery Kim. Eckhart Texts and Studies, vol 6, Leuven: Peeters, 77–96.
- 2016: Einleitung „Meister Eckhart interreligiös", in: Büchner, Enders Mieth (Hg.) Meister Eckhart – interreligiös, IX–XXIII.
- 2016: „Meister Eckhart und Luther: ein Annäherungs- und Differenzierungsversuch", in: Mariano Delgado, Volker Leppin (Hg*.), Luther: Zankapfel zwischen den Konfessionen und „Vater im Glauben", Historische, systematische und ökumenische Zugänge*, Fribourg/Schweiz-Stuttgart: Kohlhammer, 52–74.
- 2016: „Perfektionierung und Meliorisierung (enhancement) – ein Versuch über Menschenbilder", in: hg.v. Paul Lissmann, *Neue Menschen, bilden, optimieren, perfektionieren*, Wien, 220–252.
- 2017: „Demut bei Meister Eckhart", in *Wort und Antwort* 58 (2017) Heft 3, 197–111.
- 2017: „Deutsche und Lateinische Werke Meister Eckharts. Ein kurzer Überblick", *Theologische Quartalschrift 197, Heft 1*, 96–100.
- 2017: „Experiential Ethics and Religious Experience with Reference to Meister Eckhart" in: Patrick Cooper – Satoshi Kikuchi (eds.), *Commitments to Medieval Mysticism within Contemporary Contexts*, Leuven-Paris-Bristol: Peeters, 195–222.
- 2017: „Geflügelte Motive und Leitbilder. Meister Eckhart liest Marguerite Porete", in: Mieth, Vannier, Vinzent, *Meister Eckhart Erfurt Paris Straßburg*, Meister Eckhart, Texts and Studies, vol. 5, Leuven: Peeters, 1–19.
- 2017: „Gewissen", in: Christine Büchner, Gerrit Spallek (Hg.), *Auf den Punkt gebracht, Grundbegriffe der Theologie*, Ostfildern: Grünewald, 77–90.
- 2017: „Innerlichkeit ohne Weltgestaltung? Der Weg von der ‚devotio moderna' zu den ‚Stillen im Lande'" (Pietismus), in: Marie-Anne Vannier (Hg.), *Mystique rhénane et Devotio Moderna*, Paris, 267–282.
- 2017: „Leben und Leben oder: Lebensführung und Lebensforschung. Folgerungen für eine ‚neue' Metaphysik im Sinne Hermann Deusers. Ein Essay", in: hg. v. Matthias Kleinert und Heiko Schulz, *Natur, Religion, Wissenschaft, Beiträge zur Religionsphilosophie Hermann Deusers*, Tübingen, Mohr Siebeck, 421–438.
- 2017: „Meister Eckhart, Predigt 67: Deus Caritas est", in *Lectura Eckhardi* IV, hg.v. Georg Steer und Loris Sturlese, Stuttgart: Kohlhammer, 95–122.
- 2017: „Über Mystik reden. Joseph Bernhart und Meister Eckhart", in: Rainer Bendel, Josef Nolte (Hg.), *Befreite Erinnerung, Teilband 2: Region-Religion-Identität: Tübinger Wege. Beiträge zu Theologie, Kirche und Gesellschaft* Bd. 26, Berlin: Lit, 35–50.
- 2017: „Zu den Diskursen über Individualisierung, bezogen auf das Spätmittelalter", *Theologische Quartalschrift 197, Heft 1*, 4–34.

- 2018: „Contemplativus post actionem", „contemplativus in actione" ou „contemplativus sine actione"? In: Marie-Anne Vannier (éd.), Les chemin spirituels dans la mystique thénane et la Devotio Moderna, Paris 2018, 53–78.
- 2018: „Perfektionierung und Meliorisierung („Enhancement") – ein Versuch über Menschenbilder. Religiöse und ethische Perspektiven". In: *Die Perfektionierung des Menschen*, hg. v. Thomas Bahne und Katharina Waldner (Vorlesungen des Interdisziplinären Forums Religion der Universität Erfurt, Bd. 13) Münster: Aschendorff, 19–42.
- 2018: „Migranten und Flüchtlinge. Solidarität als Anspruch an die Verteilung von Rechten und Pflichten". In: Marie Jo Thiel, Marc Feix (Hg.), *The Challenge of Fraternity – Die Herausforderung der Geschwisterlichkeit,* Berlin: Lit 2018, 113–125.
- 2018: „Meister Eckhart, Opus tripartitum". In: *Religionsphilosophie und Religionskritik, Ein Handbuch*, hg. v. Michael Kühnlein, Berlin: Suhrkamp, 126–137.
- 2018: „Christliche Sozialethik – Orientierung zu welcher Praxis?" In: Bernhard Emunds (Hg.), *Christliche Sozialethik – Orientierung zu welcher Praxis? Festschrift für Friedhelm Hengsbach*, Baden-Baden: Nomos 2018, 201–218.
- 2018: „1968 – ein theologisches Jahr an der Universität Tübingen. Hans Küng zum 90. Geburtstag". In: *Revolte in der Kirche? Das Jahr 1968 und seine Folgen.* Hg. im Auftrag des Theologischen Forschungskollegs der Universität Erfurt von Sebastian Holzbrecher, Benedikt Kranemann, Julia Knop und Jörg Seiler. Freiburg-Basel-Wien: Herder, 167–184.
- 2018: „‚Exodus' – Ein Exempel für ein mediales Missverständnis und ein religionskritischer Ertrag". In: *Ethik in Serie*, hg. v. Cordula Brand und Simon Meisch, Festschrift zu Ehren von Uta Müller (Materialien zur Ethik in den Wissenschaften, Bd. 13). Tübingen 2018, 61–76.
- 2018: „Für Viele und für alle. Gegen die Opfertheorie im Christentum". In: Hans-Gerd Janßen, Julia D.E. Prinz, Michael J. Rainer (Hgg.), *Theologie in gefährdeter Zeit, Stichworte von nahen und fernen Weggefährten für Johannes Baptist Metz zum 90. Geburtstag*, Berlin: Lit, 325–327.
- 2018: „Autonomie und Selbstbestimmung an den Polen des Lebens". In: Wolfgang Beer u.a. (Hgg.), *Weichenstellungen an den Polen des Lebens*. Frankfurt a.M.: Wochenschau-Verlag, 77–96.
- 2018: „Die individuelle Unmittelbarkeit der Mystik als Herausforderung der Religionen?", in: Erdal Toprakyaran, Hansjörg Schmid, Christian Ströbele (Hg.), *Dem Einen entgegen, Christliche und islamische Mystik in historischer Perspektive* (Transliminale Diskurse der Islamischen Theologie, Bd. 2), Berlin: Lit, 9–26.
- 2019: „Der Aufstieg des ‚gewerbes': Meister Eckhart, Martin Luther und Max Weber. Historisch-systematische Betrachtungen". In: Volker Leppin, Freimut Löser (Hg.) *Meister Eckhart und Martin Luther,* Jahrbuch der Meister Eckhart Gesellschaft, Bd. 13. Stuttgart: Kohlhammer 2019, 139–168.
- 2019: „Die Entstehung des Bildungsgedankens bei Meister Eckhart". *Theologische Quartalschrift 199* (2019) Heft 2, 75–96.
- 2019: „Dynamische Stabilisierung und resonante Weltbeziehung. Laudatio für den soziologischen Diagnostiker Hartmut Rosa". In: *Gefangen in der Gesellschaft*, FrommForum 23, Tübingen 2019, 133–143. Auch in: *Resonanz, Im interdisziplinären Gespräch mit Harmut Rosa*, hg. v. Jean Pierre Wils, Frankfurt a.M. 2019, 179–190.
- 2019: „‚Herz' bei Meister Eckhart". In: Jens Haustein, Regina D. Schiewer, Martin Schubert, Rudolf Kilian Weigand (Hgg.), *Traditionelles und Innovatives in der geistlichen Literatur des Mittelalters, Freimut Löser zum 65. Geburtstag,* Meister-Eckhart-Jahrbuch, Beiheft 5, hg. v. Regina Schiewer, Stuttgart: Kohlhammer, 1–24.
- 2019: „Narrative Ethik als Moralische Verunsicherung durch Literatur". In: Volker Sühs (Hg.), Die entscheidenden Fragen der Zukunft, Theologen und Theologinnen nehmen Stellung, Essays anlässlich 100 Jahren Matthias Grünewald Verlag, Ostfildern: Grünewald, 117–123.

- 2019: „Meister Eckhart: Kontemplation und Gottesgeburt. Die religiöse Erfahrung des Christentums und die christliche Erfahrung des Religiösen". In: Marie-Anne Vannier (Hg.), *Meister Eckhart und die Kirchenväter*, Paris: Beauchesne 18–44.
- 2019: „‚Gefährliche Religion(en)'. Die Ambivalenz religiöser Narrative und die weitere Entwicklung eines ‚Weltethos'". In: Daniel Bogner (Hg.), *Moraltheologie im Disput*, Fribourg: Echter.
- 2019: „Religiöse Individualisierung und Selbstbestimmung. Soziale Plurivalenzen und Widersprüche der Selbstbestimmung, damals und heute". In: Dietmar Mieth, Regina Schiewer (eds.), *Religiöse Selbstbestimmung, Anfänge im Spätmittelalter, Beiheft 7 zum Meister-Eckhart-Jahrbuch*, Stuttgart: Kohlhammer.
- 2019: „Marguerite Poretes Lebenswende als Modell religiöser Selbstbestimmung". In: Dietmar Mieth, Regina Schiewer (eds.), *Religiöse Selbstbestimmung, Anfänge im Spätmittelalter. Beiheft 7 zum Jahrbuch der Meister Eckhart Gesellschaft*, Stuttgart: Kohlhammer.
- 2019: „Selftranscendence in Meister Eckhart", in: Martin Fuchs *et al.* (eds.), *Religious Individualisation: Historical Dimensions and Comparative Perspectives*, Berlin: de Gruyter, 73–98.

Müller-Schauenburg, Britta

- 2013: Benedikt XIII., in K.-H. Braun et al. (eds.), *Das Konstanzer Konzil. Essays*, Theiss: Darmstadt, 121–125.
- 2013: Person, Sammlung, Kollektivität. Die Schutzmantelmadonna als Bild einer Versammlung mit spirituellem Gemeinschaftspunkt, in: G. Jähnert *et al.* (eds.), *Kollektivität nach der Subjektkritik*, Bielefeld: transcript, 197–219.
- 2014: Der Heilige Geist und das Ritual. Das Scheitern der Verhandlungen Sigismunds mit Pedro de Luna (Benedikt XIII.) 1415 in Perpignan, in: A. Büttner *et al.* (eds.), *Grenzen des Rituals. Wirkreichweiten – Geltungsbereiche – Forschungsperspektiven*, Köln: de Gruyter, 209–228.
- 2014: Erfolglos zu Recht schreiben. Die Pariser Handschriften des Traktats Quia nonulli Benedikts XIII. mit Britta Müller-Schauenburg, den Responsa, in: R. Berndt (ed.), *Eure Namen sind im Buch des Lebens geschrieben. Antike und mittelalterliche Quellen als Grundlage moderner prosopographischer Forschung*, (Erudiri Sapientia 11), Münster: Aschendorff, 381–412.
- 2017: Benedikts XIII. antihäretische Profilierung einer konservierten Einheitsfiktion – Die Handschrift BnF latin 1478 aus der Bibliothek des Papstes als Exempel, in: H. Müller (ed.), *Der Verlust der Eindeutigkeit. Zur Krise päpstlicher Autorität im Kampf um die Cathedra Petri (Schriften des Historischen Kollegs. Kolloquien 95)*, Berlin: de Gruyter, 147–162.
- 2018: Einleitung, in R. Berndt (ed.), Der Papst und das Buch im Spätmittelalter (1350–1500). Bildungsvoraussetzung, Handschriftenherstellung, Bibliotheksgebrauch (Erudiri Sapientia 13), Münster: Aschendorff, 13–21.
- 2019: „The lonely antipope – or why we have difficulties classifying Pedro de Luna [Benedict XIII] as a religious individual", in: Martin Fuchs *et al.* (eds.), *Religious Individualisation: Historical Dimensions and Comparative Perspectives*, Berlin: de Gruyter, 1351–1380.
- Forthcoming: Perpignan 1415. The negotiations and the role of Benedict XIII, in: A. Catafau et al. (eds.), Perpignan 1415. Ein europäisches Gipfeltreffen in der Konzilszeit/Perpignan 1415. Un sommet européen à l'époque des consiles.

Mulder-Bakker, Anneke B.

- 2019: Lived religion and eucharistic piety on the Meuse and the Rhine in the thirteenth and fourteenth centuries, in: Martin Fuchs *et al.* (eds.), *Religious Individualisation: Historical Dimensions and Comparative Perspectives*, Berlin: de Gruyter, 719–736.

Mulsow, Martin

- 2012. Prekäres Wissen: Eine andere Ideengeschichte der Frühen Neuzeit. Berlin: Suhrkamp.
- 2015. *Enlightenment underground: Radical Germany, 1680–1720*, trans. H. C. Erik Midelfort (Studies in early modern German history). Charlottesville: University of Virginia Press.
- ; Eskildsen, Kasper Risbjerg and Zedelmaier, Helmut (eds.). *Christoph August Heumann (1681–1764): gelehrte Praxis zwischen christlichem Humanismus und Aufklärung* (Gothaer Forschungen zur Frühen Neuzeit). Stuttgart: Steiner.

- 2012: „Joseph – Fracois Lafitau und die Entdeckung der Religions- und Kulturvergleiche". In: Maria Effinger, Cornelia Logemann and Ulrich Pfisterer (eds.), *Götterbilder und Götzendiener in der Frühen Neuzeit – Europas Blick auf fremde Religionen*. Heidelberg: Universitätsverlag. 37–47.
- 2014. „The radical enlightenment: problems and perspectives". In: *Concepts of (radical) enlightenment: Jonathan Israel in discussion*. Leipzig: Mitteldt. Verl. 81–94.
- 2014: „73. Eine Konversion zum Islam: Adam Neuser (ca. 1530–1576)". In: Aus erster Hand: 95 Porträts zur Reformationsgeschichte: aus den Sammlungen der Forschungsbibliothek Gotha: Katalog zur Ausstellung der Universitäts- und Forschungsbibliothek Erfurt/Gotha vom 6. April bis 25. Mai 2014. Erfurt: Universität Erfurt. 146–7.
- 2015: „Vorwort". In: Marten, Maria: Fogels Ordnungen: aus der Werkstatt des Hamburger Mediziners Martin Fogel (1634–1675). Frankfurt/M.: Klostermann. 11–2.
- 2015: „Vor Adam: Ideengeschichte jenseits der Eurozentrik". Zeitschrift für Ideengeschichte: Marbach, Weimar, Wolfenbüttel, Grunewald 9 (1), 47–66.
- 2015: „Impartiality, individualisation, and the historiography of religion: Tobias Pfanner on the rituals of the ancient church". In: *History and religion: narrating a religious past*. Berlin: de Gruyter. 257–68.
- 2016: „Ökonomie des Wissens, Wissen der Ökonomie und Wissensökonomie." In *„Eigennutz" und „gute Ordnung": Ökonomisierungen der Welt im 17. Jahrhundert*. Wiesbaden: Harrassowitz. 295–300.
- 2016: „Wissen am Hof: ‚Gesamternestinische' Gelehrte zwischen Weimar und Gotha um 1700." *Mens et Manus: Kunst und Wissenschaft an den Höfen der Ernestiner*. Göttingen: Wallstein. 35–54.
- 2016: „Die Gothaer Illuminaten als fortgeführte ‚gemeinnützige Privatgesellschaft'? Die Aufsatzpraxis der Gothaer Sozietät von 1778 und die Minervalkirche von 1783–1787". In: *Aufklärung: interdisziplinäres Jahrbuch zur Erforschung des 18. Jahrhunderts und seiner Wirkungsgeschichte 28*, 343–60.
- 2017: „Hausenblasen: Kopierpraktiken und die Herstellung numismatischen Wissens um 1700." In: *Objekte als Quellen der historischen Kulturwissenschaften: Stand und Perspektiven der Forschung*. Köln: Böhlau. 261–344.
- 2017: „Vincent Placcius: Freundschaftsethik, gemeinsame Forschung und moralphilosophische Lehre am Akademischen Gymnasium in Hamburg". In: *Das Akademische Gymnasium zu Hamburg (gegr. 1613) im Kontext frühneuzeitlicher Wissenschafts- und Bildungsgeschichte*. Berlin: de Gruyter. 87–101.
- 2017: „Der Verbesserer Heumanns Poecile im Kontext seiner Korrespondenz mit der Gelehrtenrepublik: Mit einem Inventar von Heumanns Briefwechsel". In: *Christoph August Heumann (1681–1764): gelehrte Praxis zwischen christlichem Humanismus und Aufklärung*. Stuttgart: Steiner. 39–70.
- 2017: „Global intellectual history and the dynamics of religion". In: Dynamics of religion: past and present: Proceedings of the XXI World Congress of the International Association for the History

of Religions, Erfurt, August 23–29, 2015, edited by Christoph Bochinger and Jörg Rüpke; in cooperation with Elisabeth Begemann. Berlin: de Gruyter. 251–72.
–; Roling, Bernd 2016: „Wissenstransfer und Wissensverflechtungen: Wie Gelehrte der Frühen Neuzeit sich dem Orient näherten". In: Engel, Christa (Hg.). *Kulturen im Dialog: Das HERA-Förderprogramm „Cultural Encounters"* Berlin: Bundesministerium für Bildung und Forschung, 32–3.
–; Linkenbach, Antje, 2019: „The Dividual Self: Introduction to Part 2", in: Martin Fuchs et al. (eds.), *Religious Individualisation: Historical Dimensions and Comparative Perspectives*, Berlin: de Gruyter, 323–344.
– 2019: „Dividualisation and relational authorship: from the Huguenot *République des lettres* to practices of clandestine writing", in: Martin Fuchs et al. (eds.), *Religious Individualisation: Historical Dimensions and Comparative Perspectives*, Berlin: de Gruyter, 475–496.

Murphy, Anne

– 2013. *The Materiality of the Past: History and Representation in Sikh Tradition.* New York: Oxford University Press, 2012; New Delhi: Oxford University Press, 2013.
– 2019: „Configuring community in colonial and pre-colonial imaginaries: Insights from the Khalsa Darbar records", in: Martin Fuchs and Vasudha Dalmia (eds.), *Religious Interactions in Modern India.* Delhi: Oxford University Press. doi:10.1093/oso/9780198081685.003.0006.
– 2019: „Sufis, Jogis, and the question of religious difference: Individualization in early modern Punjab", in: Martin Fuchs et al. (eds.), *Religious Individualisation: Historical Dimensions and Comparative Perspectives*, Berlin: de Gruyter, 289–314.

Nijhawan, Michael

– 2016. The Precarious Diasporas of Sikh and Ahmadiyya Generations: Violence, Memory, Agency. New York: Palgrave Macmillan.

– 2013: „Lullabies for Broken Children: Diasporic Citizenship and the Dissenting Voices of Young Sikhs in Canada", Co-authored with Kamal Arora, *Sikh Formations: Religion, Culture, Theory* 9(3), 299–322.
– 2014: „1984 and the Diasporic Politics of Aesthetics: Reconfigurations and New Constellations among Toronto Sikh Youth", *Diaspora: A Journal for Transnational Studies* 17(2), 196–219.
– 2019: „Constructing a Genuine Religious Character: The Impact of the Asylum Court on the Ahmadiyya Minority in Germany", in: Fuchs, M. et al. (eds.), *Religious Individualisation: Historical Dimensions and Comparative Perspectives.* Berlin: de Gruyter, 1139–1164.
– 2019: „Migrant Precarity and Religious Individualization", in: Fuchs, M. et al. (eds.), *Religious Individualisation: Historical Dimensions and Comparative Perspectives*, Berlin: de Gruyter, 737–758.

Otto, Bernd-Christian

–; Michael Stausberg (eds.) 2013. *Defining Magic. A Reader*, [Critical Categories in the Study of Religion], Sheffield: Equinox.
–; Susanne Rau and Jörg Rüpke (eds.) 2015. *History and Religion: Narrating a Religious Past*, [Religionsgeschichtliche Versuche und Vorarbeiten; 68], Berlin: de Gruyter.

–; Daniel Bellingradt 2017. *Magical Manuscripts in Early Modern Europe. The Clandestine Trade in Illegal Book Collections*, [New Directions in Book History], Basingstoke: Palgrave MacMillan.
–; et al. (eds.) 2019. Religious Individualisation: Historical Dimensions and Comparative Perspectives. Berlin: de Gruyter.

– 2013: „Discourse theory trumps discourse theory: Wouter Hanegraaff's Esotericism and the Academy", in *Religion* 43/2 (2013), 231–40.
–; Jörg Rüpke and Susanne Rau 2013: „Tagungsbericht: Historiography of Religion: New Approaches to origins of narrating a religious past", in: H-Soz-u-Kult, 30.01.2013, online available at: http://hsozkult.geschichte.hu-berlin.de/tagungsberichte/id=4609-2013.
– 2013: „Towards historicizing 'Magic' in Antiquity", in: *Numen* 60, 2/3 (2013), 308–47.
– 2013: „Zauberhaftes Ägypten – Ägyptischer Zauber? Überlegungen zur Verwendung des Magiebegriffs in der Ägyptologie", in: Florian Jeserich (Hg.), *Ägypten, Kindheit, Tod. Gedenkschrift für Edmund Hermsen*, Wien, 39–70.
– 2015: „A Catholic 'magician' historicizes 'magic': Éliphas Lévi's Histoire de la Magie", in: Otto, Bernd-Christian et al. (eds.), *History and Religion: Narrating a Religious Past*, Berlin: de Gruyter, 419–43.
–; Susanne Rau and Jörg Rüpke 2015: „History and Religion", in: Idd. (eds.), *History and Religion: Narrating a Religious Past*, Berlin: de Gruyter, 1–18.
– 2016: „Historicising 'Western learned magic': preliminary remarks", in: *Aries 16 (2016)*, 161–240.
– 2017: „Magic and Religious Individualization: On the construction and deconstruction of analytical categories in the Study of Religion", in *Historia Religionum* 9 (2017), 29–52.
– 2018: „Das Motiv der Perfektionierung im gelehrtenmagischen Diskurs des 20. Jahrhunderts", in: Thomas Bahne and Katharina Waldner (eds.), *Die Perfektionierung des Menschen? Religiöse und ethische Perspektiven*, [Vorlesungen des Interdisziplinären Forums Religion; 13], Münster: Aschendorff 2018. 81–105, 305–19.
– 2019: „A discourse historical approach towards medieval 'learned magic'", in: Sophie Page and Catherine Rider (eds.), *The Routledge History Handbook of Medieval Magic*, London: Routledge 2018. 37–47, 60–64.
– 2019: „'Magie im Islam' aus diskursgeschichtlicher Perspektive", in: Sebastian Günther and Dorothee Lauer (eds.), *Die Geheimnisse der höheren und der niederen Welt: Magie im Islam zwischen Glaube und Wissenschaft*, Leiden: Brill. 515–546.
– 2019: „If people believe in magic, isn't that just because they aren't educated?", in: Wouter Hanegraaff, Marco Pasi, Peter Forshaw (eds.), *Hermes Explains: Thirty-Five Questions about Western Esotericism. Celebrating the 20-year anniversary of the chair for History of Hermetic Philosophy and Related Currents at the University of Amsterdam*, Amsterdam: Amsterdam University Press 2019. 198–206.
–; Parson, Rahul Bjørn 2019: „Introduction: conventions and contentions", in Martin Fuchs *et al.* (eds.), *Religious Individualisation: Historical Dimensions and Comparative Perspectives*, Berlin: de Gruyter, 633–642.
– 2019: „The Illuminates of Thanateros and the Institutionalization of Religious Individualization", in: Martin Fuchs *et al.* (eds.), *Religious Individualisation: Historical Dimensions and Comparative Perspectives*, Berlin: de Gruyter, 757–794.

– 2013: (Rev.) „Gideon Bohak, Yuval Harari, Shaul Shaked (eds.), Continuity and Innovation in the Magical Tradition", [Jerusalem Studies in Religion and Culture; 15], Leiden: Brill 2011, 396 pages, in *ARIES: Journal for the Study of Western Esotericism* 13/2 (2013), 308–13.

- 2018: (Rev.) „Edward Bever, Randall Styers (eds.), Magic in the Modern World: Strategies of Repression and Legitimization", [The Magic in History Series], University Park: Pennsylvania University Press 2017, 207 pp., in *Jahrbuch für Kommunikationsgeschichte* 20 (2018).
- 2018: (Rev.) „Marco Frenschkowski, Magie im antiken Christentum. Eine Studie zur Alten Kirche und ihrem Umfeld", [Standorte in Antike und Christentum; 7], Stuttgart: Hiersemann 2016, 338 S., in *Zeitschrift für antikes Christentum* 22/1 (2018).

Parson, Rahul Bjørn

- 2019: Individualisation and democratisation of knowledge in Banārasīdās' *Samayasāra Nāṭaka*, in: Martin Fuchs *et al.* (eds.), *Religious Individualisation: Historical Dimensions and Comparative Perspectives*, Berlin: de Gruyter, 865–894.

–; Otto, Bernd-Christian 2019: Introduction: conventions and contentions, in: Martin Fuchs *et al.* (eds.), *Religious Individualisation: Historical Dimensions and Comparative Perspectives*, Berlin: de Gruyter, 633–642.

Patera, Ioanna

–; H. Bernier-Farella (eds.) 2014. L'objet rituel. Méthodes et concepts croisés = Special issue Revue d'histoire des religions 2014/4.

–; H. Bernier-Farella 2014: „L'objet rituel: concepts et méthodes croisés. Avant-propos", *Revue d'histoire des religions* 2014/4, 531–538.
- 2015: „Objects as substitutes in ancient Greek ritual", *Religion in the Roman Empire* 1.2, 181–200.
- 2019: „Individuals in the Eleusinian Mysteries: choices and actions", in: Martin Fuchs *et al.* (eds.), *Religious Individualisation: Historical Dimensions and Comparative Perspectives*, Berlin: de Gruyter, 669–694.

Quero-Sánchez, Andrés

- 2019: ‚Go from your country and your kindred and your father's house!' (Gen. 12:1): Schelling's Boehmian redefinition of idealism, in: Martin Fuchs *et al.* (eds.), *Religious Individualisation: Historical Dimensions and Comparative Perspectives*, Berlin: de Gruyter, 223–243.

Raja, Rubina

- 2019: Dining with the gods and the others: the banqueting tickets from Palmyra as expressions of religious individualisation, in: Martin Fuchs *et al.* (eds.), *Religious Individualisation: Historical Dimensions and Comparative Perspectives*, Berlin: de Gruyter, 243–256.

Ramelli, Ilaria

- 2013. The Christian Doctrine of Apokatastasis: A Critical Assessment from the New Testament to Eriugena, Leiden: Brill, Vigiliae Christianae Supplements 120.

– (ed.). 2015. Tempo ed eternità in età antica e patristica: filosofia greca, ebraismo e cristianesimo, Assisi: Cittadella.
– (ed.) 2015. Early Christian and Jewish Narrative: The Role of Religion in Shaping Narrative Forms, edited by Ilaria Ramelli and Judith Perkins, Tübingen: Mohr Siebeck.
– (ed.) 2016. Social Justice and the Legitimacy of Slavery: The Role of Philosophical Asceticism from Ancient Judaism to Late Antiquity, Oxford: Oxford University Press.
–; Svetla S. Griffin (eds.) 2019. Lovers of Souls, Lovers of Bodies: Philosophical and Religious Perspectives in Late Antiquity. Cambridge, Mass.: Harvard University Press.

– 2014: „The Stoic Doctrine of Oikeiosis and its Transformation in Christian Platonism", «Apeiron» 47 (2014), 116–140.
– 2015: „Ancient Jewish and Christian Exegeses of the ‚Curse of Ham': Divergent Strategies against the Background of Ancient Views on Slavery", in: David Nelson and Rivka Ulmer (eds.), „It's better to hear the rebuke of the wise than the song of fools" (Qoh 7:5). Select Proceedings of the Midrash Section, Society of Biblical Literature, Volume 6, with Contributions by Ilaria Ramelli, Steven Sacks, Jonathan Kaplan, Piscataway: Gorgias, Series: Judaism in Context 18, 1–51.
– 2015: „Ethos and Logos: A Second-Century Apologetical Debate between „Pagan" and Christian Philosophers", Vigiliae Christianae 69.2 (2015), 123–156.
– 2015: „Reply to Professor Michael McClymond", Theological Studies 76.4 (2015), 827–835.
– 2017: „Origen and the Platonic Tradition", Invited article, in: Plato and Christ: Platonism in Early Christian Theology, special topics issue of Religions, guest editor J. Warren Smith, Religions 2017, 8(2), 21, 1–20.
– 2017: „Divine Power in Origen of Alexandria: Sources and Aftermath", in: Anna Marmodoro and Irini Fotini Viltanioti (eds.), Divine Powers in Late Antiquity, Oxford: OUP, 177–198.
– 2017: „Christian Apokatastasis and Zoroastrian Frashegird: The Birth of Eschatological Universalism", Religion and Theology 24, 3–4 (2017), 350–406.
– 2018: „Origen to Evagrius", in: Harold Tarrant, Dirk Baltzly, Danielle A. Layne, and François Renaud (eds.), Brill's Companion to the Reception of Plato in Antiquity, Leiden: Brill, 271–291.
– 2019: „Institutionalisation of Religious Individualisation: Asceticism in Antiquity and Late Antiquity and the Rejection of Slavery and Social Injustice", in: Martin Fuchs et al. (eds.), Religious Individualisation: Historical Dimensions and Comparative Perspectives, Berlin: de Gruyter, 695–718.

Reinhardt, Nicole

– 2016. Voices of Conscience. Royal confessors and political counsel in seventeenth century Spain and France, Oxford: Oxford University Press.

– 2013: „Betrachtungen eines Unpolitischen? Überlegungen zur Geschichte der politischen Ideen im Kirchenstaat", in: B. Emich and C. Wieland (ed.), Kulturgeschichte des Papsttums (Beiheft der Zeitschrift für historische Forschung 2013), 99–125.
– 2013: „Das königliche Gewissen im Prisma jansenistischer Kritik", in: D. Burkard/T. Thanner (eds.), Der Jansenismus– eine 'katholische Häresie'? Das Ringen um Gnade, Rechtfertigung und die Autorität Augustins in der Neuzeit; Münster: Aschendorff, 349–73.
– 2014: „Introduction: War, Conscience, and Counsel in Early Modern Catholic Europe", Journal of Early Modern History 18 (2014), 435–46.
– 2014: „Just War, Royal Conscience and the Crisis of Theological Counsel in the Early Seventeenth Century", Journal of Early Modern History 18 (2014), 495–521.

- 2015: „How individual was conscience in the early modern period? Observation on the development of Catholic moral theology", *Religion* 45, no. 3 (2015), 409–28.
- 2017: „Hernando de Mendoça, General Acquaviva, and the Controversy over Confession, Counsel, and Obedience", *Journal of Jesuit Studies* 4 (2017), 209–29.

Renzi, Beatrice

- 2015: „Anti-caste radicalism, Dalit movements and the many critiques of secular-nationalism in India", in: M. Burchardt, M. Wohlrab-Sahr, M. Middell (eds.), *Multiple Secularities Beyond the West: Religion and Modernity in the Global Age*, Berlin: de Gruyter, 63–94.

Rüpke, Jörg

- 2013. De Júpiter a Cristo: Cambios religiosos en el Imperio Romano, Santa Maria: eduvim.
- 2013. *Tra Giove e Christo: Trasformazioni religiose nell'impero romano*, Trad. Roberto Alciati. Brescia: Morcelliana.
- 2014. From Jupiter to Christ: On the History of Religion in the Roman Imperial Period. Oxford: Oxford University Press.
- 2014. Il crocevia del mito: Religione e narrazione nel mondo antico, Trad. Giovanni Cerro, Bologna: EDB.
- 2014. *Religion: Antiquity and Modern Legacy*, London/New York: Tauris/Oxford University Press.
- 2014. Römische Religion in republikanischer Zeit: Rationalisierung und ritueller Wandel, Darmstadt: Wissenschaftliche Buchgesellschaft, 2014.
- 2014. *Superstitio: Devianza religiosa nell'Impero romano*, Trad. Elisa Groff. Roma: Carocci.
- 2015. *Superstition ou individualité ? Déviance religieuse dans l'Empire romain*. Collection Latomus 352. Traduction par Ludivine Beaurin. Bruxelles/Leuven: Latomus/Peeters.
- 2016. On Roman Religion: Lived Religion and the Individual in Ancient Rome, Townsend Lectures. Ithaca, NY: Cornell University Press.
- 2016. *Pantheon: Geschichte der antiken Religionen*, Historische Bibliothek der Gerda-Henkel-Stiftung, München: Beck.
- 2016. Religious Deviance in the Roman World: Superstition or Individuality, Cambridge: Cambridge University Press.
- 2016. *Superstición o individualidad. Desviaciones religiosas en el imperio romano.* Trad. María Teresa, Josefina González, Micaela van Muylem. Madrid: UNED.
- 2018. *Pantheon*, trad. di Roberto Alciati, Maria dell'Isola, Biblioteca Einaudi, Torino: Einaudi.
- 2018. *Pantheon: A New History of Roman Religion*, trsl. by David M.B. Richardson, Princeton: Princeton University Press.
- 2018. Religiöse Transformationen im römischen Reich: Urbanisierung, Reichsbildung und Selbst-Bildung als Bausteine religiösen Wandels (Hans-Lietzmann-Vorlesung 16), Berlin: de Gruyter, 2018.

–; Wolfgang Spickermann (eds.) 2012. *Reflections on Religious Individuality: Greco-Roman and Judaeo-Christian Texts and Practices* (Religionsgeschichtliche Versuche und Vorarbeiten 62), Berlin/New York: de Gruyter.
–; Nicola Cusamano, Valentino Gasparini, Attilio Mastrocinque (eds.) 2013. *Memory and Religious Experience in the Greco-Roman World* (Potsdamer Altertumswissenschaftliche Beiträge 45). Stuttgart: Steiner.

–; Bärbel Kracke, René Roux (eds.) 2013. *Die Religion des Individuums* (Vorlesungen des Interdisziplinären Forums Religion 9). Münster: Aschendorff
–; Martin Jehne, Bernhard Linke (eds.) 2013. Religiöse Vielfalt und soziale Integration: Die Bedeutung der Religion für die kulturelle Identität und politische Stabilität im republikanischen Italien. Studien zur Alten Geschichte 17. Heidelberg: Verlag Antike.
–; Greg Woolf (eds.) 2013. Religious Dimensions of the Self in the Second Century CE, Tübingen: Mohr Siebeck, 2013.
– (ed.) 2013. The Individual in the Religions of the Ancient Mediterranean, Oxford: Oxford University Press.
–; Raja, Rubina (eds.) 2015. A Companion to the Archaeology of Religion in the Ancient World. Boston: Wiley-Blackwell.
–; Eric Rebillard (eds.) 2015. *Group Identity and Religious Individuality in Late Antiquity*, CUA Studies in Early Christianity, Washington: Catholic University of America Press
–; Bernd-Christian Otto, Susanne Rau (eds.) 2015. *History and Religion: Narrating a Religious Past.* (Religionsgeschichtliche Versuche und Vorarbeiten 68). Berlin: de Gruyter.
–; Rubina Raja (eds.) 2015. *Individual Appropriation in Lived Ancient Religion* = Religion in the Roman Empire 1.1 (2015).
–; Christopher Degelmann (eds.) 2015. Narratives as a lens into lived ancient religion, individual agency and collective identity = Religion in the Roman Empire 1.3 (2015).
–; Clifford Ando (eds.) 2015. Public and Private in Ancient Mediterranean Law and Religion: A Historical and Comparative Conference. RGVV 65. Berlin: de Gruyter.
–; Martin Fuchs (eds.) 2015. Religious Individualization in Historical Perspective = Religion 45,1 (2015).
–; Christoph Bochinger (eds.) 2016. *Dynamics of religion: Past and Present*, Religionsgeschichtliche Versuche und Vorarbeiten 67, Berlin: de Gruyter.
– (ed.) 2015. The gods of the others = Archiv für Religionsgeschichte 15 (2014), 143–222.
–; Petridou, Georgia, Richard Gordon (eds.) 2017. *Beyond Priesthood: Religious Entrepreneurs and Innovators in the Roman Empire*, Religionsgeschichtliche Versuche und Vorarbeiten 65, Berlin: de Gruyter.
– *(ed.) 2018. Construing religion(s) by historiography*, = Archiv für Religionsgeschichte 20 (2018), 1–178.
–; Marlis Arnhold, Harry O. Maier (eds.) 2018. *Seeing the God: Image, Space, Performance and Vision in the Religion of the Roman Empire*, Culture, Religion, and Politics in the Greco-Roman World 2, Tübingen: Mohr Siebeck.
– et al. (eds.) 2019. Religious Individualisation: Historical Dimensions and Comparative Perspectives. Berlin: de Gruyter.

– 2012: „Religion in der Antike", in: Wolfgang Hameter, Sven Tost (Hgg.), *Alte Geschichte: Der Vordere Orient und der mediterrane Raum vom 4. Jahrtausend v. Chr. bis zum 7. Jahrhundert n. Chr.*, vgs Studientexte 3, Wien: StudienVerlag, 283–300.
– 2013: „Archaic Roman Religion through the Republic", in: Michele R. Salzman, Marvin A. Sweeney (eds.), *Cambridge History of Religions in the Ancient World 1: From the bronze Age to the Hellenstic Age*, Cambridge: University Press, 336–363.
– 2013: „Fighting for differences: Forms and limits of religious individuality in the ‚Shepherd of Hermas'", in: id. (ed.), *Religious individuation in the Ancient Mediterranean*, Oxford: Oxford University Press, 315–341.
– 2013: „Heiliger und öffentlicher Raum: Römische Perspektiven auf private Religion", in: Babett Edelmann-Singer, Heinrich Konen (Hgg.), *Salutationes: Beiträge zur Alten Geschichte und ihrer Diskussion. Festschrift Peter Herz zum 65. Geburtstag*, Berlin: Frank & Timme, 159–168.

- 2013: „Individuals and Networks", in: Corinne Bonnet, Laurent Bricault (eds.), *Panthée: Religious Transformations in the Graeco-Roman Empire*, (Religions in the Graeco-Roman World 177), Leiden: Brill, 261–277.
- 2013: „Individuelle Religion", in: Alfred Schäfer, Marion Witteyer (Hgg.), *Rituelle Deponierungen in Heiligtümern der hellenistisch-römischen Welt: Internationale Tagung Mainz 28.–30. April 2008*, Mainz: Generaldirektion Kulturelles Erbe, 25–34.
- ; Valentino Gasparini, Attilio Mastrocinque, Ennio Sanzi 2013: „Introduction", in: idd. (eds.), *Religious Memory and Experiences*, PawB 45, Stuttgart: Steiner, 2013. 7–10.
- 2013: „Introduction: Individualisation and individuation as concepts for historical research", in: Jörg Rüpke (ed.), *Religious individuation in the Ancient Mediterranean*, Oxford: Oxford University Press, 3–28.
- 2013: „On Religious Experiences That Should not Happen in Sanctuaries", in: Valentino Gasparini, Attilio Mastrocinque, Jörg Rüpke, Ennio Sanzi (eds.), *Religious Memory and Experiences*, PawB 45, Stuttgart: Steiner, 137–144.
- 2013: „Polytheismus und Monotheismus als Perspektiven auf die antike Religionsgeschichte", in: Christoph Schöbel (Hg.), *Gott – Götter – Götzen: XIV. Europäischer Kongress für Theologie (11.–15. September 2011 in Zürich)*, Leipzig: Evangelische Verlagsanstalt, 56–68.
- 2013: „Regulating and Conceptualizing Religious Plurality: Italian Experiences and Roman Solutions", in: Martin Jehne, Bernhard Linke, Jörg Rüpke (eds.), *Religiöse Vielfalt und soziale Integration*, 275–295.
- ; Attilio Mastrocinque 2013: „Religious experience in the Roman World", in: Valentino Gasparini, Attilio Mastrocinque, Jörg Rüpke, Ennio Sanzi (eds.), *Religious Memory and Experiences*, PawB 45, Stuttgart: Steiner, 135–136.
- 2013: „The others' god(s).", *Archiv für Religionsgeschichte 15* (2013), 245–248.
- 2013: „Two cities and one self: Transformations of Jerusalem and reflexive individuality in the Shepherd of Hermas", in: id., Greg Woolf (eds.), *Religious Dimensions of the Self in the Second Century CE*, Tübingen: Mohr Siebeck, 49–65.
- 2013: „Überlegungen zur öffentlichen Festkultur aus ritualtheoretischer Perspektive", in: Horst Groschopp (Hg.), *Humanismus – Laizismus – Geschichtskultur* (Schriftenreihe der Humanistischen Akademie Berlin 6), Aschaffenburg: Alibri Verlag, 123–138.
- 2013: „Was ist ein Heiligtum? Pluralität als Gegenstand der Religionswissenschaft", in: Oliver Freiberger (Hg.), *Alternative Voices: A Plurality Approach for Religious Studies. Essays in Honor of Ulrich Berner* (Critical Studies in Religion/Religionswissenschaft 4). Göttingen: Vandenhoeck & Ruprecht, 211–225.
- 2014: „Ethnicity in Roman Religion", in: Jeremy McInerney (ed.), *A Companion to Ethnicity in the Ancient Mediterranean*, Boston: Wiley, 470–482.
- 2014: „Historians of religions and the space of law", in: Salvo Randazzo (ed.), *Religione e diritto Romano: la cogenza del rito*, Tricase (LE): Libellula, 43–49.
- 2014: „Historicizing Religion: Varro's Antiquitates and History of Religion in the Late Roman Republic", *History of Religions* 53.3 (2014), 246–268.
- 2014: „Im Rhythmus von Sonne und Mond: Die astronomischen und kulturellen Grundlagen der Zeitrechnung", *Welt und Umwelt der Bibel* 19,4 (2014), 40–45.
- 2014: „Is history important for a historical argument in religious studies [Rev.article A. Norenzayah, Big Gods ... 2014] ", *Religion* 44,4 (2014), 645–648.
- 2014: „New Perspectives on Ancient Divination", in: Veit Rosenberger (ed.), *Divination in the Ancient World* (Potsdamer altertumswissenschaftliche Beiträge 46), Stuttgart: Steiner, 9–19.
- 2014: „Religiöses Handeln: Kommunikation mit göttlichen Mächten", in: *Imperium der Götter: Isis – Mithras – Christus. Religionen im römischen Reich*, hg. Badisches Landesmuseum, Stuttgart: Theiss, 32–39.

- 2014: „Religiöse Individualität: Historische Befunde", *Jahrbuch der Meister-Eckehart-Gesellschaft* 8 (2014), 1–9.
- 2015: „3.3. Religion: 3.3.1 Zentraler und westlicher Mittelmeerraum", in: Anne-Maria Wittke (Hg.), *Frühgeschichte der Mittelmeerkulturen: Historisch-archäologisches Handbuch* (Der Neue Pauly Supplemente 10), Stuttgart: Metzler, 889–903.
- ; Raja, Rubina 2015: „Archaeology of Religion, Material Religion, and the Ancient World", in: Rubina Raja, Jörg Rüpke (eds.), *A Companion to the Archaeology of Religion in the Ancient World*, Malden: Wiley, 1–25.
- ; Rubina Raja 2015: „Appropriating Religion: Methodological Issues in Testing the 'Lived Ancient Religion' Approach", *Religion in the Roman Empire* 1.1 (2015), 11–19
- 2015: „Construing 'religion' by doing historiography: The historicisation of religion in the roman Republic", in: Bernd-Christian Otto, Susanne Rau, Jörg Rüpke (eds.), *History and Religion: Narrating a Religious Past*, (Religionsgeschichtliche Versuche und Vorarbeiten 68), Berlin: de Gruyter, 45–62.
- 2015: „Das Imperium Romanum als religionsgeschichtlicher Raum", in Richard Faber, Achim Lichtenberger (Hg.), *Ein pluriverses Universum: Zivilisationen und Religionen im antiken Mittelmeerraum* (Mittelmeerstudien 7), München: Fink, 333–351.
- ; Christoph Bochinger 2015: „Dynamics of religion – past and present: Looking forward to the XXI World Congress of the IAHR", in: Tim Jensen, Armin W. Geertz (eds.), *Numen, The Academic Study of Religion and the IAHR: Past, Present, and Prospects*, Leiden: Brill, 283–300.
- ; et al. 2015: „Editorial", *Religion in the Roman Empire* 1.1 (2015), 1–7.
- 2015: „Geteilte und umstrittene Geschichte: Der Chronograph von 354 und die Katakombe an der Via Latina", in: Hartmut Leppin (Hg.), *Antike Mythologie in christlichen Kontexten der Spätantike*, Berlin: de Gruyter, 2015. 221–238.
- ; Bernd-Christian Otto, Susanne Rau 2015: „History and Religion", in: Bernd-Christian Otto, Susanne Rau, Jörg Rüpke (eds.), *History and Religion: Narrating a Religious Past*, (Religionsgeschichtliche Versuche und Vorarbeiten 68), Berlin: de Gruyter, 1–18.
- 2015: „Individual Choices and Individuality in the Archaeology of Ancient Religion.", in: Rubina Raja, Jörg Rüpke (eds.), *A Companion to the Archaeology of Religion in the Ancient World*, Malden: Wiley, 437–450.
- ; Clifford Ando 2015: „Introduction", in: idd. (eds.), Public and Private in Ancient Mediterranean Law and Religion: An Historical and Comparative Conference. RGVV 65. Berlin: de Gruyter, 2015. 1–9.
- ; Eric Rebillard 2015: „Introduction: Groups, Individuals, and Religious Identity", in: Eric Rebillard, Jörg Rüpke (eds.), *Group Identity and Religious Individuality in Late Antiquity*, Catholic University of America Studies in Early Christianity, Washington: Catholic University of America Press, 2015. 3–12.
- 2015: with the assistance of Christopher Degelmann, „Narratives as a lens into lived ancient religion, individual agency and collective identity", *Religion in the Roman Empire* 1.3 (2015), 289–296.
- 2015: „Öffentliche Festkultur und Ritual", in: Doron Kiesel, Ronald Lutz (Hgg.), *Religion und Politik: Analysen, Kontroversen, Fragen*, Frankfurt/Main: Campus, 271–286.
- ; Bernd-Christian Otto, Susanne Rau 2015: „Origins and Developments: Introduction", in: Bernd-Christian Otto, Susanne Rau, Jörg Rüpke (eds.), *History and Religion: Narrating a Religious Past*, (Religions-geschichtliche Versuche und Vorarbeiten 68), Berlin: de Gruyter, 21–25.
- ; Fuchs, Martin 2015: „Religion: Versuch einer Begriffsbestimmung", in: Christoph Bultmann, Antje Linkenbach (eds.), *Religionen übersetzen: Klischees und Vorurteile im Religionsdiskurs* (Vorlesungen des Interdisziplinären Forums Religion der Universität Erfurt), Münster: Aschendorff, 17–22.

- 2015: „Religione e guerra: Sulla relazione tra i sistemi politici e religiosi di una società", in: Carlo Altini (ed.), *Guerra e pace: Storia e teoria di un'esperienza filosofica e politica*, Brescia: Il mulino, 53–81.
- 2015: „Religious agency, identity, and communication: reflections on history and theory of religion", *Religion* 45.3 (2015), 344–366.
- –; Martin Fuchs 2015: „Religious individualization in historical perspective", *Religion* 45.3 (2015), 323–329.
- 2015: „Roles and Individuality in the Chronograph of 354", in: Eric Rebillard, Jörg Rüpke (eds.), *Group Identity and Religious Individuality in Late Antiquity*, Catholic University of America Studies in Early Christianity, Washington: Catholic University of America Press, 247–269.
- 2015: „Roma imparatorlugu'nda dinî çogulculuk ve avrupa din tarihine etkileri" [Religiöse Pluralität im Römischen Reich und ihre Folgen für die europäische Religionsgeschichte], *Sabah Ülkesi* 44 (2015), 18–21.
- 2015: „Rituelle Uniformität und religiöse Distinktion: Ein ritualtheoretischer Blick auf Altarweihungen", in: Alexandra Busch, Alfred Schäfer (Hgg.), *Römische Weihealtäre im Kontext*, Friedberg: Likias, 2014 [2015], 19–25.
- 2015: „The 'Connected Reader' as a Window into Lived Ancient Religion: A Case Study of Ovid's Libri fastorum", *Religion in the Roman Empire* 1.1 (2015), 95–113.
- 2015: „The role of priests in constructing the divine in ancient Rom", in: Nicole Belayche, Vinciane Pirenne-Delforge (eds.), *Fabriquer du divin: Constructions et ajustements de la représentation des dieux dans l'Antiquité,* Collection Religions: Comparatisme – Histoire – Anthropologie 5, Liège: Presses Universitaires de Liège, 79–92.
- –; Bernd-Christian Otto, Susanne Rau 2015: „Transforming narratives: Introduction", in: Bernd-Christian Otto, Susanne Rau, Jörg Rüpke (eds.), *History and Religion: Narrating a Religious Past*, (Religionsgeschichtliche Versuche und Vorarbeiten 68), Berlin: de Gruyter, 327–331. 2016: „Ancient Lived Religion and the History of Religion in the Roman Empire", *Studia patristica* 74 (2016), 1–20.
- –; Bernd-Christian Otto, Susanne Rau 2015: „Writing histories: Introduction", in: Bernd-Christian Otto, Susanne Rau, Jörg Rüpke (eds.), *History and Religion: Narrating a Religious Past*, (Religionsgeschichtliche Versuche und Vorarbeiten 68), Berlin: de Gruyter, 205–8.
- 2016: „Creating Groups and Individuals in Textual Practices", *Religion in the Roman Empire* 2.1 (2016), 3–9. doi: 10.1628/219944616X14537295637718.
- –; Casteigt, Julie, Mieth, Dietmar 2016: „Der Träger der Erfurter Riesenthorarolle: Eine religionsgeschichtliche Hypothese zu einem übersehenen Judaicum.", *Zeitschrift für Religions- und Geistesgeschichte* 68,2 (2016), 97–118.
- 2016: „Discourses and narratives, experiences and identities", *Religion in the Roman Empire* 2.2 (2016), 149–151.
- 2016: „Divi Augusti oder: Wozu braucht man die neuen Götter?", *Latein und Griechisch in Berlin und Brandenburg* 60.3 (2016), 46–51.
- 2016: „Erinnerung", in: Daniel Weidner (Hg.), *Handbuch Literatur und Religion*, Stuttgart: Metzler, 28–33.
- 2016: „Historisierung von Religion", in: Giovanni Casadio, Attilio Mastrocinque, Clauida Santi (eds.), *Apex: Studi storico-religiosi in onore di Enrico Montanari*, Roma: Quasar, 143–150. ISBN 978-88-7140-742-5
- 2016: „History and Theory", *Religion* 46.3 (2016), 439–442.
- 2016: „Individual appropriation of sacred space", in: Yves Lafonds, Vincent Michel (ed.), *Espaces sacrés dans la Méditerranée antique, de l'âge du Bronze à l'Antiquité tardive,* Rennes: Presses universitaires de Rennes, 69–80.

– 2016: „Individualization and privatization"; in: Steven Engler, Michael Stausberg (eds.), *The Oxford Handbook of the Study of Religion*, New York: Oxford University Press, 702–717.

–; Christoph Bochinger 2016: „Introduction", in: id. (eds.), *Dynamics of Religion*, RGVV 67, Berlin: de Gruyter, 1–8. doi: 10.1515/9783110450934-001.

– 2016: „Knowledge of religion in Valerius Maximus' *exempla:* Roman historiography and Tiberian memory culture", in: Karl Galinsky (ed.), *Roman Memory*, Oxford: Oxford University Press, 89–111.

–; Sylvie Estienne, Valentino Gasparini, Anne-Françoise Jaccottet 2016: „La religion romaine: une fabrique de la norme?", in: Tanja Itgenshorst (ed.), *La norme sous la république et l'haut empire romains*, Bordeaux: Ausonius, 201–216.

– 2016: „Starting sacrifice in the Beyond: Flavian innovations in the concept of priesthood and their repercussions in the treatise 'To the Hebrews'", in: Gabriella Gelardini, Harold W. Attridge (eds.), *Hebrews in Context*, Ancient Judaism and Early Christianity 91, Leiden: Brill, 109–132.

– 2016: „Textgemeinschaften und die Erfindung von Toleranz in der römischen Kaiserzeit (2./3. Jh. n.Chr.)", in: Martin Wallraff (Hg.), *Religiöse Toleranz. 1700 Jahre nach dem Edikt von Mailand* (Colloquium Rauricum 14), Berlin: de Gruyter, 141–157.

– 2016: „The Role of Texts in Processes of Religious Grouping during the Principate", *Religion in the Roman Empire* 2.2 (2016), 170–195.

– 2016: „Warfare and ritual, Roman", *Encyclopedia of Ancient History*, Malden: Wiley, online.

– 2016: „Warum es keine interreligiöse Beziehungen in der Antike gab", in: Gabel, Michael, Malik, Jamal & Okolowicz, Justyna (Hgg.), *Religionen in Bewegung: Interreligiöse Beziehungen im Wandel der Zeit*, VIFR 12. Münster: Aschendorff, 253–262.

–; Marlis Arnhold, Jörg Rüpke 2017: „Appropriating and Shaping Religious Practices in the Roman Republic", in: Matthias Haake, Ann-Cathrin Harders (Hgg.), *Polititsche Kultur und soziale Struktur der Römischen Republik: Bilanzen und Perspektiven*, Stuttgart: Steiner, 413–427.

– 2017: „Cult and identity", *Politica antica* 7 (2017), 121–137.

– 2017: „Doubling religion in the Augustan Age: Shaping time for an empire", in: Jonathan Ben-Dov, Lutz Döring (eds.), *The Construction of Time in Antiquity: Ritual, Art and Identity*, Cambridge: Cambridge University Press, 2017. 50–68. 49.300 LZ.

– 2017: „Essen in religiösen Zusammenhängen im antiken Mittelmeerraum: Sakrale Mähler zwischen Euphrat und Tiber", *Welt und Umwelt der Bibel*. 2017, 1. 32–39.

– 2017: „Etruskisches Denken in Zeitaltern", in: Badisches Landesmuseum Karlsruhe (Hg.), *Die Etrusker: Weltkultur im antiken Italien*, Darmstadt: Theiss/Wissenschaftliche Buchgesellschaft, 337.

– 2017: „Georg Wissowa als Bearbeiter des 'Sacralwesens'", in: Kai Brodersen (Hg.), Joachim Marquardt, Georg Wissowa, *Römische Staatsverwaltung 3*, ND der 2. Aufl. 1885, Darmstadt: Wissenschaftliche Buchgesellschaft.

–; Paul Lichtermann, Rubina Raja, Anna-Katharina Rieger 2017: „Grouping together in lived ancient religion: individual interacting and the formation of groups", *RRE* 3.1 (2017), 3–10.

– 2017: „Der Hirte des Hermas: Visionsliteratur als Anleitung zu religiöser Praxis in Textproduktion und -rezeption", in: Juan José Ferrer Maestro et al. (eds.), *Entro los mundos: Homenaje a Pedro Barceló/Zwischen den Welten: Festschrift für Pedro Barceló*, Besançon: Presses universitaires de Franche-Comté, 247–260.

–; Richard Gordon, Georgia Petridou 2017: „Introduction", in: Richard Gordon, Georgia Petridou, Jörg Rüpke (eds.), *Beyond Priesthood: Religious Entrepreneurs and Innovators in the Roman Empire*, RGVV 66, Berlin: de Gruyter, 5–11.

– 2017: „Mut zur Religion", *Interjekte* 10 (2017), 8–15.

–; Federico Santangelo 2017: „Public priests and religious innovation in imperial Rome", in Richard Gordon, Georgia Petridou, Jörg Rüpke (eds.), *Beyond Priesthood: Religious Entrepreneurs and Innovators in the Roman Empire*. RGVV 66, Berlin: de Gruyter, 15–47.
– 2017: „'Religion' as conceptualised in a Roman perspective", *Social Imaginaries* 3.2 (2017), 37–56.
– 2017: „Römische Priestermähler", in: David Hellholm et al. (eds.), *Sacred Meal, Communal Meal, Table Fellowship, and the Eucharist*, Wissenschaftliche Untersuchungen zum Neuen Testament. Tübingen: Mohr Siebeck, 1527–37.
– 2017: „Sukzessionen in römischen Priesterschaften", in: Almut-Barbara Renger, Markus Witte (Hgg.), *Sukzession in Religionen: Autorisierung, Legitimierung, Wissenstransfer*, Berlin: de Gruyter, 375–391.
– 2018: „Caesar: Priesthoods, Gods, and Stars", in: Luca Grillo, Christopher Krebs (eds.), *Cambridge Companion to the Writings of Julius Caesar*, Cambridge: University Press, 58–67. 2018: „Creating Religion(s) by Historiography", *ARG* 20 (2018), 3–6.
– 2018: „Gifts, votives, and sacred things: Strategies, not entities", *RRE* 4.2 (2018). 207–236.
–; Marlis Arnhold, Harry O. Maier 2018: „Introduction", in: idd. (eds.), *Seeing the God: Image, Space, Performance and Vision in the Religion of the Roman Empire*, Culture, Religion, and Politics in the Greco-Roman World 2, Tübingen: Mohr Siebeck, vii–xix.
– 2018: „Not gods alone: On the visibility of religion and religious specialists in ancient Rome", in: Marlis Arnhold, Harry O. Maier, Jörg Rüpke (eds.), *Seeing the God: Image, Space, Performance and Vision in the Religion of the Roman Empire*, Culture, Religion, and Politics in the Greco-Roman World 2, Tübingen: Mohr Siebeck, 81–94.
– 2018: „Reflecting on Dealing with Religious Change", *RRE* 4.2 (2018), 132–154.
– 2018: Janico Albrecht, Christoph Degelmann, Valentino Gasparini, Richard Gordon, Georgia Petridou, Rubina Raja, Jörg Rüpke, Benjamin Sippel, Emiliano Urciuoli, Lara Weiss, „Religion in the Making: The Lived Ancient Religion Approach", *Religion* 48,4 (2018), 568–593.
– 2018: „Religious agency, sacralisation, and tradition in the ancient city", *Istrazivanya* 29 (2018), 22–38. doi: 10.19090/i.2018.29.22-38
– 2019: „Narratives as factor and indicator of religious change in the Roman Empire (1st and 2nd centuries)", *Studia Patristica* 99 (2019), 35–53.
– 2019: „Introduction: authorities in religious individualisation", in: Martin Fuchs *et al.* (eds.), *Religious Individualisation: Historical Dimensions and Comparative Perspectives*, Berlin: de Gruyter, 971–981.
– 2019: „Ritual objects and religious communication in lived ancient religion: multiplying religion", in: Martin Fuchs *et al.* (eds.), *Religious Individualisation: Historical Dimensions and Comparative Perspectives*, Berlin: de Gruyter, 1201–1222.

Sander, Sabine

– (ed.) 2015. Language as Bridge and Border: Linguistic, Cultural and Political Constellations in 18th to 20th Century German-Jewish Thought. Berlin: Hentrich & Hentrich.
– 2017. Dialogische Verantwortung: Konzepte der Vermittlung und des Fremdverstehens im jüdisch-deutschen Kontext des 19. und 20. Jahrhunderts, Paderborn: Fink.

– 2013: „Menschenrechte im Judentum", in: Hamid Reza Yousefi (Hg.), *Menschenrechte im Weltkontext. Geschichten – Erscheinungsformen – Neuere Entwicklungen*, Wiesbaden: Springer 2013, S. 79–84.

- 2015: „Between Acculturation and Self-Assertion. Individualization in the German-Jewish context of Prussia and the Weimar Republic and its Contribution to Culture and Social Theory of Modernity", *Religion. Journal of Religious Studies, vol. 45 (3) 2015*, 429–450. doi: 10.1080/0048721X.2015.1024041.
- 2015: „Introduction. Language as a Border and a Bridge", in: Sabine Sander (ed.), Language as Bridge and Border. Linguistic, Cultural and Political Constellations in 18th to 20th Century German-Jewish Thought, Berlin: Hentrich & Hentrich, 11–30.
- 2015: „Messianic Universalism: The Social Ethics and Dialogue Philosophy of Hermann Cohen, Martin Buber, and Karl Löwith", in: Sabine Sander (ed.), *Language as Bridge and Border. Political, Cultural and Social Constellations in the German-Jewish context*, Berlin: Hentrich & Hentrich, 119–136.
- 2018: „Variations of the Embodied Self: George H. Mead, Ernst Cassirer, and Lawrence Krader on Human Being between Nature and Culture", in: Cyril Levitt and Sabine Sander (ed.), *Beyond the Juxtaposition of Nature and Culture: Lawrence Krader, Interdisciplinarity, and the Concept of the Human Being* (Series: History and Philosophy of Science: Hersey, Crossroads, and Intersections, ed Paolo Palmieri), New York: Peter Lang, 99–130.
- 2019: „Jewish Emancipation, Religious Individualization, and Metropolitan Integration: A Case Study on Moses Mendelssohn and Moritz Lazarus", in: Martin Fuchs *et al.* (eds.), *Religious Individualisation: Historical Dimensions and Comparative Perspectives*, Berlin: de Gruyter, 939–962.

Sangari, Kumkum

- 2019: Singular individuals, conflicting authorities: Annie Besant and Mohandas Gandhi, in: Martin Fuchs *et al.* (eds.), *Religious Individualisation: Historical Dimensions and Comparative Perspectives*, Berlin: de Gruyter, 1065–1096.

Sangmeister, Dirk

- 2017. *Vertrieben vom Feld der Literatur*, Verbreitung und Unterdrückung der Werke von Friedrich Christian Laukhard. Bremen: edition lumière (= Presse und Geschichte, 104).

Scheid, John

- 2013. Les dieux, l'État et l'individu. Réflexions sur la religion civique à Rome, Paris, Seuil, 2013.
- 2015. The Gods, the State, and the Individual. Reflections on Civic Religion in Rome, Philadelphia: University of Pennsylvania Press, 2015.

- 2013: „Priests and prophets in Rome", in: Dignas, B., Parker, R., Stroumsa, G. (éds.), *Priests and Prophets among Pagans, Jews and Christians*, Leuven: Peeters, 15–28.
- 2013: „Religion collective et religion privée", *Dialogues d'histoire ancienne, 39/2, 2013*, 19–31.
- 2014: „Opferaltar und Weihaltar in Rom und in Italien", in: Busch A. W., Schäfer A. (éds.), *Römische Weihaltäre im Kontext* (Tagung Köln 2009), Friedberg, 27–35.
- 2014: „I sacerdozi „arcaici" restaurati da Augusto. L'esempio degli arvali", in: Urso G. (éd.), *Sacerdos. Figure del sacro nella società romana, Cividale del Friuli, 26–28 settembre 2012*, Pisa, (I convegni della Fondazione Niccolò Canussio 12) Edizioni ETS, 177–189.

- 2015: „Auguste et la Religion" in: Paolo Fedeli, Hans-Christian Günther (éds.), *Augustus und Rom: 2000 Jahre danach*, Rome, 19. 9. 2014 (Akten des Symposions, Studia Classica et Mediaevalia, vol. 9), Nordhausen 2015, 217–242.
- 2015: „Des dieux qui se fâchent mais ne connaissent pas le repentir. Le cas romain", in: Durand J.-M., Marti L., Römer Th. (éds.), *Colères et repentirs divins* (Actes du colloque organisé les 24 et 25 avril 2013), Paris, 65–70.
- 2015: „Gaetano Marini et les frères arvales", in: *Gaetano Marini (1742–1815)*, Città del Vaticano 2015 (ST 492–493), 1187–1210.
- 2015: „Les *Augustea* et le culte des empereurs. Réflexions sur les rites célébrés dans ces lieux de culte", in: P. Gros, E. Marin, M. Zink (éds.), *Auguste, son époque et l'Augusteum de Narona*, Paris: Académie des inscriptions et belles-lettres, 17–30.
- 2015: „Religious Practice un a World without Revelation: the Example of the Roman Empire", in: Almqvist K., Linklater A., *Religion. Perspectives from the Engelsberg seminar 2014*, Stockholm, 45–52.
- 2015: „Spéculation érudite et religion. L'interaction entre l'érudition et les réformes religieuses à Rome", in: Belayche N., Pirenne-Delforge, V. (éds.), *Fabriquer du divin. Constructions et ajustements de la représentation des dieux dans l'Antiquité*, Liège, 93–104.
- 2016: „Le *lustrum* et la *lustratio*. En finir avec la ,purification'", in: V. Gasparini (éd.), *Vestigia. Miscellanea di studi storico-religiosi in onore di Filippo Coarelli nel suo 80 anniversario*, Potsdamer Altertumswissenschaftliche Beiträge, vol. 55, Stuttgart, 203–209.
- 2016: „Moerae, Ilithyiae, Terra mater, des Grecques très romaines", in: Bonnet C., Pirenne-Delforge V., Pironti G. (éds.), *Dieux des Grecs, dieux des Romains. Panthéons en dialogue à travers l'histoire et l'historiographie*, Bruxelles/Rome, 37–43.

Scheuermann, Leif

- 2013. Religion an der Grenze. Provinzialrömische Religion am Neckar- und äußeren obergermanischen Limes, Rahden/Westf.: Leidorf.
- –; Spickermann, Wolfgang (eds.) 2013. *Keltische Götternamen als individuelle Option? /Celtic Theonyms as an Individual Option?*, Akten des 11. internationalen Workshops „Fontes Epigraphici Religionum Celticarum Antiquarum" vom 19.–21. Mai 2011 an der Universität Erfurt, Rahden/Westf.: Leidorf.

Schlette, Magnus

- 2019: The inward sublime: Kant's aesthetics and the Protestant tradition, in: Martin Fuchs *et al.* (eds.), *Religious Individualisation: Historical Dimensions and Comparative Perspectives*, Berlin: de Gruyter, 99–140.

Spickermann, Wolfgang

- (ed.) 2013. *Keltische Götternamen als individuelle Option? /Celtic Theonyms as an Individual Option?*, Akten des 11. internationalen Workshops „Fontes Epigraphici Religionum Celticarum Antiquarum" vom 19.–21. Mai 2011 an der Universität Erfurt, Rahden/Westf.: Leidorf.
- –; Scheuermann, Leif (eds.) 2016. Religiöse Praktiken in der Antike. Individuum, Gesellschaft, Weltbeziehung, Graz: Uni Press Graz.

–; Waldner, Katharina; Gordon, Richard (eds.) 2016. Burial Rituals, Ideas of Afterlife, and the Individual in the Hellenistic World and the Roman Empire, Stuttgart: Steiner.

- 2013: „Kultisches und Religiöses bei Polybios", in: V. Grieb/C. Koehn (Hrsg.) (Hg.): *Polybios und seine Historien*, Stuttgart: Steiner, 301–318.
- 2013: „Lucian of Samosata on Oracles, Magic and Superstition", in: Veit Rosenberger (Hg.): *Divination in the ancient world: religious options and the individual*, Stuttgart: Steiner, 139–151.
- 2013: „Lukian von Samosata und die Leibesübungen", in: P. Mauritsch/Chr. Ulf (Hrsg.) (Hg.), *Kultur(en) – Formen des Alltäglichen in der Antike. Festschrift Ingomar Weiler zum 75. Geburtstag*, Grazer Universitätsverlag Allgemeine wissenschaftliche Reihe 33, Nummi et Litterae VII, Bd. 2, Graz, 509–522.
- 2013: „Philosophical claim and individual lifestyles: Lucian's Peregrinus/Proteus – charlatan and Heros", in: J. Rüpke/G. Woolf (Eds.) (Hg.): *Religious Dimensions of the Self in the Second Century CE, Studien und Texte zu Antike und Christentum" (STAC) 76*, Tübingen, 175–191.
- 2013: „Women and the cult of Magna Mater in the Western provinces", in: E. Hemelrijk/G. Woolf (eds.), *Woman and the Roman City in the Latin West*, Leiden, Boston: Brill, 147–168.
- 2014: „Arianische Vandalen, katholische Provinzialrömer und die Rolle kirchlicher Netzwerke im Nordafrika des 5. Jh. n.Chr", in: Daniel Bauerfeld/Lukas Clemens (Hg.), *Gesellschaftliche Umbrüche und soziale Netzwerke*. Bielefeld: transcript, 65–86.
- 2014: „Kultplätze auf privatem Grund in den beiden Germanien", in: Benedikt Kranemann/Christof Mandry/Hans-Friedrich Müller (eds.), *Religion und Recht*, Münster: Aschendorff, 167–196.
- 2014: „Neue epigraphische Zeugnisse gallo-römischer Götternamen aus den beiden Germanien". in: Eck, Werner; Funke, Peter (eds.), *Öffentlichkeit-Monument – TextXIV Congressus Internationalis Epigraphiae Graecae et Latinae 27.–31. Augusti MMXII Akten*. Berlin: de Gruyter, 568–570.
- 2015: „Das Ende der Weiheinschriftenkultur in den beiden Germanien", in: Lukas Clemens, Hiltrud Merten & Christoph Schäfer (Hg.), *Frühchristliche Grabinschriften im Westen des Römischen Reiches. Beiträge zur Internationalen Konferenz „Frühchristliche Grabinschriften im Westen des Römischen Reiches", Trier, 13.–15. Juni 2013*, Trier: Kliomedia, 75–85.
- 2015: „Eine Weihung an Mars Equitum aus Ravna, Serbien", in: Sabine Panzram, Werner Riess und Christoph Schäfer (Hrsg.) (Hg.), *Menschen und Orte in der Antike. Festschrift für Helmut Halfmann zum 65. Geburtstag*, Rahden/Westf.: Leidorf, 257–272.
- 2015: „Lukian und die (Götter)bilder", in: D. Boschung/A. Schäfer (Hg.), *Römische Götterbilder der mittleren und späten Kaiserzeit*, Paderborn: Fink, 87–107.
- 2015: „Monumental Inscriptions", in: Rubina Raja/Jörg Rüpke (Hg.), *A Companion to the Archaeology of Religion in the Ancient World*, Chichester: Wiley Blackwell, 412–424.
- 2015: „Trauer und Tod in der 2. Sophistik am Beispiel des Lukian von Samosata", in: Beate Ego, Ulrike Mittmann (Hg.), *Evil and Death. Conceptions of the Human in Biblical, Early Jewish, Greco-Roman and Egyptian Literature*, Berlin/Boston: de Gruyter, 275–293.
- 2016: „Regionale Zentren und „Stammes"heiligtümer in Nordgallien und Germanien", in: Manfred Lehner/Bernhard Schrettle (Hg.), *Zentralort und TempelbergSiedlungs- und Kultentwicklung amFrauenberg bei Leibnitz im VergleichAkten des Kolloquiums im Schloss Seggau am 4. und 5. Mai 2015*, Wien: Phoibos, 197–209.
- 2016: „Tod und Jenseits bei Lukian von Samosata und Tatian", in: Waldner, Katharina; Gordon, Richard; Spickermann, Wolfgang (Hg.), *Burial Rituals, Ideas of Afterlife, and the Individual in the Hellenistic World and the Roman Empire*, Stuttgart: Steiner, 67–81.
- 2017: „Inschriftlich bezeugte Stiftungen von Theatern und Kultgebäuden in Gallien und Germanien", in: Thomas Hufschmid (Red) (Hg.), *Theaterbauten als Teil monumentaler Heiligtümer in den nordwestlichen Provinzen des Imperium Romanum: Architektur – Organisation – Nutzung*, Augusta Raurica, 37–47.

- 2017: „Kulte, Religion und Heiligtümer in der Zeit des Marc Aurel", in: Grieb, Volker (Hg.), *Marc Aurel – Wege zu seiner Herrschaft*, Gutenberg: Computus, 325–342.
- 2017: „Mogontiacum/Mainz als Zentrum der Romanisierung", in: Claudia Horst/Tassilo Schmitt (Hg.), *Die antike Stadt. Begriff – Imagination – Soziale Realität*, Bremen: edition lumière, 79–112.
- 2017: „Religion in contact, Germany", in: Roger S. Bagnall, Kai Brodersen, Craige B. Champion, Andrew Erskine (Hg.), *The Encyclopedia of Ancient History (online)*, Chichester: Wiley, 1–3. doi:10.1002/9781444338386.wbeah3015
- 2017: „Überlegungen zum Kult der Magna Mater und des Attis im Westen des Imperium Romanum", *Carnuntum Jahrbuch 2016*, 23–38.

Stuckrad, Kocku von

- 2015. *The Scientification of Religion: An Historical Study of Discursive Change, 1800–2000*, Berlin & Boston: de Gruyter, Paperback edition published November 2015.

- 2013: „Discursive Study of Religion: Approaches, Definitions, Implications", *Method and Theory in the Study of Religion 25/1 (2013)*, 5–25.
- 2016: „Religion and Science in Transformation: On Discourse Communities, the Double-Bind of Discourse Research, and Theoretical Controversies", in: Frans Wijsen & Kocku von Stuckrad (eds.): *Making Religion: Theory and Practice in the Discursive Study of Religion*, Leiden & Boston: Brill, 203–224.

Suitner, Riccarda

- (ed.) 2016. *First Results of the Second Funding Period of the Research Group 'Religious Individualization in Historical Perspective'. A Reader*, with Contributions by Martin Fuchs, Jörg Rüpke, Angelika Malinar, Rahul Parson, Richard L. Gordon, Dietmar Mieth, Bernd-Christian Otto, Nicole Reinhardt, Cristiana Facchini, Sabine Sander, Vera Höke, and Dorit Messlin, Erfurt.

- 2016: „Reformation, Medicine, and Religious Dissent in the Late Renaissance: the Case of the University of Padua", in: *Nuncius. Journal of the Material and Visual History of Science (XXXI)*, 2016, 11–31.
- 2017: „Radykalny reformator czy uczen Telesia? Przypadek Agostina Doniego", in: Michał Choptiany and Piotr Wilczek *(ed.), Reformacja w dawnej Rzeczypospolitej i jej europejskie konteksty. Postulaty badawcze* [The Reformation in the Polish-Lithuanian Commonwealth and Its European Contexts: Research Proposals], Warsaw, Wydawnictwa Uniwersytetu Warszawskiego: Warsaw University Press, 123–142.
- 2019: „Reformation, Naturalism and Telesian Philosophy: the Case of Agostino Doni", in: Pietro Daniel Omodeo (ed.), *Bernardino Telesio and the Natural Sciences in the Renaissance*, Leiden: Brill.
- 2019: „The Good Citizen and the Heterodox Self: Turning to Protestantism and Anabaptism in Sixteenth-Century Venice", in: Martin Fuchs *et al.* (eds.), *Religious Individualisation: Historical Dimensions and Comparative Perspectives*, Berlin: de Gruyter, 459–474.

van Hove, Rebecca

- 2019: „A Dream on Trial: The Contest of Oracular Interpretations and Authorities in Hyperides 'In Defence of Euxenippus'", Mnemosyne 72, 405–36.

Vannier, Marie-Anne

- 2015. Cheminer avec maître Eckhart. Au cœur de l'anthropologie chrétienne, Paris: Artège.
- (ed.) 2013. La christologie chez Eckhart et Nicolas de Cues, Paris: Cerf, coll. «Patrimoines».
- (ed.) 2014 Intellect, sujet, image chez Eckhart et Nicolas de Cues, Paris: Cerf.
- ; H. Schwaetzer (eds.) 2015. Der Bildbegriff bei Meister Eckhart und Nikolaus von Kues, Münster: Aschendorff.
- (ed.) 2015. Maître Eckhart, Commentaire du Livre de la Sagesse, Introduction, notes, Paris: Les Belles Lettres.
- ; D. Mieth, M. Vinzent, C.M. Wojtulewicz (eds.) 2016. Meister Eckhart in Paris and Strasbourg, Leuven: Peeters.
- (ed.) 2017, Mystique rhénane et Devotio moderna, Paris: Beauchesne, coll. «Mystiques d'Orient et d'Occident».

- 2013: „La christologie d'Eckhart: une réalité à redécouvrir", in: M.-A. Vannier (dir.), La christologie chez Eckhart et Nicolas de Cues, Pars: Cerf, coll. «Patrimoines», 9–15.
- 2013: „L'Un et la relation chez Eckhart", in: R. Cazalis (éd.), Monade, Dyade, Triade. Des approches de la réalité, Namur: Presses Universitaires de Namur, 59–75.
- 2014: „Sujet, intellect, image chez Eckhart", in: Intellect, sujet, image chez Eckhart et Nicolas de Cues, Paris: Cerf, 17–39.
- 2015: „Die Bedeutung der Frage des Bildes bei den Rheinischen Mystikern", in: H. Schwaetzer, M.-A. Vannier, Der Bildbegriff bei Meister Eckhart und Nikolaus von Kues, Münster: Aschendorff, 9–17.
- 2015: „Eckhart, lecteur d'Origène", Irénikon LXXXVIII (2015), 483–496.
- 2015: „L'expérience mystique chez Eckhart", in: D. Cohen-Levinas, G. Roux, M. Sebti, Mystique et philosophie dans les trois monothéismes, Paris: Hermann, 91–108.
- 2015: „L'originalité de l'interprétation eckhartienne des Noces de Cana", in: J.-M. Vercruysse, Les Noces de Cana, Arras: Graphè, 103–113.
- 2016: „Eckhart et Augustin", Théophilyon XXI (2016), 39–52.
- 2016: „Eckhart, une lecture de Genèse 1, 1", in: B. Bakhouche (éd.), Science et exégèse. Les interprétations antiques et médiévales du récit biblique de la création des éléments (Gn 1, 1–8), Turnhout: Brepols, BEHE, 347–354.
- 2016: „L'humilité", in: ead. (éd.), L'humilité chez les mystiques rhénans et Nicolas de Cues, Paris, Beauchesne, 7–15.
- 2017: „D'Erfurt à Strasbourg. L'arrivée d'Eckhart à Strasbourg, il y a 700 ans", D. Mieth, M.-A. Vannier, M. Vinzent, C. Wojtulewicz, Meister Eckhart in Paris and Strasbourg, Leuven, Peeters, 325–334.
- 2017: „Eckhart or the actuality of a classic", in: P. Cooper, S. Kikuchi S. (ed.), Commitments to Medieval Mysticism within Contemporary Contexts, Leuven: Peeters, Bibliotheca Ephemeridum Theologicarum Lovaniensium, 290, 177–194.
- 2017: „Introduction", in: D. Mieth, M.-A. Vannier, M. Vinzent, C. Wojtulewicz, Meister Eckhart in Paris and Strasbourg, Leuven, Peeters, XI–XXII.

- 2017: „Les rapports entre la mystique rhénane et la *Devotio moderna*", ead. (éd.), *Mystique rhénane et* Devotio moderna, Paris: Beauchesne, 13–19.
- 2017: „L'écriture d'Eckhart. L'exemple de sa théologie trinitaire", in: E. Boncour, P. Gire, E. Mangin, *Maître Eckhart, une écriture inachevée,* Grenoble: Jérôme Millon, 125–133.
- 2017: „L'essor des études eckhartiennes en France", D. Mieth, ead., M. Vinzent, C. Wojtulewicz, *Meister Eckhart in Paris and Strasbourg,* Leuven, Peeters, 157–175.
- 2017: „Présentation", D. Mieth, M.-A. Vannier, M. Vinzent, C. Wojtulewicz, *Meister Eckhart in Paris and Strasbourg,* Leuven, Peeters, 321–322.
- 2017: „Présentation de Mystique rhénane et Devotio moderna", in: ead. (éd.), *Mystique rhénane et* Devotio moderna, Paris: Beauchesne, 11–12.
- 2018: „Der Freie Geist/Das ledige Gemüt bei Meister Eckhart", in: *Meister-Eckhart-Jahrbuch 12 (2018)*, 201–212.
- 2018: „Origen, a Source of Meister Eckhart's Thinking", in: M. Vinzent, *Studia Patristiica.* Vol. XCVII – Papers presented at the Seventeenth International Conference on Patristic Studies held in Oxford 2015 Volume 23: From the Fourth Century Onwards (Latin Writers), Nachleben, Leuven: Peteers, 345–354.

Vinzent, Jutta

- 2013: „Challenging the abstract in late 1930s Britain", in: Jordana Mendelson (ed.), *Encounters with the 1930s,* exhibition catalogue, Museo Nacional Centro de Arte Reina Sofía, Madrid, 3 October 2012-7 January 2013 (ISBN 978-84-15691-01-3), 140–147.
- 2016: „Austria in *Die Zeitung*: The Instrumentalisation of Émigré Newspapers during WWII and the Subversive Power of Cartoons", in: Mark Stocker and Phillip G. Lindley (eds.), *Tributes to Jean Michel Massing. Towards a Global Art History,* London: Harvey Miller, 323–343.
- 2016: „Space and Form in String Sculptures: Naum Gabo, Barbara Hepworth and Henry Moore", in: Hans Aurenhammer and Regine Prange (eds.), *Das Problem der Form. Interferenzen zwischen moderner Kunst und Kunstwissenschaft,* Berlin: Gebrüder Mann Verlag, (Neue Frankfurter Forschungen zur Kunst, 18), 355–381.
- 2016: „Space, Time and Body in Performance Art and Meister Eckhart", in: ead., Christopher M. Wojtulewicz (eds.), *Performing Bodies. Time and Space in Meister Eckhart and Taery Kim,* Leuven: Peeters, 2016 (Eckhart: Texts and Studies, 6), 217–265.
- 2017: „in conversation with Tim Ingold 2017, 'Representations on the line. From lines as geometrical form to lines as meshwork rather than network", in: Sebastian Dorsch and Jutta Vinzent (eds.), *SpatioTemporalities on the Line. Representations – Practices – Dynamics,* Berlin/Boston: de Gruyter, (SpatioTemporality. Practices – Concepts – Media, 3), 13–19.
- 2019: „Challenging Personhood. The Subject and Viewer of Contemporary Crucifxion Iconography", in Martin Fuchs *et al.* (eds.), *Religious Individualisation: Historical Dimensions and Comparative Perspectives,* Berlin: de Gruyter, 603–624.

Vinzent, Markus

- 2019: Monism and dividualism in Meister Eckhart, in Martin Fuchs *et al.* (eds.), *Religious Individualisation: Historical Dimensions and Comparative Perspectives,* Berlin: de Gruyter, 363–382.

von Wyss-Giacosa, Paola

–; Isler, Andreas (eds.) 2017. Gemachte Bilder. Derwische als Orient-Chiffre und Faszinosum, Zürich: VMZ.

– 2013: „Henri Michaux und die Idolatrie Indiens", in: Schwarz, Dieter (ed.), *Henri Michaux, Momente*, Düsseldorf: Richter, 26–33
– 2014: „Confronting Asia's ‚Idolatrous Body', Reading some Early Modern European Sources on Indian Religion", in: Höpflinger, Anna-K./Ornella, Alexander D./Knauss, Stefanie (eds.), *Commun(icat)ing Bodies, Body as a Medium in Religious Systems*, Zürich/Baden-Baden: Pano/Nomos, 387–423.
– 2015: „Western imaginaries between fascination, colonial construction and appropriation. The Lore of a Mysterious India, of Kali, the Black Goddess, and of her Evil Devotees", in: Pezzoli-Olgiati, Daria (ed.), *Religion in Cultural Imaginary. Explorations in Visual and Material Practices, Religion – Wirtschaft – Politik, Vol. 13*, Zürich/Baden-Baden: Pano/Nomos, 79–115.
– 2017: „Ein thailändischer Buddha in Gottorf. Zur Bedeutung materieller Zeugnisse im frühneuzeitlichen Idolatrie-Diskurs", in: Cremer, Annette Caroline/Mulsow, Martin (eds.), *Objekte als Quellen der historischen Kulturwissenschaften. Stand und Perspektive der Forschung*, Wien: Böhlau-Verlag, 211–224.
– 2017: „Gemachte Bilder. Einige Beobachtungen zur visuellen Repräsentation des „Derwischs" in europäischen Berichten seit der frühen Neuzeit", in: von Wyss-Giacosa, Paola/Isler, Andreas (eds.), *Gemachte Bilder. Derwische als Orient-Chiffre und Faszinosum*, Zürich: VMZ, 49–100.

Wildberger, Jula

– 2019: „Cosmic Beauty in Stoicism: A Foundation for an Environmental Ethic as Love of the Other?", in: Hunt, Ailsa/Marlow, Hilary (eds.), *Ecology and Theology in the Ancient World: Cross-Disciplinary Perspectives*, London: Bloomsbury, 63–74.

Woolf, Greg

–; Hemelrijk, E. (eds.) 2013. *Women and the Roman City in the Latin West*, (Mnemosyne Supplements). Leiden: Brill.
–; Rüpke, J. (eds.) (2013). *Religious Dimensions of the Self in the Second Century CE*. (Studien und Texte zu Antike und Christentum; 76). Stuttgart: Mohr Siebeck.

– 2013: „Female Mobility in the Latin West", in: Hemelrijk, Emily & Greg Woolf (eds.), *Women and the Roman City in the Latin West*, (Mnemosyne, Supplements, History and Archaeology of Classical Antiquity), Leiden: Brill, 351–368.
– 2013: „Ritual and the Individual in Roman Religion", in: Rüpke, J. (ed.), *The Individual in the Religions of the Ancient Mediterranean*, Oxford: Oxford University Press, 136–160.
– 2014: „Isis and the evolution of religions", in: Bricault, L., & Versluys, M. J. (eds.), *Power, Politics, and the Cults of Isis*, (Religions of the Graeco-Roman World), Leiden: E. J. Brill, 62–92.
– 2015: „Mars and memory", in: K. Galinsky and K. Lapatin (eds.), *Cultural memories in the Roman Empire*, Los Angeles: Getty Publications, 206–224.
– 2015: „Ritual Traditions of Non-Mediterranean Europe". In: Raja, R., & Rüpke, J. (eds.), *A Companion to the Archaeology of Religion in the Ancient World*, Wiley-Blackwell, 465–477.

- 2016: „Only Connect? Network Analysis and Religious Change in the Roman World" in: Cláudia Beltrão (ed.), *Revista Hélade de História Antiga 2.2, Religiões no Mundo Antigo*, 43–58.
- 2016: „Polis religion", in: Orlin, E. (ed.), The Routledge Encyclopedia of Ancient Mediterranean Religions, Routledge.
- 2017: „Empires, diasporas and the emergence of religions", in: J. Carleton-Paget and J. Lieu (eds.), *Christianity in the Second Century. Themes and Developments*, Cambridge University Press: New York, 25–38.

Zwierlein, Cornel

–; Vincenzo Lavenia (eds.) 2018. The Fruits of Migration. Heterodox Italian Migrants and Central Europe – 1550–1620, Leiden: Brill (Intersections Nr. 57).

- 2017: „,Konfessionalisierung' europäisch, global als epistemischer Prozess: Zu den Folgen der Reformation und zur Methodendiskussion", in: Christoph Strohm (Hg.): *Reformation und Recht. Zur Kontroverse um die Kulturwirkungen der Reformation*, Tübingen: Mohr Siebeck, 1–51.
- 2017: „Herrschaft und Reziprozität: Vom Sichtbarwerden der Gegenseitigkeit in Krieg und Konflikt (Paris-Rom 1589)", in: *Zeitschrift der Savigny-Stiftung für Rechtsgeschichte. Germanistische Abteilung 134 (2017)*, 71–98.
- 2018: „Historicizing Environmental Security", in *European Journal of Security Research 3 (2018)*, 1–13.
- 2018: „Security, Nature and Mercantilism in the Early British Empire", in *European Journal of Security Research 3 (2018)*, 15–34.
- 2018: „Tyrannenmord, Majestätsverbrechen und Herrscherwechsel bei Shakespeare: Resonanzen konfessioneller Polarisierung um 1600", in *Shakespeare-Jahrbuch 154 (2018)*, 31–53.